International economics

Related titles from Macmillan

A Jacquemin and H. de Jong: *European Industrial Organisation*
I. Pearce: *International Trade*
W. M. Scammell: *International Monetary Policy: Bretton Woods and After*
W. M. Scammell: *The International Economy since 1945* (second edition)

International economics

Second edition

Bo Södersten

University of Lund

M
MACMILLAN
EDUCATION

First published in the USA 1970
First published in the UK 1971

First edition 1971
Reprinted 1971, 1972, 1973, 1974, 1977 (twice), 1978, 1979

Second edition 1980
Reprinted 1981 (twice), 1982, 1983, 1984, 1985 (twice), 1988

Published by
MACMILLAN EDUCATION LTD
Houndmills, Basingstoke, Hampshire RG21 2XS
and London
Companies and representatives
throughout the world

Printed in Hong Kong

British Library Cataloguing in Publication Data
Södersten, Bo
International economics. — 2nd ed.
1. International economic relations
I. Title
382.1   HF1411
ISBN 0-333-23641-6
ISBN 0-333-23642-4 Pbk

To Astrid, Anna, Henrik, Erika and Viktor

Contents

Preface to the Second Edition

The first edition of *International Economics* was published in Swedish in 1969. The American edition came out in 1970 and the British in 1971. An Italian translation was published in 1976.

The first edition of the book was well received and has been used in many countries. The purpose of the book was to present a reasonably rigorous, modern treatment of international economics which should still be accessible to undergraduate students and persons with a general interest in economics and international affairs. The emphasis was on theory, even though problems of economic policy were discussed throughout. The book tried to provide the reader with theoretical tools that could be applied to various kinds of problems, not just those that happened to be at the forefront of discussion just when the book was published.

This basic outline and approach has been kept in the second edition. However, as almost a decade has gone by since the first edition was originally published, the second edition has been thoroughly revised, both in order to take into account new theoretical developments and to bring the exposition up to date and take account of the changes in institutional settings and of new policy perspectives.

Parts I and II, on the pure theory of trade and on economic growth and trade, have been organized around the standard trade barter model. This is the area where standard theory is most firmly rooted. Hence the outline of the first edition has been kept. However, the exposition has been tightened, condensed and also simplified. More emphasis has been given to the testing of trade theories and a new chapter on alternative trade theories has been added to Part I to review alternative approaches to the Ricardo and Heckscher–Ohlin models. In Part II the empirical survey has been revised to take recent trends into account.

Part III now deals with trade policy. The chapters on institutions have been altered to keep pace with facts and changing perspectives on policy problems. Two new chapters have been added to strengthen the book's emphasis on the theory and policy of trade and development. One of the chapters is on import substitution versus export-push, and the other is on the quest for a new international economic order. The section on effective rates of protection has been changed to take care of new theoretical insights.

Part IV now comprises the balance of payments and problems of international economic monetary policy. In this area major theoretical advances have been made. This has led to the addition of a new chapter on the monetary approach to the balance of payments and to complete revisions of the chapters on fixed versus flexible exchange rates and on how to achieve external and internal balance.

Part V, on the international monetary system, has been completely rewritten as the institutional scene has completely changed following the breakdown of the Bretton Woods system and the introduction of floating exchange rates.

HOW TO USE THE BOOK

There is no one best way of organizing the subject of international economics. Some will prefer to start with macroeconomic aspects, others with micro-economic or pure-theory parts. Each part of this book has a logical structure, and it might prove difficult to break up a part, though it is unnecessary to study all the material in any one part before turning to the next. The sequence in which one chooses to cover the parts is to some extent a matter of taste and interest. For example, if one starts with pure theory, perhaps it would be logical to continue with the theory of growth and trade.

But whether one wishes to take Part III, on trade policy, next, or Part IV, on the balance of payments, is a matter of preference. The part on trade policy has been placed before the part on international monetary economics because the theoretical structure of the analysis underlying trade policy problems has more logical connections with the pure theory of trade. But it might also be argued that insights into balance-of-payments problems will enhance the understanding of problems of trade policy. I have instead chosen to concentrate the exposition in the first three parts of the book to problems connected with the 'real' side of the economy and to concentrate the analysis of monetary aspects of the international economy to Parts IV and V. However, the five parts are intended to be self-contained.

ONE-SEMESTER COURSES

Instructors who wish to use the book in one-semester courses on international economics may find it too voluminous. For one-semester courses I would suggest the following fifteen chapters: 1–4, 7, 8, 9, 14, 17–19 and 22–25. But other combinations are equally possible.

ACKNOWLEDGEMENTS

The conception and execution of this book have been considerably influenced by discussions with students and colleagues. I cannot mention them all. Alan Harkess has been especially helpful in updating empirical material. Arne Bigsten, Göte Hansson, Lennart Pettersson, Robert M. Stier and Bo Walfridsson assisted me in various ways. Harold Dickson, K. G. Löfgren, Mats Lundahl, Inga Persson-Tanimura and Bo Sandelin read parts of the manuscript and gave valuable comments. Greta Fridmar, Agnetta Kretz and Maja Lisa Johansson typed the manuscript in an effective and cheerful manner.

I gratefully acknowledge research support during the work on this book from the Swedish Social Science Research Council and from the Swedish Agency for Research Co-operation with Developing Countries.

Lund,
March 1979   BO SÖDERSTEN

International economics

Introduction: international economics and economic theory

Today the national state is the dominant political entity. Most countries, from an economic point of view, are still intimately linked with others. A few - the United States, the Soviet Union, and China - could conceivably withdraw from the world economy without disastrous consequences to themselves. For other countries such an act would border on the unthinkable. It would bring about not only a drastic lowering of economic welfare but also a complete change of ways of life. For practical purposes, all countries must accept the fact that they are part of a world economy. No country can escape its role in the system of interdependent trading nations.

It is debatable whether the degree of interdependence among nations is increasing or not. It is true that world trade has grown exceptionally fast in the post-war years. The forces behind the internationalization process have been strong. Technical progress in transport and communication has played an important role. Increased returns to scale in production and high income elasticities for differentiated products have also had their impact. These and many other factors have favored international specialization and trade. The forces working for economic interdependence among nations seem irresistible.

At the same time, we should not forget that the nation-state is still in the 1970s the dominant entity. However, there are forces working against interdependence. The possibilities for the advanced industrial countries to control their own economies and isolate themselves from international repercussions are considerable. While it is true that the increase in oil prices in 1973 played havoc with the world economy and induced an international depression, many countries, notably Japan and some of the stronger Western European economies, have not been so greatly affected by international business cycle fluctuations as they were in the interwar period.

Labor markets, especially those in Western Europe, have been influenced by regional migration, but we have not witnessed any migrations on the scale of those which took place in the nineteenth century from Europe to the United States.

Many less developed countries have tried to establish a policy of self-reliance. They have tried to isolate themselves from international influences by a policy of import-substitution. When speaking about integration a word of caution should be inserted. The really important integration is between parts of the world economy. There is still, for instance, a very definite dividing line between the Soviet Union and the East European communist countries on the one hand, and the United States and the Western European capitalist countries on the other. What has been said so far really applies to parts of the world economy; the world economy as a whole is not and never was integrated in any qualified sense of the word.

It is therefore an open question if the degree of interdependence is increasing or not. There are undoubtedly many economists who would argue that the forces behind the internationalization process are strongest and that the national state will wither away. I am not convinced that this will be the case. The forces working for a national identity – perhaps a new type of identity, be it from dominating neighbours or a new type of changed social and political system – are also strong in many countries. Whether existing trends toward internationalization or new forms of nationalism will get the upper hand is impossible to say. This is primarily a political question.

To be able to reach an informed opinion about these matters, it is necessary to study international economics.

INTERNATIONAL ECONOMICS AS A SUBJECT

Even if most people agreed that international economic relations are of great importance for most countries, it does not necessarily follow that international economics should be studied as a subject independent of other branches of economics.

International economics is often referred to as 'applied economics', and there are certainly many policy problems and problems of an empirical nature within international economics that the use of economic theory can elucidate. But there are more deep-seated reasons why international economics has a long tradition as a subject in its own right.

Many theorems and insights central to economic theory have been developed by economists working within international economics. The theory of comparative advantage and the factor-price equalization theorem are examples. Both belong to the area usually called the *pure theory* of international trade. The pure theory of trade can be said to be part of price theory, the terms used in a broad sense. But price theory or microtheory *per se* seldom pursues the subject to such a degree that all the aspects of the theory which are of interest to a trade theorist are revealed in its full implications. Trade theory is a distinct part of modern economic theory with a rich body of theorems. These results are not part of general economic theory as it is commonly understood and taught.

Analogous conditions hold, though perhaps to a less degree, for the macroeconomic parts of international economic theory. Some of its results, for instance those about income determination in open economies, are quite straightforward applications of the corresponding parts of the theory for closed economies. But other parts, for instance exchange-rate theory, can hardly be obtained except from a study of the specific theory.

When it comes to the policy aspects of the subject, it is quite obvious that international economic relations give rise to problems not encountered in other fields of economics. The nation is not only a distinct political entity, it also has many important economic characteristics that set it apart from the larger integrated areas that make up the world economy: the mobility of the factors of production is much larger within the nation than among nations, there are tariffs and taxes on imported goods, different currencies give rise to specific problems, etc. All these lead to international economic policy problems that are different in nature from national policy problems.

There are, therefore, from both theoretical and policy points of view, good reasons why international economics is dealt with as a specific branch of economics. Modern economics is a large and diversified subject. A training in general economic theory is the best background for a study of international economics. But it can be regarded only as a background. To obtain a real understanding of the field, the student will have to study international economics directly.

Now we shall look at some characteristics of international economics and preview some of its problems and results.

COMPARATIVE ADVANTAGE AND PURE THEORY

One of the basic questions facing international trade theory is why trade takes place. The classical economists saw labor as the only factor of production and said that differing labor productivity among countries caused trade.

A closely linked question is: Why do countries gain by trading? The classical economists said that as long as cost conditions differ between two countries, at least one and probably both will gain by trading.

These questions and answers contain the essence of the theory of comparative advantage. The first can be said to state the positive side and the second the normative side. The normative aspect is perhaps the most interesting to the modern student. It demonstrates, on very weak assumptions, that trade will be beneficial to all countries involved in trade. It is important to understand the nature of this theory. It has often been attacked and is often misunderstood. It is still frequently argued that trade is detrimental to countries, today especially in connection with less developed countries. Right from the outset, therefore, we will enter disputed territory. Whatever the student's final opinion is, he will have to undertake a certain amount of theoretical work before he can reach an informed judgement.

One of the central assumptions of the classical economist was that factors of production were fully mobile within countries but not at all mobile between countries. Labor could move freely from New York to Arizona, but it could not cross the border into Mexico. This is an assumption that modern trade theorists have stuck to in elaborating the modern theory of trade. It might seem to be too strong. Some four million workers, for instance, have since 1945 moved north from Portugal, Spain, southern Italy, Greece and Turkey to France, West Germany and Switzerland. But the movements of labor have taken place primarily within somewhat integrated areas. The movement of workers from the United States to Europe, or from Eastern Europe to Western Europe, is still insignificant.

For many purposes the assumption that labor is immobile between countries is valid. Using this (and some other fairly stringent assumptions), modern trade theory has proved some quite startling theorems. One is that trade alone will lead to a complete equalization of factor prices. Even in the absence of factor movements, if only goods can be traded freely, wages will be equalized.

A study of modern trade theory will also help the student understand one of the basic principles of economics, that of *general equilibrium*. Trade theory is essentially a branch of general-equilibrium analysis. It is firmly embedded in the Walrasian tradition. From there stems the preoccupation with creating a theory that is self-contained, where all variables of importance enter and where all variables are interdependent. Such a theory will of necessity be of an abstract and simplified nature. It works with a few well-defined variables and relies on simplifying assumptions, some of which are of a drastic nature. Its strength lies in the fact that it creates a picture of the world which in important ways is complete.

At the heart of general-equilibrium theory are the notions of determinateness and completeness: the relations which describe an economy must form a complete whole where all the variables of the system can be determined. The viewpoint that all factors which make up an economy hang together and are dependent on one another has had a very strong place in economic theorizing. It might even be said to have been *the* distinctive feature of economics as a science. It had also had important policy implications as it has forced policy-makers to try to view the economy as a whole and not simply try to focus the attention on the effect of a parameter change on one or two obvious variables. The pure theory of trade offers the student an excellent illustration of one of the basic notions of economics as a science.

COMPARATIVE STATICS: THE QUESTION OF CHANGE

The pure theory of trade is fundamentally a static theory. It studies some aspects of trading economies in the setting of static equilibrium. It abstracts from one fundamental aspect, that of change.

The simplest way to study the effects of change is by the use of comparative statics. We take an economy in a given equilibrium and then introduce a change in some of the basic variables. This is done in Part II, which studies the effects of economic growth on international trade. The theory in Part II is based on the same type of model as is used in Part I for the pure theory of trade. It is the so-called 'two-by-two-by-two model', i.e. a model with two countries, using two factors of production, labor and capital, to produce two goods, one export commodity and one import commodity.

Growth of production and trade in the world economy was very rapid in the 1950s and 1960s. The more precise theory of growth and trade was also primarily developed during these two decades. From a methodological point of view, this type of theory is also interesting because it illustrates clearly how the static models used in Part I can be developed in a comparative-static way. It clearly demonstrates also some of the basic effects of economic growth on the variables in the trade model. One question it answers is the following. Let us assume that economic growth occurs in two trading economies. What will be the effects on the terms of trade (the ratio of export prices to import prices) and on national income? The answer will depend on which sectors growth occurs in and what the income elasticities are.

The effects of increases in factor endowments and technical progress are also studied. These effects can be handled clearly by the use of geometry. An understanding of this type of theory therefore does not involve very advanced or difficult methods. The effects of technical progress, for instance, are quite striking. An understanding of this kind of theory is essential also for a broad group of problems outside the field of international trade, so it seems appropriate to treat the theory of economic growth and trade rigorously and explicitly.

TRADE POLICY: IS TRADE GOOD OR BAD?

The book is based on the principle of decreasing abstraction. The most theoretical parts are in the beginning, especially in Parts I and II; then, as the exposition develops, it becomes more and more policy oriented – it assumes more of an 'applied' nature. This is because theory is needed to appreciate all the facets of a policy problem. It is logical to start with theory and then proceed to policy, though it perhaps seems that policy problems are sometimes 'easier' to deal with than theoretical questions.

Part III is devoted to problems of trade policy. It both demonstrates principles of trade policy, for example the effects of tariffs on trade, and analyzes the factual development of trade policy. One thing it shows is that free trade, in a world of sovereign states, is practically never the best policy. However, some trade is always better than no trade.

The trade problems of the developed countries and the less developed countries are seldom of the same kind. One of the trade problems confronting less developed countries is the stabilization of commodity prices. Together with the question of tariff preferences, this problem has dominated the few UNCTAD conferences held so far. These questions are also intimately linked with the strivings for a new economic world order.

The proposals for stabilization of commodity prices are of different kinds. The object of some is to stabilize terms of trade between less developed and industrial countries; others, less far-reaching, aim at stabilizing export prices or export proceeds. To understand the true nature of some of these plans, they should be considered against the models of growth and trade developed in Part II.

These models show explicitly the basic factors that determine the development of commodity prices in international trade. Therefore, they show clearly which factors have to be controlled if international prices are to be controlled. They give an example of how recent developments in trade theory can be used to elucidate long-standing policy problems.

Part III analyzes the real content of, and conflicts surrounding, the proposals for a new economic world order. It also treats another important feature of the present era: the development of regional trade groupings.

MACROECONOMIC ASPECTS: DIFFERENT CURRENCIES

One of the obvious differences between trade within a country and international trade is that the latter involves different currencies. If a New Yorker trades with a Californian, they both use the same currency, but trade between a New Yorker and a Canadian involves different currencies.

One essential complication in connection with foreign trade is that the relative values of currencies change. One year, £1 sterling could be worth $2.00 U.S., the next, 1.50. This concerns the balance of payments between countries.

Disequilibria in the external balances of countries give rise to changes in exchange rates. The policy problems surrounding disequilibria in the balance of payments and changes in exchange rates are among the most pertinent ones in the world economy. It anything, they also seem to become more important and to attract increasing attention as the years go by.

Part IV is devoted to these macroeconomic aspects of international economics. The basic principles of foreign exchange markets are discussed and an explanation is given of how a country's balance of payments can be in disequilibrium and how it can be kept in equilibrium.

International monetary matters have been at the forefront of economic theory in recent years. Important reformulations of theory have taken place. They center around what is commonly called the *monetary approach to the balance of payments*. This theory states (to put it somewhat bluntly) that the exchange rate will primarily be determined by changes in the money supply. An increase in the money supply will cause inflation. This in turn will cause a depreciation of the exchange rate. This is an illustration of 'the law of one price': if the price level increases, the value of the currency will fall proportionately.

A critical evaluation of the new theories will be given in Part IV.

INTERNATIONAL MONEY: CAN THE SYSTEM SURVIVE?

The international monetary system has undergone great changes in the 1970s. Up until 1971 the Bretton Woods system reigned, which meant that exchange rates were fixed. During the 1960s this system was put under greater and greater strain. Finally, it broke down. It has now been replaced by a system of floating exchange rates.

The 1970s have been very eventful times. In October 1973 the so-called 'oil crisis' occurred, caused by the drastic increase of oil prices. The oil crisis has had a very large impact on the world economy. It was probably fortunate that the international monetary system operated with floating rates when the increase in oil prices came, so that its effect was somewhat cushioned. A system of floating rates does not, however, solve all balance-of-payments problems. On the contrary, the world economy has seen very large imbalances during the years of floating rates.

Exchange-rate changes have also been very large. Some would argue that this is due to speculation in currencies. Some might take an ominous view on the future of the system: the days of relatively free trade and unregulated capital markets might soon be over. Others are more optimistic.

Part V, which concludes the book, will be devoted to an analysis of the international monetary system.

SELECTED BIBLIOGRAPHY: INTRODUCTION

Each bibliography in this book covers the chapter or chapters that precede it.

The purposes of the bibliographies are to let the reader know which works the author has especially consulted, and to guide the reader for further studies. The bibliographies are selective, but that does not imply that omitted works are not useful. The reader can easily find extensive bibliographies in survey works, especially the ones by Bhagwati, Caves and Chipman listed below. I have been quite selective in my bibliographies because, though selectivity might in some cases be arbitrary, I find that long reading lists often tend to be inefficient: instead of giving the student real guidance, they can drown him in a multitude of works without distinguishing the important, path-breaking articles from the elaborations and repetitions.

International economics, especially in its theoretical parts, has been excellently surveyed in recent years. The most outstanding of these surveys, all containing excellent bibliographies, are:

J. Bhagwati, 'The Pure Theory of International Trade', *Economic Journal,* vol. 74, March 1964, pp. 1–84.

R. E. Caves, *Trade and Economic Structure,* Cambridge, Mass., Harvard University Press, 1960.

J. Chipman, 'A Survey of the Theory of International Trade, Parts I – III', *Econometrica,* vols 33 and 34, July 1965, October 1965, and January 1966, pp. 477–519, 685–760, and 18–76.

When one comes to the monetary parts of international economics, no survey of the same calibre exists. The standard work in this area is still:

J. E. Meade, *The Balance of Payments,* London, Oxford University Press, 1951.

One work that contains a survey of a more personal kind is:

R. E. Mundell, *International Economics,* New York, Macmillan, 1968.

Two collections of readings published by the American Economic Association are of great interest. They are:

R. E. Caves and H. G. Johnson (eds), *Readings in International Economics,* Homewood, Ill., Irwin, 1968.

H. S. Ellis and L. M. Metzler (eds), *Readings in the Theory of International Trade,* Homewood, Ill., Irwin, 1949.

These two books will be referred to in subsequent bibliographies by the abbreviations *RIE* and *RTIT.* Two older books that contain interesting material from the point of view of the development of the subject are:

G. Haberler, *The Theory of International Trade,* London, William Hodge & Co., 1936.

J. Viner, *Studies in the Theory of International Trade,* London, Allen & Unwin, 1938.

Among textbooks of about the same level of difficulty, the following ones can be mentioned:

R. E. Caves and R. W. Jones, *World Trade and Payments,* Boston, Little, Brown, 1973.

H. G. Grubel, *International Economics,* Homewood, Ill., Irwin, 1977.

R. H. Heller, *International Trade: Theory and Empirical Evidence,* 2nd ed., Englewood Cliffs, N.J., Prentice-Hall, 1973.

R. H. Heller, *International Monetary Economics,* Englewood Cliffs, N.J., Prentice-Hall, 1974.

C. Kindleberger, *International Economics,* 5th ed., Homewood Ill., Irwin, 1973.

W. M. Scammell, *International Trade and Payments,* Toronto, Toronto University Press, 1974.

Among graduate-level books, using more mathematics, are the following:

M. C. Kemp, *The Pure Theory of International Trade and Investment,* Englewood Cliffs, N.J., Prentice-Hall, 1969.

T. Negishi, *General Equilibrium Theory and International Trade,* Amsterdam, North-Holland, 1972.

I. F. Pearce, *International Trade,* London, Macmillan, 1970.

R. M. Stern, *The Balance of Payments: Theory and Economic Policy,* Chicago, Aldine, 1973.

A. Takayama, *International Trade,* New York, Holt, Rinehart & Winston, 1972.

The student who is interested in finding data can go to the statistical yearbooks and international trade statistics published by various countries and international organizations. Two standard monthly sources for data are:

International Monetary Fund, *International Financial Statistics.*

United Nations, *Monthly Bulletin of Statistics.*

A useful reference book is:

R. G. D. Allen and J. S. Ely (eds), *International Trade Statistics,* New York, Wiley, 1953.

The exposition in this book builds primarily on articles published in the leading scientific journals. These journals will be referred to by the following abbreviations in the bibliographies:

AER – *American Economic Review*
EJ – *Economic Journal*
Ec – *Economica*
JPE – *Journal of Political Economy*
MS – *Manchester School of Economic and Social Studies*
OEP – *Oxford Economic Papers*
QJE – *Quarterly Journal of Economics*
RES – *Review of Economic Studies*
RE&S – *Review of Economics and Statistics*
SP – *Staff Papers* (of the International Monetary Fund)

PART I

The pure theory of international trade

1
The theory of comparative advantage and the gains from trade

One of the basic questions that the theory of international trade has to answer is what determines trade. Put another way, why do countries gain by trading? Economics does have an answer – one that goes back more than 150 years – in the theory of comparative advantage. This theory, formulated around 1815, is usually connected with the name of David Ricardo.[1] The theory of comparative advantage, or, as it is sometimes called, the theory of comparative costs, is one of the oldest, still unchallenged theories of economics.

Before tackling the theoretical aspects of this concept it might be worth while to take a quick look at its historical background – at the kind of setting out of which the theory of comparative advantage developed.

The economic doctrine that prevailed during the first two centuries of the development of the modern national state – the seventeenth and eighteenth centuries – was *mercantilism.* The doctrine of mercantilism had many modern features: it was highly nationalistic, it viewed the well-being of the own nation to be of prime importance, it favored the regulation and planning of economic activity as an efficient means of fostering the goals of the nation, and it generally viewed foreign trade with suspicion.

The most important way in which a country could grow rich, according to the doctrine of mercantilism, was by acquiring precious metals, especially gold. Single individuals, however, were not to be trusted: they might also like gold, but perhaps they liked other things even more. Left to themselves, they might exchange gold for satin and linen, spices from India, or sugar from Cuba, or indulge in whatever private pleasures they preferred, to the detriment of the stock of precious metals stored in the nation. To prevent such undertakings, the nation had to control foreign trade. Exports were viewed favorably as long as they brought in good, solid gold, but imports were viewed with apprehension, as depriving the country of its true source of richness – precious metals. Therefore, trade had to be regulated, controlled and restricted, no specific virtue being seen in having a large volume of trade.

It was against this background that English classical economics developed, for mercantilism was the credo that Adam Smith and David Ricardo rebelled against.[2] English classical economics was an offspring of liberalism and the Enlightenment – of a general philosophy that stressed the importance of the individual and viewed the nation as nothing more than the sum of its inhabitants.

For Smith, as for Ricardo, the supreme subject of economics was the consumer: man labored and produced in order to consume. And anything that could increase consumption, or, to use Ricardo's picturesque phrase, 'the sum of enjoyments', ought to be viewed with favor.

ADAM SMITH AND THE ABSOLUTE ADVANTAGE OF TRADE

Adam Smith saw clearly that a country could gain by trading. The tailor does not make his own shoes; he exchanges a suit for shoes. Thereby both the shoe-maker and the tailor gain. In the same manner, Smith argued, a whole country can gain by trading with other countries.

If it takes 10 labor units to manufacture 1 unit of good A in country I but 20 labor units in country II, and if it takes 20 units of labor to manufacture 1 unit of good B in country I but only 10 labor units in country II, then both countries can gain by trading.

If the two countries exchanged the 2 goods at a ratio of 1 to 1, so that 1 unit of good A is exchanged for 1 unit of good B, country I could get 1 unit of good B by sacrificing only 10 units of labor, whereas it would have to give up 20 units of labor if it produced the good itself. Likewise, country II would have to sacrifice only 10 units of labor to get 1 unit of good A, whereas it would have to give up 20 units of labor if it produced it itself. The implication of this is clearly that both countries could have more of both goods, with a given effort, by trading.

This was a simple and powerful illustration of the benefits of trade, and on it Adam Smith rested his plea for non-interference – for free trade as the best policy for trade between nations. Smith's argument seems convincing, but it is not very deep. It was left to Torrens[3] and Ricardo to produce the stronger and more subtle argument for the benefits of trade contained in the theory of comparative advantage.

DAVID RICARDO AND THE THEORY OF COMPARATIVE ADVANTAGE

Ricardo did not object to Smith's analysis. It is obvious that if one country has an absolute advantage over the other country in one line of production and the other country has an absolute advantage over the first country in a second line of production, both countries can gain by trading. A great deal of trade, perhaps most trade, is governed by such differences.

But what if one country is more productive than another country in all lines of production? If country I can produce all goods with less labor cost than country II, does it still benefit the countries to trade? Ricardo's answer was yes. So long as country II is not equally less productive in all lines of production, it still pays both countries to trade.

We will spend some time elucidating this principle, as it is of basic importance to the theory of trade. We may as well start with Ricardo's own model before going on to more modern means of demonstration.

Ricardo used England and Portugal as examples in his demonstration, the two goods they produced being wine and cloth. Being a courteous Englishman, and living in an era when no one had heard about 'under-developed countries', Ricardo assumed that Portugal was more efficient in making both cloth and wine. Table 1.1 shows how Ricardo summed up the cost conditions in the two countries.

TABLE 1.1

Cost comparisons

	Labor cost of production (in hours)	
	1 unit of wine	1 unit of cloth
Portugal	80	90
England	120	100

According to this model, Portugal has an *absolute advantage* in the production of wine as well as in the production of cloth, because the labor cost of production for each unit of the two commodities is less in Portugal than in England.

To demonstrate that trade between England and Portugal will, even in this case, lead to gains for both countries, it is useful to introduce the concept of *opportunity cost*. The opportunity cost for a good X is the amount of other goods which have to be given up in order to produce one (additional) unit of X. Table 1.2 gives the opportunity costs for producing wine and cloth in Portugal and England. These costs have been constructed on the basis of the information given in Table 1.1.

TABLE 1.2

Opportunity costs

	Opportunity costs for	
	Wine	Cloth
Portugal	80/90 = 8/9	90/80 = 9/8
England	120/100 = 12/10	100/120 = 10/12

A country has a *comparative advantage* in producing a good if the opportunity cost for producing the good is lower at home than in the other country. Table 1.2 shows that Portugal has the lower opportunity cost of the two countries in producing wine, while England has the lower opportunity cost in producing cloth. Thus Portugal has a comparative advantage in the production of wine and England has a comparative advantage in the production of cloth.

We should now further clarify the meaning of the term 'comparative advantage'. In order to speak about comparative advantage there must be at least two countries and two goods. We compare the opportunity costs of the production of each good in both countries. As long as the two countries' opportunity costs for one good differ, one country has a comparative advantage in the production of one of the two goods, while the other country has a comparative advantage in the production of the other good. As long as this is the case, both countries will gain from trade, regardless of the fact that one of the countries might have an absolute disadvantage in both lines of production.

RICARDO ON THE GAINS FROM TRADE

Let us assume that Portugal and England do not trade but produce and consume in isolation. The prices of cloth and wine in the two countries are then determined by their respective costs of production.

If in England it takes 120 hours of labor to make 1 unit of wine, while it takes only 100 hours to make 1 unit of cloth, clearly wine must then be more expensive per unit than cloth – 1 unit of wine will cost 120/100, or 1.2, units of cloth.

If in Portugal it takes 80 hours of labor to make 1 unit of wine and 90 hours to make 1 unit of cloth, cloth will be more expensive than wine – 1 unit of wine will cost 80/90, or 0.89, units of cloth.

Let us now open the possibility of trade. If England could import 1 unit of wine at a price less than 1.2 units of cloth, she would gain by doing so. If Portugal could import more than 0.89 units of cloth for 1 unit of wine, she, too, would gain. Therefore, if the international price of 1 unit of wine is somewhere between 1.2 and 0.89 units of cloth, both countries will gain by trading.

Let us assume further that in the international market 1 unit of wine exchanges for 1 unit of cloth. It is then advantageous for England to export cloth and import wine, because in the absence of trade England would have to give up 120 hours of labor for every unit of wine she wants. By trading she can, instead, with 100 hours of effort, produce 1 unit of cloth and then exchange this unit of cloth for 1 unit of wine. Under *autarky* – i.e. a country producing and consuming in isolation – she would have to give up 120 hours of labor for every unit of wine she wanted, whereas with trade she only needs to give up 100 hours. With each 20 hours left over she can produce more cloth and enjoy a higher level of consumption – or the workers can rest, and trade will make possible more leisure with a given amount of consumption.

Portugal will also gain from trading. In isolation she would have to give up 90 hours of labor to get 1 unit of cloth. Now she can make 1 unit of wine with the effect of 80 hours of labor and exchange this unit of wine for 1 unit of cloth in the international market. Every 10 hours of labor freed by this process can then be used for either increased production or increased leisure.

Thus trade offers each country the possibility of specializing in the line of its comparative advantage and then exchanging these products for those in which she has a comparative disadvantage. Both countries can reallocate their factors of production to the line where their comparative advantage lies and then export this product and import the other product. In short, with a given amount of resources each country can consume more by trading than in isolation.

Let us now see how the gains from trade can be illustrated by geometric means. We will begin by introducing the concept of a *production-possibility curve*.

FIGURE 1.1
Production-possibility curves

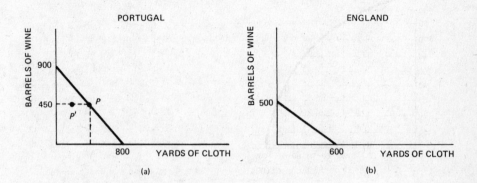

(a)

(b)

THE PRODUCTION-POSSIBILITY CURVE

The quantity of each good a country produces will depend on her factor endowments and on her technical knowledge. By 'factor endowments' we mean the amounts of factors of production the country possesses. If we were to go on thinking in Ricardian terms, how much each country could produce would depend on how much labor she had with the production techniques available to her.

Assume that each day Portugal has 72,000 working hours at its disposal and England 60,000. According to the information that we already have about how much labor is required to produce wine and cloth in the two countries, we find that Portugal can produce 900 units (barrels) of wine if she specializes completely in wine production and that England can produce 500 units of wine if she does the same. Analogously, Portugal can produce 800 (yards) units of cloth if she specializes completely in this line of production, while England, under complete specialization in cloth, can product 600 units.

Table 1.2 lists the opportunity costs for producing wine and cloth in the two countries. These costs are independent of the production volume. For example, one always has to sacrifice 8/9 units of cloth in Portugal to get one more unit of wine. Given, as in the present case, constant opportunity costs, the production-possibility curve will be a straight line. The production-possibility curves for Portugal and England are illustrated geometrically in Figure 1.1.

In isolation or autarky, the country ought to produce and consume at some point on the production-possibility curve. By definition, she cannot reach a point in the commodity space outside the curve. The reason for this is that with the amounts of factors of production the country has, plus her knowledge, she can only produce some combination of goods indicated by the production-possibility curve. The country can, on the other hand, produce any combination

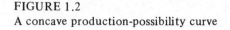

FIGURE 1.2

A concave production-possibility curve

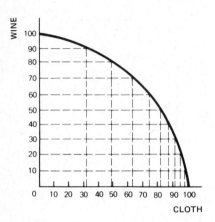

of goods represented by a point inside the curve such as point P' in Figure 1.1(a). This, however, is clearly not an efficient point, because by moving out to point P on the curve, the country can produce the same amount of wine as at P' and a larger amount of cloth. Therefore, assuming as always that more of any commodity – wine or cloth – is preferred to less of it, point P is preferable to point P'. In fact, *any* point inside the curve is less desirable than a point on the curve.

VARIABLE OPPORTUNITY COSTS: A CONCAVE PRODUCTION-POSSIBILITY CURVE

The economic meaning of constant opportunity costs, or a straight-line production-possibility curve, is that all factors of production are equally efficient in all lines of production. This is not a very realistic assumption. If, for simplicity's sake, we think in terms of only one factor of production – labor, for example – we would expect some workers to be especially efficient in the production of wine and others more efficient in making cloth. If this is the case, the production-possibility curve will resemble the one shown in Figure 1.2 which illustrates variable opportunity costs.

    Let us say that we, as a country, start by being completely specialized in wine, producing 100 units of wine. If we give up production of 10 units of wine by shifting the workers most suited for production of cloth to the cloth industry, we can produce over 30 units of cloth; by giving up still 10 more units of wine, we can produce almost 20 additional units of cloth; and so on. We can see that the amount of extra cloth we can produce by decreasing production of wine with a given amount is steadily decreasing as we move downward along the production-possibility curve. The *opportunity cost* of cloth in terms of wine is

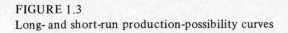

FIGURE 1.3
Long- and short-run production-possibility curves

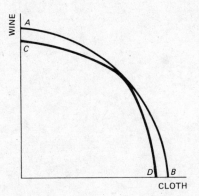

therefore steadily *increasing* as we increase the production of cloth and decrease the production of wine.

So far we have been considering only one factor of production, labor. The law of increasing opportunity cost, however, does not in any way hinge upon the number of factors of production. If we had instead three factors of production – labor, land and capital, for example – we would still expect some factor to be more suited for production of wine than for production of cloth. Whenever this is the case, the opportunity cost for increasing production of a certain good increases, and the production-possibility curve will be concave to the origin, as it is in Figure 1.2.

As the shape of the production- possibility curve is determined by production conditions, the ease with which factors of production can be moved from one industry to another is one important element in determining it. In the short run we would expect the adaptability of the economy to be low and that an increase in the production of one good from a given position on the curve would be possible only with sharply rising opportunity costs. In Figure 1.3 the production-possibility curve *CD* illustrates this situation. In the long run, given opportunities for retraining workers, readjusting the capital stock, etc., we would expect the substitution possibilities in the economy to be larger; the curve *AB* illustrates this situation. Commodity prices also play a significant part in a situation where there are variable opportunity costs, and if prices shift, the producers adjust production to obtain the greatest advantage. Figure 1.4 illustrates this interplay between shifting prices and shifting production.

Let us assume that at any given moment relative commodity prices in an economy are indicated by the line P_0P_0. With these prices, producers will produce at point A, i.e. they will produce OQ of wine and OR of cloth. This is because the price ratio P_0P_0 is tangential to the production-possibility curve at A, which means that opportunity cost in production equals relative prices. If, with the same prices, the country were to produce at some other point, say

FIGURE 1.4
Role of shifting prices

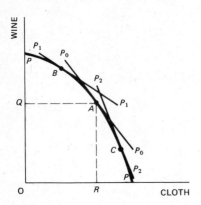

B, the opportunity cost of producing more cloth would be lower than its price, and producers could increase their profits by making more cloth. Only at A are relative prices and opportunity costs equal and profits maximized.

If prices were to change to P_1P_1, for example, and wine thus became more expensive, producers would again reallocate factors of production, produce more wine, and move to point B, which is the new optimal point. Likewise, if the price of wine fell and the new price line were P_2P_2, they would move to point C.

COMMUNITY INDIFFERENCE CURVES

If we are referring to the demand of only one consumer, we can use indifference curves to illustrate demand factors. In international trade, however, we are concerned with a whole community or a whole nation, and things become more complicated. As it is not possible to draw an easy analogy when going from one to many, we cannot say that indifference curves can be used to illustrate the demand of a whole nation in the same way as they can be used to illustrate the demand of a single consumer unless some very restrictive assumptions are used.

Let us now see how a *community indifference curve* can be derived. We take the simplest possible example by assuming that we have a community with only two members, a and b. Each of the two consumers have been given a certain amount of wine and a certain amount of cloth to begin with. They trade with each other until they reach the best possible point of exchange, given their initial resources. This can be called an 'efficient' point. Such an efficient point is P_1 in Figure 1.5. At P_1, consumer a has, say, the utility level u_a, and consumer b the utility level u_b.

If we now take away a certain amount of wine from the original commodity bundle (or national incomes of a and b), how much more cloth must we give the two consumers to make both of them as well off as at P_1? Doing this, we learn

FIGURE 1.5
Community indifference curves

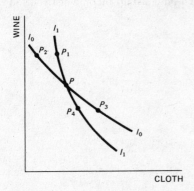

that P and P_4 are indifferent to point P_1. Combining these three points, we get the curve $I_1 I_1$, which is an example of a community indifference curve. The utility levels u_a and u_b are thus assumed to be constant along the curve, so that the two consumers separately get the same utility, or level of satisfaction, along the curve.

Let us again take the two consumers and the commodity bundle represented by point P on the indifference curve $I_1 I_1$. But now we make an experiment: suppose we change the income distribution. Let us assume that P is still an efficient point even with this new income distribution between a and b. We once more ask: how much less wine and more cloth need we give the consumers to keep their respective utility levels constant? (We can call the new utility levels u_a^* and u_b^*, where, say, $u_a^* > u_a$ and $u_b^* < u_b$.)

We now find that P_2 and P_3 are indifferent to P and that the new community indifference curve is given by $I_0 I_0$.

From this we can see that it is possible for community indifference curves to intersect. The commodity bundle represented by point P in Figure 1.5 could for one income distribution be equivalent to the commodity bundle represented by P_1, but for another income distribution it could be equivalent to the commodity bundle represented by P_2. In other words, for a certain income distribution P_1, P and P_4 could be indifferent to each other, whereas for another income distribution P_2, P and P_3 could be indifferent. Curves that represent different income distributions can thus cross each other.

It can also be added that if all the consumers had the same preferences and if individual incomes were identical at all national income levels, community indifference curves would also be well behaved. To find a society characterized by such a degree of complete communism is not, however, an easy task.

The main point to keep in mind when using community indifference curves is that concerning the constancy of income distribution. Only if we assume a constant income distribution can we vindicate the use of community indifference curves and make meaningful comparisons. Making this assumption means that we can get community indifference curves such as those shown in Figure 1.6 which obey the same rules as ordinary indifference curves, so we can say that

FIGURE 1.6
Community indifference curves
based on constant income distribution

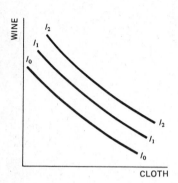

every point on $I_1 I_1$ is superior to every point on $I_0 I_0$, and so on. This means that as we move along the production-possibility curve with changes in production conditions, the changes in income distribution thus induced are being neutralized by an appropriate redistribution policy.

THE GAINS FROM TRADE RESTATED

We can now restate the meaning of gains from trade, combining supply and demand factors. By combining the supply and demand sides of the economy we can illustrate how equilibrium is reached under autarky in an economy with perfect competition. This is shown in Figure 1.7. The optimum point is the one where an indifference curve is tangential to the production-possibility curve. This happens at point S, where the indifference curve $I_2 I_2$ is tangential to the production-possibility curve TT. Drawing the tangent line to this point on the two curves we obtain the price line PP. At point S the national income is maximized, because the marginal rate of substitution in consumption equals the opportunity cost in production. Given the shape of the indifference curves and given the production-possibility curve, S is the optimum point. This is demonstrated by the fact that if the society chose to produce at some other point on the production-possibility curve, that choice would place the consumers on an indifference curve to the left of $I_2 I_2$ (for instance, $I_1 I_1$), which represents a lower level of utility.

The possibility of trading means that the country can produce and consume at prices that differ from those prevailing in isolation. Figure 1.8 illustrates this situation. The international terms of trade are given by the price line $P_2 P_2$. That means that cloth is more expensive in the international market than it is in the home market. Domestic producers will take advantage of this fact and move some factors of production from wine to cloth. The country will then reallocate its factors of production and move to point Q, where $P_2 P_2$ is tangential to the production-possibility curve. This means that the marginal rate of transformation

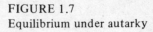

FIGURE 1.7
Equilibrium under autarky

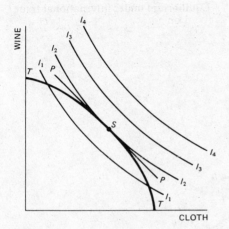

in production equals the international terms of trade. The country will then export AQ of cloth in exchange for CA of wine, moving to point C, where the terms of trade are tangential to the indifference curve I_4I_4. Thereby, the marginal rate of substitution in consumption is made equal to the terms of trade. Given the production-possibility curve and the international price ratio, point C represents the best point in the commodity space the society can achieve.

It might be useful to think of the gains from trade as consisting of two parts: one depending on the possibility for exchange, the other on the possibility for specialization in production. If for some reason the country could not change its pattern of production, it would have to continue producing at point S. It could still gain from trade by exchanging at the new price ratio, moving from S to C' (the price line P_1S is parallel to P_2P_2). This would place the country on the indifference curve I_3I_3, which represents a higher level of utility than does I_2I_2. The gains from exchange could thus be said to consist of the movement from S to C'.

This, however, would not represent an optimal situation, because the ratio of transformation in production at S is not equal to the ratio of substitution in consumption at C'. Therefore, the country would be better off by changing its production and moving to Q, and from there to C. The move from C' to C can be said to represent the gain from specializing in production.

THE FLAW IN RICARDO'S ARGUMENT

It is important to remember that community indifference curves such as the ones in Figure 1.8 can be constructed only if the income distribution is kept unchanged. When moving from S to Q the income distribution will move in favor of the factors of production especially well suited for the production of cloth, the country's export good, while it will move against those engaged in wine

FIGURE 1.8
Equilibrium under international trade

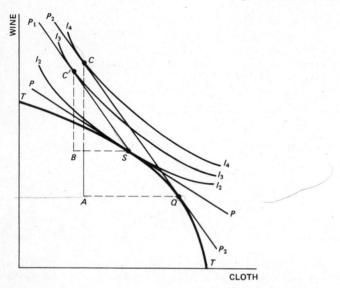

production. Somehow the wine producers will have to be compensated so that they are at least as well off as they were at point *S*. Only if this is done and something is still left over to make the cloth producers better off than at *S* can we say that the country gains from trade in an unambiguous sense.

This was the main point that Ricardo and the classical economists overlooked in their argument about the benefits from trade, and one that has been raised by modern welfare economics. The classical economists thought in terms of each individual's utility. So does modern welfare economics. There is no guarantee that every consumer will be better off under free trade than under no trade, even though the country as a whole will be better off. Only if a policy of redistribution is pursued can free trade guarantee such an outcome. Thus free trade leads to a potential increase in welfare for everyone.[4]

As we mentioned earlier, the doctrine of free trade was one of the cornerstones of economic liberalism. We have now arrived at the slightly paradoxical situation that this doctrine can be saved only if a policy of intervention is pursued concomitantly with it. Hence it follows that economic liberalism, in the sense of letting market conditions determine production and consumption, can be justified on welfare grounds without reservations, only if a policy of redistribution goes with it.

OFFER CURVES

Before concluding this chapter, we should also introduce another standard tool

FIGURE 1.9
Price ratio under autarky

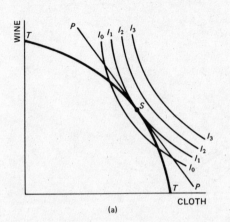

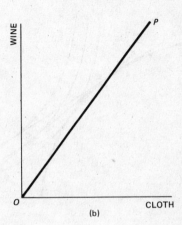

(a)

(b)

of analysis in international economics, the *offer curve,* and show how gains from trade can be illustrated by the use of this tool.

We have seen how, when countries trade with each other, international terms of trade are established by the interaction of supply and demand. Another way of stating this interaction is by the use of offer curves, first used by Edgeworth and Marshall, and since then often used in international economics, especially for pedagogical purposes. Some perhaps doubt the efficacy of using offer curves, especially for direct analytical purposes. They are not very easy to derive in a clear and simple way. As they are regarded as standard tools, however, we will now show one way in which they can be derived, using the geometric tools we are familiar with.

Figure 1.9(a) shows a production-possibility curve and a set of community indifference curves that characterize demand in the country. In the absence of trade, equilibrium will be established at point S, where an indifference curve is tangential to the production-possibility curve. At this point, the marginal rate of transformation in production equals the marginal rate of substitution in consumption. The highest level of satisfaction that the country can enjoy under autarky is that symbolized by the indifference curve $I_1 I_1$. The price ratio that will be ruling under autarky is given by the line PP, which is tangential to the production-possibility curve and the indifference curve at S.

In Figure 1.9(a) we have depicted the relative price by the line PP, which has a negative slope. We could, however, also depict the same relative price ratio by a line with a positive slope. This is done in Figure 1.9(b) by the ray OP.

Suppose now that we open up the possibility of international trade. Production and demand conditions in country I are as shown in Figure 1.9(a). Which commodity country I will export and import depends on the international terms of trade that are established. Let us suppose that country I has a comparative advantage in production of wine and that the new terms of trade established under

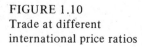

FIGURE 1.10
Trade at different
international price ratios

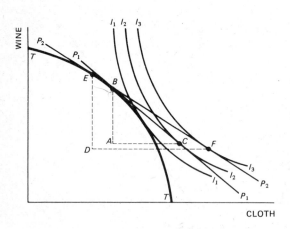

CLOTH

trade are as shown by the line P_1P_1 in Figure 1.10. Country I will then produce
at point B and consume at point C, and export AB of wine in exchange for AC imports of cloth. By trade, country I can move to the indifference curve I_2I_2, which
represents a higher level of satisfaction than does I_1I_1, the highest one obtainable
under autarky. Had the terms of trade been even more favorable, for instance
such as represented by P_2P_2 in Figure 1.10, the country could have reached indifference curve I_3I_3 by trading DE of wine for DF of cloth.

We can now show how country I's volume of exports and imports change as
the terms of trade change. This is done in Figure 1.11. On the vertical axis we
have net exports of wine and on the horizontal axis we have net imports of cloth.
The triangle OAc in Figure 1.11 corresponds to the trade triangle BAC in Figure
1.10. It shows that if the terms of trade are OA (these terms of trade are the
same as those depicted by P_1P_1 in Figure 1.10), Ow of wine will be exchanged
for Oc of cloth. If the terms of trade instead should change to OB (which corresponds to P_2P_2 in Figure 1.10), Ow_1 of wine would be exchanged for Oc_1 of cloth
(the triangle OBc_1 corresponds to the trade triangle EDF in Figure 1.10.

In this way we can trace out a pattern of points that show how the traded
volumes change when the terms of trade change. If we join together all these
points for country I, we get a curve such as OC in Figure 1.11. OC is an example
of an offer curve. Thus an offer curve shows how the volumes traded change
when the terms of trade change.

By analogous reasoning we can construct an offer curve for country II. An
example of such an offer curve is OD in Figure 1.11. The offer curves of the two
trading countries intersect at point R. This is the only equilibrium point and the
equilibrium terms of trade are given by the ray OR from the origin. Only at
these terms of trade will exports of wine (Ow_2) from country I equal imports of
wine from country II and imports of cloth into country I (Oc_2) equal exports of
cloth from country II, and hence markets be cleared.

FIGURE 1.11
Offer curves

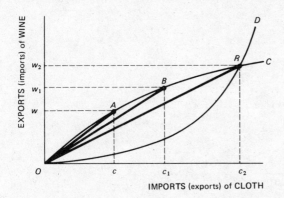

The shape of the offer curves are determined by both supply and demand conditions in the respective countries. The limits within which they will fall are given by the autarky terms of trade in the two countries (shown by the slope of the respective offer curve as it starts from the origin). With improving terms of trade, a country is willing to offer more and more of its exports for more imports. After a certain amount of trade, however, the country could become more and more unwilling to accept an increase in the amount of imports, even though they are offered at improving terms of trade. An example of this is given in Figure 1.12, where country I's offer curve becomes inelastic after point P. After this point, country I is willing to offer only a decreasing amount of its exports (wine) even though its terms of trade are improving.

It is not possible to infer anything *a priori* about a country's offer curve. One has to study a given country's supply and demand conditions and then derive an offer curve in the way described. The exact shape of the curve depends on the given empirical conditions that prevail.

When we derived the other curve, we argued as though the terms of trade were changing for some exogenous reason and then derived the shape of the curve. This was a pedagogical device and must not be misunderstood. The offer curve is a general-equilibrium concept. It is determined jointly by production and consumption conditions. It is more appropriate to say that these conditions determine the shape of the trading partners' offer curves, which in turn determine the terms of trade.

Offer curves might seem to be simple concepts but they are, in fact, the result of a complicated interplay of factors. This makes them somewhat hard to deal with, as it is difficult to see how a change in more basic concepts – supply and demand – exactly influences an offer curve. Some economists use offer curves extensively. We use them very sparingly. Only on one occasion, in Chapter 13, when dealing with the theory of tariffs, will offer curves be used. In the rest of the analysis we have preferred to use other types of instruments. However, by

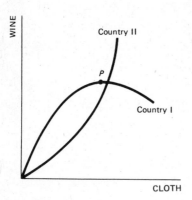

FIGURE 1.12
Inelastic offer curve

now the student should have a basic understanding of the meaning of offer curves.

Before coming to some basic theorems of international economics in Chapter 3, we will, in Chapter 2, introduce some of the geometric tools that will be used extensively throughout the book.

SELECTED BIBLIOGRAPHY: CHAPTER 1

Classical expositions of the theory of comparative advantage are contained in:

G. Haberler, *The Theory of International Trade*, especially ch. 10.

J. Viner, *Studies in the Theory of International Trade*, ch. 8.

The surveys by Bhagwati and Chipman also contain excellent parts on the theory of comparative costs. Chipman, part I, contains the definitive exposition of this theory. Among empirical tests of the theory of comparative advantage one should especially mention:

G. D. A. MacDougall, 'British and American Exports: A Study Suggested by the Theory of Comparative Costs, Parts I and II,' *EJ*, December 1951 and September 1952 (Part I reprinted in *RIE*).

A survey of the concept of gains from trade among the classics and early neoclassics is found in Viner, ch. 9. A classical article is:

P. A. Samuelson, 'The Gains from International Trade', *Canadian Journal of Economics and Political Science*, May 1939 (reprinted in *RTIT*).

Later contributions are contained in:

J. M. Grandmont and D. McFadden, 'A Technical Note on Classical Gains From Trade', *Journal of International Economics*, vol. 2, May 1972.

M. C. Kemp, 'The Gain from International Trade', *EJ*, December 1962.

P. Kenen, 'Distribution, Demand and Equilibrium in International Trade: a Diagrammatic Analysis', *Kyklos,* vol. 12, 1959.

E. Olsen, 'Udenrigshandelens Gevinst', *Nationalökonomisk Tidsskrift,* vol. 96, 1958.

P. A. Samuelson, 'The Gain from International Trade Once Again', *EJ,* December 1962.

The two articles that introduced the use of production-possibility curves are:

W. W. Leontief, 'The Use of Indifference Curves in International Trade', *QJE,* May 1933 (reprinted in *RTIT*).

A. P. Lerner, 'The Diagrammatical Representation of Cost Conditions in International Trade', *Ec,* 1932 (reprinted in Lerner, *Essays in Economic Analysis,* London, Macmillan, 1953).

For a discussion of the signification of community indifference curves see:

T. Scitovsky, 'A Reconsideration of the Theory of Tariffs', *RES,* Summer 1942 (reprinted in *RTIT*).

2
Production functions in international trade: the box diagram

In Chapter 1 we discussed the theory of comparative advantage in terms of a one-factor model, where the only factor of production was labor. What gave rise to trade was different cost ratios in production. It is now time to go a step further and look into what determines these cost ratios.

We did not dwell at any length on the causes of trade in Chapter 1. However, what determines trade in the Ricardian setting is quite obvious. If there is only one factor of production, labor, and the cost of production of any good is determined by how much labor it takes to produce a unit of the good, differences between countries in the relative productivity of labor will determine trade.

If we want to use modern jargon, we can say that different countries have different production functions and that differences in production functions are the causes of trade. This might be called the *positive* side of Ricardo's theory of comparative advantage, as it contains a scientific proposition about the causes of trade. The theory of comparative advantage can also be viewed as a proposition about gains from trade. This we might call its *normative* side, because, as we have seen, it contains a value judgment, at least by implication.

Modern trade theory, however, offers another explanation for the causes of trade. This is contained in the so-called Heckscher–Ohlin theory of trade, which says that trade is caused by the fact that different countries have different factor endowments.[1] This is a more fruitful approach than Ricardo's, as it brings factors of production explicity into the picture and forces us to study in a detailed fashion the interrelationships between commodity and factor prices, between amounts of input and output. We will have to take a general-equilibrium approach to the study of the trading relationships between countries. By so doing, we will train ourselves in the application of the first principle of economics, the notion that 'everything in an economy hangs together'.

To understand the Heckscher–Ohlin theory of trade, we need to introduce additional geometric tools. We do so in this chapter, which is primarily devoted to a derivation of different tools of analysis. We start by presenting the type of production function that we are going to use in the following chapters of this book, namely linearly homogeneous production functions.

THE MEANING OF LINEARLY HOMOGENEOUS PRODUCTION FUNCTIONS

A production function shows the relationship between input of factors of production, in the following analysis capital and labor, and output of a good (or output of several goods, if we assume joint production). For many reasons it would be advantageous if we would use unspecified production functions. This means that to derive the results we wanted, to prove certain theorems, we would need to assume only that a relationship exists between inputs and outputs, but we would not have to assume anything specific about the nature of this relationship.

As a matter of fact, when we come to the effects of technical progress on international trade we will refer to results that have been derived using only this weak assumption. But for most of the theorems of trade theory a more specific relationship between inputs and outputs has to be assumed.

The standard constraint on the production function that we will have to assume is that the production function is homogeneous of the first degree, or, another way of expressing the same fact, that the production function is linearly homogeneous.[2] By this is meant that the production function is such that if the inputs are increased by a certain proportion, output is increased by the same proportion. If, for instance, both labor and capital are doubled, output is also doubled. If labor and capital are increased by 10 per cent, output is also increased by 10 per cent, and so on.

The reader is probably familiar with the concept of *marginal productivity* from elementary production theory. By marginal productivity of labor is meant the increase in output caused by an increase of 1 unit of labor, assuming that the amount of capital is held constant. Analogously, the marginal productivity of capital is defined as the increase in output we get if we increase the amount of capital by 1 unit, keeping constant the other factors of production – in our case labor.

Let us assume that the marginal productivities of labor and capital are positive. This means that if the labor force increases, with a given stock of capital, total output will increase. There is nothing unusual about this assumption. If we increase labor with a given stock of machinery, we certainly would expect to be able to produce more, as we would if we were to increase the number of machines with a given labor force.

We further assume that the marginal productivity of labor is a decreasing function of the amount of labor used. It is easy to see the common-sense reasoning for the declining marginal productivity of labor. As we keep increasing labor with a given stock of capital, the workers will have relatively fewer and fewer machines to work with. Therefore, the more workers we add, the lower will be the productivity of the last-added worker. By analogous reasoning, we assume that the marginal productivity of capital is a decreasing function of the amount of capital used.

Assuming that the production function is homogeneous of degree 1 and that the marginal productivities of labor and capital are positive, we can state that the marginal productivity of labor increases when the stock of capital used increases. The reason is that if we add more and more machines with a given number of workers, the workers will become more and more productive. Likewise, if we add more workers to a given stock of machinery, they can tend the machines better, and the marginal productivity of capital will go up. Thus the marginal productivity of capital is an increasing function of the amount of labor used.

It is now time to observe another important and useful feature of a linearly

FIGURE 2.1
Isoquants

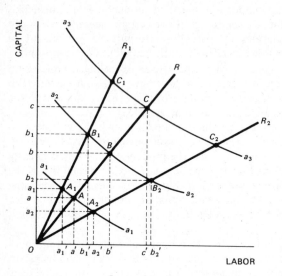

homogeneous production function: <u>as long as the two factors of production are</u> <u>combined in the same proportion, the marginal productivities of the two factors</u> <u>stay unchanged.</u> Another way of expressing this fact is by saying that the marginal productivities depend only on the ratios in which the two factors are combined. It is important to understand this fact, and we illustrate it geometrically in Figure 2.1.

Along any ray from the origin, such as OR, the two factors are combined in the same proportion. Thus Oa of capital divided by Oa' of labor at A equals Ob of capital divided by Ob' of labor at B, which also equals Oc of capital divided by Oc' of labor at C, and so on. Therefore, the marginal productivity of labor is the same along all of OR, as is the marginal productivity of capital.

The same holds for OR_1, so the marginal productivity of labor is the same at A_1, B_1, and C_1, and analogously for the marginal productivity of capital. In the same vein, the marginal productivities of the two factors of production are constant along OR_2.

We can now compare the marginal productivity of labor along the isoquant $a_1 a_1$, for instance at the three points A_1, A and A_2. It is then immediately clear that the marginal productivity of labor is higher at A_1 than it is at A, and that it is higher at A than at A_2, because the ratio of capital to labor – the capital intensity – is higher at A_1 than at A, and higher at A than at A_2. This means that each worker has more capital, more machinery to work with, at A_1 than at A. The same holds for A as compared with A_2. <u>The more capital-intensive the</u> <u>methods of production are, the higher is the marginal productivity of labor.</u> In

FIGURE 2.2
Equilibrium in production under free competition

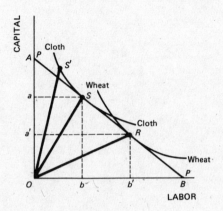

the same way, the more labor-intensive the methods of production, the higher is the marginal productivity of capital.

But what will determine which methods of production are used? How will labor and capital actually be combined? This cannot be inferred from Figure 2.1. To say something about this we have to know something about factor prices.

THE MEANING OF COMPETITIVE FACTOR MARKETS:
FACTOR PRICES AND FACTOR INTENSITIES

Let us assume that our economy is characterized by free competition. If two goods, cloth and wheat, are produced with different production functions, a possible equilibrium situation is as shown in Figure 2.2. At points S and R the factors of production are allocated so that the ratio of marginal productivities in the two lines are equal, and both lines equal the relative factor-price ratio PP.

We know that the ratio of marginal productivities changes as we move along an isoquant. The slope of the cloth isoquant at S is equal to the slope of the wheat isoquant at R. If we combine Oa of capital with Ob of labor in cloth production, the ratio of marginal productivities in this line will be the same as the corresponding ratio for wheat production combining Oa' of capital with Ob' of labor.

We can now get a deeper understanding of the nature of our assumption about free competition. We start by having two different production functions, given by the technology prevailing in the economy. Also given is a set of factor prices. The factor-price ratio is assumed to be given by supply and demand

FIGURE 2.3
Factor intensity changes

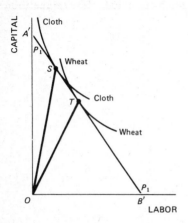

conditions in the factor market. The point here is that because a single producer cannot influence factor prices, as far as he is concerned they are given. The question to be answered is: given production functions and given factor prices, how will the producer combine labor and capital in the two lines of production?

We assume free competition, so we find that he will have to use *OS* capital/labor ratio in the production of cloth and *OR* capital/labor ratio in the production of wheat, because only at *S* and *R* are the ratios between marginal productivities of capital and labor in the two lines of production equal to the factor-price ratio. If he were producing somewhere else, for instance at point *S'*, using the capital/labor ratio *OS'* in cloth production, the marginal productivity of the last unit of capital (in value terms) would be lower than its price, and the marginal productivity of labor (in value terms) would be higher than its wage. Hence he could increase profits by employing more labor and less capital. Only at points *S* and *R* is the marginal productivity of labor equal to its price (i.e. the going wage), and the marginal productivity of capital equal to *its* price (i.e. the rental price for 1 unit of capital during the adequate time period).

The essence of the assumption of free competition is, therefore, that it is an assumption about rationality. It is not an assertion or a postulate about market forms in the real world. It is best viewed as an approximation of a reasonable behavior pattern that facilitates formulation of economic models. There is no reason to believe, *a priori*, that, for instance, if oligopolistic or monopolistic market forms were prevailing, the basic theorems we are about to derive would not stand up. Only a vulgar view on economic theorizing could claim such a thing. Only if we believed for some reason that resources were systematically misallocated, or completely randomly allocated, would we have to be suspicious about the assumption of free competition. As long as this is not the case, we would expect our results on this score to hold for any type of economy, be it capitalistic, socialistic, or whatever.

If for some reason factor prices were to change, factor intensities would also

FIGURE 2.4
Isoquants cut twice: identical factor intensity

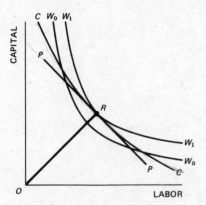

change. Let us assume that the price of labor compared with the price of capital increases. Then more capital-intensive methods of production will be used in both lines of production, as shown in Figure 2.3. We have the same type of cloth and wheat isoquants in Figure 2.3 as in Figure 2.2. The only difference is that labor is now relatively more expensive. Earlier, OA of capital exchanged for OB of labor, whereas now OA' of capital exchanges for OB' of labor. This difference is illustrated by the fact that the factor-price line P_1P_1 in Figure 2.3 is steeper than the factor price line PP in Figure 2.2.

As labor is now more expensive and capital is cheaper than before, producers will use less labor and more capital by substituting capital for labor. Thus methods of production become more capital-intensive in both cloth and wheat production. This is shown by the fact that the factor ratios OS and OT in Figure 2.3 are steeper than the corresponding ratios OS and OR in Figure 2.2.

So far we have assumed that the cloth and wheat isoquants cut only once. This is a very important assumption, because if it is true, cloth will always be capital-intensive and wheat will always be labor-intensive, regardless of what the factor prices are.

This amounts to assuming that production functions differ between commodities and that there is a one-to-one relationship between factor prices and factor intensities, in the sense that one of the goods is always labor-intensive and the other always capital-intensive, irrespective of what the factor prices are. The reason this assumption is important is that if we can classify goods in this way, so that we can say that good A will always be capital-intensive while good B will be labor-intensive, we can show that, given some extra assumptions, trade will have some very definite effects on factor prices. We will be able to show that trade will lead either to a complete factor-price equalization (so that wages will be the same in both trading countries), or else to a complete specialization in production. All this will be carefully spelled out in due course. But before that, there is some more groundwork to be done.

FIGURE 2.5
Differing factor intensities

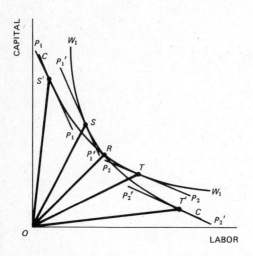

FACTOR REVERSALS

What if the assumption just described did not hold? What would happen if the isoquants cut twice? This situation is depicted in Figure 2.4. We can see from Figure 2.4 that the wheat isoquant $W_0 W_0$ cuts the cloth isoquant CC twice. As both these isoquants are each members of families of isoquants, each member having the same shape, we can find another isoquant, such as $W_1 W_1$, which at some point is tangent to the cloth isoquant CC. This happens at point R. If the factor-price ratio is represented by the line PP that is tangent to the two isoquants at R, then R is the equilibrium point, and the factor intensity in both lines of production is OR.

But out of infinitely many factor-price ratios there is only one that gives the same factor intensity in both lines of production. If labor were more expensive (or less expensive), how would labor and capital then be combined? The answer is contained in Figure 2.5. In the figure we have the same cloth isoquant CC and the same wheat isoquant $W_1 W_1$ as in Figure 2.4 with a common point of tangency at R.

If labor becomes more expensive than in our earlier example the factor-price line will become steeper. The factor-price ratio $P_1 P_1$ and $P_1' P_1'$ (these lines are parallel) illustrates this case. We know that both lines will use more capital-intensive methods of production as labor becomes relatively more expensive. The factor intensity used in wheat will be OS, and in cloth it will be OS'. Thus, at this price ratio, cloth will be the capital-intensive good and wheat will be the labor-intensive good. By analogous reasoning, we find that at all factor-price ratios where labor is relatively more expensive than at PP in Figure 2.4, cloth will be the capital-intensive good and wheat the labor-intensive good.

But what happens if labor is relatively cheaper than at the ratio *PP*? This case is also illustrated in Figure 2.5. Then the factor-price ratio has to be less steep than *PP*. An example is P_2P_2 and $P_2'P_2'$ (they are parallel). We find that the factor intensity is *OT* in wheat production and *OT'* in cloth production. Thus wheat is now the capital-intensive line of production and cloth the labor-intensive good. By analogous reasoning, we find that at any factor-price ratio where capital is relatively more expensive than at *PP*, wheat is capital-intensive and cloth is labor-intensive.

From this it follows that there is no longer a one-to-one correspondence between factor prices and factor intensities. Whether cloth is the labor-intensive good or the capital-intensive good will depend on which factor-price ratio is ruling.

The economic meaning of the fact that isoquants cut twice is that possibilities of substitution differ significantly between the two industries. We can see this from Figure 2.4 and 2.5, where we find that the wheat isoquant is more convex to the origin than is the cloth isoquant. This means that the two factors of production are better substitutes for each other in cloth production than in wheat production. This is a fact derived from the shape of the production functions, something given to us from the state of the art.

With any change in factor prices, the two industries will substitute the relatively cheaper factor for the more expensive. But their possibilities of doing this in a profitable way depend on technological factors.

Let us assume first of all that the factor-price ratio *PP* is the ruling one, and hence *OR* is the factor intensity in both lines of production. If factor prices change and labor becomes more expensive, capital will be substituted for labor. But this is more easily done in cloth than in wheat production. Therefore, cloth will be more capital-intensive than wheat. Analogously, if capital becomes more expensive relative to labor, labor will be substituted for capital, but as this still is more easily done in cloth than in wheat production, cloth will become labor-intensive. From this it follows that the new equilibrium factor-intensity ray in wheat will be closer to the ray *OR* than the new equilibrium factor-intensity ray in cloth, regardless of the way factor prices change relative to the ratio *PP*.

Thus we have established the proposition that if factor reversals exists, there is no longer a one-to-one correspondence between factor prices and factor intensities. We will be able to show, however, that once we have specified the total amounts of the factors of production a country has, only a limited number of factor-price ratios are compatible with economic equilibrium. And, given that, it will turn out that there is a one-to-one correspondence between this set of possible factor price and factor intensities, so that we will be able to classify one good as being always labor-intensive and the other as being always capital-intensive.

But the proof of this proposition involves a little bit of tricky reasoning and the need for more tools. Therefore, we will postpone it to Chapter 6, where we will give a detailed treatment of the implications of factor reversals for the effects of trade on factor prices. Before we end this chapter, however, we should introduce another important tool of analysis, the *box diagram*.

FIGURE 2.6
Box diagram

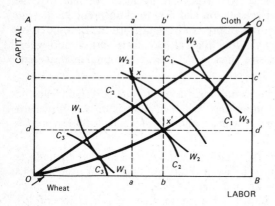

THE BOX DIAGRAM

So far we have not said anything about a country's total factor endowments. The box diagram permits us to study the interrelationships between production functions and total amounts of factors of production and to derive optimal factor inputs and outputs.

A box diagram is illustrated in Figure 2.6. The sides of the box measure labor and capital. In the figure we have capital on the vertical side and labor on the horizontal side. The dimensions of the box give total factor endowments, so that OA measures the total amount of capital available to the economy and OB gives the total amount of labor. The diagonal OO' gives the over-all factor intensity of the economy.

Furthermore, we are producing two goods, wheat and cloth, and their production functions are illustrated by two sets of isoquants. These are of the same kind as the ones illustrated in Figure 2.2. The only difference is that we now measure wheat production from the lower left-hand corner, whereas we measure cloth production from the upper right-hand corner. We can then draw two sets of isoquants, one for wheat with the origin at O, and another for cloth with the origin at O'.

We still assume the production functions to be homogeneous of degree 1. The isoquant $W_2 W_2$ is twice as far from the origin as the isoquant $W_1 W_1$ and therefore represents twice as much wheat as does $W_1 W_1$. Likewise, $W_3 W_3$ is three times as far from the origin as $W_1 W_1$ and therefore represents three times as much wheat. Analogous conditions hold for the cloth isoquants. For the sake of reasoning, let us assume that $W_1 W_1$ represents 1 unit of wheat, $W_2 W_2$ represents 2 units of wheat, and so on, and that the same is true for the cloth isoquants.

Any point in the box, for instance x, represents a certain combination of outputs of the two goods. In our present example, x represents 2 units of wheat and between 1 and 2 units of cloth. But it also represents a certain input combination. To produce x of wheat we have to combine Oa of labor with Oc of capital. And to produce x of cloth we have to combine what is left of labor, $O'a'$, with what is left of capital, $O'c'$. This is an application of the assumption that the economy is fully employed, so that all labor and all capital are used up in production.

The output combination represented by x is not efficient, however, This is shown by the fact that if we move along the isoquant W_2W_2 to the point x' we can still get the same amount of wheat but a greater amount of cloth, because at x' the cloth isoquant C_2C_2 is tangential to the wheat isoquant W_2W_2. This, then, is an efficient point because here the ratio between the marginal productivities is the same in both lines of production. Therefore, the relative efficiency of the two factors of production is the same in both lines of production and the factors of production are allocated in an optimal way. Another way of stating this is by saying that it is impossible to produce more of one commodity without decreasing production of the other commodity.

Thus by combining Ob of labor with Od of capital in wheat production and $O'b'$ of labor with $O'd'$ of capital in cloth production, the ratio between the marginal productivities in the two lines of production are equalized. Therefore, x' is a possible equilibrium point.

If we combine all the points in the box where two isoquants are tangential to each other, we get a curve such as OO' in Figure 2.6. This curve is usually called the *contract curve*. All the points on the contract curve are efficient in the sense just described, i.e. they represent efficient output and input combinations. Any point off the contract curve can be shown to be inferior to a point on the curve by the type of reasoning we have just used. So far, however, we have no way of judging which point on the contract curve is preferred to any of the other points. This can be done only after we know something about demand conditions, and we will have to wait to introduce these. The contract curve is derived exclusively from technical conditions in production.

In concluding this chapter it might be worth while to make a couple of comments about the box diagram. Figure 2.7 illustrates the same kind of production conditions as did Figure 2.6. We are still measuring production of wheat from the lower left-hand corner and cloth production from the upper right-hand corner, etc.

First, it is observed that wheat is the labor-intensive commodity and cloth is the capital-intensive one, because the contract curve is below the diagonal. If the contract curve had gone above the diagonal, wheat would have been the capital-intensive good.

Let us assume that S in Figure 2.7 illustrates the initial equilibrium position in the economy. Then we know how the factors of production will be allocated. By drawing a ray from O to S we find that OS is the factor intensity in wheat production, and by drawing a ray from O' to S we find that $O'S$ is the factor intensity in cloth production.

What would happen if the demand for wheat increased? The relative price of wheat would go up and more of it would be produced. That means that we would move away from S along the contract curve toward O'. A new possible

FIGURE 2.7
Box diagram

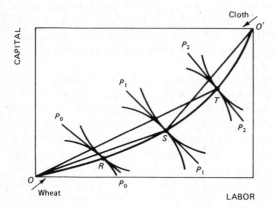

equilibrium point could be T, which represents more wheat and less cloth.

At point T we find that the factor intensities in both lines of production differ from those at S. In wheat production the new factor intensity is OT, which shows that the new method of production is more capital-intensive than the old one. Likewise, we find that the new method of production in cloth, $O'T$, is more capital-intensive than the old method of production $O'S$. But how is it possible that both lines of production can become more capital-intensive when the over-all amounts of capital and labor have not changed?

The answer to this apparent paradox is that the output mix at T differs from that at S. At T more wheat and less cloth is produced. When cloth production is decreased, both capital and labor are released. Cloth is the capital-intensive good, so relatively much capital and little labor is freed. Part of this capital will be used in wheat production, so the method of production there will be more capital-intensive. But part of it will also be re-engaged in cloth production, so the method of production will be more capital-intensive there, too.

Obviously, the movement from S to T will also have some implications for factor prices. The relative factor-price ratio is shown by the slope of a line which is tangential to the point of tangency between two isoquants. The slopes of the lines P_0P_0, P_1P_1 and P_2P_2 show relative factor prices at R, S and T, respectively. We can see that these lines *become steeper and steeper* as we move along the contract curve from the lower left-hand corner to the upper right-hand corner. This means that the relative price of labor increases as we move from O to O'.

The economic explanation of this is as follows. As we move from O toward O' we increase production of wheat and decrease production of cloth. This means that the relative price of wheat is going up. But wheat is the labor-intensive commodity. To produce more wheat, entrepreneurs need larger amounts of the factors of production, and as wheat is labor-intensive, they are especially eager to get more labor. To hire more labor they bid up its price, so

FIGURE 2.8
The box diagram and the
production-possibility curve

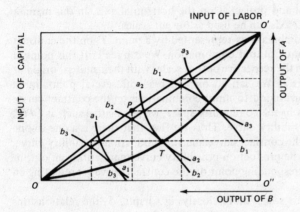

the relative price of labor rises. But as this occurs, producers in both lines of production try to economize on labor and to use capital instead. Therefore, as the wage increases, more capital-intensive methods are used in both lines of production.

THE PRODUCTION-POSSIBILITY CURVE DERIVED
FROM THE BOX DIAGRAM

In a general sense, we know already that any movement along the production-possibility curve must correspond to a movement along the contract curve in the box diagram. The time has come to spell out explicitly the connection between the two tools of analysis and to show how the production-possibility curve can be derived from the box diagram.[3]

Figure 2.8 shows a slightly modified box diagram. On the left-hand vertical side and on the upper horizontal side we still measure factor inputs, capital and labor, respectively. Inputs into the two goods are still measured in the usual way: inputs into good A from the lower left-hand corner and inputs into good B from the upper right-hand corner. The difference that we now introduce is that we measure outputs along the two remaining sides. The right-hand vertical side $O''O'$ is used to represent an index for measuring output of good A, and the lower horizontal side $O''O$ is used to measure output of good B. The O'' corner is the origin for both the output scales.

We draw the diagonal OO' in the box. Because of the fact that the production functions are homogeneous of the first degree, we know that if an isoquant cuts the diagonal twice as far away from the origin O as $a_1 a_1$, it represents twice as large an output as $a_1 a_1$. Likewise, if a b isoquant cuts the diagonal twice as far away from the O' corner as another b isoquant, it represents double the output of the latter. We can therefore find where the a isoquants cut the diagonal and then project them on the vertical axis. Analogously, we can find where the b isoquants cut the diagonal and project it on the horizontal axis. In this manner the $O'' O'$ axis and the $O'' O$ axis can be used as output scales.

Therefore, the input combinations represented by a point, T, on the contract curve correspond to a unique output combination. We can read off this point in the commodity space from the respective output scales with their mutual origin at O'', and we find that it is P. We can go on and read off several points in an analogous fashion that correspond to input combinations on the contract curve. If we join all these points in the commodity space, we get a curve such as OPO'. This is the production-possibility curve. Thus we find that there is a one-to-one correspondence between the contract curve and the production-possibility curve, so that for every point on the production-possibility curve representing an output combination there is a corresponding point on the contract curve representing an input combination.

We will use this fact to study more closely, in Chapter 5, the relationships between commodity and factor prices, as well as the connection between the gains from trade and income distribution.

3
Comparative advantage in the Heckscher–Ohlin trade model

In Chapter 1 we studied the theory of comparative advantage in terms of a one-factor model. In this setting differences in the productivity of labor were the cause of trade. It is now time to take a closer look at the Heckscher–Ohlin theory of trade. According to this theory, trade results from the fact that different countries have different factor endowments.

The Heckscher–Ohlin theory is usually formulated in terms of a two-factor model, with labor and capital as the two factors of production. We will use this model, and in the following we will be concerned only with this case. It would be possible in some instances to generalize the result to the case in which there are many factors of production. Attempts at such generalizations, however, would require the use of fairly advanced mathematics and therefore fall outside the scope of this book. The two-factor case will give us an understanding of all the essentials of the Heckscher–Ohlin theory.

As we have said, according to the Heckscher–Ohlin theory, what determines trade is differences in factor endowments. Some countries have much capital, others have much labor. The theory now says that countries that are rich in capital will export capital-intensive goods, and countries that have much labor will export labor-intensive goods.

The terms 'rich in capital' and 'rich in labor' are not very precise at the moment. Before we can get much further, we have to define our terms and give them a more precise meaning. First, however, we will comment upon and explain some of the more general assumptions for this type of analysis. Since the exposition in Chapter 2 has paved the way for us, we can do this briefly.

The following five assumptions are essential to the analysis: (1) there are no transport costs or other impediments to trade; (2) there is perfect competition in both commodity and factor markets; (3) all production functions are homogeneous of the first degree; (4) the production functions are such that the two commodities show different factor intensities; and (5) the production functions differ between commodities, but are the same in both countries, i.e. good A is produced with the same technique in both countries and good B is produced with the same technique in both countries.

The meaning of these should not be too difficult to understand. The first assumption is an abstraction to facilitate the analysis. It implies that commodity prices under trade will be the same in both countries. The meaning of the second assumption should be clear from Chapter 2. It implies that the factors of production will be allocated in an optimal way.

The last three assumptions all refer to characteristics of the production functions. The meaning of a production function being linearly homogeneous was explained in Chapter 2. The fourth assumption means that different techniques of production are used in the two industries. Furthermore, we assume that there is a one-to-one correspondence between factor intensities and factor prices; another way of stating this fact is by saying that there are no factor reversals.

The fifth assumption, that production functions are the same in both countries, is quite a strong one. What it amounts to is assuming that knowledge travels freely. In other words, the best techniques of production in the world are known to everyone.

These are the assumptions used in connection with the Heckscher–Ohlin theory of trade. They are necessary to state the meaning of comparative advantage in the 'two-by-two-by-two' model, and to prove the factor-price equalization theorem. They are quite strong assumptions, and one might think that they are rarely fulfilled in the real world. Sometimes, however, strong assumptions are needed to prove interesting theorems. The conclusions of the theorems can still be empirically valid, even though some of the assumptions are only approximations of conditions existing in the real world. Simplifying assumptions have to be made in theoretical studies. The theorems built on such assumptions can still be important.[1] The theorems we are about to derive will give us a most useful insight into the general-equilibrium character of economics. In this way we will be able to see that a change in one variable in our trading system necessarily implies changes in all the other variables.

FACTOR ABUNDANCE DEFINED BY FACTOR PRICES

We will now try to demonstrate the proposition that capital-rich countries export capital-intensive goods and that labor-rich countries export labor-intensive goods. It is, however, not yet clear what is meant by a country being rich in capital. At least two alternative definitions can be given.

One of these definitions runs in terms of factor prices. This definition says that country I is capital-rich compared with country II if capital is relatively cheaper in country I than in country II. The second definition compares overall physical amounts of labor and capital. It says that country I is rich in capital if the ratio of capital to labor is larger in country I than in country II.

These two alternative definitions are not equivalent. We will now show that the Heckscher–Ohlin proposition follows if we use the first definition but that it does not necessarily follow using the second definition. Ohlin himself defined richness in factor endowments with the help of factor prices. According to his definition country I is abundant in capital if $P_{1C}/P_{1L} < P_{2C}/P_{2L}$, where P_{1C} is the price of capital in country I, P_{1L} is the price of labor in country I, and P_{2C} and P_{2L} are the prices in country II of capital and labor, respectively. In other words, if capital is relatively cheap in country I, the country is abundant in capital, and if labour is relatively cheap in country II, country II is rich in labor.

It now remains for us to show that country I will export the capital-intensive good and that country II will export the labor-intensive good. This is easily done, as is demonstrated with the help of Figure 3.1. We start with two isoquants, *aa* and *bb*, which characterize the production functions and are the same in both countries. According to these isoquants, B is the labor-intensive good and A is

FIGURE 3.1
Factor abundance defined in terms of factor prices

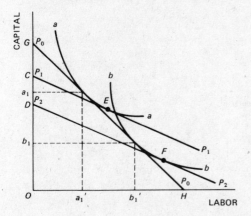

the capital-intensive good. Relative factor prices in country I, where capital is cheap, are given by the line P_0P_0. Let us assume that the isoquants represent 1 unit of the respective good. Then 1 unit of good A will be produced with Oa_1 of capital and Oa_1' of labor. But capital and labor can be exchanged for each other in a ratio shown by the factor-price line P_0P_0. Therefore, Oa_1' of labor is worth a_1G of capital, and Oa_1 of capital is worth $a_1'H$ of labor.

We said that 1 unit of good A would be produced with Oa_1 of capital and Oa_1' of labor. But now we can view the line GH as a budget line, or a cost line, and we can express the cost of producing 1 unit of A in terms of capital alone, or of labor alone. Doing so, we find that the cost of producing 1 unit of A is OG measured in capital or OH measured in labor.

By applying exactly the same kind of reasoning we also find that the cost of producing 1 unit of good B in country I is the same as that for producing 1 unit of A, i.e. it is OG measured in capital and OH measured in labor.

The next step is to find out the cost of producing 1 unit of each good in country II. The only information we have about country II is that capital is relatively more expensive there than in country I. This means that the slope of the line representing the ratio of factor prices in country II will be less steep than the slope of P_0P_0.

A possible factor-price line in country II is P_1P_1. It is tangential to the aa isoquant at E. A parallel factor-price line is P_2P_2, which is tangential to the bb isoquant at F. It is obvious that P_2P_2 must lie below P_1P_1. From this it follows that the cost of producing 1 unit of good A in country II is OC measured in capital, whereas it is OD measured in capital for 1 unit of good B. Thus in country II it is more expensive to produce a given amount of good A than it is to produce the same amount of good B.

FIGURE 3.2

Factor abundance defined
in physical terms

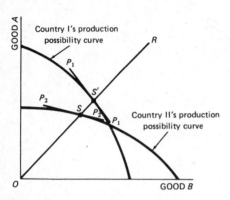

If we now compare production costs in the two countries, we find that it is relatively cheap to produce good A in country I and relatively cheap to produce good B in country II. From this it follows that country I will export good A and country II will export good B. This establishes the Heckscher–Ohlin theorem that the country abundant in capital will export the capital-intensive good and the country abundant in labor will export the labor-intensive good.

Thus, starting from the definition of factor abundance in terms of factor prices, it is easy to establish the Heckscher–Ohlin theorem. We might mention in passing that the reverse of the theorem also holds, i.e. if a country exports the capital-intensive good, capital is its relatively cheap factor of production.

One could argue, however, that stating the theorem in terms of factor prices is not very interesting, because factor prices are themselves results of a complicated interplay of economic forces. They are, for instance, not only determined by supply factors but are also influenced by demand factors. It is not possible to say anything about factor prices from the knowledge of factor endowments alone. To state the Heckscher–Ohlin theorem in terms of factor prices gives perhaps not the most interesting version of the theorem.

A more natural definition, it seems, would run in terms of physical amounts. Let us now use this definition and see what the result will be.

FACTOR ABUNDANCE DEFINED IN PHYSICAL TERMS

Defining factor abundance in physical terms, we say that country I is rich in capital and country II is rich in labor if $C_1/L_1 > C_2/L_2$, where C_1 is the total amount of capital in country I, L_1 is the total amount of labor in country I, and C_2 and L_2 are the total amounts of capital and labor, respectively, in country II.

We will now show that if country I is abundant in capital according to this definition, it implies that country I has a bias in favor of producing the capital-

FIGURE 3.3

Demand factors offsetting production bias

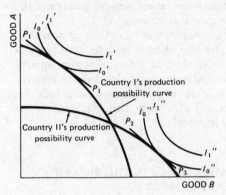

intensive good. The nature of this bias is best illustrated by Figure 3.2. It is assumed in the figure that good A is the capital-intensive good and good B is the labor-intensive good. If both countries were to produce the goods in the same proportion, say along the ray OR, country I would be producing at point S' on its production-possibility curve and country II would be producing at point S on its production-possibility curve. The slope of country I's production-possibility curve at S' is steeper than the slope of country II's curve at S. This implies that good A would be cheaper in country I than in country II, and that good B would be cheaper in country II than in country I, were the two countries producing at the respective points. This is also illustrated by the fact that the commodity price line P_1P_1 is steeper than the line P_2P_2. The opportunity cost of expanding production of good A is therefore lower in country I than in country II, and vice versa for good B. This shows that country I, the capital-rich country, has a bias in favor of the capital-intensive good from the production side, and that the country abundant in labor, country II, has a bias in favor of producing the labor-intensive good.

It does not follow from this, however, that the labor-rich country will export the labor-intensive good. It might be the case that demand factors more than offset the bias from the production side. Such a case is illustrated in Figure 3.3, which contains the same production-possibility curves as Figure 3.2, and good A is still the capital-intensive good and good B the labor-intensive good. The difference is that now we have taken demand into account. Demand in the two countries is characterized by two sets of indifference curves, where the curves $I'_0I'_0$, $I'_1I'_1$, etc., represent demand in country I and the curves $I''_0I''_0$, $I''_1I''_1$, etc., represent demand in Country II. Demand in country I is obviously biased toward the capital-intensive good and demand in country II is biased toward the labor-intensive good. Thus in isolation good A is relatively more expensive in country I than in country II. This is shown by the fact that the commodity price line P_2P_2 in country II is steeper than the line P_1P_1 representing relative commodity prices in country I.

From this it follows that when trade is opened up between the two countries, country I will export good *B* and country II will export good *A*. In other words, the country abundant in capital will export the labor-intensive good, and the country abundant in labor will export the capital-intensive good.

In conclusion we can say that factor abundance can be defined in two ways in the Heckscher–Ohlin trade model. The two alternative definitions are not equivalent. Only according to one of them does it follow that the country abundant in capital will export the capital-intensive good and that the country rich in labor will export the labor-intensive good. Let us, before we conclude this chapter, compare and contrast the meaning of comparative advantage in the Ricardian and in the Heckscher–Ohlin trade models.

A COMPARISON OF COMPARATIVE ADVANTAGE IN THE RICARDIAN AND IN THE HECKSCHER–OHLIN TRADE MODELS

In Chapter 1, where we treated comparative advantage in the Ricardian model, the only factor of production was labor. In the Ricardian model, comparative advantage was determined by production conditions alone. We also learned that if a country had a comparative advantage in the production of a good, it would export that good.

In the neoclassical, two-factor model these two conditions are no longer met. Speaking in terms of the first definition of factor abundance, i.e. in terms of factor prices, we can see that the second condition is fulfilled and that if a country is abundant in capital, it will also export the capital-intensive good. But the first condition is not met, because we cannot infer from production conditions alone anything about factor prices.

Then, going to the second definition of factor abundance – the definition in terms of physical amounts of factors of production – we find that it is the other way around. This definition takes into account only production conditions; here the first condition of the Ricardian model is fulfilled, but the second is not, because we cannot infer anything about comparative advantage. We cannot, for instance, use this definition to say that the country abundant in capital will export the capital-intensive good.

One thing which does hold, however, is that even though the country that is abundant in capital according to the second definition might export the labor-intensive good, it will still produce relatively more of the capital-intensive good than the other country. If *A* is the capital-intensive good and *B* is the labor-intensive good, and if country I is abundant in capital and country II in labor, we know that country I will always produce *A/B* in a higher ratio than country II. In this sense we can say that country I has a comparative advantage in the production of the capital-intensive good and that country II has a comparative advantage in the production of the labor-intensive good.

4
Commodity and factor prices under trade: factor-price equalization

We have studied the meaning of comparative advantage in the two-factor trade model. To get a more complete understanding of the interrelationships between the variables in a general-equilibrium system, we now turn our attention to the effects that trade will have on factor prices.

We have assumed that there are no impediments to trade. Then when trade is introduced, commodity prices will be the same in both countries. But what about factor prices? What effects will trade have on factor prices?

One assumption central to the theory of international trade is that factors of production are completely immobile between countries. This has also been tacitly assumed in the preceding chapters. We have assumed that factors of production are completely mobile within each country but that they cannot cross borders. There is no cost involved for labor or capital in moving from Florida to California, but it is impossible for labor or capital to move from Florida to Cuba, or from Arizona to Mexico.

Let us for a moment give up this assumption and instead assume full mobility internationally for factors of production: that capital and labor can move freely without cost. Then it is quite obvious that factor prices would be the same in all countries: if workers in Haiti had lower wages than workers in the United States, they would move to the United States, as there are no costs of transportation and no impediments to migration of labor. In this process wages in the two countries would be equalized. In an analogous manner, capital would move to the countries where returns to capital are highest. Thereby, returns to capital would be equalized and the rental price for 1 unit of capital would be the same everywhere.

We will now demonstrate that in a world where factors of production cannot move between countries but where goods can move freely, trade in goods can be viewed as a substitution for factor mobility. In a model built on the type of assumptions that we have already set out in earlier chapters we will find that free trade leads to a complete equalization of factor rewards or to a partial equalization combined with complete specialization in production.

THE BOX DIAGRAM WITH THE SAME PRODUCTION FUNCTIONS IN THE TWO COUNTRIES

We will, as usual, couch our argument in terms of the two-country, two-good model with two factors of production. We retain all the assumptions that were

FIGURE 4.1

Factor endowment
comparison

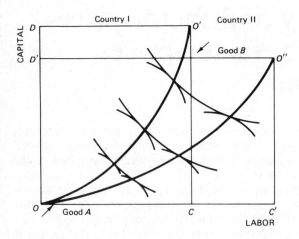

listed at the beginning of Chapter 3 and explained there and in Chapter 2. One
of these assumptions was that production functions differ between goods but
are the same in both countries.

It might be useful to give a geometric illustration of this fact (Figure 4.1). The
box $OCO'D$ represents total factor endowments in country I, and the box
$OC'O''D'$ represents total factor endowments in country II. From this we can
read that country I is abundant in capital, measured in physical amounts as
$C_1/L_1 > C_2/L_2$, and country II is abundant in labor, using the same measure.

We measure production of good A from the lower left-hand corner and production of good B from the upper right-hand corner. As production functions
are the same in both countries, the aa isoquants are identical for both countries.
This can easily be seen from Figure 4.1 for good A, because production of this
good is measured from the O corner in both countries. The bb isoquants are also
the same, in the sense that they both illustrate the same production function,
even though production of this good in country I is measured from the O' corner
and production in country II is measured from the O'' corner.

As can be seen from the figure, labor is measured on the horizontal axis of
the box and capital on the vertical axis. From the ways the isoquants are drawn,
it follows that good A is the labor-intensive good and good B is the capital-
intensive good.

FACTOR PRICES UNDER AUTARKY

In isolation, before trade, the two countries can produce anywhere on the contract curve in their respective boxes. Figure 4.2 illustrates the same situation as

FIGURE 4.2
Factor prices under autarky

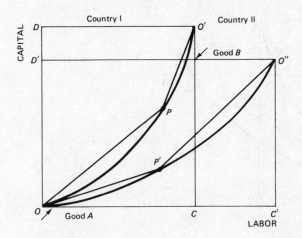

Figure 4.1, but for convenience the isoquants are omitted here. Let us assume, for the sake of reasoning, that country I produces at point P on its contract curve and that country II produces at point P'. What will then be the implication for factor prices?

We can see immediately from Figure 4.2 that country I uses more capital-intensive methods of production than country II in both lines of production. Production functions are the same in both countries and they are homogenous of the first degree. We know that the marginal productivities are determined exclusively by the factor intensities used in production. Because country I uses more capital per unit of labor than country II, the marginal productivity of capital at P in country I will be lower than the marginal productivity of capital at P' in country II. Factor prices are determined by marginal productivities. From this it follows that the relative price of capital will be lower in country I than in country II and that the return for labor, i.e. the wages, will be higher in country I than in country II.

This holds when each country produces and consumes in isolation. Let us now introduce the possibility of trade and see what happens.

COMMODITY AND FACTOR PRICES UNDER TRADE: FACTOR-PRICE EQUALIZATION

If the equilibrium situation before trade is the one that we have depicted in Figure 4.2, it follows that $P_{1C}/P_{1L} < P_{2C}/P_{2L}$. Then we know from Chapter 3 that country I, where capital is relatively cheap, will export the capital-intensive good when the countries start to trade and that country II will export the labor-

FIGURE 4.3

Factor-price equalization

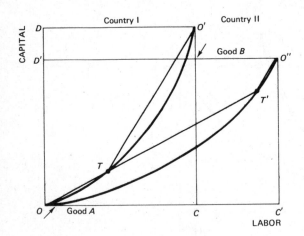

intensive good. This follows from a straightforward application of the Heckscher–Ohlin theorem.

Good B is the capital-intensive good and good A is the labor-intensive one. Hence, when trade starts, country I will move along its contract curve from point P toward the O corner and country II will move from point P' along its contract curve toward the O'' corner. Possible equilibrium points when the two countries trade are shown in Figure 4.3. The boxes and the contract curves are, of course, the same. The difference is that country I now produces at point T and country II produces at point T'. These are obviously production patterns which are possible under trade. What are the implications for factor prices?

Because of the assumption about constant returns to scale, the marginal productivity of labor and capital will be constant along any ray from the origin, such as OTT'. Denote the marginal productivity of labor and capital in country I in industry A and in industry B with, respectively, MPL_{1A}, MPC_{1A}, MPL_{1B}, and MPC_{1B}. Analogously, denote the marginal productivities in the respective industries in the second country with MPL_{2A}, MPC_{2A}, MPL_{2B}, and MPC_{2B}.

We can see that labor and capital are used in the same proportions in industry A in both countries at T and T'. From this it follows that $MPL_{1A} = MPL_{2A}$ and that $MPC_{1A} = MPC_{2A}$. Furthermore, the line $O'T$ is parallel to the line $O''T'$. Hence the factors of production are combined in the same proportions in both countries in industry B, too. From this it follows that $MPL_{1B} = MPL_{2B}$ and that $MPC_{1B} = MPC_{2B}$.

One of our assumptions is that factor markets are perfectly competitive and that factors of production are fully mobile within each country. This means that the payment for labor, the wage, must be the same in both industries and that the payment for 1 unit of capital also must be the same in both industries. But the factor reward equals the marginal productivity of the factor multiplied by the price of the good produced. From this it follows that $MPL_{1A} \times P_{1A} = MPL_{1B} \times P_{1B}$ and that $MPC_{1A} \times P_{1A} \doteq MPC_{1B} \times P_{1B}$. This gives $P_{1A}/P_{1B} = MPL_{1B}/MPL_{1A}$ and $P_{1A}/P_{1B} = MPC_{1B}/MPC_{1A}$. Analogously, we get for the second country, $MPL_{2A} \times P_{2A} = MPL_{2B} \times P_{2B}$ and $MPC_{2A} \times P_{2A} = MPC_{2B} \times P_{2B}$. Hence $P_{2A}/P_{2B} = MPL_{2B}/MPL_{2A}$ and $P_{2A}/P_{2B} = MPC_{2B}/MPC_{2A}$.

But P_{1A}/P_{1B} and P_{2A}/P_{2B} are nothing but relative commodity prices in the two countries. Under trade, disregarding all impediments to trade, they must be the same, and hence $P_{1A}/P_{1B} = P_{2A}/P_{2B}$. We already know that at points T and T' $MPL_{1A} = MPL_{2A}$, $MPC_{1A} = MPC_{2A}$, $MPL_{1B} = MPL_{2B}$, and $MPC_{1B} = MPC_{2B}$. This gives $MPL_{1A} \times P_{1A} = MPL_{2A} \times P_{2A} = MPL_{1B} \times P_{1B} = MPL_{2B} \times P_{2B}$. In other words, factor prices will be completely equalized in the two countries.

This demonstration shows that as long as we can find trading points such as T and T' in Figure 4.3 the implication is that factor prices will be the same in both countries. Given our present assumptions, this means that as long as both countries are incompletely specialized – i.e. as long as both countries produce both goods – trade will lead to a complete factor-price equalization.

Let us now examine the common-sense explanation of factor-price equalization. We start out with the situation illustrated in Figure 4.2. In isolation, capital is cheap in country I and labour is cheap in country II. Therefore, country I has a comparative advantage in the capital-intensive good (good B) and country II has a comparative advantage in the labor-intensive good (good A).

When the two countries start to trade, it is obvious that country I will export good B and country II will export good A. To increase its production of good B, country I has to move its factors of production from industry A to industry B. But industry B is the capital-intensive industry. To produce more of good B, the producers in country I need, especially, more capital. Therefore, the price of capital is bid up, and the relative price of what was the cheap factor before trade rises.

In an exactly analogous manner, the producers in country II start to produce more of good A, in order to export it. This is the labor-intensive good. As more of it is produced, more labor is needed and the relative price of labor goes up. Hence trade leads to an increase, in both countries, in the price of the abundant factor – the relatively cheap factor – until factor prices are the same in both countries.

But are we always able to find trade points such as T and T' in Figure 4.3? Not necessarily. The alternative is that one of the countries, or possibly both, might be completely specialized and produce only one good. Let us look into this case.

COMPLETE SPECIALIZATION

Figure 4.4 can be used to illustrate the conditions that must be fulfilled if trading points are to be found with production of both goods in both countries. First we draw a line tangent to country I's contract curve. This line is OE', which meets country II's contract curve at E'. Then we draw the diagonal OO'' for country II's box. This line cuts country I's contract curve at E. Then any point

FIGURE 4.4

Complete specialization

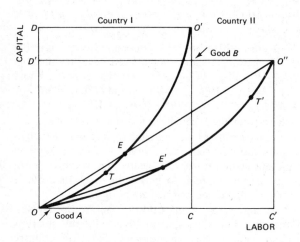

between OE on country I's contract curve can be paired with any point between $E'O''$ on country II's contract curve. But only if both countries produce on these segments of their contract curves will we be able to find corresponding trading points and incomplete specialization, which are conditions for full factor-price equalization.

Figure 4.4 also illustrates the fact that only if the factor-endowment ratios in both countries lie between the factor intensities used in the two lines of production will there by incomplete specialization. This was obviously the case for points T and T', for example, and therefore we had incomplete specialization at these points.

Let us assume that we have the situation depicted in Figure 4.4, so that country I is producing at point T and country II is producing at point T', and let us see how complete specialization can be brought about. This equilibrium situation might be disturbed by, for instance, an increase in the demand for good A brought about by a change in tastes. Both countries will then produce more of good A, and both will move up and to the right, country I toward O' and country II toward O''. This can be done only by shifting factors of production from good B to good A.

But country II was already producing much of good A at T'. After a while the country will therefore reach point O'', where it will produce only good A. Country I will then be producing at point E. If the demand for A, and at the same time the relative price of A, keep on increasing, country I will increase its production of good A. This means that it will be producing somewhere on the contract curve between E and O'. But country II has already shifted all its factors of production to good A. Even if the price of A goes up, it cannot produce more of it. Therefore, the factor intensities used in the same line of production in the two countries will no longer be the same.

FIGURE 4.5

Changes in factor endowment and complete specialization

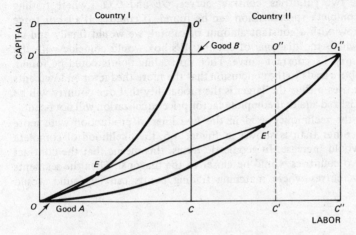

The implications of such a development for factor prices are easy to see. At T and T' factor prices were equalized in the two countries. When the demand for good A – the labor-intensive good – increases, the demand for labor increases concomitantly. This leads to an increase in the relative price of labor. As this happens, producers try to substitute capital for labor and go over to more capital-intensive methods of production. It can also easily be seen from Figure 4.4 that as we move up and to the right, the methods of production in both lines of production become more and more capital-intensive.

But at point O'' country II has pulled all its factors of production out of industry B and put them into industry A, and the capital-intensity in industry A at O'' equals the over-all capital-intensity of the country. Country I, which is abundant in capital, uses the same capital intensity in the production of good A but still has enough capital to use methods even more capital-intensive in the production of good B. At points E and O'' factor prices are still equalized. If the relative price of good A goes up even higher, so does the relative price of labor in country I. But it cannot go higher in country II. Factor intensities will no longer be the same in the two countries, the relation between marginal productivities will no longer be the same, and factor prices will no longer be completely equalized.

However, there will still be a tendency to factor-price equalization because of trade: if capital is relatively cheap in country I, the country will export the capital-intensive good and the price of capital will go up, and if labor is relatively cheap in country II, the country will export the labor-intensive good and the wage will go up, because of trade.

We might now make a couple of comments on which factors determine whether countries under trade will be completely or incompletely specialized. If there were a greater difference between factor endowments than in Figure 4.4, the probability for complete specialization would increase. This can be seen from Figure 4.5. The figure shows a situation where country II has relatively more labor than in Figure 4.4. The amount of labor $C'C''$ has been added, and country II's new box consists of $OC''O''_1D'$. This leads to a diminution of the segments of the two countries' contract curves, OE and $E'O''$, where trading points with incomplete specialization can be found. If country II's labor force continued to grow with a constant amount of capital, we would finally end up in a situation where the diagonal of country II's box would coincide with the tangent to country I's contract curve. Then no trading points could be found. The reasoning above leads to the conclusion that the more the factor endowments in the two countries differ, the larger is the probability that one country will be completely specialized and that complete factor-price equalization will not occur.

Likewise, if the techniques used in the two lines of production were more similar to each other than is shown in Figure 4.5, the likelihood of complete specialization would increase. In geometric terms, this means that the contract curves in the two countries would be closer to the diagonal. Then the segments of the contract curves where matching trading points can be found would diminish.

FACTOR PRICES, POVERTY, AND INCOME EQUALIZATION

We have now proved that given certain rather strict assumptions, trade will equalize factor prices. But we live in a world where wide divergences in wages can be observed. Does not experience contradict the results of the factor-price equalization theorem? Before we conclude this chapter it is appropriate to make a few comments on this question.

First, we must observe what the factor-price equalization theorem does *not* say. It does not say that trade will equalize incomes. Wages are not the only source of income. Someone must own the capital, and capital also commands its factor reward. Therefore, the more capital a country has for a given amount of labor, the higher the average income will be. So even if factor rewards were completely equalized, as long as the capital stocks differ, incomes will also differ.

Second, the factor-price equalization theorem is a completely static type of theory. It only studies some characteristics of a given equilibrium situation at a given point in time. It says only what the effects of trade will be with a given technique, with given factor endowments, and so on. But the real world is not in a given equilibrium forever; all sorts of changes occur. It could very well be the case that trade does have the effects on factor prices which the factor-price equalization theorem predicts, but that other factors, disregarded by this type of theory, work in an opposite direction.

Furthermore, of course, we have to keep in mind that the factor-price equalization theorem, and static theorizing in general, should not be viewed as directly amenable to or geared toward empirical testing. It gives us, however, indispensable tools and insights into the general-equilibrium nature of economics. It is the necessary background for all further theorizing. As we go along, for instance in Part II, on economic growth and international trade, we will see how the theory can be developed and how testable hypotheses of considerable interest can be derived from it.

SELECTED BIBLIOGRAPHY: CHAPTERS 3 AND 4

The basic sources for the Heckscher–Ohlin theory of international trade are:

E. F. Heckscher, 'Utrikeshandelns verkan på inkomstfördelningen', *Ekonomisk Tidskrift*, 1919 (reprinted in English translation in *RTIT*).

B. Ohlin, *Interregional and International Trade*, Cambridge, Mass., Harvard University Press, 1933, especially chs 5 – 7 and 8.

There exists a vast literature on the Heckscher–Ohlin model and the factor-price equalization theorem. The following essays are but a few gleanings from the existing literature. An article that the author has found most useful and on which much of the exposition in Chapter 3 is founded is:

R. W. Jones, 'Factor Proportions and the Heckscher–Ohlin Theorem', *RES*, January 1956.

The first published proofs of the factor-price equalization theorem are found in:

P. A. Samuelson, 'International Trade and the Equalization of Factor Prices', *EJ*, June 1948.

P. A. Samuelson, 'International Factor-Price Equalization Once Again', *EJ*, June 1949 (reprinted in *RIE*).

Another important essay by the same author is:

'Prices of Factors and Goods in General Equilibrium', *RES*, vol. 21, no. 1, 1953.

A stringent proof of the theorem was given already in 1933 by A. P. Lerner in a paper given to the Robbins seminar at the London School of Economics. But the exposition was not published until 19 years later:

'Factor Prices and International Trade', *Ec*, February 1952.

Other essays that can be mentioned are:

H. G. Johnson, 'Factor Endowments, International Trade and Factor Prices', *MS*, September 1957 (reprinted in *RIE*).

K. Lancaster, 'The Heckscher–Ohlin Trade Model: A Geometric Treatment', *Ec*, February 1957.

An excellent survey of the discussion about the factor-price equalization theorem is given in Chipman, Part 3.

5

The gains from trade and the income distribution

In this chapter some of the general-equilibrium aspects of the standard model will be studied more closely. We will start by looking into how a change in one variable in the general-equilibrium system necessarily implies changes in the other variables. We will then go on and study the interrelationships between gains from the income distribution. But we will start by seeing how, in general equilibrium, 'everything hangs together'.

'EVERYTHING HANGS TOGETHER'

We demonstrated in Chapter 2 the precise relationship between the production-possibility curve and the box diagram. We will now apply this knowledge.

Figures 5.1 and 5.2 can be used to demonstrate the interrelationships between the variables in the general-equilibrium system. The production-possibility curve RR in Figure 5.2 has been derived from the box in Figure 5.1 in the way that we have shown in Chapter 2. The only difference from Figure 2.8 is that we have changed it in a mirror-like fashion, so that in Figure 5.2 the origin is at O.

Let us assume that we start with an equilibrium situation with production at point S' in Figure 5.2. This means that the country produces Oa of good A and Ob of good B. This implies that relative commodity prices are as shown by the line $P_0 P_0$, which is tangential to the production-possibility curve at S'.

A unique point on the contract curve in the box diagram corresponds to this point on the production-possibility curve. This unique point is S. This tells us that in order to produce Oa of good A the country has to use Ol of labor combined with Oc of capital, as can be seen from Figure 5.1. It also says that in order to produce Ob of good B the country has to use $O'l'$ of labor combined with $O'c'$ of capital in industry B. It also implies that a certain relative factor price ratio, $P'_0 P'_0$, corresponds to a certain relative commodity price ratio, $P_0 P_0$.

Let us now see what happens if there is a disturbance – if something happens that induces the system to move away from points S and S' to a new equilibrium. There are many factors that could disturb the system. Examples are changes in the factor endowments, innovations that change the technology, changes in demand, and so on. Some of these changes, such as technical progress, are so important that they deserve to be studied at length. This we will do in coming chapters, when we come to the theory of economic growth and trade. For the time being we are only interested in understanding the basic features of the general-equilibrium system. Therefore, we choose the simplest possible type of disturbance as an example: a change in demand, caused, for instance, by a change in tastes.

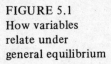

FIGURE 5.1
How variables
relate under
general equilibrium

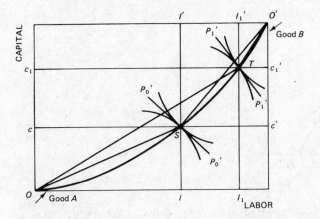

If tastes change so that consumers want more of good A and less of good B, the relative price of A will go up. Let us say that the relative price of A increases from $P_0 P_0$ in Figure 5.2 to $P_1 P_1$. This will induce producers to produce more of A and less of B, so that they move to point T', where the price line $P_1 P_1$ is tangential to the production-possibility curve RR.

What are the implications for factor inputs? First we have to find the point on the contract curve in the box that corresponds to point T'. This point is T. As T lies to the right and above S, it implies more of good A and less of good B. We can directly read off the factor inputs and find that Ol_1 of labor combined with Oc_1 of capital is used in production of good A, and that $O'l_1'$ of labor combined with $O'c_1'$ of capital is used in production of good B. Therefore, we can see that a change in relative prices induces a change in outputs, entailing a change in inputs as well.

It was the labor-intensive good that became relatively more expensive. This implies that the factor intensities in production will change. From Figure 5.1 we can immediately see that the methods of production at T are more capital-intensive in both lines of production compared with what they were at S.

The implications for factor prices are clear. We can read off directly from the box diagram that the relative price of labor has gone up, because the factor-price line $P_1' P_1'$ at T is steeper than the factor-price line $P_0' P_0'$ at S. The explanation for the rise in wages is simple. As more of good A is demanded, the demand for factors of production increases. The good is labor-intensive, so the demand for labor increases, and there is an excess supply of capital as factors are released from industry B, causing an increase in the price of labor and a fall in the price of capital. The change in relative factor prices can also be inferred from the fact that the marginal productivity of labor is higher at T than at S, whereas the marginal productivity of capital is lower at T than at S.

Thus we can see that a change in one of the variables in our general-equilib-

FIGURE 5.2

How variables relate under general equilibrium

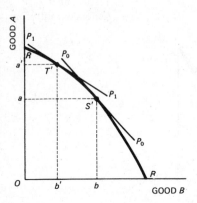

rium model implies a change in all other variables. Once we know which good is labor-intensive and which is capital-intensive, we can infer from a change in commodity prices the direction in which factor inputs, factor intensities and factor prices will change.

THE GAINS FROM TRADE AND THE INCOME DISTRIBUTION

In Chapter 1 when we studied the gains from trade, we found that trade would make a country as a whole better off, but that it need not necessarily make every citizen better off. Therefore, some citizens might need to be bribed into accepting the change from autarky to free trade, so that some could earn much on the transition, while others, by being compensated for eventual losses, at least would not get hurt by it.

We are now equipped to study this matter in detail and to see exactly what effect the introduction of trade will have on the income distribution. Let us again use the box diagram and a production-possibility curve derived from this box diagram as the means of exposition.

Figure 5.4 shows a production-possibility curve RR derived from the box diagram in Figure 5.3. Before trade, under autarky, the country produces and consumes at point S' on its production-possibility curve. Relative commodity prices before trade are given by the line P_0P_0, tangential to the production-possibility curve at S'. The point on the contract curve in the box diagram that corresponds to S' is S.

Let us now assume that a possibility for trade is introduced and that the international terms of trade are given by the line P_1P_1. As good B is relatively more expensive, the country changes its pattern of production and produces more of good B, thus moving to point T' on its production-possibility curve, where the international price line P_1P_1 is tangential to the production-possibility curve. The country can then trade along the international price line. Let us

FIGURE 5.3

Gains from trade and
resource allocation

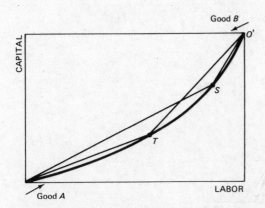

assume that the country moves to point T'' by trading. T'' is obviously better than the point S' because it represents more of both goods. This establishes the fact that the country as a whole can be made better off by trading.

But what about factor prices, and what happens with the income distribution? Can we infer anything about the income distribution from the movement along the production-possibility curve from S' to T'?

Yes, we can. With the tools we have at hand it is easy to see what happens. The point on the contract curve in the box that corresponds to point T' on the production-possibility curve is point T. We then have to compare factor prices at points S and T on the contract curve. We can easily see that at point T the methods of production are more labor-intensive in both industries than they are at S. This implies that the marginal productivities of labor are lower and those of capital higher at T than at S. Therefore, wages are lower and returns to capital higher at T than at S. Thus the income distribution has moved against labor and in favor of the owners of capital.

Another way of stating the same fact is as follows. At point T every worker in both industries has less machinery to work with than he had at point S as the methods of production become more labor-intensive. This means that the marginal productivity is lower, and because the marginal productivity determines the wage, the wage is also lower. The wage times the amount of labor employed determines the income that goes to labor. As there is full employment both before and after trade, there is no change in the volume of employment. Hence the income going to labor decreases when the country goes from autarky to free trade.

From this it follows that the ones who gain from free trade – in our example the owners of capital – will have to compensate the workers for their loss of income in order for us to be sure that all citizens are at least as well off at point T'' as they were at point S'. Only if this is done can we say unconditionally that free trade is better than no trade. This was the point that Ricardo and the classical economists failed to see.

FIGURE 5.4

Gains from trade and resource allocation

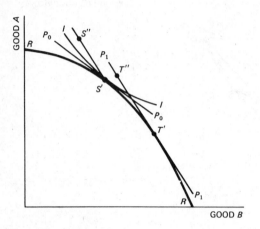

It is no accident that one factor of production gets hurt, as it did in our example, when going from autarky to free trade. In the two-factor model, the factor that is used intensively in the import-competing industry will always suffer when going from autarky to free trade. Therefore, a policy of free trade will generally have to be accompanied by measures of redistribution in order to make sure that free trade will be an advantage over no trade.

But what if those who gain from free trade are not willing to compensate those who suffer? Could some degree of trade still be advantageous?

Yes, it could be. This situation, too, can be illustrated with the help of Figure 5.4. If the capital-owners are not willing to compensate the workers, the workers could refuse to move into the other industry. Then we would have the same pattern of production after trade as before trade and the country would still be producing at point S' on the production-possibility curve. The country would still have the option, however, to trade according to the international terms of trade. She could trade along the price line $S'S''$ (which is parallel to P_1P_1). She would then produce at point S' but consume, for instance, at point S''. This would clearly be advantageous, as point S'' lies to the right of the indifference curve *II*, which is tangential to the production-possibility curve at S' and represents the highest level of utility obtainable under autarky. This shows that restricted trade is better than no trade. But restricted trade is potentially less advantageous than free trade.

6
Factor reversals and factor prices: empirical testing and the Leontief paradox

One of our assumptions in Chapters 3 and 4 was that there was a one-to-one relationship between factor intensities and factor prices, so that regardless of factor prices one good could always be classified as labor-intensive and the other good could always be classified as capital-intensive. Another way of stating this fact is by saying that the isoquants cut only once.

This is a critical assumption for proving factor-price equalization. If this condition is not fulfilled, we have the case of factor reversals, as explained in Chapter 2. The meaning of factor reversals is that at a certain set of factor prices one good is labor-intensive, whereas at another set of factor prices the same good is capital-intensive. This situation is illustrated in Figure 6.1.

For a given factor-price ratio, illustrated by the price line $P_0 P_0$, both industries in the same ratio, the λ ratio. If factor prices were to change, so that capital, for example, became relatively cheaper, both industries would go over to more capital-intensive methods of production. But as the possibilities for substitution are easier in industry B than in industry A, good A would now be labor-intensive and good B would be capital-intensive. Analogously, if factor prices changed in the opposite direction, so that labor became relatively cheaper, good A would become the capital-intensive industry and good B would become the labor-intensive industry. Again, this is because it is easier to substitute labor for capital in industry B than in industry A. Therefore, the factor-intensity ray in industry A will always be closer to the λ ratio than will the factor intensity ray of industry B. (This was already explained in Chapter 2, with the help of Figures 2.5 and 2.6.)

We do not know *a priori* if industry A, for instance, is labor-intensive or capital-intensive. It depends on factor prices. We hinted in Chapter 2 that if factor endowments are specified, only a limited number of factor prices are compatible with economic equilibrium. And at this limited set of possible factor prices one good is always labor-intensive and the other is always capital-intensive. The time has come to establish this fact.

FACTOR REVERSALS, FACTOR PRICES, AND ECONOMIC EQUILIBRIUM

We use Figure 6.2 to establish the proposition that, given factor endowments, one good is always labor-intensive and the other is always capital-intensive. We have the same kind of isoquants as in Figure 6.1 – isoquants which are tangential to one another at the point where they are cut by the critical λ ratio. The only difference is that now we have specified the country's factor endowments. They

FIGURE 6.1

Factor reversal

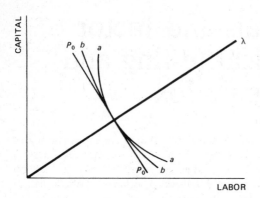

are given by the box *OBO'A*. The diagonal of the box is the line *OO'*. We measure good *A* from the lower left-hand corner and good *B* from the upper right-hand corner.

If factor prices are depicted by the P_0P_0 price line in Figure 6.1, the factor intensity in industry *A* will be the one depicted by the λ ratio. What will then be the factor intensity in industry *B*?

If, for instance, industry *A* were producing at point *C*, the factor intensity in industry *B* would be *O'C*. But at point *C* the relative factor prices must be given by the price line P_0P_0; only then can *C* be a possible equilibrium point, i.e. a point on the contract curve. This presupposes that factor intensities are the same in both lines of production, because we know that at this given factor-price ratio both industries use the same factor intensities. But the factor intensity *OC* in industry *A* is obviously not the same as the factor intensity *O'C* in industry *B*. Hence point *C* cannot be on the contract curve.

The explanation of why *C* cannot be on the contract curve is simple. Given that industry *A* uses the factor intensity shown by the λ ratio – i.e. uses the factor intensity *OC* – industry *B* would also have to use the same factor intensity. But this is not possible, because the total factor endowments do not suffice for this. It would be possible only if the country had more labor than it has – if the box was *OB'O''A* instead of *OBO'A*. As long as factor endowments are what they are, *C* cannot be on the contract curve.

Nor can the contract curve go below the λ ray from the origin. For it to do so would imply that industry *A* could use production methods even more labor-intensive than those illustrated by the λ ratio. Then factor prices would be such that industry *B* also would use a factor intensity more labor-intensive than the one shown by the λ ratio. But the all-over factor endowments do not suffice for this. For this reason the contract curve must be wholly above the λ ray.

But if the contract curve goes above the λ ray, we know that factor prices will have to be such that capital is relatively cheaper than what is shown by the factor-price ratio P_0P_0 in Figure 6.1. And at any set of factor prices where

FIGURE 6.2

Factor reversal
with factor
endowment specified

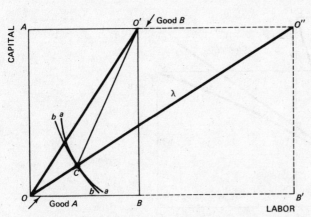

capital is relatively cheaper than it is at the factor-price ratio depicted by P_0P_0, good B will be capital-intensive and good A will be labor-intensive. Therefore, once the total factor endowments are specified, the set of factor prices compatible with economic equilibrium will be restricted. At this restricted set of factor prices one good will always be labor-intensive and the other will always be capital-intensive.

We have now cleared the ground for showing the effects of trade on factor prices in the case of factor reversals.

TRADE AND FACTOR PRICES WITH FACTOR REVERSALS

We assume that we have the situation illustrated in Figure 6.1, so that factor reversals do exist. We now have to distinguish carefully between two cases – one in which factor reversals, though existing in theory, do not play a practical role, and another case in which they will destroy all the earlier results for the effects of trade on factor prices.

The first case is easy to deal with. It is the one in which the endowment proportions in both countries lie on the same side of the critical λ ratio. If, for instance, the diagonals in both countries' box diagrams lie to the left of the λ ray, the only factor-price ratios compatible with economic equilibrium in both countries will be ones with the relative price of capital lower than shown by the price ratio P_0P_0 in Figure 6.1. At this set of possible factor-price ratios good A will be labor-intensive in both countries and good B will be capital-intensive in both countries.

If, on the other hand, the endowment proportions are to the right of the λ ray, good A will be capital-intensive in both countries and good B will be labor-intensive in both countries.

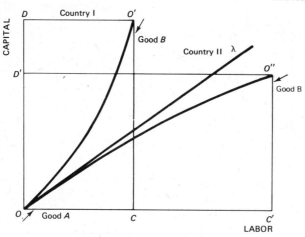

FIGURE 6.3

Factor reversal under
differing factor endowments

From this it follows that if the endowment proportions in both countries are on the same side of the critical λ ratio, there will be the same one-to-one relationship between factor prices and factor intensities in both countries. Although factor reversals exist in theory, they will have no practical importance.

This being the case, we have the same situation in practice as when we assumed that no factor reversals existed, with the strong assumption about a one-to-one relationship between factor prices and factor intensities. Therefore, the same analysis that was used in Chapter 4 can be applied to this case, with the conclusion that trade will lead either to a complete equalization of factor prices or to a tendency to factor-price equalization combined with complete specialization in one or both countries.

The interesting case in connection with factor reversals is therefore the one in which factor endowments differ significantly between the two countries, so that the endowment proportions in the two countries are on different sides of the critical λ ratio. We will now examine this case, which is illustrated geometrically in Figure 6.3 in detail. The factor endowment of country I is given by the box $OCO'D$, and the factor endowment of country II is given by the box $OC'O''D'$. In terms of physical endowments country I is capital-rich and country II is labor-rich.

We assume the isoquants to be of the same kind as those illustrated in Figures 6.1 and 6.2. As the diagonal of country I lies to the left of the critical λ ratio, its contract curve has to lie wholly above the λ ratio. This implies that in country I good A is labor-intensive and good B is capital-intensive.

The diagonal of country II's box, on the other hand, lies to the right of the critical λ ratio. This implies that the only factor-price ratios compatible with economic equilibrium are the ones at which good A is capital-intensive. Therefore, the contract curve for country II has to go above the diagonal of its box.

FIGURE 6.4

Commodity prices and factor prices under factor reversal

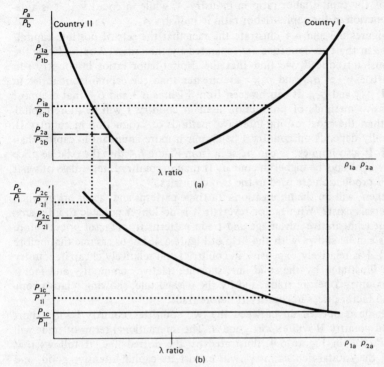

From this it follows that good A is labor-intensive in country I and capital-intensive in country II, and that good B is capital-intensive in country I but labor-intensive in country II.

The next step is to look into the interrelationships among commodity prices, factor prices, and factor intensities in the two countries. If the relative price of good A increases, country I will move along its contract curve from the O corner toward the O' corner. As good A is the labor-intensive good in country I, the relative price of labor will rise and producers will go over to more capital-intensive methods of production. If we use ρ_{1a} to denote the capital/labor ratio in industry A in country I (i.e. $\rho_{1a} = C_{1a}/L_{1a}$), we find that Pa/Pb is an increasing function of ρ_{1a} in country I.

Country II, by analogy, will move along its contract curve from the O corner toward the O'' corner if the relative price of good A goes up. However, in country II good A is the capital-intensive good. Therefore, the relative price of capital will increase and the producers will go over to more labor-intensive methods of production. Using the notation introduced above, we find that in country II Pa/Pb is a decreasing function of ρ_{2a}.

These interrelationships are illustrated in Figure 6.4. On the vertical axis in Figure 6.4(a) we have relative commodity prices, Pa/Pb, and on the horizontal axis we have the capital/labor ratios ρ_{1a} and ρ_{2a} in industry A. Figure 6.4(a) illustrates the fact that in country I the relative price of good A is an increasing function of the capital/labor ratio in industry A, while in country II it is a decreasing function of the capital/labor ratio in industry A.

Both Figures 6.3 and 6.4 illustrate the fact that the sets of possible capital/ labor ratios in the two countries are separated by the critical λ ratio. Using the notation just introduced, we find that the capital/labor ratios in country I in both industries – i.e. ρ_{1a} and ρ_{1b} – are greater than the capital/labor ratios in country II, ρ_{2a} and ρ_{2b}. It can be seen from Figures 6.3 and 6.4 that the most labor-intensive methods of production used in country I will be more capital-intensive than the most capital-intensive methods of production in country II. This naturally depends on country I being much more abundant in capital than country II. It also implies, as can be seen from Figure 6.4 that the relative price of capital will always be higher in country II than in country I, regardless of what methods of production are used in the two countries.

What, then, will be the implications for trade patterns and factor prices when factor reversals exist? With factor reversals it is no longer possible to infer anything about comparative advantage and trade patterns from factor prices before trade. This can be shown with the help of Figure 6.4. Let us assume that before trade good A is relatively expensive in country I and relatively cheap in country II. This is illustrated by the solid line, showing relative commodity and factor prices in country I before trade, and by the dashed line, showing relative commodity and factor prices in country II before trade.

When trade is opened up between the two countries, country I will export good B and country II will export good A. The international terms of trade will move to Pia/Pib in Figure 6.4, illustrated by the dotted line. It follows that country I, the capital-rich country, will export its capital-intensive good, and country II, the labor-abundant country, will also export *its* capital-intensive good. Hence both countries will export their respective capital-intensive goods.

This follows from the simple fact that both countries will not export the same good. But with factor reversals, if good A is labor-intensive in one country, it is capital-intensive in the other country, and vice versa. Hence it follows that either both countries export their respective capital-intensive good or else both countries export their respective labor-intensive good.

In our example, country I, which is abundant in capital, exported its capital-intensive good. There is, however, nothing that prevents it from exporting instead its labor-intensive good. Had good B been relatively expensive in country I before trade, the country would have exported good A, its labor-intensive good. Hence with factor reversals it is fully conceivable that the capital-rich country exports its labor-intensive good and the labor-abundant country exports its capital-intensive good. This holds true even if we define capital abundance and labor abundance in terms of factor prices. Hence the Heckscher–Ohlin theorem does not hold when factor reversals exist.

In a way, however, this is only a superficial objection to the Heckscher–Ohlin theorem. The theorem does not hold true in the literal interpretation given above, but it still holds in a deeper sense. It is true that the country abundant in capital might export its labor-intensive good. It is also true, however, that even in the production of this good, the capital-rich country will use methods of production that are more capital-intensive than any of the methods of production used by the labor-abundant country.

In other words, even though the capital-rich country might export its labor-intensive good, its methods of production even in the labor-intensive industry will be more capital-intensive than will the labor-rich country's methods of production in its capital-intensive line of production. Analogously, the labor-rich country will always use more labor-intensive methods of production in both its industries than will the capital-rich country in either of its industries. In this deeper sense, therefore, the Heckscher–Ohlin theorem will still hold.

What about the factor-price equalization theorem? Will it still hold? No: the factor-price equalization theorem will not hold, given factor reversals. This can easily be seen from Figure 6.4. Country I will export good *B*, its capital-intensive good. This will increase the relative demand for capital and the relative price of capital will increase because of trade. Country II will export good *B*, *its* capital-intensive good. Therefore, in country II also the demand for capital will increase relatively and its relative price will go up. Hence the relative price of capital will go up in both countries.

We have no way of knowing in which country the relative price of capital will increase more. It might increase more in country I; then there will be a tendency to factor-price equalization. But it might just as likely increase more in country II; then there will be a tendency to increase the difference between relative factor prices in the two countries. With factor reversals, however, there is no possibility for factor-price equalization in the two countries. This can easily be seen from Figure 6.4. The relative price of capital will always be lower in the capital-rich country than in the labor-rich country, and the return for labor will always be relatively lower in the labor-rich country than in the capital-rich country.

Perhaps the most interesting empirical test of the Heckscher–Ohlin theorem that has been made so far is a study undertaken by Wassily Leontief in the early 1950s.[1] A very intensive debate followed publication of Leontief's somewhat paradoxical findings. One way of explaining his result is by reference to factor reversals. Before concluding this chapter and the part of the book that deals with the pure theory of trade, it might be worthwhile to discuss briefly Leontief's findings and some of the more important aspects of the discussion of the Leontief paradox.

THE EMPIRICAL RELEVANCE OF THE HECKSCHER–OHLIN THEOREM: THE LEONTIEF PARADOX

Leontief starts from the observation that a country will tend to export those commodities which use its abundant factors of production intensively and import those which use its scarce factors intensively. By common consent the United States is the one country that is most abundantly endowed with capital. Therefore, one would expect the United States to export capital-intensive goods and import labor-intensive ones.

Leontief tests his hypothesis with the help of an input–output table for the United States for 1947. He assumes that the United States decreases its production of exports and its imports by an equal amount, $1 million. This can be achieved, for instance, by an increase in tariffs, making the relative price of imports go up, thereby stimulating production of import-competing goods and making the relative price of exports fall, thereby curtailing production of exports.

Leontief then goes on to see what effects this change in the production pattern will have on the use of the factors of production. He only takes two factors explicitly into account, labor and capital. When exports are decreased, both labor and capital are released. When production of import-competing goods is increased, both more labor and capital are needed. According to Leontief's hypothesis, we would expect relatively more capital to be released from the export industries and relatively more labor to be needed by the import-competing industries.

His finding, however, is that it is the other way around. Export industries use relatively more labor than do import-competing industries. Hence the United States exports labor-intensive goods and imports capital-intensive goods!

How are we to explain Leontief's paradoxical results – that the most capital-rich of all countries, the United States, exports labor-intensive goods?

Like all empirical findings, Leontief's paradox can be explained in a number of ways. We can in this context only touch on what we regard as some of the main contributions to the heated controversy that Leontief's findings gave rise to.

To start with, we might mention that several writers questioned the accuracy and the appropriateness of the data. N. S. Buchanan criticized Leontief's measurement of capital: he argued that Leontief's capital coefficients were 'investment requirement coefficients' which did not take into account the durability of capital.[2] G. A. Loeb argued that the differences in capital intensity between the export sector and the import-competing sector were not statistically significant.[3] B. C. Swerling contended that 1947 (the year for which the input – output table was constructed) was an atypical year.[4]

Leontief refined his measurements and tried to answer this and some other criticisms in a paper published in 1956.[5] This paper hardly settled all the points about measurements and the like. This was not to be expected. There are too many difficulties involved for any completely unambiguous conclusions to come forward. Renewed measurements for later years might reveal a picture other than the one given by Leontief. Until then it seems reasonable to accept Leontief's measurements as basically correct. Let us then go on to the theoretically more interesting question of what explanations can be given for the Leontief paradox, provided we are willing to accept the data on which it is founded.

Several alternative explanations of the Leontief paradox have been given, including the ones forwarded by Leontief himself. We will now briefly discuss the most interesting of these explanations.

One explanation is fully compatible with the Heckscher–Ohlin theory. We know from Chapter 4 that in the case of consistent factor intensities, differential factor endowments establish a comparative advantage in each country for the production of the good using its intensive factor. But demand conditions might offset this predisposition. If the capital-rich country, for instance, prefers capital-intensive goods, it might import these and export labor-intensive goods instead. From data relating to factor coefficients in export goods and import-competing goods alone, no inference can be made about factor endowments.[6]

There is, however, little empirical evidence to support this view. Studies made by H. S. Houthakker show that there is a considerable similarity in demand functions among countries.[7] To date there is little evidence that capital-rich countries have a disproportionate tendency to consume capital-intensive goods. This type of explanation is a theoretical possibility but it does not seem to be a very likely one in view of existing evidence; it is more a theoretical *curiosum* than a very likely empirical possibility.

Leontief himself tried to explain his findings along two different lines. The one he gave priority to ran in terms of differences in labor productivity. Leontief argued that American labor could not really be compared with labor in other countries, because the productivity of an American worker is substantially higher (three times higher, suggested Leontief) than that of a foreign worker. This would be one way, according to Leontief, by which his findings could be reconciled with the Heckscher–Ohlin theorem.

If production functions are identical between countries, if factor reversals are ruled out, and if factors of production are homogeneous and identical between countries except for a multiplication constant (Leontief suggested a constant of 3 for labor in the United States), Leontief's explanation might be valid.

These are quite strong assumptions to accept. Most economists might acknowledge the superior quality of American labor. Leontief quotes a study by I. B. Kravis indicating that wages are higher in U.S. export industries than in its import-competing industries as supporting evidence.[8] This, however, conflicts with Leontief's assumption of labor being a homogeneous factor of production, which would imply the same wage irrespective of occupation.

Difficulties such as these are easily encountered if one is willing to accept Leontief's explanation. It is not easy to swallow the multiplicative constant 3 without further ado. This, then, would also have to be explained. It could be explained by the fact that skilled workers have capital embedded in them by being a product of capital-intensive institutions. Then it might be argued that the United States is still exporting capital-intensive goods but goods intensive in human capital.

Explanations like these, however, easily become somewhat far-fetched. They are not easily compatible with the assumptions of identical production functions between countries and the homogeneity of factors of production, two assumptions that are critical for reaching the Heckscher–Ohlin result. Leontief's explanation is a little too good to be true. It is possible, but it rests on very stringent assumptions. It has a flair of being an *ad hoc* justification of a puzzling result.

Another explanation for which Leontief has shown a certain understanding is connected with the two-factor framework and the broad use of the term 'capital'. The only two factors explicitly taken into account are labor and capital. But, as Leontief notes:

"Invisible in all these tables but ever present as a third factor or rather as a whole additional set of factors determining this country's productive capacity and, in particular, its comparative advantage *vis-à-vis* the rest of the world, are natural resources: agricultural lands, forests, rivers and our rich mineral deposits."[9]

By taking into account this third factor an explanation to the Leontief paradox can be found. It might be the case, for instance, that imports require more capital to labor than exports; it is still, however, possible that imports are intensive in the third factor, say land. If capital and the third factor (land) are substitutes but both are complementary with labor, it might be the case that import-competing goods are capital-intensive in the United States but land-intensive abroad. By bringing a third factor into account in this way, possible explanations might be found.

The analytically most interesting explanation is perhaps the one that invokes factor reversals. We have already discussed the theoretical meaning of factor reversals in the beginning of this chapter. Let us now look into the implications of the existence of factor reversals for Leontief's results.

Leontief took only one country into account. He only computed factor requirements for marginal changes in the production of American exports and import-competing goods. In the beginning of this chapter we have, however, demonstrated that if factor reversals exist, it is fully possible for a capital-rich country to export its labor-intensive goods. The country will still use more capital-intensive methods in its export industries than any other country.

Leontief never brought a second country into the picture. Had he done so and compared, for instance, the factor intensities in American export industries with those of Japan or West Europe, he might well have found that American exports were capital-intensive compared with Japanese or Western European exports. By invoking factor reversals we can thus explain Leontief's puzzling results.[10]

An interesting empirical study of the possibility of factor reversals has been made by B. S. Minhas.[11] Minhas has, together with some other economists, derived a new form of production function, the so-called C.E.S., or *homohypallagic*, production function.[12] When estimating this production function for different countries Minhas finds that factor reversals are quite common because the elasticity of substitution differs between industries, and that these factor reversals occur in the empirically relevant range of relative factor prices (i.e. factor-price ratios prevailing in such diverse countries as the United States and India).[13] This result would tend to reinforce the theoretical possibility of factor reversals as an explanation of the Leontief paradox. Minhas's findings would, alas, also tend to minimize the practical relevance of the factor-price equalization theorem and the Heckscher–Ohlin theorem about capital-rich countries exporting capital-intensive goods, as both these theorems build on the assumption of a one-to-one correspondence between factor prices and factor intensities.

Minhas's study is, therefore, of considerable empirical relevance. His findings have, however, been criticized on econometric grounds, primarily by Leontief. Leontief has recalculated some of Minhas's results using additional information. He then finds that the possibility of factor reversals is much less than Minhas suggests.[14]

Leontief's argument carries a great deal of conviction. This is not to say that the controversy is thereby closed. On the contrary, the empirical relevance of factor reversals is still a very open question. Pending further research, it seems wise not to express a firm opinion in this matter.

Another explanation to the Leontief paradox has been given by Erik Hoffmeyer.[15] He argues that if products relying to a large extent on natural resources are excluded from Leontief's list of goods, the normally expected picture that the United States exports capital-intensive goods and imports labor-intensive goods will prevail.

Hoffmeyer's conclusion is still not completely satisfactory. Some of the products that the United States imports are highly capital-intensive, e.g. petroleum, copper and newsprint. These products are probably as capital-intensive in other countries as in the United States. At the same time, production of these goods might be more efficient outside the United States and hence require a smaller quantity of inputs per unit produced.[16]

Hoffmeyer's conclusion raises some questions. Why is it that the United States does not import more of these resource-rich products if they are cheaper abroad than at home? Why should just these products be excluded? Are they the only ones in which the United States has comparative disadvantage?

An answer to these questions has been suggested by William P. Travis.[17] All the economists who have examined the Leontief paradox have so far implicitly assumed that the law of comparative advantage determines the existing pattern of trade. Travis takes the opposite view. He wants to explain the Leontief paradox with the help of U.S. trade policy.

He refers to the fact that U.S. trade is highly protected, a fact even more true when Leontief made his study than it is today. Travis explains the Leontief paradox as merely a quirk of nature. When Leontief made his study, most competitive imports consisted of crude oil, paper pulp, primary copper and lead, and metallic ores. These products were imported because the United States simply could not produce them. These products are more capital-intensive than any other products. According to Travis, U.S. protective policies alone, therefore, are sufficient to explain the Leontief paradox.

THE ROLE OF HUMAN CAPITAL

Research in more recent years has especially focused on investment in human capital as an explanation for trade flows. The basic idea is simple. Human capital is created by schooling, i.e. by investment in human beings. As such investment takes time and as its fruits are long-lasting, the productivity of labor in which it is invested increases substantially.

Leontief touched on the idea when he referred to the greater productivity of American labor as a possible explanation for the Leontief paradox. Later, in an interesting paper, P. B. Kenen tried to estimate the value of human capital involved in U.S. exports and import-competing products.[18] Using a 9 per cent rate of discount, he estimated its value by capitalizing the income difference between skilled and unskilled labor. He then added the estimates of human capital to those of physical capital and found, indeed, that the Leontief paradox was reversed.

R. E. Baldwin subsequently confirmed the finding that U.S. export industries used more skilled labor than did its import-competing industries.[19] Using costs of education and earnings forgone, he obtained a different measure of human capital. His findings were somewhat ambiguous, to the extent that he found that his measure of human capital was not enough to reverse the paradox except when products using natural resources intensively were excluded.

An alternative to devising measures for human capital is to measure the skill component of labor. This has been done by several writers, notably D. B. Keesing.[20] He showed that there was a rather high correlation between U.S. *net* exports of various commodities and the amount of skilled labor used in their production, so that the United States especially exported goods using a high percentage of skilled labor. The use of human capital as an explanation of the pattern of U.S. trade is generally regarded as a vindication of the Heckscher–Ohlin model. There seems to be little doubt that the United States exports goods which are intensive in the use of human capital and imports goods which are intensive in 'raw' labor. These results have been solidified by the econometric investigations of W. H. Branson and N. Monoyios.[21] The general results do not seem to hinge on whether one estimates human capital by discounting wage differentials or by dividing labor into classes of various skills.

Whether or not human and physical capital can be aggregated into a single measure is a question which can be debated. Both H. B. Lary, in his book *Imports of Manufactures from Less Developed Countries,*[22] and Kenen, in the study aforementioned, used such an aggregate. In their study Branson and Monoyios raise doubts about such a procedure and maintain that human and physical capital should not be combined into one single factor of production to be used in explaining trade patterns.

The latter point of view questions the strict interpretation of the Heckscher–Ohlin model as a two-factor model. Introducing human capital as an explanation of trade seems to necessitate having at least three factors of production: raw labor, physical capital and human capital. Empirical findings are not always easy to reconcile with the simple general-equilibrium models of pure trade theory; they tend to point in the direction of more complicated models whose implications are, unfortunately, often rather vague.

The Heckscher–Ohlin theory is essentially static. Explanations running in terms of human capital and changing technology have a more dynamic flavor. We will return to some alternative explanations of trade in terms of availability, imitation gaps and product cycles in the next chapter. Before that we should also review some empirical results based on the Ricardian theory of comparative advantage.

LABOR PRODUCTIVITY AND COMPARATIVE ADVANTAGE

The discussion about the Leontief paradox is interesting from two points of view. First, it shows that it is not easy to reformulate simple analytical models so that they will be suited to empirical testing. It is easy to mis-specify a model. Second, empirical research is in itself fruitful as it will undoubtedly give rise to reformulations and extensions of the model used as a starting-point for the empirical investigations. The reason we have treated the Leontief paradox and the discussion following Leontief's original paper at some length is that they provide excellent illustrations to the above propositions.

According to our point of view, static theories like the Heckscher–Ohlin theory or the theory of comparative advantage should not primarily be viewed as geared to empirical testing. They are first and foremost means of studying the general-equilibrium characteristics of open economics. Nevertheless, they have been tested and it might be appropriate to end by some comment on these tests.

The Ricardian theory of comparative advantage suggests that labor costs will be the determinant of trade: the country with the lower labor cost in the production of a good will be the exporter of that commodity. A pioneering attempt at empirical testing of this theory was made by Donald MacDougall, and was published in 1951 and 1952.[23] MacDougall used data from 1937 to compare labor productivity and exports for the United States and Great Britain. The bilateral trade between them was only a small fraction of their total trade. What MacDougall then tested was whether their relative exports to third countries was connected with their labor productivities.

Wage rates in the manufacturing sector were roughly twice as high in the United States as in Britain. Therefore, MacDougall argued, the United States should be the dominant exporter in markets where her labor productivity was more than twice as high as in Britain. Britain, on the other hand, should be the dominant supplier in any line of production where her labor productivity was more than 50 per cent of the American. Whenever labor productivity in U.S. industry was twice that of its British counterpart, we should expect export shares of the two countries to be roughly equal in third markets.

MacDougall had data for twenty-five products. His test seems to have come off well, and his findings did not refuse his hypothesis. In most cases the ratio of U.S. to British exports was higher whenever her ratio of labor productivity was higher: here his correlation was high. However, the dividing line between British and American exports in third markets was not where U.S. productivity was twice as high as in Britain. In these markets Britain had still a comparative advantage (we should remember that the test used figures from 1937). The American industries needed even a larger productivity advantage, roughly 2.4, to be even with the British in third markets. The basic explanation for this phenomenon seems to be in terms of demand factors and political preferences. MacDougall himself suggested that imperial preferences and other tariff advantages that were enjoyed by countries which were close to her politically could be possible explanations for the advantage that Britain at the time enjoyed in her export markets. Other reasons could be that Britain had been the pioneering industrial nation and that her dominance in international finance and her commercial reputation still gave her certain advantages which were difficult to measure but which were still important.

MacDougall's study gave support to the Ricardian theory of comparative advantage. One might have thought that factors other than labor costs, such as the presence of capital costs, demand factors, political ties, various types of trade impediments, etc., could have broken the link between labor productivity and export shares. This was not the case. Hence the simple Ricardian model of comparative advantage seems to be a good explanation of the empirical pattern of trade.

Follow-up studies of MacDougall's work have been made by Stern and by Balassa.[24] Stern's study is of special interest. He repeats MacDougall's procedure with data from 1950 instead of from 1937. His general findings confirm the earlier results. But in markets where the higher American labor productivity and the lower British wages offset each other, the British predominance has now diminished so that U.S. procedures now have about 80 per cent of the British exports as compared with 40 per cent before. This suggests that Britain is losing some of the 'immaterial' comparative advantages that she enjoyed before and that export shares in these markets will be determined purely on economic grounds.

SUMMARY AND CONCLUSIONS

The first six chapters of the book have covered the static part of the pure theory of international trade. We have thereby been able to give an explanation of the causes of trade. We have also seen why countries will gain by trading.

By studying the trade model connected with the names of Heckscher and Ohlin we have also been able to get a good understanding of the meaning of general equilibrium. We have seen how the possibility of trade causes a change in commodity prices, giving rise to a change in factor prices, to a reallocation of factors of production, and to a change in the production structure. All these variables are intimately linked together and it is not possible to change one of them without changing all the others. We should by now have a good grasp of how the essential variables in a trading system are interrelated with one another.

Along the way we have introduced economic concepts and geometric tools. We are now familiar with the use of production-possibility curves, indifference curves and box diagrams in the exposition of trade theory.

Our study has been geared towards theoretical aspects of international trade. The pure theory of trade should give us the background for further analysis for development, policy and monetary aspects of international economics, into which we will now go.

Some empirical tests of the Ricardo and Heckscher–Ohlin theories of trade have also been made.

MacDougall and others have confirmed that labor productivity has a high predictive value for explaining a country's export pattern. Enquiries into British and American trade patterns demonstrated that the countries primarily exported the goods in which their labor productivity was the highest.

In a broad sense applications of the Heckscher–Ohlin model have shown that factor proportions can be used to explain a country's trading pattern. As factor proportions change over time, so will the trading pattern: a country that accumulates capital and skill over time will proceed to export more labor-intensive products which use a refined technology, while a pre-existing comparative advantage in simpler industrial products will be eroded as other countries with more abundant labor and lower labor costs will move in to take over these export matters.

Leontief tested the factor proportions theory on U.S. trade but found that the United States exported relatively labor-intensive goods. Several explanations have been forwarded to explain the Leontief paradox. One is that the model was not correctly specified and that Leontief's measurement did not take into account the fact that U.S. labor is more skilled and thereby more productive than labor in other countries. Other possible explanations to the paradox are that tariffs may distort the picture by stopping labor-intensive imports. Factor reversals may also be present and offer an explanation that is fully consistent with the Heckscher–Ohlin theory of the trade.

Research in recent years has especially stressed the importance of investment in human capital as an explanation for trade flows and demonstrated that the United States exports goods which are intensive in the use of human capital and imports goods which are intensive in 'raw' labor.

SELECTED BIBLIOGRAPHY: CHAPTERS 5 AND 6

Important works that should be mentioned in connection with general-equilibrium models of international trade are:

J. L. Mosak, *General Equilibrium Theory in International Trade,* Bloomington, Indiana, Principia Press, 1944.

T. Negeshi, *General Equilibrium Theory and International Trade,* Amsterdam, North-Holland, 1972.

For a discussion of the role of factor reversals which has influenced the exposition in Chapter 6, see:

R. W. Jones, 'Factor Proportions and the Heckscher–Ohlin Theorem', *RES,* January 1956.

M. C. Kemp, *The Pure Theory of International Trade and Investment,* Englewood Cliffs, N.J., Prentice-Hall, 1969.

For a critical discussion of the factor price equalization theorem see:

I. F. Pearce, *International Trade,* London, Macmillan, 1970, book II, ch. 16.

M. Clement, F. L. Pfister and K. J. Rothwell, *Theoretical Issues in International Economics,* Boston, Houghton, Mifflin, 1969.

Material on the Leontief paradox and empirical testing of trade theories are provided in the references mentioned in the text. Excellent survey articles dealing with the testing of trade theories are:

J. Bhagwati, 'The Pure Theory of International Trade', *EJ,* vol. 74, March 1964, pp. 1ff.

Robert M. Stern, 'Testing Trade Theories in International Trade and Finance', in P. Kenen (ed.), *International Trade and Finance: Frontiers for Research,* Cambridge, Cambridge University Press, 1975.

A book of readings that contains important papers on the structure of international trade is:

R. E. Baldwin and J. D. Richardson (eds), *International Trade and Finance: Readings,* Boston, Little, Brown, 1973.

Apart from the papers cited in this and the following chapter, one may mention:

Robert E. Baldwin, 'Determinants of the Commodity Structure of U.S. Trade', *AER,* March 1971.

K. E. Hansson, 'A General Theory of the System of Multilateral Trade', *AER*, vol. 42, March 1952, pp. 52ff.

J. Vanek, 'The Natural Resource Content of Foreign Trade, 1870–1955. and the Relative Abundance of Natural Resources in the United States', *RE&S*, vol. 41, May 1959, pp. 166ff.

7
Alternative theories of trade

ALTERNATIVE THEORIES OF TRADE

The preceding chapters have given a thorough exposition of the established theory of trade. But apart from this mainstream theory there also exist other explanations for trade of a less comprehensive kind. We will now, for the sake of completeness, give a brief exposition of some of these theories.

One such theory is the so-called *vent-for-surplus approach*. It is especially applicable to less developed countries and states that such a country often has some commodity for which domestic demand is already satisfied and which it can readily export or that some idle resources are at hand which can be used for export purposes once trade is opened up. Another approach emphasizes 'availability': it says that Saudi Arabia exports oil because it has rich oil deposits. Monopolistic market forms can provide other important influences on a country's trade pattern. Other theoretical explanations for trade take technological factors as their point of departure. Increasing returns to scale in production may be one reason why a country exports a certain commodity. Demand factors may also be important in explaining international specialization. More sophisticated versions of the technological explanations are the so-called *imitation gap* and *product-cycle* theories.

VENT FOR SURPLUS

The vent-for-surplus approach has mostly been used for explaining how colonial countries were drawn into trade. At the heart of this approach lies the idea that a country has 'free' some commodity or some unused resources which it can use to generate export earnings. Traditional trade theory presupposes that production takes place on a country's production-possibility curve both before and after trade. The vent-for-surplus approach, on the other hand, is most readily interpreted in terms of a country producing inside its production-possibility curve.

It is not exactly easy to explain why this should be the case. A possible explanation runs along the following lines. Let us assume that the country produces two goods, handicrafts and food. According to conventional views, the country ought to be producing somewhere along the line *HF*, its production-possibility curve, in Figure 7.1. Instead it is producing at point *A* inside the curve. Why is this so?

The handicraft sector has a very low productivity both in absolute terms and in comparison with the food sector. Food, however, is relatively plentiful. Hence its relative price is low. Because of the unfavorable terms of trade, the food producers do not worry about producing at maximum capacity. Hence the production-possibility curve becomes inoperative and they will instead be producing at point A, exchanging food for handicrafts at the same relative price ratio as

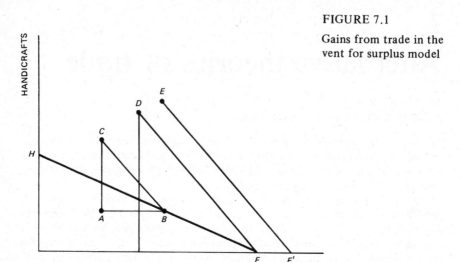

FIGURE 7.1

Gains from trade in the vent for surplus model

that depicted by the *FH* line. We can say that the economic explanation for this behavior is, on the one hand, that land is fertile and plentiful so that the peasants can easily produce the food they need and that leisure is valued fairly highly as its opportunity cost is low. Therefore, due to existing relative prices, the economy is left with a surplus capacity that could be used if economic conditions changed.

The possibility of trade with a mature industrial economy offers the country such a change. It can now obtain much better terms of trade in terms of food products than it could if it were to rely on domestic technology. There would be an increase in the relative price of 'lying in the sun'. Previously, the peasants would only have forgone a few hand-made baskets. Now, each hour in the sun would mean the sacrifice of a greater number of industrial products. The opportunity cost of leisure would rise. The economy would move out to its production-possibility curve, with production taking place at *B*. By trading at the new improved terms of trade it can move to *C*. The slope of the line *BC* measures the international terms of trade and we have assumed that point *C* is tangential to the country's highest feasible community indifference curve.

We have now demonstrated some essential points in the vent-for-surplus theory of trade. Trade does not only lead to a reallocation of resources, as it does in the traditional case. First and foremost it gives rise to a 'vent' or an outlet for the surplus labor and land that existed in the traditional economy. Through the improvement in the terms of trade these productive factors are given incentives to become gainfully occupied. This is demonstrated in Figure 7.1 by the substantial increase in consumption that is represented by the movement from *A* to *C*.

After some time local handicrafts will be ousted from the market and the economy would become completely specialized in the production of food, producing at point *F* in Figure 7.1. We assumed that to begin with the country had both a surplus of fertile land and of labor (which will also be released from the handicraft sector). As trade is opened up, labor will be fully employed at point

B. The next stage is that labor is being reallocated as the country completely specializes in food production. This will bring us to point *F*. If production increases from then on, the production-possibility curve will expand outwards, to point *F'*, as illustrated in Figure 7.1, where the slope of the lines *FD* and *F'E* show the favorable terms of trade. Once all land has been drawn into production the country may enter a difficult period. Then it would be difficult to increase food production, at least in the absence of land-saving technical improvements. With food production constant, the increase in population would eat into the exportable surplus. Exports would fall, and so would imports as imported manufactures would have to be exchanged for food. The pressure on food exports would be combined with the existence of a surplus of labor. The country would then have a difficult policy problem on its hands.

In fact it has been asserted that trade has contracted in former colonial economies.[1] The vent-for-surplus models offer an explanation for this phenomenon that is not easily explicable in terms of the Heckscher–Ohlin model, where we would instead expect a change in factor proportions to take place so that exports would become more labor-intensive and could still expand even if the population expanded.

AVAILABILITY

Why does Saudi Arabia export oil, or Chile copper? The simple-minded answer to the question is that it is because Saudi Arabia has oil fields and Chile has copper deposits. An American economist, I. B. Kravis, has put forward the availability of scarce resources like the ones mentioned above as a rival doctrine to the theory of comparative advantage.[2]

The availability theory has a great deal of plausibility in certain cases. However, it is not a very deep-seated theory and does not take us very far. An example might be taken to demonstrate its usefulness. Let us assume that there are four countries, I, II, III and IV. There are two goods, food *(F)* and manufactures *(M)*. Labor and capital are required for production of both goods but production of *F* furthermore requires land while production of *M* requires technical 'know-how'. The first three countries possess land, while the last three countries possess know-how. Hence country I can only produce *F*, while country IV can only produce manufactures. The other two countries can produce both goods.

From the way the above example is set up it follows immediately that 'availability' will govern the exports of countries I and IV. These countries can only produce one good and must export that good if they are going to acquire anything at all of the other product which they then will have to import. Countries II and III can, however, produce both goods. What they will export will depend on relative prices.

Let us assume that the marginal rate of transformation is constant in both countries and that in country II 5 units of food exchanges for 1 unit of manufactures, while in country III 3 units of food exchanges for 1 unit of manufactures. World demand conditions and production possibilities will determine the price ratio between *M* and *F*. If the price ratio is less than 3*F* for 1*M*, then both countries will export food. If it is greater than 5*F* for 1*M*, then both countries will export manufactures. If the price ratio is between $5F$ for $1M$ and $3F$ for $1M$, say $4F$ for $1M$, then country II will export food and country III will export manufactures.

Summing up, exports from country I of food to country IV and of manufactures from the latter country I can be explained completetely in terms of availability. Trade between countries II and III requires, however, comparative cost theory being brought forward as an explanation, as both countries can produce both goods. Trade between countries I, II and III requires an explanation in terms of availability for country I, while comparative costs have to be taken into account for the rest of the trade; analogous conditions hold for trade between countries II, III and IV, where availability will have to be used to explain trade with country IV.

The above model should serve to highlight the essence of the availability theory. Its fruitfulness, as compared with the traditional comparative cost theory, is an empirical matter. If a large proportion of world trade is of the type taking place between countries II and III in the above example, availability will play a limited role in explaining the pattern of international trade. If, instead, trade is of the country I and IV type, the scope for availability as an explanation will increase. So far as we know, no empirical study of these questions exists.

Another type of availability sometimes referred to has to do with special consumer preferences and is used to explain the cases of Scotch whisky and Swiss watches. Here, foreign consumers have an 'irrational' attachment to the source of a particular product, be it for past excellence, compelling advertising, or some other reason. Consumers are willing to pay more for a commodity for the preferred country than for an objectively identical article from some other country. A country that can produce a commodity of this type will enjoy more favorable terms of trade than potential competitors.

Is this type of availability sufficient as an explanation for trade? No, it is not. It could very well be the case that a country would still be exporting the commodity in question but in a smaller quantity if the special foreign attachment to it did not exist; or it could be the case that the country could switch to the production of some other commodity where its resources could be used even more profitably even though no special consumer preferences were present in foreign markets. What Kravis has in mind seems to be trade in certain articles to which a snob value is attached and which should not otherwise enter world trade as cost differences are too small to warrant international trade. When it comes to trade in certain raw materials like oil or scarce mineral deposits, or commodities whose production requires very specific input factors, availability might be a good explanation. For explaining trade in goods whose production requires a technique that is commonly known or input factors which are readily available, traditional trade theory will prove superior. Which type of trade is most prevalent or most important is basically an empirical question.

MONOPOLISTIC COMPETITION AND INTERNATIONAL TRADE

We have, in the preceding chapters, assumed that competitive market conditions prevailed. Theory means abstraction. Details and all inessential clutter of reality

FIGURE 7.2

Trade and monopolistic
competition

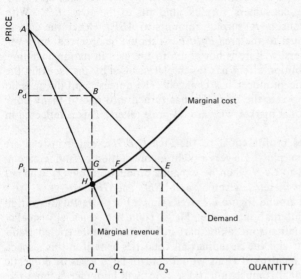

has to be disregarded in order to focus attention on essential points and important
interrelationships. It was in this spirit that we assumed that perfect competition
ruled in commodity and factor markets so that the interactions between a few
important variables could be studied in detail.

In reality, all markets are not competitive. Various forms of monopolistic
competition can play important roles. International trade and market forms
interact in important ways. Monopolistic market forms can have a great impact on
prices and volumes traded. International trade can also influence the organization
of markets, and formerly monopolistic domestic markets can be turned into competitive markets through foreign trade. This is especially important for small and
middle-sized countries where various types of natural monopolies would flourish
were it not for international trade.

It is now time to demonstrate how international trade can influence behavior
under monopolistic market forms. For this we will use the standard graph showing
a simple case of monopolistic pricing. Figure 7.2 illustrates the behavior of a
profit-maximizing monopolist. Given the demand curve, and the marginal revenue
curve that can be derived from it, and given his marginal cost curve, the monopolist will charge the price P_d in his domestic market and sell the quantity OQ_1.
This happens if foreign exporters do not have access to the domestic market, and
when the domestic producer cannot export his product. Let us now assume that
the protection for the domestic monopolist is removed. Foreign exporters will
now move into the market and the internationally ruling competitive price P_i
will also prevail in this market. The quantity sold in the market will increase to
OQ_3.

What is the welfare effect of this change in competitive conditions? Consumers'
total satisfaction from the consumption of the good in question is given by the

area AEQ_3O if the price is P_i. For this they have to pay the amount P_iEQ_3O, which goes to the producers as a remuneration for the resources used up in producing the good. Hence 'consumers' surplus' amounts to the area AEP_i.[3] With monopoly pricing the consumers' surplus amounts to ABP_d. Hence the gain in consumers' welfare is equal to the area P_dBEP_i. It should be observed, however, that the gain in consumers' welfare is not equal to the gain in national welfare, as an important redistribution effect has taken place caused by the fact that the situation of the domestic producer has changed. The domestic producer is no longer a monopolist who sets the price. He has turned into one of many competitors in the international market who are all price-takers. This is reflected in his welfare.

The monopolist loses profits equal to the area P_dBGP_i, which instead are turned into consumers' surplus.[4] He gets a slight compensation by an increase in producer's surplus equal to GFH when he expands production to OQ_2. The net gain in national welfare is therefore given by areas BEG and GFH.

The analysis centered around Figure 7.2 gives a simple but powerful illustration of the importance of international trade. Many countries, especially smaller countries, reap great benefits from taking part in reasonably unrestricted trade. Belgium, the Netherlands and the Scandinavian countries benefit in this respect. Without foreign trade a handful of firms would control large areas of domestic markets. With international competition, these firms will be under competitive pressures and resources will be allocated far more efficiently than what would be the case in the absence of foreign trade. The impact of international competition on market organization is a form of gain from trade that should be added to the traditional ones that we dealt with in preceding chapters.

What has been said so far should not, however, lead us to believe that various types of monopolistic practices are not being used in international trade. The large international corporations are powerful. Often a few of them even control international markets.

Technology and production conditions sometimes give rise to only a few firms operating in a certain market. The presence of only a few sellers in more than one country can be accounted for by the fact that production conditions do not vary that much. Oligopoly at home is met by oligopoly abroad. Firms working under such conditions at home watch each other closely and often cooperate. For firms of this type, international cooperation is quite natural.

An interesting case of monopolistic practices in *international* markets is the case of 'dumping'. This is a phenomenon that is poorly understood by both politicians and laymen. Dumping means that different prices for the same product are charged at home and abroad. The use of the word 'dumping' is somewhat unfortunate – to the extent that it evokes the picture of a producer who dumps some unsold supply in a foreign market. There is, however, nothing vicious or peculiar about dumping. It is simply an example of price discrimination. Two prerequisites for it is that the producer can exert monopolistic control over the domestic market while the demand abroad is more elastic than that at home. These conditions are met quite often. It is not uncommon that a seller has a domestic monopoly but has to face free competition in the international market. A piece of geometry should be useful for illustrating the case of dumping (see Figure 7.3).

FIGURE 7.3

The case of dumping

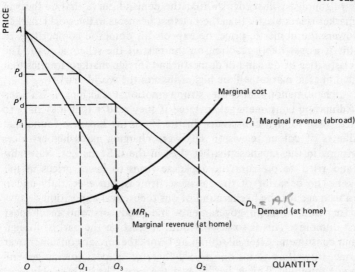

In the domestic market the producer has monopoly power (because of protectionist policies, collusion, or some other reason). The demand curve facing the producer in the domestic market is given by ADh and the marginal revenue curve derived from it is given by the line $AMRh$. In the international market the producer is a price-taker and his demand and marginal revenue curves (which coincide) are given by the line P_iD_i. If our producer had no opportunity to sell abroad, he would maximize profits in the home markets by equating marginal revenue with marginal cost and charge the price P'_d in the domestic market and sell the quantity OQ_3. Now, however, he has the opportunity to sell both at home and abroad. The guiding principle will be that he will maximize his profits by equating marginal revenue with marginal cost in each of his two markets. This can be done by producing the amount OQ_2. At this amount his marginal cost equals his marginal revenue in the international market. He still has the possibility, however, to charge a higher price than P_i in the domestic market. There he will charge the price P_d, where his marginal revenue in the domestic market equals his marginal cost (which is determined by his total volume of production). Out of his total production OQ_2 he will sell OQ_1 in the domestic market and export the rest, i.e. Q_1Q_2. We can observe that, because of dumping, the price in the domestic market will be higher than it would have been if no exports had taken place. Another interesting observation is that the domestic price will move jointly with the international price level. If the international price increases and the producer can increase his profits, one might think that he could compensate the domestic consumers (who will always have to pay a price above the international price) by lowering the domestic price. This will not occur. On the contrary, if the price abroad goes up, so will the price in the domestic market. If the traded price falls, however, the domestic price will also go down.

To illustrate dumping we have used the case of pure monopoly. The general argument is equally applicable to other forms of monopolistic competition like oligopoly. The oligopolist will recognize that the demand curve that he faces in the domestic market is less elastic than the one that he meets in the world market. Hence, if he lowers the domestic price, he expects his domestic competitors to react, while this is a less likely reaction on the part of the sellers abroad. The difference in elasticities of demand in domestic and foreign markets implies that the price in the domestic market will be higher than in the world market.

Dumping is a phenomenon that causes strong emotional reactions. It is understandable that domestic consumers get irritated if they realize that they have to pay higher prices than foreign consumers. In the 1960s the Japanese found that Japanese producers of colour television sets were charging much higher prices for their televisions in the Japanese market than in the U.S. market. Naturally they reacted and tried to pressure the Japanese firms to lower prices in the domestic market. The behavior of the Japanese firms is, however, fully understandable when seen against the background of our theoretical exposition.

It is most frequently foreign governments and producers who react most strongly against dumping. This is somewhat odd, at least on the part of foreign governments and consumers. After all, dumping favors the foreign consumer over the domestic one. In welfare terms one would therefore expect foreign governments to welcome dumping. This is hardly ever the case. The basic explanation seems to be that the foreign governments regard dumping as an unstable situation. Sooner or later, it is expected that domestic producers would be wiped out. Then the foreign firms would again increase their prices in their export markets. Whether this is correct or not is debatable. Probably xenophobia plays its role in explaining the aversion that is raised by the type of price differentiation that goes under the name of 'dumping'.

In modern markets a large proportion of the products are not standardized but are differentiated. A car is not a car, it is a Cadillac, a Volvo, or a Renault. Product differentiation is an important factor in international trade. This is confirmed by the experience of the countries of the European Economic Community. When tariff protection between the Western European countries was removed, trade between the countries increased. But the changes in net trade were not very large. Gross exports rose substantially, however. This suggests that countries penetrate one another's markets, and that foreign trade to an important extent consists of exports and imports of the same class of products which are not complete substitutes but which are differentiated products of the same type.

However, the law of comparative advantage still has an important role to play. The development during the 1970s has again vindicated that proposition. Cost levels have increased quite differently between countries. Competition has become fiercer in the wake of the oil crisis and its deflationary impact. The countries that have experienced difficulties in keeping their cost levels down have had to pay the penalty of losing their share of the market.

The presence of differentiated products has an important impact on trade flows. Generally, domestic producers have a strong position in their own markets as they know the local scene and cater to majority tastes. Foreign producers can, however, find pockets of minority tastes, consumers with special needs or tastes, who will prefer imported products. This is especially important for producers in small countries who often can find a niche in a large country which is very important to them but which is of limited interest to the large producer in the large country. Countries that have similar economic structures and similar cultures swap large volumes of substitutable but differentiated products between one another.

INCREASING RETURNS TO SCALE

In earlier chapters, when examining the neoclassical pure theory of trade, we assumed that returns to scale were constant and production functions homogeneous of the first degree. Increasing returns to scale can, however, be an interesting source of trade. They imply that the real unit cost of production of a good decreases as production expands. Increasing returns to scale are somewhat cumbersome to deal with from an analytical point of view. They are not compatible with competitive market forms. They usually have important implications for the stability of an industry and generally give rise to some form of monopolistic market structure.

Figure 7.4 gives a simple illustration of the effects of increasing returns to scale. Suppose that we have two countries (I and II) that have identical production functions for wheat and cloth and that both are characterized by increasing returns to scale. This gives rise to a transformation curve that is convex to the origin like the curve TQT' illustrated in Figure 7.4. Suppose that each one under autarky produces at point Q and that the terms of trade are given by the line PP. Let trade be opened up. Any slight deviation from the existing terms of trade will lead to complete specialization. Let us say that country I specializes in wheat and country II in cloth. If they were to exchange the goods at the same terms of trade as before trade was opened up, they could still both be better off (the line TCT' is parallel to the PP line). This is demonstrated by the fact that the point C is outside and to the right of Q. Increasing returns to scale will naturally lead to complete specialization as the countries reap the benefits of large-scale production. The example given above is primitive. Nevertheless, it captures some of the essence of increasing returns to scale. The man in the street, if he reflects on the causes of trade, would probably say that international specialization is due to the fact that unit costs of production fall as the scale of production increases. Increasing returns to scale can also play an important role for trade.

In particular, small countries should be able to benefit from international trade if increasing returns to scale are present. As it is no longer confined to small-scale production of its exportables, it can increase capacity and lower production costs. Economies of scale can be of importance in the production of standardized products. They can, however, also play a role in connection with differentiated products. The length of the production run of a differentiated good within a plant might be important for its production costs. Before European integration, European unit costs were usually distinctly higher than U.S. costs for the same product. This has been explained by the fact that the average European plant was producing more ranges, styles and sizes than its American counterpart. An increase in the length of run made possible by increased exports can then have important cost-reducing effects.[5]

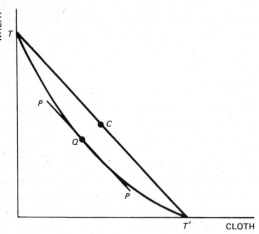

FIGURE 7.4

Trade and increasing returns
to scale

An argument that runs counter to the general trend of thought has been advanced by the Belgian economist Jacques Drèze. He argues that many goods are effectively differentiated between countries and geared for a special national market. This has less to do with the fact that tastes, etc., may differ than with the presence of specific national standards and various safety regulations (for electrical equipment, special measure requirements, etc.). Such non-tariff barriers to trade will especially impede producers in small countries. They will not reach an efficient scale of production in the home market, and they will not have access to markets abroad. Therefore, Drèze suggests, the best way out for small countries may be to specialize in undifferentiated products, often of an intermediate type, like wood products, metals, minerals, paper and pulp, etc., and instead import differentiated products.[6]

Dynamic scale effects have long been recognized as important for trade. It may take time for an industry to acquire skill and capacity. The work-force might have to be trained for a long time to learn industrial skills. 'Learning by doing' can be an important factor in reaping increasing returns to scale which only come through time and experience. We will return to some of these questions when discussing infant-industry arguments for protection in Chapter 16.

TECHNOLOGY, IMITATION GAP, AND PRODUCT CYCLES

In the first six chapters technology was regarded as being stable. They were concerned with the long run determinants of trade. We studied primarily general-equilibrium aspects of trade of the stable, long-run kind.

But the world is not stable. One important source of change is technology. Availability, for instance, can be interpreted in terms of availability of a special technology that can give a country a comparative advantage in that line of production. Monopoly power is often based on the possession of a superior technology.

Hence technology can be important for explanations of trade patterns that emphasize technology or monopolistic competition.

The most interesting explanations of trade where technological improvements play an essential role are the so-called *imitation gap* or *product-cycle* theories.

Innovation is at the heart of modern production. New products and new production methods are constantly developed. This process can have a profound influence on the pattern of international trade.

When a firm develops a new product it first tests it in the domestic market. If the product proves successful, it is natural that the firm tries to expand production of it by trying to introduce it in foreign markets. Analogously, a new production process for an established product may be invented. The new process lowers cost. It is embodied in a new piece of machinery. The firm that has the new type of equipment can either use it to lower prices on the final product and increase its market share or it can export the new equipment.

In both these cases, the country in question will have a comparative advantage and an imitation gap with the rest of the world will be created. For a time the innovating country enjoys a monopoly and others have to import the good or the new technology. Trade is created during the period of the imitation gap. But naturally, producers abroad will want to imitate the new product or to learn the new production process. But it may take time before they can do this.

M. V. Posner has made an interesting test and elaboration of the imitation gap theory.[7] He breaks up the imitation lag into three components. The first is 'the foreign reaction lag', which is the time it takes for the first foreign firm to try to produce the new good. The second is 'the domestic reaction lag', which is the time that is required for other domestic producers to follow suit and to be able to establish a hold on the domestic market. The third is 'the demand lag', which is the time it takes for the domestic consumers to acquire a taste for the new product. If local producers are on the alert and take up production of the new good quickly, and if consumers in the country are slow in their response to the new product, the imitation lag will be shortened. If the contrary holds, so that domestic consumers are eager to get the good but local producers are not able to produce it, the imitation lag will be prolonged. In principle it can become eternal.

A dynamic country in international trade is characterized by the rate at which it innovates, which includes both the number of new commodities and production processes that it introduces per unit of time, and the speed with which it imitates foreign innovations. If one of two trading partners have a higher degree of dynamism than the other country, the second country will find its markets being eroded and its balance of trade to be in deficit. The more sluggish partner will then have to try to redress the balance by exporting more traditional products. Usually this will have to be done at deteriorating terms of trade. Classic illustrations of the operation of this mechanism from the post-war era are given by the performances of the British and the Japanese economies. The British economy has been lacking in dynamism. It has tended to be caught in a vicious circle. The lack of dynamism has caused deficits in the balance of payments as exports have lost their competitiveness. Deflationary policies have had to be used to curb the deficits. They, in turn, have prevented the country from investing on a large scale in modernizing plants and equipment which alone could have raised the degree of dynamism. The Japanese economy, on the other hand, has had a high ratio of investment to

G.N.P. and a fast rate of innovation. This created a highly competitive economy which has led to a strong balance of trade. Presence of dynamism tends to give rise to cumulative processes: if a country has a high degree of dynamism, it usually has a strong external position.

Another theory of technological change that is rather closely related to the imitation-gap model is the product-cycle theory. This model develops the imitation-gap approach by suggesting that changes occur in the input requirements of a new product as it becomes established in a market and standardized in production. As the product cycle develops, the cost advantage will also change, and a comparative advantage in innovative capacity may be offset by a cost disadvantage. A standard example for explaining the product-cycle theory is the case of the radio.

When the radio was invented its market success was uncertain. To begin with, it did not appeal to many customers. Production was small scale, and of a handicraft type that demanded large amounts of skilled labor. The price was high and the good had to be produced close to the market as the commodity was far from perfect. Repairs and improvements of existing radios were necessary to make them work and a quick feedback from the consumers was important for the producers in order that they could get the essential information required to perfect the product.

After an initial period of trial and error, the radio became an established product suitable for mass production. Demand for the product increased as the networks expanded and the usefulness to the consumers became obvious. Soon it developed into an export item as the innovating firms started to test foreign markets. At the end of the Second World War the radio was a well-established product. In the early stage of its history U.S. producers dominated the international market for radios built with vacuum tubes. Soon, however, Japan took over a large share of this market as the production technique became known. Japan could exploit her low labor costs and start to expand production and take over a large part of the international market. Then the U.S. industry developed the transistor, and for a number of years the U.S. radio competed successfully with the Japanese industry, which continued to be based upon the old technology. Eventually, the Japanese learned the transistor technology and again, taking advantage of its low labor costs, started to compete with American producers. Later developments on the part of the U.S. industry with miniaturized transistor technology has again given the U.S. industry a technological advantage. It remains to be seen if the cycle of innovations and erosion of comparative advantage will continue or if the technology is approaching its state of maturity. If the latter is the case, it will be interesting to see if the technology in the end will be capital or labor-intensive.

The theory of the product cycle helps to explain changes in production and trade in new product lines. The case of the radio and electronics industry is instructive. It seems that the most advanced industrial nation, the United States, has been the principal innovator. But production has spread rather rapidly to other countries that have been technically alert and which have had a comparative advantage in terms of cheap labor. Two interesting observations can be made in connection with product cycles. First, the export performance of the mature, principal innovating country is better for new products than it is for those approaching maturity. Second, technology becomes simplified as the maturing process continues, and products which are at first produced with skilled labor can later be produced by an increased use of automatic processes combined with the use of unskilled labor.

The relationship between technically advanced and less advanced countries does not remain stable forever. Countries which once were the principal innovators might fall into relative decline. There is a phenomenon that is sometimes referred to as 'the penalty of taking the lead'. A classic illustration of this can be taken from railway history. Britain was the first country to produce railways. At the time it was done with a narrow gauge and small goods wagons. Later, this proved to be a drag on progress and subsequent imitators like Germany and the United States could adapt their railways more successfully to new technological and economic conditions. This helped them to challenge the British supremacy and compete with the earlier principal innovator in many lines of production.

Demand factors can also be important in connection with the product cycle. As a consumer good matures and incomes rise, many products pass from being a luxury to become a necessity; what is a necessity is, after all, a relative thing depending on standards of living and preferences. (The effect of technical progress on any commodity or group of commodities is generally to lower its relative price.) General growth of *per capita* incomes broadens the market for mass production. This leads to a general increase of international trade in the later stages of the product cycle.

Demand factors can also be important in determining trade flows. New commodities often appear in rich countries. Scarcity of labor in relation to capital prompts the searching for labor-saving devices and generates a stream of automatic machinery and appliances that will facilitate household work. Once these products have appeared in a country, they tend to be exported to countries with similar demand conditions. The Swedish economist Staffan B. Linder has argued that a country tends to specialize in production and exports of products for which there is a large demand from the majority of the population, while goods in demand at the upper or lower spectrum of demand would be imported. Linder found some support for his hypothesis in the case of Sweden, but efforts to replicate his results for other countries have generally not been successful.[8]

The product-cycle theory is interesting to the extent that it points to the importance of changing technology as an important determinant of trade. It thereby also involves time in an essential way. It also points to the fact that human knowledge and technical ingenuity are important determinants of international trade apart from land, labor and capital.

SUMMARY AND CONCLUSIONS

In this chapter we have introduced some alternative explanations of trade. We have also modified some assumptions that were used in the previous chapters and taken imperfect competition into account and dealt with some aspects of technological change.

The vent-for-surplus theory was primarily applicable to less developed countries. It suggested that if a country has some 'free' commodity or some unused resources that can be used for export purposes, it can readily gain by engaging in foreign trade. The theory also points to some risks connected with trade. If a country's traditional handicraft sector is wiped out because of international competition, and if a population increase eventually eats into the exportable surplus of food, trade might in the end contract and development come to a halt.

The availability theory points to the existence of some specific commodities or scarce resources as a cause of trade. The theory is easily applicable to the case of oil or mineral deposits. When it comes to trade in goods where input factors are generally available, traditional factor proportions theory offers a superior type of explanation.

International trade can have important effects on market forms, and market forms can influence trading patterns significantly. When the domestic market is dominated by a monopolist, opening up the market to international competition can give the country great benefits. This case is especially applicable to small and middle-sized countries whose markets are prone to be riddled by various forms of monopolistic competition.

Monopolies and oligopolies in one country often come into competition with the same market forms in other countries. However, firms working under monopolistic competition will naturally try to collaborate internationally to divide markets and decrease competition. However, they often find it harder to collude with their foreign than with their domestic rivals. This fact helps to explain *dumping*, which is a form of price differentiation built on the fact that the domestic market is monopolistic or oligopolistic while there is more competition in the international market. Dumping implies that export prices are lower than domestic prices and that, therefore, foreign consumers will be at an advantage.

Under product differentiation countries may export and import the same goods (or goods which are close substitutes). However, the domestic producer should be at an advantage as he knows the domestic market better. With product differentiation, international trade will be larger than it would be if products were completely homogeneous and costs alone determine the production pattern.

Increasing returns to scale can influence the location of production both in static and dynamic ways ('learning by doing'). Their presence can profoundly influence production through trade and will often lead a country to specialize completely in one or several lines of production.

Technology factors point to the importance of changing production patterns through time. Innovations are an important source of trade. The theory of the innovation gap suggests that the country that is a leading innovator will have a comparative advantage in the exports of new, technically advanced products. The product-cycle theory helps to explain how the export pattern changes as a product matures. In the early stages the innovating country has a lead. Then the product is usually produced with the help of skilled labor. As the production process becomes rationalized, other countries, in which labor is inexpensive, will come in as serious competitors and take over parts of the international market.

SELECTED BIBLIOGRAPHY: CHAPTER 7

For the vent-for-surplus theory of trade, see:

H. Myint, 'The Classical Theory of International Trade and the Underdeveloped countries', *EJ,* vol. 68, June 1958.

R. E. Caves, 'Export-led Growth and the New Economic History', in J. Bhagwati *et al.* (eds), *Trade, Balance of Payments and Growth,* Amsterdam, 1971.

R. E. Caves, ' "Vent for Surplus" Models of Trade and Growth', in R. E. Baldwin *et al.* (eds), *Trade, Growth and the Balance of Payments,* Chicago, Rand McNally, 1965.

R. Findlay, *Trade and Specialization,* Baltimore, Johns Hopkins University Press, 1970, ch. 4.

S. A. Resnick, 'The Decline of Rural Industry under Export Expansion: a Comparison among Burma, Philippines and Thailand, 1870 – 1938', *Journal of Economic History,* March 1970.

For availability theory, see the work cited in the text by Kravis.

For works on monopolistic competition and international trade, see:

M. A. Adelman, *The World Petroleum Market,* Baltimore, 1973.

C. Edwards, *Control of Cartels and Monopolies: an International Comparison,* New York, Dobbs Ferry, 1966.

D. L. McLachlan and D. Swann, *Competition Policy in the European Community,* London 1967.

An early analysis of the imitation gap theory is the work quoted by Posner. The product cycle theory has been discussed in:

R. Vernon, 'International Investment and International Trade in Product Cycle', *QJE,* May 1966.

W. Gruber, D. Mehta and R. Vernon, 'The R + D Factor in International Investment of United States Industries', *JPE,* February 1967.

G. Hufbauer's book *Synthetic Material and the Theory of International Trade,* Cambridge, Mass., Harvard University Press 1966, contains a thorough study of product cycles in the chemical industry.

A major source for theoretical and empirical investigations on technology and trade is:

R. Vernon (ed.), *The Technology Factor in International Trade,* New York, National Bureau of Economic Research, 1970.

The influence of demand factors on the trade pattern are treated in:

S. B. Linder, *An Essay on Trade and Transformation,* New York, Wiley, 1961.

PART II

Economic growth and international trade

8
Economic growth and international trade during the nineteenth and twentieth centuries

In the first seven chapters we studied the theory of international trade under static conditions. The only exceptions were some aspects of dynamic trade theory dealt with in Chapter 7. We took an economic system characterized by no trade, introduced the possibility of trade, and studied in a careful way the characteristics of the new equilibrium with trade. This part of trade theory is completely static.

Now we have to go on and see what happens to two countries' trading relationships given economic growth, i.e. provided that some fundamental variables in the trading system change. New methods will have to be used to do this. We then no longer study only the characteristics of a static, never-changing situation. The methodology that we will use is that of comparative statics. We now start from a given equilibrium situation, introduce a change in one of the variables – for instance, in the amount of capital available to an economy – and study the implications for the new equilibrium, given this change.

Before we go into the theoretical aspects of economic growth and international trade, it is appropriate to say a few words about the long-run development of the world economy.

THE GROWTH OF WORLD TRADE DURING THE NINETEENTH AND TWENTIETH CENTURIES: A BIRD'S-EYE VIEW

The nineteenth century, from an economic point of view, is remarkable. Earlier centuries had witnessed economic development, but on a slow and modest scale. The limited amount of empirical evidence that exists shows that, for instance in Great Britain, probably the most vigorously expanding country during the eighteenth century, total product grew by 5 per cent per decade from 1700 to 1780, and that income *per capita* increased by 2 per cent per decade during the same period.

This shows that an economic transformation of the British society took place during the eighteenth century, and that the change occurred at a slow pace. The nineteenth century, by contrast, showed very high rates of growth in several fields. The growth of the British economy, for instance, was spectacular: Britain's population more than trebled during the nineteenth century, despite heavy

TABLE 8.1

World foreign trade from 1750 to 1889

	Approx. 1750	1820– 1830	1830– 1840	1840– 1850	1850– 1860	1860– 1870	1870– 1880	1880– 1889
World trade, at 1865 – 85 prices (millions of £)	153	315	410	662	1058	1616	2483	3497
Rate of growth per decade (%)		10.1	30.2	61.5	59.8	52.7	53.7	43.4

SOURCE: S. Kuznets, *Modern Economic Growth: Rate, Structure, and Spread*, New Haven, Conn., Yale University Press, 1966, pp. 306–307.

emigration, and the national income seems to have increased more than seven-fold at current prices.

Britain was not the only country to experience rapid economic growth. The United States showed an even higher rate of growth, especially during the latter half of the nineteenth century. Several European countries, and some countries overseas, too, especially those colonized by Britian, also showed rapid economic development.

The growth of world trade is an important aspect of economic development during the nineteenth century. Tables 8.1 and 8.2 summarize this development. The tables contain some important and interesting information. First, the rate of growth of world trade was quite low from around 1750 to 1820. During this period, trade seems to have increased by about 10 per cent per decade, or 1 per cent per annum.

Needless to say, the statistical information for this period is not too reliable. Trade between the relatively developed countries and the more isolated parts of the world could possibly have been measured inadequately. Smuggling, which at this time was not insignificant, is not taken into account, and so on. It is hardly probable, however, that factors such as these would influence the broad trend, which shows that foreign trade grew at a very moderate pace from the middle of the eighteenth century up to approximately 1820.

After the Napoleonic wars, from around 1820, world trade started to grow at a brisk pace. During the 1820s and 1830s, trade speeded up, international trade growing at an astonishingly steady rate during most of the nineteenth century. The rate of growth, by roughly thirty year periods, was 50 per cent per decade between 1820–30 and 1850–60, and between 1850–60 and 1880–89.

The next thirty year period, from the 1880s to the beginning of the First World War, also show a very marked increase in world trade, though the relative rate of growth was somewhat lower: from 1881–85 to 1911–13, world trade grew at a rate of 37 per cent per decade. For the long period as a whole, i.e. from the 1820s to 1913, the rate of growth of world trade was 46 per cent per decade.

Another interesting fact is the trend in foreign trade ratios. We have seen that

TABLE 8.2

World foreign trade from 1881 to 1913

	1881–1885	1886–1890	1891–1895	1896–1900	1901–1905	1906–1910	1911–1913	1913
World trade, at 1913 prices (billions of $)	15.69	18.13	19.97	22.54	27.52	32.88	39.07	40.50
Rate of growth per decade (%)		42.0	27.3	24.2	37.8	45.9	47.6	

SOURCE: Kuznets, *Modern Economic Growth,* pp. 306–7.

trade grew rapidly. For most countries, their foreign trade grew faster than their national income. This led to an increase in the foreign trade quota. Around 1840, the proportion of foreign trade to the British national product was roughly 20 per cent; at the outbreak of the First World War, this proportion had grown to over 40 per cent.[1]

Other European countries experienced a similar development. The foreign trade proportion of France was 21.9 in 1859; around 1910 it had risen to 35.2. Italy and the Scandinavian countries also showed a marked increase in their dependence on foreign trade. Germany is the only exception, showing a more or less stable foreign trade quota during the later half of the nineteenth century.

Other 'new' countries which underwent a rapid economic development showed a diverse picture in this respect. Japan followed the general European pattern and had a rapidly growing foreign trade ratio: Around 1880 it amounted to only 10 per cent of GNP; at the outbreak of the First World War it had risen to 30 per cent. Other 'new' countries, such as the United States, Canada and Australia, showed a steady, or even falling, foreign trade ratio. For Canada, the ratio showed some fluctuations, but the trend was on the whole steady. Australia and the United States showed a slight fall in their ratios: the United States had a foreign trade ratio of 13 per cent in the 1840s; at the beginning of the twentieth century, it had fallen to 11 per cent; apart from showing a declining trend, the foreign trade ratio of the United States was remarkably small.

In a general way, the changes in the foreign trade proportions could be regarded as the result of two competing sets of forces: on the one hand, those that induce growth of domestic output, and, on the other, those that induce growth of exports and imports. It is obvious that the trade-generating growth factors were very strong during the nineteenth century. For most countries, trade grew faster than domestic output. The main European countries, especially Britain, economically the most important, showed an export-biased type of growth. The major exception is the United States, which even during the nineteenth century showed an import-biased type of growth.[2]

To explain the pattern of growth and trade is a large and involved undertaking. This chapter presents only a broad outline of this process; therefore we will merely point to some of the most important causes of this development.

One is that the nineteenth century was dominated by a great revolution in transport connected with the development of railroads and ocean transport. The railroads led to an opening up of new territories such as the west of the United States, and of formerly underdeveloped parts of Canada, Argentina and Australia, which then became exporting areas of agricultural products. In Europe, the introduction of railroads led to an increase in both foreign and domestic trade. The development of ocean transport made possible an increase in the trade between Europe and the countries overseas.

It seems that for the 'new' countries, such as the United States, Australia, Canada and Argentina, the improvements of transport had the strongest effects on domestic trade. These countries also showed high rates of growth during the nineteenth century. In Europe, on the other hand, improvements in transport mostly favored foreign trade.

Another important aspect was the continuous absorption of previously closed areas into the network of world trade: Japan is the most conspicuous example. Apart from Japan and the 'new' countries referred to above, foreign trade did not induce any strong domestic growth. The other less developed countries remained underdeveloped and had mostly the character of trade posts of the developing countries.

Economic policy also played an important role. For most of the nineteenth century, Britain was the world's leading economic nation. It was there that the industrial revolution started in the middle of the eighteenth century, and consequently she became the center of the world economy. Britain was an island with limited resources, so it was natural for her economy to be geared to trade. The classical British doctrine of comparative advantage developed by Ricardo and others in the early nineteenth century stressed, as we have seen, the gains from trade. The doctrine of free trade was the cornerstone of Britain's economic policy, and the British economists preached the virtues of free trade. At least until the last quarter of the nineteenth century, there was also a marked lowering of trade barriers. This could hardly have done other than have greatly favored the growth of world trade.

Britain's economic growth was centered around manufacturing. It was of an export-biased kind, and Britain was the main supplier of industrial products to the rest of the world. As the British economy grew, it became increasingly specialized. It depended more and more on imports, of which agricultural goods and raw materials were the most important. Britain's imports came from the United States, to some extent from Central Europe, from what have been called 'regions of recent settlement' - i.e., Canada, Argentina, Uruguay, South Africa, Australia and New Zealand - and from the Scandinavian countries. All these countries experienced a great impetus for economic growth through an increased demand from Britain for their exports. They could start to grow by exporting food products and raw materials to Britain, and they could continue to grow because Britain's demand for their exports kept growing.

A significant fact to bear in mind is that countries which could be classified among the less developed at this time - the regions of recent settlement and the Scandinavian countries - especially benefited from this type of growth. Table 8.3 gives a hint of this.

TABLE 8.3

Percentage distribution of British imports by countries of origin

	1857–59	1911–13
United States	19	19
Other 'new' countries*	8	18
Industrial Europe†	21	23
All other areas	52	40
	100	100

*Canada, Argentina, South Africa, Australia and New Zealand.
†Germany, France, Italy, Belgium and the Netherlands.

SOURCE: R. Nurkse, *Patterns of Trade and Development,* Oxford, Blackwell, 1962, p. 16.

We know that Britain's imports grew rapidly during the nineteenth century. Table 8.3 indicates that the 'new' countries increased their share of British imports very substantially. For these countries, and for some others, such as the Scandinavian countries, trade truly served as *an engine of growth.*

From the point of view of theory, we can observe the following. We know that international trade along the lines of comparative advantage brings about an improved allocation of existing resources and gains from trade. But static trade theory has no implications for growth; it can only tell how resources ought to be allocated at a given point in time. At a time when transport improved greatly in efficiency, when policy barriers to trade were removed and countries entered into trade with each other, static trade theory did have a great deal of relevance. But once the countries in question had started to trade and had reallocated their resources, what happened?

On this, the static theory has little to say. What happened was that the central country of the world economy, Britain, grew at a steady pace. Her imports grew even faster. Her trading partners, the 'peripheral countries' saw their exports expand rapidly; they could continue to grow along a pattern suggested by the theory of comparative advantage. The theory itself did not promise any growth, but it so happened that the demand for the products in which the 'peripheral' countries had specialized grew rapidly.

The first half of the twentieth century did not show any comparable expansion of world trade. Table 8.4 illustrates that trade between countries continued to grow but on a much more modest scale. However, as Table 8.4 also shows, a rapid increase in the growth of world trade took place during the 1950s and 1960s. This has meant that despite the markedly lower rate of expansion of world trade during the first half of the century, the growth rate of world trade from 1913 to 1970 has been approximately 37 per cent per decade or about 3.7 per cent per annum, i.e. only slightly lower, than that experienced during the nineteenth century. Indeed, if allowance is made for the First World War, which was an abnormal period, the growth rate for the period 1928 to 1970 was 44 per cent, or almost identical to that of the period from 1820 to 1913.

TABLE 8.4

World foreign trade 1913 to 1974

	1913	1928	1937	1950	1960	1970	1974
Index of volume of world exports (1913 = 100)	100	113	114	131	244	525	732
Rate of growth per decade (%)		8.5	1.0	11.3	86.0	115	(119)

SOURCE: Kuznets, *Modern Economic Growth*, p. 308.

Another important aspect of the development of world trade since the First World War is its unevenness. During the 1920s there was a modest growth of around 1 per cent per annum; in the 1930s there was a complete standstill. During the 1940s there was again a modest growth, and during the 1950 and 1960s a very rapid rate of growth.

Much of this development is explained by the upheavals of the first half of the twentieth century. During the sixty years since 1913, a full decade was taken up by the two world wars. Another decade was characterized by deep depression. Several years were taken up by recovery after the wars; these were painful years, especially for the countries that had suffered heavy damage in the wars. On the other hand, the period since 1950 has been markedly free from disruption.

The upshot, therefore, is that development during the twentieth century has been characterized by two very different periods. Trade increased at a slow pace among industrial countries during the interwar period. The two world wars impeded foreign trade more than output and the capacity to produce. The effects of the prolonged depression of the 1930s were also more harmful to trade than to domestic production; this was due to the fact that the depression induced protectionist policies.

Since the beginning of the 1950s international trade has increased at a very rapid rate. During a quarter of a century leading up to the middle of the 1970s the volume of trade has expanded by around 8 per cent on an annual basis. Production has also expanded at a rapid rate, but the increase of trade has outstripped that of production, and hence the degree of international interdependence has increased. The above description applies primarily to the developed industrial countries. The basic pattern also applies to many less developed countries, even though there are marked differences between various groups of countries.

We have seen that world trade and trade among industrial countries increased at a relatively slow pace during the first half of the twentieth century. This period of slow growth has been followed by two decades of rapid expansion in world trade. This pattern has also applied to the less developed countries in so far as the retardation of world trade was even more pronounced for them. However, they have not shared to the same extent in the rapid growth of world trade

TABLE 8.5

Foreign capital investments and the shares of three major countries before 1914 (absolute figures in billions of dollars)

| | Gross foreign investment outstanding | | | | |
	Ca. 1874	Ca. 1880	Ca. 1890	Ca. 1900	Begin. 1914
Great Britain	4.6	5.8	9.5	11.7	19.6
France	n.a.	3.0	4.0	5.6	9.0
Germany	n.a.	1.2	2.8	3.4	5.6
TOTAL	6.0	10.0	16.3	20.7	34.2
Volume per year, 1913 prices		0.62	0.68	0.52	1.09
Total foreign investment, 1913 prices	4.9	8.6	15.4	20.6	35.3

SOURCE: Kuznets, *Modern Economic Growth*, p.322.

during the 1950s and 1960s. We will return to their situation and to the development of world trade since the second World War at the end of this chapter. First, we will briefly examine capital movements and take a somewhat closer look at one case where trade functioned as an engine of growth along the standard nineteenth-century pattern, the case of Sweden.

INTERNATIONAL CAPITAL MOVEMENTS

International capital movements played an important role during the nineteenth century. They provided an outlet for savings in the mature, industrial countries and helped to finance development in countries then emerging from a traditional, agricultural economy. They also helped to ease the balance-of-payments problems of the rapidly developing 'new' countries. Table 8.5 summarizes some of the information about the major lending countries.

Table 8.5 shows the position for only three major credit countries. These, however, had a dominating position at the time: together, they accounted in 1913 for about three-quarters of the total gross debt outstanding. Table 8.5 is therefore quite a good indicator of the amount and importance of international lending during the period in question.

The annual value of world trade in 1913 prices amounted in 1881–85 to about $6 billion per year; it increased to about $13 billion per year in 1913. The capital outflows for the 1874–1914 period averaged between $0.5 and 1.1 billion per year. The outflow of foreign capital seems therefore to have amounted to roughly 10 per cent of the trade volume. This is quite a substantial figure and shows that capital movements played an important role during the forty-five years before the First World War.

TABLE 8.6

Shares of debtor areas in outstanding gross investment in 1913-14 (%)

Europe	28
United States and Canada	24
Oceania	5
Latin America	i9
Asia and Africa	24

SOURCE: Kuznets, *Modern Economic Growth*, p. 322.

There was no marked rise in the annual flow of capital according to Table 8.5 (with a possible exception of the last few years before 1914). Yet the increase in the cumulative total of foreign capital invested was striking. The total amount invested rose from $4.9 to 35.3 billion (in 1913 prices) from 1874 to 1913-14. The growth rate per decade was 64 per cent, which is higher than the rates of growth of both foreign trade and national income. The explanation of the phenomenon must have been that these foreign investments earned a good return, and that these earnings were reinvested on the spot. On top of this came the net flow of capital illustrated in table 8.5. The result of this development was that the stock of foreign capital increased in relation to the national income. This applied to both lending and borrowing countries.

Most of these capital exports seem to have gone to fairly developed countries. The available statistics relate to 1913-14 only. Table 8.6 shows the distribution of the outstanding foreign gross investments at that time.

It shows that at least half of the foreign capital then outstanding had been invested in developed countries. Of the 28 per cent invested in Europe, most had been investe : in the developed parts of Europe. To this has to be added the United States, Canada and Oceania. Then the share going to these parts of the world is well over 50 per cent. If Argentina and Japan are also added, the share going to developed countries increases to over 60 per cent.

It seems, however, as though the share of investments going to the less developed parts of the world could have risen during the period 1870-1913. It seems especially as though foreign investments in Europe were declining relatively, whereas investments in the less developed parts of the world – both in colonies and independent nations in Africa, Asia and Latin America – were on the increase. Figures for Britain seem to confirm this view, as shown in Table 8.7.

Around the middle of the nineteenth century and up to 1870, the bulk of British foreign investment went to Europe. During the latter part of the century and in the years leading up to the First World War, British capital went instead mostly to the 'new' countries, i.e. Argentina, Canada, South Africa, Australia and New Zealand. It was investments in these countries that expanded by far the most rapidly. But there was also an increase, both absolutely and relatively, in capital going to the colonies; this was, after all, the heyday of European imperialism.

TABLE 8.7

Percentage distribution of total British capital invested overseas

	1870	1913
United States	20	20
Other 'new' countries	10	45
Europe	50	5
All other areas	20	30
	100	100

SOURCE: Nurkse, *Patterns of Trade and Development*, p.17.

Capital movements were substantial both in absolute and relative terms during this period. The proportion of the annual outflow of capital to national output varied between 1 and 4 per cent for the major credit countries. During its peak periods, in 1880–89 and 1905–14, Britain sent 5 and 7 per cent, respectively, of its G.N.P. as capital exports abroad. In terms of capital formation generated within the country, the share was, of course, much higher. During the peak periods, it was close to 50 per cent, and during the whole period 1860–1913, between 25 and 40 per cent of gross domestic savings were invested abroad, a high figure indeed. Germany and France also exported a substantial share of their savings as capital exports abroad. These figures show that the world economy had reached a high degree of integration at this time.

Viewed from the angle of the debtor countries, there is little doubt that these capital imports played a critical role for speeding up the rate of domestic investment. The United States had already at this time developed a high degree of autarky, but it still financed about 10 per cent of its capital formation by capital imports. Towards the end of the century, this position changed, however, and the United States, from being a debtor country, became a creditor country, exporting capital, instead.

Japan, the other large country that import capital, showed a more varied picture. During the time when it imported capital on a massive scale, from 1897 to 1906, it financed about 30 per cent of its domestic investment by imported capital.

Capital imports played the largest role for a group of smaller countries. To this group belonged primarily the 'regions of recent settlement', i.e. Canada, South Africa, Australia and New Zealand, the Scandinavian countries, and Argentina. Canada, for instance, financed between 30 and 50 per cent of her investments by capital imports. Australia similarly, during the period from 1860 to 1900, financed between 20 and 50 per cent of her domestic capital formation by imported capital. The bulk of Argentina's capital imports seem to have come during the first two decades of the twentieth century. During this period, roughly 40 per cent of investments in Argentina were financed by foreign capital. The Scandinavian countries had also substantial deficits in their balance of payments, which they financed by capital imports. During

TABLE 8.8

Foreign capital investments since 1914, all countries
(absolute figures in millions of dollars per year)

	1921–1929	1930–1938	1921–1938	1951–1955	1956–1961
Total per year, flows from all creditor countries	1547	-706	421	4279	7145
Same flows, in 1913 prices	1067	-728	170	2038	3226
Shares of major creditors, flows in current prices (%)					
Great Britain	27.7	14.1	39.1	10.5	10.2
France	21.8	1.3	38.9	2.5	6.2
Germany	Net debtor			2.2	9.2
United States	43.0	78.1	13.6	78.4	67.4

SOURCE: Kuznets, *Modern Economic Growth*, p. 323.

1870–1910, foreign capital financed around 20 per cent of total investments in these countries.

All these countries were 'peripheral' with respect to the leading European industrial nations, especially Britain. Their exports to Britain and other mature industrial nations grew, as we have seen, very rapidly during this period. They needed to invest both in the traditional export lines and in various forms of social overhead capital to meet the increased demand for their export products. The original increase in demand led to more investments which, in their turn, through a multiplier effect, led to higher income and a still higher increase in demand, which led to more investments, and so on. The well-known *accelerator - multiplier mechanism* was at work guaranteeing growth. Slowdowns and crises occurred, but the over-all world economy grew rapidly, and world trade grew even faster. Then, as now, the less developed and semi-developed countries of the era needed capital to invest in order to grow. Being poor, they had difficulties in generating enough savings by themselves. To speed up their growth process they needed to import capital. We have just seen for several of these 'peripheral' countries both trade flows and capital flows formed an integral part of their growth process.

Capital movements played a very small role during the interwar period. This is illustrated in Table 8.8.

We know that the growth of world trade was slowed down during the interwar period. The disruptive effects on the international capital market was even stronger. Before the First World War, a net flow of about $1.1 billion went to debtor countries. During the period between the two world wars, only a fraction of this amount was invested abroad. During the 1920s, capital movements still played a role that was not unimportant. During the 1930s, the net flows completely stopped; what happened was that capital was repatriated. During the interwar period as a whole, the importance of capital movements drastically diminished.

Since the Second World War capital movements have again been substantial. However, they have to a considerable extent changed their nature. They no longer consist only of private capital flows geared by market considerations. They have to a large extent consisted of government grants and loans. About 30 per cent of capital export during this period has been in the form of government grants and another 20 per cent has consisted of government loans. The major credit nation has been the United States. The Soviet Union and France have also been active in exporting capital.

Private capital flows, especially in the form of direct investments, however, have also played an important role, especially in the years since 1955. We return to this topic in Chapter 21, which is devoted to the theoretical and material aspects of direct investments.

We now have a general understanding of the importance of trade and capital movements, especially for the countries on the periphery during the nineteenth century. Trade during this period functioned as an engine of growth for several countries. It might now be useful to illustrate this general principle by taking a brief look at how it worked in a specific case.

GROWTH AND TRADE DURING THE NINETEENTH CENTURY: THE CASE OF SWEDEN

Sweden was, in the beginning of the 1870s, a poorly developed country with more than 70 per cent of the population employed in agriculture. Certain prerequisites for growth were at hand: a compulsory school system had been introduced as early as 1842; the administration was honest and competent; and there was a tradition of manufacturing simple products from iron. Nevertheless, the country was poor and primitive in many respects, and it would have been no great surprise if it had remained so.

By the 1870s a sustained growth process had begun. The growth that took place was geared especially towards exports. The dominating export branch up to the beginning of the 1890s was timber and wood products, which made up around 35 per cent of total exports. Total exports expanded fast; the export volume rose, on the average, 4 per cent a year from 1870 to 1890. The terms of trade also showed a favorable development. Exports of timber and wood products went primarily to England, and the performance of Swedish exports during this period is a good example of how a country could grow by specializing in the production of raw materials that it sold in an expanding market at rising prices.

Another interesting feature of Swedish exports during 1870–90 was the export of butter. This export group expanded most rapidly of all exports; it comprised 20 per cent of the total in 1895. This reflects an important transformation that took place in Swedish agriculture during this time.

Around 1850 Swedish agriculture produced mainly grain, of which it had a considerable export surplus. During the following decades Swedish grain exports were outcompeted, especially by American and Russian producers. Swedish farmers turned instead to production of animal products, concentrating on butter, for which it found an expanding market in Britain. Some other of the traditional export branches, such as bar iron, were less lucky and underwent a drastic decline, especially in relative terms.

By the beginning of the 1890s a new export pattern emerged. Exports of timber and wood and agricultural products lost their momentum and were no longer focal in the growth process. New products took their place. For example, Swedish iron-ore deposits were rich in phosphorus. Technical progress in steel production (the application of the Thomas process) made it possible to extract the phosphorus from the iron. Thereby the rich iron-ore deposits in Lapland, in the north of Sweden, could be profitably mined. From the 1890s iron-ore became one of the expanding export branches.

Other emerging export branches which built on the application of innovations were paper and pulp and engineering products. Innovations made it possible to use spruce and pine as raw material for the production of paper and pulp. Swedish forests provided these trees in abundance, and paper and pulp became one of the rapidly expanding export industries.

Swedish economic history shows many examples of unsuccessful ventures in the engineering industries during the latter part of the nineteenth century. By the end of the century the audacity and innovative spirit of many Swedish engineers and small entrepreneurs started to pay off, and some highly successful companies began to exploit home-made innovations. Examples of such innovations were a lighthouse, separators, diesel engines, some electric products, and, somewhat later, ball bearings. All this led to the engineering industry becoming one of the most expansive export industries from 1890.

At the outbreak of the First World War the new pattern of Swedish exports was firmly established. The shift in the structure of exports that began around 1890 had matured, and by 1913 the three most expansive export industries, iron-ore, paper and pulp, and engineering products, comprised roughly 40 per cent of total exports. This pattern has since continued, with the engineering industry as the leading sector, so that over half of Swedish exports today consist of a well-diversified list of engineering products.

Another very interesting aspect of Swedish economic development in the period from 1870 to 1913 is the role of capital movements. Sweden had, almost without exception, consistent deficits in her balance of payments during the forty years from 1870 to 1910. There was only a short period from 1895 to 1897 during which Swedish trade balanced. The deficits were also quite large: they amounted, on the average, to between 15 and 20 per cent of total imports. This meant that a substantial part of Sweden's capital formation during the country's transformation from a less developed to an industrial economy was provided by foreigners. A large part of this external debt, incidentally, was paid off in inflated prices during the First World War.

This is an example of how, during the era of the classic gold standard, long-term capital movements on a large scale helped to speed up the economic growth of a less developed country by increasing her capacity to invest, and also eased her balance-of-payments problems by providing much-needed foreign currency. According to the textbooks, the gold standard mechanism, given Sweden's strained balance-of-payments situation, should have forced the country to export gold and pursue a deflationary monetary policy. On the contrary, however, the capital imports led to an inflow of gold, which in turn led to an increase in the money supply and made possible an expansionary economic policy. A study of economic history could prove useful for those who are overly worried about the balance-of-payments problems of today's less developed countries.

It would be premature, however, to treat this topic at length at this stage. We will discuss the role of capital movements in detail when we come to the parts of the book which deal with the theory of the balance of payments and with the problem of international liquidity.

The economic development of any country is a complicated and many-faceted process. It is not possible to give more than a glimpse of it in a couple of pages. Nevertheless, the exposition above should have illustrated the fact that for many of the countries which could be classified as less developed in the nineteenth century or as being on the periphery, trade functioned as an engine of growth. Sweden is a case in point, but its experience is in no way unique.

Today's less developed countries seem faced with more difficult problems. To grow by specializing according to comparative advantage and to concentrate on promoting export industries is, to many, a dubious proposition. Let us now look into the role of trade in the twentieth century.

WORLD TRADE SINCE 1945: THE LESS DEVELOPED COUNTRIES

We have seen that during the first half of the twentieth century, world trade grew at a slow rate. During the following twenty-five year period from 1950, the growth of world trade has been strikingly rapid.

However, this rapid rate of development has been lopsided. Table 8.9 shows that the expansion has been primarily concentrated on the exports of the industrial developed countries, the oil producers and a few less developed manufacturing countries.

The industrial countries have benefited from the rapid increase in world trade that has taken place during the last twenty-five years. For them, trade has grown faster than national income. Trade in manufactured products, especially, has expanded during the post-war period. Exports of these products have grown rapidly in many developed countries. This, in turn, has had a favorable effect on the growth of national income in these countries.

Most underdeveloped countries have not experienced a similar stimulus from trade. A few of the less developed countries have been able to show a rapid increase in exports of manufactured products. Among these countries are Mexico, South Korea, Hong Kong and Singapore. Table 8.9 also shows that the oil-producing countries have experienced a very rapid expansion in the value of their exports. But the majority of less developed countries have continued to export traditional products, such as raw materials and agricultural products, demand for which has grown at only a relatively low rate. The result has been a continual fall in their share of world exports, as indicated in Table 8.9. The share of world exports of the less developed countries (disregarding the oil

TABLE 8.9

Growth and export shares, 1960–74

Average annual percentage growth rate of the volume of exports, 1960–74

	1960–5	1965–70	1970–4
(1) Developed market economy countries	8.6	11.6	10.0
(2) Developing countries			
OPEC producers	5.2	6.0	4.8
Fast-growing exporters of manufactures	5.0	13.8	12.5
Other developing countries	4.0	4.0	4.8

Percentage share of the value of world exports

	1960	1970	1974
(1) Developed market economy countries	66.8	71.9	65.5
(2) Developing countries			
OPEC producers	6.6	5.5	14.9
Fast-growing exporters of manufactures	2.2	2.3	2.7
Other developing countries	12.6	9.1	7.6
(3) Socialist countries			
Europe	10.1	9.9	7.9
Asia	1.6	0.8	0.7

SOURCE: United Nations Conference on Trade and Development (UNCTAD), *Handbook for International Trade and Development Statistics*, New York, United Nations, 1976, Sales No. E/F, 76, II D.3.

countries) was 25 per cent in 1950; in the middle of the 1970s it was down to roughly 10 per cent.

How fast the national incomes of the less-developed countries have expanded is a difficult question to answer in a precise and meaningful way. The paucity and unreliability of data is one reason. The multitude of less-developed countries and the lack of homogeneity among them should also be kept in mind when attempting generalizations.

It seems, however, as if most of the less developed countries would have shown a definite and positive growth rate during the past twenty-five years.[3] This is illustrated by Table 8.10.

Table 8.10 covers only a short period. If the information it contains can be taken at face value, it says that national income grew at roughly the same rate

TABLE 8.10

Average annual percentage growth rate of real G.D.P. at market prices, 1950 – 74.

	Total real produce			Per capita real produce		
	1950– 1960	1960– 1970	1970– 1974	1950– 1960	1960– 1970	1970– 1974
Developed market economies	4.1	5.1	4.2	2.8	4.1	3.2
Developing countries	4.7	5.2	6.4	2.4	2.6	3.8
United States	3.2	4.5	3.7	1.5	3.5	2.7
E.E.C.	5.0	4.6	3.9	4.3	3.9	3.2
Sweden	3.4	4.3	2.8	2.8	3.7	2.2
Latin America	5.2	5.5	6.6	2.2	2.6	3.7
Africa	4.5	4.7	5.2	2.3	2.0	3.5
South and South-east Asia	4.1	4.6	4.2	2.0	2.2	1.8

SOURCE: UNCTAD, *Handbook for International Trade and Development Statistics.*

for both industrial and less developed countries during the 1950s and 1960s. During the 1970s, and particularly following the energy crisis and the recession which it induced, real G.D.P. has tended to grow somewhat faster in the developing countries taken as a whole, i.e. including oil-producing countries. However, an energy-importing development area such as South-East Asia has experienced a fall in its growth rate compared with the previous decade. The difference in the growth of *per capita* income is primarily caused by differences in the growth of population. It also tells us that no 'pauperization' has taken place, at least not during the time in question: *per capita* income in the underdeveloped countries has grown, though at a modest rate.

The implication of the information contained in Tables 8.9 and 8.10, however, is that trade hardly seems to have played any propulsive role for the growth in these countries. Expansion of trade seems at best to have kept pace with the growth in national income.

For several of the developing, 'peripheral' countries of the nineteenth century, trade functioned, as we know, as an engine of growth. It seems that this has not been the case to anything like the same extent for the underdeveloped countries of today. Their difficulties in this respect seem to have started with the slowdown of the growth of world trade that took place in the interwar period. Table 8.11 gives an indication of this.

A few of the less developed countries, especially those that happen to be oil producers, have done quite well, but the majority of them have seen their share of world exports fall. This is not only a recent phenomenon. It dates back to the 1920s. Then, the less developed countries lost out at a time when world trade

TABLE 8.11

Percentage share of developing countries in the value of world trade

	Including oil-exporting countries				Excluding oil-exporting countries			
	1928	1950	1960	1974	1928	1950	1960	1974
Exports	33.8	30.5	21.4	25.2	32.2	24.3	14.7	10.3
Imports	28.0	26.8	22.0	17.8	26.9	22.7	17.5	13.8

SOURCES: GATT, *Trends in International Trade*, Geneva, 1958; UNCTAD, *Handbook for International Trade and Development Statistics.*

was stagnating, and they have been unable to recover their share at a time when trade has been rapidly expanding. This development has resulted in the overwhelming share of trade today being carried on between industrial countries. This is illustrated by Table 8.12.

One important fact that must be kept in mind is that trade among themselves is most important for the industrial countries. When formulating trade policies, it is only natural for them to be primarily interested in measures that concern trade in industrial products, which to them is the most important part of their trade. Although their trade with less developed countries is by no means negligible, its value is less than one-third of *intra-industrial* trade. For the less developed countries, the reverse applies: for them, trade with industrial countries is much more important than trade among themselves.

A complaint often voiced by representatives for the less developed countries is that the terms of trade of these countries deteriorate. We remember from Chapter 1 that the terms of trade were defined as export prices divided by import prices. Not only has the volume of exports declined relatively, but the prices for the exports of the less developed countries have fallen relative to the prices they must pay for their imports, according to these spokesman.

It is not easy to give adequate measures of the development of the terms of trade for large groups of countries. Differing results can usually be obtained depending upon what time periods are chosen, how countries are grouped, etc. It seems that the terms of trade went against the less developed countries during the interwar period.[4] For the postwar period the evidence is less clear-cut. Table 8.13 shows indices for the terms of trade since 1960 for developed market economy countries, oil-exporting, and other developing countries. The table shows that for the developed countries the period up until 1974 was one of markedly stable terms of trade. The terms of trade of the developing countries improved during the 1960s. During the 1970s the non-oil-exporting countries have experienced a decline in their terms of trade and this trend was reinforced by the substantial rise in the price of oil during 1973–4. The oil-producing countries, on the other hand, have had a tremendous improvement in their terms of trade during the 1970s.

TABLE 8.12

Total trade, 1974 ($ U.S., billions)

Destination → Origin ↓	World	Developed market economy countries	Developing		Socialist Europe	Socialist Asia
			OPEC	Non-OPEC developing		
World	845.350	595.940	34.720	137.130	62.960	8.320
Developed market economy countries	542.520	398.610	29.000	84.760	21.130	5.560
OPEC	135.100	110.330	350	20.710	2.120	150
Non-OPEC developing countries	96.850	63.350	3.820	22.170	5.190	1.010
Socialist Europe	64.270	19.770	1.490	7.620	33.300	1.640
Socialist Asia	5.950	2.700	165	1.900	1.190	–

SOURCE: UNCTAD, *Handbook for International Trade and Development Statistics.*

The export volume of the less developed countries has not been growing very fast, as we have seen. We might expect that these countries would have been able to sell their exports at increasing prices, but that is not the case. The result is that trade has not transmitted growth from the developed, industrial countries to the less developed countries the way it did in the nineteenth century. Income *per capita* has been growing quickly in the industrial countries, but it seems not to have led to a proportional increase in the demand for primary products.

How are we to explain this development? One answer has been suggested by Ragnar Nurkse.[5] He gives the following six factors as reasons:

(1) The emphasis of industrial production in the advanced economies is shifting away from 'light' industries toward 'heavy' industries (such as engineering and chemicals) – that is, from industries where the raw-material content of finished output is high to those where it is low.

(2) The share of services in the total output of advanced industrial countries is rising, which tends to cause their raw-material demand to lag behind the rise in their national product.

(3) The income elasticity of consumer demand for many agricultural commodities tends to be low.

(4) Agricultural protectionism has adversely affected imports of primary products.

TABLE 8.13

Term of trade (1970 = 100)

	Developed	Other Developing	OPEC
1960	96	97	98
1961	97	92	98
1962	98	93	100
1963	97	94	100
1964	97	99	102
1965	90	99	100
1966	98	105	104
1967	99	100	104
1968	99	103	107
1969	99	105	105
1970	100	100	100
1971	99	90	115
1972	100	90	113
1973	99	97	127
1974	87	96	337
1975	89	88	318

SOURCE: UNCTAD, *Handbook for International Trade and Development Statistics.*

(5) Substantial economies have been achieved in industrial uses of natural materials.

(6) The leading industrial centers have tended more and more to displace natural raw materials by synthetic and other man-made substitutes.

It sounds extremely plausible that the factors Nurkse refers to should have played a role in causing the adverse demand conditions that many primary-producing countries have faced during recent decades. The type of explanation that Nurkse proposes, however, is not very systematic. It has too much the character of being invented on the spot, of being *ad hoc* in nature. We would like to develop a more systematic framework for studying the effects of economic growth upon international trade. This is now what we will set out to do. We will then be able to derive hypotheses to explain the development of the terms of trade. We will seek to state under what conditions countries can be expected to develop favorably by trading and under what conditions growth by trade will lead to an impasse. By continuing to build on the general-equilibrium framework that was developed in the first part of the book, we will also be able to see more clearly how the different variables are related to each other. In Chapter 16 we will further analyze trade strategies for development.

SELECTED BIBLIOGRAPHY: CHAPTER 8

The main sources for Chapter 8 are:

S. Kuznets, *Modern Economic Growth: Rate, Structure, and Spread*, New Haven, Conn., Yale University Press, 1966, especially ch. 6.

United Nations Conference on Trade and Development (UNCTAD), *Handbook for International Trade and Development Statistics*, New York, United Nations, 1976, Sales No. E/F, 76, II D.3.

See also:

S. Kuznets, 'Level and Structure of Foreign Trade: Long Term Trends', *Economic Development and Cultural Change*, 1967.

Another source of interest is:

R. Nurkse, *Patterns of Trade and Development*, Oxford, Blackwell, 1962.

For a discussion of underdeveloped countries, see:

J. Pincus, *Trade, Aid and Development*, New York, 1967.

G. Myrdal, *Asian Drama. An Inquiry into the Poverty of Nations*, London, Allen Lane, The Penguin Press, 1968.

W. A. Lewis, *Aspects of Tropical Trade 1883–1965*, Uppsala, Almqvist & Wiksell, 1969.

G. Helleiner, *International Trade and Economic Development*, Harmondsworth, Penguin, 1972.

K. Morton and P. Tulloch, *Trade and Developing Countries*, London, Croom Helm, 1977.

The information about Swedish economic growth and trade is taken from the author's unpublished manuscript:

'Studier över den långsiktiga utvecklingen av svensk utrikeshandel.'

See also:

L. Jörberg, 'Structural Change and Economic Growth: Sweden in the Nineteenth Century', *Economy and History*, vol. 7, 1965.

G. Fridlizius, 'Sweden's Exports 1850–1960: A study in Perspective', *Economy and History*, vol. 6, 1964.

Among the standard works in economic history are:

W. Ashworth, *A Short History of the International Economy*, 3rd ed., London, Longman, 1976.

H. J. Habakkuk and M. Postan (eds), *The Cambridge Economic History of Europe. Volume VI: The Industrial Revolutions and After*, Cambridge University Press, 1965.

A. G. Kenwood and A. L. Lougheed, *The Growth of the International Economy 1820 – 1960*, London, Allen & Unwin, 1971.

9
A model of economic growth and international trade where growth is unspecified

Most parts of the pure theory of international trade dealt with in the first part of the book were quite old. Some of the rigorous proofs of certain theorems may be recent, but the basic ideas had been known for a long time. The theory of economic growth and international trade, on the other hand, has been developed only in recent years.

Classical and neoclassical economists did not take much interest in the subject, at least not in its theoretical aspects. The question of the long-run development of the terms of trade had already in the early nineteenth century been posed as a problem in economic policy. We will come back to this aspect in Chapter 12. But little had been said about it on a more theoretical level. An exception was John Stuart Mill, when he formulated the strikingly modern question 'What will be the effect of technical progress in the export industries? But he devoted only one page to the question in his *Principles of Political Economy* and then went on to other fields.

As the starting-point for the modern theory of growth and trade, one can turn to a paper by J. R. Hicks published in 1953.[1]

HICKS ON GROWTH AND TRADE

The topic Hicks dealt with in his paper was the long-run development of Great Britain's terms of trade and balance of trade. In the late 1940s and the early 1950s, Britain, like the rest of Western Europe, had experienced persistent deficits in her balance of trade. Hicks tried to explain these deflicits with reference to a change in the nature of economic growth in the United States.

Hicks couched his reasoning in terms of the standard two-country trade model. Let us assume, he said, that there are two countries, A and B, and that only A grows, while B is stagnant. What will happen?

If productivity grows uniformly in A – i.e. if all its industries expand at the same rate – the likelihood is that this will benefit B. The simplest way to see this is to assume that money incomes rise to the full extent of the productivity increase in A, while incomes remain unchanged in B, because nothing has happened there. Then the cheapening of A's products would have been erased by the rise in incomes, and prices would remain unchanged in A. Prices would also remain unchanged in B, as nothing has happened there. Money income has not changed in B, so there is no reason why B should buy a larger or smaller quantity of A's products than before. But A's income has risen and that will lead to an increase in demand for imports. This implies that the balance of trade will turn in *B*'s favor. To restore balance, the relative price of *B*'s exports would increase, and she would get improved terms of trade. This would also mean an improvement in her real national income.

Naturally, the picture becomes more complicated if incomes in *A* do not rise at the same rate as productivity increases. In that case the outcome might be different. For the present we are only concerned with the main drift of the argument and will lay these complications aside.

The case in which productivity increases uniformly in all industries might be called the *neutral* case. Let us go on and assume that the productivity increase instead is concentrated in the export sector and that we have what Hicks called an *export-biased* growth. What will happen then?

This case is extremely favorable for country *B*. Suppose that incomes remain constant in both countries. The prices of *B*'s exports will then remain constant, because nothing has happened in this country, whereas the prices of *A*'s exports will fall. The terms of trade will, therefore, turn in favor of *B*. What happens to the volume of *A*'s export to *B* will depend mainly on demand conditions. If *B*'s demand for *A*'s exports is inelastic, it might happen that the value of *A*'s exports would fall while the volume would increase. Under such circumstances *A*'s whole productivity gain might be exported away to *B*. Export-biased growth is clearly the type of growth that is most detrimental to *A* and most favorable to *B*.

But what if the productivity increases in *A* are concentrated in the import-competing sector and *A* has *import-biased* growth? This is the case which is most favorable to *A* and least favorable to *B*, and can be demonstrated in the same manner as before. If incomes in both countries remain the same, the prices of import-competing goods in *A* would have to fall. This would mean that a larger share of the market would be taken over by goods produced in *A*, because imports would be substituted with import-competing goods. The demand for exports from *B* would therefore fall. This would create a deficit in *B*'s balance of trade, and to restore it and be able to compete, *B* would have to lower her export prices. Thus *B*'s terms of trade would deteriorate, and *A* would be able to keep all her productivity gains and on top of that get improved terms of trade.

Hick's analysis provided a good start by giving a rough formulation of the problem, but his analysis is of a very tentative nature. It is difficult to see how the different factors he discusses hold together. Sometimes Hicks argues in real terms, as for instance when he talks about the terms of trade, and other times in monetary terms, as when he talk about the balance of payments. How one moves from one framework to the other is not easily discernable. His argument is also very sketchy: the demand side, for instance, is virtually ignored. In order to come to grips with the problem of economic growth and international trade, we therefore have to go beyond Hicks's formulation and introduce a more formal kind of analysis.

A MODEL OF ECONOMIC GROWTH AND INTERNATIONAL TRADE: THE BASIC FORMULA[2]

In order to study the effects of economic growth on international trade in a more thorough manner than, for instance, Hicks did, we have to use a more formal approach and set out a well-specified model. We can then derive a formula that in a neat way captures the effects of growth in two trading countries on critical variables such as the terms of trade. This will also give us a more precise insight into the interrelationships among critical variables in a general-equilibrium framework.

In the text of this chapter we will only set out the main formula and discuss the assumptions and results of the model in a verbal way. The formal presentation of the model and the derivation of the principal result will be presented as an appendix to this chapter. The model is, however, a simple one indeed, and the reader who is not strongly averse to the use of simple mathematics will probably find it very useful to go through the appendix. The main drift of the argument should, however, be clear from the text.

The argument is set up in terms of the standard trade model, with two countries and two goods. Both countries produce both goods so that specialization is incomplete. We know that economic growth occurs, but at this stage we do not specify the sources of it. Later on, in Chapters 10 and 11, we will study the effects of increases in factor endowments and of technical progress. But for the time being we shall simply take growth for granted: as time goes by, the productive capacity of both countries increases.

The model works roughly in the following way. Economic growth means that the productive capacity in one or both countries increases. This leads to an increase in the supply of one or both goods. But it also implies an increase in income. The increase in income will lead to an increase in demand.[3] The point is, however, that supply and demand of each good will not, in all likelihood, increase with the same amount. Therefore, relative prices will have to change in order to clear the markets. If, for instance, supply of country I's export good increases more than the demand for it, there will be an excess supply of the good and its price will have to fall.

But a change in relative prices is, of course, nothing but a change in the terms of trade. The object of the model is to show how economic growth affects both the direction and the size of the changes in the terms of trade. We shall then also go on to show that once we know something about the effects of growth on the terms of trade, we also know a great deal about its effects on the real national income. We will discuss these effects in a verbal way, as a formal analysis would be too complicated.

It is now time to set out the basic formula that captures the effects of economic growth in the two trading countries on their terms of trade. This is done in equation (9.1).

$$\frac{dP}{dt} = \frac{(R_{1m}\,S_{1m} - R_1 E_{1m}\,C_{1m}) - (R_2\,E_{2x}\,C_{2x} - R_{2x}\,S_{2x})}{\dfrac{C_{1m}}{P}\,e_1 + \dfrac{C_{2x}}{P}\,e_2 + \dfrac{S_{1m}}{P}\,s_1 + \dfrac{S_{2x}}{P}\,s_2} \qquad (9.1)$$

Before analyzing the model we will explain the notations briefly (exact definitions are given in the appendix). Figures in the subscripts stand for countries, x denotes export and m import magnitudes, C denotes consumption and S supply. Thus S_{1m} denotes supply (output) of the import-competing good in country I. S_{2x} stands for supply of the export good in country II. C_{1m} denotes consumption of the imported good in country I and C_{2x} denotes consumption of country II's export good. Economic growth is symbolized by t. P_x is the price of country I's export good and P_m of its import good. Country I's terms of trade are given by P. ($P = P_x/P_m$). It is then obvious that country II's terms of trade are equal to $1/P$.

R_{1m} denotes the growth rate of the import-competing sector in country I, and R_1 denotes the growth rate of the national income in country I; R_{2x} and R_2 have analogous meanings. The four symbols e_1, e_2, s_1, and s_2 denotes demand and supply elasticities. Country I's elasticity of demand for its import good with respect to the terms of trade is given by e_1, its elasticity of supply of importables with respect to P is given by s_1, etc. E_{1m} denotes the income elasticity of importables in country I. E_{2x} stands for the income elasticity of exportables in country II.

AN ANALYSIS OF THE MODEL

Formula (9.1) indicates that the outcome for the terms of trade depends on quite a number of factors. The growth rates of the national incomes in the two countries are important. Which sector experiences growth is also very important. The development of demand, measured by income elasticities, also plays a role. These are the factors which have the stage, and they are depicted in the numerator.

The interrelationships between volumes and prices, measured by demand and supply elasticities, are important. They lay, so to speak, the frame within which the determining forces work. They are depicted in the denominator. We will start by looking at the factors pictured in the denominator.

The denominator will be positive provided that the two goods are substitutes (so-called 'gross substitutes') for each other in consumption in both countries. This hardly seems a very strong assumption to accept. The first elasticity, e_1, shows, as already stated, how demand for importables in country I changes if relative commodity prices change. If P increased, it would imply that the imported good had become relatively cheaper. Then we would expect consumers to buy more of the cheaper good (importables) and substitute this good for the other good (exportables) in consumption; if this happens, e_1 will be positive.

Analogous reasoning can be applied to e_2. This elasticity measures how demand for exportables in country II changes if the terms of trade change. If P would increase, it means that country II's terms of trade deteriorate, i.e. the relative price of its export good falls. This implies that consumption of exportables in country II increases. Then the sign of e_2 is positive (see the appendix). The only assumption needed for this result is that the two goods are substitutes (gross substitutes) for consumers in country II.

The other two elasticities in the denominator are supply elasticities. The first one, s_1, shows how production of importables in country I changes as relative prices change. Let us say that P increases. This implies that the relative price of importables falls. If the price of importables falls, its supply will also fall, because producers will transfer resources out of the sector. This means that s_1 will have a positive sign (for the exact definition, see the appendix).

We assume in this model that competitive conditions prevail both in commodity and factor markets. This implies that the production-possibility curve is concave to the origin. (For a discussion of the shape of the production-possibility curve, see Chapter 2.) This means that producers are going to behave the way we expect them to behave, — i.e. if the relative price of a good falls, they are never going to increase production of it.

For analogous reasons, s_2 is also non-negative. This elasticity measures how production of the export good in country II changes if relative prices change. If a change in P had a negative sign, it would mean that the terms of trade had deteriorated for country I but had improved for country II. As the price of exportables in country II goes up, producers in this country will produce more of its export good. Provided that this happens, s_2 will always be positive.

If we are willing to accept the quite weak assumptions of competitive conditions in production and gross substitutability in consumption, the denominator will be positive. The magnitudes of the elasticities which make up the denominator are very important for the adaptability of the two trading economies. The direction of change in the terms of trade will depend, as we shall soon see, on the factors depicted in the numerator. But just how much the terms of trade will have to change in order to get to a new equilibrium depends critically on the supply and demand elasticities in the denominator. The larger they are, i.e. the more adaptable the two trading economies are, the less the terms of trade will have to change in order for a new equilibrium to be reached.

It is easy to see why this is true. High values on the demand elasticities suggest that the two goods are easily substituted for each other in consumption. Any change in relative prices will therefore lead to a substantial change in quantities consumed. Analogously, high values on the supply elasticities also make for an easy adjustment. The higher the values on these elasticities are, the more willing and able the producers in the two countries are to change the pattern of production if relative prices change.

Generally speaking, we can say that the larger the value of the denominator, the smaller the change in the terms of trade arising from any disturbance, and the easier the adjustment to price changes by producers and consumers in the two countries. Therefore, the elasticities in the denominator are very important, their values being a measure of the degree of the adaptability and the reallocative capacity of the two trading economies. In the extreme case, when the values of the elasticities tend to infinity, the change in the terms of trade is negligible.

If the denominator in equation (9.1) is positive, the outcome for the terms of trade depends on whether $R_{1m} S_{1m} - R_1 E_{1m} C_{1m} \gtreqless R_2 E_{2x} C_{2x} - R_{2x} S_{2x}$. If the left side of this expression is larger than the right side, the terms of trade will improve for country I; she will then find that some gains from improving terms of trade will be added to her autonomous growth because of her participation in foreign trade. If the right side is the larger, the terms of trade will improve for country II. If the two sides are equal, the terms of trade will not change during the growth process.

The important factors are obviously the sectoral growth rates and the income elasticities in the two countries. In them are captured the effects of economic growth on supply and demand in the two countries. In order to emphasize the implications of equation (9.1), let us for the sake of reasoning assume that country II is stationary and the country I is the only growing country. Then both R_2 and R_{2x} are zero, and only the left part of the numerator in equation (9.1) is of interest.

Given these assumptions, the result for the terms of trade depends on whether the weighted growth rate of import production ($R_{1m} S_{1m}$) is larger or smaller than the weighted income elasticity of demand for importables ($R_1 E_{1m} C_{1m}$). If the former is larger than the latter, i.e. $R_{1m} S_{1m} > R_1 E_{1m} C_{1m}$, the terms of trade will improve for country I. Growth under these conditions will lead to an increase in the supply of importables which is larger than the increase in demand. This will create an excess supply of importables in country I at existing prices. In order to clear the markets, the price of importables has to fall, i.e. the terms of trade will improve. We can also think of this process as leading to a condition in which more of the home market for importables is captured by producers in country I. The demand for imports falls. The exports in country II find a decrease in demand for their exports. Therefore, they have to lower their prices in order to clear the markets; in other words, the terms of trade move in favor of country I.

If it were the other way around, i.e. if $R_1 E_{1m} C_{1m} > R_{1m} S_{1m}$, then the terms of trade would deteriorate for country I, because in this event the demand for importables would grow faster than the supply of importables. There would be an excess demand for importables in country I at existing prices. The exporters in country II would find that demand for their product had increased; to clear the markets the price of country II's exports would have to rise. In short, country I's terms of trade would deteriorate.

We can now compare these results with the ones suggested by Hicks. His results lie in the same general direction, but because he never took demand factors into account, his analysis was, from a rigorous point of view, indeterminate. Hicks said that export-biased growth would turn the terms of trade against a country, and that import-biased growth would improve a country's terms of trade. With our terminology we interpret export bias in Hick's sense to mean that $R_{1x} S_{1x} > R_{1m} S_{1m}$ and import bias to mean that $R_{1m} S_{1m} > R_{1x} S_{1x}$. That is, we simply compare the weighted growth rates in the two sectors, and if the growth in the supply of exportables is larger than the growth in the supply of importables, growth is said to be export-biased. If it is the other way around, growth is said to be import-biased.

It is, however, easy to see that Hicks's definitions of export and import bias do not necessarily imply a definite change in the terms of trade. It is fully conceivable to have an export-biased growth in Hicks's sense and still have improving terms of trade. According to formula (9.1), country I will get improving terms of trade if $R_{1m} S_{1m} > R_1 E_{1m} C_{1m}$. Let us assume that the income elasticity of demand for importables, E_{1m}, is equal to zero. As long as there is any growth at all in the import-competing sector, the terms of trade will always improve for country I. In such a case it is possible that $R_{1x} S_{1x} > R_{1m} S_{1m}$, or that the growth is export-biased in Hicks's sense, and that the terms of trade will still improve for the country. This is explained by the simple fact that all the increased income caused by the economic growth will be spent on exportables, and as long as some growth occurs in the import-competing sector, economic growth will always give rise to an excess supply of importables and to excess demand for exportables at existing prices. To clear the markets and reach a new equilibrium the relative price of importables will have to fall, i.e. the terms of trade will improve for the country.

If we would like to use the notions of export bias and import bias and have a definite connection between bias and a change in the terms of trade, we will have to redefine the terms. If we define export-biased growth as one in which the supply of exportables is increased more than the demand for exportables, i.e. if $R_{1x} S_{1x} > R_1 E_{1x} C_{1x}$, then export-biased growth will lead to deteriorating terms of trade. Analogously, if we define import-biased growth as $R_{1m} S_{1m} > R_1 E_{1m} C_{1m}$, then import-biased growth will always imply improving terms of trade.

Up to this point we have assumed country II to be stationary. If we instead assume that country I is stationary and that country II grows, exactly analogous results hold. Export-biased growth in country II, i.e. $R_{2x} S_{2x} > R_2 E_{2x} C_{2x}$, leads to a deterioration in her terms of trade, and import-biased growth, i.e. $R_{2m} S_{2m} > R_2 E_{2m} C_{2m}$, leads to an improvement in her terms of trade.

If both countries grow, the outcome for the terms of trade will depend on the type of growth which occurs. If both countries tend toward import-biased growth, i.e. if $R_{1m} S_{1m} > R_1 E_{1m} C_{1m}$ and $R_{2m} S_{2m} > R_2 E_{2m} C_{2m}$, the country with the greatest degree of import bias will get improving terms of trade. If both countries have export-biased growth, the country with the greatest degree of export bias will have deteriorating terms of trade. If country I has an export-biased growth and country II and import-biased one, the terms of trade will always turn against country I; the faster the growth rates and the larger the bias (regardless of country), the faster the terms of trade will deteriorate. This also holds, *mutatis mutandis,* for country II.

These are the kinds of results that can be obtained by a model with unspecified growth. Its strength lies in the fact that we, with the help of the model, are able to see the basic interrelationships between supply and demand factors in the growth process. We have now achieved a fundamental understanding of how economic growth affects prices and volumes of the trading countries. It is now possible to specify growth and see what the effects of increases in the factor endowments and of technical progress will be. Before doing this, however, we will say something about the effects of growth on the national income and touch briefly in some policy implications of the development of the terms of trade.

GROWTH, TRADE, AND THE NATIONAL INCOME

If the growth rate of a country's national product is 3 per cent per annum and if the terms of trade do not change, the country's national income will also increase by 3 per cent. If the growth is of such a kind as to make the terms of trade deteriorate, what might be called the 'autonomous' growth rate – the growth rate at pre-growth prices – will be higher than the realized growth rate because some of the growth will be exported away in the form of falling terms of trade. On the other hand, if growth is of a type to improve the terms of trade, the realized growth rate will be higher than the autonomous one, because besides the home-generated growth, the country's real income will improve because of improving terms of trade.

Therefore, if one knows something about how growth affects a country's terms of trade, one also knows a great deal about its effect on national income. Analogous to the method in treating the terms of trade, a formula can be derived for the effects of growth on the real national income.[4] To do this would, however, require a more elaborate formal analysis. We will therefore be content with some verbal commentary.

If a country has its growth possibilities confined to the export sector, she might get adverse terms of trade. But this depends on the situation in the second country. If the second country also grows and if her income elasticity of demand for importables is high, demand for imports can be expected to grow quickly, and the first country is able to increase her exports at only slightly lower prices. In this way the first country can grow and prosper by concentrating on increasing production of exports.

But if the second country does not grow, or if its income elasticity of demand for importables is low, the first country might be in trouble. Under these conditons the demand for imports in the second country might increase only slightly or not at all, and in order to sell an increased amount of exports the first country will have to lower its prices, i.e. to accept falling terms of trade. Now the price elasticity of demand for importables in the second country (depicted in the denominator in equation (9.1)) will be important. If this elasticity is low, it may be impossible for the first country to increase its revenue from exports. In such a case, growth by means of export is a dead-end.

The ultimate case on the pessimistic side is that of so-called 'impoverishing' or 'immiserizing' growth. This is the case in which a country ends up having a lower real income after growth because the loss due to deteriorating terms of trade has outweighed the gain due to increased production.

The possibility of impoverishing growth was first contemplated by F. Y. Edgeworth, who, upon reading John Stuart Mill's analysis of the effects of improvements of production in export industries, drew the conclusion that under certain conditions 'the exporting country is damnified by the improvement; and by parity of reasoning may be benefited by a restriction of its exports'.[5]

Edgeworth established the conditions for impoverishing growth with exceedingly simple reasoning. He used a model of complete specialization both in consumption and production whereby each of the two trading countries produced only one good, all of which it exported but did not consume, and whereby each country imported all of the good which it consumed. Under these very special conditions the foreign demand elasticity is all-important, and the condition for impoverishing growth is simply that this elasticity be less than unity. If the first country grows and the second country is stationary, and if the foreign demand elasticity for the first country's exports is less than unity, total export earnings will fall because of growth; and as the national income equals total export earnings, the country will become poorer because of growth.

If a less specific model than the one Edgeworth had in mind is used, the probability for impoverishing growth diminishes.[6] Then either production of importables has to decrease because of growth, or the sum of all the elasticities which appear in the denominator in equation (9.1) has to be less than unity.[7] These are both quite stringent conditions. There is no reason to expect the former to occur unless some non-reproducible factor is used in the production of importables. The implication of the sum of all the above-mentioned elasticities being less than unity is obviously that there are no possibilities of substitution, neither on the demand nor the supply side, in either of the trading economies.

Perhaps the case of impoverishing growth should be viewed as a curiosity. But it brings in focus the factors that may make growth through trade an impasse for a country. That is, if a country is faced with sluggish demand in her export market, if her growth is confined to the export sector, and if her adaptability is low, growth by means of trade might be a fruitless venture.

Import-biased growth, on the other hand, will always be beneficial to a country. This kind of growth improves the country's terms of trade, and her national income will increase by more than the autonomous growth. The favorable effects of import-biased growth will be reinforced if the country has a high income elasticity of demand for her own export good and if the trading partner's economy has a low degree of adaptability.

We have now seen some of the basic factors that determine the effects on the national income of economic growth in open economies. Before we conclude this chapter it might be appropriate to say a few words about the policy aspects of the development of the terms of trade.

THE TERMS OF TRADE AS A POLICY PROBLEM

The interest economists have shown in the long-run development of the terms of trade has always been great, at times almost obsessive. One line of thought, inaugurated by the classical English economists, claimed that the development of the terms of trade would be detrimental to the industrial countries and benefit the primary-producing countries. Keynes was a proponent of this school, and it has had its advocates even in our day. Another line of thought widely discussed during the 1950s and the 1960s is connected with the names of Singer and Prebisch. It claims that the development of the terms of trade for different reasons had, and would have, to be detrimental to the less developed, primary-producing countries and beneficial to the industrial countries.

These various explanations for the development of the terms of trade have been both loose and intricate. It should be clear by now that the type of theorizing set forth in this chapter can generate hypotheses for the development of the terms of trade. We know that these hypotheses are internally consistent, because they have their foundation in a general-equilibrium type of theory. Because the theory on which they build is explicitly formulated, it is also easy to see what assumptions they rest on. It would be premature to evaluate and criticize the theories mentioned above now; this will have to wait until later, after we have dealt with the effects on the terms of trade of specified growth. But even at this point it should be clear that it is easy to set out a set of conditions which would lead to deteriorating or, for that matter, improving terms of trade for a country.

APPENDIX: A FORMAL MODEL OF ECONOMIC GROWTH AND INTERNATIONAL TRADE

We will now set out the simple general-equilibrium model that was used in the text of Chapter 9. It is a model with five equations in five unknowns (S_{1m}, S_{2x}, C_{1m}, C_{2x}, and P) and with an exogenous variable t. The model is rudimentary but it suffices for pedagogical purposes.[8]

The variables used in the model are as follows. Y_1 and Y_2 denote national income in counties I and II, respectively. S_{1m} denotes, as was stated in the text, output (supply) of the import-competing good in country I. S_{2x} stands for supply of the export good in country II. C_{1m} denotes consumption of the imported good in country I and C_{2x} denotes consumption of country II's export good. Economic growth is symbolized by t. P_x is the price of country I's export good and P_m of country I's import good. The import good of Country I is used as the *numéraire,* and P_m equals 1. We then indicate country I's terms of trade by P.

We can then set out the following system of equations:

$$S_{1m} = S_{1m}(t, P(t)) \tag{9A.1}$$

Equation (9A.1) shows that supply of country I's import-competing good is a function of economic growth and of relative prices.

$$C_{1m} = C_{1m}(Y_1(t), P(t)) \tag{9A.2}$$

Equation (9A.2) shows that consumption of importables in country I is a function of its national income and of relative prices. Equation (9A.2) is, in other words, a simple type of demand function.

We can then set out analogous functions for the second country.

$$S_{2x} = S_{2x}(t, P(t)) \tag{9A.3}$$

This equation illustrates that the output of exportables in country II is a function of economic growth and relative prices.

$$C_{2x} = C_{2x}(Y_2(t), P(t)) \tag{9A.4}$$

Equation (9A.4) shows that consumption of exportables in country II is a function of its national income and of relative prices.

Finally, we have the following equilibrium condition:

$$S_{1m} + S_{2x} = C_{1m} + C_{2x} \tag{9A.5}$$

Let us call country I's import good, good I. Good I is thus also country II's export good. Equation (9A.5) simply says that, in equilibrium, demand for good I must equal its supply.

We assume the above system of equations to have a solution for t. By differentiating the equilibrium condition, equation (9A.5) with respect to t we get:

$$\frac{d(S_{1m} + S_{2x})}{dt} = \frac{d(C_{1m} + C_{2x})}{dt} \tag{9A.6}$$

which gives:

$$\frac{\partial S_{1m}}{\partial t} + \frac{\partial S_{1m}}{\partial P}\frac{dP}{dt} + \frac{\partial S_{2x}}{\partial t} + \frac{\partial S_{2x}}{\partial P}\frac{dP}{dt}$$

$$= \frac{\partial C_{1m}}{\partial Y_1}\frac{dY_1}{dt} + \frac{\partial C_{1m}}{\partial P}\frac{dP}{dt} + \frac{\partial C_{2x}}{\partial Y_2}\frac{dY_2}{dt} + \frac{\partial C_{2x}}{\partial P}\frac{dP}{dt} \tag{9A.7}$$

Solving for dP/dt gives:

$$\frac{dP}{dt} = \frac{\left(\dfrac{\partial S_{1m}}{\partial t} - \dfrac{\partial C_{1m}}{\partial Y_1}\dfrac{dY_1}{dt}\right) - \left(\dfrac{\partial C_{2x}}{\partial Y_2}\dfrac{dY_2}{dt} - \dfrac{\partial S_{2x}}{\partial t}\right)}{\dfrac{\partial C_{1m}}{\partial P} + \dfrac{\partial C_{2x}}{\partial P} - \dfrac{\partial S_{1m}}{\partial P} - \dfrac{\partial S_{2x}}{\partial P}} \tag{9A.8}$$

Expression (9A.8) shows the effects of economic growth on the terms of trade. It might be convenient to rephrase it in terms of growth rates and elasticities. To do so we need to introduce the following definitions:

$R_{1m} = \dfrac{\partial S_{1m}}{\partial t}\dfrac{1}{S_{1m}}$ — The growth rate of the import-competing sector at given terms of trade.

$R_1 = \dfrac{dY_1}{dt}\dfrac{1}{Y_1}$ — The growth rate of the national income in country I.

$E_{1m} = \dfrac{\partial C_{1m}}{\partial Y_1}\dfrac{Y_1}{C_{1m}}$ — The income elasticity of importables in country I.

$R_2 = \dfrac{dY_2}{dt}\dfrac{1}{Y_2}$ — The growth rate of the national income in country II.

$E_{2x} = \dfrac{\partial C_{2x}}{\partial Y_2}\dfrac{Y_2}{C_{2x}}$ — The income elasticity of exportables in country II.

$R_{2x} = \dfrac{\partial S_{2x}}{\partial t}\dfrac{1}{S_{2x}}$ — The growth rate of the export sector in country II at constant terms of trade.

$e_1 = \dfrac{\partial C_{1m}}{\partial P}\dfrac{P}{C_{1m}}$ — Country I's elasticity of demand for its import good with respect to the terms of trade.

$e_2 = \dfrac{\partial C_{2x}}{\partial P}\dfrac{P}{C_{2x}}$ — Country II's elasticity of demand for its export good with respect to the terms of trade.

$$s_1 = -\frac{\partial S_{1m}}{\partial P} \frac{P}{S_{1m}}$$ Country I's elasticity of supply of importables with respect to the terms of trade.

$$s_2 = -\frac{\partial S_{2x}}{\partial P} \frac{P}{S_{2x}}$$ Country II's elasticity of supply of exportables with respect to the terms of trade.

Using these definitions we can rewrite equation (9A.8) as follows:

$$\frac{dP}{dt} = \frac{(R_{1m} S_{1m} - R_1 E_{1m} C_{1m}) - (R_2 E_{2x} C_{2x} - R_{2x} S_{2x})}{\dfrac{C_{1m}}{P} e_1 + \dfrac{C_{2x}}{P} e_2 + \dfrac{S_{1m}}{P} s_1 + \dfrac{S_{2x}}{P} s_2}$$

This, then, is the model that has been used and analyzed as equation (9.1) in the text of the chapter.

10
Increases in factor endowments and international trade: the Rybczynski theorem

In Chapter 9 economic growth was unspecified. As time went by both countries grew, but we did not try to examine the causes of growth. In this chapter we will go a step further. Two factors of production, conventionally called labor and capital, will be introduced and we will study what happens to the trading relationships of the two countries if one of the countries has an increase in the labor force or in the stock of capital.

In Chapter 9 we studied the effects of simultaneous growth in both countries. It will now suffice to take only one country explicitly into account, because we already know the basic interrelationships between the two countries, as expressed by the elasticity factor in the denominator of equations (9A.8) and (9.1).

We will start by giving an exposition in geometric terms of the so-called Rybczynski theorem.[1] This theorem states that if one of the factors of production increases, the other one being constant, the output of the good using the accumulating factor intensively will increase and the output of the other good will decrease in absolute amount, provided that commodity and factor prices are being kept constant. We will then do away with these assumptions and look into the general-equilibrium implications of the Rybczynski theorem. After having dealt with the effects on commodity and factor prices, we will also give a verbal treatment of the effects of increases in factor endowments on some other factors in the trade model, especially on the national income.

THE RYBCZYNSKI THEOREM

It will now be useful to apply the geometric tools developed in the first part of the book. We will make the by-now familiar assumptions that commodity and factor markets are characterized by competitive conditions and that the production functions are homogeneous of the first degree. These assumptions are necessary to establish our results. It is, however, not necessary to assume that production functions are the same in the two countries.

We begin by assuming that the two countries are trading and that country I is in the equilibrium depicted in Figure 10.1. The country's original factor endowments before growth are measured by the box $OAO'B$. Capital is measured on the vertical side and labor on the horizontal side. The production of the country's export good, S_{1x}, is measured from the lower left-hand corner and the production of its import-competing good, S_{1m}, from the upper right-hand corner.

FIGURE 10.1

Factor growth at constant commodity prices

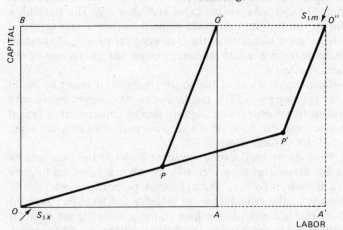

It follows that the export good is labor-intensive and that the import-competing good is capital-intensive.

Let us assume that country I before growth produces at point P on its contract curve. The factor intensity used in production of exportables will then be OP and the factor intensity used in production of importables will be $O'P$. Country I now gets an increase in its labor force with a constant capital stock. The increase in the labor force is measured by the distance AA', so that the new box, after the increase in the labor force, will be $OA'O''B$. What will be the effects on volumes produced, the terms of trade, and so on?

To deal with these questions we start by assuming that commodity prices are kept constant. To keep commodity prices constant, we also have to keep factor prices constant. To keep factor prices constant, the marginal productivities in each line of production have to stay fixed. Since the production functions are homogeneous of the first degree, the ratio of marginal productivities is a function only of factor intensities. As long as factor intensities do not change, the ratio of marginal productivities does not change either. The only point in the new box at which factors of production are combined in the same proportions as at P is P'. The factor intensity OP' is obviously the same as the factor intensity OP and the factor intensity $O'P$ is the same as $O''P'$.

But what about point P'? Is it on the contract curve in the new box? Yes, it is, because the ray OP' cuts the isoquants of the export industry (not shown) at points where they all have equal slope. As $O'P$ and $O''P'$ are parallel they also cut the isoquants of the import-competing industry (not shown) at points where they have equal slope. Therefore, the ratios of the marginal productivities are the same at P and P'. Hence P' fulfills the optimum condition and is on the contract curve in the box $OA'O''B$.

It is now clear what the consequences of keeping commodity prices constant are for outputs. Because of the property of linear homogeneity of the production functions, the amount of a commodity produced can be measured by the distance along any ray from the origins in the box. The distance $O''P'$ is obviously shorter than the distance $O'P$. Therefore, less of the import-competing good is produced at P' than at P. Analogously, P' is farther away from the O origin than is P. Therefore, more of exportables are produced at P' than at P. This establishes the fact that if one of the factors is increased while the other is kept constant, the production of the good intensive in the increasing factor will, at constant commodity prices, increase in absolute amount, whereas the production of the other good decreases absolutely.

To see the economic implications of the above argument, it might be useful to reiterate it in the following way. The assumption about constant commodity prices implies constant factor prices, which in turn implies constant labor/capital ratios in the two industries. But how can we keep the two ratios constant when the amount of one of the factors increases?

This can only be done by reallocating resources between the two lines of production. When the amount of labor increases, all the new labor has to go to the labor-intensive industry. To keep the old factor proportions, we have to release some capital from the capital-intensive industry and let it be combined with the new labor. But not only do we have to move some capital from the capital-intensive industry, we also have to move some workers from the capital-intensive to the labor-intensive industry. As long as the labor force keeps increasing, we have to move factors of production over from the capital-intensive to the labor-intensive line of production. This means that the production in the labor-intensive industry has to expand while production in the capital-intensive industry contracts. If this process were to continue indefinitely, the country would obviously become completely specialized.

But keeping commodity prices constant is only a device for tracing the logic of the argument; it is hardly compatible with general equilibrium. It is now time to give up that assumption and to see what the implications are for all the important variables in the general-equilibrium framework.

Let us for the moment, however, ask the question: Under what conditions would point P' be a true general equilibrium point?

An increase in the labor force of Country I increases the productive capacity of the country and leads to an increase in the national income. But at point P' less importables are consumed. In other words, an increase in income causes a fall in the demand of one of the goods. This implies, obviously, that the import good is an inferior good. P' can therefore be a possible equilibrium point only with the provision that one of the goods is inferior. If we stay with the assumption from Chapter 9 and bar inferior goods, we also rule out P' as a possible new equilibrium point. In other words, assuming constant commodity prices is not compatible with general-equilibrium theorizing.

To continue the argument it is convenient to use another geometric illustration. In Figure 10.2 the production-possibility curve TT is derived from the box diagram $OAO'B$ in Figure 10.1. The international terms of trade are given by the price line P_0P_0, which is tangential to TT at point S. What about the new production-possibility curve? What shape will it have? All we can say is that a price line such as P_1P_1, which is parallel to P_0P_0, must be tangential to the new production-possibility curve below the line SB, because, as we have just shown, at constant prices more exportables will be produced and less importables will be produced. So if we derive the new production-possibility curve $T'T'$ from the

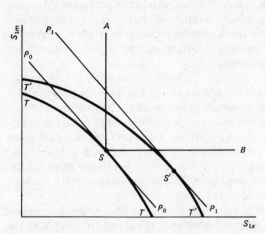

FIGURE 10.2

Equilibrium situation for terms of trade after factor growth

box $OA'O''B$ in Figure 10.1 it will appear as it does in Figure 10.2.

Barring inferior goods, S' cannot be an equilibrium point. The increase in the labor force implies an increase in the national income. Demand for both goods will increase. Therefore, the new equilibrium point will lie somewhere on the new production-possibility curve $T'T'$ between where it is cut by the lines SA and SB. The slope of this segment of the production-possibility curve is not as steep as the slope of the production-possibility curve TT at S. That implies that the relative price of the import-competing good, S_{1m}, will be higher in the new equilibrium situation, or that, in other words, an increase in the labor force will lead to a deterioration in the country's terms of trade.

We have now established that factor growth leads to a deterioration in the terms of trade for that good which uses the accumulating factor intensively. Because labor increased and the country's export good was the labor-intensive good, the terms of trade deteriorated for the country. Had the import-competing good instead been the labor-intensive good, the terms of trade would have moved in favor of the country, because in that event, assuming unchanged commodity prices, the output of importables would have increased and the output of exportables would have decreased. This would have created an excess demand for exportables at unchanged prices, and in order to clear the markets the relative price of exportables would have had to increase; i.e. the country's terms of trade would have improved.

We will now go on and make some remarks about some generalizations of the Rybczynski theorem.

MORE GENERAL REMARKS ABOUT FACTOR GROWTH AND TRADE

A critical assumption for establishing the Rybczynski theorem is that production functions are homogeneous of the first degree. Then the effects on commodity prices hinge, as we have seen, in a critical fashion on which industry is labor-intensive and which is capital-intensive. It is not possible to generalize this result to the case of less -constrained production functions. For the case of unspecified production functions, no clear-cut result about the change in relative commodity prices can be established. The outcome depends on a set of second derivatives about which nothing *a priori* can be said.[2]

In what follows production functions are therefore assumed to be linearly homogeneous. The results for the volumes and for the national income again depend on which factor it is that accumulates and on factor intensities.

If, for instance, the increasing factor is used intensively in the export industry, the volume of exportables will always increase. The result for the volume of importables is not determinate. The volume of importables will probably also increase, especially if the income elasticity of demand for importables is high. The same results hold, *mutatis mutandis,* if the increasing factor is used intensively in the import-competing sector.

If the accumulating factor is used intensively in the import-competing industry, growth will have a strongly beneficial effect on the real national income. Then positive effects on the real national income will come from both sectors of the economy. If the increasing factor is used intensively in the export industry, the effects on the growth of the national income are less clear-cut. Then a negative influence will come from the export sector and the positive effects on the national income from growth might not be very large. These risks are enhanced if the share of exports in the national income is large. A large export share means that the country has a substantial amount of new exportables to offer to its trading partner. Since the terms of trade in this case go against the country, it implies a relatively strong negative influence on the growth of the real income.

Another important element in this situation is the elasticity factor (measured by the denominator in equations (9A.8) and (9.1). If its value is large, the negative influences coming from the export sector will tend to be neutralized, because the economy is sensitive to price changes and responds to them with changes in the production and demand patterns without much friction. The greater the possibilities for substitution in the two countries, the smaller the risks that the growing country will be hurt by its export-biased growth.

The effects on factor rewards are clear-cut. If capital accumulates while the labor force is constant, the real wage will always increase and the return to capital will fall. The income distribution will also usually turn in favor of labor under these circumstances. Wicksell pointed to these results in his *Lectures,* with the famous dictum:

The capitalist saver is thus, fundamentally, the friend of labor, though the technical innovator is not infrequently its enemy. The great innovations by which industry has from time to time been revolutionized, at first reduced a number of workers to beggary, as experience shows, while causing the profits of the capitalists to soar. There is no need to explain away this circumstance by invoking 'economic friction', and so on, for it is in full accord with a rational and consistent theory. But it is really not capital which should bear the blame; in proportion as accumulation continues, these evils must disappear, interest on capital will fall and wages will rise – unless the labourers on their part simultaneously counteract this result by a large increase in their numbers.[3]

Thus if one factor of production increases in amount, the reward to the other factor, which has been kept constant, will increase. This is what Wicksell meant when he pointed out that the capitalist, by saving and investing, is increasing the stock of capital, the workers have more machines to work with, the marginal productivity of labor increases and the wage goes up. As long as the workers are not reproducing themselves at a faster rate than capital accumulates, their real wage will increase in the growth process.

The second part of Wicksell's statement refers to the fact that certain types of technical progress – some kinds of innovations – might have a negative effect on the marginal productivity of labor, thereby reducing the real wage. In this sense the technical innovator can be the enemy of labor. This will be made clear in Chapter 11, where we will deal with the effects of technical progress on international trade.

11
Technical progress and international trade

We have just dealt with the effects of factor growth on trade. Another perhaps more important element in modern economic life is technical progress. Innovations of different kinds – technical progress, in short – have transformed the agricultural economies of the eighteenth century into the modern industrial economy. The study of the effects of technical progress on international trade needs no justification.

Again, classical and neoclassical economists showed no great interest in the study of the effects of technical progress. It is significant that many leading classical and neoclassical economists were so preoccupied with one type of factor growth – the increase in population – that they failed completely to grasp the importance of technical progress for economic development.[1]

We shall now study how technical progress affects international trade. To do this it is convenient to illustrate geometrically how technical progress affects the production function and how technical progress can be classified into different subgroups.

THE CLASSIFICATION OF TECHNICAL PROGRESS

In order to classify technical progress we use the same type of production function used in earlier parts of the book, i.e. a production function with two inputs, labor and capital. We also assume the production function to be homogeneous of the first degree. Technical progress means that more output can be produced with a given amount of inputs – or, to use a different but equivalent formulation, that a given output can be produced with less inputs.

In the classification of technical progress we will, in this chapter, follow Hick's way of classifying technical progress.[2] There technical progress is classified according to the effect it has on the marginal productivities of the factors of production. A neutral innovation is one which increases the marginal productivity of both factors of production in the same proportion. Labor-saving technical progress increases the marginal productivity of capital more than it increases the marginal productivity of labor. And capital-saving innovations increase the marginal productivity of labor more than they increase the marginal productivity of capital.

We will now show how the effects of technical progress can be illustrated in a geometric fashion.[3] The effects of neutral innovations on the production function are illustrated in Figure 11.1. Isoquant aa shows in a familiar way how labor and capital can be combined before any technical progress has taken place to produce 1 unit of good A. If factor prices are as depicted by the line P_0P_0, entrepreneurs will combine factors of production along ray OR and use Oc_1 of

FIGURE 11.1

Effects of neutral innovations
on the production function

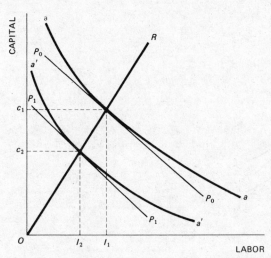

capital combined with Ol_1 of labor. The isoquant $a'a'$ depicts the new production function for good A after technical progress has taken place. The new isoquant lies completely below the old one, which shows that less labor and capital are needed to produce 1 unit of good A after the innovation.

If relative factor prices are the same (P_1P_1 is parallel to P_0P_0), it is obvious from Figure 11.1 that the factors of production even after the innovation will be combined in the same ratio as before. This is indicated by the fact that P_1P_1 is tangential to the new isoquant $a'a'$ at the point at which this isoquant is cut by the ray OR. Hence, after the technical progress has taken place, Oc_2 of capital will be combined with Ol_2 of labor to produce 1 unit of good A. This is an example of neutral innovation. That the innovation is neutral is shown by the fact that both marginal productivities have increased in the same proportion. At constant factor prices there is therefore no reason to change factor proportions, and at constant factor prices the same capital/labor ratio will be used both before and after the innovation.

It is pure coincidence that the isoquant has changed in a neutral way as in Figure 11.1. Technical progress can change the production function in any way. The only thing we know is that more output can be produced with constant inputs, or the same output with less inputs, i.e. that the new set of isoquants characterizing the production function after technical progress will be closer to the origin than was the old set of isoquants characterizing the production function before the innovation.

Labor-saving technical progress is illustrated in Figure 11.2. We start out with a pre-improvement isoquant aa and a ruling factor-price ratio P_0P_0. The capital/labor ratio used in production will then be OR. After the innovation we get a new isoquant $a'a'$. That the innovation is labor-saving – the marginal productivity

FIGURE 11.2

Labor-saving technical progress

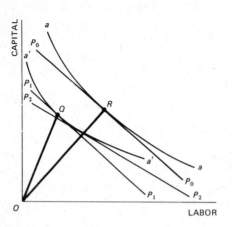

of capital is higher relative to the marginal productivity of labor in the new situation – can be seen in either of the two following ways. If the same factor-price ratio were to prevail in the new situation, the factors of production would have to be used in the ratio OQ instead of OR, and the production method would be more capital-intensive (P_1P_1 is parallel to P_0P_0). The marginal productivity of capital is higher than before the innovation but the relative price of capital is the same, so producers will find it advantageous to use relatively more capital than before. If, instead, we assume that the same capital/labor ratio were to prevail both before and after the innovation, the price of capital, to achieve a new equilibrium, would have to increase, compared with the price of labor, because at the old capital/labor ratio, capital would be more efficient and its price would be bid up. This is illustrated by the fact that the factor-price line P_2P_2, which is tangential to the new isoquant where it is cut by OR, is less steep than the original factor-price line P_0P_0.

In an analogous way, Figure 11.3 demonstrates a change in the isoquants caused by a capital-saving innovation. Here the marginal productivity of labor has increased relatively. If the factor-price ratio which existed before the innovation were to be the same after the innovation, we would get a more labor-intensive method of production, OQ instead of OR, as P_1P_1 (parallel to P_0P_0) is tangential to the new isoquant $a'a'$ at Q. This is explained by the fact that the marginal productivity of labor is higher than before. But the relative price of labor is the same. Hence producers try to use more labor and the methods of production become more labor-intensive, until the marginal productivity of labor is again equated to the going wage, which happens at Q.

Another way of viewing the effects of a capital-saving innovation is to assume that the same capital/labor ratio prevails both before and after the innovation. Because the marginal productivity of labor has increased relatively, labor is now more attractive to the producers and they will try to hire more

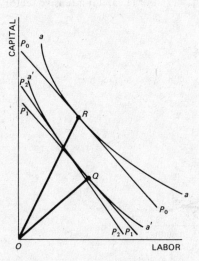

FIGURE 11.3

Capital-saving technical progress

labor. As they do this its relative price goes up. This is indicated by the fact that a factor-price line P_2P_2, which is steeper than the original factor-price line P_0P_0, is tangential to the new isoquant at the point where it is cut by the capital/labor ratio OR. This demonstrates that labor is relatively better paid than it used to be.

We have now seen how technical progress can be classified, and we should have an understanding of the meaning of the different kinds of innovations. It is now time to see what the effects of different types of technical progress will be on the terms of trade and on other variables in the trade model.

NEUTRAL TECHNICAL PROGRESS AND THE TERMS OF TRADE

To study the effects of technical progress on trade we will again use the standard trade model, with two countries consuming and producing two goods and using two factors of production. We have already studied the basic interrelationships between the two countries in Chapter 9, so we need only take one country explicitly into account in this chapter.

Let us assume that we have a country with two sectors, manufacturing and agriculture. Manufacturing is the capital-intensive sector and agriculture is the labor-intensive sector. The isoquants of the two sectors are illustrated in Figure 11.4. We assume that they only cut once.[4] Manufacturing is supposed to be the innovating industry.

We start from an equilibrium situation in which relative factor prices are given by the factor-price line P_0P_0. The pre-improvement isoquants are *mm* for manufacturing and *aa* for agriculture. The capital/labor ratio used in manufacturing is OR and in agriculture it is OQ.

FIGURE 11.4

Neutral technical progress
in the capital-intensive sector

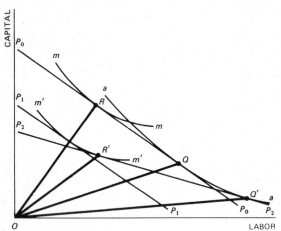

A neutral innovation takes place in manufacturing, so that the production function is now characterized by the isoquant $m'm'$. That the innovation is neutral can be seen from the fact that at unchanged factor prices (P_1P_1 is parallel to P_0P_0) the same capital/labor ratio will be used after as before the innovation.

Let us assume, for the sake of reasoning, that commodity prices are kept constant. Then what will the effect of neutral technical progress in the manufacturing sector be on outputs?

To keep commodity prices constant, factor prices will have to change. The new factor-price ratio is obtained by drawing a factor-price line that is tangential to the new manufacturing isoquant and the old agricultural isoquant. This line is P_2P_2 in Figure 11.4. It shows that the relative price of capital will increase because of neutral innovation in the manufacturing sector. The economic explanation of this phenomenon is that because of the innovation, the marginal productivity of both factors of production has increased in manufacture. Producers in this sector will bid, therefore, at constant factor prices for more factors of production. Because the industry is capital-intensive they are especially eager to attract more capital, and its relative price will go up. As capital becomes more expensive, producers in both sectors will try to substitute labor for capital in production, and the methods of production in both sectors will become more labor-intensive. The new capital/labor ratio in manufacture will be OR', and the new capital/labor ratio in agriculture will be OQ'.

To study the effects on outputs, it is convenient to use the box diagram. In the box diagram in Figure 11.5 agricultural production is measured from the lower left-hand corner and manufacturing is measured from the upper right-hand corner. The contract curve is given by the curve OO'. Since agriculture is the labor-intensive sector, the contract curve goes below the diagonal.

FIGURE 11.5

Effects on outputs of neutral
technical·progress in the
capital-intensive sector

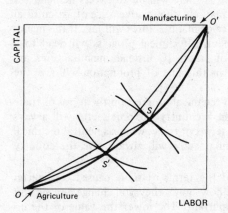

We start from an equilibrium position at S, where two isoquants are tangential to each other before any technical progress has taken place. The capital/labor ratio used in agriculture will be OS and in manufacturing it will be $O'S$. The first question we might ask is whether point S will also be on the new contract curve which will be established after technical progress has taken place. The answer is yes, it will be.

The reason is as follows. Technical progress is of a neutral type, so the new $m'm'$ isoquant at S will have the same slope at S as the old mm isoquant. The isoquants for agriculture will, of course, be the same as before the innovation, because nothing has happened in this sector. Therefore, the two isoquants will be tangential to each other at S after, as well as before, the innovation, and S will be a point on the new contract curve.

We now have to infer what happens to outputs. We saw in Figure 11.4 that to keep commodity prices constant, factor prices would have to change and production methods would become more labor-intensive in both lines of production. This means that the new point of production will have to be somewhere on the contract curve to the left of S. A possible such point of production is S' in Figure 11.5. At S' fewer agricultural products are produced. This is because less capital and labor are used in agriculture and no technical progress has taken place in the sector. But more manufactures are produced at S', partially because more labor and capital are used in this sector, and partially because neutral technical progress has taken place, so that both labor and capital are more efficient. Neutral technical progress in manufacturing will therefore result, at constant commodity prices, in the larger production, in absolute terms, of manufactured goods, and in the smaller production, in absolute terms, of agricultural good. (The reader might observe the similarity between neutral technical progress and factor growth in this respect.)

Point S' is, however, not a genuine new general-equilibrium point. We still assume that Say's Law holds and that everything produced is consumed.

Technical progress will lead to an increase in the national income. Barring the existence of inferior goods, the demand for both products will increase. This implies that at constant commodity prices there will be an excess demand for agricultural goods. In order to clear the markets, the relative price of agricultural products will go up and the relative price of manufactures will fall. If the manufacturing sector is the export sector, neutral technical progress will lead to a deterioration in the country's terms of trade. If, instead, manufactures are importables, neutral technical progress in this line of production will give the country improving terms of trade.

We can sum up the effects of neutral technical progress on the terms of trade as follows. Neutral technical progress in a country's export sector will always lead to a deterioration in the country's terms of trade, whereas neutral technical progress in a country's import-competing sector will always give the country improving terms of trade.

Thus the direction in the change of the terms of trade caused by neutral technical progress is unambiguous. Just how much they will change depends on several factors. Demand factors are important. The lower the value of the income elasticity of demand for importables, the less the deterioration in the terms of trade in the unfavorable case and the more the improvement in the favorable case. The explanation for this is that if the import elasticity is low, it implies that the increase in income caused by the innovation will primarily give rise to an increase in demand for exportables; this means, everything else being equal, that the export surplus at given terms of trade will be smaller in the unfavorable case and that the excess supply of importables, again at given terms of trade, will be larger in the favorable case.

The degree of adaptability of the two trading economies, as measured by the supply and demand elasticities pictured in the denominator of equations (9A.8) and (9.1) is also important. The greater the degree of adaptability, i.e. the higher the values of these elasticities, the less the change will be in the terms of trade.

We have now seen the effects of neutral technical progress. It is time to consider the effects of biased innovations.

CAPITAL-SAVING TECHNICAL PROGRESS IN THE CAPITAL-INTENSIVE INDUSTRY

The effects of a capital-saving innovation in manufacturing, the capital-intensive industry, is shown in Figure 11.6. We start out from an equilibrium situation where the isoquant *mm* depicts the production function for manufacturing and the isoquant *aa* characterizes the production function for agriculture. Relative factor prices are given by the line P_0P_0. The capital/labor ratio used in manufacturing is OR, and in agriculture OQ.

Then a capital-saving innovation takes place in the manufacturing sector, which is the capital-intensive line of production. That the innovation is capital-saving can be seen from the fact that the method of production has, at unchanged factor prices (P_1P_1 is parallel to P_0P_0), become more labor-intensive (OR' is to the right of OR), for now the marginal productivity of labor has increased more than that of capital.

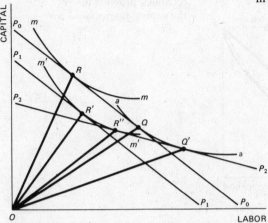

FIGURE 11.6

Capital-saving technical progress
in the capital-intensive sector

For the sake of reasoning, commodity prices are assumed to be constant. In that case, factor prices must change in favor of capital. This is illustrated by the new factor price line P_2P_2, which is less steep than the original factor-price line. When capital becomes relatively more expensive, more labor-intensive methods of production are used in both sectors. The new capital/labor ratio in manufacture is OR'', and in agriculture OQ'.

To see the effects on outputs of a capital-saving innovation in manufacturing, it is convenient to use the box diagram. A box diagram illustrating the situation is set out in Figure 11.7. At the outset, the point of equilibrium is T on the pre-improvement contract curve, OT being the capital/labor ratio used in agriculture and $O'T$ being the capital/labor ratio in manufacturing. We know, as was demonstrated in Figure 11.6, that at constant factor prices after the innovation, manufacturing will become more labor-intensive, while the factor intensity in agriculture will not change, of course, as long as factor prices do not change, because nothing has happened in this sector. At point T' the new capital/labor ratio in manufacture meets the original capital/labor ratio in agriculture. Because production functions in both sectors are assumed to be homogeneous of the first degree, we can conclude that one of the aa isoquants must be tangential to one of the new $m'm'$ isoquants. From this it follows that T' must be on the new contract curve that is established after technical progress has taken place.

At point T' the production of manufactures has increased, both because more capital and labor are used in this sector, and because at least labor is more efficient than before because of technical progress. Fewer agricultural products are produced, however, because fewer factors of production are devoted to this sector and because the technique of production is the same as it was before.

We reached point T' by assuming that factor prices remained constant. But factor prices could not stay fixed. In order for commodity prices to remain un-

FIGURE 11.7

Effects on outputs of capital-saving
technical progress in
the capital-intensive sector

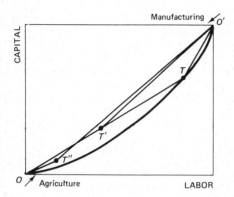

changed, it was necessary for factor prices to change, and thus capital became
more expensive. This would cause methods of production to become more labor-
intensive in both sectors, and we are taken farther toward the O corner let us say
to the point T''. At this point two isoquants are again tangential to each other,
and T'' is therefore on the post-innovation contract curve.

The implication of this process for outputs is clear. At point T'' even fewer
agricultural products are produced than at T' and more manufactures are
produced. Hence, assuming constant commodity prices, capital-saving technical
progress in manufacture will lead to an absolute increase in output of manufactured goods and an absolute decrease in the output of agricultural products.

Keeping commodity prices constant is just a device used to trace through the
argument. It ought to be easy now to see the implication for the new general-
equilibrium situation. Technical progress leads to an increase in the national income and, if we disregard inferior goods, to an increase in demand for both
goods. This implies that, at constant commodity prices, there will be an excess
demand for agricultural goods, because demand for these goods has risen but
supply of them has decreased. Hence the relative price of agricultural products
has to go up in order to clear the markets.

The implications for the terms of trade are immediate. If manufactures are
exported, the terms of trade will turn against the country; if they are imported,
there will be an improvement in the country's terms of trade.

To sum up, capital-saving technical progress in the export sector will always
turn the terms of trade against the country when the export sector is the
capital-intensive line of production. If, on the other hand, the capital-saving
innovation occurs in the import-competing sector, which is the capital-intensive
sector, the terms of trade will improve for the country.

The effects of capital-saving technical progress in the capital-intensive line of
production are thus unambiguous in the sense that we know in just what
direction the terms of trade will change in the case of such an innovation. But
the amount of this change in terms of trade depends on several factors. Demand

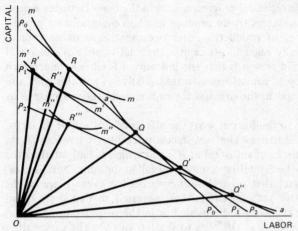

factors and the degree of adaptability in the two countries will play a role exactly analogous to the role they played in the case of neutral technical progress. The lower the income elasticity of demand for importables is in the innovating country and the higher it is in the other country (assumed to be stationary), the better off the innovating country will be. The higher the degree of adaptability in the two countries, the less the terms of trade have to change in order to reach a new equilibrium.

We now have to treat the third and last possibility to be elaborated – that of labor-saving technical progress in the capital-intensive line of production.

LABOR-SAVING TECHNICAL PROGRESS IN THE CAPITAL-INTENSIVE INDUSTRY

The effects of labor-saving technical progress in manufacturing, the capital-intensive industry, can be illustrated in a manner analogous to that of our previous discussion of the other types of technical progress. In Figure 11.8 we begin with the pre-innovation isoquants mm and aa and a given factor price line, P_0P_0. The capital/labor ratios are then OR in manufacturing and OQ in agriculture.

A labor-saving innovation takes place in manufacturing. The new isoquant is given by $m'm'$. That the innovation is labor-saving can be seen in that, at unchanged factor prices, the new capital/labor ratio in manufacture is given by OR', as a factor-price line (not drawn) parallel to P_0P_0 is tangential to $m'm'$ at R'. This shows that because of the innovation, the marginal productivity of capital has increased more than that of labor, and that producers therefore use, at unchanged factor prices, a more capital-intensive method of production, because capital is now relatively more efficient than it used to be.

We assume that commodity prices are kept unchanged and will try to infer the effects on outputs. To keep commodity prices fixed, factor prices will have to change, so capital becomes relatively more expensive. There are two reasons for this. The first is that as technical progress occurs in the manufacturing sector, costs are lowered and producers try to produce more to increase their profits. They will demand factors of production, and because the sector is capital-intensive, they are especially eager to get capital, the relative price of which will then be bid up. The second reason is that the innovation is labor-saving, which means that the efficiency of capital has increased relatively, and this gives rise in turn to a relative increase in the demand for capital and hence to a rise in its relative price.

The next step consists of finding out what the effects of this will be on factor intensities in the two industries. The new factor-price line is given by P_1P_1, which is tangential to the isoquant $m'm'$ at R'', and which is tangential to the isoquant aa at Q'. Hence the capital/labor ratio will fall in the agricultural sector. This follows from the fact that no technical progress has taken place in the sector but that the relative price of capital has increased so that more labor-intensive methods of production will be used. But in the manufacturing sector, the capital/labor ratio will rise, as OR'' lies to the left of OR. The explanation is as follows. The relative price of labor has fallen. This provides an inducement to producers to use more labor-intensive methods of production. But the marginal productivity of capital has increased relatively because of the labor-saving innovation. This provides producers with an inducement to use more capital-intensive methods of production. In our case the latter tendency will be stronger than the former, so that even though capital is relatively more expensive, a more capital-intensive method of production will be used.

This is not, however, a necessary result. If the innovation had reduced costs even more and the new isoquant had been closer to the origin, the outcome would have been different. This case is also illustrated in Figure 11.8. The new, post-innovation isoquant is given by $m''m''$. Commodity prices are still assumed to be constant, and for this to be possible, factor prices will have to change in favor of capital for the same reasons as in the other case. The new factor-price line is given by P_2P_2. Because capital is more expensive and no technical progress has taken place in agriculture, a more labor-intensive method of production will be used in this sector; this is shown by the fact that the new capital/labor ratio OQ'' is to the right of the original capital/labor ratio OQ. The new factor-price line P_2P_2 is tangential to the isoquant $m''m''$ at R'''. The capital/labor ratio in manufacture will be OR''', which is to the right of the pre-improvement capital/labor ratio OR. Hence the new method of production will be more labor-intensive in the manufacturing sector as well. This is explained by the fact that even though the marginal productivity of capital has increased relatively because of the innovation, this increase is outweighed by the fact that capital has become relatively more expensive, so the end-result will be a more labor-intensive method of production.

It is now time to infer the results for outputs. To do so we will again use the box diagram. The same type of box diagram as that used in the earlier parts of the chapter is constructed (Figure 11.9). Production of agricultural goods is measured from the lower left-hand corner, production of manufactures is

FIGURE 11.9

Effects on outputs of labor-saving
technical progress in the
capital-intensive sector

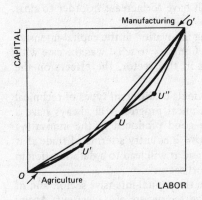

measured from the upper right-hand corner, and so on. Before any technical
progress has taken place, the point of equilibrium of production is at point *U*,
with *OU* being the capital/labor ratio used in agriculture and *O'U* being the
capital/labor ratio in manufacturing.

We now have to study the effects on outputs of technical progress, assuming
commodity prices to be constant. We start with the second case discussed above.
This was the case in which the highest degree of technical progress led to the
new isoquant *m"m"* in manufacturing, as depicted in Figure 11.8. In this case the
capital/labor ratio in both sectors fell, so that both lines of production became
more labor-intensive. This situation is compatible with a movement from point
U to point *U'* in Figure 11.9.

In this case the implications for outputs is clear. At point *U'* fewer
agricultural goods and more manufactures are produced. This implies, in exactly
the same manner as was the case with capital-saving technical progress, that there
will be an excess demand for agricultural products at given prices. Hence the
relative price of agricultural goods will increase to clear the markets. If manufactures are exported, the terms of trade will deteriorate for the innovating
country; if agriculture is the export sector, the terms of trade will improve.

But this is not a necessary outcome of labor-saving technical progress in the
capital-intensive industry. In the first case we dealt with, the effect of the
innovation was to increase the capital/labor ratio in manufacturing but to lower
it in agriculture. Labor-saving technical progress in the capital-intensive industry
will always lead to an increase in the relative price of capital and to a fall in the
capital/labor ratio in the labor-intensive industry. The smaller the reduction in
cost caused by the innovation, the more the capital/labor ratio will increase in
manufacturing and the less it will fall in agriculture. Point *U"* in Figure 11.9
shows a situation in which there is an unchanged capital/labor ratio in agriculture
and an increasing capital/labor ratio in manufacture. This is not a possible
general-equilibrium point, but a point infinitesimally close to it is consistent
with a new point of equilibrium characterized by a higher capital/labor ratio in-

manufacture and a lower one in agriculture. At such a point, output of agricultural products will have increased, and output of manufactures will have decreased, at constant commodity prices. Hence there will be an excess demand for manufactures, and their relative price will have to increase in order to clear the markets.

The implication of this is that a labor-saving innovation in the capital-intensive sector can have any effect on relative prices. Contrary to what was the case with neutral and capital-saving technical progress in this sector, the effects on the terms of trade are indeterminate.

Let us now sum up the discussion of the effects of different types of technical progress on the terms of trade. Neutral technical progress will always have a negative effect on the relative price of the good produced in the innovating sector. Neutral technical progress will improve a country's terms of trade if it takes place in the import-competing sector, and it will lead to a deterioration in the terms of trade if it is confined to the export sector.

The effects of capital-saving innovations in the capital-intensive sector, and of labor-saving innovations in the labor-intensive sector, are also clear-cut. Again, relative commodity prices of the innovating product will fall. Hence if export-ables are capital-intensive, and capital-saving technical progress takes place in this sector, the terms of trade will deteriorate for the country. Analogously, if the import-competing sector is labor-intensive and if labor-saving technical progress takes place within it, the terms of trade will improve for the country.

The effects of labor-saving innovations in the capital-intensive industry and of capital-saving innovations in the labor-intensive sector, finally, are indeter-minate. The relative price of the innovating product might increase or it might decrease, but no specific conclusions can be drawn from a theoretical point of view.

One of the critical assumptions for the analysis has been the assumption that production functions in the two sectors are homogeneous of the first degree. We learned, in Chapter 10, that this assumption was necessary for reaching qualitative conclusions about the effects of factor growth on the terms of trade. It is, however, not a necessary assumption for reaching clear-cut results about the effects of technical progress. Here it is possible to get results with more general, unspecified production functions. It is also easier to interpret these results in economic terms. To give a rigorous presentation of the results, a mathematical approach is needed. If the exposition is confined to the use of geometry, it is necessary to assume that the production functions are linearly homogeneous. A full-fledged mathematical exposition would take us outside the scope of the present book, so we will be content to give some verbal comments on the more general results.

REMARKS ON TECHNICAL PROGRESS AND THE TERMS OF TRADE WITH UNSPECIFIED PRODUCTION FUNCTIONS

In Chapter 2 we studied some of the characteristics of a production function with two factors of production. Technical progress leads to a shift in the production function. With given inputs a larger output will be produced. As an analytic expression for a production function with technical progress we can write

$$Q = f(L, K, t) \tag{11.1}$$

where Q stands for output, L and K for labor and capital, respectively, and t signifies technical progress. In Chapter 2 we studied the marginal productivities of labor and capital. The marginal productivities are mathematically represented by partial derivatives of the production function with respect to capital and labor respectively. We can go on and take second partial derivatives, which show how the marginal productivity of labor changes with a constant stock of capital, etc. Also such changes have been studied in Chapter 2.

In a similar fashion we can now take partial derivatives with respect to t.[5] We can take $\partial f/\partial t$, for instance. This partial derivative describes the shift in the production function. It is a measure of the technical progress to the extent that it shows how much more can be produced with given inputs because of the technical progress. By definition, this partial derivative is always positive, because we take technical progress to mean an increased capacity to produce.

We can also take two other partial derivatives with respect to t, $\partial^2 f/\partial L\, \partial t$ and $\partial^2 f/\partial K\, \partial t$. The first shows the effect of technical progress on the marginal productivity of labor, and the second the effect of technical progress on the marginal productivity of capital.

These three partial derivatives are very important in determining the effects of technical progress on the terms of trade and on other variables in the trade model. Once we know something about the sign of these derivatives, we also know a great deal about the effects of technical progress on the terms of trade. Other factors are, of course, also important, but the sign of the second partial derivatives illustrated above determines the direction of change in the terms of trade.

Let us assume that we have technical progress only in the export sector. We know that this means that more exportables can be produced with given inputs, or, in other words, that $\partial f/\partial t$ is positive. If technical progress has a positive effect on the marginal productivity of both factors of production, it means that both $\partial^2 f/\partial L\, \partial t$ and $\partial^2 f/\partial K\, \partial t$ are positive. This implies that the terms of trade will deteriorate for the country.

It is easy to understand why this must be so. Technical progress itself, symbolized by $\partial f/\partial t$, will have a positive effect on outputs of exportables at constant prices, because more will be produced with given inputs. If the marginal productivity of labor goes up because of the innovation, more labor will be attracted to the sector and this will also have a positive effect on output. If the marginal productivity of capital increased by the technical progress, more capital will be attracted to the sector in an exactly analogous manner, and this will again have a positive effect on output. Hence all three factors will go in the same direction, and there will be an excess supply of exportables at constant commodity prices. In order to clear the markets, the price of exportables has to fall; i.e. the terms of trade will turn against the country.

Technical progress in the import-competing sector will have completely analogous effects, provided that both marginal productivities increase because of the innovation. In that case the three factors work in the same direction. More importables will be produced at constant commodity prices. The country's own producers will capture a larger share of the market for importables. The demand for the other country's exports will fall, and in order to clear the markets, the price of the innovating country's importables will fall; i.e. its terms of trade will improve.

What is of importance, therefore, is the change in the absolute values of the marginal productivities. As long as the marginal productivity of a factor increases because of technical progress, more of this factor will be attracted to the innovating sector from the non-innovating sector. The change in the absolute value of the marginal productivities, therefore, is what is important for the reallocation of factors of production.

The Hicksian classification of technical progress concerned itself only with relative changes in the marginal productivities. To understand Hicks's classification we must take into consideration the fact that it was originally introduced to study the effects of technical progress on the income distribution. It is not difficult to understand that for the income distribution the relative change in marginal productivities is of prime importance. But for the effects on outputs, commodity prices, and allocation of factors of production, it is the absolute changes in the marginal productivities that count.[6]

Hence as along as technical progress is of a kind which increases the marginal productivity of both factors of production, the effects on outputs and relative prices are clear-cut. But there is no guarantee that innovations will have this effect. *A priori* it is fully possible that the marginal productivity of one, or perhaps both, factors of production will fall because of technical progress.[7] If this happens, the result for the terms of trade is no longer determinate.

If, for instance, there is technical progress in the export sector, and if the innovation is of such a kind as to increase the marginal productivity of labor but decrease that of capital, we will have two forces pulling in opposite directions. At constant commodity and factor prices, labor will be attracted to this section, because the marginal productivity of labor is now above the going wage. This will tend to increase output of the good. At the same time, capital will be released from the sector, because the marginal productivity of capital is below the going return to capital. This will have a negative influence on the output of the good. To this must be added the upward shift in the production function itself, symbolized by $\partial f/\partial t$, which, of course, will always have a positive effect on the supply of the good. Hence there are two positive effects and one negative effect on output of this kind of technical progress, and it is no longer possible to infer anything about the effects on outputs and relative prices.

We should now have a fairly firm grasp of how technical progress affects the terms of trade and outputs in the standard trade model. Before we conclude this chapter it might be useful to comment upon how other factors, such as the national income and the income distribution, are affected by innovations. To derive formal expressions for these effects would take us outside the scope of this book. Against the background of this chapter it should, however, not be too difficult to grasp the main drift of the argument concerning the effect on these variables.

TECHNICAL PROGRESS, THE NATIONAL INCOME, AND THE INCOME DISTRIBUTION

The effects on the real national income are closely linked with those on the terms of trade. Technical progress which improves the terms of trade has a strongly positive effect on the growth of real income. With innovations that lead to deteriorating terms of trade, the case becomes more complex. If the losses in the terms of trade are large, they might cancel out most of the prospective gains in the growth of income.

If there is technical progress in the export sector, and if this progress is of such a kind as to decrease or leave unchanged the marginal productivity of the factors of production, it is bound to have a positive effect on national income. But if the innovation (which is perhaps more likely) leads to an increase in the marginal productivities, a certain negative effect on real income will come from the export sector. This negative effect will play a larger role if the country's export share is large. (The reader should, however, observe that technical progress in the export sector also gives rise to a potential increase in the production of importables, as the model is of a neoclassical type and the factors of production are substitutable.)

Technical progress in the import-competing sector, on the other hand, will always have positive effects on real income. Thus it is of critical importance whether the progress occurs in the export- or in the import-competing sector.

The most favorable case one could construct would be that in which most technical progress would be concentrated in the import-competing industry and where any innovations in the export sector would be of a type which would lower the marginal productivity of the factors in that industry. Then all the strategic variables, i.e. the rise in the production functions and the change in the marginal productivities, would exert a positive influence on real income. In this case a large dependence on foreign trade would benefit the country. Especially if the two trading economies have small possibilities of reallocating resources and adapting demand to price changes, so that the value of the elasticity factor would be low, technical progress of this kind would imply large increases in the terms of trade for the innovating country and a fast growth of real income.

In the opposite case, that in which the innovations are concentrated to the export sector and the marginal productivity of labor and capital are rising sharply because of technical progress, the contributions to real income from the innovations might easily be dispersed through trade. The chances that this will occur are especially high if the export share of the economy is large and if the adaptability of the economy is low. Technical progress of this kind might lead to a situation such as that discussed in Chapter 9 in which impoverishing growth takes place.

Thus the same general factors which tend to increase the volume of importables and to give rise to improving terms of trade will also exert a strong positive influence on the growth of national income. Those factors, on the other hand, which increase the volume of exportables and make for deteriorating terms of trade might also, under certain circumstances, cause the positive effects of innovations on real income to be comparatively weak. It should be stressed, however, that the effects depend to a large extent on the adaptability of the two economies, measured by the elasticities set out in the denominators of equations (9A.8) and (9.1). If the value of the weighted sum of these elasticities is large, the terms of trade might be said to act as an excellent steering mechanism, and small changes in relative prices will give rise to rapid and efficient reactions from consumers and producers. In these circumstances, the changes in the terms of trade might be small during the growth process, whereas the effects on volumes and incomes would be large. This should, however, not obscure the fact that it is extremely useful to know which factors influence the terms of trade in the growth process. (To say that the steering-wheel of a car might not move much during a trip is not to say that it is an unimportant part of the car.)

Technical progress also affects factor rewards and income distribution. If technical progress is neutral, the effect on factor rewards depends on factor intensities in the innovating sector. If the industry is labor-intensive, neutral innovations will lead to a relative increase in the wage. If, on the other hand, the sector is capital-intensive, neutral innovations will lead to an increase in the return to capital.

The effects of biased innovations are quite clear. Labor-saving technical progress will benefit capital, because it primarily increases the marginal productivity of capital, and capital-saving progress will benefit labor, because it increases the marginal productivity of labor.

Capital-saving innovations in the labor-intensive line of production are therefore the type of progress most beneficial to labor. Analogously, labor-saving progress in the capital-intensive line of production should have the most favorable affects on the return to capital.

It is easy to see intuitively the economic meaning of these results. Capital-saving innovations increase the marginal productivity of labor more than they do that of capital. This gives a stimulus to producers to use more labor, because it is now relatively more efficient. If the sector in which the innovation occurs is also labor-intensive, this will reinforce the demand for labor, so the wage will be bid up even more than it would be otherwise.

Against this background it is easy to understand Wicksell's statement, given in Chapter 10 to the effect that the capitalist is the friend of the worker, whereas the innovator is not infrequently his enemy, at least in the short run. If the labor force is constant and capital accumulates, this is bound to have a positive influence on the real wage. In this sense, the capitalist-saver is the friend of the worker. But certain types of innovations can easily have a negative effect on the real wage. A labor-saving innovation of a kind which would decrease the marginal productivity of labor, especially if it were to occur in a capital-intensive line of production, could very well lead to a lowering of the real wage. In this sense the good engineer might be an enemy of the worker.

Obviously, a good many cases of different effects of techncial progress on income distribution can be constructed. We will satisfy ourselves for the present by merely pointing out those factors which will lead to a fast growth of the real wage and leave the task of figuring out the other cases as an exercise for the reader.

If we also take factor growth into account, it is clear that if capital accumulates faster than the population grows, the real wage will increase faster than the real rent and the income distribution will turn in favor of labor. The higher the degree of capital-saving innovations and the faster the rate of technical progress, the more the real wage will rise. This development will be further increased if the innovations occur in the labor-intensive lines of production and if the possibilities of substituting factors of production for each other are limited.

We should by now have certain insights into the theoretical aspects of economic growth and international trade. In Chapter 12 we will deal with more empirical and policy-oriented questions in this realm. We will see that many of these policy issues can be clarified by the kind of theorizing we have done in Chapters 9, 10 and 11.

SELECTED BIBLIOGRAPHY: CHAPTERS 9, 10 AND 11

The model developed in Chapter 9 was originally set out in the author's paper:

'Utrikeshandel och ekonomisk tillväxt: den marginella aspekten', *Ekonomisk Tidskrift*, no. 1, 1961. An English translation was published in *International Economic Papers*, no. 11, London, Macmillan, 1962.

Otherwise the three chapters build primarily on the author's book:

A Study of Economic Growth and International Trade, Stockholm, Almqvist & Wiksell, 1964.

Important papers on growth and trade are:

J. R. Hicks, 'An Inaugural Lecture', *OEP*, June 1953 (reprinted under the title 'The Long-Run Dollar Problem', in *RIE*).

H. G. Johnson, 'Economic Development and International Trade', *Nationalökonomisk Tidsskrift*, vols 5–6, 1959 (reprinted in *RIE*).

R. Findlay and H. Grubert, 'Factor Intensities, Technological Progress, and International Trade', *OEP*, February 1959.

T. M. Rybczynski, 'Factor Endowment and Relative Commodity Prices', *Ec*, November 1955 (reprinted in *RIE*).

J. Bhagwati, 'Immiserizing Growth: A Geometric Note', *RES*, June 1958 (reprinted in *RIE*).

These articles together give a good overview of the growth and trade problem treated in a verbal and geometric way. An alternative treatment of technical progress is given in:

M. C. Kemp, *The Pure Theory of International Trade*, 2nd ed., Englewood Cliffs, N.J., Prentice-Hall, 1969 (first published 1964).

For a criticism of Kemp, see:

K. G. Mäler and B. Södersten, 'Factor-biased Technical Progress and the Elasticity of Substitution', *Swedish Journal of Economics*, no. 1, 1967.

For extensions of the analysis and attempts at treating the effects of trade on growth, see:

W. M. Corden, 'The Effects of Trade on the Rate of Growth', in J. Bhagwati *et al.* (eds), *Trade, Balance of Payments and Growth*, Amsterdam, 1971.

H. G. Johnson, 'Trade and Growth: A Geometrical Exposition', *Journal of International Economics,* 1971.

Papers that aim at a dynamic treatment and deal with problems specific to the less-developed countries are:

D. M. Bensusan-Butt, 'A Model of Trade and Accumulation', *AER*, September 1954.

W. A. Lewis, 'Economic Development with Unlimited Supplies of Labor', *MS*, May 1952.

H. Oniki and H. Uzawa, 'Patterns of Trade and Investment in a Dynamic Model of International Trade', *RES*, January 1965.

The reader can also consult:

G. M. Meier, *The International Economics of Development*, New York, Harper & Row, 1968.

12
The terms of trade and the international income in the growth process

The development of the terms of trade has, at least since the beginning of classical economics, held great sway over the imagination of economists. A case might be made for a theory about this concern being an offspring of the plague of the last two centuries: nationalism. We will, however, not go into the intricacies of the interrelationships between nationalism and the theories of the development of the terms of trade. This we will leave to the reader who is interested in intellectual history to think about in his own time. What we shall do, in this chapter, is to consider, against the background of the neoclassical theorizing developed in the last three chapters, two of the main types of theories about the development of the terms of trade which have dominated the thought of economists during the last two centuries. We will also deal with its implications for the development of the national income in real terms. At the end of the chapter we will appraise the theory of comparative advantage against the background of the theory of economic growth and international trade.

The first kind of theory we will deal with, concerning the long-run development of the terms of trade, we will call the *British school,* as it has been primarily the concern of British economists. This school held that the terms of trade would go against the developed, industrial nations. The other theory, or set of theories, about the terms of trade we will deal with is connected with the names of Singer and Prebisch, especially that of Prebisch. This theory maintains that the terms of trade will go against the less developed countries and will continue to do so unless some specific policy measures are taken.

THE BRITISH SCHOOL

The beginnings of the British school date back to the heyday of the English classical economists. One of their firm beliefs was that of decreasing returns in agriculture. This belief was one of the cornerstones upon which Ricardo founded his theory of income distribution. To explain the income distribution was, according to Ricardo, the main object of economics. Because of decreasing returns to scale in agriculture, the income distribution would move in favor of the landlords: population would increase and keep the wage at a subsistence level, the capitalists would be squeezed, and the landlords would reap an increasing land rent and live forever in leisure at the expense of the others.

The decreasing returns to scale in agriculture would also have ominous consequences for England's terms of trade. Robert Torrens wrote in 1821:

> As the several nations of the world advance in wealth and population, the commercial intercourse between them must gradually become less important and beneficial . . . the species of foreign trade which has the most powerful influence in raising profits and increasing wealth, is that which is carried on between an old country in which raw produce bears a high value in relation to wrought goods, and a new country where wrought goods possess a high exchangeable power with respect to raw produce. Now, as new countries advance in population, the cultivation of inferior soils must increase the cost of raising raw produce, and the division of labor reduce the expense of working it up. Hence, in all new settlements, the increasing value of raw produce must gradually check its exportation, and the falling value of wrought goods progressively prevent their importation; until at length the commercial intercourse between nations shall be confined to those peculiar articles, in the production of which the immutable circumstances of soil and climate give one country a permanent advantage over another.[1]

This quotation indicates quite clearly that Torrens believed that the terms of trade would go against the industrial countries, of which England was the most important at the time Torrens wrote the above paragraph. The price of manufactured goods in terms of food products and raw materials would steadily diminish, and the developed, industrial nations which exported manufactured, 'wrought' goods would suffer from this development until finally the volume of trade would diminish to such an extent that every country would be self-contained.

This theory is primitive, but it is, in an odd way, complete. It builds on very narrow assumptions and drastic simplifications. From the vantage point of the middle of the twentieth century it is clear that its most crippling defect is the failure to take into account technical progress. But judged on its own terms it is quite logical. If one is willing to disregard technical progress and to assume that there are constant returns to scale in the production of manufactures but decreasing returns to scale in agriculture, and that the prime movers in the growth process are increases in capital and labor, Torren's result is quite likely to occur. Its chief fault lies not in defective deductive reasoning but in the narrow and unrealistic assumptions upon which the analysis is built. The emphasis put on a few strategic factors is so great that the basic model is, at least for all practical purposes, transformed from a general-equilibrium to a partial model by leaving out the demand side.

The line of thought that Torrens inaugurated was virtuously upheld by English economists during all of the nineteenth century, and its remnants can be seen to this day. Its chief proponent during this century was no one else but John Maynard Keynes. As a commentary to the development of Britain's terms of trade during the first decade of this century, Keynes wrote the following in the *Economic Journal* of 1912:

> The deterioration – from the point of view of this country . . . is due, of course, to the operation of the law of diminishing returns for raw products which, after a temporary lull, has been setting in sharply in quite recent years. There is now again a steady tendency for a given unit of manufactured

product to purchase year by year a diminishing quantity of raw product. The comparative advantage is moving sharply against industrial countries.[2]

The quoted paragraph makes quite clear that Keynes adheres, on this score, to the old, classical tradition. His rebelliousness was to be saved for other causes. The notion that the terms of trade will go against the industrial countries he seems even to be willing to give the stature of a law of nature.

This line of thought was to play a great role in some of his later writings. It dominated the economic argument contained in the book which first made Keynes known to a greater public, *The Economic Consequences of the Peace,* published in 1920. The industrial nations of Europe had, before the war, relied upon imports of food and raw materials from the rural parts of Europe and from countries overseas. But they had only been able to do this at relatively increasing costs. The affluence of industrial Europe before the First World War depended, according to Keynes, on an intricate and delicate balance and division of international labor:

> Much else might be said in an attempt to portray the economic consequences of the Europe of 1914. I have selected for emphasis the three or four greatest factors of instability - the instability of an excessive population dependent for its livelihood on a complicated and artificial organization, the psychological instability of the laboring and capitalist classes, and the instability of Europe's claim, coupled with the completeness of her dependence, on food supplies of the New World.[3]

The tragedy of the Treaty of Versailles, according to Keynes, was that it disrupted the economic organization of Europe and the intricate network of international trade on which it was built. The terms at which Europe could trade were critical for her well-being. If she would have to pay too dearly for the food necessary to feed the 'excessive' population, and if the raw materials needed to produce industrial goods became too expensive, the era of progress might come to an end.

There is little doubt that when Keynes wrote about Europe he had Britain primarily in mind, and that the two tended to be synonymous for him. The fear of a long-run deterioration of the terms of trade, which would cause foreign trade to be of little advantage to Europe (Britain) and would jeopardize its future economic progress, haunted his mind. The development of the terms of trade during the heyday of the British Empire (1870–1900) had not substantiated this fear, but Keynes somehow felt that this had been an abnormal period, and in *The Economic Consequences of the Peace* he again reiterated his belief in the inevitability of deteriorating terms of trade for the industrial countries:

> Up to about 1900 a unit of labor applied to industry yielded year by year a purchasing power over an increasing quantity of food. It is possible that about 1900 this process began to be reversed and a diminishing yield of nature to men's effort was beginning to reassert itself.[4]

This is not the place to make a whole-scale evaluation of all the political and economic beliefs and ideas contained in *The Economic Consequences of the Peace.* We will content ourselves with the chief idea expressed by Keynes and other members of the British school about the development of the terms of trade.

Keynes's main idea seems to have been that Britain's (Europe's) population would continue to grow and that this would cause a deterioration in her terms of trade. It is easy to evaluate this idea against the background of the theories developed in Chapters 9, 10 and 11.

Let us start by thinking in terms of a two-by-two-by-two model and assume that Europe is exporting industrial products which are produced with capital-intensive methods of production and that the production functions are homogeneous of the first degree. If population were to increase with other factors remaining constant, that would lead to a result opposite to that of Keynes: the terms of trade would go in favor of Europe.

The assumption about constant returns to scale is critical for obtaining this result. It might be added that this is an assumption Keynes would not have found acceptable, because he instead viewed constant returns to scale in industry but decreasing returns to scale in agriculture as being somehow embedded in nature. If this were the case, things would become more tricky; then the effects of a population increase would no longer be clear-cut but would depend on the exact shape of the production function.[5] The general presumption would still be, however, that, given all other assumptions, the terms of trade would go in favor of Europe.

The general conclusion to be drawn seems, therefore, to be that Keynes was not very careful in theorizing about the development of the terms of trade and that he drew very far-reaching conclusions from an incomplete, weak and intuitive type of reasoning. There is little doubt that Keynes himself, in his thinking about international trade, belonged to the neoclassical tradition. However, a consistent application of neoclassical theorizing would, if anything, have led him to conclusions quite opposite from those he drew. One might also observe that his dark prophecies were not fulfilled, at least not in a literal sense. Britain might have had difficult economic problems during the interwar period, but her terms of trade improved considerably during the 1920s.

Classical thought on the subject – the theories of Ricardo and Torrens about the development of the terms of trade – can also be elucidated by our earlier theorizing. To think in terms of two-sector models was not uncommon for their economists. They did not take technical progress into account. Their case, then, seems to be best approximated by a situation in which both labor and capital increase in the industrial country but where capital is the prime mover in economic development and is the factor which increases fastest. If the manufacturing sector is the exporting, capital-intensive sector, we would expect the terms of trade to go against the industrial country, or, in other words, that even in our type of theorizing the classical result would follow from the classical assumptions.

The main criticism to be raised against the British school is that it tends to oversimplify matters. The stress on one or two factors at the expense of others made the outlook of the British school narrow and rigid. Torrens is a good example of this. The unrealistic assumptions both about the causes of growth and about production functions made the classical analysis quite sterile. Keynes and quite a few of his followers do not come off much better, even though they in principle at least had the neoclassical apparatus to fall back upon.[6] An uncritical acceptance of the classical line of thought is clearly discernible, and the dominant impression left by their writings is one of worry that things are no longer what they used to be and that somehow, as the afternoon grows late, things are not going to get better.

It is, of course, not difficult to construct examples (against the background of our earlier theorizing) which would lead to a deterioration of the terms of trade of the industrial countries. For the sake of concreteness it might be useful to give a couple of such examples. One example is the one mentioned in connection with Torrens. If the second, agricultural country is stationary, and if capital accumulates in the industrial country, her export sector being capital-intensive, the terms of trade will deteriorate for the industrial country. Another example would be the case in which the industrial country has technical progress in her export sector leading to increases in the marginal productivities of the factors of production. Such progress will also cause a deterioration in her terms of trade. A third example is the one in which the export sector, the industrial sector, is capital-intensive, and capital-saving technical progress occurs in it. Again, the terms of trade will go against the country.

There is obviously no difficulty in constructing hypothetical examples that will lead to a worsening in the terms of trade of industrial countries. The causes that members of the British school had in mind are by no means the only ones which might lead to a worsening in the terms of trade for industrial countries. But to prophesy the future course of the terms of trade is not our task. We have to be satisfied with having gained a certain insight into the interrelationships between the variables in the trade model in the context of economic growth.

SINGER, PREBISCH, AND THE TERMS OF TRADE

To analyze the British school in its main outline was a comparatively simple affair, because the members of this school argued within a fairly well-known and reasonably well-defined frame of reference. It was not difficult to understand what they were trying to say or to follow the logic of their reasoning. Indeed, their tendency toward oversimplification constituted one of the chief flaws in their argument. They upheld too faithfully the Ricardian tradition, with its emphasis on deduction from a few simple premises.

When we turn to the Singer–Prebisch case we move into another world.[7] The structure of the Singer–Prebisch theory of development and trade is much more complicated. The basic part of it, which refers to growth, is simple enough, it runs in terms of productivity gains, development of demand, etc. But intertwined with this basic theory are hypotheses about the influence of the business cycle on the terms of trade, the interrelation between factor rewards and the terms of trade, the effects of different market forms on the terms of trade, and so on. These different theories or hypotheses are neither clearly expressed nor rigorously formulated. Tacked on to the main theory, they are difficult to deal with for at least two reasons. First, it is often hard to tell what the theories really intend to say and how the interconnections are supposed to work. Second, it is often difficult to see their significance for the main line of argument: what role, for instance, can the labor unions possibly have in the development of the terms of trade?

It goes without saying that it is difficult to present an exposition and an examination of theories of this type. Perhaps Singer and Prebisch would claim that we are writing about something other than the Singer–Prebisch case, but that is a risk they have taken by their implicit and incomplete theorizing.

Genetically speaking, the Singer–Prebisch case starts as an *ad hoc* explanation of the hardships of the South American economies and as a rationalization for certain policy conclusions. In 'Commercial Policy in the Underdeveloped Countries' Prebisch begins by saying that the only way for South America to speed up its rate of economic growth is by attempting industrialization. If the South American states try to increase their primary production – their supply of raw materials and food products – they will meet falling terms of trade, because the income and demand elasticities facing them in their export markets are so low, but they need rising export incomes in the development process, because their own marginal propensities to import are so high.[8]

This is the core of the Singer–Prebisch case. If the income elasticity facing the exports of the underdeveloped (or 'peripheral', as Prebisch calls them) countries is low and if, furthermore, the demand and supply are inelastic with regard to price, little is to be gained from pushing these exports. However high the domestic growth rate within the export industry may be, most of the productivity gains within the export sector will be exported away through falling terms of trade. This is exactly what we would expect from our theorizing in earlier chapters.

If this were as far as the Singer–Prebisch case were to go, it could claim a good foundation in orthodox economic theory. But in itself this proposition has to be regarded as a very simple, even trite one, and it is astonishing that such claims of novelty and revolutionary thinking could have been made for such a simple argument. However, although this is in our view the core or, to put it even more bluntly, the only meaningful part of the Singer – Prebisch case, there are also other theories or propositions attendant to it. It is now time to discuss this 'superstructure' of the Singer–Prebisch case.

One of Prebisch's arguments is concerned with the effects of business cycles on the terms of trade. In boom times, profits, wages and prices rise. But profits rise more than wages, and prices in the peripheral countries rise more than prices in the industrial countries, so profits among primary producers rise even more than profits in industrial countries. On the downswing, however, asymmetry enters the picture. Profits, wages and prices now ought to fall, but because of the downward rigidity of wages there, they will not fall in industrial countries. Profits in the center (the industrial countries) will be squeezed, and entrepreneurs in these countries restore their profits from the periphery. The workers in the primary-producing countries do not have strong organizations, and consequently wages and profits are squeezed more in these countries to ensure that profits in the center are kept at a level which is not regarded as abnormally low.[9]

It is hardly possible to analyze this line of argument closely. The suggested relationships are so nebulous that it is almost impossible to discern how his theory might function. Why is it that prices in the peripheral countries decrease relatively more on the downswing than they improve on the upswing, so that the end-result is a deterioration in the terms of trade of these countries? How can the behavior of wages and prices hang together? This theory is very hard to fit into our frame of reference, which works with a few, well-defined variables. It can also be a relief to realize that this theory is of a typical short-run nature and consequently does not merit so much attention in the context of growth. We shall go on, therefore, and deal with a part of the Singer–Prebisch case which has attracted both more attention and more support: the theory about market forms and the terms of trade.

Prebisch stresses as an important fact that while in industrial countries monopolistic market forms are common, the export industries in most less-developed countries work under competitive conditions.[10] It is hard to say whether this assertion is right or wrong.[11] This is, however, of no great importance from our point of view, because we are primarily interested in the consistency of Prebisch's reasoning and in the implications of his assertions. In other words, would monopolistic market conditions tend in the long run to improve the terms of trade for a country and would free competition tend to worsen them?

Many economists seems to take for granted that monopoly gets better terms of trade than competition for a country. They reach this conclusion by applying a simple comparative-static price theory which assumes that under unrestricted competition supply will expand faster than it would under monopolistic conditions, because the monopolist can restrict his output to maintain price, whereas under free competition supply will always expand until price equals costs and profits have been competed away.[12]

Such a simple type of theory does not seem a fruitful approach to the question at hand. What is needed is a theory of market forms and the growth of output, or, to put it in a more general form, a theory of market forms and economic growth. Such a theory could not take the change in productivity – the lowering of the cost curves – as a datum and derive a result applying the simple maximization principle; rather, it would have to offer a hypothesis about the effect of different market forms on productivity.

There exists no such rigorous and well-established theory. Attempts to tackle the question have, however, been made by Baumol, Galbraith, Sylos-Labini, and others.[13] It might be worth while to give a short review of the relevant aspects of these attempts.

The argument of these authors is essentially simple. They start with the observation that the size of the firm under competitive conditions is much smaller than under monopolistic or oligopolistic conditions. But the possibility of innovations, of introducing and applying technical progress, is intimately connected with the size of the firm. Technical progress is no longer a matter of the ingenuity of the small man. Or, to quote Galbraith:

> Most of the cheap and simple innovations have, to put it bluntly and unpersuasively, been made. Not only is development now sophisticated and costly but it must be on a sufficient scale so that successes and failures will in some measure average out. Few can afford it if they must expect all projects to pay off.[14]

This leads to the conclusion that the rate of technological progress tends to be higher under monopolistic market conditions than under competition.[15] Even if, in the short run, cost reductions might be kept within the firm and not lead to any reduction in price, output in the long run will expand, and the growth rate of supply will be higher under monopolistic and oligopolistic conditions than under free competition.[16] Only those firms that operate on a large enough scale can afford the research and development needed to introduce systematically cost reductions and new products.[17]

The implications of these arguments are clearly contrary to the hypotheses of Prebisch. What is of interest are not the market forms themselves but their influence on the growth of supply. The faster output grows, all other things being equal, the more adverse the development of relative commodity prices of the firm will be. Therefore, if one tries to isolate the effects of market forms on the terms of trade, the conclusion, according to this view, must be that the more monopolistic and oligopolistic market forms a country has in its export sector, the worse the prospects are for the terms of trade, a result which is opposite to Prebisch's assertions.

The point of our argument is not necessarily to say that Prebisch is wrong. This is an area in which no conclusive evidence is available. What can be said, however, is that the implications of what seem to be the dominant views are not on Prebisch's side. These are complicated matters, and Prebisch's slightly extravagant assertions do not stand up too well under closer scrutiny.

Another explanation of the deterioration in the terms of trade of the underdeveloped countries lies, according to Singer and Prebisch, in the fact that the industrial countries have much stronger labor organizations than the peripheral countries. In the absence of labor unions wages can be depressed, which leads to falling product prices and deteriorating terms of trade.

This argument seems to have a certain plausibility. The difficulties with institutional arguments of this sort is that they are hard to fit into a consistent theory. We want our theories to be general equilibrium in nature in order that we can have a certain confidence in their self-consistency. From a practical point of view, the variables entering a general-equilibrium model must, when it is rigorously formulated, be limited. Therefore, it is almost impossible to construct a model which is consistent and at the same time takes into account the effects of different institutional arrangements.

Having said this, we may proceed to look into this aspect of the Singer-Prebisch case. A good exposition of it has been given by Werner Baer. In one of the key passages of his paper he says:

The complications arising from an increase in productivity in the export sector can now be fully appreciated. If productivity in the domestic sector does not change, and hence the general wage level in both sectors remains the same, the fruits of this productivity increase will be transferred to the Center, since prices of exports will drop in about the same proportion as the productivity increases. But the productivity increase and the inelastic international demand will cause employment to shrink in the export sector. The resulting manpower surplus can only be employed in domestic industries if wages will shrink so that industries with a lower productivity ratio can exist (i.e. a lower international productivity ratio). This lowering of wages in order to increase employment will cause more international transfers of income through the export industries; it might also stimulate the older domestic industries into the export sector, since wages for them are now lower than productivity, but this will occur at the cost of still more international income transfers.[18]

It should, first of all, be remarked that this passage takes technical progress as the factor which sets the machinery in motion. In the context of less-developed countries, one might perhaps think the origin of economic growth to be an increase in population. We shall return to this question shortly. First, we shall consider the effects of technical progress.

Technical progress will lower the cost at constant output and increase the profit. Under competitive conditions, this will lead to an expansion of output. The effect on prices depends on demand conditions, which have two significant aspects. One is the growth of demand for exportables, which will be a function primarily of the growth of income in the importing country (or countries). If the incomes of the trading partners do not grow very fast or if the marginal propensity to import the product in question is very low (or perhaps zero), the demand for the products of the innovating industry will not increase very much. The second aspect is the demand elasticity. If it is small (lower than unity), it is not possible to make the demanded volume expand through price decreases. Under conditions like these it might be possible that the total income of the export industry might fall, even though output has increased. Growth under these circumstances might even become impoverishing.

A development like the one sketched above will lead to a decrease in the number of workers employed in the export sector, unless the progress is heavily biased in a capital-saving direction. The wage will fall, and the unemployed workers will hopefully find employment in other industries whose costs will now decrease, and consequently they might become export industries. If the demand facing these industries is also inelastic, there might be further decreases in the terms of trade.

If this sounds like a sad story, we must keep clearly in mind that the basic reason for all these hardships is the adverse demand conditions. This is the *sine qua non* without which the difficulties described above would not occur. Trade unions would not be able to do much about the demand conditions in the international market, though their presence might modify the situation to some degree.

However, the presence of labor unions could conceivably make a difference. It might be useful to think in terms of a two-sector model with one capitalist, export sector where innovations occur and one domestic subsistence sector which uses traditional methods of production. If the workers are well informed about technical progress and have strong unions, they might be able to raise wages at the same rate as the productivity increases. This will increase the costs of the industry more than would be the case otherwise. Profits will tend to decrease, as will the rate of capital accumulation in the industry, assuming that most profits are reinvested. The growth of output of the industry will be slowed down, and if the demand conditions are analogous to the ones described above, export prices will not fall as much as they otherwise would. It should be observed that the above reasoning implies that there is a wage difference between the domestic and the export sector, which essentially amounts to assuming that the supply of labor has no effect on wages. Given the above assumptions about technical progress, this wage differential would be an ever-widening one.

It is obviously not easy to make more precise statements about how wages would behave in the long run in factor markets with and without labor unions. The influence different wage patterns would have on output and relative prices is even more difficult to establish. There is no reason to deny that labor unions might make a difference in the development of relative prices, but it is extremely difficult to have any more definite notion about what the consequences for the terms of trade would be.

We might conclude our reasoning about this aspect of the Singer–Prebisch case by saying that it is not impossible to think of cases where labor unions could affect the terms of trade in a favorable way. But it it extremely difficult to fit the possible effects of labor unions on wages into a full-fledged theory of growth and trade. In all cases we have considered, and in all the meaningful interpretations of the Singer–Prebisch argument, demand conditions are already so unfavorable that any growth of export industries can only lead to nothing. Under such conditions, an explanation of deteriorating terms of trade in less developed countries requires no reference to the absence of labor unions.

The chief difficulty one encounters in analyzing the Singer–Prebisch approach to growth and trade is its looseness. If we take the Singer–Prebisch case in its simplest variant, i.e. as a simple statement that the terms of trade will go against the less developed countries, it is not difficult to make a highly plausible case for it. But economists of this school are not satisfied with just that. They want also to give very special and intricate explanations for the deterioration in the terms of trade of the peripheral countries.

The reasons we are critical of these explanations have just been given. The theorizing of Chapters 9, 10 and 11 can now be used as an Occam's razor. There is no need to fall back upon highly· dubious theories about the influences of market forms, of labor unions, etc. Simpler reasons can be given for why the terms of trade might go against the less-developed countries and why growth through trade might prove a fruitless venture for these countries. If we consider this the core of the Singer–Prebisch case, there are three conditions necessary for reaching their conclusions. These are that growth must be confined to the export sector, that the degree of adaptability must be low (so that the value of the respective demand and supply elasticities will be small), and that the demand for the country's export products must only grow slowly. Usually the first two conditions – the export-biased growth and the low adaptability – are taken for granted, if only implicitly. Then the decisive circumstance is the growth of demand. If this is sluggish, the Singer–Prebisch result will follow. This is the critical condition without which no valid version of the Singer–Prebisch case can be constructed.

It might now be useful to construct a few examples which will lead to results along the Singer–Prebisch lines and view them against the background of the theorizing of Chapters 9, 10 and 11.

We can apply the two-country model and think in terms of one less developed agricultural country and one developed industrial country. Let us start by thinking in terms of the model of unspecified growth set out in Chapter 9. If, for instance, the income elasticity facing the less developed country is only one-third of that facing the industrial country, and if the export sector is large in both countries, then the over-all growth rate of the less developed country can be roughly only one-third of that in the industrial country. If it is higher, the agricultural country will get deteriorating terms of trade. Such a development will, of course, also have implications for volumes and the real national income. The volume of exportables will grow and the country's dependence on foreign trade will increase. With export-biased growth in both countries, the factors of the greatest importance for the growth of real national income are the size of the export sector and the value of the income elasticities. The larger the export share in the agricultural ('peripheral') country, and the lower the income elasticity of importables in the industrial country, the more the terms of trade will go against the peripheral country and the less its real income will grow. How much the terms of trade will deteriorate, given these conditions, depends primarily on the demand and supply elasticities (which enter the denominator in equation (9.1)). One can expect their values to be low in this case. The smaller they are the more the terms of trade will deteriorate.

The less developed country will, in a situation such as this one, to a large extent have its possibilities of growth determined by the development of the rich country. The faster the growth of the industrial country, the greater the possibility for growth without impediments in the agricultural country. At a certain limit, the growth rates in the two countries will match so as to yield a 'balanced' development with no tendency for a change in the terms of trade. The exact conditions for this case can be found in equations (9A.8) and (9.1). If the growth rate of the poor country should fall below this rate, she will get an inducement for growth by improving terms of trade; if, on the other hand, she tries to increase her own autonomous growth rate above this level, she might find it to be a self-defeating undertaking, because the losses from her falling terms of trade will erase the gains of the extra effort.

We can then specify the source of growth and treat the case of increases in factor endowments against the background of the theorizing of Chapter 10. Here the assumption about production functions being homogeneous of the first degree is critical. The effects of an increase in labor or capital on the terms of trade depended then on factor intensities. Let us now discuss an example of a kind of factor growth that could lead to results along Singer–Prebisch lines.

Many less developed countries have a rapidly growing labor force. Such a country, therefore, is abundantly endowed with labor, so we would expect it to export labor-intensive goods. If this is the case, an increase in the labor force will lead to a deterioration in the country's terms of trade. Again, much will depend on the country's elasticity of demand for imports. If this is high, it will have a negative effect on the terms of trade, because it implies that as the country grows, more and more of its demand will be directed toward imported goods. This is a situation in which many less developed countries find themselves, because they need to import capital goods to get their development process under way. As usual, the possibilities for substitution, both on the demand and supply sides, are important. If they are small, the negative effects on the terms of trade will be reinforced.

Export-biased growth, where the source of growth is an increase in the factor endowments, will always increase the volume of exports and lead to an increased dependence on foreign trade. The effects on the real national income will depend on the behavior of the terms of trade. If the negative influences on the terms of trade are strong, most of the prospective gains of growth will be exported away. The risk of such an outcome is enhanced if the country's export share is substantial, making the country dependent on its foreign trade.

Let us see, finally, what the effects will be if technical progress is the source of growth. We know from Chapter 11 that the effects of technical progress depend to a large extent on which sector it occurs in. Singer and Prebisch focus their attention on the export sector; if this is the leading sector, the only 'modern' sector in the economy, it is natural to regard it as being the one where innovations occur. We know from our geometric exposition in Chapter 11 that most innovations in the export sector will have negative effects on the terms of trade.

We also know that for the most general case, the one where production functions are unspecified, three stratergic factors determine the upshot for the terms of trade: the upward shift in the production function associated with technical progress, the way the marginal productivity of labor changes, and the way the marginal productivity of capital changes because of the innovation. The first effect will always have a negative influence on the terms of trade. So will the other two under normal circumstances (provided, that is, that the marginal productivities increase because of the innovation). Therefore, we would expect the terms of trade to deteriorate because of technical progress in the export sector.

How much they will deteriorate depends on several more factors. The more the marginal productivities increase because of the improved technique, and the more the production function is lifted by the innovation, the more the terms of trade deteriorate. As usual, demand conditions play an important role. The larger the income elasticity of imports and the smaller the value of the elasticity factor, the less hopeful are the prospects for the terms of trade. A rapid growth of the export sector, combined with a high marginal propensity to consume importables and a low degree of response on the supply and demand sides in both countries to changes in relative prices, make for a rapid deterioration of the terms of trade.

How the real national income is affected by technical progress depends to a large extent on the course of the terms of trade. If the terms of trade deteriorate heavily for the progressing country, the increments to the real income will be small. This will be the case especially if the country has a large export share. If the adaptability of the country is low, and if it is so dependent on trade that the export sector is the only progressive part of the economy, the risk is great that the country will export away most of its productivity gain. Growth in these circumstances easily becomes self-defeating.

We have, with these example based on the theory of growth and trade set out in Chapters 9, 10 and 11, tried to substantiate the Singer–Prebisch thesis in its basic version and to show that under quite realistic conditions the terms of trade can move against a less developed country and make growth along established lines (i.e. confined to the traditional export sector) a very frustrating undertaking. After some time there simply will be no additional gains to be made in pushing ahead in this direction. There is no need for deep and impenetrable theories to explain such a situation; nor do we have to resort to theories of conspiracy among the rich. A careful application of established, neoclassical theory will suffice.

Before we end this chapter it will be useful to take a look at the theory of comparative advantage against the background of the theory of growth and trade.

GROWTH, TRADE, AND THE THEORY OF COMPARATIVE ADVANTAGE

In the first part of the book we expounded the theory of comparative advantage and we demonstrated that countries could gain by specializing according to comparative advantage and trade. In the second part of the book we have showed that growth under trade can have quite different effects on a country's well-being and that there might be cases in which growth with trade might even be detrimental to a country. Is there not a contradiction between these two statements – between, on the one hand, the theory of comparative advantage, and, on the other hand, the case of impoverishing growth?

To resolve this apparent paradox we have to think carefully about the kind of theory the doctrine of comparative advantage is and what the theory of growth and trade says.

It is not unusual to find statements to the effect that there is something wrong with the theory of comparative advantage because it is not useful for development economics. Prebisch provides us with an example of this. Comparative advantage should not be the ruling principle; rather, one should consider marginal income increments when trying to decide which sector or industry a country should develop:

> It is not really a question of comparing industrial costs with import prices but of comparing the increment of income obtained in the expansion of industry with that which could have been obtained in export activities had the same productive resources been employed there.[19]

This statement is fallacious to the extent that it suggests that what Prebisch is saying contradicts the theory of comparative advantage. The mistake lies in imputing something to the theory of comparative advantage which is not there. The theory of comparative advantage is completely static. It only compares two countries in a given static setting and says that if prices before trade differ in the countries, they can gain by trading. But it implies nothing whatsoever about economic development. If production conditions change – if, for instance, population were to increase, or if technical progress were to occur – there is nothing in the theory of comparative advantage which says that the same pattern of specialization ought to prevail after, as well as before, the change in production conditions. The new situation has to be assessed again after the change and the pattern of comparative advantage calculated again. The theory of comparative advantage does not imply that the same goods which were exported before the change in production conditions also ought to be exported after the change.

Prebisch, in the quotation above, is therefore right when he says that the fact that a country at a certain time had a comparative advantage in exporting a certain good does not imply that she ought to expand the production of that very good, if, for instance, factor supplies were to increase. It is true that the prospective marginal income increments of different lines of production ought to be considered before any one of them is expanded. But this is no objection to the theory of comparative advantage, which was never intended to answer that kind of question.

The theory of comparative advantage does not guarantee that because a country has a comparative advantage in a certain line of production at a given time she should grow and expand along those lines. We have seen from the theory of growth and trade that economic growth can have quite varied effects on the real national income of the trading country. Certain types of growth will lead to increasing terms of trade and strongly positive effects on the growth of the country's national income; here the country's participation in trade will bring strong advantages. But other types of growth might lead to heavily deteriorating terms of trade and to little, if any, positive effect on her national income; in these instances growth via trade in established lines is not a rewarding venture.

It may be that during the nineteenth century most national economies had durable, stable characteristics, such as the possession of specific raw materials and primary products or skills, the knowledge of which spread only slowly to other countries. Therefore, trade was grounded in typical and only slowly changing characteristics which gave rise to a situation of durable comparative advantage. A great deal of trade is of this nature even today. But it seems that comparative advantage is increasingly founded in superior technology, the possession of which can only be kept a secret for a very limited time. This leads to a more shifting pattern of comparative advantage. Only countries which are adaptable, willing and able to develop and learn new techniques can reap the full benefits of trade.

Part I gave us an understanding of the determinants of trade and of the gains from trade. We have now seen in Part II how economic growth affects trade. We have spent a great deal of effort in studying basic theoretical aspects of international economics. It is now time to go on to more applied, policy-oriented questions and to deal with the balance of payments, trade policy, and the problem of international liquidity.

SELECTED BIBLIOGRAPHY: CHAPTER 12

The main sources for the discussion of the theories concerning the development of the terms of trade are given in the notes and references to the chapter. For empirical facts about the actual development of the terms of trade and a discussion of these facts, see:

M. L. Dantwala, 'Commodity Terms of Trade of Primary Producing Countries', and H. M. A. Onitiri, 'The Terms of Trade', both in E. A. G. Robinson (ed.), *Problems of Economic Development,* New York, St. Martin's Press, 1965.

R. E. Baldwin, 'Secular Movements in the Terms of Trade', *AER*, Papers and Proceedings, May 1955.

J. Bhagwati, 'A Sceptical Note on the Adverse Secular Trend in the Terms of Trade of the Underdeveloped Countries', *Pakistan Economic Journal*, December 1960.

C. P. Kindleberger, *The Terms of Trade: A European Case Study*, New York, Wiley, 1956.

T. Morgan, 'Trends in Terms of Trade, and their Repercussions on Primary Producers', in R. F. Harrod and D. C. Hague (eds), *International Trade Theory in a Developing World,* New York, St. Martin's Press, 1963.

W. A. Lewis, *Aspects of Tropical Trade 1883-1965,* Stockholm, Almqvist & Wiksell, 1969.

R. C. Porter, 'Some Implications of Post-war Primary-product Trends', *JEP*, May–June 1970.

For a discussion of the Prebisch case see:

M. June Flanders, 'Prebisch on Protectionism: An Evaluation', *EJ*, June 1964.

PART III
Trade policy

13
Tariffs under optimal market conditions

In Part III we shall discuss questions of trade policy, and the first chapter will deal with the theory of tariffs under optimal conditions. We shall study what the effects of tariffs are, assuming that competitive conditions prevail in commodity and factor markets. Tariffs are, however, not the only means of trade policy that a country can use. Other important means are quotas and quantitative restrictions. They will be dealt with in Chapter 14. Some other specific aspects of trade policy which deserve some special attention are the participation of governments in international trade, and trade between Eastern and Western economies; both of these topics will also be discussed in Chapter 14.

Markets may not always be fully competitive. A time-honored argument for tariffs is the infant-industry argument, which states that tariffs may be needed to give an industry time to develop and become competitive. This argument will be discussed in Chapter 15, which will be devoted to tariffs under sub-optimal conditions. Chapter 15 will also deal with the use of tariffs to foster economic development, and with a comparison of tariffs with other policy means for correcting distortions in commodity and factor markets. The chapter also deals with the case of tariffs being levied on input goods, and the theory of the effective rate of protection.

Tariffs and the numerous other forms of protectionism provide important means of directing a country's trade and development. In Chapter 16 we will extend our studies to include various strategies of trade and development. An account will be made of the attempts of different countries at carrying out policies of import substitution. These methods are then contrasted with methods of encouraging exports.

Chapters 17 and 18 are devoted to a discussion of some current problems in trade policy. One of the central international organizations for trade policy is GATT (General Agreement on Tariffs and Trade). We will deal with the philosophy behind GATT and the economic realities behind the Kennedy Round and the Tokyo Declaration.

An important element in post-war economic development is the growth of common markets. The most spectacular of these is the European Economic Community. The development of regional trade groupings is also described in Chapter 17. The economic theory of customs unions is surveyed in Chapter 20. UNCTAD (the United Nations Conference for Trade and Development) tackled some important issues of trade policy from the point of view of the less-developed countries at the four conferences that have been held up to 1979. Examples of issues dealt with by UNCTAD are policies for stabilizing raw-material prices and tariff preferences for developing countries. We shall look at these problems in Chapters 18 and 19.

Chapter 21, finally, is devoted to another important issue in international economics, that of direct investment. For some, direct investment is the most important way of speeding up economic development and bridging the gulf between industrial and less developed countries; others view it as a vehicle of imperialism and neo-colonialism. In Chapter 21 we shall deal with the economic significance of direct investment and multinational corporations.

There are many reasons a country applies tariffs, and tariffs have long been used. Classical economics taught, as we have seen, the blessings of free trade. During the eighteenth and the beginning of the nineteenth century, tariffs were used primarily to raise government revenue. The taxing of imports is probably the easiest existing means by which a government may acquire income. In the 1840s the teaching of the classical economists started to bear fruit in their home country, England. Income taxes were introduced, protection of agriculture was abolished, and the famous corn laws were repealed in 1846. Capitalists and workers joined forces against the landowning class, and the tariffs which helped English agriculture were abolished. England continued its course toward free trade and was, from the 1850s to the First World War, for all practical purposes, a free trading nation.

Other European countries, especially France and Germany, followed England's path and lowered already low tariffs in the 1860s. The United States alone stood as a fairly protectionist nation, though a trend towards the liberalization of trade was also predominant. World trade grew at an extremely fast rate during this period, as we learned in Chapter 8.

Soon, however, demands for a more protectionist policy were heard. There were two specific factors in the 1870s which helped protectionism. One was the invasion of the European Continent by cheap grain from the United States and Russia, made possible by railways, steamships and innovations in agriculture. The other was the depression of 1873–79, the longest and deepest period of stagnant trade the world had yet known. Distressed farmers in Germany and France started to ask for protection. At first Bismarck in Germany did not want to listen to them, but as the need for government income grew, he gave in, and during the 1880s tariffs on iron and food products were introduced. France also, revised her trade policy in the 1890s and increased tariffs.

The period between the world wars saw a drastic increase in tariffs and other trade impediments; the 1930s especially was a period when protectionism increased. Since the Second World War the trend, especially among leading industrial nations, has been towards trade liberalization. Many impediments to trade have been abolished and the average level of tariffs has fallen.

We shall now examine the effects of tariffs.

THE THEORY OF TARIFFS: SOME PARTIAL ASPECTS

Tariff theory is quite complicated. To begin with, therefore, it may be useful to study the effects of a tariff in a simple geometric fashion in a partial way, i.e. disregarding all its secondary effects.

The effect of a tariff is to raise the price of the good on which duty is levied. This is illustrated in Figure 13.1. Before the tariff, the price is p, and Oq_s of the

FIGURE 13.1

Effects of a tariff:
the partial aspect

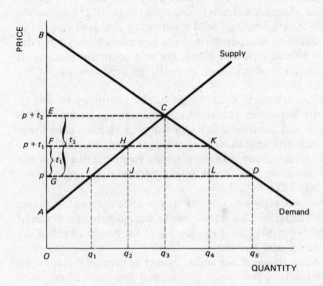

good is consumed; of this amount Oq_1 is produced within the country and q_1q_5 is imported. We then say that the tariff t_1 is levied on the good. This raises the price to $p + t_1$. Consumption falls to Oq_4, as the price of the good in the domestic market has increased. Domestic production at the same time increases with q_1q_2 to Oq_2 and imports fall to q_2q_4.

If a higher tariff, t_2, were levied on the good, the price would increase even further, to $p + t_2$. Domestic production would then increase to Oq_3 and consumption would fall to Oq_3. Hence consumption would equal domestic production and imports would fall to zero. The tariff t_2 is an example of a prohibitive tariff, i.e. a tariff high enough to curtail all imports of the good.

We have now seen that a tariff affects prices, consumption, production and imports. It is now time to study the economic costs of a tariff. Implicit in the argument for free trade is a proposition that a situation with a tariff is worse than one with free trade. A tariff must then involve a cost for society, and we shall now examine the nature of this cost, the *cost of protection*, as it is often called.

We can use the tariff t_1 to illustrate the cost of protection. The increase in the domestic price of the good due to the tariff has caused a loss in consumers' surplus of $FKDG$.[1] This is a loss which the consumers of the good have to bear. Part of this loss in consumers' surplus goes to the government in the form of tariff revenue. This part equals $JHKL$. Another part of the loss in consumers' surplus goes to producers in the form of an increase in producers' surplus.[2] This part is $GIHF$. This leaves the two triangles IJH and KLD unaccounted for, and together these two measure the cost of protection for society as a whole.

The first of these two triangles, IJH, measures the production cost of protection. If the country had imported the amount q_1q_2 of the good, instead of producing it at home, its cost would have been $q_1 q_2 JI$. Now when the country chooses to produce it in its domestic industry the cost will be $q_1 q_2 HI$. The difference IJH represents a misallocation of resources brought about by the tariff. The economic reason for this is that if the country had used resources to a value of $q_1 q_2 JI$ in its export industry, it would have produced enough exports to buy $q_1 q_2$ of the imported good. When it instead produces it at home in a protected industry, it has to devote a larger amount of resources, $q_1 q_2 HI$, to produce $q_1 q_2$ of the imported good.

The second of the two triangles, KLD, measures the consumption cost of the protection. The tariff introduces distortion in consumption. Because of the tariff, the value to the international producer of a unit of the good will be lower than the value to the domestic consumer. For the consumer, the tariff on the good will raise the price in comparison with other goods, giving rise to a distortion of consumption for the consumers. The size of this consumption cost of protection is measured by the triangle KLD.

It was assumed in the preceding analysis that the price of the good increased by the whole amount of the tariff. This is the same as assuming that the terms of trade are not affected by the tariff. This is an example of the partial aspect of the analysis, but it is hardly a realistic assumption.

When a tariff is levied on the good, we would expect its price in the domestic market to increase, decreasing consumption of the good and causing imports to fall. When imports fall, foreign exporters probably decrease the price of the good to try to recapture part of their lost sales. This means that the terms of trade of the country levying the tariff will improve, implying that the price of the good in the domestic market will increase by less than the full amount of the tariff. Only if the country levying the tariff is so small that a change in its demand will have no effect on international prices, or if the foreign supply elasticity is infinitely large, will the terms of trade not be affected by the tariff.

An improvement in a country's terms of trade implies an improvement in the country's real income. Cannot this gain from a tariff be so large as to outweigh the cost of protection we have just been discussing? Yes, it can be. We shall return to this question shortly when discussing the optimum tariff.

For the time being, however, we shall sum up what we have learned from a partial analysis of the effects of tariffs. The price of the good on which a tariff is levied will be raised in the domestic market. Imports will fall and the domestic production of the good will increase. The government will receive an increased income in the form of tariff revenue. The national income of the country, however, will fall in the normal case because of the greater inefficiency in production and the distortion of consumption which the tariff entails.

All these results are by and large true even within the context of a more refined, general-equilibrium type of analysis, as we shall soon demonstrate.

Tariff policy has in most countries been a widely discussed political issue, because the tariff has been felt to have a very direct impact on the well-being of the citizens. If a tariff can save the livelihood of some citizens, it is understandable that they are interested in the existence or removal of that tariff.

Classical and neoclassical economists by and large advocated the virtues of free trade, but their success was limited. One of the reasons may have been that they did not fully understand the effects of a tariff on income distribution.

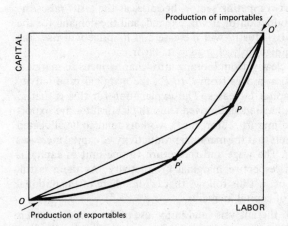

FIGURE 13.2

The Stolper – Samuelson
theorem

Modern economics has achieved a very striking result in this respect, the so-called
Stolper–Samuelson theorem, which is easily demonstrated with the tools at
hand. As it is also the easiest result to verify in general-equilibrium tariff theory,
we shall therefore begin to study the effects of tariffs in a framework of general
equilibrium by looking into the effects of tariffs on income distribution.

TARIFFS AND INCOME DISTRIBUTION: THE STOLPER–SAMUELSON THEOREM

The Stolper–Samuelson theorem is best studied with the help of a box diagram.
In Figure 13.2 we have the usual box diagram, with a contract curve OO'. (For
the sake of convenience the isoquants are omitted.) Input of labor is measured
on the horizontal axis and input of capital is measured on the vertical axis. Output of exportables is measured from the lower left-hand corner and output of
importables from the upper right-hand corner. We start from a situation with free
trade, when the country is producing at point P.

A tariff on the import good means, as we have seen, that the domestic price
of importables rises. Domestic producers then change their production, increasing production of the import good and decreasing production of the export
good. This is illustrated in the diagram by a movement from point P to point P'.
What are the implications for factor prices?

We see immediately from the diagram that the production method in the
export sector becomes more labor-intensive. Labor-intensity also increases in the
import-competing sector, the reason being that as producers start expanding production of importables (which are capital-intensive), they are especially eager to
get more capital. Hence the relative price of capital is bid up. Producers then try
to substitute labor for capital and the production methods become more labor-

intensive. The result is that the rent for capital goes up and the wage falls. The tariff causes income distribution to turn in favor of capitalists and against labor.

With a more general formulation we can say that a tariff favors the factor used intensively in the import-competing sector, because, as the tariff raises the price of the import good, production of it will expand, and the demand for the factor used intensively in this industry will increase and its price will rise: the income distribution will unambiguously change in its favor.

We can also see this very clearly from looking into what happens to marginal productivities. When production moves from P to P', the marginal productivity of labor falls and that of capital increases. The explanation for this is that as factors of production are reallocated and moved from the labor-intensive export sector to the capital-intensive import sector, more workers tend to be allocated to each machine, with the result that the marginal productivity of capital increases while that of labor decreases. The wage and the return to one unit of capital is determined, however, by its respective marginal productivity. As there is full employment in both situations, it thus follows that labor's share of the national income has to fall while that of capital increases.

One of the assumptions in the analysis (and in the use of the box diagram) is that production functions are homogeneous of the first degree. This implies that the factor rewards exhaust that total product, in other words, that all the income generated in production is divided between the factors of production (in our case labor and capital) and that profits are zero, as they have been competed away in the equilibrium situation.[3]

Let us denote the total labor force by L, the total amount of capital by C, the wage by w, and the return to capital by r. The national income, Y, is then

$$Y = L w + C r \tag{13.1}$$

Labor's share of the national income is then $L w$ and capital's share is $C r$. Let us say that equation (13.1) denotes the situation under free trade, i.e. the situation at P in Figure 13.2. The situation at P' can then be denoted by

$$Y^* = L w^* + C r^* \tag{13.2}$$

where Y^* is the new national income and w^* and r^* the new wage and the new return to capital, respectively.

The marginal productivities, and hence the wage and the return to capital, are a function of the factor intensities alone. We know that with a tariff, at P', $r^* > r$ and $w^* < w$. From this follows that $L w^* < L w$ and that $C r^* > C r$, and that labor's share of the national income has fallen while that of capital has increased.

Yet could it not be the case that the national income has fallen because of the tariff, that Y^* is smaller than Y, and that although capital's share has increased, the capitalists will receive a larger share of a smaller national income and hence possibly suffer in absolute terms? But this is impossible. It is possible that the national income falls because of the tariff, a question to which we shall shortly return. But the return to the scarce factor, in our case capital, must increase in both relative and absolute terms. Because of the reallocation of resources, the methods of production will become more labor-intensive in both lines of production, and the marginal productivity of capital will increase in both sectors. Hence, in whichever good we measure the return to capital, its reward will increase and the capitalists will receive a larger income in real terms.

The Stolper–Samuelson theorem demonstrates that the effects of a tariff are unambiguous within the context of the standard trade model. Following the Heckscher–Ohlin reasoning, we can say that a country exports the good which it produces primarily with the help of its abundant factor of production. A tariff will decrease production of exportables and lead to an increase in production of the import-competing good, and benefit the scarce factor – that used intensively in the import sector. Thus a tariff will benefit a country's scarce factor of production in an unambiguous fashion and cause the real income of the abundant factor to fall.

The Stolper–Samuelson theorem is based on some rather stringent assumptions; most of those needed to reach the Heckscher–Ohlin results, set out and discussed in Chapters 3 and 4, are also required for the Stolper–Samuelson theorem. Competitive conditions in commodity and factor markets are assumed, production functions are homogeneous of degree one, and there is always full employment. Furthermore, the theorem was only proved for the standard case with only two goods and two factors of production. But it can be generalized and some of the assumptions erased. The assumption of two goods is not critical. As long as we can classify the goods according to factor intensities, we are able to establish the results, though there are many goods. To increase the number of factors and still get the main result is more problematic; it is then difficult even to define what is meant by 'factor intensity'. The assumption about linearly homogeneous production functions is also crucial. But the assumption about competitive markets can probably be released without the main result being more than at the most slightly changed.

In practice the theorem can therefore also be said to provide valuable insight into the effects of a tariff on income distribution. It is no longer possible to believe simply that free trade will benefit all groups in society. On the contrary, the presumption is that a tariff will benefit one of the factors of production at the expense of the other. History has many examples of economic groups which have tried to foster their cause by demanding tariffs. It is quite probable that they often were right in the sense that they had a correct understanding of the fact that tariffs would further their own economic interests.

Thus the general result of economic theory is that a tariff lowers the national income but benefits the country's scarce factor of production. We studied the dual result of this in Chapter 5, when we saw that free trade generally increases a country's national income but harms the factor of production used intensively in the import-competing sector of production.

In establishing the Stolper–Samuelson result, we assumed that a tariff will always increase the price of the import good in the domestic market. This amounts to assuming (as did Stolper and Samuelson) that the terms of trade are not affected by the tariff, which is a rather strong assumption, because in the normal case we would expect the terms of trade to improve through the tariff. Yet as long as the improvement in the terms of trade is no larger than the tariff, the domestic price of the import good will still increase, and this is the only factor necessary for the country to have a movement in the 'right' direction along its contract curve, i.e. in the direction from P to P' in Figure 13.2. Could it not, however, be the case, that the improvement in the terms of trade is so large that it is larger than the tariff? This implies that a tariff will lead to a fall in the price of the import good in the domestic market, and the result for the income distribution would

FIGURE 13.3

Effect of a tariff
on the terms of trade
and domestic prices

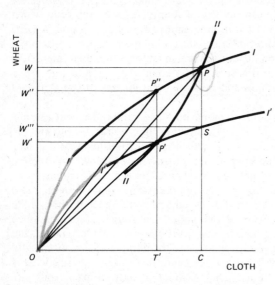

ie: Metzler paradox

then be the opposite to the Stolper–Samuelson theorem. To deal with this
question we have to study the effects of a tariff explicitly on the terms of trade
and domestic prices.

TARIFFS, THE TERMS OF TRADE, AND DOMESTIC PRICES

We assumed at the beginning of this chapter that a tariff increased the domestic
price of a good by the whole amount of the tariff, and it was later stated that
this was hardly a realistic assumption. It is true that the immediate effect of a
tariff is to increase the price of a good, but a tariff will also trigger a series of
secondary events. It will affect not only the consumption and production of the
good itself, but also production and consumption of other goods, thereby affecting
all relative prices.

Introduce offer curves

It is now time, to study the effects of a tariff on prices in a general-equilibrium
setting, and for this offer curves are convenient. Figure 13.3 shows offer curves
for countries I and II in a situation of free trade. Country I has a comparative
advantage in wheat and country II in cloth. The free-trade offer curves are given
by *I* and *II*, respectively. Equilibrium is established at point *P*, and *OC* of cloth is
exchanged for *OW* of wheat. The equilibrium terms of trade are given by the ray
OP from the origin.

Country I now introduces a 50 per cent tariff. This means that there will be
a downward shift in the country's offer curve. The new offer curve is *I'*. As importers in country I now have to pay a 50 per cent tariff, they are only willing
to give *OW'''* of wheat for *OC* of cloth; the additional amount *PS* (= *WW'''*)
they will have to pay as a tariff. This amount, which is 50 per cent of *CS*, and
which formerly went to the exporters in country II, will now go to the government in country I in the form of tariff revenue. *PS* is one-third of *PC* or 50 per

cent of *SC*. A 50 per cent tariff will, analogously, cause all the points on the new, tariff-ridden offer curve to lie one-third closer to the horizontal axis than a corresponding point on the free-trade offer curve. In this way the exact shape of country I's new offer curve can be derived.

After the imposition of the tariff, a new equilibrium is established. This is at point P', where country I's new offer curve intersects country II's offer curve. The volumes traded have decreased because of the tariff, and the terms of trade have improved for country I. This can be seen from the fact that the ratio of exports divided by imports has decreased, as $T'P'/W'P'$ is smaller than CP/WP, which implies that country I now receives more imports per unit of exports, also illustrated by the fact that the ray from the origin measuring the new terms of trade, OP', falls to the right of OP, the ray measuring the terms of trade under free trade.

This is also the standard result. Only if country II's supply elasticity of exports were infinitely large, and the country's offer curve a straight line, would the terms of trade be unaffected by the tariff. Then the only result would be a decrease in the volume of trade, but at unchanged terms of trade.

Hence the terms of trade will improve for the tariff-imposing country except in the limiting case in which the foreign country has a completely elastic offer curve, when the terms of trade are not affected by the tariff. In general it can be said that the larger the price elasticities of demand and supply in the foreign country, the smaller is the change in the terms of trade.[4] Large values on any one of these elasticities imply that either consumers or producers (or both, if the two elasticities are large) are sensitive to changes in relative prices. If the demand elasticity is large, it means that consumers are easily able to substitute exportables for importables in consumption; if the supply elasticity is large, it means that producers can move factors of production easily from one sector to the other. In other words, the larger the adaptability in a country's economy, the smaller the chances are that it will suffer deteriorating terms of trade because of tariff increases in other countries. (The reader may observe that essentially the same mechanism is at work here as in Chapter 9 in connection with the effects of economic growth on the terms of trade. The factors set out in the numerator of expressions (9A.8) and (9.1) play the same role here as they did in connection with economic growth there.)

For the income distribution it is, however, not the effect on the terms of trade that is important but the effect on domestic prices. In the international market, the country will exchange OW' of wheat for OT' of cloth, but domestic importers will have to pay more in the domestic market: they will have to give OW'' of wheat to acquire OT' of cloth, because they must also pay a tariff amounting to $W'W''$. Hence the price of the import good will increase in the domestic market, as is seen from the fact that the fraction OW''/OT' is larger than the fraction OW/OC, or from the fact that the ray from the origin representing the new domestic price, OP'', falls to the left of the ray OP. (Under free trade, before the tariff was introduced, the international terms of trade and the relative domestic price of goods were, of course, the same.)

The result of our investigation so far is that a tariff improves the terms of trade for the country, but that this improvement in the terms of trade is not large enough to offset the tariff. Hence the domestic price of the import good will

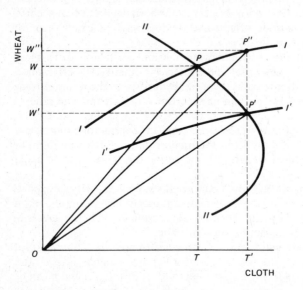

FIGURE 13.4

Effect of a tariff
on domestic prices:
inelastic offer curve

increase. This implies that the Stolper–Samuelson result holds good, and that the tariff will benefit the factor of production used intensively in the import-competing sector.

The results just referred to for the effects of a tariff on the terms of trade and on domestic prices are standard. No one seems to doubt that a tariff will improve a country's terms of trade, or, in the limiting case, leave them unchanged. The effect on domestic prices is a more disputed question in economic literature. We will, therefore, go on to relate a case according to which the effect on domestic prices ought to be the opposite of the one just stated.

It is again convenient to use geometry to present the argument. Figure 13.4 illustrates offer curves for country I and country II, denoted by *I* and *II*, respectively. The difference is now that country II has an inelastic offer curve. Under free trade the equilibrium is at point *P*. Country I still has a comparative advantage in the production of wheat, and exchanges *OW* of wheat for *OT* of cloth at the terms of trade *OP*. When country I introduces a 50 per cent tariff, there is a downward shift in its offer curve from *I* to *I'*. The new point of equilibrium is at point *P'*, and *OW'* of wheat is traded for *OT'* of textiles. Because of the fact that country II's offer curve is inelastic in the relevant range, a large improvement is produced in the terms of trade of country I. The improvement is, in fact, so large that the country with the tariff receives a larger amount of imports for a smaller amount of exports. The new terms of trade are given by the ray *OP'* from the origin.

In the domestic market the relative price of wheat will be higher, and domestic consumers will have to pay *OW''* of wheat for *OT'* of cloth; thus in the domestic market the relative price of imports has also fallen. This can be seen from the fact that the ratio *OW''/OT'* is smaller than the fraction *OW/OT*, and hence domestic consumers, even when the tariff is included in the domestic price of importables, will get more of the imported good for one unit of exportables than they did under free trade. This can also be seen from the fact that the ray from origin representing domestic price, OP'', is to the right of OP.

If the price of the imported good falls in the domestic market because of the tariff, then the effects on income distribution are the opposite to the ones suggested by the Stolper–Samuelson theorem. As the relative price of import falls, the relative price of exports rises. This means that production of exportables will be more profitable because of the tariff, and resources will be transferred from the import-competing sector to the export sector. The factor reward of the factor used intensively in the export sector will increase and the income distribution will turn in favor of the country's abundant factor of production, i.e. the one used intensively in the export sector.

This is a quite striking result, first set out in a classic article by Lloyd A. Metzler.[5] He admitted that the result to be expected was an increase in the relative price of importables in the domestic market, but he argued that if the following condition were fulfilled, the relative price of imports would instead fall in the domestic market:

$$\eta < 1 - k \tag{13.3}$$

where η is defined as country II's demand elasticity for country I's (the tariff-imposing country's) exports, and $1 - k$ is defined as country I's marginal propensity to consume its export good. Condition (13.3) says, in other words, that only if the trading partner's (i.e. the rest of the world's) demand elasticity for the tariff-imposing country's exports is larger than that country's marginal propensity to consume exportables, will the price of the import good increase in the country which has levied the tariff. If the country's marginal propensity to consume its export good is larger than the foreign demand elasticity confronting its exports, the domestic price of imports will instead fall because of the tariff. We observe that the country's marginal propensity to consume its exportables can never be larger than unity. If the foreign demand elasticity (η) is larger than unity, an orthodox result always follows.

It is fairly easy to understand the economics behind Metzler's result. The larger a country's marginal propensity to consume exportables, the larger is the amount of its tariff revenue spent on demanding the good exported by the country. Hence an excess demand for exports may come from this source. If the foreign country's demand elasticity for the first country's exports is low, it means that its demand for this good will fall only slightly, though its relative price increases. Under such circumstances, a tariff could create an excessive demand in the tariff-imposing country's market for its export good. If this happens, the price of imports will fall because of the tariff.[6]

We should now have gained a certain insight into the effects of a tariff on prices and income distribution in a general-equilibrium setting. The time has now come to deal with another standard problem in tariff theory, the effects of a tariff on national income.

TARIFFS AND THE NATIONAL INCOME: THE OPTIMUM TARIFF

The effect of a tariff is to improve a country's terms of trade and to restrict

FIGURE 13.5

The optimum
tariff

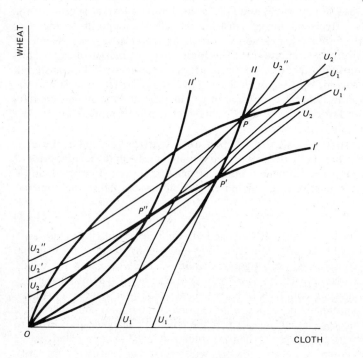

trade by decreasing the volume of imports and exports. Often we would expect
the negative effect of the misallocation of resources in production and of the distortion of consumption to be larger than the positive effect connected with the
improvement in the terms of trade. There is then a cost involved in protection,
the nature of which we discussed at the beginning of this chapter. It might, however, be that the positive effect on terms of trade is the larger; then there is a
gain in protection. And if a country is in a situation of free trade, it can always
improve its welfare by applying the 'right' tariff. This tariff, the tariff that maximizes a country's welfare, is called the *optimum tariff*. The optimum tariff is
illustrated in Figure 13.5.

We start from a free-trade situation where the curve I is country I's offer
curve and II is country II's offer curve. Equilibrium under free trade is reached at
point P, and the terms of trade are given by the ray OP (not shown) from the
origin. There are also two sets of community indifference curves, $U_1 U_1$, $U_1' U_1'$,
etc., for country I and $U_2 U_2$, $U_2' U_2'$, etc., for country II, which characterize the
two countries' preference systems.

By applying a tariff, country I will change its offer curve to I'. The new
equilibrium will be at point P', where country I's new, tariff-ridden offer curve
cuts country II's original, free-trade offer curve. The new terms of trade are

FIGURE 13.6

A case when a tariff
is not beneficial

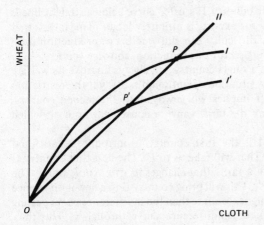

given by the ray OP' (not shown) from the origin. This tariff, which changes
country I's offer curve from I to I', is the country's optimum tariff. This is shown
by the fact that at point P' one of country I's community indifference curves,
$U'_1 U'_1$, is tangential to country II's offer curve. This is the highest indifference
curve that country I can reach. The optimum tariff is, in other words, a tariff
that maximizes the real welfare of a country.

We should observe, however, that the optimum tariff only potentially maximizes a country's welfare. The optimum tariff will, like any tariff, affect the income distribution. It will make some better off but make others worse off. To
increase a country's welfare in an unambiguous sense, therefore, the optimum
tariff has to be accompanied by a redistribution policy to compensate those who
are hurt by the tariff. As the optimum tariff, by definition, increases a country's
total welfare, this will be possible and there will still be something left over for
those who directly benefit from the tariff. It is in this sense that the optimum
tariff is a proposition in welfare economics.

We can also see from Figure 13.5, that country I's optimum tariff will have a
negative effect on country II. At point P, country II was on the indifference
curve $U''_2 U''_2$. It will now be forced to point P' and will fall on to a lower indifference curve, $U_2 U_2$. The economic explanation for this is that country II
will both suffer deteriorating terms of trade and a decrease in its volume of foreign
trade.

The only case in which country I will not benefit from levying a tariff is when
country II's offer curve is a straight line from the origin, such as is illustrated
in Figure 13.6

Country II's offer curve is given by II and country I's free-trade offer curve
by I. Under free trade, equilibrium will be at P and the terms of trade are given
by OP. A tariff will change country I's offer curve to I'. The new equilibrium
will be at P'. The volume traded will be reduced, but the terms of trade stay un-

changed. As country I can only gain from a tariff if its terms of trade improve, its optimum tariff in this case will be a zero tariff. Hence free trade will maximize its welfare in this special case.

The economic explanation for country II's offer curve being a straight line is that its price elasticity of supply for exports is infinitely large.[7] This means that the country without any cost or difficulty can shift factors of production from the export to the import-competing sector of production, and vice versa.

Leaving this special case aside, a single country can always improve its welfare by changing from free trade to a situation of optimum tariff, yet the restriction of trade that the optimum tariff implies will always hurt the second country. Both countries of course can play the tariff game, a convenient note on which to return to Figure 13.5.

Let us assume that country I is the first country to introduce a tariff and that it levies an optimum tariff. That will take us to P'. The best that country II can do in this situation is to levy a tariff that changes its offer curve to II'. The new trade equilibrium will be at P''. This will bring country II to a new indifference curve, $U_2'U_2'$, which represents higher welfare than the indifference curve passing through P' but a lower one than the indifference curve through P. This thus demonstrates that country II can reach a higher level of welfare by retaliation, but that it cannot reach as high a level as that enjoyed under free trade.

Point P'' is not a stable equilibrium point according to the diagram. We would therefore expect the two countries to go on raising their tariffs until either all trade is killed off or a stable situation is reached, i.e. a situation in which both countries at the same time are levying what for each of them is the optimum tariff, taken the other country's tariff as given.

The moral of the story is that a country taken as a single unit can always gain by levying a tariff, provided that the other country does not retaliate. It could under specific circumstances gain, even if the other country did retaliate. From the individual country's point of view tariffs must therefore produce great attraction. It is only if both countries can jointly cooperate that we can hope for free trade. If we take both countries together, viewing them as a unit, free trade will be the optimal policy, since one country's gain from an optimum tariff will always be smaller than the other's loss from it. Free trade is in this sense the best policy, though it presupposes an internationalist point of view in order to be implemented.[8]

We should now have gained an insight into the meaning of the optimum tariff, though this concept can be still somewhat elusive. What determines, for instance, the height of the optimum tariff? To find an explicit answer to this question we would have to take a more formal approach and develop a full algebraic model, and this would take us outside the scope of the present book.[9] We can, however, touch on some of the factors determining the height of the optimum tariff.

The higher a country's share of foreign trade, the larger is the scope for its optimum tariff, explained by the fact that the larger the share of national income which the country exports, the more effective will a given improvement in a country's terms of trade be. Otherwise the important factors stem from the second country (the rest of the world). Of the greatest importance are the effects produced by a change in relative prices on quantities consumed and supplied. The larger they are, the lower country I should set its optimum tariff. A tariff in country I will turn the terms of trade against country II. If the second country's price elasticity of supply is high, the country has a flexible structure of production. Producers can easily switch their factors of production from one line of production to another. If this is the case, then the terms of trade will not change much because of the tariff and country I will not stand to gain much by levying one. If the value of the supply elasticity is very large, there will be no change at all in relative prices because of a tariff, and country I's best policy will be one of free trade. A high value of country II's elasticity of demand for exports (or imports) with respect to a change in relative prices will play much the same role. It means that the goods are good substitutes and that consumers will easily adapt their habits of consumption to a change in relative prices.[10]

Thinking in terms of developed and less developed countries, we observe that industrial, developed countries usually have a high degree of flexibility in their economies as far as both supply and demand are concerned. Poor, less developed countries often show a low degree of adaptability in their economies. This means that less developed countries usually cannot expect to gain much from high tariffs and that their optimum tariffs are probably quite low. The developed countries might, from this point of view, have more to gain from exploiting a monopoly position by applying high tariffs. We could expect the optimum tariffs for these countries to be quite high at times; this applies especially to their trade with the less developed countries.

The optimum tariff argument is important. Leaving dynamic considerations aside and assuming optimal market conditions, it is, from a welfare point of view, the only valid argument for a tariff. We have now seen how the main variables in a general-equilibrium framework, i.e. prices, the national income, and the income distribution, are affected by a tariff. Before we conclude this chapter we will also mention in passing their effects on other variables.

OTHER EFFECTS OF TARIFFS

If a country has unemployment, a tariff can be used to produce an expansionary effect on the national income. A tariff means, as we have seen, that imports will decrease and that the demand for home-produced goods will increase. This is illustrated in Figure 13.7.

Tariffs can be seen as a device switching demand away from international to home goods. We start, in Figure 13.7, with an export schedule X and an import schedule M, so that the national income will be Y_0. Because of the tariff the import schedule is moved down to M'. This implies that less imports and more home-produced goods will be demanded and that there will be an expansionary effect on the national income, which increases to Y_1. If there were unemployment at Y_0, it will obviously decrease as the national income expands.

The use of a tariff for eradicating unemployment is an example of what is sometimes called a 'beggar-my-neighbor' policy. If there is unemployment in both trading countries, the country levying the tariff will export part of its unemployment to its trading partner, producing a negative effect on its national income and an increase in its rate of unemployment. It is therefore very likely that it will retaliate and in turn increase its tariff. Trade warfare could break out

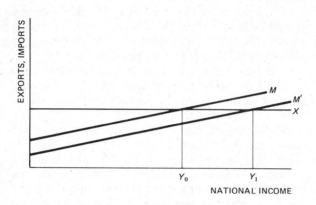

FIGURE 13.7

Effect of a tariff
on national income

and the likely result be that no one will benefit from the gradual increases in tariffs.

It should be observed that only if the country levying the tariff has unemployment will the tariff produce a positive effect in real terms. Otherwise the tariff will only cause an increase in the national income in monetary terms.

If a country has unemployment, and provided that no retaliation occurs, a tariff can bring about a decrease in unemployment. The same effect can be brought about more efficiently, however, by means of monetary and fiscal policy.

A tariff will usually also have a positive effect on a country's balance of trade. The initial effect of an increase in tariffs is to cut imports but to leave exports unchanged, thus improving the balance of trade. At the same time the national income will expand, negatively affecting the balance of trade. Much now depends on the behavior of the trading partners. If repercussions are small and no retaliations occur, the trade balance may improve; but if imports in the tariff-increasing country go up very much because of the increases in income caused by the tariff, and if foreign repercussions are great, then the temporary improvement in the balance of trade may quickly be destroyed.

A more efficient way of improving a country's balance of trade is the appropriate use of monetary and fiscal policy, or devaluation, as will be described in Chapters 25 and 26.

SUMMARY

We have now studied some of the main effects of a tariff under competitive conditions. A tariff will improve a country's terms of trade and increase the domestic price of the imported good. This implies a reallocation of resources so that more home-produced and fewer traded goods will be produced. The import-competing industry will benefit and the income distribution will move in favor of the factor used intensively in the import-competing line of production.

A tariff will, at least if the starting-point is free trade, lead to an increase in the income of the government. The national income will also be affected and an optimum tariff exists which will maximize a country's real income. A tariff will usually stimulate employment and lead to an improvement in a country's balance of trade.

SELECTED BIBLIOGRAPHY: CHAPTER 13

For a discussion of the concept of 'cost of protection' see:

W. M. Corden, 'The Calculation of the Cost of Protection', *Economic Record*, April 1957.

H. G. Johnson, 'The Cost of Protection and the Scientific Tariff', *JPE*, August 1960.

The standard essay on the effect of a tariff on the income distribution is:

W. F. Stolper and P. A. Samuelson, 'Protection and Real Wages', *RES*, November 1941 (reprinted in *RTIT*).

See also:

J. Bhagwati, 'Protection, Real Wages and Incomes', *EJ*, December 1959.

Two classical papers on the price effects of a tariff in a general-equilibrium model are:

L. A. Metzler, 'Tariffs, the Terms of Trade, and the Distribution of National Incomes', *JPE*, vol. 57, February 1949 (reprinted in *RIE*).

L. A. Metzler, 'Tariffs, International Demand and Domestic Prices', *JPE*, vol. 57, August 1949.

For a critical view of Metzler's results and a generalization and integration of the theory of tariffs, see:

B. Södersten and K. Vind, 'Tariffs and Trade in General Equilibrium', *AER*, June 1968.

Concerning the optimum tariff see:

T. Scitovsky, 'A Reconsideration of the Theory of Tariffs', *RES*, no. 2, 1942 (reprinted in *RTIT*).

For later works see:

J. de V. Graaff, 'On Optimum Tariff Structures', *RES*, no. 1, 1949.

H. G. Johnson, *International Trade and Economic Growth*, London, Allen & Unwin, 1958, ch. 2.

Works presenting a comprehensive survey on the theory of tariffs are:

W. M. Corden, *The Theory of Protection,* London, Oxford University Press, 1971.

W. M. Corden, *Trade Policy and Economic Welfare,* London, Oxford University Press, 1974.

A valuable collection of essays on different aspects of the theory of tariffs is:

H. G. Johnson, *Aspects of the Theory of Tariffs,* London, 1971.

14
Quotas and quantitative restrictions: state trading

Tariffs are the most widely used means of trade policy for influencing prices and volumes in international trade, but there are other means. Quantitative restrictions and quotas are examples. We will deal with some implications of such means for the balance of payments in Chapter 25, under the heading of *direct controls*. We now give a somewhat more systematic account of their effects, and deal with the effects on 'real factors' such as prices and volumes. We also touch briefly on another matter of interest in international trade: state trading.

THE USE OF TRADE RESTRICTIONS

We saw in Chapter 13 that the history of tariffs goes back to the beginnings of the national state. The principal reason for the use of the tariffs in its early days was the need for government revenue. The use of tariffs is probably the simplest means that a government has for raising revenue.

Quotas and other direct trade restrictions do not yield any income for the government, at least not directly. They came into practice later than tariffs. Direct trade restrictions are primarily used for protecting domestic industries and improving the balance of payments.

A brief summary of the history of trade regulations is far from easy. Wars and depressions seem to inspire an increase in protection. Otherwise, few generalizations are possible: regulations developed differently in different countries.

By and large, it can be said that the period from 1750 to 1850 saw a decline of trade restrictions. After the First World War, the trend was in the opposite direction; the interwar period especially was characterized by an intensification of trade restrictions. After the Second World War, the international organizations for dealing with international trade and monetary policies, GATT and the I.M.F., have sought to turn the tide. The developed, industrial countries have agreed not to use restrictive trade practices as an ordinary policy measure. The less developed countries, however, use them frequently to deal with the balance-of-payments problems created by their own development efforts.

The attempts at liberalizing world trade and at dismantling trade restrictions have been quite successful since the Second World War; world trade has also grown at an unprecedented rate. Trade restrictions, however, are still used to a considerable extent. Several industrial countries have resorted to them on occasion when pressed by balance-of-payments difficulties. For less developed countries, quotas and quantitative restrictions are very important policy means for controlling imports. There is no sign that these countries will change their policies in this respect.

FIGURE 14.1

Effects of a quota: the partial aspect

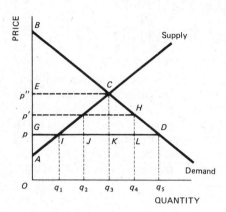

THE EFFECTS OF QUOTAS

The effects of a quota have almost exclusively been analyzed under partial conditions, so we start with the partial case. As the effects of a quota have important
similarities to those of a tariff, it is convenient to follow the analysis of tariffs
quite closely, and Figure 14.1 is like Figure 13.1.

The world market price of the good is p. At this price, the country demands
Oq_5 of the good and produces Oq_1. Thus, imports amount to q_1q_5. The country
now decides that it will have to lower imports of the good. The authorities
decide that imports will have to be reduced from q_1q_5 to q_2q_4.

A quota that reduces imports to q_2q_4, as in our example, will in many respects
be equivalent to a tariff such as the one in Chapter 13, which increased the
domestic price of the good from p to $p + t_1$ (the reader should note that the
price p' in Figure 14.1 equals the price $p + t_1$ in Figure 13.1). The effect on
domestic production and consumption will be the same, the effect on the home-
market price and the international terms of trade will be the same, and the effect
on imports will be the same. In one important respect, however, there is a
difference: a tariff will give rise to a tariff revenue that will go to the government,
whereas the quota will give rise to a gain of equal size that will go to the quota
holders. If we assume that competitive conditions prevail in the import industry,
a monopoly profit will accrue to the quota holders.

If the effects of a tariff are equivalent to those of a quota that limits imports
by the same amount, why should the government use a quota instead of a tariff,
only to deprive itself of a tariff revenue?

Part of the answer is that the equivalence depends in a critical way on market
conditions. Only on condition that there are competitive market conditions
abroad, that there is free competition in the domestic import-competing industry,

and that there is perfect competition among quota holders, will a tariff be equivalent to a quota that limits imports to the same amount as the tariff.

But competitive conditions do not always hold in all the relevant markets. Quotas have typically been used to limit imports of agricultural products. They especially flourished in the 1930s because the supply of many products was very inelastic then. A country confronted with an inelastic supply of exports of certain goods would find it difficult to limit imports of the goods by way of a tariff. Under these circumstances, a tariff would primarily give the tariff-imposing country a large improvement in its terms of trade, but it would fail to protect domestic production of the goods by a limit of imports. A tariff would have little or no effect on the domestic price of the goods, which would remain low despite the tariff, and domestic production would be outcompeted.

The foreign export supply of agricultural products is often inelastic, especially in the short run. In this situation, a quota is often the only way by which imports can be limited and the domestic price of the goods upheld. An important aspect of domestic agricultural policy in several countries is price support for agricultural products that guarantee farmers a 'fair income', so agricultural products are typically the ones for which import quotas have been used. The French were pioneers in the use of quotas in the 1930s, and since the Second World War quotas have been an integral part of the agricultural policy of the United States, where they have been used to limit and control imports of such products as sugar. The United States has an important domestic sugar industry, but for various reasons it has wanted to import from abroad. The question whether to use quotas or tariffs to control imports from less developed countries has been debated in recent years. We return to this in Chapter 18 in connection with a discussion of UNCTAD.

It is therefore important to remember that if markets abroad and at home are not perfectly competitive, the effects of tariffs can be quite different from quantitative restrictions. Another important aspect of a quota is that it can have important repercussions on the market structure in the country that imposes it.

Assume that there is an emerging industry in a country and that the authorities decide to help it by establishing a quota on imports that compete with the products of the industry. This secures a market for the domestic industry, and a domestic monopoly could be established, one profiting from the higher domestic price that the quota implies. Had a tariff been used instead, imports would have been permitted freely at the tariff-inclusive price. If the foreign supply is quite elastic, the domestic industry would eventually be in a perfectly competitive situation. If quantative restrictions are used, a domestic producer can benefit from them to establish a domestic monopoly, whereas if tariffs had been used, he would have had to accept full international competition.

Besides limiting competition in domestic markets, quantitative restrictions attach a scarcity value to imports, and the scarcity value gives rise to an economic rent. Who will capture this rent? It depends on market conditions and on the way the quantitative restrictions are organized.

If the government merely introduces a quota, and if domestic producers are organized, and foreign producers are not, the domestic producers will capture the rent by increasing profits and prices. But if foreign producers are organized and domestic ones are not, then the foreign producers can get a substantial part of the rent by increasing their prices and turning the terms of trade against the country.

The government, however, might not be content merely to announce the introduction of a quota without further ado. It might want to capture the rent for itself, which it can do by auctioning off import licenses. If the auctioning is done efficiently, and if market conditions are fully competitive, the effects of a quota can be precisely the same as those of a tariff, including the revenue going to the government in the form of an income from auctions.

This is a theoretical possibility that is difficult to put into practice. Quantitative restrictions invariably seem to benefit some specific groups in society. Who benefits largely depends on how the system is organized. In India, for instance, import licenses are divided into established importers (E.I.), actual users (A.U.) and capital goods (C.G.). E.I. licenses, used for imports of consumption goods and other commodities, are allocated to traders, A.U. licenses are allocated to producers, and C.G. licenses to investors with approved investment projects.

The reason for using quantitative restrictions seems to be that they give a sense of certainty. With them, a country can then be sure it can limit imports of the good. But this certainty is often bought at quite a high price and often at the cost of introducing uncertainties of other kinds, for instance effects on the production and cost structures within the country.

QUANTITATIVE RESTRICTIONS AND THE BALANCE OF PAYMENTS

We will deal with some implications of quantitative restrictions for the balance of payments under the heading of *direct controls* in Chapter 25, so we can be brief here.

It is true that quantitative restrictions are often introduced to improve a country's balance of payments. They have an immediate visible impact on a country's imports. But they also have secondary effects. When these are taken into account, the total impact of quantitative restrictions could be considerably less beneficial than an untrained observer might suppose.

In a general way, quantitative restrictions might be thought of as an expenditure-switching type of policy. Like any other expenditure-switching type of policy, quantitative restrictions will improve a country's balance of trade only if they decrease a country's total absorption (or, given unemployment, if they increase total production).

The most important ways in which this can be done are as follows. The general price level of the country will in all probability increase because of the restrictions. If the supply of money is kept constant, a *real balance effect* will come into play as consumers and firms try to restore the real value of their cash holdings. This will lead to a fall in total absorption in the same way as happened in connection with a devaluation. Savings can also be affected in several ways. The restriction of imports might lead to forced savings, for instance through purchases being postponed if the public expects the restrictions to be temporary. The income distribution might be changed in favor of profits (if entrepreneurs and traders reap the rent connected with the restrictions). If savings out of profits are less than savings out of wages, total absorption will fall. Investment, too, might be affected, for instance if imports of capital goods are curtailed.

All these effects, however, are quite subtle in character. Quantitative restrictions cannot be expected to lead to an improvement of the balance of payments equal to the amount by which imports are cut. In all normal circumstances, they will lead to a change in demand: goods that were earlier exported will now be demanded by domestic consumers. The net effect on the balance of payments of quantitative restrictions is therefore often much smaller than the amount by which imports are originally cut.

It should be stressed, however, that all ways of curing a deficit in the balance of payments contain some costs and painful adjustments. Expenditure-reducing policies can sometimes be regarded as too costly in terms of unemployment. If, for some reason, a country cannot or will not devalue, quantitative restrictions can be the best solution.[1] It must be realized, however, that in such a case the equilibrium in the balance of payments is bought at the expense of a certain misallocation of resources.

STATE TRADING

The state also plays a direct role in international trade by making its own purchases and sales. It is difficult to define state trading precisely; it can take many forms. It can take the form of a government agency or monopoly operating more or less according to the same principles as a private firm, or it can be a ministry or an organization that completely controls the country's international trade, as in most Communist countries. We will discuss the latter under the separate heading of *East–West trade*.

The government sector is increasing in most developed, industrial countries, so state purchasing for direct government use is increasing. Thus one would expect states to become more and more directly engaged in international trade, but most governments tend to be quite chauvinistic in this respect: they prefer to buy at home.

This tendency was especially strengthened during the depression in the 1930s, but it is still prevalent. Governments pay no tariffs. A certain preference for domestic producers (say 10 per cent of the price) can therefore seem natural, to enable the domestic producers to compete on the same terms as foreign producers. In recent years, much larger preferences have been granted to domestic producers by certain governments. The United States, for instance, had during the interwar period a 25 per cent preference, which was lowered to 10 per cent during the 1950s. For balance-of-payments reasons, this was increased to 50 per cent during the 1960s. This helped to insulate the U.S. balance of payments from the effect of the Vietnam war.

In times of balance-of-payments pressure, governments often introduce rules about buying home products, so that government officials are urged to use only domestic airlines, embassies to serve only domestic wines, etc. Thereby a double standard is used: no tariffs or quantitative restrictions for balance-of-payments reasons for the private sector, but near autarky as far as government purchases are concerned. This might be understandable, but it is hardly rational economically.

Some products, such as tobacco and alcohol, are frequently handled as government monopolies. In Sweden, for instance, the state liquor authority is the sole importer of wine and liquor and the largest single buyer of French wines in the world. In many countries, a tradition of state trading has long existed. State trading expanded greatly during the 1930s when several countries started to engage in direct trading in connection with schemes for supporting domestic industries, especially agriculture. Nazi Germany pioneered some new arrangements in this field, especially in its trade with the Balkan countries. So-called bulk buying was one example of this. It meant that Germany imported all, or the larger part, of a country's export crop, for instance tobacco from Greece. Arrangements of similar kinds were also discussed after the Second World War. The thought was that if the seller had an assured market, he could plan production, utilize economies of scale, and lower costs. The benefits reaped could then be shared with the purchaser by a lowering of prices.

Until the oil crisis of 1972–5 bilateral trade deals between governments were almost exclusively associated with Communist countries trading within COMECON. However, in the wake of the rising price of oil a number of bilateral trading arrangement have been established between oil-exporting and oil-importing countries, e.g. between India and Iran. For the oil importers, it was a means of securing oil supplies as well as also creating the opportunity to offset partially the balance-of-payments burden of increased oil prices by increasing exports to the oil producers. As far as the oil exporters are concerned, the arrangement offers the opportunity of a cheaper supply of imports secured under usually favorable conditions.

State trading has also played an important role for many less developed countries in recent years. These countries have often tried to organize market boards for important agricultural products. This has been done with the double intention of rationalizing the internal market structure and helping to improve agricultural techniques. Another important objective has been to get some control over the country's foreign trade and to improve the terms of trade by taking advantage of monopoly power.

Thus state trading plays and is likely to continue to play an important role in many of the developing countries. Although it has diminished in importance since the Second World War in the developed industrial countries of the West, the resurgence of a more protectionist climate of world trade may lead to the increasing involvement of governments in the arrangement of bilateral trade deals.

EAST–WEST TRADE

Until the mid-1960s the foreign trade of the centrally planned economies of Eastern Europe were state monopolies directed by the Ministry of Foreign Trade and conducted through central agencies known as 'foreign trade corporations'. Accordingly, trade flows were integrated within the general scheme of planning requirements rather than being guided by relative prices which in any case were not determined with respect to market conditions.

The pattern of foreign trade within Eastern Europe was also strongly influenced by the network of trading relationships within COMECON – the Eastern European 'Common Market'. Set up by Stalin in 1949, it sought to establish a flourishing trade in machinery, equipment and industrial raw materials amongst member nations, reflecting the rapid industrialization programme being carried out in each country. In the first five years of COMECON, the proportion of trade carried out between COMECON members increased from 30 to 73 per cent. However, this trade diversion was not accompanied by a similar degree of trade creation. There was considerable duplication in the industrialization effort, with member countries trying to sell similar types of machinery to each other while simultaneously competing for the region's (usually Soviet) raw materials. At first, the more industrialized members, Czechoslovakia and East Germany, found a ready market for their export of machinery, but with the growth of industrial production in the less developed member countries, surplus industrial capacity began to develop. At the same time as it became more difficult to sell machinery within COMECON, exports to Western markets suffered due to a failure to keep up with technological developments in production and marketing.

In response to these problems, several of the more trade-oriented COMECON countries – Hungary, Poland and Romania – introduced a series of trade reforms in the mid-1960s which allowed productive enterprises greater freedom to participate in foreign trade. At the same time, the obstacle to trade provided by highly unrealistic exchange rates was somewhat modified with the adoption of more realistic policy instruments such as shadow exchange rates.

The 1960s was also a decade during which Western European countries tended to reduce their list of embargoed goods in trade with Eastern Europe and to offer improved credit facilities.

Hence, from an admittedly low level, the rate of growth of East–West trade experienced a marked increase during the 1960s. Eastern European imports from developed countries rose at an average rate of 12 per cent, while their exports to developed countries averaged 10 per cent per annum. In fact, East–West trade expanded more rapidly than intra-COMECON trade and world trade in general.

Trade with the West was not only important as a source of foreign exchange, it also became a vital element in the economic strategies of a number of Eastern European countries following the economic reforms introduced in the mid-1960s. Unable to maintain growth rates by further large inputs of capital and labor, the emphasis shifted to raising productivity via a programme of industrial modernization which required expanded trade with the West and access to American and Western European technology.

However, the expansion of East–West trade remains beset by a number of problems. First, due to a shortage of foreign exchange as well as a need to protect planning targets, the currencies of Eastern European countries are almost completely inconvertible. Since domestic currencies are not exchanged for other currencies, their exchange rates seldom reflect, at the official exchange rate, the real purchasing power of these currencies in terms of Western currencies. Perhaps the most serious aspect of this problem is that balance-of-payments pressures and planning constraints have tended to restrict trading opportunities to a series of bilateral trade agreements specifying the total volume of trade and the categories of goods to be exported to, and imported from, the country in question. However, the expansion of credit support for exports to Eastern Europe by banks and Western governments has tended to reduce this obstacle to trade.

A further factor which has tended to restrict East–West trade stems from the fact that Eastern European planning has not been adapted to meet the changes in Western tastes for consumer goods. The range of products is often limited and tends to be concentrated on products for which demand grows relatively slowly, e.g. foodstuffs, shoes, wooden toys.

However, the impediments to trade are not all in one direction. Eastern European criticism is increasingly levelled at the protectionist policies inherent in Western import quotas (e.g. on shoes and textiles), the E.E.C.'s Common Agricultural Policy, as well as the American denial of most-favored-nation status to certain Eastern European countries.

These institutional obstacles have nevertheless not prevented the growth of new forms of East–West trade. Perhaps the most common is the coproduction operation under which each side supplies components for the finished product with the Western firm frequently undertaking the provision of technical assistance and marketing. Another type of East–West business venture is the so-called 'joint venture', where Western firms are responsible for the supply of plant design, technology and some of the sophisticated equipment while the Eastern European firm is responsible for construction and assembly. An example of the latter would be the U.S. development of Soviet natural gas.

The growth of East–West trade has undoubtedly been hampered by the institutional obstacles discussed above. However, cooperative ventures, agreements to share science and technology and joint enterprises are all indications of a growing awareness of economic interdependence between Eastern and Western Europe. To the extent that such agreements are based on the principal of comparative advantage, the benefits gained can be considered to be of mutual value.[2]

SUMMARY

Under competitive market conditions there are important similarities between quotas and tariffs. If imports are curtailed by the same amount, the effects on prices and volumes will be the same. An important difference is that a quota will not give the government any tariff revenue but will instead give rise to an economic rent.

Under monopolistic market conditions, the effects of quotas and tariffs will differ. An important effect of a quota might be to help establish a domestic monopoly.

The advantage of quotas and quantitative restrictions is often claimed to be certainty: using a quota, a country can be certain that its imports will fall. When all secondary effects are taken into account, the certainty proposition is less valid. The balance of payments will improve only if quotas lead to a fall in total absorption.

State trading used to be confined to certain state monopolies, such as tobacco and alcohol. Nowadays it is widely used within the centrally planned economies and to an increasing extent within less developed countries. Within the developed market economies, state trading tends to be limited to periods characterized by economic and political crisis.

SELECTED BIBLIOGRAPHY: CHAPTER 14

For the theory of quotas, see:

R. E. Baldwin, *Non-Tariff Distortions of International Trade,* Washington, D. C., Brookings Institution, 1970.

J. Bhagwati, 'On the Equivalence of Tariffs and Quotas', in R. E. Caves, H. G. Johnson and P. B. Kenen (eds), *Trade, Growth and the Balance of Payments,* Chicago, University of Chicago Press, 1965.

Other interesting contributions are:

G. and V. Curzon, *Hidden Barriers to International Trade,* Thomes Essays No. 1, London, Trade Policy Research Centre, 1970.

J. M. Fleming, 'On Making the Best of Balance of Payments Restrictions on Imports', *EJ,* March 1951 (reprinted in *RIE*).

F. D. Holzman, 'Comparison of Different Forms of Trade Barriers', *RES,* May 1969, pp. 159–65.

W. B. Kelly jr, 'Non-Tariff Barriers', in B. Balassa (ed.) *Studies in Trade Liberalization,* Baltimore, Johns Hopkins Press, 1967, pp. 265–314.

The use of auctions in connection with quotas is discussed in:

J. Bhagwati, 'Indian Balance of Payments Policy and Exchange Auctions', *OEP,* no. 1, 1962.

On state trading, and the development of East–West trade, see:

F. D. Holzman, 'Foreign Trade Behavior of Centrally Planned Economies', in H. Rosovsky (ed.) *Industrialization in Two Systems,* New York, Wiley, 1966, pp. 237–65.

M. Kaser, *COMECON:* Integration Problems of the Planned Economies, London, Oxford University Press, 1967.

15
Tariffs, subsidies, and distortions in commodity and factor markets

We learned in Chapter 13 that from a welfare point of view the only valid argument for tariffs is the optimum tariff. In arriving at this result we assumed that both the factor and commodity markets worked under fully competitive conditions. But this might seem to be quite a drastic assumption. In many countries, especially perhaps in the less developed ones, markets do not work under optimal conditions. Distortions of different kinds exist.

Distortions may exist in commodity markets, and examples of such are external economies. It can be the case, for instance, that farmers do not realize that, through their farming methods, erosion takes place and the soil is destroyed. The private cost of producing agricultural goods may therefore underestimate the true social cost. Another factor which could complicate matters is the existence of economies of scale which for some reason or other are not reaped. Distortions in the factor market could also exist. Producers in industry may have to pay a higher wage than agricultural producers, for instance. If such distortions exist, free trade would no longer be the optimal policy.

We will now discuss these problems. We should, however, note that this part of tariff theory differs not only in its assumptions from the tariff theory which we dealt with in Chapter 13. It differs also in the questions asked. In Chapter 13 we asked what the effects of tariffs were in prices, income distribution, etc. Here we are concerned with less ambitious questions. This type of tariff theory evaluates, on the one hand, the effects of tariffs compared with free trade on the welfare of a country and, on the other hand, compares tariffs and other means (subsidies, taxes) available for best correcting distortions.

At the end of the chapter, we will also analyse a relatively new and interesting concept in tariff theory, the notion of effective rates of protection (E.R.P.).

THE INFANT-INDUSTRY ARGUMENT FOR PROTECTION

The oldest existing argument for protection is the infant-industry argument. It was forwarded in the 1840s by the German economist and politician Friedrich List.[1] The core of the infant-industry argument is the existence of some kind of internal economies. A firm cannot compete if it is small. It has to be large before it can harvest all the economies of scale in production and become competitive. Therefore, it has to be protected for some time, and be permitted to grow, without meeting immediate competition from abroad.

When the firm has become fully developed, the tariff can be dismantled and free trade can be allowed. This is the essence of the argument.

The country List had in mind when he developed the infant-industry argument was Germany of the mid-nineteenth century. Great Britain was then the leading industrial state and German industry had difficulty competing with the older, more established British industry. List was modern in his views in so far as he saw industry as a prerequisite of progress. On this score he had no doubts: 'Manufactories and manufactures are the mothers and children of municipal liberty, of intelligence, of the arts and sciences, of internal and external commerce, of navigation and improvements in transport, of civilization and political power.'[2]

Free trade was good for Britain, whose position was already established. For young, emerging German industry, however, tariffs were necessary. The infant-industry argument soon won acceptance, and even the dean of classical economies in the 1850s, John Stuart Mill, gave it a niche in his exposition of classical economic theory.[3] List was, in other words, the first successful German economist.

Figure 15.1 is a geometric illustration of the infant-industry argument for protection. To start with, the country has the production-possibility curve SS. The international terms of trade are given by the line P_iP_i, which is the tangential to the production-possibility curve at P. The country produces at P and moves by trade to T. This depicts the country's situation under free trade.

The country now wants to protect its industry. It introduces a tariff (assumed to be prohibitive) so that the price for domestic consumers and producers now becomes P_hP_h. This price line is tangential to the production-possibility curve at P', and under protection the country will produce and consume at this point. Protection lowers the country's welfare, as seen from the fact that P' is to the south-west of T.

This is, however, only what happens in the short run. Protection gives rise to a substantial increase in production of industrial goods. Thereby internal economies can be reaped, industrial skills can be learned, etc., and this will lead to an increase in productive capacity, there will be an outward shift in the country's production-possibility curve. After some time of protection, the new production-possibility curve will be $S'S$. The country can then start free trade again. If the same international terms of trade prevail as before protection, the country will produce at P''. ($P'_iP'_i$ is parallel to P_iP_i.) Through trading, the country can then move to T'. As T' is to the north-east of T, it represents higher social welfare. By nurturing an infant industry for some time, the country has thus been able to reach a higher level of welfare than would have been possible if it had been engaged in free trade all the time.

A protectionist policy initially implies a lowering of welfare. In the usual manner a tariff will cause a production and consumption cost. For protection to produce social benefits, the infant industries must grow up. They must eventually be able to compete at world market prices. They must pass what is sometimes called 'Mill's test'[4] Not only, however, do they have to grow up; for a protectionist policy to be profitable, they will also have to be able to pay back the losses due to protection during the infant-industry period. They will have to pass what is sometimes called 'Bastable's test'. Only then is there a clear-cut case

FIGURE 15.1

The infant-industry argument for protection

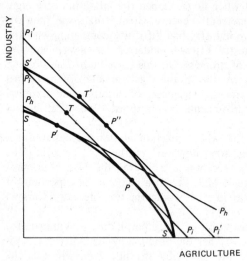

for infant-industry protection.

We now have to look somewhat more closely into the circumstances causing an industry to be of an infant-industry type. We did not say why the production-possibility curve in Figure 15.1 expanded. One reason could be the existence of internal economies. Let us say that the production function in the industry shows increasing returns to scale. This means that, as production expands, the unit cost will fall. Investment will have to take place at some period and production expand until the optimum size is reached. During this time the industry will have to be protected. This, therefore, is the main argument.

In reality this argument is less convincing than it may at first sound. It is not enough to show that present losses have to be incurred if future gains are to be had. This is, in itself, no argument for protection, because if a capital market exists and functions properly, and if domestic producers have a correct view of the profitability of the investment, they will invest in the industry even without a tariff. The existence of internal economies is not, by itself, a sufficient reason for protection. The infant-industry argument has to be built on a more intricate case than this.

It might be the case, for instance, that the capital market does not function properly. This is a common feature in many less developed countries. They have small and poorly developed credit markets, and it can be difficult for a single investor to raise the money needed to make the investment, or it could be that investors are not properly informed about the prospects of investment. They might be unduly pessimistic about the future or unwilling to take chances in an unprotected market. The case for infant-industry protection will then be strengthened.

An important reason why the social return of the investment in an infant industry may exceed the private return is connected with education. This phenomenon is usually of special importance for less developed countries. One of the results of the investment may be the acquisition of knowledge, for instance in the form of experimenting with a suitable technique of production. Once acquired by one firm, this technique can usually be bought at minimal cost by competing firms. Another factor is that part of the cost of the investment may comprise instructing workers, for instance in the form of on-the-job training. Once the workers have gained these skills they can go to another industry and use them there. These could contribute to the reasons an investment, although socially profitable, may not be undertaken by a private firm in an unprotected market. Protection, therefore, can give the added incentive necessary for undertaking the investment.

We have now shown examples of the economics behind the expansion of the production-possibility curve as illustrated in Figure 15.1. We now have to ask the question: Is a tariff the most suitable policy means for achieving this increase in productive capacity? We have to admit that there are cases in which protection for some time will give better results than free trade. Are there, however, other policy means which would be more efficient than tariffs for promoting the desired increase in productive capacity?

The answer is yes. On a somewhat abstract level we say that an optimum solution implies equality between the foreign rate of transformation (FRT), the domestic rate of transformation in production (DRT), and the domestic rate of transformation in consumption (DRS).[5] From this point of view we can say that if a country has 'monopoly power' in trade, i.e. can influence its own terms of trade, the situation under free trade will be that DRS = DRT ≠ FRT. Hence there is scope for the optimum tariff. Only that can give DRS = DRT = FRT.

In the presence of infant industries, the true domestic rate of transformation in production is not equal to the domestic rate of transformation in consumption. Hence we have a situation where DRS = FRT ≠ DRT, though a tariff cannot here bring equality between all three rates of transformation. It would give equality between DRT and FRT but inequality with DRS. In this case only a policy combination of taxes and subsidies can produce equality between all three rates of transformation.

This means that tariffs are not the most suitable means of dealing with the problem created by infant industries. It is always possible to reach a better solution by using subsidies, perhaps in combination with taxes.

In the case first discussed, internal economies were present. If the entrepreneurs were not able to reap them because of risk aversion or an imperfect capital market, the state should deal with these imperfections directly. It could for instance, help the entrepreneurs to acquire correct information or underwrite some of the risks; or it could give loans on favourable conditions. Thereby the private rate of transformation in production can be made to coincide with the true social rate of transformation, and no disturbance on the consumption side will occur. A tariff would always distort consumption by making the home-market price higher than the international price of tariff-ridden goods.

Analogous conditions hold if external economies in education exist. If private entrepreneurs are unwilling to undertake some investment because they cannot get profitable returns on their investment in education, the state should subsidize them. This the state can do in the form of starting trade schools or by compensating the entrepreneurs for the cost of on-the-job training. The appropriate policy in this connection is some sort of subsidy or tax concession, not a tariff. Tariffs are only efficient if, for some reason, the country also wants to decrease its dependence on foreign trade.

The infant-industry argument for protection is essentially dynamic.[6] It is an argument for a tariff (or if properly formulated, a subsidy) during a transient period. For some reasons original free trade will not permit a country's true comparative cost situation to develop. Therefore, trade has to be protected for a period of time to enable the country's real pattern of comparative advantage to be established.

Sometimes the existence of external economies and diseconomies are given as reasons for infant-industry protection. These are, however, better dealt with in connection with distortions in commodity markets. We will now discuss this case.

DOMESTIC DISTORTIONS IN COMMODITY MARKETS

If external economies or diseconomies exist, they could cause the private cost of production to differ from the social cost. If monopolistic or oligopolistic market conditions prevail in parts of the industry, they may have the same effect. External economies is probably the most interesting case. Let us, therefore, deal with that.

Economists often speak about the importance of external economies. Some even go as far as to say that they are the most important basis for state intervention in markets: the theory of socialism should be based on them. Be that as it may, it is often difficult to visualize them and find good examples of external economies. Bees and flowers could do, but somehow they convey no sense of urgency.

Let us think in terms of a two-sector economy, with one agricultural and one industrial sector. An example of an external diseconomy in agriculture could be that farmers do not realize that they impoverish the soil by their farming methods – that, for instance, erosion and soil destruction could be the consequences. This implies that the private cost of producing a certain amount of agricultural products is lower than the social cost, because farmers in their calculations of price do not reckon on the impoverishment of the soil. Then relative prices in the domestic market will not reflect the true marginal cost of transformation in production.

Figure 15.2 is a geometric illustration of this fact. Production of agricultural goods is measured on the vertical axis and the production of industrial goods on the horizontal axis. The 'true' production-possibility curve reflecting the social marginal rate of transformation is given by SS. Because of the distortions in the commodity market caused by the external diseconomies in agriculture, relative prices in the domestic market are given by the price line P_hP_h. At these prices the country will produce at point P. The international terms of trade are given

FIGURE 15.2

Domestic distortion in the market
for agriculture: a tariff increases welfare

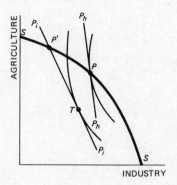

by the price line P_iP_i. This shows that the country has a comparative advantage
in agriculture (at distorted prices), as agricultural products are more expensive
on the international market than in the distorted domestic market. With free
trade the country will produce at P'. It will trade according to international
terms of trade and consume at T. As T is to the south-west of P (and lies on an
indifference curve representing a lower level of welfare), the country will be
worse off because it is trading.

Figure 15.2 exemplifies the possible detrimental effect of trade on a country
when domestic distortions exist in the commodity market and shows how the
country specializes in the wrong commodity. If all the external effects were
taken into account, the country would have exported industrial goods instead
of agricultural products. Free trade accentuates the importance of the external
diseconomies. In this case, a policy of protection would stimulate production
of the industrial goods, in which the country's true comparative advantage lies,
and lead to an improvement in welfare.

The tariff introduces a distortion of the usual kind for consumers, because
the domestic price will differ from the world market price. This will entail a
loss of welfare for consumers. At the same time it will lead to an improvement
in the allocation of resources, because it will curtail the production of agricultural goods and decrease the impoverishment of the soil. In the case illustrated
in Figure 15.2, gains on the production side are larger than losses on the
consumption side, and the tariff leads to an improvement in welfare.

This outcome is, however, not necessarily so. Figure 15.3 illustrates the
opposite possibility. The assumptions and the situation in this case are the same
as in that illustrated in Figure 15.2. To start with, the country produces at point
P. With trade, production will move to P', and trade will take the country to T.
Even in this case the country specializes in the wrong commodity. Trade will
lead to a worsening in resource allocation and a loss on the production side.
But consumers will gain and the gain on the consumption side will outweigh the

FIGURE 15.3

Domestic distortion in the market
for argriculture: a tariff decreases welfare

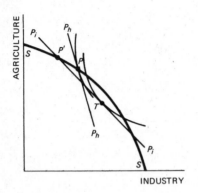

loss on the production side, as seen from the fact that T lies on a higher indifference curve than P.

The result of the discussion so far is thus that protection can improve a country's welfare if distortions exist in a country's commodity market. This is, however, not a definite outcome. It could also lead to a deterioration in a country's welfare. Whether it does or does not depends on the relation between production gains and consumption losses.

A tariff is not the optimal policy instrument if distortions exist. By applying the general principles exposed earlier in this chapter, we find that better results can be reached by a combination of subsidies and taxes. This is illustrated in Figure 15.4. Under free trade and with no interventions in the market, the country will produce at P and consume at T. At point P, however, the international terms of trade are not equal to the country's social cost of transformation in production. Because of distortions, the real cost of producing agricultural goods is underestimated. A tariff might make the country better or worse off, depending on conditions just outlined. The best policy is a combination of taxes and subsidies. A tax on agriculture combined with an industrial subsidy should make the private cost of transformation equal to the social cost of transformation. Such a policy takes the country to point P', where the social cost of transformation equals the international terms of trade ($P_i'P_i'$ is parallel to P_iP_i). Then the country can engage in free trade at undistorted prices, thus taking the country to T', the best point the country can reach with the given technique, preference system and international prices. This point can never be reached by means of tariffs. Hence a policy of subsidies *cum* taxes is superior to tariffs when dealing with distortions in commodity markets.

DISTORTIONS IN FACTOR MARKETS

It is often argued that industry in less developed countries has to pay a higher

FIGURE 15.4

Domestic distortion in the market
for agriculture: the optimal policy

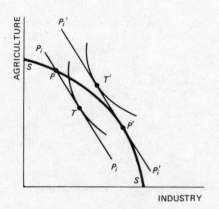

wage than agriculture in order to get labor. This may be a reason why industry
in these countries is placed at a disadvantage and why it should be protected.
We then have a distortion in the factor market. We now have to examine
whether protection is an appropriate policy or not for the case where distortions in the factor markets exist.

One sometimes hears the assertion that in underdeveloped countries the
marginal productivity of labor in agriculture is zero. Yet the peasants and
agricultural workers earn a positive wage. If this is the case, then there will
always be a distortion in factor markets, as long as the marginal productivity
and the wage in industry is positive. Whether the marginal productivity in
agriculture is in reality zero is a question which we shall not discuss here. We
shall simply assume that some distortion in the factor market exists.

One cannot, however, from the simple existence of a wage differential
between industry and agriculture, draw the implication that a distortion
exists. There may be many rational explanations for such a wage differential.
One could be that workers prefer to work in agriculture, where they are
therefore willing to accept a lower wage. Another could be that work in
industry requires specific training and that the higher wage reflects a return to
this investment in human capital. A third reason may be that work in industry
requires a movement for which the worker has to be compensated. All these,
and several other reasons, are examples of wage differentials with rational
economic foundations. Hence no distortions are involved.

One can also find examples that reflect a true distortion. One could be that
labor unions exist in industry but not in agriculture and that they force the
employers in industry to pay a certain minimum wage. Another could be that
employers pay 'decent' wages on humanitarian grounds. If this is the case,
labor will not be optimally allocated between industries, and total production
will be lower than it would otherwise be.

FIGURE 15.5

Distortion in the factor market:
a tariff increases welfare

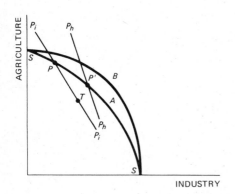

There are also other more intricate factors that could entail distortions. One could be that industry might have to pay a higher wage to get labor because of 'dynamic' reasons. Another may be that industry cannot give employment to the non-adult members of a family the way agriculture can. Hence a higher wage for the head of the household is needed in order to make him move.

Despite the fact that all that may look like distortion is in reality not distortion, one can certainly think of conditions reflecting true distortions. We will now go on and give a geometric illustration of factor-market distortions and see what the effects of protection will be, given that such distortions exist.

Figure 15.5 illustrates the case where distortions exist in the factor market. The production-possibility curve in the prevailing distorted market is given by *SAS*. If the distortions did not exist, the production-possibility curve would be given by *SBS*. Factor-market distortions lead, in geometric terms, to a position where the production-possibility curve is pulled in toward the origin. The reason for this is that factors will not be optimally allocated if distortions exist. The relation between marginal productivities in the two industries will not be the same. The marginal productivity of labor in industry, for instance, will be higher than the marginal productivity of labor in agriculture. This means, in geometric terms, that the country will not be on the contract curve in the box diagram. (The country will produce on the contract curve only if it is completely specialized, i.e. only if it is producing at one of the two ends of the box diagram). In general, the country will produce somewhere off the contract curve. The production-possibility curve which could be derived if the country were producing along the contract curve in the box is *SBS*. The production-possibility curve that can be derived from the combination of points where the country will produce under distortions is *SAS*.

Let us assume that we start off with free trade. The country is then producing at *P* and consuming at *T*. Protection in the form of a tariff on industrial

FIGURE 15.6

Distortion in the factor market: the optimal policy

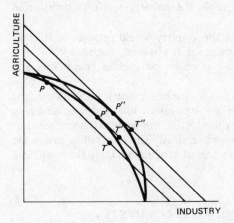

goods would take the country to P'. This point is obviously preferable to T, and hence protection is advantageous for the country.

This is, however, not a necessary result. The situation here is completely analogous to the one with distortions in commodity markets. Protection might give a better result than free trade, but it might also lead to a lowering of welfare. It all depends on the specific case and the relationship between production gains and consumption losses implied by a tariff if distortions exist in commodity or factor markets.

If distortions exist in the factor market, a tariff can, however, never be an optimal solution. This is illustrated in Figure 15.6. The international terms of trade are given by the three parallel price lines. Under free trade the country will produce at P and consume at T. Because of the distortion in the factor market, the social marginal rate of transformation will not coincide with the terms of trade. The real cost of producing agriculture at P will be higher than that shown by the market price. A tariff may in this case lead to an improvement, or it may not. (The student can easily convince himself that a combination of tariff-ridden price lines and indifference curves can lead to a deterioration in welfare). A tariff can, however, never bring the true domestic marginal rate of transformation in production to coincide with the international terms of trade.

A subsidy could do that, in a specific sense. It could bring the marginal rate of transformation along the distorted curve to coincide with the international prices. A subsidy to industry could take the country to P'. Through trade it could then move to T', which is obviously superior to T. Hence a policy of subsidies on production is better than free trade, if factor market distortions exist.

A subsidy on production is, however, not the best policy. It is still the case that the relation between marginal productivities in the two lines of production differs. What is needed is a tax or subsidy on the use of the factor of production. A subsidy to labor in industry could lead to greater employment within industry and to the equalization in both sectors of the marginal productivity of labor. A tax on the use of labor in agriculture would have the same effect. Only by such a policy could the country reach its undistorted production-possibility curve.

This would mean, in our case, that the country would produce at P'', and through trade could move to T''. This point is obviously superior to T' and represents the best the country can do, given its production possibilities and the international terms of trade.

Summing up, if distortions in the factor markets existed, protection might give a better result than free trade or a worse result, but it will never be an optimal policy. Subsidies and taxes on production are more efficient means of economic policy, but neither will they be optimal. The best policy means are taxes and subsidies on the use of the factors of production. Only these will lead to optimal results.

TRADE POLICY FOR DEVELOPMENT: FIRST COMMENTS

We now have met two serious arguments for tariffs. The first was the optimum tariff argument which we met in Chapter 13. The second, or rather second group of arguments, is that dealt with in this chapter. In a nationalistic world a protectionist policy will always hold appeal. It is quite natural that protectionism has been tried by less developed countries as a means of speeding up their economic development. The difficulties involved in fostering economic growth are now well known. Many countries are in desperate situations, and their possibilities of meeting population pressure with increased production are limited. There are cases where the *per capita* income is stagnant or even falling.

Against this background it is easy to understand why protectionism is a tempting alternative. It is usually heavily backed by certain domestic interests: a policy of increasing tariffs is also often easy to implement. Protectionism seems to give a lot of mileage for a little effort.

A protectionist policy also contains very real dangers. It is doubtful, as we have already hinted, whether the optimum tariff argument has much relevance for most underdeveloped countries. A tariff can only increase a country's welfare if the adaptability of supply and demand for the country's exports in the rest of the world is low. This is probably not the case for most of the less developed countries. This implies that the value these countries can derive from a tariff must, on this score, be limited. Consequently, the relevance of the optimum tariff argument for less developed countries is probably small.

The infant-industry argument can very well be applicable in some instances to underdeveloped countries. Distortions in commodity and factor markets also presumably exist. These could be reasons for using a protectionist policy. In both these cases, however, tariffs are not the optimal means of economic policy. Yet tariffs are often easy to implement, as they are usually easier to use than taxes and subsidies. This argument, incidentally, should not be carried too far. Even most underdeveloped countries have a set of taxes which can be adapted to deal with the distortions.

Protectionism ·could, however, be a defensible policy under these circumstances, at least as a second-best solution. If tariffs are used to correct distortions and foster development, they should be used with great discrimination and against the background of a carefully worked out policy. Many less developed countries have used tariffs to implement a policy of import-substitution.

The problems connected with different trade strategies such as export-push and import-substitution will be treated in the next chapter.

EFFECTIVE RATES OF PROTECTION

Empirical estimates have shown that a large share and perhaps most of international trade consists of trade in intermediate goods which are used as inputs in the production of other goods. Most of trade theory, however, has been concerned only with trade in final goods. Economists have viewed the neglect of intermediate goods in trade theory differently. Jagdish Bhagwati suggests, for instance, that it constitutes one of the central limitations of trade theory, while Murray Kemp has argued that the neglect of intermediate products in the earlier literature can be defended on the grounds that most results derived in the absence of these products are also valid in their presence.

The idea of the effective rate of protection is that when inputs are taken into account the nominal tariff of a good may differ from the rate of protection given to the value added in the production of the good. According to the proponents of the theory, it is the protection to the value added that is of importance, not the nominal tariff on the final good.

Assume that the final tariff on a good is 10 per cent, and that inputs (raw material, intermediate goods, etc.) used in the production of the good amount to 50 per cent of the value of production and that these inputs are imported without duty. The effective rate of protection accorded to value added is then 20 per cent, not 10 per cent as the manifest duty implies.[7]

The value added is created by the factors of production. (We disregard profits, for simplicity's sake.) The purpose of a tariff is to protect the factors of production, and hence the effective rate of protection is a more meaningful concept than the manifest tariff. This is the argument of the proponents of the effective rate of protection.

It might be assumed that capital is available for industries in different countries on more or less the same conditions. What a tariff then really aims at protecting is labor. Let us assume, in the above example, that half of the value added was created by capital and half by labor, and that we deduct capital and take labor to be the only original factor of production to be protected. The effective rate of protection for labor in the above example is then 40 per cent. Hence a manifest tariff of 10 per cent in reality gives an effective rate of protection to labor of 40 per cent. Using this argument it is easy to see that the implicit tariffs, especially if calculated in the form of the effective rate of protection given to labor, can differ very significantly from nominal or manifest tariff rates. Empirical calculations have also shown large discrepancies of this kind.[8] It should be observed that, everything else being equal, the smaller the value added in an industry, the larger will be its effective tariff (provided it is positive). Empirical estimates have shown that effective rates of protection can differ greatly from nominal tariff rates. Often value added can be protected by several hundred and in certain cases several thousand per cent when final tariffs can be quite modest. Balassa found, for instance, that the nominal tariff on processed food in Chile was 82 per cent in 1961. However, the effective rate of protection was 2884 per cent![9]

Empirical findings of this kind are quite common. The notion of the effective rate of protection is certainly interesting – but it is also a very elusive concept. It is one thing to measure a concept, it is something entirely different to give this measurement a well-defined meaning and fit it into a coherent theory.

The theory of the effective rate of protection differs from standard tariff theory to the extent that it uses a partial-equilibrium approach. It is assumed that the general-equilibrium repercussions of tariffs do not exist or are negligible. However, a tariff obviously changes relative prices. It is then questionable whether one can assume that these tariff-induced price changes will not lead to any repercussions for volumes, factor intensities, etc. Second, it is assumed that factors of production are used in fixed proportions. This is also an assumption of doubtful validity.

In order to gain some insights into the economic significance of effective tariff theory, we will go on with some geometric analysis. We will demonstrate some aspects of effective tariff theory by using a simple model where inter-mediate goods enter in explicitly.[10] Thereby a somewhat more precise understanding of the role of intermediate products should be gained. The meaning of 'cascading' of tariffs will be illustrated and we should get an improved understanding of the importance of input-output relationships for the tariff structure.

We assume that the economy is endowed with fixed supplies of two primary factors, labor (L) and capital (C). There are two final goods, X and Y, and two intermediate goods, A and B. The intermediate goods are produced by labor and capital. Each has a production function that is homogeneous of the first degree. The intermediate goods are then used to produce final goods. In order to produce one unit of each of the final goods there is a fixed amount of A and B that is required. (the amount is fixed for each final good but different for X and Y). Labor and capital are, of course, also needed to produce final goods. Again, we assume that the production functions are of the neoclassical kind and show constant returns to scale.

Hence labor and capital can be substituted for each other in the production of final goods but the input coefficients for intermediate goods into the final goods are fixed. A further assumption about the technology is that the strong factor-intensity assumption holds, which means that there is a one-to-one correspondence between factor prices and factor intensities for all four goods irrespective of relative factor prices.

We can now distinguish between *net* and *gross* production functions for X and Y. The net production functions show the combinations of labor and capital that are needed to produce one unit of each of the two goods given the required inputs A and B (when the labor and capital that has gone into A and

FIGURE 15.7

Tariffs on intermediate goods

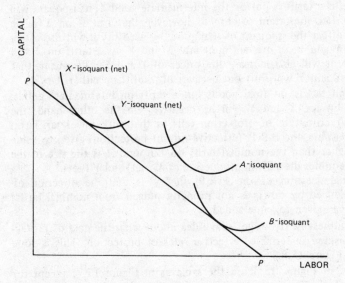

B have been deducted, so to speak). The gross production functions show both the necessary amounts of the primary factors, labor and capital, as well as the required inputs, *A* and *B*, used in making one unit of each final good. Suppose that there is free trade at fixed world prices for all the four goods. Then we can determine the amounts of *A* and *B* that are equal in value to the *value added* in the goods *X* and *Y*. Let us choose *B* as the common denominator and say that the amounts are equal to one unit of *B*. If we want to express the value added in terms of world prices of *X*, for example, it is determined by converting the value of one unit of *X* in terms of *B* at world market prices. Then we deduct the value of the fixed inputs of *A* and *B* that are needed to make one unit of *X*, evaluated in terms of *B*.

Figure 15.7 illustrates a configuration of four isoquants for the four goods. World prices and factor endowments will determine relative factor prices. In Figure 15.7 they are shown by the line *PP*. Under free trade all four commodities will be produced only in the exceptional circumstance that all the isoquants would all be tangential to the factor price line *PP*. According to Figure 15.7 only two goods, the final good *X* and the intermediate good *B*, will be produced under free trade. Some of *A* must be imported, as it is an input into *X*. Some of *Y* will also have to be imported if it is to be consumed at all. Either *X* or *B* or both will be exported. This will depend on the relation between supply and demand in the domestic market.

We can now study the effects of tariffs explicitly on both final and intermediate goods. A tariff on a final good, such as *Y*, means that its domestic price will increase. Fewer units of *Y* will be worth one unit of *B* (our common denominator or standard of account). In a way, this can be expressed as an increase in the marginal productivities of labor and capital used in the production of Y. It means that the Y-isoquant will shift inward, in the direction of the PP-line. Likewise, if a tariff is put on the intermediate good A, its isoquant will also shift inward. It is important to observe, however, that a tariff on A (or on B) will not only affect the isoquant of that good; by necessity it will also affect the isoquants of X and Y, as A is an input into X and Y. As a tariff on A will increase its price, it will also increase the prices of X and Y. This means that the isoquants of X and Y will shift out because of a tariff on either A or B.

If there are no tariffs on final goods but a tariff on intermediate goods, effective protection for X and Y will be negative. On the other hand, the theory of the effective rate of protection tells us that with lower tariffs on inputs than on outputs, the E.R.P. (effective rate of protection) given to value added will be higher than the nominal tariff on outputs. It is the size of the E.R.P. which determines the shift in production of X (net) and Y (net).

One interesting assertion of the E.R.P. theory is that the direction of resource flows induced by tariffs is not properly judged from nominal tariffs but from the E.R.P. given to value added.

It is also of interest to try to get some idea about what the cost of protection is when measured in terms of effective rates of protection. This is done with the help of Figure 15.8.

The isoquants in Figure 15.8 are the same as in Figure 15.7, except for isoquants Y' and A'. These two new isoquants show how much the original isoquants have to be shifted in order to induce domestic production of the two goods. These shifts have been induced by the use of tariffs. How much domestic prices have to be raised to make domestic production possible will depend on the excess domestic cost of production. This is measured by the distance the original Y- and A-isoquants have to be moved to become tangential to the factor-price (or cost) line PP. This shift is the distance PP' for the Y-good and PP'' for the A-good.

We can observe that the production cost of protection is larger for A than for Y. We have to remember that the nominal tariffs were set so that the E.R.P. which was afforded the activities was just sufficient to make them competitive in the domestic market. The ranking of processes by their levels of effective protection is equivalent to ranking them according to their current competitiveness in world markets.

In our case X and B were competitive in the world market even without protection. Hence the country has a comparative advantage in the production of these two goods. The next most competitive activity is the production of Y. It has been given support, which in real terms amounts to PP' capital (measured along the vertical axis) or PP' labor (measured on the horizontal axis) per unit of output in order to make it competitive in the domestic market. The least competitive line of production is A, which has to be given a support of PP'' to make it competitive in the domestic market.

It should be observed that when protection is given to good A it also has to be given to good X. Originally good X was competitive on the world market in the free-trade situation, but if a tariff is levied on one of its inputs compensation must be made for the consequent price increase on an input factor by

FIGURE 15.8

The effective rate of protection

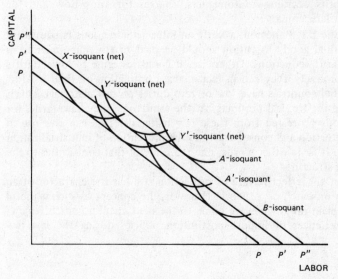

granting a tariff on the value-added process for good X. This also demonstrates the important fact that it is often difficult to trace the repercussions of tariff changes because of the complex input – output relationship which characterize modern industry.

Under the assumption that relative factor prices do not change, and given the other assumptions that this type of analysis rests on, it is, thus, possible to give a measure of the effective rate of protection that is to a certain extent meaningful: that is, one which tells us that the most protected industry is the least effective one. If, however, relative factor prices change because of tariff changes (which is quite probable), then things get more complicated and no simple classifications are possible.

The basic idea behind E.R.P. is sound and interesting. But it is also very easy to put too much emphasis on the concept, and the empirical estimates that have been made of different E.R.P.s certainly have to be viewed cautiously. In order to interpret them correctly they have to be judged against the background of the specific conditions of any given country.

In practice most countries have a 'cascading' tariff structure in the sense that there are high tariffs on final goods, and successively lower tariffs, the lower the degree of processing. At the same time, we have to remember that the smaller the value added, the higher is the E.R.P. This leads to the somewhat ironic result that the E.R.P. tends to vary inversely with the proportion of value added in gross output. Because of this, assembly operations and 'finishing touches' to consumer goods and consumer capital goods like cars, refrigerators, etc., can be extremely profitable. For many less developed countries such industries can even end up depleting foreign exchange reserves. These industries are often controlled by foreign firms, and apart from an inducement to consumers to demand luxury goods they can lay claim to valuable foreign exchange for profits accruing to foreigners, charges for know-how and for earnings of expatriate employees.

According to the E.R.P. notion, a tariff on intermediate goods is equivalent to a tax on the final good. Attention should be paid to this phenomenon in negotiations on tariff reductions. Otherwise, if countries agree to lower tariffs on intermediate products, they can in fact increase protection on final production. Most industrial countries have low or zero duties on raw materials. This is especially the case for tropical products. At the same time, they have tariffs for manufactured goods processed from these raw materials. This can give rise to high effective protection and consequently to the prevention of industrialization in poor countries. It is, in other words, one more factor that contributes to the cascading of tariff structures.

The concept of the effective rate of protection still has the character of an interesting notion in search of a theory. However, the concept as such is useful and should be kept in mind when we come to the next chapter, which reviews some of the experiences of import-substitution policies during the last few decades.

APPENDIX: THE FORMULA FOR THE EFFECTIVE RATE OF PROTECTION

The idea behind the notion of the E.R.P. is to take intermediate goods into account. If this is done, the nominal tariff rate on a good can differ from its implicit or effective tariff rate. Let us think in terms of an input – output system. Then the E.R.P. can be derived in the following way:

$$v_j = 1 - \Sigma \ a_{ij} \tag{15A.1}$$

Where v_j is the value added (or income earned by the factors of production) in the jth industry and a_{ij} is the value of the input from the ith industry into the jth industry, all at world market prices.

If there is a system of tariffs, domestic prices and values will differ from the international ones. The value added in the domestic industry is then

$$v_j' = 1 + t_j - \Sigma \ a_{ij} \ (1 + t_i) \tag{15A.2}$$

Where v_j' is the domestic value added in the jth industry, t_j is the nominal tariff in that industry, and t_i is the nominal tariff in the ith industry.

Let us now define the effective rate of protection as:

$$v_j' = (1 + \tau_j) \ v_j \tag{15A.3}$$

Then we obtain

$$\tau_j = \frac{t_j - \Sigma \ a_{ij} \ t_i}{v_j} = \frac{t_j - \bar{t}_j \Sigma \ a_{ij}}{v_j} = t_j + \frac{(t_j - \bar{t}_j) \Sigma \ a_{ij}}{v_j} \tag{15A.4}$$

Where $\bar{t}_j = \Sigma \ a_{ij} \ t_i \ / \ \Sigma \ a_{ij}$ is the weighted average tariff rate on inputs of commodities into the jth industry.

We can observe from equation (15A.4) that if $t_j = \bar{t}_j$, then the nominal tariff rate and the effective tariff rate are the same. If $t_j > \bar{t}_j$, then the effective rate of protection is higher than the nominal tariff rate. If $t_j < \bar{t}_j$, then the implicit tariff is smaller than the nominal or manifest tariff rate. If $t_j < \Sigma \ a_{ij} \ t_i$, then the effective rate of protection is negative. This is usually the case with exports, but it can also happen with imported goods that have a positive nominal tariff.

SELECTED BIBLIOGRAPHY: CHAPTER 15

Two works which attempt to prove that protection is to be preferred to free trade are:

M. Manoilesco, *The Theory of Protection and International Trade*, London, King, 1931.

E. Hagen, 'An Economic Justification of Protection', *QJE*, November 1958.

A classic essay discussing tariffs versus free trade under different market imperfections is:

G. Haberler, 'Some Problems in the Pure Theory of International Trade', *EJ*, June 1950 (reprinted in *RIE*).

Two excellent papers on tariffs and subsidies as means of correcting market imperfections, and on which the exposition in Chapter 15 draws quite heavily, are:

J. Bhagwati and V. K. Ramaswami, 'Domestic Distortions, Tariffs and the Theory of the Optimum Subsidy', *JPE*, February 1963 (reprinted in *RIE*).

J. Bhagwati, 'The Generalized Theory of Distortions and Welfare', in J. Bhagwati *et al.*, *Trade, Balance of Payments and Growth*, Amsterdam, North-Holland, 1971.

Among other works in this field are:

P. K. Bardhan, 'External Economies, Economic Development, and the Theory of Protection', *OEP*, March 1964.

H. G. Johnson, 'Optimal Trade Intervention in the Presence of Domestic Distortions', in R. E. Caves, H. G. Johnson and P. B. Kenen (eds), *Trade, Growth and the Balance of Payments*, Chicago, University of Chicago Press, 1965.

J. E. Meade, *Trade and Welfare*, London, Oxford University Press, 1955.

H. Myint, 'Infant Industry Arguments for Assistance to Industries in the Setting of Dynamic Trade Theory', in R. F. Harrod and T. D. C. Hague (eds), *International Trade Theory in a Developing World*, London, Macmillan, 1963.

W. P. Travis, *The Theory of Trade and Protection*, Cambridge, Mass., Harvard University Press, 1964.

A standard work on effective rates of protection is:

W. M. Corden, *The Theory of Protection,* London, Oxford University Press, 1971.

A valuable paper on which the presentation in the chapter draws is:

R. Findlay, 'Comparative Advantage, Effective Protection and Domestic Resource Cost of Foreign Exchange', *Journal of International Economics,* No. 1, 1971.

Other works in this area are:

H. G. Grubel, 'A Non-specialist Guide to the Theory of Effective Protection', in H. G. Grubel and H. G. Johnson (eds), *Effective Tariff Protection,* Geneva, United Nations, 1971.

W. M. Corden, 'The Structure of a Tariff System and the Effective Rate of Protection', *JPE,* June 1966.

H. G. Johnson, The Theory of Tariff Structure with Special Reference to World Trade and Development', in H. G. Johnson and P. B. Kenen (eds), *Trade and Development,* Geneva, United Nations, 1965.

H. G. Johnson, 'A Model of Protection and the Exchange Rate', *RES,* 1966.

For empirical estimates of effective rates of protection, see:

B. Balassa, 'Tariff Protection in Industrial Countries: An Evaluation', *JPE,* December 1965 (reprinted in *RIE*).

G. Basevi, 'The U.S. Tariff Structure: Estimate of Effective Rates of Protection of U.S. Industries and Industrial Labor', *RE&S,* December 1966.

B. Balassa *et al., The Structure of Protection in Developing Countries,* Baltimore, Johns Hopkins University Press, 1971.

16
Import-substitution versus export-push

Part II gave us some insights into the effects of economic growth on international trade. The preceding chapters have treated some aspects of the theory of trade policy. It is now opportune to analyze some strategies for trade and development and survey some experiences that the last few decades have provided. Growth with trade can provide a wide variety of consequences for a country's real income. It is not difficult to find types of growth which might lead to deterioration in the terms of trade and to export losses. Influential economists and international organizations – like Raúl Prebisch as head of the Economic Commission for Latin America – stressed these possibilities. Many countries, especially those among the less developed, felt that trade was disadvantageous to them. They did not view trade as a possible engine of growth.

Many countries became 'trade-pessimistic'. They often viewed industrialization as the road to development and held a rather dim view of agricultural development, especially as a base for export growth. Arguments for an inward-looking type of industrialization, for a policy of import-substitution, became prevalent. We will now review some of the results of this approach and some of its implications.

THE BACKGROUND FOR IMPORT-SUBSTITUTION

The drive for import-substitution in many less developed countries has to be explained by reference to economic experiences during the interwar period and the Second World War. The great depression at the beginning of the 1930s hit the bulk of less developed countries very hard. These countries were dependent on exports of primary products for their earnings of foreign exchange. The dollar price of primary products fell by 50 per cent from 1929 to 1932; the value of exports fell even more, by some 60 per cent. It is true that prices of industrial products also fell; however, the less developed countries were subjected to a heavy deterioration in their terms of trade.

Furthermore, these countries usually had large foreign debts. These had to be serviced in fixed amounts in foreign currency; hence the real burden of debt service increased as prices fell. The inflow of capital to which these countries had become accustomed was also cut off, often in quite an abrupt fashion.

There were even more deep-seated reasons for the view, on the part of the less developed countries, that they were at the mercy of the major developed, industrial countries. Not only did their incomes and export earnings fall, relative to those of the developed countries, the causes of the slump emanated basically from the developed countries themselves. In (Keynesian) hindsight it seems that the developed countries would have been able to deal better with the economic crisis by applying economic policies to dampen the deflation. These options did not exist for the less developed countries. On the contrary, by existing institutional arrangements they were prevented from pursuing independent economic policies; this is underlined by the fact that practically none of the less developed countries had an independent central bank and hence no possibilities existed for applying an independent monetary policy.

It is not astonishing that the traumatic experiences of the 1930s left deep scars in the memories of the less developed countries and made them opt for policies which would free them from the type of economic dependence to which they earlier had been subjected.

Experiences during the Second World War also drove home this point, even though by this time their problems were very different from what they had been during the 1930s. During the war the demand for exports from the less developed countries increased drastically. Now it was imports that were lacking. The less developed countries had no difficulty selling their export products at good prices, but they could not import industrial goods, especially capital equipment. This hampered the expansion of industrial capacity in these countries. At the same time, the export boom led to a build-up of foreign reserves, and demand was directed toward domestically produced goods. This brought with it better use of domestic manufacturing capacity; industrial output increased substantially in many less developed countries during the war years, ranging from a 20 per cent increase in India to an almost 50 per cent increase in Mexico.

Hence it is understandable that a large group of less developed countries opted for a policy of self-reliance based on import-substitution. By so doing, they showed their distrust for the arguments of gains from trade on which we have placed such stress in this book so far.

ECONOMIC RESULTS OF IMPORT-SUBSTITUTION

One of the great advantages of import-substitution is that domestic producers can take over markets which are already established in the country. Thus, by shutting off imports, domestic producers can get a flying start in certain, already established lines of production.

Import-substitution is usually most successful in the final stages of production, in producing consumers' goods. Here technology is often rather simple and the demand for the product is easily identifiable. In some countries, like Brazil, Mexico and India, which started early on the road to import-substitution, the share of consumers' goods which were imported was already low at the beginning of the 1950s.[1] By the end of the 1960s these countries imported practically no consumers' goods whatsoever. In other countries, like Pakistan and the Philippines, where import-substitution came later, imports of consumers' goods fell drastically during the 1950s and 1960s.

To the extent that it reduced imports of consumers' goods, import-substitution obviously achieved one of its goals. It also, however, created a need

TABLE 16.1

Imports·in per cent of G.D.P. at current prices

Country	1950–2	1957–9	1964–6
Argentina	9	11	7
Brazil	12	10	8
Mexico	12	11	8
India	8	7	7
Pakistan	8	7	10
Philippines	14	13	19
Taiwan	13	14	19

SOURCE: Little, Scitovsky and Scott, *Industry and Trade in Some Developing Countries*, p. 63.

for increased imports in other areas. Final production in any economy using modern technology depends upon raw materials and inputs from other sectors of the economy or on imported items through a system of complex input-output relationships. As domestic production of consumer goods increased, the dependence on imported inputs like machinery, spare parts and semi-fabricated goods increased. In a strategic sense a country's reliance on the world economy can increase, at least for some period, through a policy of import-substitution. A lack of foreign exchange which earlier could have caused a temporary fall in imports of consumer goods could now lead to disturbances in the functioning of the economy with work stoppages, temporary lay-offs of workers due to lack of imported inputs, etc. Import-substitution, therefore, offers no easy road to self-reliance.

Import-substitution seems, however, to have been successful in several countries to the extent that it has decreased the ratio of imports to the gross domestic product (G.D.P.). Table 16.1 gives an illustration of this.

In countries like Argentina, Brazil and Mexico the ratio of imports to total production fell. In other countries, like the Philippines and Taiwan, which also practised a policy of import-substitution, the ratio went up. In interpreting figures like those given in Table 16.1 one has to be careful. Some countries might have a higher 'natural' marginal propensity to import than others. It is likely that small countries like Taiwan and the Philippines have a higher propensity to import as they grow than larger countries like Brazil, Mexico and India. The figures in Table 16.1 should also be judged against what would have been the case had some kind of policy other than import-substitution been attempted. Obviously, such comparisons are difficult to make. Estimates demonstrate, however, that for Mexico – to take an example – imports would have been 22 per cent higher in 1960 than they were had the same proportions of consumers' goods, intermediate goods and capital goods been imported in 1960 as in 1950.

When it comes to economic growth, countries like those mentioned in the table varied in their performance. Looking at the growth rate of G.D.P. at constant prices, Taiwan had the highest rate, growing at over 8 per cent annually from the beginning of the 1950s to the end of the 1960s. Mexico, Brazil and the Philippines showed growth rates of 5–6 per cent, while India, Pakistan and Argentina grew at 3–4 per cent. As population grew rapidly during this period, figures for *per capita* growth rates are substantially lower, being 2–3 per cent for countries like Brazil and Mexico and 1–2 per cent for countries like Argentina, India and Pakistan.

Industrial production grew faster than G.D.P. in most countries but not so much faster as to make industry the dominant sector. Only in countries such as Argentina, Brazil and Mexico was the share of manufacturing industry as high as 25–30 per cent of G.D.P. toward the end of the 1960s; in countries like India and Pakistan it was 10–15 per cent. After two decades of promoting industry through import-substitution, agriculture and services were still by far the most important sectors of the economy.

How successful the import-substitution policies were is a matter of dispute. It is certainly possible to argue that such policies raise as many problems as they solve for the dependent, less developed countries. At the same time, it might be argued that the results presented above are not necessarily so bad and that in the longer run important substitution policies might achieve their aim. In any case, to get a deeper understanding of the process of import-substitution, we should look at other aspects of it.

THE ANATOMY OF EXCHANGE CONTROLS

Exchange controls are at the heart of import-substitution. There exist many types of restrictive measures. They differ between countries. They usually also vary over time. It is, however, important to get some grasp over the means used. It is also convenient to characterize a country's control over foreign trade according to the policy instruments used. Usually a country's protectionist policies can be characterized by various phases with respect to the degree of liberalization of its protectionist policies.[2] There is a logic in the use of restrictive measures that is instructive to study.

Tariffs and surcharges are common protectionist devices. (See Chapters 13–15 for a theoretical treatment of tariffs and quantative restrictions.) Other instruments are import licenses. There can be a large variety of licenses: for users or for wholesalers they can be obtained by direct permission from some ministry or the central bank, or they can be sold at official auctions; they can be combined with specific import programmes and they might be combined with lists of prohibited import products. Other means are guarantee deposits which have to be made by the importer for the right to import an item. Foreign firms can be restricted in their right to repatriate dividends and profits. Domestic exporters, on the other hand, may be allowed to resell part of their foreign earnings at advantageous exchange rates. Multiple exchange rates may exist, with, for instance, special tourist rates.

Thus the policy instruments are numerous. In order to see how exchange controls work and to understand some of their logic and consistency it is useful to characterize them according to phases *à la* Bhagwati and Kreuger.

Phase I is characterized by an imposition of heavy and undifferentiated quantitative controls. Often it entails a sharp itensification of some controls which might have been operative previously. They can be regarded as a response to hardships brought about by, for example, crop failures, adverse terms of trade, or international depressions. Chile was greatly hit by the depression of the 1930s. Hence it started to apply exchange controls of the Phase I type. Brazil is another case in point. After a fairly liberal exchange regime at the end of the 1940s, it started to apply stricter quantitative measures at the beginning of the 1950s. This development was intensified through the abrupt decline in coffee prices which occurred in 1953. Phase II is characterized by a continuation of quantitative restrictions. The restrictiveness of the control system tends to become more pronounced. The system also becomes more complex as two new features are added. The first is that the operation of the system becomes more discretionary as *ad hoc* measures increase. The second is that price measures start to be used. Both these phenomena can be regarded as stemming from the fact that the authorities want to streamline the control system and make it more flexible as time goes by.

During Phase I the control system is operated in a rather heavy and undiscriminating fashion. As the authorities perceive special interests and want to increase the effectiveness of the system, rules, regulations and special cases tend to proliferate. Often cabinet·ministers and other decision-makers feel that they lose control over the system.

The reasons for manipulating prices are also easy to comprehend. The continuation of quantitative restrictions creates shortages of foreign exchange. To relieve that shortage it is often deemed desirable to induce exporters to export more by the use of export rebates, 'import replenishment' schemes, special credits, and the like. Price incentives are also used on the import side. Tariff increases, surcharges and guarantee deposits are often applied. These measures are aimed both at checking imports and at taxing away the various rents and windfall gains which go together with rationing systems and quantitative restrictions.

The prevalence of various types of controls during Phase II implies that the exchange rate is overvalued. Were it not for the restrictions, the demand for foreign exchange would be much larger than the supply. Phase III therefore starts with a change of the exchange rate, i.e. a devaluation. Connected with the devaluation is a loosening up of exchange controls.

Phases I and II can be of long duration. Usually Phase III is of shorter duration. It can either be a tidying-up operation to take care of previous distortions on the way to a more liberal trade regime; or it can be a period of abortive attempts at liberalization which after some time will be deemed futile and the country in question will then slide back to Phase II again. There are, however, also instances when Phase III has lasted for several years as the economy has taken considerable time to adjust its relative price structure to the new more liberal trade regime. In general Phase III has the character of a disequilibrium period of adjustment.

Phase IV starts when foreign exchange earnings grow at a reasonably rapid rate so that the liberal measures of Phase III can be sustained. If the supply of foreign exchange matches the demand, there is no need to restrict trade further. It is true that quantitative restrictions may still apply but they are of a reasonably non-distortionary kind. Thus premia that might exist on import licenses do not increase. Phase IV continues as long as the controls of trade are unchanged or diminishing.

Phase V is characterized by full liberalization of the exchange regime. The currency is fully convertible. Hence Phase V is not an exchange-control regime but an alternative to the first four phases dealt with above.

Naturally, the characterization of exchange regimes into phases contains moments of arbitrariness. Nevertheless, it may still be useful. Countries in Phases I and II are in a position very different from those in Phases IV and V. Phase III is also interesting as an interregnum between regimes of strict controls and those characterized by liberal trade policies.

It is interesting to study how countries move from the first two phases to the last two. Classical cases of such transitions are offered by Brazil and South Korea.

From the early 1950s up to 1963 Brazil was in Phase II, interspersed with brief lapses into Phase III. Brazil undertook a devaluation and a stabilization programme in 1964. Several years of adjustment of a Phase III type followed, but in 1968 quantitative restrictions of the Phase IV kind were established and from then on to the mid-1970s Brazil has had an exchange regime which has become increasingly liberal.

From the end of the Korean war in 1953 up to 1961 South Korea was in Phase II. Two attempts at liberalizing her trade policies were made in the early 1960s. The first proved abortive, but the second, in 1964–5, was more successful. From 1966 South Korea's exchange regime has been fairly liberal (of Phase IV type) even though some quantitative restrictions have been used. South Korea's growth of exports have been extremely rapid in the last decade and the growth of G.D.P. has also been fast (9.1 per cent in real terms during the 1960s).

Examples of countries which have more or less constantly been in Phase I and II are Chile and India. Chile was hit hard by the 1930s depression and applied restrictive trade policies from then up to the mid-1950s. Several attempts at devaluation have been made and 'stabilization programmes' have been launched in connection with them. They have all been of short duration. Although many alterations of the exchange-rate regime have been made, the escudo has remained overvalued most of the time. Chile has been characterized by high inflation and heavy use of quantitative restrictions. Chile's export performance has not been impressive. It has been tied closely to the vagaries of the world market for copper, as copper is the country's dominant export product. During the latter half of the 1960s its export earnings grew rapidly as copper prices rose. Chile did not, however, alter the bias of its exchange regime and the country could not use its export earnings effectively for development purposes.

India entered its first five-year plan in 1951 with large currency reserves that had been accumulated during the Second World War. An investment boom in the mid-1950s led to large increases in imports and a deterioration in her balance of payments. Restrictive measures of the Phase I type were applied. By the end of the decade the country entered Phase II. Since then India has worked out a very intricate system of quantitative restrictions and has almost continuously remained in Phase II.

INCOME DISTRIBUTION AND SAVINGS

The most important aim of import-substitution is to promote domestic industry at the expense of foreign industry. Seldom, however, are foreign interests seriously hurt by import-substitution. A country pursuing this policy might also hope to get imports more cheaply, i.e. by an improvement in the terms of trade. However, in most cases imports to the less developed countries trying to pursue a policy of import-substitution form only a small part of world imports. Therefore, a decrease in these imports will have only a slight effect on world prices. Hence less developed countries will not gain much on this score and foreign exporters will not be harmed much by import-substitution.

Domestic price levels will, however, usually be heavily influenced by import-substitution. Prices of industrial goods will go up. This will have important effects on the income distribution within the country. Primarily it is the domestic income distribution that will be affected by import-substitution, not the world income distribution.

Import-substitution aims to protect the domestic manufacturing sector. What this sector gains, other sectors within the economy will lose. The effect of import-substitution is basically to shift domestic income distribution in favor of entrepreneurs and workers within industry at the expense of farmers. As farmers are often among the poorest groups in a country, the effect of import-substitution will be to increase income inequality.[3] In Pakistan, for instance, farm incomes have been estimated to be 11–13 per cent lower because of import-substitution than they would have been otherwise. When import substitution was at its height in Argentina in 1947–55 the distortion of prices it brought about was equivalent to a tax of 30–40 per cent of incomes in the agricultural sector.[4]

Attempts to change income distribution in favor of the industrial sector were often quite deliberate. Increased savings were needed to increase investment and spur the development effort. As the entrepreneurs in the industrial sector were regarded as having a large propensity to invest, it was deemed favorable to shift the income distribution in their favor. This argument has some merit. At the same time, it should be pointed out that high prices might lead not only to high profits but also to high costs. Moreover, there are alternative ways of providing savings for a developing economy. One major alternative is to encourage household saving. This presupposes a well-functioning credit market with the power to inspire confidence and to create safe financial instruments that households can acquire.

Most countries seem to have relied on the first method. In Pakistan and Brazil, for instance, industrial investments were almost completely generated out of profits. Very high rates of protection were used to secure high profits for the domestic industry.

Mexico is an example of a country where household savings played an important role for the financing of industry. The country used a policy of comparatively high interest rates to stimulate household savings; as the rate of inflation was low, this meant that the rates were also positive and quite high in real terms. To guarantee stability, some bonds were even denoted in U.S. dollars. This was contrary to the experience of Brazil, where the rate of inflation was high and where, furthermore, usury laws did not permit interest rates to rise above a certain level. This implied that interest rates in real terms were negative for long periods of time. The Mexican policy was successful: around 5 per cent of household incomes were channelled to industrial investments. In Brazil, on the other hand, household savings played a negligible role in industrial investments.

Mexico's policy has some distinct advantages. First, it can be pursued without relying on a very uneven income distribution. It is enough to count on the positive time preference that many households have, even though their average income might be quite low. Second, domestic prices need not be as distorted *vis à vis* world market prices, for the degree of protection can be lower when excessive profits are no longer needed to fund investments in the industrial sector. Mexico was not the only country that successfully stimulated household savings and channelled them into investments for industrial expansion. Taiwan applied the same type of policy in the 1950s and South Korea followed suit in the mid-1960s.

We must conclude that the policy of import-substitution created problems from the point of view of economic justice. It tended to discriminate against agriculture and thus sharpen the inequality of an already very uneven income distribution. It also tended to restrict the market for industrial goods because large groups of workers, especially small farmers and farm workers, were too poor to be able to buy industrial products.

CHOICE OF TECHNOLOGY AND EFFECTS OF EMPLOYMENT

One of the primary aims of a policy of import-substitution is to create employment in the industrial sector. Even here, import-substitution has not been too successful. Perhaps the most pressing social problem in the less developed world today is the influx of migrants to the cities. Industrial employment has not increased fast enough to absorb the increase in urban population. Besides, the policy of import-substitution might be seen as a major factor in creating this disequilibrium situation, which in turn is a source of constant social and economic tensions.

In most of the less developed countries the rate of growth of industrial employment is quite low. Some countries, like Mexico and Taiwan, had an annual increase in their industrial labor force of around 5 per cent yearly from 1950 to 1960, as did Pakistan, which had a very small industrial base to start from. Other major countries, such as India, Brazil and Argentina, had much lower growth rates of industrial employment: in India and Argentina the rate was less than 2 per cent, and in Brazil it was 2.6 per cent. As the increase in urban population was much faster in these countries, unemployment increased. Some of the reasons for the increase in unemployment were intimately linked to the process of import-substitution.

The influx of people to the cities created a demand for investment. The investment needed was of an 'unproductive' kind, especially in infrastructure like roads, drainage, transportation, schools and housing. This type of investment can be viewed as 'capital-widening' of a kind. When referring to them as 'unproductive', it is not to be inferred that they were not needed or that they did not improve the standard of life for city-dwellers. However, had migration to the cities been slower and had more of the would-be city-dwellers stayed in agricultural areas, the same infrastructure could have been provided at lower cost.

Import-substitution discriminated against agriculture and favored industry. It led to stagnation and impoverishment in rural areas. This, in turn, led to migration to the cities, necessitating the 'unproductive' type of investments we have referred to above. When judging aggregate investment figures one should therefore keep in mind that they might overstate the efficiency of investment. Had export-promoting policies instead been applied, such policies could have led to larger growth of employment from a given amount of investment.

Another consequence of import-substitution is the capital-deepening it induces. The protection given to industry stimulates investment in industry. It is quite clear that most countries pursuing import-substitution policies opted for investments which were far too capital-intensive according to the existing factor-price ratios, had these been allowed to reflect true social costs. Why firms in these countries opted for a capital-intensive type of technique is a complex issue; there is little doubt, however, that a policy of import-substitution favored this choice of technique.

We have already pointed out that import-substitution forced most countries to import the capital goods needed to speed up the process of industrialization. Most of the imported capital equipment tended to be highly capital-intensive. This was to a degree not the fault of the importing countries themselves but of the fact that this equipment had been constructed for a completely different set of factor prices than the ones prevailing in the less developed countries. Administrators and politicians in less developed countries often failed to grasp the significance of this point; they often insisted on importing the most advanced machinery available, instead of importing machinery which, though it did not necessarily embody the most modern technology, was less capital-intensive. This led to waste of resources, especially through underutilization of the cheap labor available.

There were also other factors which worked in the same direction. Prices of imported capital goods were often kept artificially low by means of low, or no, tariffs and an overvaluation of domestic currency. Furthermore, interest rates were often kept low, even to the extent of making real interest rates negative. This naturally led to capital-rationing, which usually benefited larger firms at the expense of small businesses. Very liberal depreciation allowances lowered the relative price of capital even more and encouraged investment.

Another reason firms in these countries might have chosen to overcapitalize had to do with *discrimination*. Machines do not talk back and they never strike – at least not to get higher wages. For entrepreneurs, used to reaping easy profits behind high walls of protection, it might have been tempting to substitute machines for labor. This could also be a rational policy, because wages in the industrial sector in several countries seemed to be affected more by profits than by supply and demand conditions in the local labor markets. In order to counteract the influence of unions, which fought militantly for the interests of small groups of elite workers, entrepreneurs might have deliberately tried to minimize the wage bill, even though that implied using capital-intensive methods of production.

One of the striking facts about industry in the less developed countries is its low capacity utilization. It is well known that urban unemployment rates are high in these countries. The unemployment rate of machinery is also very high. Reliable figures are not easy to come by in this area, but it is quite clear from the ones that exist and from available experience that capacity utilization is much lower in less developed countries than it is in developed industrial countries.

In Argentina, for instance, the capacity utilization of industry in the mid-1960s was estimated to be around 65 per cent. In India, taking capacity utilization on a two-shift basis as a measuring-rod, most industries worked at less than 50 per cent of their capacity.[5] Figures naturally differed from industry to industry but it seems certain that most less developed countries used their industrial capacity far less intensively than did the industrial, developed countries. By way of comparison it can be mentioned that in 1964 capacity utilization in U.S. manufacturing was estimated to be close to 90 per cent and that average capacity utilization in Western European industry was around 95 per cent.

Contributing to this low capacity utilization is the fact that shift work seems to be rare in less developed countries. With labor being cheap and machinery expensive one would think that the developing countries would use their machinery intensively, with shift work. This is not the case. Again, strictly comparable data do not exist to any great extent, but estimates for Mexico and the United States show that shift work is more common in the United States than in Mexico: the shift coefficient for Mexico is 1.07, while it is between 1.2 and 1.3 in the United States.[6] It is also well known that most industries in the less developed countries work only one shift.

We have pointed to several mechanisms that all worked to create too much capital for industry which was then not used in an effective fashion. Import-substitution fostered these mechanisms and hence led to overcapitalization of industry and underutilization of existing capacity. It also probably fostered attitudes on the part of domestic producers not conducive to expansion and growth.

Import-substitution meant protection for domestic industry behind high tariff walls. It implied a policy of high profits. With foreign competition gone, high and easily reaped profits tended to create lax attitudes on the part of domestic producers. They could get by even if they let costs rise and even if they did not use capacity very efficiently. High profits encouraged waste, in terms of unused capacity, and made life easy for the domestic producers.

EXPORT-PESSIMISM AND DISCRIMINATION AGAINST AGRICULTURE

The main sector which import-substitution discriminated against was agriculture. As a poor country develops, one would expect demand for food to grow. Increases in *per capita* consumption of food, however, have been extremely slow or non-existent in most less developed countries from the mid-1930s. Low growth of production contributed to this, and this in turn was caused to a large extent by the discrimination implicit in the policy of import-substitution.

According to information provided by GATT, *per capita* consumption of agricultural goods in Argentina was practically stagnant from the mid-1930s to the mid-1960s: it increased from 121 dollars *per capita* to 129 dollars; at the same time agricultural production *per capita* actually fell, from 223 dollars to 188 dollars.[7] In India the situation was practically the same. Here consumption levels were much lower *per capita* consumption amounting to 31 dollars *per capita* in the mid-1930s and falling to 28 dollars in the mid-1960s. The decline in consumption went together with a decline *per capita* production.

Again, during the same period, the story was very much the same in countries like Pakistan and Brazil. There is little doubt that the adverse development in agriculture was caused by the discrimination inherent in the policy of import-substitution. The high degree of protection offered to industry turned the terms of trade and the income distribution against agriculture. Controls on imports and on overvaluation of the currency, usually associated with import-substitution, made matters worse. Returns to agriculture became depressed and an air of export-pessimism prevailed. The best illustration of this is Argentina. Argentina had held a very strong position in the world market in the early 1930s in many important agricultural commodities. This position was much eroded thirty years later. From the early 1930s to the early 1960s, her share in world exports decreased drastically for a long list of important commodities: fresh meat from 40 to 18 per cent, wheat from 23 to 6 per cent, maize from 64 to 17 per cent, and linseed from 79 to less than 7 per cent.[8] Brazil and India had much the same experience with their major export crops, coffee and tea.

Export-pessimism certainly seems justified against the background of figures such as these. However, this pessimism was to a large extent policy-induced. It was created by the less developed countries themselves in their efforts to foster domestic industry at the expense of the traditional agricultural exports. High degrees of protection, amounting to heavy taxation of agriculture, combined with an overvaluation of the domestic currency, served to depress economic conditions in agriculture while at the same time making imported goods look cheaper than they really were.

Mexico, with a much milder form of protection of domestic industry and less discrimination against agriculture, fared better. Here consumption of agricultural goods increased by almost 50 per cent *per capita*: from 36 dollars *per capita* in the mid-1930s to 50 dollars *per capita* thirty years later. During the same period, production increased by more than 50 per cent and exports of agricultural products went up substantially.

In recent years a re-evaluation of the importance of agriculture as a source of export earnings has also taken place in some countries. A case in point is Argentina. The country has a very strong comparative advantage in agriculture. By lowering discrimination against the agricultural sector, the country has been able to take advantage of the booming demand conditions in world agricultural markets in the early 1970s. Her exports of agricultural products, around 1500 million dollars in the 1960s, more than doubled during the agricultural boom that occurred in the early 1970s. It remains to be seen if Argentina can overcome its export-pessimism and start growing again through sustained exporting of her agricultural products.

Brazil also appears to have a comparative advantage in some agricultural products. With the shift over to more export-promoting policies during the 1960s the country was more likely to exercise her comparative advantage in certain agricultural sectors. Outputs and exports of soya bean and corn increased, while domestic demand for wheat could be satisfied through imports as the foreign exchange constraints became less binding.

South Korea is also an interesting case for study, in that she has combined agricultural policies with an export-promoting strategy. During the 1950s agricultural growth was satisfactory. In the 1960s it increased sharply. In the early years of Korean development poor harvests had very negative effects on the economy: 1961 was a year of bad harvest, and that year South Korea devalued her currency. The devaluation failed as prices increased sharply in connection with the poor harvest. Later on, the export-push strategy became more successful. Agricultural production increased rapidly. At the same time, the phenomenal increase in industrial exports increased export earnings. The country became less dependent on the short-term fortunes of the agricultural sector. In times of bad harvests food could be imported to supplement domestic supplies. The 1964-5 devaluation was also successful and paved the way for a more liberal exchange-rate regime.

India, on the other hand, has a relatively weak agricultural base. The policy of import-substitution seems to have put the country in prolonged difficulties. India does not seem willing to reverse her policy of high protection and severe controls over trade. The country has hardly been able to increase agricultural production in any decisive way. Developments in recent years have been somewhat uneven, but the country remains quite heavily dependent on imports of agricultural goods.

CONCLUDING REMARKS ON DEVELOPMENT STRATEGIES

The question of the success of the policy of import-substitution in less developed countries cannot be answered categorically. Among other things, this is due to the fact that import-substitution is only part of a more general economic policy of any country and can have different effects depending upon the other economic policies associated with it. The reader should also beware that this is an area that is ideologically charged and that the positions taken can be influenced by value judgments. Nevertheless, some general conclusions should be warranted.

We should also be careful not to make strategies of export-push and import-substitution into complete opposites. In fact, countries which have at later periods in their history gone for export-push policies have started by applying import-competing policies for considerable amounts of time. Brazil and South Korea are cases in point. An argument could even be made for the view that import-substitution policies will eventually have to give way to export-push methods if a high rate of development is to be sustained.

There are several examples of countries where import-substitution has not been very successful, such as India, Pakistan and Argentina. In such countries it was accompanied by low rates of growth of *per capita* income – consumption levels of food were stagnating. In these countries the policy of inward-looking industrialization seemed to hold little hope for the great mass of people.

For other countries, such as Brazil, Mexico, the Philippines and Taiwan, import-substitution was more successful, at least in terms of growth of their G.D.P.s: they all had annual growth rates ranging from around 6 to 8 per cent during the twenty-year period from the beginning of the 1950s to the end of the 1960s. In two of these countries, Brazil and the Philippines, income distribution was very uneven and large segments of the population were not touched by the improvement in the standard of living.

Of special interest are the experiences of South Korea and Brazil. Despite all countries being different, there are, however, some similarities between the two countries which should be pointed out.

A common trait in export-push strategies is that they are market-oriented. Reliance will be placed on pricing incentives rather than on quantitative controls. We have also seen that an outward-looking strategy had to be accompanied by realistic exchange rates, such as those prevailing in Bhagwati and Kreuger's Phases IV and V, which were the phases of liberalized exchange regimes. The essence of the export-push strategy is that it is geared to the international market. Import-substitution works under an umbrella of controls. Buyers and sellers will be oriented toward the domestic market. The outcome of economic activities will be greatly determined by government decisions.

No politician or civil servant thinks, however, that he can control international markets. Exporters will be in a strong position. They will be the ones who have the information about foreign markets, and government officials will have to accept the statements of exporters most of the time. For example, if exporters claim that they need to import input factors because eventual domestic substitutes would be inferior, these claims will generally have to be accepted as the alternative might be export failure.

In general, protectionist policies might create large windfall gains for importers and those domestic producers who can benefit from such policies. It is much more difficult to create artificial gains under an export-push strategy. Here the successful firms are usually those which can succeed in the international market-place. Thereby they will achieve a strength of their own that is not directly related to government policy. This will give a pluralistic tinge to society, as the business sector will become an independent source of power.

Among factors which have been put forward for explaining the development of the South Korean economy is its proximity to Japan. However, too much emphasis should not be put on this factor. Several south-east Asian countries have expanded their exports to Japan rapidly. Indonesia, Thailand and the Philippines have all had access to the Japanese market. These countries have also experienced a satisfactory growth of their exports but none has achieved the high over-all growth of South Korea.

A common feature for Brazil and South Korea is that financial reforms were undertaken. Thereby capital markets became more efficient. The foreign exchange rate became more stable and the greater assurance about the future of the real exchange rate had positive effects on export performance.

On the real side of the economy, it is a fact that economies of scale can be reaped more effectively in the context of export-promoting policies. The argument carries special weight for small countries. It should be noted, however, that markets in most less developed countries are small in economic terms, even though the population may be large, as the purchasing power of the large majority of the population is minimal. To take an example, markets in India are usually smaller than in South Korea, and comparisons of industry-specific output levels show that they are typically much larger in South Korea. Export-push strategies are aimed at realizing economies of scale by making it possible to establish plants of optimal size in an industry. On the contrary, import-substitution often discourages output expansion in existing lines of production. Import-substitution policies are often motivated by a wish for self-reliance. Countries pushing such policies want to cut themselves off from the vagaries of international markets. Although this wish is understandable, import-substitution strategies often seem to be counter-productive.

An export-push strategy places emphasis on activities geared toward earning foreign exchange. Exports will become the leading growth sector. When export industries slow down their rate of growth, so does the rest of the economy. Demand for foreign exchange will be adapted to the supply of foreign exchange. Moreover, an export-oriented strategy implies that a realistic exchange rate has to be kept. If domestic inflation occurs, the exchange rate will usually be devalued rather quickly. Reliance on exports usually leads to a rather comfortable balance-of-payments position. Hence temporary short-falls in export earnings can often be handled in a smooth manner.

Economies which rely upon import-substitution are generally plagued by a shortage of foreign exchange. The lack of external reserves can have very negative effects on the rate of development. Disruptions in exchange earnings will have an immediate impact on development efforts, leading at the micro level, to partly finished projects standing idle and, at the macro level, to ineffectiveness in planning and difficulties in carrying out desired programmes. Recent experiences have tended to confirm the above arguments and to cast further doubts on the possibility of increased self-reliance through import-substitution. It seems that the group of countries that have been hardest hit by the drastic increase in oil prices that occurred in 1973 were poor countries that had relied on inward-looking strategies, countries like India, Pakistan, Bangladesh, Sri Lanka, and many of the black African countries. The export-oriented economies of the Far East, and Brazil, seem to have fared less badly. Although their terms of trade have also deteriorated drastically, they seemed nevertheless to have shown a greater flexibility in adjusting to the shock.

The countries relying on import-substitution strategies had very low reserves on foreign currencies. They had to cut back their imports immediately. The impact on production, for instance because of reduced fertilizer supplies, was sharp and immediate. Countries that had relied upon promotion of exports were better able to adjust to the new circumstances. They had a better foreign exchange situation to start with, their knowledge of international markets was better, and they could push their exports further to at least offset partially the adverse terms of trade.

The upshot is, ironically, that the countries which had tried to sever themselves from the vagaries of the international markets were in the end most dependent on these markets. Countries opting for a policy of export-push had provided themselves with a certain cushion in the form of knowledge of foreign markets and a greater degree of flexibility in dealing with changing the economic fortunes.

Sometimes it has been asserted that export-promoting strategies are dependent on 'strong' governments. Countries like Brazil and South Korea have also had strong governments in the form of dictatorships with strong ties to the military. They have been able to control undue increases in wages and to promote export expansion in a systematic way. However, other countries, like Turkey during the 1950s, Ghana up to 1966, and Egypt during the 1950s and 1960s have also represented 'strong' governments in the sense that they were able to impose the economic policies that they deemed desirable. It is true that Brazil and South Korea are not democracies and that in political terms economic development might have implied a high price as far as human and political liberties are concerned. A 'strong' government is no prerequisite for economic development; nor is it a guarantee for strategies of export promotion.

The views on inward- versus outward-looking policies of development differ. The mainstream of academic research seems to favor export-promoting strategies. They argue for policies to enhance each country's particular advantages relative to world economic conditions. By disregarding world market prices countries pursuing import-substitution have not taken the opportunity to import goods cheaply and instead have produced them domestically at higher costs; by the same token, they have also abstained from taking advantage of existing export opportunities. Proponents of this argument maintain that behind high walls of protection such countries have created economic distortions leading to several of the problems touched on in this chapter.

Another line of argument reaches different conclusions: import-substitution is the best policy available for the less developed countries. The advocates of this line are primarily spokesmen – often in a policy-making capacity – of the less developed countries themselves. They point to the fact that the protectionist agricultural policies of the less developed countries, and the selective protectionist policies of the developed countries (which discriminate against labor-intensive, low-technology exports), have left little scope for outward-looking policies on the part of the less developed countries. Furthermore, they emphasize industrialization as the major avenue for development. Hence they claim that import-substitution is the superior development strategy for the less developed countries. Some radical exponents of this line are critical of import-substitution policies as actually carried out even though they favor them in general. They tend to stress that more direct attacks on uneven income distribution and mass unemployment should accompany any inward-looking development strategy.

The question of inward- versus outward-looking development strategies is one of heated controversy filled with poignant political overtones. We will have to be satisfied with having surveyed some of the main approaches which have so far been put forward.

SELECTED BIBLIOGRAPHY: CHAPTER 16

The two standard works in this area are the already mentioned studies made by the O.E.C.D. (published by Oxford University Press) and the N.B.E.R. (published by Columbia University Press). The former contains the following six volumes:

J. Bergsman, *Brazil: Industrialization and Trade Policies,* London, 1970.

T. King, *Mexico: Industrialization and Trade Policies since 1940,* London, 1970.

J. Bhagwati and P. Desai, *India: Planning for Industrialization,* London, 1970.

S. R. Lewis jr, *Pakistan: Industrialization and Trade Policies,* London, 1970.

M. H. Hsing, J. H. Power and G. P. Sicat, *Taiwan and the Philippines: Industrialization and Trade Policies,* London 1970.

I. Little, T. Scitovsky and M. Scott, *Industry and Trade in Some Developing Countries: A Comparative Study,* London, 1970.

The latter contains the following ten country studies and two synthesis volumes:

A. O. Kreuger, *Turkey,* New York, 1975.

J. C. Leith, *Ghana,* New York, 1975.

M. Michaely, *Israel,* New York, 1976.

B. Hansen and K. Hashashibi, *Egypt,* New York 1976.

R. E. Baldwin, *The Philippines,* New York, 1976.

J. N. Bhagwati and T. N. Srinivasan, *India,* New York, 1976.

C. R. Frank jr, K. S. Kim and L. Westphal, *South Korea,* New York, 1976.

J. R. Behrman, *Chile,* New York, 1976.

C. F. Diaz-Alejandro, *Columbia,* New York, 1976.

A. Fishlow, *Brazil,* New York, 1976.

J. N. Bhagwati, *Anatomy and Consequences of Exchange Control Regimes,* New York, 1977.

A. O. Kreuger, *Liberalization Attempts and Consequences,* New York, 1977.

For discussions on development strategies see:

M. J. Flanders, 'Agriculture versus Industry in Development Policy: the Planner's Dilemma', *Journal of Development Studies,* April 1969.

I. Livingstone, 'Agriculture versus Industry in Economic Development', *Journal of Modern African Studies,* no. 3, 1968.

D. T. Healey, 'Development Policy: New Thinking about an Interpretation', *Journal of Economic Literature,* September, 1972.

G. M. Meier gives summaries of several contributions and comments on trade strategies in his:

Leading Issues in Economic Development, 3rd ed., New York, Oxford University Press, 1976.

17

GATT, the EEC, the Kennedy Round, and the Tokyo Declaration

In the period between the First and Second World Wars there was a marked deterioration in international economic relations. In the 1920s an attempt was made to go back to 'normal' conditions. This meant the gold standard, as far as international monetary cooperation is concerned. An attempt was also made to organize world trade on a liberal basis.

This system did not function well. Great Britain, for instance, had difficulties because of an overvalued currency, and when the depression came at the beginning of the 1930s, the system broke down. Competitive devaluations followed, and trade restrictions were introduced. Many countries reverted to an autarkic pattern of production, and trade on a bilateral basis was introduced.

At the end of the Second World War the interwar period was still fresh in memory. When the victorious countries (especially Britain and the United States) started to plan for new, more viable relations in the international economy, they were determined to avoid the mistakes of the past. The Bretton Woods conference (named after the meeting place, Bretton Woods, New Hampshire) held in 1944 was the starting-point for a new order. The world economy would be organized around three cornerstones: the International Monetary Fund (I.M.F.), the International Trade Organization (I.T.O.), and the International Bank for Reconstruction and Development (I.B.R.D.).

The I.M.F. was designed to take care of short-term problems in connection with international liquidity. It would help to smooth out and to solve difficulties that the respective countries would perhaps have with their balances of payments. The I.T.O., on the other hand, would deal with the 'real' side of trading relations. It would help to create a liberal system of regulations governing world trade; it would, in the long run, be the vehicle that carried the world toward a system of free trade. The I.B.R.D. would help to channel international investments along desired lines. It would especially help the countries most in need of capital, the less developed countries, to get capital from the more developed, industrial countries.

Attemps at guiding the world economy have met with varying degrees of success. The problems of international liquidity have at times been acute; as the international monetary system in recent years has been characterized by floating rates the system has worked in a reasonably efficient manner; the I.M.F. has also become more active in trying to steer the system. The debate about trade policy is intense. Protectionist tendencies among the industrial countries have been checked reasonably successfully so far, even if the presence of non-tariff barriers have played a role that should not be neglected. The I.B.R.D. has hardly been able

to solve the problems of the less developed countries. Most international investment has taken place outside its scope. Only a handful of less developed countries
have been successful in promoting their exports of industrial goods. A majority
of poor countries still remain very poor, and their share of international trade is
lagging. The oil-producing countries have done extremely well on their own since
the sharp increases in oil prices since 1973.

We will deal with some of the main problems that the three organizations were
given to solve. In Part V we shall deal at length with the international monetary
system. Chapter 22 will be devoted to direct international investments. This
chapter and the next will deal with some of the most pressing problems of trade
policy.

GATT AND THE PRINCIPLE OF NON-DISCRIMINATION

The International Trade Organization was the least successful of the above-
mentioned three organizations; it never actually came into existence. A conference
in Havana in 1947–8 established a charter for the I.T.O. This charter, however,
was never ratified by the U.S. Senate. Nor did any other country ratify it; thus
the I.T.O. was never established. Instead, GATT came into being. GATT was a
less ambitious organization with headquarters in Geneva. It would serve as a sort
of clearing house between nations. Instead of bargaining on a bilateral basis, the
member countries of GATT would meet in Geneva and negotiate jointly at the
same time on matters of trade policy. Thereby, it was hoped, a more orderly and
just result could be achieved.

There are today more than eighty countries that are contracting parties to
GATT, and an additional twenty-four belong to GATT on a 'provisional' basis.
The Soviet Union and China are notable absentees, though Czechoslovakia,
Hungary, Poland, Romania and Yugoslavia are all full members.

The basic principle of GATT is that of *non-discrimination*. Countries that belong to GATT accept the so-called *most-favored-nation clause*. This means that a
country agrees not to give better treatment to any single nation than it gives to
all the contracting parties of GATT. The clause of most-favored nation in principle
rules out any preferential treatment among nations as far as trade policy is concerned.

The United States in particular has shown an almost fanatical attachment to
the principle of most-favored nation in its trade policy. This goes back to the
1930s when Cordell Hull, Secretary of State in the Roosevelt administration,
made it the leading principle in his crusade against the rising tide of protectionism
and for a more liberal trade policy. It seemed to be a principle characterized by
justice and equality, it harmonized with high-minded American principles, and it
gave the American line an air of moral superiority. This principle also played a
large role in the planning of a post-war trade organization.

Principles that might appear simple and just from a moral or legal point of view
often fail to give the same impression when viewed from an economic angle. That
is the case with the most-favored-nation principle. What appears just and equitable
is not necessarily anything of the sort.

If the United States, for instance, has a certain tariff structure and applies it equally to all countries, it means that the country does not discriminate between producers, but it does not necessarily follow that the United States does not discriminate between nations. If it has a high tariff on cocoa but a low one on Scottish sweaters, it means that Britain is given better treatment than Ghana. Any change in a tariff structure can also be geared so that it favors some countries over others. It avails the African states little if the United States makes tariff concessions on industrial goods only, it these nations cannot produce and export industrial goods. Then what is a non-discriminatory policy in principle becomes for all practical purposes a policy of discrimination. It should also be borne in mind that a change in a given nominal tariff rate can differ widely in effects, depending on circumstances. The discussions in Chapters 14 and 16 have indicated that the effects of a change in tariffs depend on the interplay of all the economic forces in the general-equilibrium framework. The lawyer's play of equal treatment can turn out to be something quite different when studied from an economist's point of view.

The principle of most-favored nation is also somewhat peculiar if regarded from a more general, political point of view. It is a case of extreme nationalism. It lumps all foreigners together in one big pack and contrasts them to the members of one's own nation. The home producer, for some reason, has a moral right to be protected. And all foreigners, regardless of neighborhood, political ties, common cultural background, etc., should be treated equally, i.e. all foreign producers should have a right to enter the country's home market on the same conditions as all other foreign producers. If anything, the principle of most-favored nation seems to build on a combination of extreme and opposing political philosophies.

Experience has also shown that a policy built on the most-favored-nation clause has not been very realistic. Little progress has been made along its lines. GATT has also made important exceptions from the principle of non-discrimination. Customs unions and free-trade areas are thus permitted among groups of countries. A customs union means that a group of countries renounces all tariffs between the members of the union but has a common outer tariff wall. A free-trade area means also that no tariffs exist among the member countries but that they each have different outside tariff rates; i.e. these exceptions imply that discrimination within GATT is allowed provided it is a 100 per cent discrimination.

We can also observe that, even in principle, there is nothing specifically advantageous about a policy of non-discrimination. It could well be that a discriminatory trade policy is more efficient and leads to a larger improvement in welfare than a non-discriminatory one. We will return to this point in this chapter and also in Chapter 20.

GATT was slow in getting started and played little role in the immediate post-war period. Apart from non-discrimination, the leading principle of GATT was that only tariffs would be tolerated as a means of trade policy. The reason was that tariffs are a 'honest' means of protection. If exporters in foreign countries know what the tariffs are and if these are kept stable (or perhaps lowered), they know what they have to deal with. Other forms of trade restrictions, especially quotas, exchange controls, etc., are more difficult to deal with and their effects are often very hard to calculate and to foresee; usually they are also prone to frequent alterations and should therefore be avoided.

The difficulties that many GATT members encountered in the first post-war years, however, were so great that the GATT rules could not be strictly kept. The countries in Western Europe, especially, had to be granted exceptions; they used different types of direct controls to deal with their balance-of-payments problems. Frequent rounds of trade negotiations took place under auspices of GATT, but to begin with it seemed as if the United States and Canada had to grant genuine tariff reductions and in return mostly got empty gestures from the Western European countries. The United States, however, obtained a very important concession: the granting of a waiver that agricultural policies and trade in agricultural goods should be exempted from the GATT rules. This was a time when the United States pursued a policy of extensive farm subsidies that kept American agricultural prices high, a policy that led to a development of very considerable farm surpluses. By the GATT waiver, the United States ensured that this policy would not have to be complicated and endangered by competition from foreign producers of agricultural products.

The negotiations within GATT seemed to produce meagre results. The exceptions for agricultural goods also implied a trend in a protectionist direction. But apart from that, some improvement took place, especially concerning the dismantling of direct controls. Trade expanded rapidly in the 1950s, and the trend in trade policy was in a liberal direction. The relatively slow and painstaking development toward a lowering of tariffs through non-discriminatory tariff changes on a world-wide basis, however, soon became overshadowed by the very rapid development of regional trade groupings.

THE DEVELOPMENT OF REGIONAL TRADE GROUPINGS

The European Economic Community (E.E.C.)

The state of Western Europe in the late 1940s, after the Second World War, gave no cause for optimism. The productive machinery of the countries had been greatly damaged by the war. Many problems were encountered when trying to rebuild the economies, not least those concerned with external imbalances. A general feeling was that the reconstruction could not follow traditional national lines, but that cooperation on a wider scale was necessary.

Soon, two competing lines for a Western European integration developed. One argued for close and compact integration of a small group of countries. The other approach aimed at cooperation among a larger group of countries on less specific terms.

Already, at the beginning of the 1950s, the proponents of the first approach made some substantial progress. In 1950 France took the initiative in bringing about an economic integration of the steel and coal industries in Belgium, France, Italy, Luxembourg, the Netherlands and West Germany. The year after, in April 1951, the European Coal and Steel Community (E.C.S.C.) was created. The aim of the E.C.S.C. was to regulate the production of steel and coal in a way that would benefit the six countries. By close cooperation in an area such as this, the six countries demonstrated a new view on common problems; a war among these countries would now be impossible.

The other approach worked for closer cooperation among the group of countries belonging to the Organization for European Economic Cooperation

(O.E.E.C.), founded in 1948. The O.E.E.C. comprised all the European countries outside the Communist bloc. It was first created in connection with the launching of the Marshall Aid programme, and was then an important forum for economic cooperation between the United States and Western Europe in the first half of the 1950s. Britain was the leading proponent of this approach, which aimed at a less far-reaching cooperation in the form of a European free-trade area.

The conflict between the two approaches became manifest in 1955. That year saw the start of a period of intense and prolonged negotiations which were to lead to the establishment of the European Economic Community (E.E.C.). The British argued for a European free-trade area for industrial goods. Their interests at this time lay primarily outside Europe. They desired close cooperation with the United States and also a comparatively free hand in dealing with the overseas members of the British Commonwealth. This approach also suited the Scandinavian countries since they were primarily interested in free trade but cared less for close political cooperation with central Europe. On the other hand, France, especially after de Gaulle came to power, was less interested in larger, freer forms of cooperation, preferring instead closer cooperation among 'the Six'. The result of the negotiations was the Treaty of Rome, signed in 1957, which laid down the ground-rules for the formation of a common market. The inaugural date for the E.E.C., or the Common Market as it is often called, can be set at 1 January 1959.

The core of the Common Market is the *customs union* (discussed in more detail in Chapter 20). The partners started immediately to dismantle the tariff barriers between themselves. Progress was rapid, and by January 1966 the internal tariffs on industrial products were abolished. Simultaneously with the elimination of internal tariffs, the Community erected a common external tariff, which was to be equal to the unweighted arithmetical mean of the duties on imports from third countries which were operative in 1957. This meant, by and large, an increase in the West German and Benelux tariffs and a decrease in the French and Italian tariffs.

With the breakdown of negotiations for a broader European free-trade area, the seven countries outside the Common Market, Austria, Denmark, Great Britain, Norway, Portugal, Sweden and Switzerland, negotiated for formation of a trade grouping amongst themselves. In 1959 they signed the Stockholm Treaty, which formed the European Free Trade Association (EFTA). However, the aims of EFTA were limited to the abolition of internal tariffs and the creation of a free-trade area in industrial products, a process which was completed by 1967. At the same time, each country was to retain its own separate tariffs with the outside world. Moreover, no attempt was made to harmonize social and economic policy nor to pursue a joint agricultural policy. From the outset EFTA was conceived as a basis for bargaining with the E.E.C. In 1967 three EFTA members, Great Britain, Norway and Denmark, along with Ireland, applied for full membership in the Common Market, while the remaining members sought a free-trade agreement.

In addition to the reduction of tariffs the other important area of Community activity during the 1960s was the attempt made to harmonize agricultural policies. This proved to be much more difficult. All six members agreed that their agriculture had to be protected. The French, who had the most competitive agriculture, argued in favor of low subsidies. An agreement on common agricultural prices was achieved only after prolonged discussion, in 1967. The effect has been that the Community has adopted a high price protectionist policy in which the degree of self-sufficiency has tended to increase and which in some cases – butter, wine – has led to the Community becoming more than self-sufficient.

The Hague summit in 1969 can be viewed as a milestone in the evolution of the European Economic Community. First, it set the stage for direct negotiations with those countries who had sought full membership. At the same time, negotiations could also begin with the remaining EFTA countries on a free-trade agreement. Second, important decisions were made regarding the financing of the Common Agricultural Policy. Third, there was agreement on the need to reform the European Social Fund, which is a major instrument for the encouragement of labor mobility in the Community. Finally, The Hague summit committed member countries to the drawing up of plans for economic and monetary union and the harmonization of the foreign policies of individual member countries.

The expectations raised by The Hague summit have only been partially fulfilled. On the positive side, full membership of the Community was extended to Britain, Ireland and Denmark from 1 January 1973.[1] At the same time, free trade in industrial products was established with the other EFTA countries. Tariffs on certain 'sensitive' products such as pulp, paper and special steel were, however, to be phased out more slowly (seven to eleven years) than other industrial products covered by the free-trade agreement. The introduction of three new members and the free-trade agreement were considered as further important steps toward the economic and political integration of Western Europe.

E.E.C. trade policy towards less developed countries has also undergone important changes. In 1975 negotiations were successfully completed – the Lomé Convention – between the E.E.C. and the A.C.P. group which comprises forty-six countries from Africa, the Caribbean and the Pacific. This agreement effectively builds on the earlier trade agreement with Francophile African countries (the Yaoundé agreement) and grants duty-free access for most of the less developed country exports to the E.E.C. along with certain other concessions on trade and aid. On the other hand, E.E.C. members' exports to the A.C.P. are only guaranteed most-favored-nation treatment (for further discussion, see below).

Other areas of Community operations which can be considered to have benefited from the stimulus of The Hague summit are agricultural and social policy. A considerable measure of agreement has been achieved on the financing of agriculture, though it has been accompanied by the overproduction of certain commodities and a slow rate of structural improvement. The reform of the Social Fund presented in 1970 has meant that expenditure has been channelled into well-defined areas which fit in with Community policies rather than just the re-funding of a host of uncoordinated national schemes to aid workers suffering from, or threatened with, unemployment.

These improvements in the areas of trade, agriculture and social policy contrast with the lack of progress in the E.E.C.'s plans for economic and political union. Both the Werner plan (1970) for economic and monetary union and the Davignon report (1970) on political union have remained very much on paper. This lack of progress can be partly explained by the difficulty of coordinating economic policy during a period which has seen a rapid rise in the rate of inflation and in unemployment and the departure from a system of fixed exchange rates. Unemployment and inflation have affected E.E.C. members in varying degrees. Some countries have had a surplus on their balance of payments, while others have had substantial deficits. Some governments have given priority to fighting inflation, while others have given greater importance to the reduction of unemployment. In other words, the conditions favoring a common economic policy have deteriorated rather than improved.

However, underlying these differences in approach to economic policy are basic disparities in the economic and social structure of the nine member countries of the E.E.C. It is these fundamental structural differences which constitute the major obstacle to far-reaching plans for economic, monetary and political union.

The Tindemans report (1976) appears to accept the reality of these obstacles to economic and political cooperation. In the view of this author, economic cooperation should be intensified amongst the most developed members of the community, while the somewhat weaker members should be allowed to take a slower route towards economic union. However, this view has run up against the criticism that it scarcely touches upon the basic structural and social problems confronting the member countries of the Community.

Other regional trade groupings

Europe was not the only continent where regional cooperation developed. In recent years the movement toward greater economic cooperation has been particularly marked amongst less developed countries.[2] There is some evidence to show that intra-group trade within regional trade groupings of less developed countries has increased considerably faster than the same countries total exports or than the exports of all developing countries.[3] The same source also suggested that the main reason for this interest in the establishment of customs union and free-trade areas among less developed countries has been the rigidity of GATT rules, prior to its adoption of the non-reciprocity clause in 1969. This will be discussed more fully below.

There is a wide variation in the size, composition and objectives of these regional trade groupings. One of the oldest and largest is the Latin American Free Trade Association (LAFTA), set up in the 1961.[4] As its name suggests, it is a free-trade area with no common external tariff, though its aim is to establish a Latin American Common Market by 1985. However, the reduction of tariffs has been slow due to the wide disparity between the relatively developed countries (Argentina, Brazil and Mexico) and the underdeveloped members such as Bolivia, Ecuador and Paraguay. It is of interest to note that within LAFTA a smaller regional grouping was set up in 1969 covering the Andean states.[5] This grouping, known as the Andean Common Market, aims to establish a common external tariff by 1980 and internal free trade by 1981. Many of the Andean states have a large, foreign-owned mining sector, and this common experience undoubtedly underlies their common policy on foreign investment, which stipulates 51 per cent local control of the initial investment within fifteen years (twenty years for Bolivia and Ecuador).

Another interesting regional organization which has made rapid progress is the Central American Common Market (C.A.C.M.), consisting of Costa Rica, El Salvador, Guatemala, Honduras and Nicaragua. A common external tariff has been established and internal trade has been on a free-trade basis since 1966. Over the period 1963 – 73, intra-regional trade has increased tenfold.

As we have seen from the European experience, the establishment of a full customs union can be accompanied by a common agricultural policy, and eventually, it is hoped, by movement toward complete economic integration. This would appear to be the objective of the Caribbean Community (CARICOM) set up in 1973 following a previous free-trade association (CARIFTA). In addition to a common external tariff, a common agricultural policy has been developed which successfully exploits the comparative advantage of West Indian states in agriculture.[6]

Finally, mention should be made of the recently established (1975) Economic Community of West African States (ECOWAS), which aims at a customs union, free trade among the partners and a common external tariff within fifteen years. This grouping comprises both Anglophone and Francophone states[7] between which there had been previously little cooperation and builds upon the marked degree of unity that was established between these countries during the negotiations with the E.E.C. at the Lomé convention.

Regional cooperation has been a dominant feature in the development of trade policy since the Second World War. GATT did not play the role expected of it. The most important developments were of a discriminatory nature and took place outside GATT. The United States, the most important member of GATT and the main sponsor of a policy of non-discrimination, did not object to the formation of customs unions such as the E.E.C.; on the contrary, it gave them considerable encouragement. But customs unions usually have a protectionist aspect. If they became too successful, they could prove detrimental to outside interests. This was a risk encountered with the E.E.C. The United States saw this risk and tried to revitalize a policy of non-discrimination. This led to the important trade negotiations which took place inside GATT under the title of the Kennedy Round.

THE KENNEDY ROUND AND THE TOKYO DECLARATION

The United States had been generous in helping to establish the European Common Market. The E.E.C. was certainly not built on the principle of non-discrimination, and the GATT rules had to be amended to permit customs unions. This could never have been achieved if the United States had not granted its approval of the procedure.

As the E.E.C. developed into a full-scale customs union, the United States began to feel its protectionist slant. As a reaction to this development, and to take the sting out of it, the Kennedy administration in 1962 introduced a bill aimed at vast reciprocal tariff reductions. The idea was contained in the so-called Trade Expansion Act put before Congress in that year. From a political point of view, the bill was presented as necessary if the United States was to keep up the Atlantic alliance with Western Europe that had been the cornerstone of American foreign policy. It was also argued that it would improve the U.S. balance of payments, though why joint tariff reductions should improve any particular country's balance of payments was never explained. When American industry showed reluctance to adopt the idea, the Kennedy administration argued that it could now live up to its ideal of competition as the best foundation for a free economy.

The economic content of the Trade Expansion Act was that Congress would grant the administration the right to make a 50 per cent tariff reduction on all commodities. On top of this came 'the dominant-supplier authority'. This said that on commodity groups in which the United States and the Common Market accounted for 80 per cent or more of the trade among non-communist countries, tariffs could be cut to up to 100 per cent. Tariffs could, moreover, be completely eliminated if the U.S. tariff rate were less than 5 per cent, and on tropical products, provided the Common Market countries reciprocated. The countries' agricultural policies should also be discussed, as would be other non-tariff barriers to trade.

The concept behind the Trade Expansion Act was a bold and grand one. Since the Second World War five tariff-cutting conferences had been held under GATT's auspices. They had all been essentially performed on a bilateral basis and had consisted of bargaining on an item-by-item basis. Progress had been limited. Now it was desired to achieve a great leap forward that could match the achievement of the E.E.C. and EFTA for Europe on a regional basis.

Naturally, the self-interest of the United States was also involved. This was perhaps best seen in connection with the dominant-supplier arrangement. Although phrased in a non-discriminatory manner, it was hardly so in spirit, as it would allow the largest tariff cuts to be concentrated on goods that were especially important for trade between the United States and the E.E.C. The less developed countries would be appeased by the fact that unilateral tariff cuts by the industrial countries were foreseen on certain tropical primary products.

The Trade Expansion Act was adopted by the U.S. Congress in 1962. The enthusiasm of the European countries was less than the Americans had expected, but the negotiations, the Kennedy Round, got under way slowly in 1963.

Kennedy Round tariff reductions by developed countries averaged approximately 35 per cent and concentrated upon the manufactured goods that were of principal interest to developed countries or on the raw materials that were essential to their industry. These tariff concessions were negotiated on a reciprocal basis and were extended to all contracting parties under the most-favored-nation clause. Agricultural products were generally excluded from the Kennedy Round because of the conflict of interest between the farm exports of the United States and the drive towards self-sufficiency in farm products in the E.E.C. Other areas which received relatively little attention were tropical products and non-tariff barriers to exports.

The Kennedy Round represents probably the last attempt at large tariff reductions in a non-discriminatory fashion. The success of these rounds of mutual tariff reductions has meant that attention is concentrated upon non-tariff barriers to trade [8] (e.g. the Tokyo round of GATT negotiations) and to the granting of discriminatory or non-reciprocal tariff reductions. Indeed, it is only since the acceptance (in 1965) of the latter principle within Part IV of GATT, covering trade and development, and subsequently within the framework of the Kennedy Round itself that the less developed countries have taken part in GATT negotiations.

Trade liberalization in GATT reflected the composition of its original members, who were principally developed industrial economies. As a result, tariff reductions were concentrated on the industrial goods traded between the major industrial countries. In spite of a traditional concentration on the latter, the Kennedy Round nevertheless represented something of a watershed in the relationship between less developed countries and GATT. First, some twenty less developed countries were actively involved in the Kennedy Round negotiations. Second, the method of negotiation taken into account heeded the 'non-reciprocity' principle in Part IV of GATT, which in general terms meant that less developed countries were not required to give concessions equivalent to those exchanged among developed countries. This principle, together with the proposal for tariff preferences for the manufactured and semi-manufactured exports of less developed countries, which was presented at the first United Nations Conference on Trade and Development (UNCTAD) in 1964, has formed the basis of a new concept in world trade – the so-called 'Generalized System of Preferences' (G.S.P.). (see Chapter 18 for a full discussion of UNCTAD and the G.S.P.) These preferential tariff arrangements[9] have continued to be sponsored by UNCTAD, while multilateral trade negotiations remain under the auspices of GATT.

The latest round of these negotiations began in 1973 with the so-called 'Tokyo Declaration'. It represents both a consolidation of the concepts of preferential tariffs for less developed countries and non-reciprocity as well as a widening of the scope of GATT negotiations. It stresses that 'special and more favorable' treatment is to be granted in 'areas of negotiation where this is feasible and appropriate'.[10] In contrast to the Kennedy Round tropical products have been given priority. Moreover, for the first time GATT has made a formal commitment to the attainment of 'stable, equitable and remunerative prices for primary products'.[11] Non-tariff barriers to less developed country manufactured exports have also become an important item on the agenda for discussion.

Actual negotiations did not get under way until mid-1975. This was partly due to the delay in passing the U.S. Trade Act, without which the American delegation was unable to commence formal negotiations. However, there are a number of more substantive reasons for this delay. First, between the signing of the Tokyo Declaration in 1973 and the start of formal negotiations in 1975 most developed economies experienced a serious recession. As a result, they became increasingly reluctant to commit themselves to further liberalization of trade. In addition to the difficulties raised by a more protectionist climate of world trade, there seems to be a disagreement amongst less developed countries on the benefits to be gained from a further round of multilateral trade negotiations. It is argued that substantial most-favored-nation tariff cuts may lead to an erosion of the preferential tariff advantages negotiated under G.S.P.

On the other hand, it has to be remembered that not all developing countries or all manufactured goods are covered by these preferential arrangements.[12] Finally, there is the difficulty that in GATT negotiations, despite the changes that have taken place between the Kennedy and Tokyo Rounds, the less developed countries continue to have a relatively weak bargaining position. Trade liberalization in GATT remains dependent upon developed countries' willingness to reduce tariffs in areas of interest to less developed countries. In order to focus attention on their problems, less developed countries have increasingly tended to turn to UNCTAD as their main international pressure group on such issues. Chapter 18 will be devoted to the development of UNCTAD and to some of the problems with which it has tried to deal.

Notwithstanding the present air of pessimism surrounding the Tokyo round of trade negotiations, GATT can continue to play an important role in relation to the regulation and control of government policies which seek to restrict imports by means of quotas, taxes, subsidies and administrative procedures. This watchdog role may indeed become more important in the event of governments increasingly resorting to protectionist measures.

SELECTED BIBLIOGRAPHY: CHAPTER 17

For accounts and discussions of GATT, see:

G. Curzon, *Multilateral Commercial Diplomacy*, London, Joseph, 1965.

K. W. Dam, *The GATT, Law and International Economic Organization*, Chicago, Chicago University Press, 1970.

S. Wells, 'The Developing Countries, GATT and UNCTAD', *International Affairs*, vol. 45, no 1, 1969.

On European trade policy problems and the development of regional trade groupings, see:

Miriam Camps, *Britain and the European Community, 1955–1963*, Princeton, N.J., Princeton University Press, 1963.

S. Dell, *Trade Blocs and Common Markets*, New York, Knopf, 1963.

G. R. Denton (ed.) *Economic Integration in Europe*, London, Weidenfeld & Nicolson, 1969.

On Latin America and Africa see:

S. Dell, *A Latin American Common Market?*, New York, Knopf, 1967.

J. Grunwald, M. S. Wionzek and M. Carrioy, *Latin American Economic Integration and U.S. policy*, Washington, D.C., Brookings Institution, 1972.

A. Hazlewood, *Economic Integration: The East African Experience*, London, Heinemann, 1975.

For some aspects of the Kennedy Round, see:

R. E. Baldwin, 'Tariff Cutting Techniques in the Kennedy Round', in R. E. Baldwin *et al.*, *Trade, Growth and the Balance of Payments*, Chicago, 1965.

R. N. Cooper, *The Economics of Interdependence: Economic Policy in the Atlantic Community*, New York, McGraw-Hill, 1968, ch. 9.

See also:

B. Balassa, *Trade Liberalization Among Industrial Countries*, New York, McGraw-Hill, 1967.

B. Balassa (ed.), *Studies in Trade Liberalization*, Baltimore, Johns Hopkins Press, 1967.

P. Tulloch, *The Politics of Preferences*, London, Croom Helm, 1975.

18

UNCTAD and trade policies for less developed countries

The problems of the less developed countries have now been in the forefront of public discussion for a considerable time. In the years immediately after the Second World War when the public generally began to realize the importance of the problem, many economists had a sanguine view of the question. Capital accumulation was asserted to be at the root of the problem. If only capital could be inserted into the underdeveloped economies, they would start to grow. After years of dubious development efforts and depressing experiences, one is now less ready to offer panaceas. There are those who argue that the problem of economic development will be with us, not for years, but for decades and perhaps centuries.

We have seen that the main developments in trade policy have had little relevance for solving the problems of less developed countries. It is quite natural for the representatives of less developed countries to feel frustrated by the work done within the framework of GATT and to feel that more consideration ought to be given to their specific problems. It was the efforts roused by such feelings that led to the establishment of the United Nations Conference on Trade and Development (UNCTAD).

UNCTAD AND THE QUESTION OF TRADE PREFERENCES

In 1961 the General Assembly of the United Nations designated the decade of the 1960s as United Nations Development Decade, a period in which 'member states and their peoples will intensify their efforts to mobilize and sustain support for measures required on the part of both developed and developing countries to accelerate progress towards self-sustaining growth'.

Representatives of less developed countries soon started to press for a special trade conference within the U.N.'s Economic and Social Council. Despite certain opposition their efforts were successful, and in 1964 the first UNCTAD conference was convened in Geneva.

Since that date, three conferences have been held: New Delhi (1968), Santiago (1972) and Nairobi (1976). During this period its membership has expanded to comprise over 160 countries drawn from both the developed and less developed world. The organization of the latter within UNCTAD in the *Group of 77* (the group now numbers over 100 less developed countries) has been of considerable practical significance. Despite wide political, ideological and cultural differences, this group has not only been able to coordinate the attitudes of less developed countries within UNCTAD but has also contributed toward the adoption of a common negotiating stance in other U.N. bodies.

In contrast to GATT, the work of UNCTAD has spanned the whole field of trade investment and aid. Indeed, following UNCTAD III in Santiago, the area of interest has been further extended to include the questions of transfer of technology and the role of the multinational corporation.

The agenda for the fourth UNCTAD conference in Nairobi was more concise and tended to concentrate on the subject of the stabilization of international commodity prices and the creation of an 'integrated programme for commodities' which would help to improve the terms on which primary commodities are traded (up to that time, to the advantage of developing countries). This issue dominated the Nairobi conference. The objectives can be traced back to earlier UNCTAD conferences. Indeed, the line of argument that the terms of trade between primary products and industrial goods ought to be stabilized and that the purchasing power of a certain amount of primary-product exports should be preserved in terms of imports of industrial goods was eagerly promoted by Raúl Prebisch, the first Secretary-General of UNCTAD.[1] The wisdom of such a policy and the important questions which it raises will be discussed later in this chapter.

The other main problem of trade policy which dominated the earlier UNCTAD conferences was the subject of trade or tariff preferences for less developed countries. As we have seen in the last chapter, the Kennedy Round of GATT negotiations brought a reduction in the tariffs on industrial goods but did not significantly affect the relatively disadvantaged position of less developed country exporters. This led to a proposal for a Generalized System of Preferences being put forward within UNCTAD. It is to this whole question of tariff preferences that we shall now turn.

The demands from the less developed countries for trade preferences have grown out of their desire for industrialization. A stabilization of raw-material prices might be deemed necessary, but it is not sufficient. 'Trade not aid' has been a popular slogan. It is not perhaps meant to be taken literally, but it points to a course which the less developed countries want to take. A policy of import-substitution has not been very successful either, for reasons sketched in Chapter 16. The idea has gained ground that an 'outward-looking industrialization' is necessary. This means promoting exports, especially exports of industrial products.

It ought, parenthetically, to be stressed that aid and trade are not substitutes for each other as is sometimes suggested in popular discussion. Aid provides resources for development in the receiving country without the country having to make any efforts of its own. Trade does not in itself create any new resources for a country; it merely provides an opportunity for converting domestic resources into foreign exchange by means of exports. The confusion of the effects of trade and aid usually stems from superficial balance-of-payments considerations; they both provide foreign exchange. From a real economic point of view, it is usually more appropriate to regard aid and trade as complements instead of substitutes, as far as a country's development effort is concerned.

There are two strong reasons why exports of manufactured goods could play a critical role in the economic development of most countries. The first is that, for most countries, industrialization is the natural means of development. The second is that, in order for the development effort to be successful, the country in question needs to increase its exports, and the type of export that it can most profitably promote is that of industrial goods. But it has proved difficult for most less developed countries to gain a foothold in the import markets of the industrial countries. To achieve this, one has felt that some kind of new policy is needed. The idea of exports as an 'engine of growth' has come back into the discussion. Many believe that in tariff preferences they have found the policy means that could make such an export expansion possible.

The idea behind tariff preferences was primarily developed by Raúl Prebisch, the Secretary-General of UNCTAD, who is also the *spiritus rector* of the organization.[2] Prebisch makes a distinction between 'conventional' and 'real' reciprocity in trading relations between nations. In this view, conventional reciprocity, when an industrial and a less developed country make concessions to each other, leads to the less developed country becoming dependent on an archaic trade pattern, where it will be deemed to go on exporting primary products. Real reciprocity, on the other hand, means that the developed countries grant unilateral tariff reductions to the less developed countries. Thereby the export capacity of the latter countries will grow, their demands for imports from industrial countries will increase, and world trade will expand. There is no need for close scrutiny of this line of reasoning. We can simply accept that the demand for tariff preferences is built on political and economic wishes of the less developed countries to increase trade.

The arguments for tariff preferences proposed at the first UNCTAD conference centered to a large degree around the idea of infant-industry protection. Preferences would be granted for a limited time during which infant industries would be able to grow up by having access to large markets.

It should be observed, however, that this argument differs from the ordinary infant-industry argument. In the ordinary case, the consumers of the country in question will have to pay higher prices and subsidize the producers to enable them to learn skills that will make it possible for them later on to compete at world market prices. In the case of tariff preferences, it is the consumers of the foreign country, the one granting preferences, who will have to subsidize the producers of less developed countries, so that they will eventually be able to compete at world market prices.

Even if such an arrangement worked, we must as usual ask whether it is the most efficient means for industrialization in less developed countries. Would it not be better if the consumers of the developed countries were taxed and a certain amount of taxes given as aid? From a purely economic point of view, it seems that this would be a more rational policy, as it would avoid the distortion of consumption that a tariff preference necessarily implies. Against this, it can be argued that what the less developed countries need is to get some experience of industrialization, and that this can be facilitated by their having access to the markets of the industrial countries.

Another important question in this regard concerns the choice of industries that should be given preferences. Presumably, those industries would be chosen in which the less developed countries had, or could be expected to have, a comparative advantage. It would be hoped that these would also be the industries in which the industrial countries have substantial tariffs. This would not necessarily be the case, but, if it were, there would perhaps be scope for substantial tariff preferences. There is nothing, however, that says that these industries would also be those that are of an infant-industry type.

Two different principles for granting trade preferences can be imagined. One would be of a fairly non-discriminatory nature, at least as far as the preference-receiving countries are concerned. Here would be chosen broad groups of industries, in which the less developed countries would be expected to establish a comparative advantage, and to grant the same preferences to all less developed countries. This would amount to a general subsidy from the developed countries to industrialization in the less developed countries. Apart from the dynamic effects in the learning of skills and so on that it could have, it can also be said broadly to have the same effect as a combination of transfer of aid from the developed countries and a devaluation by the less developed countries. However, we should not disregard the political difficulties that such an arrangement could create in the developed countries: industries that are weak and highly protected in these countries are often supported by strong political pressure groups. Such an arrangement would have the advantage of being easy to comprehend and fairly easy to implement.

The other principle would be to pick the industries that would be given preferential treatment according to their prospects of becoming infant industries. To pick the right industries to qualify in this respect, to determine the duration of protection, etc., would probably be a most cumbersome undertaking. To this must be added that one cannot be sure that tariffs in industrial countries are so high, and hence a preferential treatment so effective, as to provide enough stimulus for industrialization in the less developed countries. Tariff preferences must then be accompanied by subsidies. We know from tariff theory (Chapter 13) that subsidies are a more efficient policy means than are tariffs. It can then be argued that it would be more efficient to forget about tariff preferences and to concentrate on subsidies altogether if the problem is to promote infant industries.

The idea about tariff preferences also met with criticism and resistance at the first UNCTAD conference. One line of argument was that tariffs on most industrial goods were so low in the leading industrial countries that the scope for tariff preferences was limited.[3] The tariff rates seem to average between 10 and 15 per cent. If tariff preferences of 50 per cent were granted, the price of a less developed country over competitors from a developed country would be about 5 to 7 per cent. Such a small price advantage, it is argued, would not be decisive. If the less developed countries are unable to compete without a trade preference, they will not, under these circumstances, be able to compete with a preference.

This line of argument perhaps sounds plausible; it does, however, have some weaknesses. First, it must be stated that even though average tariff rates are not too high, tariffs on individual products could be substantially higher. Second, it is quite arbitrary to presume that tariff preferences would be limited to, for instance, 50 per cent. A complete preferential treatment of certain sensitive products could perhaps give much higher price advantages than 5 to 7 per cent.

A more important objection is that what really counts is not the final or manifest tariff rates but implicit rates or effective rates of protection. Here we must refer the reader to the discussion at the end of Chapter 15. Fairly low final rates could conceal much higher effective rates of protection. If that is the case, the question of tariff preferences, it is argued, would have to be viewed in a completely different perspective. Particularly if the import content of domestic production is high, and if there is a variety of tariff rates and many exemptions, protection may be much greater than the tariff rates indicate and may vary widely from industry to industry without any logical pattern.[4]

Most countries have a 'cascading' type of tariff structure – i.e. tariffs on raw materials are lower than tariffs on semi-manufactured goods, which in turn are lower than tariffs on final products. This usually means that the effective rates of protection on final goods are substantially higher than the nominal tariff rates.[5] On most consumer goods of export interest to less developed countries, the final tariff rates in the United States, Western Europe and Japan seem to be about 13 to 18 per cent, whereas the effective rates on the same goods seem to be almost double that figure, in the 20 to 30 per cent range.[6] This would indicate that there could conceivably be substantial scope for tariff preferences on these goods.

We have to bear in mind, however, the objections raised in Chapter 15 against the use of effective rates of protection. For several reasons raised there, the vagueness about what effective rates of protection are really supposed to protect, the disregard of substitution possibilities, etc., we must be quite sceptical in trying to assess the value and implications of the empirical evaluations of effective rates of protection. Pending further research, primarily of a theoretical nature, we must leave its relevancy for the question of trade preferences very much open. It has in no way been proved that taking effective rates of protection into account will pose the problem of tariff preferences in a new light.

In general, it can be said that the theory of tariff preferences is a branch of the theory of discriminatory tariff changes, as it has primarily been developed in the form of the theory of customs unions. This is a very complex branch of general-equilibrium analysis which has been developed since 1950, and the results of a more general nature which this branch of theory has, so far, arrived at are few and not very deep. The theory of customs unions will be surveyed in Chapter 20; the ambitious reader can then try to assess the validity and relevancy of those results for the question of tariff preferences. The immediate relevancy of the results of the theory of customs unions for the question of tariff preferences, however, is probably not too great.

Broadly speaking, it can be said that discriminatory tariff changes give rise to two types of effects: trade creation and trade diversion. Trade creation means that, because of the preference, low-cost goods from the preference-receiving country will outcompete high-cost goods produced at home. This effect is beneficial, as it will mean an increase in welfare. Trade diversion means that, because of the preference, goods from the preference-receiving country produced at relatively high cost will outcompete goods from a third country produced at lower cost, but which will now be at a disadvantage because they are being discriminated against. Trade diversion will generally lead to a lowering of welfare, as it results in a misallocation of resources in production.

The results of tariff preferences can therefore be said to depend on whether they cause trade creation or trade diversion. If the former, they are beneficial; if the latter, they will lead to a lowering of the world's welfare (and most likely also of the welfare of the trading partners).

Two examples of possible effects of tariff preferences could be useful. One is where the preference-receiving country produces only a small part of the preference-granting country's total imports of the goods in question. After it has been granted the preference, the less developed country can increase its price of this export from the world market price up to the tariff-included price in the prefer-ence-granting country. This means that the producers in the less developed country will get a windfall gain. If they can expand production at not too steeply rising costs, it would possibly yield a handsome profit, which they can reinvest for further expansion, and so on. If they can acquire factors of production, for in-stance labor, at only substantially increasing costs, their profits would perhaps not increase much but, in the long run, the country would get a substantial in-crease in its volume of trained labor, and so on. In this event, the tariff-granting country would gain nothing; all the gain would go to the preference-receiving country.

An example at the other extreme is that where the tariff-receiving country is the dominant world producer of the goods in question. Then, no matter what happens in the tariff-granting country, the tariff-receiving country will have to go on selling the product at the world market price. This means that producers in the tariff-receiving country will take over the whole market in the tariff-grant-ing country, but this will in all likelihood be only of marginal concern to them, and they stand to gain little. Here the gain is concentrated to the tariff-granting country, which will benefit in two ways: first, because the consumers can buy the goods in question more cheaply; second, because the country will get the goods at a lower opportunity cost by importing it than by producing it at home. Both these effects are of a trade-creating nature.

These are two examples of how the theory of discriminatory tariff changes can be applied to throw some light on the effects of tariff preferences. Generally speaking, we might say that the former types of effects, which are primarily ben-eficial to preference-receiving countries, would probably prevail, as in most cases the less developed countries would not be large producers of the goods in question. A policy inference to be drawn from this is that there would be no great point in granting preferences for primary goods and raw materials in which the less deve-loped countries already have a dominant share of world trade.

From a strictly economic point of view, it is difficult to argue either firmly against or firmly for trade preferences. The question is also sensitive when viewed from a political angle. Some countries tend to view the problem from a primarily protectionist point of view. They do not see anything unnatural in discriminat-ing against foreigners, and some countries could be regarded as more foreign than others. This means that they can use tariff preferences to discriminate against these countries while tying other countries closer to their own sphere of influence by granting them tariff preferences.

Other countries could view the problem from what can be predominantly termed a 'free-trade angle'. They could argue that a discriminatory policy would, during a certain period, be used as an instrument for achieving freer trade. But tariff preferences should then be used in as little a discriminatory fashion as poss-ible. Especially poor or weak countries could be given extra preferential treat-ment, but otherwise preferences should be granted equally to all underdeveloped countries and should encompass broad commodity groups in which the less de-veloped countries could be expected to develop a comparative advantage.

The proposal for a Generalized System of Preferences (G.S.P.) which emerged from the first UNCTAD conference in 1964 was based on the principle that less developed countries required preferential tariff treatment without reciprocation on their part rather than substantial most-favored-nation (M.F.N.) tariff cuts. Although the latter did not discriminate between the same products exported from different sources, the exports of industrial goods from less developed countries faced higher tariffs, on average, than those exported by developed countries. The G.S.P. was also intended to counter the preferential arrangements of the type established between the E.E.C. and non-member European countries as well as a number of less developed countries under the Lomé convention (see Chapter 17).

The G.S.P. system was negotiated at length over the period 1964 – 71, with the first scheme being implemented by the E.E.C. in 1971, followed closely by Japan. The U.S. scheme did not come into operation until January 1976. These schemes generally provide duty-free entry for most manufactured and semi-manufactured products from a large number of developing countries. However, there are important limitations.

With regard to product coverage, G.S.P. tariff treatment does not extend to agricultural and fishery products. Textile products are excluded outright by the United States and Japan, while the E.E.C. only offers preferential tariff treatment to countries that abide by 'voluntary export restraints'. There are, in addition, limits on the value of imports that can receive G.S.P. tariff treatment and an initial time limit on the scheme of ten years, insufficient for many developing countries to establish a comparative advantage in a particular line of production.

The various limits on the eligibility of products for G.S.P. treatment clearly restrict its potential benefits. Using 1971 trade flows, Baldwin and Murray have concluded that developing countries stand to gain more from M.F.N. tariff cuts than they would lose from the simultaneous erosion of their G.S.P. preferential tariff margins.[7] Another study has concluded that as long as processed agricultural goods and some resource-based traditional manufactures important to the poorer less developed countries, are excluded or subject to restricted access, the G.S.P. will have a limited effect in encouraging exports from such sources.[8]

The G.S.P. schemes (in 1980) provide a limited benefit to many of the more advanced developing countries and no benefit to others.[9] However the absence of discrimination among the less developed countries was introduced explicitly into the G.S.P., it is likely that significant improvements could be made. Generally, these countries are not affected by the value limitations on G.S.P. trade and they would benefit particularly from a relaxation in the area of agricultural and fishery products.

Ultimately the strongest argument for tariff preferences will perhaps have to be of a very pragmatic nature. The need for an increase in the rate of economic development in most of the less developed countries becomes more pressing each year. It is obviously very difficult to find and implement any policy means that fosters development. Against this background it is natural to see if tariff preferences could not be an efficient means for accelerating development. This could in the end be the strongest reason for trying to work out a scheme for tariff preferences that would prove viable.

STABILIZATION OF INTERNATIONAL COMMODITY PRICES

The other big problem with which UNCTAD has been concerned is that of stabilization of international commodity prices. Exports of primary products are by far the most important source of earnings of foreign exchange for most less developed countries, accounting for 85 to 90 per cent of their export earnings. But prices on primary products fluctuate widely. This leads to instability in export earnings. The instability gives rise to many problems, including difficulties in planning development, and hampers the development process seriously. If commodity prices could be stabilized, an important obstacle to development could be eliminated. Hence the stabilization of commodity prices must be given high priority. This is the argument.

Here the ground is slippery and we must tread carefully. It is otherwise easy to perpetuate old dogmas and go on mechanically repeating old half-truths. The traditional view just paraphrased sounds convincing, but we must examine it more carefully. First, we might observe that it is not quite clear what is to be stabilized. Stabilizing prices is not the same thing as stabilizing earnings, and stabilizing export earnings is not necessarily the same thing as stabilizing real income.

As we have mentioned already, it has been argued, by Prebisch amongst others, that there ought to be a long-term stabilization of the terms of trade between less developed country primary exports and their principal industrial imports.

This argument, however, is primarily an act of wishful thinking and can claim no foundation in rational economic reasoning. We know from earlier reasoning, especially from our study of economic growth and trade in Part II, that international prices must be viewed as endogenous variables in an economic system. Variations in the terms of trade depend in a complex way on changes in production and consumption and on other basic economic variables. An aspiration to control the long-term development of the terms of trade is the same as an aspiration to control all variables in the economic system. To be effective, it would imply perfect economic planning on a world-wide scale. It is difficult to see how anyone who has grasped the core of the problem could support schemes of such a utopian nature.

To claim that a certain amount of primary products should have a stable purchasing power over industrial products in the long run is about as unrealistic a claim as that of stabilizing terms of trade. There is no reason whatsoever to expect such a development to take place, nor is there anything specifically 'just' about it. It is impossible to understand why one should try to keep stable, in the long run, a certain relation between volumes and relative prices given at an arbitrary historical moment.

We then come to more reasonable views about what to stabilize. One view is that we should try to stabilize prices on some well-defined primary products. Another is to try to stabilize export earnings of the less developed countries. These two proposals do not amount to the same thing. Stabilization of prices will not lead to a stabilization of export earnings if the supply changes. This is an important point to bear in mind, as output changes seem to be a prime cause of fluctuations in export earnings. Another point worth making is that a stabilization of money proceeds or money incomes is not the same as a stabilization of real incomes if the general price level changes.

We can take a more reasonable proposal to be that commodity prices should be stabilized in order to stabilize export earnings. This demand for stabilizing prices derives from the proposition that unstable prices cause difficulties for development policies and for plans to manage the domestic economy in a successful way.

Instability *per se* need not, however, have such disastrous consequences. In principle, the governments in these countries should be able to plan around trend values for prices and incomes and help to overcome the difficulties of lean years by building up reserves during fat years. Governments of less developed countries could for several reasons experience difficulties in doing this. Then a demand for price stabilization could be viewed as a demand from weak governments to stronger governments to help solve problems that should primarily concern only the weak governments.

It could perhaps be argued that the governments of less developed countries are afflicted with especially difficult problems in this regard. The reasons usually given for this is that supply and demand vary greatly for individual primary products, that supply and demand elasticities are low, that the exports of the less developed countries are specialized to a few products, and that, on the marketing side, they have to rely on market conditions in a few industrial countries.

These factors could potentially cause fluctuations in prices. In reality, prices on primary products do not seem to have been particularly unstable. The thought of instability has been one of the most cherished beliefs of development economics. This belief does not seem to be borne out by the facts.

In 1966 British economist, Alisdair MacBean, published a major econometric investigation on fluctuations in prices of primary products.[10] When MacBean started his investigation, he thought that the prevailing views were correct. He merely wanted to study what policy means could be used to dampen the fluctuations in export proceeds and to see how their adverse effects on the growth process could be eliminated.

But soon he started to question the basic facts. His findings can be briefly summarized as follows. Less developed countries have only insignificantly greater fluctuations in their export incomes than industrial countries. Three causes that could have been expected to result in instability – commodity concentration of exports, proportion of primary goods in total exports, and geographical concentration of exports – all have little value in explaining the fluctuations that have taken place. One extremely important finding is also that it is not fluctuating prices that have primarily caused the fluctuations in export incomes. The prime causes are on the supply side. MacBean chose twelve of the less developed countries that had had especially large fluctuations in their export incomes: Argentina, Bolivia, Ghana, Haiti, Indonesia, Iran, Iraq, Korea, Malaya, Pakistan, Sudan and Vietnam. In four of these, Malaya, Indonesia, to a certain extent Pakistan, and Vietnam, price fluctuations have had an important bearing on the fluctuations in export income. But in the others, and also to a large extent in the four countries, the primary cause of fluctuations in export proceeds is the fluctuation in output produced. The main difficulty of the less developed countries in producing primary products lies in controlling supply. It is the variations in output produced that is the prime cause of fluctuations in export incomes.[11] Part of the cause of supply changes among the twelve countries referred to also lies in political disturbances, but this does not change the main picture.

Another of MacBean's findings worthy of note is that the changes in export incomes that have taken place have not led to such adverse effects for the growth of the economies as could have been expected. Built-in stabilizers and high marginal propensities to import seem to offset fluctuations to a large extent. Therefore, fluctuations in national incomes are not so large as could be expected.

Recent work on export instability has tended to confirm MacBean's findings. Erb and Schiavo-Campo found that between 1946 and 1958, the MacBean period, and 1954 and 1966, there was an important decline in export instability both in less developed and rich countries, but in the latter more than the former.[12] Kenen and Voivodas used various methods of measuring export instability for a wide range of countries, and produced results which were in broad agreement with those of MacBean.[13] Their results do, however, seem more sensitive to the choice of time period, since, in contrast to MacBean, they found a significant negative correlation between exports and the level of investment during the 1960s.

Empirical and theoretical considerations thus lead to the scope for stabilization schemes being more limited than at first sight seems likely. Much care must be taken in defining the objective of a stabilization scheme and in studying what the causes of instability could be. If the cause is irregularity of supply, a stabilization of prices will usually aggravate instability by holding prices down when supply is short and by keeping prices up when supplies are plentiful. Stabilization schemes are usually costly to carry out. Therefore, it could be asked whether or not other means, such as provision of money reserves or borrowing facilities, could be more efficient in dealing with the problems that instability gives rise to.

The operation of international commodity agreements has been particularly difficult since 1970 due to the frequent and unpredictable movements that have taken place in international currencies. When the relative values of national currencies are constantly changing, it becomes difficult to determine the world price for the commodity in question. It would appear that the International Tin Agreement, which began in 1956 is the only one to have survived the period 1971-4 intact, and this is probably a reflection of the supply and demand conditions rather than the terms of the agreement. Demand for the metal has been strong, supply short and there is no readily available substitute. The Tin Agreement has probably contributed to smoothing out some short-term price fluctuations but has had little effect on the long-term trend, which has been consistently upwards. The International Coffee Agreement first established in 1963 has encountered serious difficulties throughout its entire existence and broke down in 1972, following a refusal by consumer countries to compensate producers for the devaluation of the U.S. dollar. In addition to the conflict between producer and consumer interests there have also been conflicts between the producers themselves, particularly between the Latin American producers and the small-scale African robusta coffee producers. The latter have little or no influence on world prices and have continually pushed for larger export quotas. However, the Brazilian crop failure of 1974-5 (and the resultant dramatic rise in world coffee prices) has reduced producer opposition to the agreement, and a new coffee agreement came into operation in October 1976. However the difference of interest within the agreement still remains.

The International Cocoa Agreement which was signed in 1973 never became operative since the threefold rise in world cocoa prices between 1972 and 1974, owing to shortages and speculation, raised the price of cocoa above its agreed ceiling. A new agreement was drawn up in October 1976, but the United States again refused to join and there was disagreement among members on the level of the ceiling price. Finally, the Wheat Agreement has been of little importance because of the dominant role played by the two main producers, the United States and Canada, while the Sugar Agreement was abandoned in 1973 having only covered 50 per cent of international trade in the commodity.

It is not surprising, against the theoretical and practical difficulties that commodity agreements entail, that they have been in little use. Instances could arise, however in which they would serve a useful purpose. Some of the theoretical considerations that will probably have to be taken into account when constructing stabilization schemes will now be discussed.

There are several types of stabilization schemes that can be constructed. One is the use of *buffer stocks*. The operators of the scheme own a stock, either of money or of a commodity. They use this stock to mitigate fluctuations in prices by selling from the stock when prices are high and buying the commodity when prices are low.

This scheme is only possible for certain products with low storage costs. There is always a cost involved in the form of interest on the capital invested in the stock. If additional costs, such as costs for warehousing space, refrigeration, and pesticides, are high, a buffer-stock scheme is obviously impracticable. The main difficulty with a buffer-stock scheme (as with stabilization schemes in general) is in foreseeing the long-term equilibrium price. If the operators are too optimistic about prices (or pressed into being too optimistic by producer interests), they will try to maintain too high a price, and the stocks will keep growing. This cannot go on indefinitely; eventually the stocks will have to be disposed of at a loss. If the price should be set too low, which is more unlikely, the stocks will instead be sold out and the price can only be kept down for a limited time. Buffer-stock schemes can only be used to mitigate short-term price fluctuations; they cannot be used to offset the damaging effects of trends in prices.

Another type of stabilization scheme is a *restriction scheme*. This means that less developed countries agree to restrict production or exports of the commodity in question in order to maintain its price. Restriction schemes can be useful, especially if competition among producers is keen and demand inelastic. Then the price might be driven down very low if nothing is done. Under these circumstances, prices can be maintained and the total revenue increased by a restriction of exports.

Restriction schemes, however, have certain drawbacks. One is that they are usually difficult to enforce for any long period. There is always a temptation for a single producer to break away from the scheme, thereby being able to sell a larger quantity at a good price. Tendencies to overproduction, which usually follow from the price-maintenance policy, can easily cause a breakdown of the system.

If the price is maintained at a high level for some time, this can also create difficulties on the demand side. The demand elasticity could be low in the short term, but it could be substantially higher in the long run. A policy of high prices could then mean that demand for the product will not expand as much as it otherwise would. It could also lead to the development of competing products, for instance of a synthetic kind, that can prove very damaging in the long run. What has happened to rubber is an illustration of this danger.

Restriction schemes, moreover, easily give rise to a misallocation of resources.

They tend to conserve a given production structure both among and within countries, and established but inefficient producers will prevail over new and more efficient ones. Restriction schemes could be useful to alleviate short-term problems, but they are rarely efficient in the long run. They build on an intrinsic conservatism and will probably eventually prove detrimental to economic growth.

Other schemes could be more useful. An interesting multilateral price-compensation scheme was proposed at the 1964 UNCTAD conference by James Meade.[14] Let us assume, says Meade, that there are two countries, Ruritania and Urbania, and that Ruritania exports a primary product, Commod, which Urbania imports. The two countries now agree on a 'normal' volume traded and a 'standard' price. The countries then devise a sliding scale whereby if the price falls below the 'standard' price, Urbania pays Ruritania a compensation which equals the short-fall of the 'standard' price on the 'normal' amount traded. Conversely, Ruritania pays Urbania an amount equal to an excess over the 'standard' price times the 'normal' volume if the price is above its normal level.

The main idea behind the Meade proposal is to try to separate the distributional effects of the price mechanism from its allocative effects. When the price of a product falls, this is a signal to producers to produce less and to consumers to consume more. This is the efficiency aspect or allocative aspect of the price mechanism, and this we usually do not want to interfere with. But price changes also have distributional implications. When the price falls. producers get hurt, because their incomes fall. So do workers in the less developed country; the tax base of the government shrinks; and so on. This can, at least partially, be avoided by a scheme *à la* Meade. It is most natural to think of the scheme as one between governments. If the price falls and the producers in Ruritania get lower incomes, the consumers in Urbania will benefit by lower prices. But they will now have to pay more in taxes, and this increase in taxes will be transferred to the government in Ruritania. The government there can then dispose of this income as it sees fit. It can directly subsidize producers of Commod, or it can invest the money for development purposes.

So far the scheme has been sketched on a bilateral basis. But it can easily be extended to a multilateral basis. Then a 'normal' volume of imports is designated for each importing country and a 'normal' volume of exports for each exporting country. A 'standard' price has to be agreed upon. Then if the actual price differs from the 'standard' price, the respective countries will have to pay and receive compensation according to 'normal' volumes.

A difficulty with this scheme, as with others, is that of forecasting the price correctly. If the price is set too high, the scheme amounts to a transfer of resources from the industrial to the primary-producing countries, and vice versa when the price is set too low. One could think of an arrangement whereby initially the price was set too high, but then would be gradually lowered. Then the compensation scheme would also entail an aid arrangement which would help the primary-producing countries to develop other sectors during a transitory period.

The Meade scheme is both simple and elegant, but it has certain drawbacks. An important one is connected with its aggregated nature. If a producer is small and a change in his output does not affect the world price of the goods, it could well be that even though the output of this producer is very low one year, prices would not exceed the 'standard' price. The country would then get no compensation, even though its export proceeds fall considerably. A scheme such as Meade's has difficulties in dealing with fluctuations caused by changes in the supply of single countries. This is a serious deficiency, as we have seen that the primary cause of fluctuations in export earnings seems to be difficulties in controlling supply conditions in the primary-producing countries themselves.

CONCLUDING REMARKS

So far the result of our discussion has tended to be on the negative side. It seems that the trend in the thinking among experts is away from commodity agreements. The theoretical and practical difficulties that they entail seem to be so great that the costs of implementing them would be greater than the eventual benefits.

Another possibility is compensatory financing of fluctuations in export earnings. Such schemes can be of two kinds. They can either be straightforward insurance schemes designed to stabilize a country's earnings over time without altering its total receipts, or they can, on top of the insurance part, also involve a transfer of real resources from the developed to the less developed countries.

The most important scheme so far is that devised by the International Monetary Fund. This is a scheme to help less developed countries whose export earnings decline to get easier loans than usual. It permits a country experiencing a decline in its export earnings below a certain moving average due to circumstances outside its control to draw up to 50 per cent of its I.M.F. quota, subject to the approval of the Fund. However, it may not draw more than 25 per cent in any twelve-month period.

This facility was welcomed by less developed countries since it was the only export stabilization measure which attempted to stabilize total export earnings. However, it is also subject to certain drawbacks from the point of view of less developed countries. First, the Fund tends to impose more stringent conditions on borrowers that have also made compensatory drawings. Second, it requires that the country's general economic policies are open to their appraisal. Finally, the actual amount of credit available remains very limited – at 1973 levels, it would have covered a mere 2½ per cent fall in less developed country total merchandise export earnings.[15]

In addition to the facility for compensatory finance, the I.M.F. established a facility for buffer-stock financing in 1969. This permitted less developed countries to draw up to 50 per cent of their quota to finance purchases of commodity buffer stocks. If the borrowing country is also drawing compensatory finance, her total borrowings cannot, however, exceed 75 per cent of her quota.

A further stabilization scheme of a preferential kind was introduced by the E.E.C. under the Lomé convention signed in 1975. It involves an export revenue stabilization scheme, known as STABEX, which aims to compensate the forty-six Lomé convention countries in Africa, the Caribbean and the Pacific for shortfalls in their export earnings in any one year compared with the average value for the preceding four years. However, the funds provided by the Community may be insufficient ($400 million over five years), particularly if prices and revenue fall markedly from their reference average levels.

Any scheme of compensatory financing will probably prove unsatisfactory from the point of view of the less developed countries. This depends on fluctuations not being their main problem, which instead is lack of resources. To get some degree of approval, a scheme of compensatory financing has to have some element of aid in it. But to tie aid to fluctuations in export earnings could easily be arbitrary and create a weakness in this type of scheme. Countries that strive successfully to control supply conditions could get the smallest amount of aid. Under such circumstances, resources could easily be transferred to countries where they are least efficiently used.

It was as a response to the limited value of individual commodity agreements and schemes of compensatory finance that the less developed countries presented their 'integrated programme for commodities' at the fourth UNCTAD conference held in Nairobi. In broad outline, the programme proposes that buffer stocks of ten key commodities be established to be financed internationally from a common fund with floor and ceiling price levels. The fund would be created partly by borrowing and partly by contributions from the participating states. The indexation of prices to compensate for the deterioration in commodity producers' terms of trade was also put forward as a key element in the programme. In return, developed countries would be ensured a stable long-run source of supply of these commodities.

In addition to the problems of the political acceptability of the proposals which dominated the discussion at Nairobi, there are a number of practical difficulties which call the scheme into question. First, not all commodities are amenable to stockbuilding. The beverage commodities, tea, coffee and cocoa, would come under this heading. Second, both the demand prospects and the extent to which the less developed countries are dominant suppliers vary markedly from commodity to commodity. Third, the existence of commodity stock-piles may in the long run tend to depress rather than raise prices. The latter would require a deliberate policy of supply restriction, and this may be very difficult to supervise on an international basis and be continually subject to internal disagreement over quotas (e.g. the International Coffee Agreement) and to problems of creating alternative employment opportunities.

The most efficient type of trade policy that the developed countries can for the time being pursue is probably to extend protectionist preferences to less developed countries. As we have seen, this has been the objective of the G.S.P. system. Although so far it has only had a limited effect, it retains an important potential particularly if the rules on product coverage can be liberalized. A study of quantitative restrictions applied by developed countries has found that 62 per cent of all restrictions fall on agricultural processed products which are of particular importance to the poorer less developed countries.[16]

None of the policies sketched above is ideal. For a believer in international competition and division of labor, they have obvious shortcomings. A policy of manipulating prices by tariffs leads to featherbedding for producers in both developed and less developed countries. Under the guise of a working price system, competition is eliminated or greatly restricted, and consumers are exploited by the use of monopolistic practices. A policy of quota arrangements will, in all probability, lead to a control of markets and the conservation of inefficient production structures. Prices will also be kept artificially high and consumption be curtailed. Still, in a world of protectionist practices, measures like these are perhaps the only practicable ones.

Our discussion has not given too much reason for hope. There are perhaps some gains to be derived for the less developed countries from a revision of trade policy in the developed countries. These gains, however, seem to be limited. In the immediate future, export earnings of the less developed countries will have to come primarily from exports of primary products. A revision of trade policies, especially of agricultural policies in the developed countries, should be of help to the less developed countries, but this help will be limited. Many less developed countries will have to try to get their industrialization under way. Tariff preferences could help in this respect, but how efficient they would prove is an open question. A certain scepticism is probably not unwarranted.

Trade policies are not unimportant, but they will have only marginal effects unless supplemented by other means. What is needed is the application of scientific methods in agriculture that can lead to control of supply conditions and give the less developed countries a firm and reliable export base in products in which they have a natural comparative advantage. Furthermore, industries will have to be built and managed rationally. Whether this can be done within the existing structure of society is an open question. Large vistas open up in which trade policy is only a detail. It is with the large vista offered by the new demands of the developing countries for the establishment of a 'New International Economic Order' that we will now be concerned.

SELECTED BIBLIOGRAPHY: CHAPTER 18

For the general development of UNCTAD, especially the political and institutional aspects, see:

D. Cordovez, *UNCTAD and Development Diplomacy from Confrontation to Strategy*, (a special publication of *Journal of World Trade Law*, 1972).

B. Gosović, *UNCTAD, Conflict and Compromise*, Leiden, Sythoff, 1972.

See also:

Brookings Institution, *Trade in Primary Commodities: Conflict or Cooperation?*, Washington, 1974.

For an analysis of trade-policy questions in connection with less developed countries, see:

G. K. Helleiner, *International Trade and Economic Development*, London, Penguin Books, 1972.

C. F. Diaz-Alejandro, 'Trade Policies and Economic Development' in P. B. Kenen (ed.), *International Trade and Finance*, Cambridge University Press, 1975.

H. G. Johnson, *Economic Policies Toward Less Developed Countries*, Washington, D.C., Brookings Institution, 1967.

For discussions of commodity arrangements see:

J. W. F. Rowe, *Primary Commodities in International Trade*, Cambridge, 1965.

A. I. MacBean, *Export Instability and Economic Development,* London, Allen & Unwin, 1966.

C. P. Braun, *Primary Commodity Control,* Kuala Lumpur, 1975.

For tariff preferences see:

H. B. Lary, *Imports of Manufactures from Less Developed Countries*, New York, National Bureau of Economic Reasearch, 1968.

S. Weintraub, *Trade Preferences for Less-Developed Countries*, New York, Praeger, 1967.

UNCTAD, *Review of the Schemes of Generalized Preferences*, TD/B/C, 5/9, 1973, and TD/B/C, 5/22, 1974.

19
A new economic world order?

A 'new economic world order' has become one of the catch-phrases of the 1970s. A demand for a new international economic order has been raised with increasing eagerness in the United Nations and by other international bodies. The demands were first formulated at extraordinary sessions of the U.N. General Assembly in 1974 and 1975. They have since been echoed in many corners of the world. Some would view the resolutions passed in the United Nations expressing the desire for a new order as primarily politically oriented. A large number of poor countries which together have a voting majority in the U.N. General Assembly have sought to convert their claims into economic rights. Important developed countries, primarily the United States, have not seen fit to give support to some of the most important of these claims.

Some would argue that the claims and desires of the less developed countries are not new, and are impossible to meet in the foreseeable future. They would regard the rhetoric surrounding the claims for a new economic world order as mere verbiage. Others would say that the struggle to achieve a new world order is one of the important issues of the 1970s that will shape the destiny of mankind in years to come. Proponents of the different theses may also disagree as to what exactly should be meant by a new international economic order.

It may now be opportune to deal with the issues surrounding a new world order. One reason for this is that parts of our earlier analysis logically pave the way for the issues that are at the heart of the quest for a new international economic order. Another reason is that a discussion of these issues naturally brings in broader political questions. The present book is primarily concerned with economics. Still, it can be useful at some point to confront the scientific analysis of more precise, narrow problems with a larger policy framework.

LOPSIDED POVERTY

The countries that make up the Third World are very dissimilar. An important group are the oil-exporting countries (OPEC). The exports of OPEC have been extremely profitable in recent years, especially since the increase in oil prices which occurred in 1973 (see Chapter 30). Even among these countries differences are marked. There are, on the one hand, two large countries, Nigeria and Indonesia, where the overwhelming majority of the population is very poor. At the other end of the scale are Saudi Arabia, Libya and the emirates of the Persian Gulf with large production of oil, small populations, and high *per capita* incomes. Somewhere in the middle are Algeria, Iran and Venezuela, with populations of a fair size among whom the oil revenues have to be shared. These countries are expanding their industries rapidly and incomes are growing. Another group is made up of those countries which have concentrated successfully on pushing their exports

TABLE 19.1

Growth of G.N.P. of four poor countries

Country	Population (million in 1973)	G.N.P. *per capita* in 1973 at 1972 prices (U.S. dollars)	Average annual growth rate of *per capita* income	
			1967–70	1970–3
Afghanistan	18	89	0.8	−1.2
Bangladesh	76	75	−0.8	−0.9
Ethiopia	27	85	1.2	−1.0
Nepal	12	84	0.3	−1.0

SOURCE: UNCTAD, *Handbook of International Trade and Development Statistics*, New York, United Nations, 1976, TD/B/AC.17, addendum 1, Table 1.

(dealt with in Chapter 16). Among these countries are South Korea, Hong Kong, Singapore, Taiwan, Brazil and Mexico.

Another group includes the exporters of raw materials, be it minerals or agricultural products: countries such as Chile, Jamaica, Zambia, Colombia, Ghana and Sri Lanka.

Yet another group among the less developed countries consists of the three large countries in South Asia: Bangladesh, India and Pakistan. These countries have large populations. Their economies are reasonably diversified, but the majority of the inhabitants are very poor.

The problem of poverty centers around the countries in the last two groups. A distinguishing feature is also that the income distribution in most less developed countries is very unequal. In forty less developed countries for which statistics are available, the 20 per cent of the population with the highest incomes receive 55 per cent of the G.N.P.; the lowest 20 per cent get only 5 per cent of G.N.P. The population of the less developed countries amount to two billion. Around 800 million of these people live in abject poverty: they have to subsist on an income of about $100 a year, or the equivalent of 30 U.S. cents a day.

For the great majority in the Third World prospects are bleak. The following reasoning might serve as an illustration. Take for concreteness the case of four countries, Afghanistan, Bangladesh, Ethiopia and Nepal, which together possess 56 per cent of the population in the countries which have been classified as the 'least developed countries'. Table 19.1 gives some information on their economic development in the late 1960s and early 1970s. The table shows that these countries have been stagnating, or even falling behind, in recent years. The international development strategy of the United Nations and its organizations has postulated a sustained growth rate of *per capita* income of 3.5 per cent per year. The poorest countries do not even come close to reaching this target. Furthermore, even if they did, would that solve their problems?

If this feat were to be accomplished, *per capita* incomes would double in approximately twenty years. However, around the year 2000, *per capita* incomes would still remain very meagre indeed. The rate of absolute income rise of the 'representative individual', an individual enjoying the *per capita* income of his or her nation, would be so slow as to be hardly perceptible. For example, the representative individual in Ethiopia would get roughly an additional 3 dollars in the first year over a base-year income of 85 dollars. This would mean an increase in monthly income of approximately 25 cents. In the eleventh year the rise in monthly income would be around 35 cents, and in the twentieth year 50 cents.

The example is based on the assumption that economic growth would take place in the very poor countries. We know that this might not be the case. For lower-income strata in vast areas of the globe the prospects look dim indeed. Much of development economics has relied on development coming about through a 'trickle-down effect'. The entrepreneurs in agriculture, industry and trade, and the political and bureaucratic elites, should be the prime-movers in the development process. Through their efforts at the top, the benefits of development should then trickle down to the masses below.

The trickle-down theory has hardly worked, at least not for the areas of the world where the large masses of the very poor live. It is natural that alternative formulas for development should be proposed. It is only to be expected that the deprivation and poverty which hundreds of millions of people have to suffer each day will arouse demands for a new economic world order.

It is doubtful whether the strategies suggested so far by proponents of a new international order have much to offer. Still, the prevalence of poverty for great masses of people and the absence of any economic progress in many areas certainly have been important factors behind the efforts to achieve a new international economic order.

THE ECONOMICS OF THE UNITED NATIONS

At its beginning in 1945 the United Nations was dominated by the major powers that had been victorious in the Second World War. The primary task of the organization was to safeguard world peace. Over the years U.N. activities have shifted over from political issues to social and economic ones. This is demonstrated by the fact that 80 per cent of the total operating budget of the United Nations is now spent on social and economic programmes.

The less developed countries now make up the majority of the nations in the United Nations. It is natural, therefore, that they will use the organization to promote their own interests. Many citizens in the advanced countries have been dismayed by the vehemence with which the representatives of the less developed countries have expressed their dissatisfaction with the existing order and pressured for reform. It has to be remembered, however, that the actual powers of the U.N. General Assembly are few. The resolutions of the Assembly carry no legal force. The General Assembly functions first and foremost as a pressure group. It is a forum where member states can express their views and where a majority of states can try to influence the behavior of others through moral suasion.

One reason for the new fighting spirit on the part of the less developed countries has to do with the prevalence of poverty and the slow progress taking place in many countries. Another source of inspiration has been the stunning success of

OPEC in raising oil prices. The OPEC story taught both developed and less developed countries several lessons.

One was that the OPEC members had engineered a vast improvement in their economic fortunes without any assistance or consent from their 'benefactors'. The trick had been done by the application of an embargo and the ruthless use of monopoly power. Another was that the OPEC venture drastically altered the perceptions of the Third World countries of their own economic prospects. Instead of hardship, savings and national sacrifice OPEC members had increased their economic fortunes through a simple act of redistribution of existing wealth (again, see Chapter 30). This way of achieving prosperity had distinct advantages over any traditional development strategy that had so far been advocated.

One aspect of the proposals for a new international economic order is also a desire to redistribute wealth from the industrial nations to the poor, less developed ones. There is a presumption on the part of the proponents of a new order that restitution or reparation is due on the part of the rich countries. Economics is viewed in terms of exploitation: what one man gains another man must lose. It is asserted that the wealth of the industrial countries has been built up at the expense of the less developed countries, many of which were once colonies. Implicit in this view is also the opinion that existing property rights are illegitimate. Therefore, they can be arbitrarily reassigned.

Behind the philosophy of a new world order is also the notion of a 'just price'. The idea about a just price crops up in various forms. A venerable conviction is the one about a long-term deterioration in the terms of trade for the producers of primary goods. A modern form of the argument is that raw-material prices ought to be indexed to some basket of industrial goods to keep their purchasing power stable in terms of those goods. All these proposals boil down to the assertion that prices, as viewed from the less developed countries, are unjust and that some form of retribution should be forthcoming.

The opinions referred to are not, however, acceptable to policy-makers in the developed countries. On the contrary, they reject the idea of a just price and maintain that prices are governed by basic economic conditions. Prices play an important role for the allocation of economic resources. They also have important implications for the distribution of incomes and wealth but it is not appropriate to view prices primarily in terms of moral notions like justice. Likewise, the critics of the new order argue that economics is not only a question of redistribution. They try to contain their adversaries by using the argument that secure property rights serve an important economic function. They maintain that the role of property rights, prices and markets are poorly understood by the advocates of a new international economic order. Progress can only be achieved if the proper emphasis is given to sound economic means for achieving development. The industrial countries have become rich through work, abstinence and innovations, they maintain. Their wealth does not rest on exploitation.

The conflict is certainly there for all to see. We now must proceed by giving a more detailed treatment to some of the issues that the efforts to establish a new economic world order are built around.

The resolutions of the U.N. General Assembly are centered around five themes: industrialization, trade policy, financial resources, science and technology, and food and agriculture.

The industrialization of the developing countries is considered by the General Assembly to be the foremost goal in a 'new economic order'. Cooperation in the field of industrial development between the developed countries and the less developed countries, especially when it comes to encouraging export industries and industries for the elaboration and refinement of the developing countries' own primary products, should be reinforced. Those industries which, when located in developed countries, are run below a satisfactory level of profitability should be transferred to less developed countries (L.D.C.s). Developed countries should also, in accordance with the terms set by the poorer countries, induce their own firms to participate in investment projects which are within the framework of the L.D.C.s' plans and development programmes.

The main wish, as far as trade policy is concerned, is one of expanding and diversifying the trade of developing countries, especially that portion which includes manufactured and semi-manufactured goods. At the same time, however, the export of primary products from L.D.C.s is to be bolstered by building up stocks of these goods in sufficient quantities to give rise to stable or increasing export prices. As an additional guarantee, the introduction of a system of compensatory financing is urged, to cover those cases where fluctuations in export prices are unusually troublesome. Another means of surmounting the inherent problems behind the export of primary products is held to be that of increasing the degree of manufacturing of L.D.C.s' export products. At the root of all the above demands is a desire to protect the purchasing power of the developing countries. It is a matter of rectifying what are considered to be the defects of the market system by increasing the developing countries' share in the transport, marketing and distribution of their products. The developed countries must, on their part, maintain their levels of import of the L.D.C.s' products, eliminate the remaining non-tariff trade barriers which impede there imports, and concede more favorable terms for the products of developing countries on their domestic markets.

In the area of finance, an increase is sought in the transfer of financial assets from privileged to less privileged countries. The flow of aid must be made uniform, untied, and guaranteed. The developed countries should do their utmost to reach a level of foreign aid corresponding to 0.7 per cent of their respective G.N.P.s. The assets of international financial institutions (the World Bank groups and those associated to the United Nations) must be augmented and supplemented by the establishment of a new international investment agency, and by the transfer of private capital. At the same time, developing countries should be given easier access to the capital markets of the developed countires. Furthermore, a method of decreasing the L.D.C.s' burden of debt should be sought, along with the proposed increases in foreign-aid flows. The General Assembly emphasized the need for a reform of the international monetary system, relating the question of international liquidity to that of increased aid to L.D.C.s. Another issue of central importance is said to be the enhancement of the developing countries' influence in the institutions of international finance and development.

In order to remedy the scientific and technological lag of the L.D.C.s, the new world order prescribes cooperation between L.D.C.s and the developed countries for the strengthening of the technical and scientific infrastructure in the developing countries. The Assembly recommends that foundations be laid for an information bank of industrial technology, while developed countries are generally expected to support the L.D.C.s' programmes for technical and scientific development. The advanced countries are also obliged to intensify that part of their research which is of direct interest to L.D.C.s. Information on technologies which correspond to the needs of L.D.C.s should be made more easily available to these countries. Finally, it is pointed out that the emigration of the educated labor force from developing countries should be curtailed.

Lastly, the new world order aims to bring about an increase in the food production of the L.D.C.s, but in order to realize this goal certain modifications of the present pattern of world production must be made. Flows of aid to agriculture and to food production in L.D.C.s must be augmented. Access must be yielded to the protected markets of the developed countries. Furthermore, L.D.C.s must be guaranteed an even flow of fertilizers and other factors of production at reasonable prices. Research in the field of agriculture should be stepped up, and finally, on the question of aid to food production, the 'gift' portion of these aid funds must increase, and the major part of this aid should be managed multilaterally.

AIMS AND MEANS OF DEVELOPMENT POLICY

The new economic world order is primarily a set of aims or desires. One of its definite weaknesses is that the proposals it puts forth do not contain any discussion of which means should be used to reach the targets. This is expecially regrettable since a discussion of aims and means is absolutely fundamental for shaping economic policies in any efficient manner. Analysis of aims and means has been most forcefully pursued in connection with short-run stabilization policy. We will return to this topic in Chapter 28, where a systematic treatment of aims – means analysis is made in connection with stabilization policies for external and internal balance. A mere statement of goals is not enough. If it is not possible to design policy means whereby the aims can be reached, the goals will usually have to be relegated to the status of utopias.

A good rule of thumb for all forms of economic policy is that the policy-maker has to have as many means at his disposal as he has aims. It is rare that one can reach more than one aim with only one means. If policy means are not sufficient, it follows that one or more of the targets must be sacrificed. The situation may be complicated by the contradictions inherent in certain aims, or by the fact that targets can only be reached partially, due to the coexistence of other aims. What has been said might seem trivial. These are, however, trivialities with a very real economic significance. As the following analysis will demonstrate, aims have often been contradictory, and targets have been set for which no policy means are available. Sometimes the aims are so vague that it is hardly possible even in theory to design the policy means whereby they could be reached.

It is now opportune to look more closely into some of the specific issues of the new international economic order. We can be brief on several of these points, as the preceding chapters have already dealt with some of the important issues on which the proposals for a new order focus.

INDUSTRIALIZATION AND TRADE POLICY

A common target for most L.D.C.s is to increase exports. They also want to diversify exports and to increase the degree of processing in their export products. At the same time, we have to remember that three-quarters of the exports coming from the L.D.C.s consist of primary products; for many countries exports of a single commodity make up the bulk of total export earnings.

For many countries there is a conflict between the efforts to push exports and another objective: that of protecting domestic markets. Many L.D.C.s have tried to promote industrialization through import-substitution. Chapter 16 demonstrated some of the difficulties which such a policy could give rise to. Import-substitution has often fostered firms that are not competitive on international markets. High profits have been attained at low capacity utilization and the incentives for lowering costs have been weak or completely absent. Protectionist policies have discriminated against traditional exports. Producers have shifted production over to the protected, domestic market. The situation has often been complicated by the fact that the exchange rate has been overvalued and that quantitative restrictions have had to be applied to guard exchange reserves. Forty years of experience indicate that it is hardly possible to protect simultaneously the domestic market, create new export products which are internationally competitive and increase traditional exports. This is an area where the aims easily become contradictory.

Another important problem in connection with industrialization concerns the multinational firms. The L.D.C.s' attitudes toward foreign direct investments differ greatly. Some governments are directly hostile, while others show cordiality and grant preferential treatment to multinational corporations. However, it is often felt that the objectives of the large international firms and national governments are conflicting. The new international order also points out that a regulation of the activities of the multinational firms (M.N.F.s) should take place. Again, things are not as simple as they may seem at first sight. All that an L.D.C. can do on its own is simply forbid an M.N.F. to establish itself in the country. However, the country may thereby have to abstain from the advantages of having a certain type of industry. Once M.N.F.s are settled in a country the problems become more complicated. These firms undoubtedly have great possibilities of counteracting official measures, for instance by manipulating internal pricing to avoid taxes. This is a genuine problem which will be dealt with more extensively in Chapter 21. One possibility here is to try to make a fair evaluation of the property of the M.N.F.s.

M.N.F.s run the risk of becoming nationalized. If that happens, they naturally want a fair compensation for the assets that are being nationalized. This makes for a high evaluation on the part of the M.N.F.s. At the same time, they usually want to avoid paying taxes. Taxes on profits are hardly satisfactory from the host country's point of view, as profits can easily be manipulated. Instead, taxes could be paid on the value of the assets located in the country. In this case it is in the interest of the host country to get a high evaluation of the assets. Thus if assets are evaluated for tax purposes, at the same time as the prospects of an eventual nationalization are kept in mind, a 'fair value' might be set at a level that is acceptable to both parties. If an international system along these lines were enforced, it could decrease the mutual suspicions on the part of both investors and host countries that otherwise easily arise.

The treatment of multinationals again illustrates the problems of aims and means. There is little sense in simply expressing a wish that the M.N.F. should be controlled. One also has to find efficient means of enforcing such control. The multinational firms are often transmitters of advanced technologies that can be useful to L.D.C.s. They also can offer contributions to the host countries' stock of capital (provided investments are not completely financed by savings from the L.D.C.s themselves). The need for control is, however, certainly present. The problem is, how can means be designed to enforce such controls without unduly hampering incentives?

Other goals of trade policy are the stabilization of prices of raw materials and of export prices. Here we can be brief. We know that this aim expresses a desire of long standing on the part of the L.D.C.s. The previous chapter has provided a thorough analysis of the essential problems connected with stabilization proposals.

The most common means of stabilizing prices and incomes is control over supply, perhaps through creation of cartels. Other means are creation of buffer stocks, multilateral contracts and compensatory financing. The analysis in Chapter 18 demonstrated that none of these means was particularly effective.

It is often extremely difficult for the L.D.C.s to control supply. On the contrary, it can be argued that the absence of control over supply factors is one of the outstanding features common to less developed countries. This has been demonstrated by several studies, as reported in the preceding chapter. The increase in oil prices engineered by OPEC highlighted the possibility of using monopoly power through the creation of cartels. Oil seems, however, to be a very special product. No other product has the specific characteristics of oil which made the maintenance of the drastic price increases possible. A few minerals like copper, bauxite, manganese and phosphate might be eligible for restrictive policies through cartels. But even with regard to products such as these, the scope for progress seems limited. Restrictions of supply tend to conserve the existing structure of production. Established producers are unduly protected. Barriers to entry are erected which in the longer run will probably lead to inefficiencies and stagnation. Thus cartels are often, the OPEC experience notwithstanding, a rather blunt weapon.

Schemes for buffer stocks are, as we know, also marred by weaknesses. Often inventory costs become prohibitive; this is the case with many tropical products. Buffer stocks cannot meet the pressures of sustained trends in the development of prices. If prices were to fall over a longer period of time, huge quantities would have to be bought. The stocks would accumulate. This would lead to untenable consequences both from financial and storage points of view. UNCTAD has worked out a scheme where buffer stocks would be maintained for as many as eighteen products. This scheme was adopted in principle at the Nairobi conference in 1976. Future negotiations will determine what the result of this scheme will be.

The multilateral contracts and the schemes for compensatory financing basically depend on the goodwill of the developed countries as they essentially involve transfers of resources above market-determined prices to the L.D.C.s. We have already analysed the essence of multilateral contracts in connection with the scheme *à la* Meade that was dealt with in the preceding chapter. Compensatory financing rests on the idea that the less developed countries should be compensated for temporary losses of export incomes. The I.M.F. already has such a scheme (basically an insurance scheme) whereby countries can borrow up to 25 per cent of their quotas in the I.M.F., provided that the export incomes have fallen below a certain average (see Chapters 29 and 30 for a discussion of the I.M.F.). UNCTAD has also worked for the proposal that compensatory financing should take the character of pure assistance. In principle such combinations are arbitrary and can be counterproductive as they will generally favor countries which do not make any efforts in controlling falls in supply at the expense of countries which consistently try to control supply conditions and thereby stabilize their export earnings.

The resolutions of the U.N. General Assembly concerning a new world order have argued for an indexation of prices that would keep the terms of trade between developed and less developed countries stable. We have already criticized the idea of fixing the terms of trade in the preceding chapter. This proposal indicates that one has not been able to deal with the problem in an effective manner. It is an eminently fantastic proposal which shows that the originators can hardly have been aware of the essence of their proposals. Terms of trade are no more than a set of relative prices. In market economies relative prices are determined by *all* supply and demand factors that affect any single good. Any proposal for indexation of the terms of trade in fact amounts to a proposal for a completely planned world economy. This would imply regulation of production and demand for hundreds of thousands of goods, obviously not a feasible proposition.

The most meaningful target for trade policy concerns the efforts at dismantling protectionist measures in the developed countries which are directed toward imports from the L.D.C.s. Previous chapters have taught us that tariff removals under the auspices of GATT have been mostly concerned with trade in industrial products among the developed countries. Tariff preferences have, as we know, been granted to the L.D.C.s, not least in connection with the work on a generalized system of preferences for the L.D.C.s which has taken place inside UNCTAD. Here, more progress should be made than has been the case so far. Important products, such as textile goods, have been set outside the scope of preferences. Likewise, argicultural and fishery products have been exempted from negotiations. These products are very important from the less developed countries' point of view.

To rid essential areas of protection, like the ones mentioned above, the L.D.C.s will have to rely on the goodwill of the developed countries. The recession which has hit the developed market economies in the wake of the oil crisis has unfortunately diminished the possibilities of dismantling protectionist measures in areas which are sensitive for the rich countries but which offer great potential for expansion in the L.D.C.s.

One can only hope that the less developed countries will in the future concentrate their forces of attack on the areas where real progress can be achieved instead of on proposals that are completely utopian and only show an embarrassing lack of sophistication and understanding of the real nature of world economic problems.

FINANCING OF DEVELOPMENT AND ASSISTANCE

The goals of development finance can be dealt with quite briefly. The proposals which the General Assembly has advanced are rather simple as a rule, all of them making clear in one way or another that the volume of aid from the industrialized countries to L.D.C.s must be raised, and that the terms of this aid must be made more favorable. We strongly sympathize with this objective, though we severely doubt whether any significant number of developed countries can meet the demands involved. International developments up to the present would certainly give reason for some doubt. However, a number of other observations can be made in this respect: the first, concerns the issues which are *not* included in the finance proposals; the second concerns the problem of indebtedness; and the third concerns the proposals relating Special Drawing Rights (S.D.R.s) to the question of aid to development.

It must be said that the theory underlying the proposals of the General Assembly on how the financing of economic development is to be carried out is strongly partial in its analysis, and thereby rather distorted. All attention is directed toward aid, while when it comes to the developing countries themselves it is merely stated that they should utilize all their resources in furthering development. It is highly unlikely that there is a single country among the L.D.C.s whose government is not prepared to testify to the fact that this is exactly what they already are doing. It would have been a good deal more interesting if this point had been cleared up, thereby obliging the developing countries to make more concise commitments toward an active development policy. It can hardly serve any purpose to conceal the simple truth that aid can never be anything else than what the meaning of the word implies: a complement to those measures which are taken by the developing countries themselves. By concentrating all one's attention on measures for international assistance, the more delicate questions about the inner structure of the L.D.C.s, about the effects of corruption and 'the soft state' on the efficacy of development policies, about the domestic income distribution, about the effectiveness and fairness of the systems of taxation, in short about all the necessary conditions for an effective utilization of an increased supply of aid, are neatly avoided. This negligence seems all the more remarkable in the light of the General Assembly's apparent willingness to accept the prospect of L.D.C.s themselves bearing the burden of development within the forseeable future, and its having contented itself with demands for an aid boost to a volume corresponding to 0.7 per cent of the G.N.P. of the developed countries by 1980.

The indebtedness of the L.D.C.s is a problem which has been a subject of concern for many years, and the General Assembly has once again unfurled the venerable idea of the reduction of the L.D.C.s' debt burden, primarily in the form of loan write-offs, or alternatively in the form of more flexible conditions of repayment on current loans. The problem of national indebtedness is one of the matters which occupies a position of priority in international agreements. However, since any reduction in the level of indebtedness undoubtably would be met by demands for some parallel measures on the part of the L.D.C.s, it would be worth while to insert a reminder about just which factors have caused the so-called debt crises, and to try to envision what the L.D.C.s could possibly do themselves in order to avoid future crises.

Debt crises arise, generally, not so much due to that fact that a country has incurred debts by making international loans so much as due to balance-of-payments problems which have entirely separate causes. One of these is that highly ambitious development programmes have been tentatively financed using loans which have proved to be all too short term, and which must be repaid before the programme has started to produce the financial returns necessary for repayment. A number of programmes have been poorly thought out, while in others corruption and wastefulness have undermined the ability to repay. Fiscal and monetary policies have in some cases been poorly administered and have led to deficient balances. At the same time, expected revenues have not materialized, due to export fluctuations or unexpected aid cuts. The role of indebtedness has most clearly been one of endowing balance-of-payments problems which would have arisen in any case with an even greater injurious force.

When seen in this light certain measures seem to be natural complements to the eventual reduction of national debt. L.D.C.s must consider submitting to a certain discipline in their development strategies. All the problems of underdevelopment cannot be resolved in the span of a couple of five-year plans. Instead, countries are forced 'to make haste slowly', and with more careful consideration. Governments should also exercise caution in taking up loans with all too imminent repayment requirements, and in using trade credits. It is all the more urgent that governments be forced to come to grips with the devastating and deeply rooted corruption which erodes the returns on borrowed capital. Finally, in those cases where fluctuations in export incomes stem from fluctuations in supply, efforts should be made to minimize the latter.

Here, a comment on the demands for increased access to the capital markets of the developed countries would be appropriate. Many L.D.C.s have already acquired bond loans and made entry on the euro-dollar market. The length of time governments can continue with this type of financing is determined to a great extent by the amount of confidence which is offered to prospective investors on these markets, which in turn depends greatly on whether a rational development policy is being followed or not.

The industrialized countries can also contribute to the prevention of 'debt crises'. Demands for even aid flows are justified. It is impossible to plan future development, counting on aid as an integral part of the means of finance, without being able to forecast the size of future aid flows. The industrialized countries can also, in those cases where it is feasible, contribute to the stabilization of exports by entering into formal agreements with the L.D.C.s.

Let us finally make a couple of remarks in this context on the proposals for coupling Special Drawing Rights with an increased aid flow to L.D.C.s by somehow distributing the benefits of the new issue of S.D.R.s to L.D.C.s. Here, it is appropriate to separate S.D.R.s and aid. The former have been instituted in order to offer greater stability in international payments, and have nothing in principle to do with aid. If a political preparedness to increase aid were present, there would surely be little difficulty in suggesting less roundabout ways of transferring it.

SCIENCE AND TECHNOLOGY

In the field of science and technology the resolutions of the General Assembly are aimed chiefly at the imperative transfer of scientific and technological know-how from the industrialized countries to L.D.C.s, with the transferred technology being made suitable for the special circumstances prevailing in the L.D.C.s. Since the proposals are formulated in relatively vague terms, it would be fitting to define and separate the different issues involved in order to understand what the angles of approach ought to be. If it is impossible to specify the objectives, it will not be easy to decide what means to use either. Three different steps in the transfer to technology can be distinguished: getting the developed nations to share their technological know-how, suiting this know-how to the economic and social systems of the L.D.C.s; and, finally, overcoming the resistance to technological change in the L.D.C.s.

The sort of know-how which it would be easiest to get the developed countries to share would be the results of pure basic research. Fundamental research is financed to a great extent by public funds, the results of which are available to all who are interested, in, say, international technical journals. There are, thus, few measures to be awaited in this area. The results of applied research are of much greater practical interest, though their 'secrets' are more closely guarded. Applied research is frequently carried out by private firms who demand some form of exclusive protection for the results of research if they are to be interested in research investment at all. These demands are met chiefly by the international system of patents. In return for the sharing of their know-how, firms exact a commission either in the form of royalties or joint ownership. A common development is that a firm based in an industrialized country establishes subsidiaries in developing countries. As far as efficiency is concerned, this is a good method. Technological know-how is most often no isolated phenomenon. Its transfer often necessitates investment in the recipient country. The multinational firms fulfill this need, and at the same time provide technical manpower, administrative personnel, etc. An entire firm is quite simply picked up and moved with all its amassed experience and know-how.

Private direct investments have infamous negative effects, however. A review of these falls beyond the bounds of this chapter. Let it suffice by stating that the principal problem in connection with the transfer of technological know-how is bound to be the question of how to control the multinationals while extracting the benefits of their unquestionable know-how.

Let us make the assumption that the industrialized countries are prepared to transfer technological know-how, and that direct investment can be controlled. The next problem to be resolved is that the superior technology which the developed countries have at their disposal has grown out of a situation where labor has been a relatively expensive factor of production, which has led to the prospering of relatively capital-intensive techniques. However, L.D.C.s have an abundance of cheap labor at their disposal.

Thus, no incentives are present for the use of technology suited to the needs of the developed countries. Technology must, then, be reshaped to fit a myriad of varying local conditions of production. being particularly problematic in the field of agriculture. It is obviously difficult to make any general recommendations as to how the problems of technical adaption should be solved, but an intensified research on behalf of the L.D.C.s would definitely seem to be a prerequisite for progress. An expansion of school systems, and a stronger emphasis on practical instruction in the schools, would have positive results.

The next critical stage in the process of the transfer of technology is overcoming resistance to new techniques. Innovations often meet bitter opposition in L.D.C.s. An important reason for this is that innovation more often than not contains strong elements of indivisibilities. 'The Green Revolution' is an excellent example of this. It is impossible to introduce new varieties of seed without simultaneously introducing irrigation and fertilization, and providing credits to make financing possible. Problems of risk and uncertainty, especially in the area of agriculture, are another difficulty. Peasants in the developing countries often find themselves in the situation of having a meagre margin between their normal incomes and utter starvation. This gives them a very negative view of risk-taking. They simply cannot take any chances.

The introduction of new techniques always implies certain elements of subjective or objective risk. It is hard to know in advance whether a certain technique will be readily adapted in any given environment, especially if its awaited effects are of a long-term nature, and new difficulties crop up when relevant information on new techniques is to be communicated to an illiterate agrarian population. The coexistence of uncertainty and low levels of income make two things quite evident: in the first place, a system of insurance must be worked out in order to guarantee that income levels will not fall to the starvation minimum due to the failure of new techniques; and second, adult education programmes should be fostered.

FOOD AND AGRICULTURE

The most urgent part of the new economic world order, at least in the short run, is that of bringing about an increase in the food production of the L.D.C.s and rendering their agricultural sectors efficient. The outlook for the near future is bleak indeed. It has been calculated that up to 10 million people died of hunger in 1980.

The problem of food production can be solved in two main ways: either the production of food is to be increased, or the number of mouths to be fed must diminish. The General Assembly has opted for the first alternative. Measures of population control are not mentioned in its resolutions. One of the reasons why birth control is left by the wayside is that the views on such measures differ radically from country to country. Chances of reaching any accord in this area are rather slim. Birth control has also proven to be difficult to implement effectively.

If birth control is out of the question, the only solution remaining is that of increasing the efficiency of food production, and of its distribution, in the developing countries themselves and in the rest of the world. The General Assembly primarily recommends that this be brought about by the industrialized countries allowing the agricultural products of the L.D.C.s freer entry to their markets, and that they step up aid to the agricultural sectors of the L.D.C.s. We have already dealt with both trade policy and aid in the preceding chapter. However, we would like to point out an extremely important measure which is totally ignored in the resolutions of the General Assembly, namely *land reform*.

There is hardly any kind of reform proposal which has been the subject of so much debate as the quest for land reform. In order to use land effectively and to secure some kind of justice and equality, land has to be redistributed. It is also true that land reform in many instances is an indispensable prerequisite for the application of other means for increasing productivity in agriculture. Credits, the utilization of new techniques, new seeds and the improvement of factors of production can all be futile unless the pattern of land ownership is changed. Few peasants are willing to take on debts for making improvements if the fruits of their efforts go to a landowner in the form of increases in land rents. Often there are strong indivisibilities connected with land reform and technical progress in agriculture. Unless a whole package of reforms and changes are applied jointly, the results might be very different from what the reformers had envisaged. Here it is only the authorities in the L.D.C.s themselves who can really see to it that the right steps are taken.

To take an example, the Swedish government has, through its development agency, SIDA, given assistance to Ethiopia for a long time. A very interesting project was the so-called CADU project which aimed at transforming traditional agriculture in the Chilalo area in Ethiopia. The project was successful from some points of view, especially in terms of increased productivity. Ownership of land, however, remained quite concentrated. The social consequences of economic progress were also very ambiguous. When yields started to rise, the absentee landlords increased their interests in their holdings. The degree of commercial farming increased. Tenants were evicted to make room for new methods of farming. Increases in incomes were accompanied by joblessness on the part of tenants, and poverty increased.

The Swedish authorities tried to pressure the feudal Ethiopian government headed by the late Emperor Haile Selassie into accepting their proposals for land reform. Some vague promises were given, but no action took place. This occurred in the late 1960s and early 1970s. Since then, the regime has changed, and Ethiopia has been at war with forces in Eritrea and Somalia. Revolutionary declarations have been made, but if the peasants are any better off is impossible to tell. No reliable information about the situation in the Chilalo area is available at the time of writing.

The example highlights one important fact that should never be forgotten. Foreign assistance can only be just that – assistance. The really important steps toward change have to be taken by local powers. Only if peasants can reach a position of power or make alliances with progressive forces that are strong enough to break prevailing feudal orders can land reform become possible. Only the authorities in the L.D.C.s themselves can see to it that the right steps are taken and new modes of behavior are instituted.

A couple of other marginal remarks should be made in conclusion. The first concerns the demands that fertilizers and other input factors should be provided at prices which are reasonable for L.D.C.s. As in the case of the proposed regulation concerning the terms of trade, we are caught up in an argument which seems highly unrealistic. Since the price structure of the world economy is the result of the interaction of a series of complicated factors, both on the demand side and on the supply side, long-range price stabilization on input factors would imply total control over both supply and demand. In order to achieve a meaningful discussion of the demands of the General Assembly, we must delve into what the requirements for such long-range planning would be; this, however, has been left undone. The problem is complicated further in the case of the prices on fertilizers, due to the vast price increases of oil made over the last few years.

The second comment has to do with the proposals for instituting grain-storage facilities to enable a famine catastrophe to be avoided. This is a praiseworthy initiative, and calculations made by the F.A.O. imply that the building of warehousing facilities could be realized at reasonable costs. It should be noted that this argument for the erection of grain-storage facilities is not the same as the argument for price stabilization through storage. Here it is not a matter of worrying about whether given export prices and incomes should be maintained.

SUMMARY AND CONCLUSIONS

An analysis of the proposals for a new international economic order in terms of aims and means is useful. It demonstrates that the advocates of a new order have formulated their aims without any thorough analysis of what these would imply in terms of means. In many cases there simply do not exist any means whereby the proposed targets could be reached.

The proponents of a new order have also shown an amazing consistency in avoiding the most pertinent of all development problems: which changes are necessary in the L.D.C.s themselves in terms of policies and structures to get the development process going.

It is probably futile to rely too heavily on reforms in the developed countries and on a change in attitude on their parts in solving the problems of the L.D.C.s. The political structure of today's world is such that the L.D.C.s can only rely on themselves for carrying out the basic tasks connected with economic progress. The will to change the world income distribution in favor of the L.D.C.s is by no means strong. Some developed countries, for instance the United States, view the demands couched under the heading of a new order as preposterous. The prospects for implementing a new international economic order are very bleak. Reforms in the relationship between industrialized and less developed countries can be expected, but they will hardly be of the kind or as all-encompassing as those envisaged by the proponents of a new economic order.

SELECTED BIBLIOGRAPHY: CHAPTER 19

Papers in which the new international economic order is discussed are:

R. McCulloch, 'Economic Policy in the United Nations: A New International Economic Order?', in K. Brunner and A. H. Meltzer (eds), *International Organization, National Policies and Economic Development*, Amsterdam, North-Holland, 1977.

M. Abdel Falil, F. Cripps and J. Wells, 'A New International Economic Order?', *Cambridge Journal of Economics*, no. 2, 1977.

R. H. Green and H. W. Singer, 'Toward a Rational and Equitable New International Economic Order: A Case for Negotiated Structural Changes', *World Development*, no. 6, 1975.

J. S. Singh, *A New International Economic Order – Toward a Fair Redistribution of the World's Resources*, New York, Praeger, 1977.

For background information, see:

C. H. Chenery, 'Restructuring the World Economy', *Foreign Affairs*, January 1975.

J. Tinbergen *et al.*, *Reshaping the International Order*, London, Dutton, 1977.

K. Brunner and A. H. Meltzer (eds), *International Organization, National Policies and Economic Development*, Amsterdam, North-Holland, 1977.

20
The theory of customs unions

We have seen that one of the major aspects of international trading relations during the post-war period has been the development of regional trade groupings, primarily in the form of customs unions. This development naturally aroused the attention of trade theorists. Standard trade theory had only been concerned with the effects of non-discriminatory tariff changes, the type of tariff theory we have studied in Chapters 13 and 15. But customs unions are by definition discriminatory. They mean a lowering of tariffs within the union and an establishing of a joint outer tariff wall. They combine free trade with protectionism.

This makes customs unions difficult to deal with from a theoretical point of view. We have seen that ordinary tariff theory is quite complicated when general-equilibrium considerations are taken into account. The theory of customs unions is even more complex.

To begin with, we tried to formulate general propositions about the welfare effects of a customs union. The free-trade aspects of customs unions were stressed, and the general consensus seemed to be that customs unions would increase welfare. This was disputed on several grounds as the theory developed; economists tended to oscillate between broad generalizations and agnosticism.

Still, the theory is quite intuitive in character, and its results tend to take the form of some propositions of the type 'if these conditions prevail, customs unions will lead to an increase (alternatively a lowering) of welfare'. These propositions are generally not very deep. No precise, neatly established theorems, built on explicit models of a general-equilibrium character, have so far been derived. It is characteristic that the discussion runs in terms of 'welfare effects'; it has not been possible to derive precise results for the effects on all the different variables in the general-equilibrium setting, terms of trade, domestic prices, volumes, national incomes, etc. Instead, an intuitive kind of reasoning has been used. The main results in customs union theory, as it stands today, will now be surveyed.[1]

TRADE CREATION AND TRADE DIVERSION

The pioneering study of the theory of customs unions was made by Jacob Viner.[2] In the beginning, customs unions had been viewed favorably. The reasoning was as follows: free trade maximizes welfare; customs unions are a move toward free trade; therefore, they will increase welfare even though they might not maximize it.

Viner showed this conclusion to be incorrect. He introduced, instead, the key concepts of *trade creation* and *trade diversion*. They might best be illustrated by Table 20.1. The table measures the production cost of a commodity in three

TABLE 20.1

Production cost of commodity X in three countries

Country	A	B	C
Production cost	50	40	30

countries. Let us disregard transportation cost, mark-ups, etc., so that production cost completely determines the supply price of the good, and tariffs are the only source of diversion between price and cost. If country A has a tariff of 100 per cent on X, there will be no imports of the good, but domestic producers will dominate the home market. If A had levied a lower tariff, say 50 per cent, and it was non-discriminatory, it would have imported the good from the lower-cost source, country C, and the price in A's home market would be 45.

Let us now assume that A and B form a customs union. A will then, instead, import X from B, and the price in A's market will be 40. Imports will be switched from the low-cost supplier, C, to the high-cost supplier, B. This is an example of trade diversion. Trade diversion takes place when imports from a more efficiently producing country are switched to a less efficiently producing country because of the customs union. Trade diversion will lead to a lowering of welfare, as it entails a less efficient allocation of resources.

We must mention here that this analysis assumes that the countries involved are fully employed both before and after the formation of the customs union. In this sense the analysis is of a neoclassical type. This being the case, it is natural to let the analysis primarily be concerned with the effects on the allocation of resources and the welfare implications of these effects.

This kind of analysis gives rise to three possibilities. First, neither of the two countries forming the union produces the good in question. The customs union would then be of no significance, as both countries would import the good from a third country just as they did before forming the union. Second, one of the countries forming the union produces the good inefficiently, i.e. is not the lowest cost available source of supply. The union partner would then import from the cheaper source and there will be a case of trade diversion. Third, both countries forming the customs union produce the good, in which case one of the countries would be more efficient than the other. The market in both countries will then be secured for the more efficient industry, and there will be trade creation.

This analysis suggests that if a customs union primarily leads to trade creation, it will lead to an increase in welfare; and if it primarily gives rise to trade diversion, it will lead to a lowering in the world's welfare. In this case, it will certainly lead to a lowering in the welfare of the third country (the rest of the world). Whether it will also lead to a lowering in the welfare of the countries forming the customs union is less certain; we will shortly return to this case.

The implication of this analysis is that customs unions will lead to detrimental effects if the countries are complementary in the list of goods they produce. If, on the other hand, the group of commodities that both countries

FIGURE 20.1

Complementarity and overlapping production structures

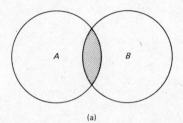 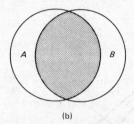

(a)   (b)

produce under tariff protection is large, the scope for positive welfare effects is large. Figure 20.1 illustrates these facts.

Figure 20.1(a) illustrates a situation where the two countries are primarily complementary. The area where the two economies overlap, shown by the shaded union of A and B, is small. Figure 20.1(b) shows a situation where the two economies are primarily competitive. The area of overlapping production, shown by the shaded union of A and B, is large.

Intuitively, one might think that an agricultural country ought to form a union with an industrial country. This is not the case. Agricultural countries should form customs unions with each other, and an industrial country should form a union with another industrial country. The scope for trade creation is then largest, and so is the scope for an improved allocation of resources and an increase in welfare. The countries within the European Economic Community are all primarily industrial countries. Therefore, we would expect them to make substantial gains from their union.

We can also observe that the larger the cost differentials between the countries in the union on goods they both produced before the union, the larger the scope for gains. We will shortly return to this point.

The Vinerian analysis of trade creation and trade diversion is useful, but it is only a beginning. Viner assumed that there are no possibilities of substitution in consumption – that all price elasticities of demand are equal to zero. On the supply side, on the other hand, he supposed the supply elasticities to be infinitely large, so that all products are produced under constant returns to scale. It is easy to understand why Viner chose these assumptions. If goods are consumed in constant proportions irrespective of prices and if costs are constant, then the only interesting thing left to study is the shifts in production between countries as given by trade creation and trade diversion. Then trade diversion, for instance, will always cause a lowering of welfare. This is illustrated in Figure 20.2.

Country A is completely specialized in production of X. It produces at point A on the X axis. It exchanges X for Y on the world market at the best terms of trade possible. They are given by the line AB. Consumers in the country consume the two goods in a constant proportion given by the ray OR from the origin. The point of consumption is then at d.

FIGURE 20.2

Effect of trade diversion on welfare
(no inter-commondity substitution)

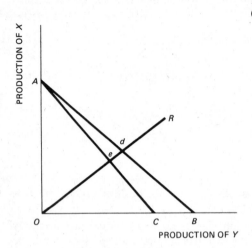

A now forms a customs union with country *C*. This leads to trade diversion. Country *A* is still completely specialized in production of *X*, which it exchanges for *Y* from *C*. Because of the customs union, *A*'s terms of trade deteriorate. The new terms of trade are given by the line *AC*. The country still consumes along the ray *OR* and consumption now will be at point *e*. This point is clearly inferior to *d* as it represents a smaller amount of both goods.

This analysis shows that, on the Vinerian assumption of no substitution in consumption, trade diversion will necessarily lower *A*'s welfare. But Viner's assumptions are very strong and quite unrealistic. A customs union will normally lead to a change in all relative prices. Will not, then, substitution take place? This is what we would normally expect. We will now look into some of the effects that substitution in consumption might give rise to.

INTER-COUNTRY AND INTER-COMMODITY SUBSTITUTION

If a country enters a customs union and trade diversion follows on some goods, it means that the country will have to pay a higher price in acquiring these goods. But at the same time the domestic consumers will no longer have to pay a duty on the goods, and its domestic price will probably fall. This will lead to an expansion in consumption of the goods, provided substitution takes place. This implies an improvement in the welfare of consumers. There are then two contradictory forces: a deterioration in the terms of trade, implying a lowering of welfare; and increased consumption, implying an increase of welfare. The result of trade diversion is then no longer given. This case is illustrated in Figure 20.3.

Country *A* is completely specialized in production of good *X* and produces at point *A* on the *X* axis. Before the union it imports good *Y* from the cheapest

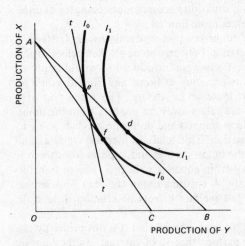

possible source, country B, at the terms of trade AB. If free trade were permitted consumption would be at point d, where an indifference curve $I_1 I_1$ is tangential to the price line AB. Now, the country prefers to have a steep duty on Y, and the domestic price ratio is indicated by line tt. Consumption is then at point e, where another indifference curve, $I_0 I_0$, is tangential to the price line tt. The tariff leads to a fall in consumption of Y, which is substituted by X, and to a lowering in consumers' welfare. The terms of trade AB are assumed not to have been effected by the tariff.

Country A now forms a customs union with country C. This leads to trade diversion and to a worsening of A's terms of trade. The country still produces at A and exchanges X for Y. The new terms of trade are given by line AC. This need not necessarily lead to a lowering in welfare for consumers, because the price ratio AC will now be ruling in A's domestic market and Y is now cheaper than at the tariff-inclusive price ratio tt. Y will therefore be substituted for X in consumption and consumption will move to point f. Point f is on the same indifference curve as e. Hence consumers are as well off after the customs union as before. This shows that a customs union, even though it leads to trade diversion, could result in consumers being as well off as before. If the deterioration in the terms of trade had been less than what is shown by AC, and the new price line had been somewhere between AB and AC, the customs union would have led to an increase in consumers' welfare and would have put them on a higher indifference curve than $I_0 I_0$. Then the customs union would have increased consumers' welfare even though it was of a trade-diverting kind.[3] This demonstrates that if substitution in consumption takes place, it implies that a customs union can lead to an improvement in welfare even if it is of a trade-diverting nature.

Thus we can speak about inter-country and inter-commodity substitution. Inter-country substitution is Viner's trade diversion and trade creation. Inter-commodity substitution is the usual substitution that takes place between commodities, both on the supply and the demand sides because of changes in relative prices. A customs union will give rise to both kinds of substitution. If both kinds are taken into account, the situation becomes more complex and the possibility of drawing inferences becomes more limited.

On a somewhat abstract level we could say that a situation with tariffs is a non-optimum situation, where the relation between home-market prices differs from international price ratios. If free trade were introduced, it would imply an improvement, as the real rates of transformation at home and abroad would be the same, and this would imply an increase in welfare. The formation of a customs union means that, as tariffs are taken away on imports from the union partner, the relative price between these imports and domestic goods is going to coincide with real rates of transformation. This tends to increase welfare. The relative price between imports from the union partner and imports from the rest of the world, however, is moved away from equality with real rates of transformation. This will tend to lower welfare. A customs union thus has both a free-trade side and a protectionist side. The welfare effects of a union depend on which is stronger.

It is important, in this connection, to bear in mind that it is not primarily the size of the imports from the union partner that is of interest, as they are involved in both a gain and a loss. What is important is the size of domestic trade in relation to imports from the outside world. The larger and more important domestic trade is, the more likely is the union to bring a gain. The reason is that 'correct' price relations will then be established on a large and important number of goods. Conversely, the smaller trade is with the rest of the world, the better, because then only a few and unimportant price relations will be disturbed by the formation of the union.

Suppose, for example, that the only import from the rest of the world is rucksacks. Then the price relation between rucksacks and imports from the union partner will be distorted, a not very important consequence, presumably, whereas prices of imports from the union partner are brought into harmony with prices of all domestically produced goods. If the country, instead, only produced rucksacks, it would be the other way around. Then 'correct' price relations between rucksacks and union imports would be established, whereas price relations between all outside imports and union imports would be distorted. The most important consequences of this reasoning is that countries heavily dependent on each other in their trade should form customs unions with each other. There are no gains to be had by forming unions with countries that, economically speaking, are of only marginal importance. Another consequence is that countries which have only a small part of their national product going in international trade can safely form customs unions. Then domestic trade is dominant and the scope for gains from a customs union substantial. Countries with a large foreign trade quota must be more careful, as they might risk important distortions in their trade with the rest of the world.

We have now seen some of the factors that are important when assessing the economic gains and losses of a customs union. The gains are primarily connected with trade creation, the losses with trade diversion. But how are these gains and losses to be measured? By volume only? Here the height of the tariffs comes in as an important factor.

FIGURE 20.4

Effect of tariff removal on welfare

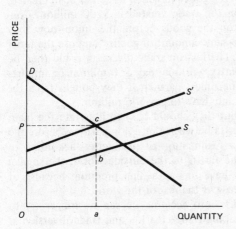

THE HEIGHT OF TARIFFS AND TARIFF REMOVALS

In a competitive world, the supply price of a good indicates the (marginal) cost to the producer and thus the opportunity cost, and the demand price indicates the utility of the good to the consumer. If no tariffs, taxes, or other distortions exist, the supply price of a good will be the same as the demand price. If taxes or tariffs exist, this is no longer the case. Suppose there is a 50 per cent tax on a product: if the cost of production of the good is $2, then the producer of the good will get $2 for it, but the consumer will have to pay $3 for it.

Since the producer is living in a competitive world, it means that the last unit of the product must be worth $2 to him – that it must cost $2-worth of resources to produce. Similarly, since the consumer is willing to pay $3 for a unit of the goods, it means that it must be worth $3 to him. A discrepancy in utility for producers and consumers thus exists, and if trade in the product could be increased, this would lead to an increase in welfare.

A tax or a tariff has completely analogous effects in this respect, and we can illustrate the effect of a tariff in a geometric fashion (see Figure 20.4). A tariff, or a tax, can be thought of as shifting the supply curve to the left. The pre-tariff supply curve is S and the tariff-inclusive supply curve is S'. Equilibrium is established at c, with p being the price and Oa the quantity consumed. The tariff rate in Figure 20.4 is cb/ba per cent, and the supply price differs from the demand price by this amount. An increase in trade of this good would, on the margin, mean an increase in welfare of an amount equal to cb.

This kind of analysis implies that the higher the initial tariffs between the countries forming the customs union, the larger the scope for gain. Conversely, the lower the tariffs with the outside world, the lower should be the losses due to trade diversion.

Assume that $100 million worth of trade is created because of the customs union and that $50 million worth of trade is diverted. Say that, before the union, the tariff was 100 per cent on the goods in which trade has been created. A rough estimate of the net gain on the trade created is $100 million. Consumers were spending $200 million on the goods before the union; now they need only spend $100 million on the same amount of goods. Suppose the tariff to the outside world is 10 per cent. The loss on trade diversion could then be approximated to $5 million. The country will now pay $50 million on imports of these goods when buying from the union partner; if they bought from the cheapest possible source, they would only have to pay $45 million.

These are very rough examples, but they should help to illustrate the main principle involved. The higher the tariffs between the union partners before the union, the larger is the scope for a reallocation of production according to comparative advantage. The lower the tariffs to the outside world, the smaller are the risks that the countries will have to pay a high premium because of subsidizing union partners at the expense of the rest of the world.

When we take the heights of tariffs into account we can no longer try to estimate gains and losses by simply taking trade creation and trade diversion at face value. We also have to weigh the values of trade created and diverted with the heights of the tariffs involved.

In practice, customs unions, such as the E.E.C., reduce tariffs gradually. The largest gains are to be had initially when tariffs are high and the distortions are important. As time goes on and tariffs become lower, so does the possibility for prospective gains. Finally, taking tariffs away completely could even entail a loss.[4]

EMPIRICAL FINDINGS AND DYNAMIC CONSIDERATIONS

We have now studied some of the main elements of the theory of customs unions. Now we must briefly look at some empirical estimates of gains and losses in connection with customs unions. A number of empirical studies have been made. One of the earliest and best known is probably one by the Dutch economist Verdoorn, later used and commentated upon by Tibor Scitovsky.[5] Another study of the same period was made by H. G. Johnson.[6] All these studies used the type of theory outlined in this chapter and tried to estimate the gains and losses from trade creation and trade diversion. There is no need here to go into any detail of how the measurements were made. It suffices for our purposes to report on the main results.

The common feature of these early empirical studies is the smallness of the estimated gains. Verdoorn, for instance, estimated that trade between the countries of the E.E.C. would increase by 17 per cent. These estimates of trade increases were then weighted with the respective tariffs. It turned out that the welfare effect of the prospective union amounted to about one-twentieth of 1 per cent of the sum of the national incomes of the original six countries. We quote Scitovsky's comments on this result:

> The most surprising feature of these estimates is their smallness. ... As estimates of the total increase in intra-European trade contingent upon economic union,

Verdoorn's figures are probably underestimates; but if, by way of correction, we should raise them five- or even twenty-five-fold, that would still leave unchanged our basic conclusion that the gain from increased intra-European specialization is likely to be insignificant.[7]

Johnson's findings tended to go in the same direction. He found that Britain, by joining a European free-trade area, can expect at the most to gain 1 per cent of national income, while Major, who examined changes in market shares over the period 1958–61, concluded that the E.E.C. did not have much effect during this early period.[8]

However, more recent studies have tended to produce substantially higher estimates for trade creation. In his analysis of the changes in the sources of supply of manufactures to E.E.C. countries, Truman estimated that by 1964, when the reduction of internal tariffs was 60 per cent complete, that intra-E.E.C. trade was something like 30 per cent higher than it would have been if the E.E.C. had not been created.[9] Moreover, he found that this increase in the share of consumption held by other E.E.C. producers had been achieved without any *net* diversion of trade from the rest of the world. The share of imports from non-E.E.C. sources had in fact risen. This external trade creation was explained by Truman as the result of tariff-cutting by former high-tariff countries to the level of the common external tariff being in excess of trade diversion which mainly occurred in the former low-tariff countries. Williamson and Bottrill lend support to Truman's estimate for trade creation for 1964 and conclude that by 1969 intra-E.E.C. trade was something like 50 per cent higher than it otherwise would have been without the E.E.C.[10] They attribute most of this increase to trade creation rather than diversion with the harm being done to other countries' exports by diversion being largely offset by positive external trade creation. A further study stated that in 1969–70 trade creation was eight times trade diversion.[11] However, there remains a wide degree of variation in the results of the published studies, and consequently it may be advisable to defer judgment on the empirical aspects of the gains from customs unions.[12]

On the other hand, it is important to understand the type of economic theory that relates to customs unions. It is of a comparative-static nature. It starts from an equilibrium with a given tariff structure. Then a discriminatory change in this structure is made, and the effects on economic welfare are estimated. The above-mentioned estimates are based on this kind of comparative-static theorizing, and no one has been able to show any serious defects in them as far as they go. Traditional economic theory would therefore tend to support the view that the welfare effects of customs unions are small.

One could argue, however, that there are other effects of a 'dynamic' or perhaps institutional kind that are more important. One such dynamic effect is the presence of unutilized economies of scale. Because of the segmentation of markets, European industry has not been able to reap the fruits of economies of scale: that is the argument. This argument, however, has the character of an unproved assertion, and it is perhaps not as convincing as it appears at first sight. First, most European industries where economies of scale could be expected are already export industries and have a larger market than the national one. Second, even though there are perhaps unused economies of scale on the production side, administration and selling costs could be rising, causing the total unit cost to rise also. For such reasons the argument for unreaped scale economies is perhaps not too valid.

Another argument of a dynamic character is that a customs union will lead to enforced competition. This argument has been applied to the European Economic Community.[13] Large parts of French industry, it is argued, consist of, on the one hand, some large efficient firms, and, on the other, several small inefficient firms, often family businesses. French big business does not want to be ruthless, so the small family firms are kept alive, competition is minimal, and economic growth is not so fast as it otherwise could have been.[14] The German pattern is different, and here competition is vivid and strong. When French industry enters into closer competition with German industry because of the E.E.C., it can no longer afford to be complacent and lenient. To survive it will have to adopt the German pattern. Competition will be enforced on French industry, and economic growth in France will be speeded up.

This could be a plausible argument. However, it is very difficult to get numerical estimates of effects such as these. Therefore, the way such an argument is evaluated is largely a matter of belief.

Other institutional aspects which could be important are those connected with increased factor movements and with rights to establish businesses within the union. Movements of labor and of capital could increase the productivity of the factors in question and foster growth. A greater freedom in establishment rights would perhaps lead not only to a greater personal freedom and increased well-being, but also to a faster spread of knowledge and thereby to faster growth. Factors such as these could be important, but it is difficult to say how important.

SUMMARY

We finish this chapter by summarizing some of the main results of the theory of customs unions. The basic conclusion is that it is impossible to pass any judgment on customs unions in general. Having said this, we find that the basic concepts of the theory are those of trade creation and trade diversion. Trade creation will lead to an improvement of welfare, whereas trade diversion generally leads to a lowering of welfare. A customs union is more likely to lead to an increase in welfare if the union partners are actually competitive but potentially complementary. The larger the cost differentials between the countries of the union in goods they both produce, the larger is the scope for gains. The higher the initial tariffs between the union partners, the greater is the scope for an increase in welfare. The lower the tariffs to the outside world, the smaller are the losses on trade diversion. The larger the part of trade originally covered by trade between the union partners, the greater is the scope for gains from the union. If a union leads to a realization of dynamic effects such as reaping of economies of scale and enforced competition, it could be important, and these effects will have to be added to the effects of a comparative-static nature.

SELECTED BIBLIOGRAPHY: CHAPTER 20

A classic work which started the modern discussion of the theory of customs unions is:

J. Viner, *The Customs Unions Issue,* New York, Carnegie Endowment for International Peace, 1953.

Two standard contributions to the theory of customs unions are:

R. G. Lipsey, 'The Theory of Customs Unions: A General Survey', *EJ,* September 1960 (reprinted in *RIE*).

J. E. Meade, *The Theory of Customs Unions,* Amsterdam, North-Holland, 1955.

Other interesting contributions are:

M. Adler, 'Specialization in the European Coal and Steel Community', *Journal of Common Market Studies,* March 1970, pp. 175–91.

C. A. Cooper and B. F. Massell, 'A New Look at Customs Union Theory', *EJ,* December 1965.

C. A. Cooper and B. F. Massell, 'Toward a General Customs Union Theory for Developing Countries', *JPE,* September 1965.

G. R. Denton, *Economic Integration in Europe,* London 1969.

H. G. Johnson, 'The Gains from Freer Trade with Europe: An Estimate', *MSS,* September 1958.

T. Scitovsky, *Economic Theory and Western European Integration,* London, Allen & Unwin, 1958.

J. Vanek, *General Equilibrium of International Discrimination: The Case of Customs Unions,* Cambridge, Mass., Harvard University Press, 1965.

For a more popular type survey see:

D. Swann, *The Economics of the Common Market,* 3rd ed., Baltimore, Johns Hopkins Press, 1975.

For a survey and critique of the empirical studies see:

W. Sellekaerts, 'How Meaningful are Empirical Studies on Trade Creation and Diversion?', *Weltwirtschaftliches Archiv,* no. 4, 1973.

21
Direct investments and the multinational firm

We touched on capital movements from various points of view earlier in the book. In Chapter 8 we studied the importance of capital movements during the nineteenth century from a historical standpoint. For several countries, imports of capital played an important role in their development process. For the lending countries, exports of capital were an important outlet for savings, which helped to smooth out business cycles and led to, if not a more rapid, at least a more stable pattern of economic growth.

In Part IV, we shall examine the significance of capital movements for balance-of-payments purposes. In this chapter we shall deal with a specific type of capital movements: direct investments. By direct investment is meant an investment in a foreign country where the investing party (corporation, firm) retains control over the investment. A direct investment typically takes the form of a foreign firm starting a subsidiary or taking over control of an existing firm in the country in question.

Direct investments are increasing in importance in the world economy. They have always attracted a good deal of attention and given rise to heated controversy; this, perhaps, is not astonishing in a world of nationalism. The Marxists saw them in the beginning of the twentieth century as the natural consequence of a maturing capitalism: the logical fruits of an ever-hardening competition, the last manifestations of a doomed system before its collapse. During recent years they have attracted renewed interest both in underdeveloped and developed countries. It is significant that one of the international best-sellers of the 1960s, *The American Challenge,* by Jean-Jacques Servan-Schreiber, was devoted to the effects of direct investments on the European economy. Resolutions at UNCTAD conferences have increasingly reflected a growing suspicion of foreign investment.

Firstly, we shall briefly discuss the differences between portfolio and direct investments.

PORTFOLIO AND DIRECT INVESTMENTS

As already stated, the main distinction of direct investments is that the investor retains control over the invested capital. Direct investments and management go together. With portfolio investments, no such control is exercised. Here the investor lends his capital in order to get a return on it, but he has no control over the use of that capital.

We saw in Chapter 9 that foreign investments played a large role in international economy in the period leading up to the First World War. The largest part of these investments consisted of portfolio investments. Great Britain provided more than 50 per cent of the total international capital outstanding in

TABLE 21.1

Composition of net flow of financial resources * from D.A.C. countries † to L.D.C.s., 1961–3 to 1971–3 (annual averages, $ billion).

	1961–3	Per cent	1966–8	Per cent	1971–3	Per cent
(1) Official development assistance	5.47	(62.5)	6.29	(53.5)	8.62	(43.8)
(2) Other official flows	0.58	(6.6)	0.56	(4.8)	1.82	(9.2)
(3) Private flows	2.71	(30.9)	4.91	(41.8)	9.26	(47.1)
a. Direct investment	1.64	(18.7)	2.44	(20.8)	4.49	(22.8)
b. Export credits	0.60	(6.8)	1.55	(13.2)	1.82	(9.2)
c. Portfolio investment	0.47	(5.4)	0.92	(7.8)	2.95	(15.1)
(4) Total disbursements	8.76		11.76		19.7	

*   Gross flows net of capital repayments but *not* interest, profits or dividends.

†   The countries which belong to the O.E.C.D.'s Development Assistance Committee: Western Europe, North America, Australia and Japan.

SOURCES: 1961–8 data, O.E.C.D., *Development Cooperation: 1972 Review;* 1971–3 data, O.E.C.D., *Development Cooperation: 1974 Review.*

1914. About 90 per cent of British investments during this period were of a portfolio type. These investments were primarily governed by interest differentials. Britain during this period generated savings that were much larger than domestic investments (25 to 40 per cent of gross domestic savings were invested abroad), and these foreign investments were primarily invested where the return on capital was high. This also applies to the other two major lending countries, France and Germany. They were also primarily engaged in portfolio investments. During a period when exchange risks were negligible and the political situation from this angle was stable, international investments were primarily governed by interest-rate differentials. Young expanding economies, which offered high returns on capital invested, could borrow money from the major lending countries.

The United States was the only country which already differed in this respect. American investors seem to have been of a more dynamic type, not content merely to reap a fairly small interest-rate differential. Even before the First World War a dominant share of U.S. capital exports consisted of direct investments.

We know from Chapter 8 that capital imports were of limited importance during the interwar period. The role and pattern of capital movements have changed considerably since the Second World War. During the 1950s the role of private portfolio investments was negligible. The most important capital flows were official gifts and loans, followed by direct investments. However, as Table 21.1 illustrates, a certain revival of portfolio investments occurred during the 1960s. These frequently took the form of international bonds associated with the finance of large infrastructure projects in less developed countries. At the same time, the role of private direct investment has also tended to increase, with the result that the share of official development assistance to less developed countries declined from about 62 per cent to around 43 per cent during the period 1961–3 to 1971–3.

This increase in the share of private capital flows to less developed countries has had a number of important consequences. First, it implies a fall in the share of concessional and grant aid, and thus represents a hardening of the terms on which less developed countries receive external finance. The problem of a growing 'debt burden' has been touched on in relation to the demands of less developed countries for a new international economic order (see Chapter 19).

The most significant feature of the era since the Second World War is, however, the growth of foreign direct investment that is intimately associated with the growth of the *multinational corporation*. An analysis of this complex and controversial subject will be the major topic of this chapter. First, however, we shall touch on a problem common to all capital movements, the so-called *transfer problem*.

THE TRANSFER PROBLEM

The transfer problem is of long standing in international economics. It is essentially a matter of international adjustment in balances of payments. It is easy to see why the transfer problem has attracted so much interest: it arises in connection with many different types of international transactions.

If a country lends $100 million to another country, it means that the lending country puts resources to the value of $100 million at the disposal of the borrowing country. The lending country will have to free resources valued at $100 million in order to export them to the borrowing country, which will import goods for $100 million more. To be successful, any long-term capital movement will have to be accompanied by a transfer of resources of equal size. This implies a change in the trade balance between lending and borrowing countries. How this comes about is studied under the heading of the transfer problem.

W. F. Taussig of Harvard University and a group of his students first studied the transfer process and the adjustment mechanism in connection with the long-term capital movements to countries such as Canada, Argentina and Australia which took place during the latter part of the nineteenth and the earlier part of the twentieth centuries.

The transfer problem, however, is not only concerned with capital movements; it also played a prominent role in connection with reparations payments for war damages. Such payments occurred, for instance, after the Franco-Prussian War in 1870–71, when France had to pay indemnities to Prussia, and after the First World War, when Germany had to pay indemnities to France. In connection with the latter payments, a heated theoretical controversy arose between Keynes and Ohlin. It is obvious why payments for war damages give rise to a transfer problem.

More recently, the transfer problem has arisen in connection with the fourfold increase in oil prices imposed by the OPEC countries at the end of 1973. The oil crisis and its impact on the international monetary system is discussed at length in Chapter 30. Here it suffices to emphasize that at the heart of the oil crisis was a transfer problem. The increase in oil prices entailed a gigantic income redistribution. It increased the world's propensity to save. The saving propensity of the OPEC countries was high as they could not spend less than half of their incomes on consumption and domestic investments. Due to their low import propensities the resource transfer implied by the income changes could not be effected by ordinary trade channels. The savings surplus of the OPEC countries had to be invested somewhere. The only countries that could swallow investments of this magnitude were the large industrial market economies. Part of capital formation in these countries (the O.E.C.D. countries) would have to be financed by oil money. This entailed a special case of the transfer problem as an organized transfer of resources from the OPEC to the O.E.C.D. countries would have been necessary to keep the world economy in equilibrium. Part of the capital formation in the West would have to be financed by the Arabs while the latter would be owners to a (small) share of the capital stock of the industrial countries. Unfortunately, the leading statesmen in the West were never able to face up to this problem. Instead of trying to apply an international solution, which would have been the only feasible one, they chose to take a nationalistic view and let each country fend for itself. The individual countries were then confronted with balance-of-payments disequilibria. In order to get rid of their external deficits they started to deflate their economies. The original disequilibria were then prolonged and the international economy was plunged into its longest recession since the early 1930s. All this happened because statesmen and politicians did not grasp the nature of the transfer problem which was at the heart of the oil crisis.

The transfer theory has been developed within the context of two theoretical models. The earliest discussion of the problem was formulated in 'classical' terms. The results of these investigations are very important. The more modern version of transfer theory is formulated in Keynesian terms. For reasons that will soon become clear, we will concentrate the exposition on the classical transfer theory and then see how this can be supplemented by taking some considerations of a Keynesian type into account.

The classical analysis cast the reasoning in the form of the standard trade model with two countries trading, producing and consuming two goods. It worked on the assumption that both countries were fully employed and that the balance of payments of both countries was in equilibrium before the transfer took place. The question now is: how could the transfer be affected and a new external equilibrium be created, given these assumptions?

Let us begin by discussing the following example. We can assume that country A lends country B $100 million. The immediate effect will be to decrease country A's income by $100 million and to increase country B's income by that amount. What will be the effect on the balance of trade? This will depend on the marginal propensity to import in the two countries. Let m_a and m_b be the marginal propensities to import in the respective countries. If $m_a = 0.3$, it means that country A will decrease its imports by $30 million when the income decreases by $100 million. If $m_b = 0.4$, it means that $40 million of the income increase in country B will be spent on imports from A. This means that the transfer will be *undereffected*.

The meaning of this term is as follows. Because of the transfer, country A will have to put resources to the value of $100 million at the disposal of country *B*, i.e. will have to increase its exports by $100 million. The income changes connected with the transfer will decrease *A*'s imports by $30 million and increase *B*'s imports from *A* by $40 million, i.e. country *A*'s trade balance will improve by $70 million because of the immediate effects of the income changes connected with the transfer. But an improvement of $100 million is needed to take complete care of the transfer. Hence country *A* will have a deficit in its balance of trade of $30 million after the transfer has taken place.

Both countries are fully employed both before and after the transfer. The only way in which the deficit in country *A*'s trade balance can be corrected is by a change in relative prices. Country *A*'s terms of trade will have to deteriorate. Such a change in the terms of trade leads to an adjustment in the balance of trade in two ways. First, it implies a fall in the real income of country *A* and an increase in the real income of country *B*. This will lead to an increase in imports in country *B* and a fall in imports in country *A*. Second, the change in relative prices will lead to substitution. As imports become more expensive in *A*, exportables are substituted for importables, and vice versa in country *B*. This will further improve country *A*'s balance of trade, and equilibrium will again be achieved but at worsened terms of trade (for *A*).

As we know from the recent experience in relation to OPEC, where the sum of the critical import propensities were considerably less than 1.0, the undereffected resource transfer implied a secondary burden for the oil-importing countries. As we know, the individual countries also had to deflate their economies to try to reach a new equilibrium in their balances of payments.

This, however, is not a necessary outcome. As we have emphasized, the critical factors are the marginal propensities to import. If the sum of the marginal propensities to import had been unity, the transfer would have been completely effected. Say that $m_a = 0.4$ and that $m_b = 0.6$. Then a loan from *A* to *B* of $100 million would decrease imports in *A* by $40 million and increase imports in *B* by $60 million. The net effect on *A*'s trade balance would be an improvement of $100 million, exactly enough to take care of the transfer. Thus the transfer would be completely effected and there would be no secondary burden.

If the sum of the marginal propensities to import is larger than unity, the transfer will be *overeffected*. This means that it will lead to a surplus in *A*'s balance of trade. To restore equilibrium the terms of trade will have to turn in favor of *A*, and part of *A*'s fall in income connected with the transfer will be restored by an increase in the real income due to improved terms of trade.

We have now set out the basic results of the classical version of the transfer theory. We have seen that the critical factors for the effects on trade balance, terms of trade, and real income are the changes in import spending induced by the transfer. We have set out the simplest version of this theory, with only two goods and involving no transport costs or impediments to trade. The theory can be extended to more complex cases, but the main drift of the argument is still the same.

If, for instance, transport costs and tariffs are introduced in the two-sector model, the transfer will be effected even though the sum of the marginal propensities is less than unity. In the case with three goods (two traded goods and one domestic, non-traded good), the result also depends on the possibilities of substitution between traded and non-traded goods in the two countries. The relative price of domestic goods will fall in the lending and increase in the borrowing country. The change in the terms of trade and the secondary effects on real incomes will therefore also depend on substitution possibilities between traded and non-traded goods. The larger these are in the lending country and the smaller they are in the borrowing country, the greater is the possibility for a favorable development of terms of trade for the lending country, and the smaller should the eventual secondary burden be.

We have now studied the main results of classical transfer theory. An essential element of this approach is that equality between income and expenditure is assumed at a level of full employment. The modern, Keynesian transfer theory is built on very different assumptions in this respect. This model is based on the assumption of underemployment: each industry in each country has an excess capacity; commodity and factor prices are therefore fixed. Hence there can be no adjustment via prices. The adjustment instead takes place by changes in national incomes (which change both in nominal and real terms).

The main finding of this type of analysis is that the result will depend on the income changes induced by the transfer. If the marginal propensities to save in the two countries (call them S_a and S_b) are positive, income changes will not suffice to take care of the transfer, and it will be undereffected. If, as the term goes, each country is stable in isolation (i.e. $S_a > 0$ and $S_b > 0$), income changes alone will not suffice to take care of the transfer.[1] Another point worth noting is that if the marginal propensity to save is larger in the lending than in the borrowing country, the transfer will have a depressive effect on world income. It is easy to see why this is so: the induced deflationary effect on country A's income will be larger than the inflationary impact on country B's income.

Summing up the discussion so far, we can say that a certain insight can be gained by combining the Keynesian transfer model with the perhaps more relevant classical model, though a certain caution must be used since the two models are based on different and not easily reconciled assumptions. The initial income changes induced by the transfer will give rise to changes in the demand for imports in the two countries. This will automatically take care of a good deal of the transfer. If the sum of the marginal propensities to import is large enough, the transfer will be completely effected by this mechanism. In most cases, however, one would expect the transfer to create a deficit in the trade balance of the lending country. Then the terms of trade will have to deteriorate for the lending country. This should work along much the same lines as a devaluation and should lead to a new external equilibrium. Income changes might also play an important role in this context. The transfer ought to have a deflationary impact in the lending country and an inflationary impact in the borrowing country. This mechanism, then, will also make for a smooth adjustment in the balances of payments of the countries taking part in the transfer.

Historical experience has shown that the adjustment mechanism works smoothly in connection with transfers. Taussig and his students found that the transfer process worked even more smoothly in the real world than the classical view would have predicted. The classical verification of the transfer process in connection with international lending is Jacob Viner's *Canada's Balance of International Indebtedness, 1900-1913*. His thorough and ingenious study showed

TABLE 21.2

Distribution of the stock of foreign direct investment (book value) by country of origin (1971)

	$ billion	Per cent
United States	86.0	52
Great Britain	24.0	15
France	9.5	6
West Germany	7.3	4
Switzerland	6.8	4
Canada	5.9	4
Japan	4.5	3
Netherlands	3.6	2
Sweden	3.5	2
Italy	3.4	2
Belgium	3.3	2
Others	7.2	4
Total	165.0	100

SOURCE: United Nations, *Multinational Corporations in World Development*, New York, 1973.

that the terms of trade really played the role it was expected to play according to the classical model.

However, the chastening experience of the oil crisis has amply demonstrated that, in a multi-country framework, a failure to agree upon an organized solution to the transfer problem can lead to a deflation of real incomes far greater than the original volume of resources transferred.

Having dealt with some of the main aspects of the transfer problem, we will continue to discuss some determinants of direct investments.

THE THEORY OF DIRECT INVESTMENTS

Direct investments have played an increasingly important role in the world economy since the Second World War. The United States is by far the most important country engaging in direct investment. This is illustrated in Table 21.2. Together with Great Britain, the United States accounted for two-thirds of the total book value of foreign direct investments at the beginning of the 1970s.

The active agents making direct investments are the developed, industrial economies. The large industrial countries are the primary investors; but even smaller, industrially advanced nations like the Netherlands, Switzerland and Sweden are home countries for important multinational firms (M.N.F.s) making large direct investments. The country whose direct investments have increased most during the last two decades is Japan.

The largest share of direct investments is carried out in the developed countries. By far the largest single recipient of U.S. direct investment is Canada.

TABLE 21.3

U.S. direct investment (billions of dollars per annum)*

Year	Total	Canada	Western Europe	United Kingdom	Latin America	Australia, S. Africa, New Zealand	Others
1950	11.8	3.6	1.7	0.8	4.4	0.4	1.7
1960	32.0	11.2	6.7	3.2	8.4	1.2	4.5
1965	48.8	15.2	14.0	5.1	10.8	2.3	6.4
1970	78.1	22.8	24.5	8.0	14.7	4.3	11.8

SOURCE: U.S. Department of Commerce, *Survey of Current Business.*

* These are book-value figures, compiled by adding annual direct investment flows and are retained earnings to census data at book values (before depreciation).

This is illustrated in Table 21.3. Canada has a long history as host for the large U.S. corporations; the Canadian market has always been closely tied to the large U.S. market.

Since about 1958, Western Europe, and the E.E.C. countries in particular, has become an increasingly important receiver of direct investments from the United States. The multinational corporations also play a major role in some less developed countries. Roughly two-thirds of all direct investments are made in developed countries and one-third in less developed countries. It is usually the latter which arouses the greatest controversy, since the M.N.F.s of the rich countries are often viewed as exploiters of the weaker, less developed economies.

The alternative form of investment, portfolio investments, were governed by a wish to maximize the rate of return and to spread risks so as to obtain an optimal portfolio mix of investments which were essentially passive; someone else made the real investments which were financed by the portfolio investments. At the heart of direct investment is *control.* The investor wants to retain the control over his direct investment himself. The most frequent emissary of a direct investment is the multinational corporation. Why should a firm want to invest in production facilities abroad? The answer to this question is rather complex. Direct investments occur essentially because a firm has some superior technology or some type of comparative advantage over which it wants to retain control. The best way to retain this control and to improve the firm's standing and profits is through direct investments.

A firm or corporation, say in the United States, working under monopolistic or oligopolistic market conditions has developed some new product or new production technique. It wants to generalize the use of its innovation and to increase its possibilities of making a profit from its superior technology. Therefore, it wants to enter foreign markets. The natural way to do this and to enjoy the benefits of its superior technology is by direct investment.

To understand the determinants of direct investments, it could be useful to set out the following production function:

$$Q = f(L, C, M)$$

where Q denotes the output produced, L and C labor and capital, and M managerial skills or organizational technique. The difference between this formulation of the production function and the formulation used in earlier parts of the book and formally set out in Chapter 2 is, therefore, that we now take management or organization explicitly into account as an argument in the production function. This is explained by the fact that we now regard management as one of the essential variables needed to explain the phenomenon we are studying.

Speaking in terms of factor endowments, we could say that the United States has a large amount of M compared with other countries. This leads to the marginal product of managerial skills, $\partial Q/\partial M$, being lower in the United States than in other countries. The United States, therefore, ought to export products which are intensive in the use of managerial skills. This might also be the case. However, we are not now primarily interested in explaining trade but in explaining factor movements. We can say that we live in a world where factors of production are at least partially mobile. Some factors, however, are more mobile than others.

The least mobile factor is labor. For legal, institutional and sociological reasons such small parts of the labor force are mobile that we can presume labor to be, for all practical purposes, immobile. Capital is more mobile than labor, but the conditions of supply of capital are not so different between countries as to make capital movements all that important. Furthermore, capital is a joint factor of production often paired with management. The most mobile factor of production is management.

Executives, or members of the technostructure, as Galbraith calls them, can fairly easily move between countries.[2] The sociological milieu of executives in developed industrial countries is not all that different; to be a director of an oil company or a computer corporation in New York, Paris, London or Frankfurt does involve certain differences in the way of life, but the resemblance in general cultural outlook, family life, and, above all, in general working conditions are also great. It might even be argued that making an executive career in an international corporation today implies a willingness to spend one's life in different parts of the world. This is also true, though to a somewhat lesser degree, for the interchange between industrial and the less developed countries of a capitalistic type.

An important reason for making direct investments is hence a willingness to increase profits by taking advantage of some technological superiority or some superior organizational form. A number of studies have produced empirical evidence of the relationship between knowledge and organizational techniques and the growth of overseas manufacturing investment. Gruber *et al.* found that U.S. overseas manufacturing investments and manufacturing exports were concentrated in research-intensive industries.[3] A similar relationship has also been established by the U.S. Tariff Commission.[4]

In a somewhat analogous manner, the international firm can be thought of as a *perfector* of markets. One can view the firm as a 'privately owned market' instead of, as is standard, seeing the market as a public coordinating function open to anyone who wants to enter it as an economic agent. The big international firm can be regarded as an international market for inputs and information. It might be more efficient, it is argued, to have market conditions equalized throughout the world with the help of big international firms in various branches of industry, than to have the same equalization process obtained by way of international trade in goods.

Before elaborating on the causes of direct investments, it should be observed that the term 'direct investment' is somewhat inadequate. As we can see, it is not so much a movement of capital that is involved in a direct investment as an international movement of techniques or organizations. This improved technique or organization is often embedded in capital, but the main thing to keep in mind is that capital, most of the time, is only the complementary factor of production in a direct investment.

The agent of direct investments is typically the large multinational corporation. Foreign investment is seldom undertaken by a firm until it has gained a strong position in the domestic market. The foreign firm is, of course, always at a disadvantage compared with the local producer who knows the language, the customs and the local markets. Why then should the foreign firm want to enter the new market?

The answer is typically explained in the terms which we have sketched above: the multinational firm possesses some superior technology or managerial skill.

Direct investment is typically industry-specific. The significance of this is that it is not so much the transfer of investment between nations as the transfer from one industry in one country to the same industry in another country. Industry-specific investments take two important forms: horizontal and vertical integration. Large corporations wish to integrate horizontally by opening new subsidiaries in various parts of the world. This is often done in a predatory way: one or several existing, competing firms in the host country are simply bought up by a large international rival. In the process competition is often reduced and markets are divided in an oligopolistic fashion.

Vertical integration is also a strong motive for direct investments. For instance, there are only a few companies that refine and fabricate copper. It is not astonishing that they also try to achieve control over copper mines by vertically integrating backwards in the production process. One obvious reason for vertical integration is a desire to reduce risk.

From the point of view of the international firm, both horizontal and vertical integration can have perfectly rational grounds. They might lead to better control over markets and/or more efficient ways of organizing production. This is, however, not the same as saying that they also are beneficial for governments and consumers in the host countries.

We will return to a discussion of some of the welfare implications of the M.N.F.s' activities later on.

About 90 per cent of all direct investments emanate from the O.E.C.D. countries. The United States is the largest direct investor but it is not the only country making such investments. Direct investments are often a two-sided affair.

Most industrial countries are both foreign investors and host countries. The balance varies, with the United States being primarily an investing country while Canada, Belgium and Italy belong more to the second category. In an intermediate position are countries such as Great Britain and the Netherlands, where in 1970 flows of direct investment were approximately the same in both directions. This is easy to understand against the background of the model just developed.

It is true that, generally speaking, the United States has the most developed technology. But the technological level within any one country varies between sectors. Some sectors are the leading ones, whereas others are relatively backward. This is true in varying degrees for all countries. Therefore, some parts of German industry or of Swedish industry are technologically more sophisticated than the corresponding parts of American industry. This being so, there is a *prima facie* case for German or Swedish direct investments in the United States. Empirical facts also show that, between industrial countries, direct investments flow in both directions. U.S. direct investments in Europe are much more important then European direct investments in the United States, but there are still flows going in both directions. No such correspondence principle holds, however, for the relations between developed and less developed countries. Here it is a one-sided relationship whereby the developed countries make direct investments in the less developed countries without any offsetting direct investments being made by the less developed countries in the industrial countries. The capital flows from less developed to developed countries are exclusively of a portfolio type.

Another observation we can make concerns the interrelations between the inputs in the production function set out in equation (21.1). An increase in any one of the three inputs, L, C, or M, will increase the marginal productivity of the other two factors.[5] It is quite easy to see why this should be so. The production function is of an ordinary neoclassical kind. The three factors of production can to a degree be substituted for one another. The more of the third factor two of the factors have to work with, the more efficient they will become.

The essence of direct investments is that it brings one of the three factors of production, managerial skills, or organizational efficiency (M), to work with the other two. Hence the marginal productivity of labor and capital increases in the country where the investment is made. This will lead to an increase in wages for the workers and to an increase in the return to capital because of the foreign investment.

In the simple model we have set out, managerial or technological superiority is the key variable. However, explanations of direct investment that are based upon these factors are often integrated with theories of industrial organization, particularly those of oligopolistic behavior. Under free competition there is no room for product differentiation, brand names, etc., and the scope for technical improvement is limited. The representative firm is small; it cannot differentiate its product, and it has few resources to devote to research and development.

On the other hand, the conditions of oligopoly, which prevent, for example in the automobile and petroleum industries, a substantial proportion of direct investment abroad, take the form of *horizontal* expansion into the same or similar lines of production.[6] The firm that successfully produces a differentiated product controls knowledge about serving the market that can be transferred to other national markets at little additional cost. However, it should be noted that although transfer costs are low, the relatively high fixed costs of securing the knowledge act as a barrier to the participation of smaller companies, who may instead prefer a licensing arrangement. At the same time, the alternative of licensing a foreign producer is limited to those cases where the information can be transferred independently of the entrepreneurial manpower or the organiz-ational framework, such as in the case of a 'one-off' technical innovation.[7]

In his work on the evolution of the firm – the so-called 'product-cycle' theory (see Chapter 7) – Vernon has emphasized that a firm tends to become multi-national at a certain stage in its growth.[8] In the early stages of the product cycle, initial expansion into overseas markets is by means of exports. Because countries are at different stages of economic development, separated by a 'tech-nology gap', new markets are available to receive new products through the *demonstration effect* of richer countries. Prior to the standardization of the pro-duction process, the firm requires close contacts with both its product market and its suppliers. However, once the product has evolved in a standard form and competing products have been developed, the firm may decide to look overseas for the lower-cost locations and new markets. It is only that factor inputs may be less expensive abroad but that considerable scale economies from longer pro-duction runs may be obtained through the allocation of component production and assembly to different plants. On the demand side, new markets can be established by price reductions, or more typically by the firm operating in an oligopolistic market situation by means of product differentiation.

The product-cycle concept offers a useful point of departure for a study of the causes of international investment but it is important to remember, as Hufbauer has emphasized, that 'the story of international oligopoly is *not* a story of aggressive expansion by giant multinational companies in a predatory effort to crowd out small local firms', but rather 'a preference for the status quo'.[9] Empirical work has shown that growth has not in fact been an increasing function of size.[10] In an uncertain world, security and counter-strategy take on an increased import-ance. It is this light that one should view the phenomenon of *vertical* integration. In order to secure their lines of supply, multinational corporations integrate 'backwards' by means of foreign investment in the production of a raw material or input. Besides the avoidance of risk, the control of input sources by a firm or a small group of firms raises substantial barriers to the entry of new competitors.[11]

Direct investments are a very complex affair. It is only natural that, in out-lining the basic theory, we seek to focus attention on some simple explanations that can take us a long way toward an understanding of the subject. However, several other factors are important. One is protectionist policies; another is closeness to the market.

The effect of protectionist policies is quite obvious. Many countries are averse to imports of industrial products. Governments with a protectionist slant often think that such products could, or should, equally well be produced by national firms. They then seek to foster domestic industries by using tariffs and other protectionist means. What such policies cannot do, however, is to deprive the foreigner of his technological or managerial advantage. Such policies, therefore, often induce foreign corporations to undertake direct investments and go directly into the protected market to which they earlier, instead, exported their products.

It is not difficult to find examples of direct investments that have been under-taken for such reasons. Countries such as Argentina and Brazil offered examples of protectionist policies that stimulated direct investments in the late 1940s and early 1950s. Some of the upsurge in direct investments which took place in the E.E.C. countries during the latter part of the 1950s could be explained along similar lines.

Protectionist policies (or beliefs about the alleged effects of such policies) were not the only reasons for the steady increase in direct investments, especially from the United States, which took place in Western Europe from the mid-1950s onward. Western Europe had experienced an unpredicted economic growth. This made the European market attractive to many American corporations. Western Europe, especially the E.E.C. countries, had emerged as politically stable industrial countries with mass markets for consumer goods. Currency restrictions were removed and full currency convertibility for non-residents was established for most European currencies at the end of 1958. All this naturally encouraged American direct investments.

Another factor worthy of note concerns size – the fact that most leading American corporations are much larger than their foreign counterparts. Not only is it true that in most fields the American firm represents the most advanced technology, it also typically commands much larger personal and financial resources. In many industries, the petroleum, electronic, and computer industries, for instance, American corporations could take over some very promising and prosperous European firms for defensive reasons – to make sure that there could be no unnecessary competition from foreign firms. It seems that a fair amount of direct investment has consisted of such placement buying of already existing assets – 'picking the plums', to use Joan Robinson's colorful phrase.[12]

DIRECT INVESTMENTS OR EXPORTS?

Direct investments and the multinational firms are controversial topics. In order to gain an increased understanding of these phenomena it might be useful to contrast direct investments with trade flows and ask the question: why do firms want to enter a foreign market by way of direct investments instead of exporting their products to the foreign country?

Let us say that there are two countries, A and B, and that a firm in country A plans to invest in country B by building a plant there. What happens if the authorities in country B pursue protectionist policies toward international investments and decide to forbid the entry of foreign firms? It all depends on certain circumstances.[13] If the *national* comparative advantage is strong but the *firm-specific* comparative advantage is weak, another firm, located in the country itself, will make the investment. The effects on trade flows, localization of production, etc., will then not be any different from the case where no protectionist policies had been followed, except for the fact that the allocation of resources on a world scale will be somewhat less efficient, as the firm in country A would have produced the goods somewhat more efficiently than does the firm in country B.

If, instead, the firm-specific comparative advantage is the important one, the outcome will be different. Then the firm in country A will build the plant (or expand the existing capacity) in its own country and then export the products to country B. In this case exports from country A will increase and the level of activity in the country will go up. Imports to country B will increase, while the demand for factors of production will decrease. In a sense we can say that this solution leads to too much trade as the impediment to foreign investment will make it impossible to utilize the national comparative advantage of country B.

A third case is the one where the planned investment will not take place at all. This occurs when both the firm-specific and the national comparative advantages are slight. The investment in country B is only profitable if it is made by the effective firm located in country A. As the foreign firm, because of the protectionist policies, will not be allowed into B, it will not make the investment at all as its firm-specific comparative advantage will be more than offset by the national comparative disadvantage if the investment has to be made in country A.

Multinational firms often work under oligopolistic market conditions. By *homogeneous oligopoly* we mean the fact that only a few large firms operate in a market, and that the firms do not differ too much from one another. One reason for such market conditions can be that very pronounced increasing returns to scale are present (see Chapter 7). Examples of such industries are steel mills, oil refineries and the sheet-glass industry. Often these industries seem to be combined with marked national comparative advantages. This is due to the fact that they are often processing industries dependent on some raw material and that they are therefore established close to the raw-material base. These industries are also often marked by vertical integration. If the national comparative advantege is strong, the industry will be established anyway, regardless of the conditions of ownership. An example on this might be the Norwegian aluminium industry, which presently is controlled by the Canadian Alcan corporation. The Norwegian comparative advantage is primarily based on the presence of cheap electric energy. Still, the Norwegian plant has preferred to become vertically integrated in a multinational corporation which controls other complementary raw materials and which has an effective marketing organization.

If increasing returns to scale are important, the industry might be footloose in the sense that it is difficult to say exactly where a firm may be located. It is still the case, however, that only a few firms will divide the international market between themselves. The sheet-glass industry seems to be an example of this. In 1979 two large corporations, the French St-Gobain and the English Pilkington, were competing for the Scandinavian market. Which of the two will gain the upper hand in the long run, and where the production will be located, for instance in Scandinavia or in West Germany, still seems to be an unresolved problem. In such cases the type of policies a country pursues *vis-à-vis* the multinationals will strategically influence the outcome.

Sometimes a country's historic comparative advantage in a branch of industry will be eroded with the passage of time. The textile industry is an example of this. In this case the established industries may still have some firm-specific comparative advantage, but they will be forced to move because of a growing national comparative disadvantage. During the 1960s and 1970s the Swedish textile industry has been forced to move to Finland and Portugal. The reason is that labor costs have been too high in the home country and that subsidiaries have therefore been started in low-cost locations. If the industry still has an effective marketing organization, it can control domestic supply even though the location of the productive activities will be determined by existing national comparative advantages.

Heterogeneous oligopoly is characterized by the fact that the firms in a market differ and that they produce goods which are clearly differentiated one from the other. Here the existence of firm-specific comparative advantage is often essential. The corporations also often want to specify the products according to the needs of the specific country, be it for reasons of safety regulations, local standards, etc. This is also a reason why firms want to be close to the market and why it is natural to establish a subsidiary in the foreign country.

We have earlier stressed that the multinational firms can be viewed as consti-

FIGURE 21.1

Comparative advantages and direct investments

Firm-specific
comparative
advantage

	Strong	Weak
Strong	I	II
Weak	III	IV

National comparative advantage

tuting a vertically integrated market. This is underlined by the fact that a substantial share of international trade consists of deliveries within the multinational firms. In 1973, for instance, 29 per cent of Sweden's foreign trade consisted of internal deliveries within individual corporations. Around 55 per cent of these deliveries went to sales subsidiaries and 45 per cent to producing subsidiary units. Swedish multinational firms often have producing units abroad, while foreign multinationals mostly have only their marketing organizations in Sweden. This is explained by the fact that Sweden is a high-cost country where labor is expensive.

It will be useful to sum up this discussion by the use of a diagram. Figure 21.1 illustrates four combinations of strong and weak firm-specific and national comparative advantages. Case I is that which demonstrates the importance – and dilemmas – of the multinational corporation most clearly. In this case the firm has a strong comparative advantage, so that no other firm can really produce the goods or services as efficiently as the firm in question. At the same time, there is also a strong comparative advantage in locating production in a specific country. Examples of such cases might be the large, well-integrated corporations working in a technologically advanced area such as the computer industry where technical progress is rapid. By letting components be produced in various countries, the corporations can take advantage of national characteristics in a way that no single country could. Strong firm-specific advantages make it difficult for any single country to avoid contact with the corporation since that would imply being excluded from access to important new technology. Firms of this category may be IBM or Philips or some of the large corporations dealing in pharmaceuticals and health technology.

Barriers to entry and to direct investments would be costly in case I and thus lead to a distinct deterioration in the efficiency of world resource allocation, the cost having to be borne by both investing and host countries.

Impediments to direct investments are less important in the other cases. In case II production will take place in the host country under any set of circumstances. As the firm-specific comparative advantages are weak, some company other than the prospective foreign investor would be expected to establish production. In case III exports can fairly easily be substituted for direct investment, and the firm can expand production in its home country and export the product to the country that raises barriers for direct investments.

Case IV is the most indeterminate case. This case is often connected with increasing returns to scale. Several firms are usually found to be competing with each other. Where production will be located will depend on chance factors, as no country offers any distinct comparative advantages over other countries. Refineries, steel mills and various petrochemical industries seem to be examples of case IV situations. It is opportune to make a comment in this context on the division of the return on direct investments between countries and corporations. The proportions in which these returns are divided depend critically, first on the nature of the investment (which of the four cases is in question), and second on the type of tax laws which are applied.

A common rule is that both home and host countries levy a tax on corporate profits of around 50 per cent of net profits. Let us presume that this is the case and that the rate of return on the investment is 16 per cent if the capital is invested abroad (in country II), while it is only 8 per cent if it is invested in the home country (country I). In this case the government of country II will retain 8 per cent of the return on the investment in taxation. Let us assume that the two countries have made an agreement not to tax their citizens or corporations twice. When the home country repatriates its profits it will receive credit for the taxes that it has already paid in the host country. Hence the net return of the corporation will be 8 per cent. If, instead, the corporation had made the investment in its home country, its gross return would have been 8 per cent, of which the domestic government would have collected 50 per cent in taxes, so that the net return would have been 4 per cent.

This can be viewed as an example of the effects of an investment of the case I type, where both strong firm-specific and national comparative advantages are present. In this case both the host country and the firm in question should lose if the investment were not to take place. The greatest loss will, however, have to be borne by the host country which forbids the foreign firm to enter its market. It should be observed that a divergence of interest between nations is implicitly present: as a matter of fact, the investing country has an interest in seeing barriers to foreign investment abroad raised, as this would increase the tax base of the investing country.

The tax issue further complicates the problems illustrated by Figure 21.1. We assumed, in the example given above, that the host country was able to collect taxes in an efficient manner. This is not always the case. The multinational firms can use means whereby taxes can be avoided and whereby profits can be directed toward countries where taxes are low. One way of doing this is by using transfer pricing. The welfare implications of the multinational firms and direct investments is an issue that has been hotly debated in recent years. It is now time to discuss more fully some of the effects of multinational firms on investing and host countries and how costs and benefits may be shared between them.

SOME EFFECTS ON THE INVESTING COUNTRY

Most of the debate about the merits and demerits of direct investments has treated

TABLE 21.4

Balance-of-payments effects of a direct investment

Balance of payments improving		Balance of payments worsening	
Export stimulus	10.6	Capital	100
Remitted dividends	8.1	Import stimulus	6.5
Royalties and fees	2.3	Loss of exports	None

the effects on the host country; we return to that shortly. Much less attention has been paid to the problems that could arise for the authorities in the investing country. We will briefly touch on some of them.

One problem is concerned with the balance of payments. We would expect, as we know from transfer theory, that a direct investment would lead to a worsening of a country's balance of payments. The extent depends on several factors, primarily on the interrelations between transferer and transferee, as expressed in the marginal propensities to import. For a typical American direct investment, a study by the Brookings Institution yields the figures given in Table 21.4. These figures suggest that the link between the investing and the host country is rather weak and that the direct effects on the two countries' balances of payments are small. Such conditions create a strong immediate negative effect on the investing country's balance of payments.

The time perspective plays an important role for the balance of payments of the investing country. If the investment in the example given in Table 21.4 was one injection, it would take six years for it to pay off, in the sense that the balance of payments of the investing country would again be positive. If the direct investment, instead, consisted of a steady flow of $100 million per year, it would take eleven years to reach equilibrium; if the flow of direct investment increased by 22 per cent per year, it would never pay off.

Against this background it is easy to understand that a large and growing volume of direct investments could be problematic from the standpoint of the investing country's balance of payments. Part of the fairly large and persistent deficit that the United States had during the 1960s can also be explained by the outflow of long-term capital (we return to this problem in Chapter 29).

In the long run, direct investments ought to have a positive effect on the investing country's balance of payments. This is especially the case if the flow of direct investments is steady or decreasing. We can see this effect today on investments from the United States and some other developed countries in their dealings with several less developed countries. If the flow sharply increases, there could be marked adverse effects on the balance of payments. Direct investments undoubtedly strained the United States' external position in the late 1950s and 1960s.

Other problems that could arise are more concerned with real factors. With the increasing internationalization of firms, the possibility of any single country pursuing its own independent economic policy becomes circumscribed. Corporations could gather in one country to work out pricing and market arrangements for another country. As long as there is no international legislation concerning

TABLE 21.5

Earnings on U.S. direct investments abroad.*
(percentage of book value at the beginning of year)

	1958	1962	1966
MANUFACTURING			
Europe	16	12	11
E.E.C.	17	14	11
Switzerland	36	11	15
TRADE AND OTHER†			
E.E.C.	20	18	6
Switzerland	42	40	16
PETROLEUM			
Europe	5	3	2
Middle East	60	71	60
Venezuela	21	18	19

* After foreign taxes.

† All direct investments other than mining and smelting, manufacturing, and
petroleum.

SOURCE: U.S. Department of Commerce, *Survey of Current Business.*

taxes, restrictive business practices, etc., any single country will have difficulties
in efficiently implementing its own laws.

Differing tax laws could create specific problems for investing countries.
Switzerland had exceptionally low taxes and favorable treatment of foreign
firms in the 1950s. (This seems still to be so even if a certain harmonization of tax
regulations has taken place.) This led to many American firms routing their sales
from all over the world through sales offices located in Switzerland. This also led
to exceptionally high earnings on investments in Switzerland. This is illustrated
in Table 21.5.

In 1962, the United States changed its tax laws. Earlier, taxes on earnings
from subsidiaries abroad were deferred until they were repatriated. In 1962 this
provision was changed so that earnings on holding companies and so-called 'tax-
haven operations' became taxable when earned. This had an immediate effect on
location of new service and sales offices: in 1961-2, 40 per cent of these were
located in Switzerland; in 1963 this figure fell to 10 per cent.

This is an example of how the investing country could try to counteract
undesirable effects of direct investments by changes in its legislation. The possibilities for such countervailing measures, however, are limited. Several countries,
especially well-developed ones with big taxes and highly developed social services,
could find their tax base shrinking as a result of direct investments. Their possibilities of implementing economic policies could also become circumscribed
by the operations of multinational firms.

There are several ways in which an international corporation could take out its profits in the most suitable place. The most important is perhaps by intra-corporate pricing practices. It has been estimated that between one-quarter and one-third of world trade now takes place within the multinational corporation and its subsidiaries.[14] This proportion is undoubtedly higher in relation to less developed countries. As a result of transactions between the foreign-owned subsidiary and the parent firm, or other subsidiaries, undeclared profits can be transferred via the over- or under-pricing of goods. Similarly, inputs of capital equipment and technology transferred from the parent company can be priced internally in such a manner that the real rate of profit is reduced. The extent to which transfer pricing can be used would appear to depend critically on the degree to which goods and services are traded within the firm rather than on the open market, at 'arm's length', to use Lall's apt phrase.[15] Consequently, consider-able scope for transfer pricing exists within the large foreign-owned enterprises which are vertically integrated with the parent company and which are typical of such industries as motor-vehicles, chemicals and electrical engineering.

Lall has put forward two forms of explanation for the use of transfer prices. First, there is the kind of transfer pricing which seeks to maximize the present value of total multinational profits in a world characterized by different rates of taxes, tariffs, subsidies, and by multiple exchange rates. However, there is also the need to protect the future level of profits against possible changes in price controls, taxation and, indeed, governments. The role of the multinationals in exacerbating the economic difficulties that confronted the Allende government in Chile between 1970–1973 is a case in point.[16]

There is little firm quantitative evidence on the actual importance of transfer pricing. It is naturally difficult to assess the extent to which the internal flow of goods and factors are over- or under-valued. However, there is no doubt that within the context of the less developed country, whose economy is heavily dependent on a small number of foreign-owned corporations, particularly of the vertically integrated variety, there is ample scope for the use of transfer pricing.

The cases referred to above will perhaps suffice to illustrate the principle that national economic policy will encounter difficulties in a world where economic integration becomes increasingly important but where the national state is still the dominant political entity. Direct investments certainly give very tangible advantages to firms in the investing countries, but they also lead to policy com-plications for governments of these countries.

SOME EFFECTS ON THE HOST COUNTRY

The problem created for the host country by direct investments have aroused by far the most intense feelings and discussion. The reason is not difficult to under-stand.

Consider first the balance of payments. It is obvious that in the short run the host country will under normal conditions improve its balance of payments and possibly also its terms of trade. This follows from a straightforward application of transfer theory.

In the long term things will turn out differently. Then, remittances of profits, etc., will be a negative term in its balance of payments. If the direct investment is of a once-for-all nature, or if the flow of direct investments into the country diminishes, the negative effects on the host country's balance of payments will soon be larger than the positive effects. This is natural; but it does not imply that the investment has proved detrimental to the country. Broadly speaking, as long as the positive effect on the host country's economic growth is larger than the negative effect on its balance of payments, the investment has benefited the country.

An essential aspect of the critique raised against direct investments has been that of control. We have already noted that the essence of direct investment is management control; this factor distinguishes it from other forms of capital movements. If direct investments take place in a country, it means that part of its industry will be controlled by foreigners. Many host countries find this difficult to accept; it has led to counter-measures in many countries.

The problem has probably been most acute in Canada. Here 59 per cent of the total capital in manufacturing is controlled by foreigners (40 per cent by Americans). Efforts have been made from time to time to increase Canada's control over foreign direct investments. In 1963, for instance, a new tax law was introduced requiring firms of less than 25 per cent Canadian ownership and with less than 25 per cent Canadian representation on the board of directors to be taxed at a somewhat higher rate than Canadian corporations.[17] Some developing countries, such as Mexico, require 50 per cent of ownership and directorship to be in domestic hands. Although wholly foreign-owned investment is permitted in the export processing sector, all foreign investment is screened, as is also the case in India, by a Foreign Investment Commission, which lays down criteria (often statutory) for the investment. These requirements usually relate to such matters as the sector and location of the investment, the extent of local participation, the transfer of technology, and disclosure of company information. A number of less developed countries have also attempted to increase their control of foreign investments by means of equity participation and joint ventures. The latter can be viewed not only as a means of control over foreign investment but as a training ground for local entrepreneurs, managers and technicians.[18]

Host countries fear direct investments for several reasons. Various types of charges are levied against foreign control. One is akin to balance-of-payments considerations. It says that the foreign firms do not export enough and that they give preference to firms in their home country or abroad (perhaps other subsidiaries of the parent corporation to which the firm in question belongs). Other charges are that foreign firms ignore local employment practices. Moreover, they could interfere with or upset domestic economic policies, for instance in the field of fiscal and monetary policy, or they could render national planning difficult. They are also often accused of having a negative effect on research and industrial development in the host country.

Before we consider the validity of these charges, advantages that direct investments can bring to the host country will be mentioned.

Some of these are implicit in the treatment we have already given to the matter when dealing with the theory of direct investment. The classical advantage is that direct investments raise world output by moving capital and managerial skills from regions where they are plentiful, and thus earn a low return, to regions where they are scarce, and thus earn a high return. We also learned that the normal effect of a direct investment is to increase the marginal product- ivity of both labor and capital in the host country and hence to have a positive effect on both the real wage and the real rate of return to capital. Comparative- static theorizing will undoubtedly tend to stress the beneficial effects of direct investments; the negative effects are concerned with more elusive arguments of a dynamic type or connected with various types of external effects.

We can now revert to our main line of argument and consider other, more important, complications that direct investment could create for the host country. Perhaps the most important argument against direct investments that a host country can raise concerns its effects on domestic research and develop- ment.

Foreign ownership of important parts of a country's industry can stifle scientific research and development work in the host country. We have seen that the main determinant of direct investments is superior technology or managerial skills. Direct investments, especially U.S. direct investments in Europe, tend to be made in technologically advanced industries whose importance for economic development is great. The research for further development of these key industries tends, however, to be located in the investing country, i.e. primarily in the United States. Thereby the host countries are deprived of the important stimulus given by research in these industries. It is this concern which motivated the demands for a Code of Conduct for the transfer of technology at the fourth conference of UNCTAD.

Thus research tends to be concentrated in the home country. The home country started with a comparative advantage in the production of goods which are intensive in research and innovating capacity. By the cumulative effects related to direct investments, this comparative advantage tends to become even more pronounced, and the host countries tend to sink into a position of second- rate economic powers.[19]

Another important point in this connection concerns external effects. It is widely believed that expenditures on research and development have important external effects. In the process of developing a certain product or improving production techniques, scientists and technicians are stimulated; new applications valuable outside the immediate project will be discovered; encouragement for, and incentives to, research in universities and other organizations outside the industry will be provided; and so on. A rational attitude geared toward experi- menting will be fostered, competent scientists will be trained, etc., and all this will have positive effects on the whole intellectual climate of the country.

If foreign firms via direct investments take over control of important parts of a country's industry, they will tend to shift research to their home country. This could be entirely rational from the point of view of the international firm, which is simply taking advantage of the economies of scale connected with the research activity. It can even be argued that this behavior is rational from the world's standpoint, because it maximizes world income. It still can have very detrimental effects on the host country, which is deprived of research activities that are perhaps comparatively inefficient but which, to the country itself, can be of great importance. How this question is viewed is largely a matter of values.

It depends, in technical language, largely on the kind of preference function used, whether international, for the home country, or for the host country. Before pursuing this, we will touch on a closely related question, that of the 'brain drain'.

The tendency, inherent in direct investments, to lead to a reallocation of research activities could also induce scientists and technicians to leave their home countries – to what has popularly been called the 'brain drain'. According to this argument, the United States will induce a 'brain drain' from Canada and Europe; Britain and France, too, will tend to siphon off scientific and technical talent from their formerly dependent areas.

It should be pointed out that such movements of educated and skilled people from the periphery to the center can be explained in rational economic terms. Education is a time-consuming activity, and teaching is a labor-intensive activity. It could therefore be expected that human capital (to use the existing jargon) should be produced in low-cost locations, as presumably the less developed or semi-developed countries are, being rich in labor. This is probably to some extent what happens. Several less developed and semi-developed countries have probably, in relative terms, quite a large supply of certain types of educated people who might have difficulty finding adequate work in their home countries. As wages are higher in the developed, industrial countries, the educated people will naturally move away from their home countries to more developed countries, i.e. a 'brain drain' will take place. This type of migration is also encouraged by laws and institutional factors, as most countries tend to favor immigration of educated persons rather than those with less training. To this should also be added the important fact that these skilled immigrants will be provided with more material capital to work with as the ratio of material to human capital is often much higher in the rich countries. Hence an English scientist will often be more efficient in the United States, and an Indian doctor will be more highly productive in England. The migrating scientist can often truthfully argue that what attracts him to move, to take part in the 'brain drain', is not the increased salary but the opportunity to work with better equipment and more assistance in more congenial surroundings.

How one views the effects on scientific activity induced by direct investments and the consequent 'brain drain' is largely a matter of values. From the world's standpoint, it can be argued that both of these effects are beneficial, as they tend to increase world income. But world income is a fairly abstract concept. There is also little reason why anybody should want to maximize world income irrespective of the effects on the world income distribution. Measures that only make the rich richer and the poor poorer can certainly be questioned.

How we view these problems, therefore, primarily depends on what type of welfare function we use. From the investing country's point of view the secondary effects on research and migration could be all to the good. From the host country's point of view it could be quite another matter.

The host country could welcome the immediate effects of a direct investment but be highly reluctant toward the secondary effects on research activity and the 'brain drain' that could be induced. If it means, for instance, that a highly promising computer program is abandoned because a domestic firm is being bought up and some very able scientists are induced to move abroad, the negative external effects are obvious. Then the country could, instead, choose to engage in a scientifically oriented infant-industry protection in the hope that, after a certain amount of development aid, the firm will become competitive on a world scale.

We cannot in this context go deeper into these interesting and many-faceted problems of direct investments. We must be satisfied with the hope of having been able to point out some of the very real problems in connection with direct investments facing a host country.

Before concluding this chapter, we should also remark briefly on another emotive aspect of direct investment, that of direct investment and exploitation.

DIRECT INVESTMENTS AND EXPLOITATION

Direct investments have in the Marxian tradition played a double role, and in both roles they have had important political implications.

In the first variant, direct investments are necessary to postpone the collapse of the capitalist system, and in the second and milder variant they are merely one of many forms of capitalist oppression.

The first line of thought was started by J. A. Hobson and taken up and developed by Lenin.[20] The essence of the argument is that capitalism needs new markets to survive. The inner forces of capitalism, primarily the relentless pursuit and application of new innovations, make it expand to new territories to find new markets and new consumers to postpone the collapse that history, according to Marx, has in store for it. The drive to technical progress also makes capitalists look for cheaper sources of raw materials in distant countries. Imperialism, according to Hobson and Lenin, is simply the logical consequence of the economic forces inherent in the capitalist system of production.

Marxists of later vintages have some difficulties in explaining this theory in its strict Leninist formulation.[21] The Marxian theories of impending collapse of the capitalist system, impoverishment of the workers, etc., are not easy to uphold in the light of the development of the capitalist system. The strong version of the Marxian theory of direct investments, which argues the necessity of these investments for the survival of the capitalist system, can hardly be sustained.[22] That capitalist countries derive profits from their direct investments abroad is one thing; it is quite another thing to argue that the industrial, capitalist nations are so dependent on the territories they in some sense dominate via direct investments that their economies would break down without them. It is hardly correct to argue that the United States, Britain, France, etc., are so dependent on their direct investments (or their trade with third countries in general for that matter) that their economic systems could not be sustained without them. A certain lowering of U.S. economic welfare would follow if, to take a drastic example, all U.S. foreign investments were nationalized overnight by the countries in question and no compensation paid. But there is no doubt that the effect of such an action would imply marginal changes in the American economy rather than a collapse of its capitalist system.

The strong version of the first line of thought which argues that direct investments are necessary for the survival of the capitalist system is not easy to uphold.

Capitalism's powers of survival should not be underestimated. However, this does not imply that part of international politics cannot be explained in economic terms, even in fairly crude terms like 'search for profits'. The second tenet of Marxist theory which relates to the need for raw materials has to a certain extent been vindicated in recent years.

This is not primarily due to the strength of Marxist methodology. However, the assumptions underlying the Marxist analysis, with its emphasis on conflict between various factors of production, on the importance of power relationships and of the natural interest on the part of the producers to try to limit competition and control markets, would seem to be more realistic than the often simple-minded, harmony-geared assumptions of neo-classical economics.

It is not difficult to find examples of varying degrees of economic exploitation. If one country has a strong economic influence over another, and couples that with an allegiance with certain ruling forces of the host country and maintains a close military cooperation with those ruling forces, the host country could be in a difficult position. Then it can certainly be maintained that both political and economic exploitation can occur.

An attempt to deal with a situation such as that just sketched would, however, quickly take us beyond the scope of the present work. Suffice it to say that, in general, we expect direct investments to benefit both the investing and the host country, for reasons set out earlier in this chapter. Nevertheless, the multinational corporation remains a topic of considerable controversy. There is no doubt that the large multinational firm, through its dominance of local markets and research and development and its ability to shift taxable income, can have substantial negative effects on the host country.

SUMMARY AND CONCLUSIONS

Portfolio investments are purely financial movements of capital, while direct investments involve international movements of technology and management rather than movements of capital.

All international capital movements give rise to a 'transfer process'. A transfer of capital from one country to another will affect the countries' incomes. Whether a transfer will be 'effected' or not will depend upon how incomes and marginal propensities to spend on imports are affected. Often a transfer will give rise to a secondary burden and the terms of trade will have to change. The transfer problem has gained a renewed topicality in connection with the increase in oil prices which occurred in 1973 and which created large imbalances in the world economy (see Chapter 30).

The main determinant of direct investment is superior technology or skill. The typical agent undertaking direct investment is the large multinational firm which wants to retain control over its investment abroad. Such a firm usually possesses superior technology or management and will naturally seek to increase profits by expanding its horizons and investing abroad.

Direct investments primarily take place under monopolistic or oligopolistic market conditions. Among developed countries it is often a two-sided affair, even if it is natural that the United States, as the leading industrial country, is also the largest direct investor.

The principal advantage of direct investments is that they raise world output by moving managerial skills and capital from regions where these factors are plentiful, and thus earn a low return, to regions where they are scarce, and thus earn a high return. Normally, direct investments will benefit both the investing country and the host country.

The immediate impact on the investing country's balance of payments can often be adverse, even though the transfer mechanism usually works smoothly. The investing country could have difficulties in controlling domestically located firms operating in international markets. National economic policies could be difficult to implement, and attempts at economic planning could be thwarted.

For the host country, the immediate impact of a direct investment will usually be an improvement in the balance of payments. In the long run, the effects could be negative. From a 'real' point of view, the effects are beneficial as long as the positive effects on the country's economic growth are larger than the negative ones on the balance of payments.

There are some effects of a secondary or external kind that could be detrimental to the host country. The most important are that direct investments could stifle scientific research and development work in the host country and that the multinational corporation could transfer a substantial part of the gains of the investment away from the host country.

Direct investments could conceivably lead to exploitation, primarily of less developed countries. The meaning of the term, however, has to be well defined and the circumstances carefully scrutinized before any such charge can be meaningfully levelled against the multinational corporations.

SELECTED BIBLIOGRAPHY: CHAPTER 21

The important theoretical papers on the transfer problem are:

P. A. Samuelson, 'The Transfer Problem and Transport Costs: The Terms of Trade when Impediments are Absent', *EJ*, June 1952 (reprinted in *RIE*).

P. A. Samuelson, 'The Transfer Problem and Transport Costs, II: Analysis of Effects of Trade Impediments', *EJ*, June 1954 (reprinted in *RIE*).

The two Samuelson papers cited above both treat the problem on 'classical' assumptions. For a treatment on Keynesian assumptions, the standard paper is:

L. A. Metzler, 'The Transfer Problem Reconsidered', *JPE*, June 1942 (reprinted in *RTIT*).

For a partial reconciliation of the two approaches see:

H. G. Johnson, 'The Transfer Problem and Exchange Stability', *JPE*, June 1956 (reprinted in *RIE*).

Two major empirical studies of the transfer problem are:

J. H. Williams, *Argentine International Trade Under Inconvertible Paper Money, 1880–1900*, Cambridge, Mass., Harvard University Press, 1920.

J. Viner, *Canada's Balance of International Indebtedness, 1900–1913,* Cambridge, Mass., Harvard University Press, 1924.

For a reworking of the Canadian material see:

R. E. Caves and G. L. Reaber, *Canadian Economic Policy and the Impact of International Capital Flows,* Toronto, Toronto University Press, 1969.

There is now a voluminous literature on the theory of direct investments and the multinational corporation. One of the most interesting which has now been published posthumously is:

S. H. Hymer, *The International Operations of National Firms: A Study of Direct Foreign Investment,* M.I.T. Press, 1976.

Amongst the leading collections of essays which survey the entire field of direct investment the following works can be mentioned:

J. Dunning (ed.), *International Investment,* Harmondsworth, Penguin, 1972.

J. Dunning, *The Multinational Enterprise,* London, Allen & Unwin, 1974.

C. P. Kindleberger (ed.), *The Interinational Corporation,* Cambridge, Mass., Harvard University Press, 1970.

F. Machlup, W. Saland and L. Tarshis (eds), *International Mobility and Movement of Capital,* New York, National Bureau of Economic Research, 1972.

R. Vernon, *The Economic and Political Consequences of Multinational Enterprises: An anthology,* Cambridge, Mass., Harvard University Press, 1972.

An interesting survey work is:

Nils Lundgren, *Internationella koncerner i industriländer,* Stockholm, Liber, 1975.

The relationship between international trade investment and imperfect markets is discussed in:

R. E. Caves, *International Trade, Investment and Market Performance,* Princeton Special Papers in International Economics, No. 10, Princeton, N.J., 1974.

W. M. Corden, *The Miltinational Corporation and International Trade Theory,* University of Reading Discussion Papers, No. 10, Reading, 1974.

G. K. Helleiner, 'Manufactured Exports from Less Developed Countries and Multinational Firms', *EJ*, March 1973.

For monographs on specific countries see:

D. T. Brash, *American Investment in Australian Industry,* Cambridge, Mass., Harvard University Press, 1966.

D. J. Forsyth and K. Docherty, *The United States Investment in Scotland,* New York, Praeger, 1972.

H. Hughes and Y. P. Seng, *Foreign Investment and Industrialization in Singapore,* Madison, University of Wisconsin Press, 1969.

M. Kidron, *Foreign Investment in India,* London, Oxford University Press, 1965.

A. E. Safarian, *Foreign Ownership of Canadian Industry,* Toronto, Toronto University Press, 1966.

C. Widstrand (ed.), *Multinational Firms in Africa,* Uppsala, Almqvist & Wiksell, 1975.

The Marxian point of view is presented in the works by Lenin and Rosa Luxemburg referred to in Chapter 21. For a neo-Marxian treatment of direct investments and imperialism see:

P. Baran, *The Political Economy of Growth,* New York, Monthly Review Press, 1957.

P. Baran and P. Sweezey, *Monopoly Capital,* New York, Monthly Review Press, 1966.

E. Mandel, *Marxist Economic Theory,* London, Monthly Review Press, 1968, vol. 2.

H. Magdoff, *The Age of Imperialism,* New.York, Monthly Review Press, 1969.

An interesting interpretation of the Marxist view of foreign investment is:

B. J. Cohen, *The Question of Imperialism: The Political Economy of Dominance and Dependence,* New York, Basic Books, 1973.

A comprehensive bibliography of the literature on direct investment is provided by:

S. Lall, *Foreign Private Manufacturing Investment and Multinational Corporations: An annotated Bibliography,* New York, Praeger, 1975.

PART IV

The balance of payments and international economic policy

22
The market for foreign exchange

In Parts I, II and III we dealt with the 'real' side of the economy. We have explained why countries trade with each other, we have studied the effects of economic growth on international trade, and we have analysed important aspects of trade policy. The standard tool of analysis has been the barter model of trade.

The time has now come to deal with monetary aspects of international economics. We will start, in this chapter, to study the market for foreign exchange. The factors that determine the demand for and supply of foreign exchange will be analyzed in the simplest possible manner, and it will be demonstrated how the market for foreign exchange is cleared under a system of flexible exchange rates.

Central to Part IV is a study of the balance of payments. To treat it in an efficient manner we have to define carefully the meaning of the balance of payments and see in what sense it will always be in equilibrium and in what sense surpluses and deficits can exist. This will be done in Chapter 23.

Chapter 24 is devoted to a study of the determination of national income in open economies. The reader is probably familiar with the Keynesian theory of income determination for a closed economy. This theory will be generalized to open economies, foreign trade multipliers will be studied, and it will be shown how international business cycles are propagated.

After that we will come to policy issues. Chapter 25 analyzes policies for dealing with balance-of-payments problems. It is important to study the effects of exchange-rate changes, especially in the form of devaluations. The standard, traditional approach to devaluation is contained in the so-called *elasticity* and *absorption* approaches, which are analyzed in the chapter.

An interesting scientific achievement in recent years has been the application of modern monetary theory to international economic problems. Chapter 26 is devoted to the new monetary approach to the balance of payments, which can be viewed as an important addition to the traditional approach.

Chapter 27 takes a look at a basic issue of long standing in international economics: the choice of exchange-rate regime. The chapter gives the arguments for and against flexible exchange rates and evaluates the advantages and disadvantages of fixed and flexible exchange rates.

Chapter 28, finally, is devoted to a discussion of aims and means in economic policy. We will study how a country can achieve jointly internal balance (full employment) and external balance under various assumptions as to what means are available to political authorities.

One of the disinguishing features of international trade is the involvement of foreign currencies. If a seller in New York sells goods to a buyer in California, he

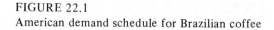

FIGURE 22.1

American demand schedule for Brazilian coffee

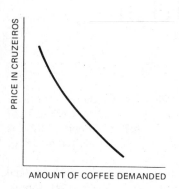

is paid in dollars. Despite the considerable regional distance between buyer and seller, they use the same currency. If a buyer in Belgium buys goods from a seller in Holland, the problem of foreign exchange occurs, because the buyer wants to pay in Belgian francs and the seller wants to receive his payment in Dutch guilders. We now look into the foreign exchange market and see how the price of one currency in terms of another currency is determined.

THE DEMAND FOR FOREIGN EXCHANGE

We shall start by treating the problem of foreign exchange in the simplest possible manner. We are interested in the question from the point of view of economic theory. We shall therefore not deal with the many technical banking aspects of the problem; readers interested in these will have to consult the specialist literature.

An importer in any one country is interested in acquiring foreign exchange with which to buy foreign goods. Figure 22.1 gives an example of the American demand schedule for Brazilian coffee. This is a very straight-forward example that needs little comment. A small amount of coffee is demanded at a high price, and at a lower price a larger amount of coffee is demanded. The demand situation for coffee is especially simple, because we assume that the United States does not produce any coffee at home but imports all that it consumes.

The demand schedule for a product, part of which is produced at home and part of which is imported, is somewhat more complicated. An illustration of this situation is given in Figure 22.2. Figure 22.2(a) shows the supply and demand for shoes in the United States. At a certain price, P_1, all the American demand is supplied by home producers. Only at a lower price does the United States start import. At price P_1 the American consumers demand q_1 of shoes. If the price low P_1, the total increase in demand is covered by imports. At the same price falls, so does the home supply of shoes. This is also taken over

FIGURE 22.2
Supply and demand for shoes in the United States

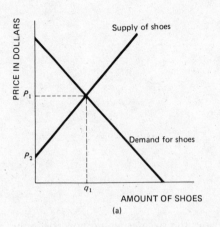
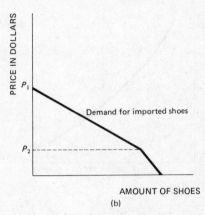

by foreign exporters. To deduce the total demand schedule for imported shoes, we therefore have to add the decrease in the domestic supply of shoes to the increase in over-all demand. If this is done, we get a demand schedule for imported shoes like that of Figure 22.2(b). This schedule is derived from the demand and supply schedules in Figure 22.2(a).

It is important to realize that if an import-competing industry exists in a country, the country's demand schedule for imports is quite different from its demand schedule for the imported good. This fact is illustrated in Figure 22.2. Above a certain price all the country's demand is covered by home production, and nothing is imported. Then follows a range where imports start to compete with home production. In this range the demand schedule for imports is much more elastic than the demand schedule for importables. If the price falls to such a low level that all domestic import-competing production has been out-competed, then the demand schedule for imports coincides with the demand schedule for importables. This fact is illustrated in Figure 22.2 when the price is below P_2.

From this it follows that in the range most often of interest, i.e. the range where some domestic import-competing production exists, the demand for imports is more elastic than the demand for the good itself.

If we add all the demand schedules for different imported goods for a country, we find the over-all aggregate demand schedule for imports. Figure 22.3 shows an example of such a demand schedule, translated into terms of demand for foreign exchange. For the sake of concreteness we have chosen to take only two countries as examples, so that Figure 22.3 shows the U.S. demand for British pounds. If the price for £1 is high, let us say $4, the amount of British pounds demanded will be small, because an article (for instance, a sweater) which costs £1 in England will cost $4 in the United States. If the price of £1 were only $2, the American demand for British pounds would increase, because

FIGURE 22.3

Aggregate demand schedule for foreign exchange

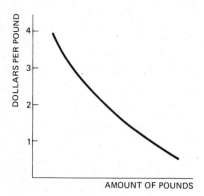

the demand for British goods would increase; the sweater would now cost only $2 in the United States. Thus it follows that we expect the demand schedule for foreign exchange to have a slope similar to that in Figure 22.3.

It is very interesting to try to deduce knowledge about the shape of the demand curve for imports so that one can remark on the elasticity of demand for imports. There are two facts of great interest in this connection. The first is the question of the elasticity of demand for importables (imported goods). If a country imports necessities and raw materials, we may expect the elasticity of demand for imports to be low and quantity imported to be insensitive to price changes. If, on the other hand, the country imported luxury goods and goods for which suitable substitutes exist, demand elasticities for imports might be high. Whether or not the country has a domestic import-competing industry is the second extremely important factor. If the country has many well-developed import-competing industries, the elasticity of demand for imports most certainly is high. This is due to the fact that if the price rises, import-competing industries will come in and take a larger share of the market, and imports will fall; if the price falls, it will be the other way around.

Time is another factor to take into account. In the short run it may be difficult to react to price changes by reallocating factors of production. In the short run, therefore, elasticity of demand for imports may not be very high. In the long run, however, it is much more probable that the production pattern will alter according to price changes, and the demand for imports will therefore be more elastic.

If we take into account different types of countries, we find that their demand for imports differs. Most well-developed, industrial countries produce and import to a large extent the same type of goods; in other words, these countries have large and well-developed import-competing industries. For these countries, the demand for imports it often very elastic. Less developed, agricultural countries often have small, poorly developed import-competing sectors. They import necessities and the industrial goods needed for their

TABLE 22.1

Supply schedule in the foreign exchange market

(1) Price of a sweater in pounds	(2) Price of $1 in pounds	(3) Price of one sweater in dollars [col. (1) ÷ col. (2)]	(4) Quantity of sweaters demanded (elas. = 1)	(5) Amount of foreign exchange supplied (in dollars) [col. (3) x col. (4)]	(6) Quantity of sweaters demanded (elas. ≈ 2)	(7) Amount of foreign exchange supplied (in dollars) [col. (3) x col. (6)]
10	7.50	1.33	750	1000	1000	1330
10	7.00	1.43	700	1000	900	1287
10	6.50	1.54	650	1000	800	1232
10	6.00	1.67	600	1000	700	1169
10	5.50	1.82	550	1000	600	1092
10	5.00	2.00	500	1000	500	1000
10	4.50	2.22	450	1000	400	888
10	4.00	2.50	400	1000	300	750
10	3.50	2.86	350	1000	200	572
10	3.00	3.33	300	1000	100	333

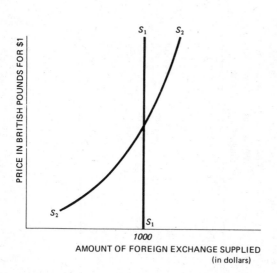

FIGURE 22.4

Elastic and inelastic supply
curves for foreign exchange

development programmes. Their demand for imports is on the whole very inelastic.

We shall find later that the question of elasticity of demand for imports has important implications for economic policy. But for the time being, we shall concentrate on the question of the supply of foreign exchange.

THE SUPPLY OF FOREIGN EXCHANGE

We have seen that the United States demands the pound sterling in order to buy British goods. Analogously, Britain supplies pounds to receive dollars in exchange. A country's supply schedule of its own currency in the foreign exchange market is therefore best viewed as an inverted demand schedule for foreign exchange. This is illustrated in Table 22.1. The first column give the price in Britain of a sweater made in Britain and exported to the United States. In the United States the price for this sweater depends on the exchange rate, i.e. the amount of pounds that an American may receive for $1. This is shown in column (2). If they receive £7.50 for $1, the price of the sweater in the United States will be $1.33. Let us assume that Americans demand 750 sweaters at this price. The amount of dollars supplied in the foreign exchange market in exchange for the import of this article is thus derived by simply multiplying the quantity demanded by its price, as done in column (5).

Let us assume that the exchange rate is such that $1 is worth £5; then the price of the sweater will be $2. We assume that 500 sweaters are demanded at this price. If the price changes, the amount demanded will also change. Table 22.1 gives two examples of how the supply of foreign exchange varies, depend-

FIGURE 22.5

Aggregate supply curve
for foreign exchange

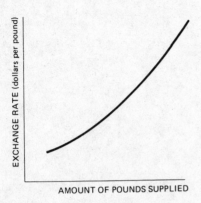

ing on demand elasticity. In column (4) the demand elasticity is supposed to be 1. Thus we see from column (5) that the amount of foreign exchange supplied by Americans is the same, regardless of price, because the total outlay on the good is constant. In column (6) the demand elasticity is supposed to be approximately 2. Thus we see from column (7) that the supply of dollars changes, so that if the price falls in the American market, a relatively larger quantity is demanded, and more dollars are supplied in the foreign exchange market for imports of this good. The two supply curves for dollars in the foreign exchange market that can be derived from Table 22.1 are illustrated in Figure 22.4.

We now see clearly that the supply curve of foreign exchange is derived from the demand for imports. If the demand elasticity for an imported article is 1, this gives rise to a completely inelastic supply curve, such as S_1 in Figure 22.4. If the demand for imports is elastic, we also get an elastic supply curve for foreign exchange, such as S_2 in Figure 22.4.

If we add all the supply curves for foreign exchange for all single import goods we will get an aggregate supply curve showing how much of its currency the country supplies at different exchange rates. An example of such an aggregate supply curve for foreign exchange is given in Figure 22.5.

Basically the same factors that are of importance for determining the elasticity of the demand curve for foreign exchange also determine the elasticity of the supply curve. As the value of the country's own currency increases, imports become relatively cheaper, and more is imported. As more is imported, more of the home currency is supplied on the foreign exchange market (provided the elasticity is larger than unity). When imports become relatively cheap, 'new' goods (goods earlier produced only at home) will start to be imported, and domestic import-competing industries will be gradually eliminated by imports. These are two important reasons why we expect the supply of foreign exchange to be quite elastic. Furthermore, the longer the time perspective we take into account, the more elastic will be the supply.

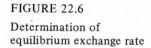

FIGURE 22.6

Determination of
equilibrium exchange rate

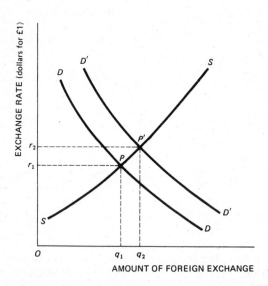

AMOUNT OF FOREIGN EXCHANGE

FLEXIBLE EXCHANGE RATES

We may now put the demand and supply schedules for foreign exchange together and see how an equilibrium exchange rate is determined. This is done in Figure 22.6, where the demand curve DD shows how many pounds the United States, for instance, demands, depending on the exchange rate, and the supply curve SS shows how many pounds the British supply as the exchange rate varies. The supply and demand curves cut each other at point P. The equilibrium exchange rate is r_1, and Oq_1 of foreign exchange is supplied and demanded. At the exchange rate r_1 the American demand for pounds equals the British supply of pounds, and the foreign exchange market is cleared.

Let us assume that a shift occurs in the American demand curve for foreign exchange from DD to $D'D'$. There may be many reasons for such a shift. One could be a change in taste, causing American consumers to demand, at any given exchange rate, more imported goods than before. Another reason could be an increase in the national income in the United States, giving rise to an increase in imports. Whatever the reason for the shift, the result is the establishment of a new equilibrium at P' with a new exchange rate r_2 and a new amount of foreign exchange Oq_2 supplied and demanded.

We now see the implications of a system with flexible exchange rates. The exchange rate varies with varying supply and demand conditions, but it is always possible to find an equilibrium exchange rate which clears the foreign exchange market and creates external equilibrium.

The American demand for foreign exchange is based on its demand for imports. If the relative price of pounds is high, so that many dollars have to be given for £1, the demand for foreign exchange to pay for imports is small. The lower the price of sterling, the larger is the demand for British imports and hence for pounds, as can be seen from the shape of demand curve *DD* in Figure 22.6. The British supply curve for pounds is determined by its imports of goods. The higher the price of pounds in the foreign exchange market, the cheaper will imports from abroad be in Britain and the more British pounds will be supplied, provided the elasticity of demand for imports is larger than unity. This is shown by supply curve *SS* in Figure 22.6. Where the supply and demand curves intersect, an equilibrium is created – at point *P*. If Americans import British goods to a value of Oq_1 pounds, the British will import American goods to a value of Oq_1 pounds, and trade between the two countries will balance.

If there is a shift in the demand curve from *DD* to *D'D'*, as illustrated in Figure 22.6, this will imply a depreciation of the American dollar and an appreciation of the British pound. By the depreciation of a currency we mean that the relative value of the currency decreases. When the dollar depreciates it means that Americans pay more dollars for £1. Analogously, an appreciation means that the relative value of a currency increases. If the pound sterling appreciates, it means that the British will have to pay fewer pounds for $1. Increase in American demand for British imports gives rise to an increase in demand for pounds and we arrive at a new equilibrium at *P'* and a new exchange rate r_2 which clears the market. This implies, as we see, a depreciation of the dollar and an appreciation of the pound. Because of the shift in demand, Americans ask for a larger amount of pounds, Oq_2, which the British supply, at the higher price. American demand for foreign exchange equals British supply, and the balance of payments is in equilibrium.

Assuming that we start from a situation in which a country has equilibrium in its balance of payments, any change from this position will, under a system of flexible exchange rates, first influence the exchange rate. If a deficit in the country's balance of payments occurs, an excess demand for foreign currency is implied. This leads to a fall in the exchange rate, so the country will have to pay more units of its own currency for a unit of foreign currency. There can be many reasons for this deficit, including an increase in imports, a fall in exports, or a decrease in the inflow of foreign capital. Whatever the reason, the effect on the exchange rate will be immediate and lead to a depreciation of the currency.

Analogously, a surplus in the balance of payments will lead to an excess supply of foreign currency and hence to an increase in the exchange rate, i.e. to an appreciation of the currency. This implies that imports now become cheaper, and the demand for imports increases. At the same time, exporters will receive less home currency for any one unit of foreign currency, producing a negative effect on exports. Hence imports increase, exports decrease, the surplus in the balance of payments is erased, and a new equilibrium in the balance of payments is established at the new exchange rate.

We should now have an understanding of how a system of flexible exchange rates work under ideal conditions. It is a very elegant system and seems to solve the problem of external equilibrium almost without effort. However, during most of the time since the Second World War, the major countries have had their exchange rates pegged. It is only since 1973 that floating rates have become more prevalent. Opinions regarding the best type of exchange-rate regime vary.

A more detailed analysis of the pros and cons of fixed versus flexible exchange rates will be given in Chapter 27, while a description of the international monetary system will be provided in Chapters 29 and 30.

SPOT AND FORWARD MARKETS FOR FOREIGN EXCHANGE

The foreign exchange market we have so far dealt with is the *spot market*. In a spot transaction the seller of exchange has to deliver the foreign exchange he has sold 'on the spot' (within two days). Likewise, a buyer of exchange will immediately receive the foreign exchange he has bought. There is also another important market for foreign exchange, the *forward market*. In the forward market, when the contract is signed, the seller agrees to sell a certain amount of foreign exchange to be delivered at a future date at a price agreed upon in advance. Analogously, a buyer agrees to buy a certain amount of foreign exchange at a future date and at a predetermined price. Usually the forward contracts are on a three-month basis, and in the following case this is assumed, though both shorter and longer contract periods exist.

Spot and forward markets are intimately linked together in at least three ways. The first way is via an interest arbitrage; the second way is by hedging or covering; the third way is by speculation.

Let us assume that the spot exchange rate is $4 for £1. This rate must be the same both in London and New York, because if the exchange rate were 4:1 in London but 3.90:1 in New York, it would pay to take dollars from New York to London and sell them there. This would continue until the rates were equalized. The forward rates might differ, however.

Let us continue to assume that the spot rate is $4 for £1. If the forward rate is higher than 4.00, for instance 4.03, we say that there is a premium on sterling. We denote the spot rate R_s and the forward rate R_f. We then get

$$R_f - R_s = \text{premium on pound sterling (if } R_f > R_s)$$

Analogously, we say that the pound sterling is at a discount if the spot rate is higher than the forward rate. This is the case if, for instance, the spot rate is $4.00 for £1 and the forward rate is $3.97 for £1. We get

$$R_s - R_f = \text{discount on pound sterling (if } R_s > R_f)$$

If the interest rates in the two countries differ, this gives rise to an interest arbitrage and a difference in spot and forward rates. Let us assume that the short-term interest rate in New York is 2 per cent while it is 5 per cent in London. We continue to assume that the spot rate is $4 for £1. So $4 in New York will yield an interest of $0.08 per year or $0.02 per three months. In London $4.00 will yield an interest of $0.20 per year or $0.05 per three months. If the forward rate in London were the same as the spot rate, the American *arbitrageurs* would place their funds in London, as the yield is higher there than in New York. This would lead to an excess supply of forward pounds, and depress the forward rate until the yield on £1 in London equalled that of $4 in New York. If we denote the British interest rate i_e, the American interest rate i_a, the discount d, and the premium p, we get the following two equilibrium conditions:

$$d = i_e - i_a \quad (\text{if } i_e > i_a) \tag{22.1}$$

$$p = i_a - i_e \quad (\text{if } i_a > i_e) \tag{22.2}$$

If we want to express the discount in per cent per year of the spot rate, we deduce that

$$d = \frac{R_s - R_f}{R_s} \; 100 \times 4 \tag{22.3}$$

If the spot rate is 4.00 and the forward rate is 3.97, the discount in per cent per year is $[(4.00 - 3.97)/4.00](100 \times 4) = 3$ per cent.

If, analogously, the premium is expressed in percent per year:

$$p = \frac{R_f - R_s}{R_s} \; 100 \times 4 \tag{22.4}$$

If the spot rate is 4.00 and the forward rate is 4.03, we see that the yearly premium is $[(4.03 - 4.00)/4.00](100 \times 4) = 3$ per cent.

Let us assume that the interest rate in New York is 2 per cent while it is 5 per cent in London, and that there is thus an interest-rate differential of 3 per cent. This will give rise to a discount on forward pounds. We assume the spot rate to be \$4.00 for £1. An interest-rate differential of 3 per cent should, in equilibrium, give rise to a discount of 3 per cent, and the forward dollar rate ought to be 3.97. If the discount were less, it would pay the arbitrageur to place his funds in London. If he placed \$4.00 in New York they would grow to \$4.02 in three months at a 2 per cent interest rate. In Britain £100 would grow to £101.25 in three months at a 5 per cent interest rate. If he had sold them in advance at the forward rate of 3.98, they would bring him $101.25 \times 3.98 = $ \$4.03, and he would make a gain.

If the short-term interest rates between two countries differed, the country with the higher interest rate would have its forward exchange rate at a discount. Let us say that country II has the higher interest rate. An arbitrageur in country I can then receive a higher return on his funds if he places them in country II. He has, however, to take into account discount on the forward rate. If the interest differential between the two countries is 3 per cent, the discount on the forward rate is also 3 per cent in equilibrium. If it is less, his gain on the interest-rate differential will be larger than the loss on the discount, and it is favorable for an arbitrageur to place his funds in country II instead of country I. This should, under normal conditions, lead to an inflow of funds to country II which would depress the forward rate in that country until the interest-rate differential was equal to the discount.

Analogously, if the short-term interest rate in country II is lower than the short-term interest rate in I, the forward rate in II should be at a premium. Let us again assume that the interest-rate differential is 3 per cent and that the spot rate is \$4.00 for £1. Then the forward rate in country II should be 4.03. The interest rate in I is, say, 5 per cent, so \$4.00 in I will grow to \$4.05 in three months, and £1 placed in II will grow to £1.005, which equals \$4.02 at the spot rate. If the forward rate equalled the spot rate and there were no premium, it would be disadvantageous to place any funds in country II, but if there is a premium, it has to be added. If the premium were 3 per cent per annum, and therefore the forward rate were 4.03, $100 invested in II would give the same return as if they were vested in I. If the premium on the forward rate were higher than 3 per cent, it would be more advantageous to place funds in II than in I. If the premium were lower than the interest-rate differential, the situation would be the opposite.

We have now set out the 'theory of interest-rate parity' in its simplest form. In reality, however, we find that the premium or discount often differs from the interest-rate differential. There are several reasons for this. Depending upon his subjective risk and liquidity considerations, an arbitrageur might not find it optimal to equalize objective return on his investments in two countries. For this reason alone the premium or discount might not equal the interest-rate differential. Interest arbitrage, however, is not the only factor influencing the forward rate.

Another important factor is *hedging* or *covering*. There is often a time difference between the signing of a contract and the delivery of the goods. An exporter, for instance, may have signed a contract to deliver goods three months hence. He knows that he will then receive, say, $1000. He may, however, fear that the exchange rate will change in the meantime. Hoping to avert a risk, he wants to know the exact sum he will receive. He is thus able to cover himself against risks by hedging. He sells $1000 forward at the going forward rate for the pound sterling. He receives no money and delivers none when he enters this contract, but three months hence, when he receives payment, he delivers the money that he has sold forward and he knows immediately what he will receive. Whatever the possible changes in exchange rates during the three months, they are of no consequence to him.

Likewise, any importer who enters a contract in the present, and knows that he will have to pay for his goods in the future, can cover himself against any exchange risks by buying forward. If the contract period is limited, three months for example, he knows exactly what the price of the goods will be when delivered to him, and he can avoid any risks connected with fluctuations in the exchange rate.

Hedging will give rise to a supply of and a demand for forward exchange. What the supply of and demand for forward exchange from this source will be depends on several factors. The volume of trade is important, and so is the risk aversion of exporters and importers. Hedging may cause the premium or discount on foreign exchange to differ from the interest-rate differential.

Hedging is important, especially in a market with flexible exchange rates, as it permits exporters and importers to protect themselves against risks connected with exchange-rate fluctuations, thus enabling them to concentrate on their pure trading functions. It should, however, be observed that the forward market is a short-run market, in which the contract period is usually three months. Longer contract periods exist, but these markets are not very well developed, and the upper limit for the contract period seems to be eight months or one year. For many contracts the period between ordering and payment is longer. In these cases hedging does not function efficiently, and risks connected with fluctuations in exchange rates can hardly be avoided.

Speculation is a third source for the supply of and the demand for forward exchange. We assume that the speculation is about the development of the future spot rate and that the speculation exclusively takes place in the forward market.[1] The speculator who expects the spot rate to increase in the future buys forward in order to sell spot when he receives his delivery of the currency that he has bought forward. On the contrary, however, a speculator who expects the spot rate to fall sells forward with the intention of buying spot when he needs currency for delivery.

We have seen that there is a close link between spot and forward rates through interest arbitrage. If speculators expect the spot rate to increase, they will buy forward, putting pressure on the forward rate, so that it, also, increases. Conversely, if they expect the spot rate to fall, they will sell forward and force the forward rate down. Therefore, speculation tends to make the spot and forward rates move together.

Under a system of flexible exchange rates there are many factors which influence movements in the exchange rates. The most important factors are connected with the supply of and demand for imports and exports. An important question is whether speculation is stabilizing or destabilizing, i.e. whether it tends to smooth out fluctuations in the exchange rate caused by trade or make them larger than they would otherwise be.

Speculation is a very important phenomenon in connection with a system of flexible exchange rates. It could, conceivably, be of critical importance for the efficient functioning of a system of flexible exchange rates. We return to this question in Chapter 27 when discussing the relative merits of different exchange-rate systems.

SELECTED BIBLIOGRAPHY: CHAPTER 22

For treatments of markets for foreign exchange, see:

F. Machlup, 'The Theory of Foreign Exchange', *Ec*, November 1939 and February 1940 (reprinted in *RTIT*).

J. E. Meade, *The Balance of Payments*, London, Oxford University Press, 1951, part IV.

L. B. Yeager, *International Monetary Relations: Theory, History and Policy*, 2nd ed., New York, Harper & Row, 1976, ch. 2.

A standard work on spot and forward markets for foreign exchange is:

P. Einzig. *The Dynamic Theory of Forward Exchange*, 2nd ed., London, Macmillan, 1961.

Other excellent works in this field are:

B. Hansen, 'Kursbildningen på valutamarknaderna', *Ekonomisk Tidskrift*, no. 3, 1961.

H. G. Grubel, *Forward Exchange, Speculation and the International Flow of Capital*, Stanford, Calif., Stanford University Press, 1966.

J. Spraos, 'The Theory of Forward Exchange and Recent Practice', *MS*, May 1953.

S. C. Tsiang, 'The Theory of Forward Exchanges and Effects of Government Intervention on the Forward Exchange Market', *SP*, April 1959.

For a discussion of international economic policy from an institutional point of view, see:

W. M. Scammell, *International Monetary Policy,* 2nd ed., London, Macmillan, 1961.

A thorough examination of the Canadian experience of flexible exchange rates is given in:

P. Wonnacott, *The Canadian Dollar, 1948-1962,* Toronto, Toronto University Press, 1965.

For a discussion of empirical estimates of price elasticities, see:

G. H. Orcutt, 'Measurement of Price Elasticities in International Trade', *RE&S,* May 1950 (reprinted in *RIE*).

A. C. Harberger, 'Some Evidence on the International Price Mechanism', *JPE,* December 1957.

23
The balance of payments

One of the most important policy issues for many countries is how to keep the balance of payments in equilibrium. Chapters 25, 26 and 28 will be devoted to policy aspects of this problem. To start with, however, we will have to understand what is meant by equilibrium and disequilibrium in the balance of payments. To do this we shall have to define carefully the meaning of the balance of payments and see in what sense there will be balance and in what way deficits and surpluses can exist. This chapter is devoted to these problems.

BALANCE OF PAYMENTS: BOOK-KEEPING

In ordinary usage one speaks of countries that have a favorable balance of payments, or a surplus, and countries that have a negative or unfavorable balance of payments, or a deficit. The most important question to be dealt with in this part of the book is how a country with a deficit can cure it. At the same time the balance of payments is merely a way of listing receipts and payments in international transactions for a country. In this sense the balance of payments is an application of double-entry book-keeping, and if we do this in a proper way debits and credits will always balance; hence in a way the balance of payments will always be in equilibrium. Our first task will be to look into this apparent paradox and understand in what way the balance of payments can be in disequilibrium and in what sense it will always be in equilibrium. The best way of treating this problem is to give a simplified example of a country's balance of payments.

The left side of Table 23.1 shows all the ways in which a country can acquire foreign currency – how it can acquire purchasing power which can be used in foreign markets. The right side of Table 23.1 shows how the foreign currency is spent and how the purchasing power over foreign goods is used. It is worth while to deal with each part to understand what is meant by it.

The most straightforward way in which a country can acquire foreign currency is by exporting goods. This is shown by row (1), which indicates that the country has exported goods to a value of 550. In an analogous way, row (5) shows that the country has imported goods to a value of 800. These two rows describe the country's visible trade.

Row (2) enumerates the receipts of the country from the sale of services to foreigners during the period in question. The most important item under this heading is usually shipping services. Exports are normally calculated f.o.b. (free on board), i.e. costs for transportation, insurance, etc., are not included, whereas imports are normally calculated c.i.f. (cost, insurance, freight), i.e. transportation, insurance costs, etc., are included. This gives rise to asymmetry, so that if we sum all countries together, the shipping services will not be cancelled out but will show a positive sign; in other words, world exports will be less than world

TABLE 23.1

Account of a country's balance of payments

Credits		Debits	
(1) Exports of goods	550	(5) Imports of goods	800
(2) Exports of services	150	(6) Imports of services	50
(3) Unrequited receipts (gifts, indemnities, etc., from foreigners)	100	(7) Unrequited payments (gifts, indemnities, etc., to foreigners)	80
(4) Capital receipts (borrowings from, capital repayments by, or sale of assets to, foreigners)	200	(8) Capital payments (lending to, capital repayments to, or purchase of assets from, foreigners)	70
TOTAL RECEIPTS	1000	TOTAL PAYMENTS	1000

imports. Any country with a merchant fleet will therefore normally have some income from shipping services to add under the heading 'exports of services'. For countries with a relatively large merchant fleet, such as Norway, this can be a very substantial item; for Norway it amounts to 30-40 per cent of total export income. Other types of earnings under this heading are interest and dividends which citizens of the country earn on investment abroad. Such payments are regarded as payments made by foreigners for current services which they derive from the capital in question. Citizens of the country whose balance of payments we are dealing with own land, shares, bonds, etc., and the foreigners who enjoy the services of this capital will have to pay for them; these payments will be registered under row (2) as exports of services, or *invisible exports,* as they often are called. Income through tourism is another example under the same heading. If a foreigner, instead of consuming a country's product at home, goes to the country and consumes it as a tourist, he will still have to pay for it in his own currency. This type of consumption, and all the services that a country offers tourists, will earn the country foreign currency. Such income will be registered under row (2) as income from export of services. Other payments registered under this heading are those for banking and insurance services made by domestic firms to foreigners.

In a completely analogous way, row (6) covers payments which residents of the country in question make to foreigners for similar services, i.e. shipping, banking and insurance services, payments the residents make as tourists abroad, and payments for capital services on foreign-owned capital.

To return to Table 23.1 we see that there are four more rows to take into account. The items enumerated in these rows are referred to as transfer items, as opposed to the trade items enumerated in rows (1), (2), (5), and (6).

The items in row (3) we have called 'unrequited receipts', i.e. receipts which the residents of a country receive 'for free', without having to make any present or future payments in return. Examples of this kind of receipt are gifts which residents receive from foreigners. It may, for instance, be the case that emigrants send money back to relatives living in the country in question. If the country whose balance of payments we study is a less developed country, it may receive gifts from a more developed one. Or it may be the case that the country came out of a war morally and physically superior, and was in a position to make the foreign country (its former enemy) pay indemnities. This kind of reparation payment played an important part after the First World War but has since fallen into relative obscurity. Transfer payments between developed and less developed countries are not negligible, however, and this type of payment seems to be on the upsurge. In a purely analogous way, row (7) describes payments which the country in question makes as gifts, assistance, indemnities, etc.

Items (1), (2), (3), (5), (6) and (7) enumerate all the payments and receipts made for the current period of time; they all have a flow dimension and refer to a certain value of exports per time period. The balance of payments of a country always refers to a certain time period, usually a calendar year. Exports and imports of goods and services, and all the other items we have discussed, are flow items. They all have the dimension of an amount per day, per month, per year, or whatever the period in question may be.

Items (4) and (8) are different. They express changes in stock magnitudes and refer to capital receipts and payments. They play a most important part, and it is critical for an understanding of the balance of payments to get a firm grasp of the nature of these items. They take many forms and it may be best to start by giving some examples.

A government, a corporation, or an individual might have borrowed money abroad, and such borrowing can be of different kinds. The government of the country in question may get a loan from another government; a firm may issue stocks abroad, or a bank might float a loan in a foreign country. In all these instances the country in question will acquire foreign currency, and these transactions will be entered as items in (4).

A government, a corporation, or an individual resident may receive sums from abroad in repayment for a loan that it had previously extended to a borrowing agency in a foreign country.

Foreigners might acquire assets in the country with whose balance of payments we are concerned. These assets can be of different kinds. They may be land, houses, productive plants, shares, etc. Changes in the country's stock of gold or reserves of foreign currency are also included in row (4).

Analogously, if residents of the country in their turn were to acquire foreign assets, for instance in the form of land abroad or foreign shares, or if the government were to lend money to a foreign government, this would give rise to an outflow of foreign currency and come as a capital transfer under row (8).

We will have more to say about the capital account in the balance of payments later in this chapter and also when studying the adjustment mechanism in later chapters. To start with, we shall say something about the somewhat puzzling use of the concepts 'capital imports' and 'capital exports'.

We have seen that if a foreign corporation buys a firm in the country we are considering, this is said to be an *import* of capital. One might expect it to be called an *export* of capital, as, after all, this firm is, so to speak 'exported' abroad, in the sense that foreigners acquire ownership of it – but this is not the case. The key factor on which to focus our attention is the fact that the country whose balance of payments we consider will get foreign currency, in other words, will acquire purchasing power abroad by selling some of its property to foreigners. Therefore, this transaction will be listed on the credit side of the country's balance of payments, as it will give rise to an inflow of foreign currency. We could say that a country can acquire foreign currency in either of two fundamental ways: by exporting goods and services, or by importing capital. Therefore, exports of goods and imports of capital both have to be listed on the credit side (i.e. on the receipt or inflow side) of a country's balance of payments.

In the same way, a country can export capital by acquiring foreign assets. This means that the country puts foreign currency at the disposal of the foreign country in which it acquires assets. Therefore, this transaction will be put on the debit side of the country's balance of payments. Again we can say that there are two fundamental ways in which a country can use its foreign currency: by importing goods and services or by exporting capital. In this sense imports of goods and exports of capital have the same effect, and therefore both have to be listed on the debit side (the outflow or payments side) of a country's balance of payments.

We said above that items (1), (2), (3), (5), (6), and (7) were flow magnitudes. Items (4) and (8) are of a different nature, because they do not have the dimensions of being flows per period of time but are instead changes in stock magnitudes during the period considered. A country has a certain capital stock consisting of land, houses, productive plants, ships, etc. If it sells part of this abroad, it engages in a stock transaction which is entered on the capital account in the balance of payments. It is important to recognize the difference in nature between a flow and a stock transaction, and for the time being this remark may suffice. We should now be equipped to say something significant about the question we started with: in what sense can the balance of payments be in equilibrium, and in what sense will it always balance? We will, however, have to answer this question in a somewhat roundabout way by introducing more concepts and definitions.

THE BALANCE OF TRADE, THE BALANCE OF CURRENT ACCOUNT, AND THE BALANCE OF PAYMENTS

There are several ways in which the balance of payments can be broken down vertically. We can first be concerned only with the export and import of goods. This gives us the balance of trade. It is obvious that the balance of trade need not always balance. If the country exports more goods than it imports, it is said to have a favorable balance or surplus in its balance of trade. If it imports more goods than it exports, it has a deficit or unfavorable balance of trade.

Row (1) of Table 23.2 shows the balance of trade for the country from our hypothetical example in Table 23.1. This country exported goods for 550 and imported goods for 800, it had a deficit in its balance of trade of 250.

Even though the country had a deficit in its balance of trade, this might be offset by items on other accounts. We can see from our example that the country has a surplus in its balance of services of 100 and a surplus in its balance

TABLE 23.2

Three external balances

(1) **BALANCE OF TRADE** [Table 23.1 rows (1) and (3)]	550 – 800 =	-250
(2) Balance of services [Table 23.1 rows (2) and (6)]	150 – 50 =	100
(3) Balance of unrequited transfers [Table 23.1 rows (3) and (7)]	100 – 80 =	20
(4) **BALANCE OF CURRENT ACCOUNT** [Sum of rows (1), (2) and (3) of Table 23.2]	800 – 930 =	-130
(5) Balance of capital account [Table 23.1 rows (4) and (8)]	200 – 70 =	130
(6) **BALANCE OF PAYMENTS** [Sum of rows (4) and (5) of Table 23.2]	1000 – 1000 =	0

of unrequited transfers of 20. This leads us to the balance of current account, which is a larger concept than the balance of trade, as it includes the balance of trade, the balance of services, and the balance of unrequited transfers. The balance of current account need not be equal but can show a surplus or a deficit. In our example the country in question has a deficit in its balance of current account of 130.

The balance of current account is a very important concept, as it shows the flow aspect of a country's international transactions. We could say that all the goods and services produced within the country during the time period in question, and exported, are entered on the credit side of the balance of current account, and all the goods and services imported and consumed (or perhaps stored) within the country during the same period are entered on the debit side of the balance of current account. We could also say that all the international transactions entering a country's system of national accounting should be listed on the country's balance of current account.

A word of warning must be inserted here. National accounting is not completely standardized among countries: different countries use different systems. This is reflected also in the construction of the balance of payments. There is agreement on the broad features; for instance, everyone agrees that exports of goods and services should be entered on the balance of current account. Differences in detail do exist, however, Some countries include such items as gifts and indemnities on the balance of unrequited transfers in the balance of capital account instead of in the balance of current account. It is hardly meaningful to say *a priori* that some of these items should be counted one way or the other. To a large extent it depends on the purpose for which the analysis of the balance of payments is used. Here we can only be concerned with the broader principles. Our aim is to understand how basic questions of economic analysis and policy can be elucidated by the use of balance-of-payments statistics and what factors one has to take into account to be able to interpret a country's balance of payments in any significant sense. A student interested in studying a specific country's balance of payments closely will have to refer to the country's balance-of-payments statistics. After having read this part of the book, one should be aware of the things to watch for.

In search of a helpful general definition we might say that all items of a flow nature should be included in the balance of current account and that all items expressing changes in stocks should enter the balance of capital account.

Let us now return to the general discussion. The sum of exports of goods, services, gifts, etc., need not equal the sum of imports of goods, services, indemnities, etc., and therefore there is no reason the balance of current account should be in equilibrium. The natural thing is to assume that it is not balanced, and in our example we saw that the country in question had a deficit of 130.

This deficit must be settled, because if a country has a deficit on the balance of current account, the country has spent more abroad during the period than it has earned. A way to settle this is by a transaction on the capital account. The country can deplete part of its stocks to an amount equal to the deficit on the balance of current account. This can be done, for instance, by borrowing abroad, i.e. by sending a loan instrument to the value of 130 abroad, by selling assets, or by depleting its reserves of foreign currency.

If we go back and look at our hypothetical example from Table 23.2, we can see that the country in question exported capital for 70 and imported capital for 200. Hence the country imported more capital than was necessary to cover the deficit in the balance on current account. This, however, is explained by the fact that it also exported capital to the value of 70. The net inflow of capital to the value of 130 was enough to offset exactly the deficit in the balance of current account and to equalize the two sides in the balance of payments. Before considering in what sense the balance of payments is in equilibrium, however, we should look more closely at the balance of capital account.

We have already said that the items on the capital account can take many forms. We might assume, in our example, that a corporation in one country acquired shares in a foreign corporation, and that the value of these shares amounted to 70. This explains the capital exports of the country which appear in Table 23.1. At the same time we might assume that a foreign company acquired shares to the value of 70 in the country whose balance of payments we are studying. This explains part of the total of 200 capital imports into the country. The rest, we can assume, consists of a loan which the government in this country receives from a foreign government, amounting to 130.

Is this, then, the deficit in the country's balance of payments? To answer this question it is no longer possible to look at the figures in the balance of payments and to think in book-keeping terms. We have to start thinking in wider economic terms.

EQUILIBRIUM AND DISEQUILIBRIUM IN THE BALANCE OF PAYMENTS

In a trivial sense the balance of payments will always be in equilibrium. Let us assume, for example, that a country has a deficit of 100 in the balance of current account. If no other transactions occur in the capital account, the country has to import capital at least to the value of 100 by, for instance, borrowing abroad (exporting a loan instrument) or depleting its reserves of foreign currency. On the other hand, if the country had a surplus in its balance of current account, it would mean that the country had exported more than it has imported (exports and imports taken in a wide sense). If no other transactions took place in the capital account, the country would still have to export capital to an extent equal to its surplus on the current account, by lending money abroad for instance. Whatever the values on other items, there will always be a residual transaction of this kind which brings the balance of payments into equilibrium. In this book-keeping sense the balance of payments will always balance.

In what sense, then, can the balance of payments be in disequilibrium? If we return to our example from Tables 23.1 and 23.2 we can see that the country has a capital inflow of 200. The critical factor is to understand the nature of this inflow. We assumed earlier that 70 was accounted for by a foreign corporation acquiring shares in a firm in the country. This meant, in other words, that some residents in the country sold assets to foreigners, thereby creating a capital inflow. The rest, 130, can be assumed to consist of a depletion of the country's reserves of foreign currency. Is this, then, the deficit in the country's balance of payments?

The answer is yes, if we assume that the country does this unwillingly and has a scarcity of foreign reserves. If, on the other hand, the country's reserves of foreign currency were plentiful and the depletion of these reserves were a consequence of a deliberate policy, it is doubtful it we could say that the country had a deficit in its balance of payments.

The inflow of capital need not take the form of a depletion of reserves. It is possible that the country has many attractive investment opportunities to offer, and that because of this, foreign investors want to invest in the country, thus covering the capital inflow. On the other hand, it is possible that an international agency is prepared to give the country a long-term loan to cover the 'deficit' of 130.

To say anything significant about a country's balance of payments, we have to study the nature of its international capital flows and also take into account its economic policy. The problem of judging the equilibrium position of a country's balance of payments becomes fairly complicated and soon takes us outside the sphere of book-keeping. The time has come to make an important distinction concerning a country's international capital flows.

AUTONOMOUS AND ACCOMMODATING CAPITAL FLOWS

We have learned that if a country has a deficit in its balance of current account, there will always be an offsetting transaction on the capital account to bring the balance of payments into equilibrium. If, for instance, a country's importers had imported 100 more than the exporters had exported, they might have to borrow 100 from the foreign exporters to pay for their purchases, and this would be registered as an inflow of capital on the capital account. There are, however, other capital flows which have no connection with the country's balance-of-payments situation. It may be, for instance, that a foreign exporter buys an

TABLE 23.3

Autonomous and accommodating transactions

Credits		Debits	
(1) Autonomous receipts	870	(3) Autonomous payments	1000
(a) Autonomous exports (visible and invisible) 700		(a) Autonomous imports (visible and invisible) 850	
(b) Autonomous unrequited receipts from foreigners	100	(b) Autonomous unrequited payments to foreigners	80
(c) Autonomous capital receipts from foreigners	70	(c) Autonomous capital payments to foreigners	70
(2) Accommodating capital receipts from foreigners	130	(4) Accommodating capital payments to foreigners	0
	1000		1000

advertising agency in the country at the cost of 100, to be able to better market his product; this would also be registered as a capital inflow of 100. The significance of these two capital flows for the country's balance of payments is very different. We therefore have to distinguish between two types of capital flow.

One type we call *accommodating* capital movements. These are capital flows that take place specifically to equalize the balance of payments in the bookkeeping sense. The other we call *autonomous* capital flows; these are 'ordinary' capital flows, and their distinguishing feature is that they take place regardless of other items in the balance of payments. To bring out the meaning and significance of autonomous and accommodating capital flows, it might be worth while to regroup the items from Tables 23.1 and 23.2 in a new way and to give some examples of the two types of capital movement.

Looking at Table 23.3 we see that the country in question exported goods and services to a value of 700. Furthermore, it received unrequited gifts, etc., to a value of 100. We assume, moreover, that the country had an autonomous capital inflow of 70. This could, for instance, be in the form of a foreign corporation buying up a subsidiary firm, thereby acquiring capital assets to a value of 70 in the country in question.

This autonomous capital inflow could take many other forms. It could have been caused, for instance, by a foreign firm or a foreign resident paying back a loan to a firm or a person in the country under discussion; or it could be that a person or a company took up a loan abroad, by issuing bonds for instance. In all these cases it is a question of private persons or firms having capital transactions with foreigners. These transactions have an effect on the country's balance of payments but they are in no way caused by balance-of-payments considerations. In fact, they are all examples of autonomous capital movements.

If we look at the debit side, i.e. the payments side, of Table 23.3, we find that the country imported goods and services to a value of 850, at the same time

TABLE 23.4

Balance of payments

---

(1)	Balance of autonomous trade [Table 23.3, rows (1a) and (3a)]	700 − 850 =	−150
(2)	Balance of autonomous unrequited transfers [Table 23.3, rows (1b) and (3b)]	100 − 80 =	20
(3)	Balance of autonomous capital movements [Table 23.3, rows (1c) and (3c)]	70 − 70 =	0
(4)	Balance of payments	870 − 1000 =	−130
(5)	Balance of foreign accommodation	130 − 0 =	130
(6)	Balance of accommodating and autonomous transactions	1000 − 1000 =	0

---

paying 80 to foreigners in the form of gifts, indemnities, etc. Furthermore, the country had an autonomous outflow of capital to the value of 70. Summing this up we find that total payments to foreigners amount to 1000, whereas the inflow only amounted to 870, a difference of 130. This difference has to be settled by an accommodating inflow of capital of the same amount.

This accommodating inflow of capital can take various forms. Foreign firms might accept short-term claims on firms in the country whose balance of payments we are studying, or perhaps a foreign government extends a loan to the country. In the case of a less developed country, it might even be possible that a foreign government is willing to ease the balance-of-payments situation of the country by making it a gift amounting to the value of the accommoding inflow. Or possibly the country in question has had to deplete its reserves of foreign currency to settle its accommodating capital inflow.

In all these cases the accommodating capital movements are a direct consequence of the balance-of-payments situation. Accommodating capital flows are unforeseen capital flows, which have to be made to bring the balance of payments into equilibrium.

We are now in a position to define a surplus or a deficit in a country's balance of payments. Looking at Table 23.4, we see that the country we have used as an example had autonomous receipts of 870 and autonomous payments of 1000. The difference comprises an accommodating inflow of 130. This is the country's deficit in its balance of payments. We therefore reach the conclusion that if a country's autonomous receipts are larger than its autonomous payments, it will have a surplus in its balance of payments. This will then be settled by an accommodating outflow of capital equal to the surplus, thereby bringing the balance of payments into equilibrium in a book-keeping sense. In a completely analogous manner we say that a country has a deficit in its balance of payments if its autonomous receipts are smaller than its autonomous payments. This deficit will have to be settled by an accommodating capital inflow which brings the balance of payments into equilibrium. If a country's autonomous payments equal its autonomous receipts, the balance of payments will be in equilibrium and no accommodating capital movements will take place.

It is useful to take into account a time perspective and think of accommodating capital movements as unforeseen or unplanned. In the capitalist or mixed type of economy prevalent in the West, the outcome of the balance of payments depends on many atomistic decisions taken by the firms and individuals that comprise the decision units of these economies. There is little reason to expect that the result of these decisions on the balance of payments will be an equilibrium in external transactions. If this is not the case, accommodating capital movements will results. Therefore, accommodating capital flows can be regarded as a residual needed to create a book-keeping equilibrium in the balance of payments.

Autonomous capital movements, on the contrary, can be regarded as planned capital movements. The different decision units – the individual, the firm, or the government for that matter – may, for different reasons, plan to engage in capital transactions with the rest of the world. These autonomous capital flows have, of course, consequences on the balance-of-payments situation of the country, but firms engage in these capital flows as a matter of course, without direct regard for the balance-of-payments consequences. It may be useful to think, in planning terms, of autonomous capital flows as being planned capital flows. Using terminology of Swedish origin, we can say that autonomous capital movements are *ex ante* in nature, i.e. the different decision units plan to engage in these capital movements at the beginning of the planning period in question.

Accommodating capital flows are, on the contrary, *ex post* in nature. Only at the end of the period can one discover whether accommodating movements have taken place. In this sense they are unplanned and appear as a result of the economic activity which has taken place during the period in question.

Accommodating capital movements have great political significance. If a country has a deficit in its balance of payments of the type just defined, and if this is settled by an accommodating inflow of capital, the accommodating inflow can be viewed as a warning signal. As has been stated, the deficit can be settled by a short-term loan or a depletion of reserves. Usually this condition cannot continue for long. Lenders are seldom willing to extend short-term loans forever, and reserves have a tendency to become depleted. If an accommodating capital inflow occurs, it is usually a sign that the government will have to change its economic policy to abolish the deficit in the balance of payments that has caused the accommodating inflow. The situation depends now to a large extent on the type of policy the country already pursues. If it works within the framework of a liberal trade policy, and if the general economic policy is not very restrictive, it may be easy to close the deficit by merely having a slightly tighter economic policy. It is possible, however, that the country already has a heavily controlled economy with many restrictions and that it still cannot avoid a balance-of-payments deficit. In that case, the country's predicament will be much more severe. Before finishing this chapter, we will say a few more words about the balance of payments within the framework of general economic policy.

Again, it could be that the country need not revise its economic policy, even though it has a deficit in its balance of payments and an accommodating capital inflow. If the country has many attractive investment opportunities to offer, it may be possible to convert the short-term, unplanned accommodating inflow to a long-term, planned, autonomous capital inflow by, for instance, issuing a long-term loan abroad. The country may receive a twenty-year loan, thus easing its balance-of-payments problems. After twenty years of foreign investment the country will perhaps be able to turn an unfavorable balance of current account into a favorable one.

THE BALANCE OF PAYMENTS AND ECONOMIC POLICY

We should now have a basic understanding of the sense in which the balance of payments is always in equilibrium and the sense in which the balance of payments might be in disequilibrium. If accommodating capital flows take place, they always have some policy implications. If a country has a deficit and an accommodating capital inflow, it must in general try to implement policy measures aimed at reducing the deficit. An asymmetry occurs here for surplus countries. A country with a surplus in its balance of payments and an accommodating outflow of capital need not take immediate measures, because it can continue to have a surplus and accumulate foreign reserves or claims on foreigners without running into difficulty. Surpluses do not usually create great problems, so we are not specifically concerned with surplus countries. We shall continue, as we have so far in this chapter, to concentrate on the balance-of-payments problems of deficit countries.

Countries can, as we have hinted, be in very different positions concerning the balance of payments, even though their deficits and accommodating capital inflows are the same, because the general economic situation in the two countries may be very different. It is, therefore, not possible to discuss a country's balance-of-payments situation intelligently without taking into account its general economic background.

To understand the nature of a deficit one has to judge it against the background of the general economic policy of a country and the policy means a country has at its disposal. The more restrictions and controls, the less scope a country has for getting rid of a deficit. If a country is already pursuing a tight monetary and fiscal policy and has high tariffs and import controls, yet still has a deficit, it may be very difficult to get rid of the deficit. We can then talk about actual and potential deficits. The actual deficit is the deficit that appears, and the potential deficit is the deficit that would appear with a more neutral, 'normal', economic policy. It is, of course, somewhat arbitrary to think of a certain economic policy as 'normal'. However, the possibility of pursuing a restrictive policy to close a deficit in the balance of payments depends on the level of tightness and restriction existing in the economy. This is important and should be kept in mind. The more restrictive a policy at the outset, the more difficult it is to get rid of a deficit.

Another important factor is the scope of policy means available. If a government has many means at its disposal and the political situation is such that the government can use any means it chooses, it is obviously in a better position than one with few means and narrowly constrained because of political reasons. We will come back to this question in Chapter 28.

The nature of capital flows is also important. We have already said that an accommodating inflow of capital can be viewed as a warning signal. It might, however, be possible for a country to convert an unforeseen accommodating import of capital into a long-term, planned capital import. This can be achieved, for instance, by issuing a long-term bond loan abroad. In such a case, the country need not change its economic policy but can continue to run a deficit for a long time, perhaps twenty years or so, without having to worry about the balance-of-payments situation.

Several examples of how a long-term import of capital has helped developing countries to solve their balance-of-payments problems are evident in history. Sweden had, as we mentioned in Chapter 8, an almost uninterrupted inflow of capital from 1870 to 1910, much of which seems to have been planned. In the 1870s capital was imported to finance the construction of railways. In the 1880s the rapid expansion in housing construction that took place in cities such as Stockholm and Gothenburg was also financed by bond issues on the international markets in Paris and London. This import of capital was a way of raising the rate of capital formation in a poor country with limited resources to devote to domestic savings. It was, however, also a way to solve the balance-of-payments problem and thus appears to have been, to a certain degree, a consciously planned policy.

Canada and Argentina are additional examples. These countries imported much capital during the period 1880-1913. Development was the main reason behind this import of capital: these countries were developing countries which were building export industries based on natural resources. To do this rapidly they needed to have a higher rate of capital formation than that possible if they had been forced to rely entirely on domestic savings. This import of foreign capital also had important implications for the balance-of-payments situation. The investment needed to open up export possibilities led to a high level of economic activity, creating a stress on the balance of payments and causing deficits. To close the deficit one had to import capital. These countries foresaw this development to a certain degree, and by planning for an import of capital were able to turn what would otherwise have been an accommodating inflow into a planned, autonomous capital import.

International capital flows play an important part in equilibrating the balance of payments. Much supersitition surrounds this subject. It is often argued that capital flows can only be of a short-run nature. As often stated, countries that cover their deficits with capital imports cannot continue for long. But this depends on the general economic situation. In a monetary system such as prevails among leading industrial countries today, capital flows have an extremely important role to play as the natural complement of other forms of adjustment. We shall have more to say on this in the following chapters, but before going on to more policy-oriented questions, we must deal with some problems of analysis. First we have to understand what determines the national income in an open economy. We should now at least have a basic understanding of what is meant by equilibrium and disequilibrium in the balance of payments and of the role played by accommodating capital flows.

24
Foreign trade and national income

One of Keynes's main contributions to economic theory was to describe how equilibrium in national income is created. As most students are familiar with the determination of national income in a closed economy, we will directly treat the case of an open economy.

THE IMPORT FUNCTION

In a closed economy consumers could spend their incomes on consumption goods or they could save them. Total consumption could then be viewed as a function of the national income. This functional relationship can be expressed in the following way:

$$C = C(Y) \tag{24.1}$$

Savings and consumption are both increasing functions of the national income.

In an open economy consumers will also demand imported goods, and imports can be expressed as a function of national income. We write the import function as

$$M = M(Y) \tag{24.2}$$

Imports are also an increasing function of income. We can illustrate the import function graphically as shown in Figure 24.1. The figure shows that even at zero national income, something would be imported (by exporting part of the country's capital stock or by borrowing abroad). As the national income increases, so do imports. A country's average propensity to import is defined as the total imports divided by the total national income, i.e. M/Y. The average propensity to import varies greatly between countries. A large country such as the United States, well endowed with resources and whose dependence on foreign trade is very small, has a low average propensity to import, 0.03, i.e. only 3 per cent of its national income is imported. The average propensity to import has fallen in the United States over the years. Early in the nineteenth century it was over 10 per cent, at the end of the century it fell to 7 per cent, after the First World War it was 5 per cent, and now it is down to 3 per cent, even though a slight tendency to increase has been discernible during recent years. Another large country, the Soviet Union, also has a very low average propensity to import, between 0.02 and 0.03; and so has a country such as India, which in national income terms is not a large country. As far as India is concerned, its low propensity to import seems to be the result of an economic policy directed toward autarky.

FIGURE 24.1

Import function

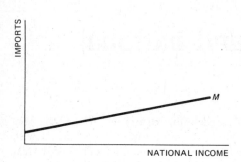

Smaller countries are usually more dependent on foreign trade and have a larger average propensity to import. Great Britain, for instance, has an average propensity to import of about 0.2 and Holland one of 0.4.

The marginal propensity to import measures how much of a change in the national income is spent on imports. Using algebraic terms it is defined as $\Delta M/\Delta Y$. If imports increase by 10 when the national income increases by 100, the marginal propensity to import will be 0.1. If the marginal propensity to import is divided by the average propensity to import, we deduce the income elasticity of demand for imports. Expressed in algebraic terms this becomes $(\Delta M/\Delta Y)/(M/Y)$. The income elasticity of imports is defined under the assumption that all other things are equal, for instance that there are no changes in prices. If the demand for imports increases by 5 per cent when the income increases by 10 per cent, the income elasticity of imports equals 0.5. If a country's average and marginal propensities to import are equal, its income elasticity of demand for imports is 1. This implies that as the country's income increases, a constant proportion of the increasing income is spent on imports, and the share of its national product which is traded is constant. If the marginal propensity to import is larger than its average propensity, this tends to increase the country's dependence on foreign trade, and if the opposite is the case, its foreign trade quota will fall.

This way of defining the propensities to import and the import elasticity should not lure the reader into thinking that these concepts are constants that do not change. A country's marginal propensity to import, for instance, is influenced by many economic factors and usually changes from year to year.

THE DETERMINATION OF NATIONAL INCOME IN AN OPEN ECONOMY: THE FOREIGN TRADE MULTIPLIER

We will now show how the national income is determined in an open economy. The difference between a closed and an open economy is that in the latter we have the possibility of foreign trade, i.e. of exports and imports. In an open economy we can write the national income identity as

$$Y + M = C + I + X \tag{24.3}$$

where the left side of the expression shows the total supply, i.e. the sum of total domestic supply (Y) and imports (M), and where the right side shows the three ways total output can be used, i.e. as consumption (C), investment (I), or exports (X).

In a closed economy we know that savings have to equal investment in equilibrium. In an open economy we have to take into account that there can be a net inflow or outflow of capital. In an open economy we can therefore write the equilibrium condition as

$$S = I + X - M \tag{24.4}$$

or

$$S + M = I + X \tag{24.4a}$$

If there is a change in any of the four variables, the change in the left side of expression (24.4a) must equal the change in the right side, as a condition for reaching a new equilibrium. Hence

$$\Delta S + \Delta M = \Delta I + \Delta X \tag{24.5}$$

Using the definitions of marginal propensity to save, s, and of marginal propensity to import, m, we can write $\Delta S = s\Delta Y$ and $\Delta M = m\Delta Y$. Then we can rewrite equation (24.5) as

$$(s + m)\,\Delta Y = \Delta I + \Delta X \tag{24.6}$$

Hence we get

$$\Delta Y = \frac{1}{s + m}\,(\Delta I + \Delta X) \tag{24.7}$$

We can now view the changes in investment and exports as the autonomous variables and see what the effects of change in, say, exports will be on the national income. From equation (24.7) we see that the effect of a change in exports on the national income equals the change in exports multiplied by the expression $1/(s + m)$, which in our formulation is the foreign trade multiplier, which we shall call k_f.

Let us for a moment assume that there is no change in investment, and see what the effect of an increase in exports will be. Assuming that the marginal propensity to consume is positive, we see that k_f will always be larger than unity and that hence the increase in exports will have some secondary effects on the national income, so that the increase in the national income will be larger than the original increase in exports.

The foreign trade multiplier, or the export multiplier as it is sometimes called, works in exactly the same way as the ordinary investment multiplier. An increase in exports gives rise to an increase in income for the exporters and those employed in the export industries. They, in turn, spend more of their increased incomes. How much more they spend on domestic goods depends on two leakages: how much they save and how much they spend on imports. The savings do not create any new incomes. An increase in import spendings does not create new incomes in the country itself, only in those foreign countries with which the

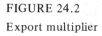

FIGURE 24.2

Export multiplier

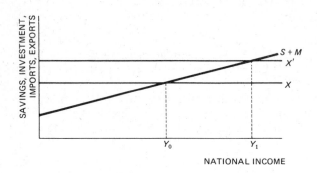

NATIONAL INCOME

first country trades. And it is the effect on the country's own national income with which we, for the moment, are concerned.

It is now easy to see that the larger the marginal propensities to save and import, the smaller will be the value of the multiplier. If the marginal propensity to save is 0.2 and if the marginal propensity to import is 0.3, the value of the multiplier will be $1/(0.2 + 0.3) = 2$, i.e. an autonomous increase in exports of 100 will lead to an increase in the national income of 200.

The reason for the original increase in exports may be one of many. It could be, for instance, that a change in tastes among foreign consumers in favor of imported goods has occurred. This gives rise to increased orders to producers of export goods. To start with, exporters may sell their stocks and receive increased incomes; in the next period they will then try to increase production and hire more workers. This creates new incomes among food and textiles producers, and so on. When the whole process has worked itself out, the increase in the national income becomes larger than the original increase in exports. How much larger depends on the value of the export multiplier, which depends in itself in a critical fashion on the values of the marginal propensities to save and import.

Figure 24.2 illustrates the export multiplier diagrammatically. The figure shows a saving – imports schedule, i.e. how much consumers plan to save and import at different values of the national income. This is arrived at by adding an import schedule to the savings schedule. We assume, furthermore, to simplify the reasoning, that there is no net investment, so that exports are the only autonomous variable. To start with, we have an equilibrium national income, Y_0, where savings plus imports are equal to exports. We now get an increase in exports, so that the export schedule rises from X to X'. This produces an expansionary effect on the national income, which increases from Y_0 to Y_1, where again we have a state of equilibrium with savings plus imports equal to exports. How large the expansionary effect on national income will be from a given increase in exports depends on the slope of the savings – imports schedule. This slope depends on the marginal propensities to save and import. The smaller the sum of these propensities, the smaller will be the slope of the schedule and the larger the expansionary effect of an increase in exports on national income.

In the same way as an autonomous increase in exports will have an expansionary effect on the national income, an increase in imports will have a contractionary effect. This is illustrated in Figure 24.3. For the sake of reason-

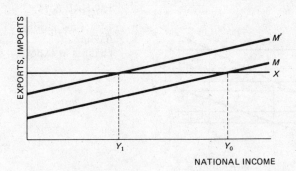

FIGURE 24.3

Effect on national income
of increase in imports

ing, we assume that there are no net savings and no net investment. The reason for the increase in imports can be one of many. The most simple explanation could be to assume that it depends on a change in tastes. The consumers consume as much as before but fewer home-produced goods and more imports. This leads to a decrease in orders for the domestic industries. Sooner or later domestic producers will have to decrease production and lay off workers. This will lead to a decrease in income for those employed in these domestic industries, and the total income will fall even more through the multiplier effect, until finally a new equilibrium is reached at a lower national income.

This process is illustrated with the help of geometry in Figure 24.3. We start from an equilibrium position at Y_0, where imports and exports are equal and where we show the original equilibrium of the national income. We then see an upward movement in the import schedule, leading to a contraction in the national income and finally to a new equilibrium at the lower national income Y_1. We might observe that this process is of exactly the same nature as the one connected with the savings paradox.

In a closed economy we have the equilibrium condition

$$I = S \tag{24.8}$$

In an open economy, investment can be broken down into two parts: domestic investment, I_d, and foreign investment, I_f. The equilibrium condition can be written

$$I_d + I_f = S \tag{24.9}$$

Foreign investment is the difference between exports of goods and services and imports of goods and services. Hence we get

$$I_f = X - M \tag{24.10}$$

Substituting equation (24.10) into (24.9) gives

$$I_d + X = S + M \tag{24.11}$$

Again it may be useful to give a geometric illustration. In Figure 24.4 we start from a situation where S is the savings schedule and $M + S$ is the added imports and savings schedule. I_d is the domestic investment schedule and $X + I_d$ denotes the schedule for exports and domestic investment. This schedule cuts

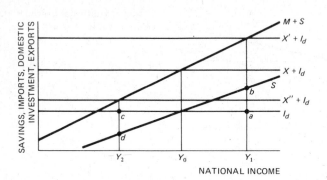

FIGURE 24.4

Effect on national
income of
changes in exports

the savings – import schedule vertically above Y_0, which is the equilibrium national income. At this level of income there is also equilibrium in the balance of current account, because savings equals domestic investment and exports equal imports.

Let us then assume that there is an autonomous increase in exports so that the combined export – investment schedule rises to $X' + I_d$. This produces an expansionary impetus on the national income, increasing it to Y_1, where again exports plus domestic investment equals savings plus imports. This is the new equilibrium in the national income, but we no longer have an equilibrium in the balance of current account because total savings are now larger than domestic investment. The difference between savings and domestic investment at Y_1 is given by the distance ab. This implies that exports are larger than imports by the same amount, and that the country exports capital.

If, on the other hand, exports fell, so that the schedule for exports plus investment fell to $X'' + I_d$, this would have a contractionary effect on the national income, which would fall from Y_0 to Y_2. At this level of income domestic investment would be larger than savings by the distance cd. This implies that imports are larger than exports by the same amount, that the country has a deficit in its balance of current account, and that an import of capital is needed to cover the given, autonomous domestic investment programme which takes place.

NATIONAL INCOME AND THE BALANCE OF PAYMENTS

We have just demonstrated in Figure 24.4 that there may be an internal equilibrium, i.e. that the national income may be in equilibrium, but that there is no external equilibrium, i.e. that there is no equilibrium in the balance of payments. The time has come to see how this can occur and to discern the effects of income changes on the balance of payments.

First we must understand clearly what is meant by equilibrium in the national income. The condition of equilibrium is for planned saving (*ex ante* savings) to equal planned investment (*ex ante* investment). This being the case, consumers will be able to carry out their plans to consume and save and producers will be able to fulfill their plans regarding production of consumer and investment goods. Production of consumer goods will equal their consumption, and savings and investment will be equal. Then there will be no change in the national income from its given equilibrium value.

In an open economy the equilibrium condition has only to be reformulated so that it takes into account the possibility of a country's not having to rely only on domestic savings but also on foreigners to provide part of the total savings by their exporting capital. Also, a country need not only invest at home but can invest abroad by exporting capital.

It is often said that the two main aims of a country's economic policy are to maintain full employment and an external balance. We shall return to the question of the aims and means in economic policy later. For the time being, we must only observe that equilibrium in a country's national income, according to the Keynesian definition just given, does not necessarily imply that the economy is fully employed. This definition says only that total planned demand equals total planned production. This equilibrium can be at any capacity level. If it happens to be at 100 per cent capacity, the economy is fully employed. If it is at a lower level of capacity utilization, there will be some unemployment in the economy, and if it is at a 110 per cent of the economy's capacity level, this will have definite implications for the balance of payments.

In this connection we must also define the way we use the terms *inflation* and *deflation*. By inflation, or an inflationary pressure in the economy, we mean simply that planned total demand is larger than planned total production, i.e. that investment *ex ante* is larger than savings *ex ante*. This does not necessarily imply rising prices, but it will, in many instances, lead to a rising price level. With deflation, or a deflationary pressure in the economy, we mean, analogously, that total production is larger than total demand, in other words, that planned savings are larger than planned investment.

Let us first assume that during the previous period of time a country achieved internal balance at a full-employment level and that the balance of payments was in equilibrium. We now get an increase in total demand. There can be many causes for such an increase. Perhaps consumers wish to save less and consume more from a given income. Or it can be a change in a policy variable, for instance a decrease in interest rates, which encourages investment. Whatever the reason, there will be an inflationary pressure in the economy. In the open economy, such pressure need not usually lead to rising prices but to a deficit in the balance of payments; it can, of course, lead to both. Consumers will consume more than before, and producers will continue to invest as much as they used to. As the economy, however, is already at full employment, there is no possibility of increasing domestic production in the short run. Exports will not change, but imports will increase to satisfy the increase in demand for consumer goods. At the end of the period, the country will find that it has a deficit in its balance of payments and that, in fact, a part of its domestic investment has been financed out of capital imports.

It is of no consequence for this process how the internal production pattern has been influenced – how the composition of goods has been affected. It may be that exports and home production of investment goods remain unchanged and that imports, only, increase. Or perhaps production of exports fall, and factors of production from this sector are drawn into domestic sectors to meet the increase in demand for consumer goods. Whichever way the production pattern changes under inflationary pressure, the main thing for us to observe is the fact that domestic investment is larger than domestic savings and that imports are larger than exports.

It is important to realize that an increase in the national income, generated on the demand side in the way just described, often leads to a deficit in the balance of payments. An inflationary pressure within the economy does not necessarily lead to rising prices but instead gives rise to a deficit in the balance of payments, which has to be covered by an unforeseen accommodating inflow of capital. This accommodating capital inflow can then be seen as a warning signal, as described in Chapter 23. This case is a classical example taken from Keynesian analysis. The policy implications in this case are also quite clear, but we shall return later to fuller discussion of these.

Let us now assume, instead, that starting from an equilibrium with full employment, a decrease in exports occurs. This produces a contractionary effect on the national income, which, through the multiplier effect, will be larger than the original decrease in exports. Imports will also fall as national income falls, but the decrease in imports will be smaller than the decrease in exports, so the country will simultaneously fall into a situation of unemployment and a deficit in balance of payments.

This is a tricky situation to escape from. An inflationary policy can return the country to full employment but only at the cost of a deterioration in the deficit in the balance of payments. A simple Keyensian policy, which works by deflating or inflating the national income, cannot alone cope with this situation. (This problem will be discussed at length in Chapters 25 and 28.)

A simpler situation is one in which, again starting from equilibrium with full employment, the country receives an autonomous upward impetus in its savings schedule. As the consumers wish to save more and consume less, deflationary pressure on national income is evolved. Income falls, resulting in some unemployment. As national income falls, so does the demand for imports, but there is no reason to expect a change in exports. Demand for exports depends primarily on incomes abroad, and these, at least to start with, have not changed. At the same time, exporters at home will be, if anything, in a better competitive position than before, as unemployment will create a downward pressure on wages, so that exporters obtain their factors of production more cheaply than previously. The country, therefore, will have a surplus in its balance of payments and be put into a situation where unemployment is combined with a favorable balance of payments.

This situation is comparatively simple to deal with. An inflationary policy will lead the country back toward equilibrium in national income at the full-employment level. This will lead to an increase in demand for imports at an unchanged level of exports, but as the country has a surplus in its balance of payments, there is little cause to worry.

We have now set out several cases of how changes in the national income affect the balance of payments. There is an intimate connection between income changes and the balance of payments, and any change in the national income will have some effect on it. To sum up, we can say that in general an inflationary change in national income will have a negative effect on the balance of payments, and a deflationary change in national income will have a favorable effect on the balance of payments. There are, however, exceptions to this general rule. An autonomous decrease in exports will have both a deflationary effect on the national income and lead to a deficit in the balance of payments. Analogously, a shift in consumption away from imports to domestically produced goods will have both an inflationary effect on the national income and lead to a surplus in the balance of payments.

The policy implications of income and balance-of-payments changes will be discussed more fully in Chapter 28, where we will deal with the question of how to achieve both internal and external equilibrium.

THE INTERNATIONAL PROPAGATION OF BUSINESS CYCLES

We have demonstrated how a change in a country's exports or imports will affect the country's national income. Countries are linked together by trade with each other, however, and a change in one country's national income will have repercussions on the income of its trading partners.

A recession in the United States which leads to a fall in its national income will also lead to a fall in American imports and thus lead to a fall in exports from its trading partners. Countries such as Britain, France and Canada will be affected by the American recession through a fall in their exports, which in turn, through a multiplier effect, will have a deflationary impact on national income in these countries. In this way all trading countries are linked together, and no country can be completely isolated from others. In a large country such as the United States, whose national income comprises approximately 40 per cent of the world's income, a change in national income will have important repercussions, even though its marginal propensity to import is small. The larger a country's marginal propensity to import, and therefore the more dependent on foreign trade it is, the more sensitive to foreign repercussions the country will usually be.

A geometric illustration of the foreign repercussions, and of how national incomes of countries are connected through trade, is given in Figure 24.5. We start off in stage 1 with an increase in domestic investment in country I, which increases from I_d to I'_d. This gives rise to a vertical upward shift in the combined investment plus exports schedule and to an expansionary effect on the national income, which increases from Y_0 to Y_1. As national income increases, so does the demand for imports. For the country's trading partners, here symbolized by country II, this means an increase in exports. We also see from the figure in stage 2 how country II receives an upward shift in its export schedule, leading to an expansion of its national income, which increases from Y_0 to Y_1. As country II's income increases, its demand for imports also increases, which in turn leads to a repercussion back to country I in the form of an increase in the demand for country I's exports. This is illustrated in stage 3, where we see that country I receives another upward shift in the $I_d + X$ schedule, so that the national income increases even more, from Y_1 to Y_2.

In this way we see how national incomes hang together and how a change in

FIGURE 24.5

International propagation of business cycles

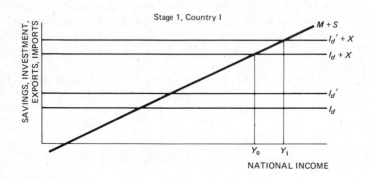

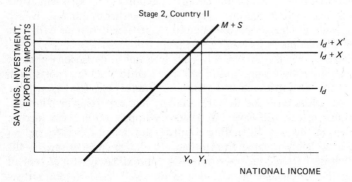

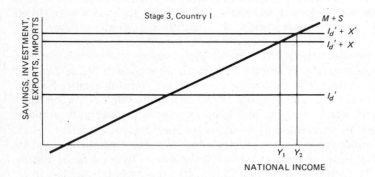

one country's national income affects another country. A disturbance in one country will, through rebounding repercussions, affect the incomes in all trading countries until a new equilibrium is achieved.

The international propagation of business cycles was once a very important problem. During the period between the world wars it even constituted *the* economic problem. After the Great Depression hit the United States in the late

FIGURE 24.6

The international propagation of business cycles

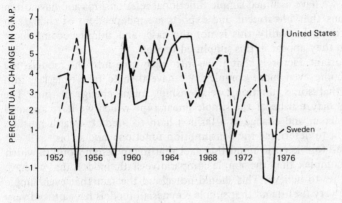

1920s it spread rapidly and began to be felt in the rest of the world. The most important factor was the fall in demand for imports in the United States, a result of the fall in national income. To this has to be added a drastic decline in American investment abroad. As a result, the number of dollars made available to the rest of the world decreased by 68 per cent between the end of the 1920s and the bottom of the depression in 1932-3. Within a short period of time, most countries began to feel the depression, and many were soon in as bad a situation as the United States itself.

The first two decades after the Second World War saw no deep recessions among the advanced industrial countries. It is true that years of boom alternated with years of recession. Figure 24.6 shows how the growth of G.N.P. varied from 1952 to 1976 in the United States and Sweden.

We can see that the years 1955, 1959, 1964, 1972 were years of boom in the United States, while the years 1954, 1958; 1967, 1974-75 were characterized by less than full capacity utilization. The figure also illustrates the fact that the United States took the lead in determining the economic rhythm of the Western world, while a smaller industrial nation, like Sweden, at least from the 1960s on, followed the American pattern with a certain lag as the international business cycle spread from the center to the periphery. The 1950s and 1960s also witnessed, however, a steady trend on growth in G.N.P. among the leading industrial nations, and even though the fluctuations were marked, they were comparatively mild. The disturbances became more pronounced during the 1970s. The oil crisis of 1973 led to a deep recession with falling G.N.P.s in many countries during 1974 and 1975. (The effects of the oil crisis are analyzed in Chapter 30.) The problems connected with the international business cycle again became acute. We will return to policy questions in connection with the control of economic activity later on.

One way of characterizing the interrelationships between countries and the sensitivity in these relationships is by means of foreign trade multipliers.

We should now have a basic understanding of how the national income is determined in an open economy and how fluctuations in one economy spread to others. It should be stressed, however, that only basic principles have been discussed. In order to derive fairly uncomplicated expressions for the foreign trade multiplier, we have assumed simple functional relationships and have often added assumptions that investment and exports are independent of changes in the national income. In reality this is not the case, and things become more complicated than they appear in this simplified version.

Another important factor is that if we introduce time into the models, the relationships become even more complex. We have then to take time lags into account, admit that some functional relationships might change in time. The savings functions may not be of the simple linear type which we have assumed but may be non-linear and change in a fashion hard to predict; wealth must be taken into account to determine the consumption functions; and so on.

We should therefore keep in mind that fact that the dynamic world in which we live is more complex than the simple comparative-static models that we have used might lead us to believe. This should not cloud the fact that even simple theorizing can be very useful and that simple Keynesian models have proved very powerful tools for economic policy.

SELECTED BIBLIOGRAPHY: CHAPTERS 23 AND 24

A standard work in this field is:

J. M. Meade, *The Balance of Payments,* London, Oxford University Press, 1951.

Chapter 23 follows Meade's chapters 1-3 rather closely. The reader should observe, however, that the use of the concepts of *autonomous* and *accommodating* capital movements does not coincide completely with Meade's use of the terms. Chapter 24 contains an exposition of income formation in an open economy, founded on Keynesian analysis. The pioneering work in this field is:

J. M. Keynes, *The General Theory of Employment, Interest and Money,* London, 1936, Macmillan, especially ch. 21.

For early generalizations and elaborations of the Keynesian theory in this field, compare:

F. Machlup, *International Trade and the National Income Multiplier,* Philadelphia, Blakiston, 1943.

L. M. Metzler, 'Underemployment Equilibrium in International Trade', *Econometrica,* April 1942.

This is a field where existing textbooks give a relatively good exposition. For example, see:

C. P. Kindleberger, *International Economics,* 3rd ed., Homewood, Ill., Irwin, 1963, chs 10-11.

For empirical estimates of marginal propensities to import and foreign trade multipliers, see:

J. H. Adler, 'U.S. Import Demand during the Interwar Period', *AER,* June 1945.

H. Neisser and F. Modigliani, *National Incomes and International Trade,* Urbana, Ill., University of Illinois Press, 1953.

J. J. Polak, *An International Economics System,* Chicago, University of Chicago Press, 1954.

25

International economic policy and the adjustment mechanism

The price of foreign exchange will, under a system of flexible exchange rates, fluctuate in such a way that the demand for foreign exchange equals the supply and the balance of payments is in equilibrium. There is no comparable mechanism that will keep the balance of payments in equilibrium under a system of fixed exchange rates. The normal situation is that the export of goods and services will not equal their import but that a surplus or a deficit will arise. Therefore, it is important to study how a country can adjust its trade flows and capital flows to get equilibrium in its balance of payments. In fact, even under a system of floating exchange rates the adjustment mechanism is important since, in practice, disequilibria often occur. A surplus in the balance of payments generally causes no problems; therefore, we will not deal with its implications at any length. A deficit in the balance of payments often entails difficult problems of economic policy. How an economy can adjust to a situation with a deficit is an important question. In this chapter we shall discuss the main policy means by which to achieve equilibrium in the balance of payments and the workings of the adjustment mechanism. During a long period of modern economic history, the gold standard set the rules of the game for countries' behavior when they had surpluses or deficits in their foreign trade. As it is an interesting example of how an adjustment mechanism can function, and is full of implications for modern policy considerations, we will start by describing how it worked, or at least how it was supposed to work.

THE GOLD STANDARD: A CASE OF AUTOMATIC ADJUSTMENT

The gold standard emerged slowly during the nineteenth century. It became more widely established about 1870 and was full fledged during the forty years from the beginning of the 1870s to the outbreak of the First World War. The leading countries tried to revive the gold standard in the 1920s. Great Britain, for instance, went back on the gold standard in 1925 and other leading countries followed. This system collapsed with the Great Depression in the beginning of the 1930s.

As the international monetary system of today closely resembles the traditional gold standard, it is instructive to see how the gold standard worked (or was supposed to work). A suitable introduction to the study of the adjustment mechanism is therefore to see how deficits were cured 'automatically' under the gold standard.

The main object of economic policy under the gold standard was to keep the balance of payments in equilibrium. The main instrument for this was monetary policy. The authority handling economic policy in those days was the central bank.

Under the gold standard a British gold sovereign, of £1, contained 113.0016 grains of pure gold. The U.S. dollar, in turn, contained 23.22 grains. As both currencies were tied to gold, it implied that £1 was worth $4.87 U.S. The dollar rate could fluctuate between an upper gold point of 4.90 and a lower gold point of 4.84. These rates were set by the cost of shipping gold from New York to London. The cost of shipping gold worth £1 amounted to 3 cents.

The stage is now set, and we can describe the workings of the gold standard. Let us assume that the United States had a deficit in its balance of payments. This implied that demand for foreign exchange in the United States was larger than the supply of foreign exchange and the price of foreign exchange tended to rise. It rose from 4.87, but it could not rise to more than 4.90, because the Federal Reserve Bank in New York had a commitment to sell and buy gold at a fixed rate. If importers found that they had to pay more than $4.90 for £1, they could, for $4.87, buy gold worth £1 in New York and ship it to London at a cost of 3 cents. Every pound sterling of gold which they shipped to London and which cost them $4.90 to buy and take there, they could sell to the Bank of England and acquire bank notes in exchange, which they could use to pay for their imports. Whatever the persistence of a deficit in the U.S. balance of payments, American importers knew that they would never have to pay more than $4.90 for £1.

What were the implications of a deficit for the U.S. authorities? Because of the deficit the country would lose foreign reserves and perhaps gold. This forced the authorities to pursue a restrictive monetary policy. The two most important means for this consist of raising the bank rate and decreasing the money supply. An increase in the bank rate has a general deflationary effect. It primarily discourages investment, because investors find it more difficult and expensive to borrow money, and if they believe particularly that the increase in the discount rate is temporary, they have good reason to postpone their investments and wait for cheaper money. The central bank also tried to decrease the money supply. The availability of credit in the banking system fell, and investors found it both more difficult and more expensive to obtain loans.

The increase in interest rates may also affect consumption, though this is less certain. The availability of all credits falls, including credits for consumption purposes, which will work in a deflationary direction. The effect of the increase in interest rates on savings, however, is less certain; it may lead to an increase in some savings because of the increase in returns, but it may also lead to a decrease in other savings, for instance those for a fixed purpose (a given sum can be reached with less savings as the interest has increased). Therefore the effect on consumption and savings is less clear cut.

Thus a tighter monetary policy leads to deflationary pressure and to a lower level of activity. It will probably also give rise to some unemployment. The general price level will fall, and probably wages, too. This benefits export industries, which become more competitive, and import-competing industries, which then will be able to compete more successfully with imports.

This was the way in which the adjustment mechanism was supposed, by the participants themselves, to work in the days of the gold standard, when stress was laid on changes in prices. For modern economists it is natural to point also to income changes as important. The tightening of monetary policy will cause a reduction in nominal incomes, and national income will fall as unemployment grows, leading to a fall in imports. If prices are sticky, it might well be that changes in income, induced by the multiplier, are the most important factor for the adjustment mechanism.

If a country had a deficit, we would expect gold to flow out of the country. Historical evidence shows, however, that deficit countries quite often had an inflow of capital even in times of deficits. The causes for such an inflow of capital were usually of two kinds, one short term and the other long term.

The country with a deficit raised its discount rate, and this tended to attract short-term capital as interest rates went up. An even more powerful way to attract capital was by price changes on short-term bonds, which went together automatically with interest-rate changes. An increase in the short-term interest rate of, for example, 1 per cent, may depress the price of a bond of short duration by, for example, 10 per cent. A foreign investor may speculate in this and place $1 million in the deficit country, hoping that the bond price would go up, after perhaps a year, when the country's foreign reserves were plentiful and the deficit erased. If his speculation were successful, he could, on top of an interest rate of, for instance, 4 per cent, make a gain of 10 per cent because of the fluctuations in bond prices.

During the nineteenth century exchange rates were generally stable. With the exception of the period of the Napoleonic wars, the pound sterling had been immovable in terms of gold since 1717. Similarly, the dollar, apart from an adjustment in 1834 and the suspension of specie payments in connection with the American civil war in 1861–5, had had a stable value in gold since 1792. Speculators were therefore not worried about changes in the exchange rate but usually acted promptly in connection with changes in interest rates.

Long-term capital movements also played an important part. As mentioned in Chapter 8, Britain and some of the richer European countries, notably France, acted as international bankers. They generated a surplus of savings which developing, 'peripheral' countries could draw on. Many of these countries offered good opportunities for investment and had a long-term inflow of capital. These capital flows were autonomous and were in no way connected with immediate balance-of-payments considerations. They eased, however, the constraint that would otherwise have been exercised on the balance of payments, by making possible a higher rate of investment than that which domestic savings only would have permitted.

International capital movements were very important during the time of the gold standard. It can even be argued that without them the system would never have worked. The adjustment of real economic factors, especially price levels, which the system prescribed was often superfluous. The situation was temporarily eased by capital flows, and a mild dampening of the activity level sufficed for curing a disequilibrium. Several countries even had long-term capital imports stretching over decades. Economic policy was geared toward external equilibrium, but one did not have to obey the rules of the game too strictly, because capital movements eased the burden of adjustment to a large extent.

THE BALANCE OF PAYMENTS AS A POLICY PROBLEM

Today most countries are more ambitious than in the days of the gold standard. Equilibrium in the balance of payments is no longer the one overriding goal of economic policy but one of several aims. The stress is, therefore, no longer on automatic adjustment. How to achieve external balance is viewed as just one of many problems for economic policy. We shall, in Chapter 28, discuss the problem of how to achieve external equilibrium jointly with full employment and also say something about the general problem of achieving a number of objectives of policy with a certain set of instruments. In this chapter we shall start by describing the main policy means at the disposal of a modern government and the way in which they work.

If, for the time being, we exlcude autonomous capital movements, the balance of payments can be viewed as the difference between total domestic output and total domestic expenditure. Using symbols, it can be written

$$B = Y - E \qquad\qquad (25.1)$$

where B is the balance of payments (net) and Y and E stand for total domestic output and expenditure, respectively.

If total output is larger than total expenditure, the country will have a surplus in its balance of payments or if, conversely, the country will have a deficit, and if output equals expenditure the balance of payments will be in equilibrium. If a country has a deficit it can, in principle, close the deficit in one of two ways: by reducing expenditure or by increasing output. It is often difficult to increase output in the short run, especially if the country already has full employment. Therefore, the chief means for reducing a deficit is usually an expenditure-reducing policy.

It is sometimes said that there are two main ways in which a deficit can be cured: by expenditure-reducing, or expenditure-switching policies. We shall keep to this terminology and divide the policy instruments into these two main categories. The terminology is somewhat inadequate, however, as it suggests that expenditure-switching could be substituted for expenditure-reducing. This is not the case. Given constant output, expenditure-switching policies must also entail some element of expenditure reduction in order to work. To put it more generally, expenditure-switching must imply either an element of reduction in expenditure or an increase of output to be effective.

EXPENDITURE-REDUCING POLICIES

We have seen, in connection with the gold standard, how monetary policies can be used to cure a deficit. Today expenditure-reducing policies can be divided into two broad categories: monetary policy and fiscal policy. Monetary policies today are in principle the same as under the gold standard, though the spectrum of policies is now broader. Fiscal policy was hardly used for this purpose before the 1930s; it has become an important policy weapon in connection with the growth of government expenditure which has occurred in most countries since the Second World War.

Changes in interest rates and open-market operations are today the most important instruments for monetary policy. To cure a deficit the natural thing to do is to raise interest rates and sell bonds.

The primary effect of an increase in interest rates is on investment. As it becomes more expensive to borrow money and as the availability of credit becomes more scarce, producers borrow and invest less.

The effects of a tighter monetary policy on investment depend to a large extent on the general economic situation. If the country is in a boom period, the result of an increase in interest rates depends to a large extent on the expectations of producers. If they expect the interest rate to fall after some time, they may postpone investments. In such a case the increase in interest may have a considerable impact, and through multiplier effects lead to a reduction in the national income or at least act as a brake in an inflationary situation. If producers, instead, expect prices to increase, they will also expect the higher interest rates to prevail in the foreseeable future. There is, therefore, no point in their postponing investment. They go ahead with their investment plans, and the effect of the higher interest rate is negligible.

Monetary policy became quite discredited in the 1930s, as it proved to be inefficient for domestic stabilization purposes during that deep depression. Even after the Second World War, in the late 1940s, many regarded it with suspicion. In the 1950s, when the overriding problem for many countries was that of inflation, monetary policy experienced a renaissance. It again became an important part of economic policy, and new variants of monetary policy were put into practice.

One aspect stressed was the availability of credit. In an inflationary climate investment returns were expected to be high. For conventional purposes interest rates were seldom higher than 7 to 8 per cent. Nominal rates such as these were often not enough to discourage investors. Banks rationed credits, and *availability* arose as an important concept.

The standard means of regulating the supply of money and influencing the availability of credit is through open-market operations. In open-market operations the central bank sells or buys bonds and securities. If it sells bonds, bond prices will be decreased and the effective interest yielded will be increased. If the central bank wants to tighten the money supply, it sells bonds and other securities to commercial banks, insurance companies, households, etc. Commercial banks and other buyers of bonds will have to pay for them with liquid money. The liquidity of the banking system falls and the availability of credit decreases. The sale of bonds will also lead to a fall in their price and to an upward pressure on interest rates.

The decrease in availability of credit, together with an increase in discounts, can have a negative influence on investment; producers may now simply find it impossible to borrow money. If this is so, investment will obviously be curtailed.

The possibility of influencing the availability of credit by open-market operations hinges on the fact that commercial banks keep a certain ratio between their liquidity and their loanable funds. If this is not the case, commercial banks may simply continue lending money, even though their liquidity has decreased.[1] In some countries banks have not adhered to strict rules in this respect, and authorities have often used less subtle means for restricting credit. They have simply put a ceiling on credits, declaring, for instance, that the banking system can only lend 80 per cent of the loanable funds available during a previous year.

New means for monetary policy were also put into practice during the 1950s. An increasing amount of funds went to finance the purchase of consumer goods, this being a natural consequence of the fact that an increasing proportion of consumption in industrial countries consists of consumer durables. Central banks have, in times of inflationary pressure, been able to restrict lending for purposes of consumption by forcing banks to ask for higher percentages in down payment and faster amortization, and to show greater selectiveness in granting loans.

Monetary policy has also proved to be a powerful instrument in the post-war period for correcting deficits in the balance of payments. The means aimed at curtailing investment have probably been most efficient. An increase in interest rates and a decrease in the availability of credit can hardly fail to affect investment. A decrease in investment will, through a multiplier effect, lead to a decrease in income and to a fall in imports. Analogously, policies that curtail consumption will also lead to a decrease in imports.

Thus a tighter monetary policy is one way of implementing a policy of expenditure reduction. It should also be stressed in this context that a 'neutral' monetary policy will automatically work to curb a deficit, because a deficit implies that payments by residents of the country are larger than receipts by residents. This means that residents are depleting their cash balances. If the deficit continues, cash balances will eventually become depleted, and payments will be brought into line with receipts; the deficit will be self-correcting.

This, however, presupposes 'neutrality' from the central bank, i.e. that it refuses to increase the money supply, even though cash balances are being depleted. Residents can only deplete their cash holdings by exchanging them for foreign reserves, and it is doubtful if the central bank has enough foreign reserves to be able to wait and let the self-correcting mechanism work itself out. One should also remember that as cash holdings become more scarce, the interest rate increases, which will also work toward curing the deficit. If, for some reason, the central bank does not want to tolerate an increase in interest rates, it must increase the money supply, and the deficit is no longer self-correcting.

Fiscal policy can also be used to reduce expenditure. We can divide the means of fiscal policy into two broad groups, depending on whether they are on the income or the spending side of the government budget.

The most important instrument on the income side is a change in taxation. An increase in direct taxes will reduce household incomes. Part of this decrease in income may lead to a reduction in savings, but part of it will most certainly lead to a reduction of consumption and a decrease in imports. An increase in indirect taxes, for instance of sales taxes, will produce much the same effect; here the effect on savings may be relatively smaller, as indirect taxes, as opposed to direct taxes, are seldom progressive.

Many countries have also used taxes against investment in the post-war period, for instance in the form of a flat-rate tax on certain types of investments. More subtle ways in which fiscal policy is used to regulate investment are in the form of so-called *investment funds*, which amounts to giving firms tax credits if they postpone investment. These means of fiscal policy have proved to be efficient in the curtailing of investment. A decrease in investment will, of course, through the usual multiplier effect, lead to a decrease in the national income and to a fall in imports.

Another form of expenditure-reducing policy is to cut government expenditure. The state budget comprises in many industrial countries 30 to 40 per cent of total G.N.P. Some of these expenditures are of a transfer type (support of children, pensions, etc.), and some of them consist of public consumption and investment. A decrease in transfer payments will usually have an immediate effect on consumption, as the groups benefiting from transfer payments are on the whole low-income groups with a high marginal propensity to consume. A decrease in public consumption will, of course, also lead to a fall in total income. A decrease in public investment produces much the same effect on national income as does a fall in private investment and leads to a fall in national income and imports.

Fiscal policy can therefore be viewed as an efficient means of implementing an expenditure-reducing policy. In certain instances there is room for doubting the efficiency of monetary policy; there can be little doubt about the efficiency of fiscal policy. It may be difficult for a government to increase taxes and keep expenditures constant, or to decrease expenditures keeping taxes constant, but if it does, there is no doubt that total expenditures will decrease and imports fall.

The balance of the budget is sometimes taken as a measure of the effectiveness of fiscal policy. If the government permits a deficit in the budget, it pursues an expansionary policy, and if it has a surplus, its policy is deflationary. One has, however, to be very careful in applying such an argument, because the total effect of the budget depends not only on the sum of tax incomes and expenditures but also on the composition of taxes and expenditures. It is quite possible that a budget with a smaller deficit has a more expansionary effect on the economy than a budget with a larger deficit. To measure the total impact of the government sector on the economy, one has to take not only the deficit or surplus but also the composition of the budget into account.

In summing up, we see that monetary and fiscal policies are the chief means of implementing an expenditure-reducing policy. If a country has a deficit in the balance of payments, it can pursue a tighter monetary policy or a more restrictive fiscal policy. This will have a deflationary effect on the national income and lead to a fall in imports, or at least act as a brake on the increase in imports. It will also have a positive effect on exports and on import-competing industries. As the activity level falls, there will be downward pressure on factor prices, wages may fall or, at least, be stable or increase less than they otherwise would. This places the export- and import-competing industries in a more competitive position. An expenditure-reducing policy will therefore have a positive effect on the balance of payments both by reducing imports and by creating space for an expansion of exports.

EXPENDITURE-SWITCHING POLICIES: DEVALUATION, THE ELASTICITY APPROACH

Expenditure-switching policies primarily work by changing relative prices. The main form for such a policy is a change in exchange rates, i.e. a devaluation or a revaluation of the domestic currency. Direct controls can also be classified under this heading and are usually applied to restrict imports. Consumers will then try to buy domestic goods instead of imported goods, and hence direct controls can be viewed as a switching device. We shall, however, concentrate on a discussion of devaluation for the time being, returning to direct controls at the end of this chapter.

We have already mentioned in Chapter 22 that a depreciation meant that the price of the domestic currency fell in terms of foreign currencies and that an appreciation meant that the value of the domestic currency increased in terms of foreign currencies. Devaluation is often used interchangeably with depreciation, and revaluation is often taken to be synonymous with appreciation. We will, however, make one distinction between the two sets of terms. Depreciation means a lowering in value with respect to other currencies, while devaluation means a lowering in value of a currency with respect to the price of gold. The same holds, *mutatis mutandis*, for appreciation and revaluation. If, as is the case with the present monetary system, the price of gold is fixed, depreciation of one currency implies devaluation of the currency in question. There exists, however, one possibility where devaluation does not imply depreciation. This is the situation where all currencies lower their value with respect to gold by the same percentage. Then there would be world-wide devaluation, i.e. the price of gold would increase by the same percentage in all countries but no currency would have been depreciated. For the time being, we are concerned with only one country, and as there can be no confusion we will use the two sets of terms interchangeably.

The immediate effect of devaluation is a change in relative prices. If a country devalues by, for instance, 20 per cent, it means that import prices increase by 20 per cent counted in home prices.[2] An increase in import prices leads to a fall in the demand for imports. At the same time, import-competing industries will be in a better competitive situation. Exporters will receive 20 per cent more in home currency for every unit of foreign currency they earn. They can therefore, lower their prices counted in foreign currency and will become more competitive. By how much they are able to expand sales abroad depends primarily on the foreign demand elasticities for their goods.

The traditional approach to the effects of devaluation on the balance of trade runs in terms of *elasticities*. We shall also start by giving an account of this view before going over to the more modern *absorption* approach.

The core of the traditional view is contained in the so-called Marshall–Lerner condition, which states that the sum of the elasticities of demand for a country's exports and of its demand for imports has to be greater than unity for a devaluation to have a positive effect on a country's trade balance. If the sum of these elasticities is smaller than unity, a country can instead improve its balance of trade by revaluation.

If we want to express this condition in terms of a formula, it can be set out as follows:

$$dB = kX_f(e_{1m} + e_{2m} - 1) \qquad (25.2)$$

where dB is the change in the trade balance, k the devaluation in percentage, X_f the value of exports expressed in foreign currency, e_{1m} the first (devaluing) country's demand elasticity for imports, and e_{2m} the second country's (the rest of the world's) demand elasticity for exports from the devaluing country. The theory behind the formula will be spelled out and the formula derived later in this chapter.

It is easy to see from expression (25.2) that the sum of the two critical elasticities has to be larger than unity for the trade balance to improve because of a devaluation. If the sum is less than unity, an appreciation should instead be used to cure a deficit in the trade balance.

We have already said that devaluation will lead to an increase in the price of imports. What the effect of this price increase will be depends on the elasticity of demand for imports. The larger it is, the greater will be the fall in the volume of imports. The value of the demand elasticity of imports depends, of course, on what type of goods the devaluing country imports. If a country primarily imports necessities, raw materials and goods needed as inputs for its industries, the demand elasticity of imports may be very low, and a devaluation may not be a very efficient means of correcting a deficit. Some less developed countries may be in this category. For most industrial countries one would expect the import elasticity to be quite high. This is especially the case if, as pointed out in Chapter 22, the country has a well-developed import-competing industry.

When the exporters, because of the devaluation, receive more for every unit of foreign currency they earn, they can lower their prices quoted in foreign currency. When they lower their prices they should be able to sell more. By how much the quantity exported increases depends on the demand elasticity confronting the country's exporters. Again, it depends to a large extent on the type of goods the country exports as well as the market conditions. If a country exports raw materials, for instance, and is the sole, or main, supplier of the product, the foreign demand elasticity for its exports may be low. If a country exports industrial goods in close competition with suppliers from other industrial countries, the demand elasticity for its products will probably be high.

There was a lively discussion among economists in the late 1940s and early 1950s about empirical measurements of demand elasticities. The first published studies, by Hinshaw and Adler, showed very low values for demand elasticities, around, or less than, unity. These studies were later criticized, mainly by Orcutt and Harberger, and two schools developed, one of 'elasticity pessimists' and one of 'elasticity optimists'.[3]

The implication of low elasticities is that a policy instrument of a 'liberal' type, such as devaluation, which presupposes a minimum of interference with trade, can hardly work, but that more direct means, such as trade controls, have to be used. Whatever the values of the demand elasticities may have been in the interwar and early post-war period, most economists seem to take the view that the relevant elasticities for most countries are now probably quite high, at least substantially higher than unity. Devaluation should then work according to the traditional elasticity approach.

Devaluation has also been used by some countries, for instance, by France in 1958, with successful results. It has, however, not been a very widely used policy instrument in the post-war period. Devaluation is viewed with suspicion, and it seems as if some economists and many politicians are of the view that it should be used only as a last resort. Devaluation has, in addition, some side effects that should be pointed out.

Devaluation can have an inflationary impact on the economy. We will deal with this question in Chapter 27, when discussing the effect of flexible exchange rates on the internal price level of a country. Suffice it to say here that the effects on the price level depend primarily on the economic policy accompanying devaluation. If a tight monetary and fiscal policy is pursued jointly with devaluation, the inflationary impact should be limited.

Another consideration to take into account is the effect of devaluation on the income distribution. It is often stated that real wages will fall because of devaluation and that there will be a redistribution of income away from the labor class to the non-labor class. The effects on income distribution are, however, very complicated, and it is difficult to state general results. A devaluation should result in a reallocation of resources away from the sector producing non-traded goods and into the export and import competing sectors. Thinking in terms of a model with linearly homogeneous production functions, and assuming that the sector producing non-traded goods is labor-intensive, we ought to have the standard result that the labor class will receive a lower real income because of devaluation. The assumptions for obtaining this result are, however, quite arbitrarily chosen. In general we can say that the factors of production employed in the export and import-competing sectors will benefit from devaluation. This holds especially true for factors that may be specific for the respective industries. In addition, the factors used intensively in these industries should receive a higher real income. In the full framework of general equilibrium we should also take into account the effects of consumption, and then the result will also hinge on the consumption patterns of labor or the specific factor of production in which we are interested. It is then almost impossible to draw clear-cut inferences. Neither should one expect that the effects of devaluation on the income distribution are any simpler or more clear cut than the effects of a change in monetary or fiscal policy.

The Marshall–Lerner condition set out in formula (25.2) is built on some drastic simplifications. It assumes, roughly, that the supply elasticities are large (approaching infinity) and that the trade balance is in equilibrium when devaluation takes place. The first may be true in times of recession, when capacity is not fully utilized, and supply can easily expand. It is, however, doubtful if it can be viewed as a close approximation to reality in times of full employment. If there were a large imbalance to start with, so that imports were much larger than exports, then imports would increase in domestic currency more than exports, although the sum of the demand elasticities is larger than unity. None of these two assumptions invalidate, however, the spirit of the Marshall–Lerner condition, which says that the larger the respective demand elasticities, the more favorable is the effect of a devaluation on the trade balance. For the sake of completeness we shall, however, also derive the complete formula for the effects of devaluation on the trade balance.

DEVALUATION AND THE TRADE BALANCE: THE COMPLETE FORMULA

The reader with a weak background in mathematics need not follow the derivation in detail. It will suffice to take a look at the final result.

We start by setting out the following equation for the trade balance:

$$B_{1f} = x_1 P_{2m} - m_1 P_{2x} = X_{1f} - M_{1f} \qquad (25.3)$$

where B_{1f} denotes the first (devaluing) country's trade balance in foreign currency, where x_1 and m_1 are country I's volume of exports and imports, respectively; P_{2m} and P_{2x} are the prices of imports and exports in country II; and X_{1f} and M_{1f} are the value of exports and imports in country I, both denoted in foreign currency.

Differentiating equation (25.3) gives

$$dB_{1f} = dx_1 P_{2m} + dP_{2m} x_1 - dm_1 P_{2x} - dP_{2x} m_1$$

$$= X_{1f}\left(\frac{dx_1}{x_1} + \frac{dP_{2m}}{P_{2m}}\right) + M_{1f}\left(-\frac{dm_1}{m_1} - \frac{dP_{2x}}{P_{2x}}\right) \qquad (25.4)$$

We then define the following four elasticities:

$$s_{1x} = \frac{dx_1}{dP_{1x}}\frac{P_{1x}}{x_1} \qquad \text{Elasticity of home export supply} \qquad (25.5)$$

$$e_{2m} = -\frac{dx_1}{-dP_{2m}}\frac{P_{2m}}{x_1} \qquad \text{Elasticity of foreign demand for exports} \quad (25.6)$$

$$s_{2m} = \frac{dm_1}{dP_{2x}}\frac{P_{2x}}{m_1} \qquad \text{Elasticity of foreign supply of imports} \quad (25.7)$$

$$e_{1m} = -\frac{dm_1}{dP_{1m}}\frac{P_{1m}}{m_1} \qquad \text{Elasticity of home demand for imports} \quad (25.8)$$

We observe from the way in which these four elasticities have been defined that they will all be positive (barring Giffen goods).

We then assume that we have price equalization between the two countries through the exchange rate, r, so that we get

$$P_{2x} = P_{1m}r \qquad (25.9)$$

Differentiating equation (25.9) totally and adding in equation (25.9) gives

$$P_{2x} + dP_{2x} = P_{1m}r + dP_{1m}r + drP_{1m}$$
$$= (P_{1m} + dP_{1m})r - k(P_{1m} + dP_{1m})r \qquad (25.10)$$
$$= (P_{1m} + dP_{1m})r(1-k)$$

In equation (25.10) we have introduced the devaluation coefficient k, which shows the relative change in the exchange rate. We can define k in the following way:

$$k = -\frac{P_{1m}}{P_{1m} + dP_{1m}}\frac{dr}{r} = -\frac{dr}{r}\frac{1}{1 + \dfrac{dP_{1m}}{P_{1m}}}$$

$$\approx -\frac{dr}{r}\left(1 - \frac{dP_{1m}}{P_{1m}}\right) \approx -\frac{dr}{r} \tag{25.11}$$

From equation (25.10) we get

$$\frac{dP_{2x}}{P_{2x}} = -k + \frac{dP_{1m}}{P_{1m}}(1-k) \tag{25.12}$$

In a completely analogous way we deduce that

$$\frac{dP_{2m}}{P_{2m}} = -k + \frac{dP_{1x}}{P_{1x}}(1-k) \tag{25.13}$$

The relative changes in volumes and prices can now be expressed in terms of elasticities and the devaluation coefficient, k. Using equations (25.6) and (25.13) we get

$$\frac{dx_1}{x_1} = -e_{2m}\frac{dP_{2m}}{P_{2m}} = -e_{2m}\left[-k + \frac{dP_{1x}}{P_{1x}}(1-k)\right] \tag{25.14}$$

But $dx_1/x_1 = s_{1x}(dP_{1x}/P_{1x})$. Substituting, we get

$$\frac{dx_1}{x_1} = e_{2m}k - \frac{e_{2m}}{s_{1x}}(1-k)\frac{dx_1}{x_1}$$

From this follows

$$\frac{dx_1}{x_1} = \frac{e_{2m}\,k}{1 + (e_{2m}/s_{1x})(1-k)} = \frac{s_{1x}e_{2m}\,k}{s_{1x} + e_{2m}(1-k)} \tag{25.15}$$

In an analogous way we can derive

$$\frac{dP_{2m}}{P_{2m}} = -\frac{ks_{1x}}{s_{1x} + e_{2m}(1-k)} \tag{25.16}$$

$$\frac{dm_1}{m_1} = -\frac{ks_{2m}e_{1m}}{e_{1m} + s_{2m}(1-k)} \tag{25.17}$$

$$\frac{dP_{2x}}{P_{2x}} = -\frac{ke_{1m}}{e_{1m} + s_{2m}(1-k)} \tag{25.18}$$

Using the last four expressions we get the effect of a devaluation on the trade balance:

$$dB_{1f} = k\left[X_{1f}\frac{s_{1x}(e_{2m}-1)}{s_{1x} + e_{2m}(1-k)} + M_{1f}\frac{e_{1m}(s_{2m}+1)}{e_{1m} + s_{2m}(1-k)}\right] \tag{25.19}$$

Expression (25.19) shows that the effects of the devaluation are somewhat more complicated than shown in equation (25.2); i.e. if we do not assume that supply elasticities are infinitely large the situation becomes somewhat more complex. If, to take an extreme example, we assumed that the supply elasticities were equal to zero there would be no improvement in the trade balance because of increasing exports but some improvement because of a fall in demand for imports. Generally speaking, we can say that if the elasticities are larger than unity, then the larger they are, both on the supply and the demand side, the larger will be the improvement in the trade balance.

The way to arrive at formula (25.2) from (25.19) is as follows: if supply elasticities tend to infinity, then

$$\frac{e_{2m} - 1}{1 + (e_{2m}/s_{1x})(1-k)} \to e_{2m} - 1$$

If, furthermore, k is small, we get

$$\frac{e_{1m}[1 + (1/s_{2m})]}{(e_{1m}/s_{2m}) + 1 - k} \to \frac{e_{1m}}{1 - k}$$

But if k is small and if we assume that trade is balanced before the devaluation, we get

$$dB_{1f} = kM_{1f}(e_{2m} + e_{1m} - 1) \tag{25.2}$$

We have now set out the main parts of the elasticity approach to devaluation. The dubious aspect of this approach is that it is built on a partial type of theorizing and that it does not take into account consideration of general equilibrium.

Demand and supply elasticities are conventionally defined *ceteris paribus*, i.e. other prices and incomes are supposed to be constant, but in devaluation prices and incomes will certainly change. Therefore, the use of partial elasticities in connection with devaluation can easily be misleading. What one would like to know is the value of the 'total' elasticities i.e. the value of an elasticity when all the factors involved in the devaluation change. Such a total elasticity measures how quantities are affected by price changes when everything likely to change has done so. This is, however, not an operational concept, as it will never be possible to know in advance the values of such elasticities. The result of a devaluation depends not only on partial elasticities but also on the aggregate behavior of the economic system.

An alternative approach to the effects of devaluation formulated in macro terms is the so-called *absorption approach*. It was first developed by Sidney Alexander in a famous paper published in 1952.[4] As it gives a very useful complement to the traditional approach, we shall now discuss it.

DEVALUATION: THE ABSORPTION APPROACH

The absorption approach runs in macro terms. Its starting-point lies in the fact that the balance of trade can be viewed as the difference between national income and total expenditure, or, as we have already stated,

$$B = Y - E \tag{25.1}$$

If we instead call total expenditure, or total demand, for total absorption, A, we can write

$$B = Y - A \tag{25.20}$$

It should be observed that total absorption includes the demand created for all purposes; in other words, it includes demand both for consumption and investment purposes. Using the simple national income identity we say that

$$A = C + I + G$$

Devaluation affects the trade balance by either affecting real national income, Y, or by affecting total absorption, A. We can write the change in the trade balance as

$$dB = dY - dA \tag{25.21}$$

Total absorption can be decomposed in two parts. First, we say that any change in the real income will induce a change in absorption. How greatly absorption will change depends on the propensity to absorb, which we shall call c. Second, we can say that devaluation has a direct effect on absorption, depending, among other things, on the level of real income at which devaluation takes place. This effect we shall call the *direct effect* on absorption, D. We can then write

$$dA = c \, dY + dD \tag{25.22}$$

Combining equations (25.21) and (25.22) gives

$$dB = (1 - c) \, dY - dD \tag{25.23}$$

Equation (25.23) is useful because it directs our attention to three basic factors important for the outcome of a devaluation. It says that the effects of a devaluation on the trade balance depend first on how devaluation affects the real income (Y), second on the propensity to absorb (c), and third on the effect on direct absorption (D).

In order to deal with the effects of a devaluation we must distinguish between two main cases, one where there are idle resources (unemployment) and one where there is full employment. Let us begin with the first case.

If there are unemployed resources when the country devalues, then production can expand in the short run. We will expect the expansionary process to start by an increase in exports, giving rise to an increase in national income via the familiar multiplier process. By how much exports will expand depends greatly on whether, because of expansion, export prices in the devaluing country rise and on the capacity (and willingness) of the rest of the world to absorb exports from the devaluing country.

The net effect of the recovery or the increase in income on the balance of trade does not comprise the total amount of increase in production but, rather, the difference between this and the induced increase in total absorption. This difference between increase in real production and real absorption can be called *real hoarding*. The effect on the trade balance is, then, equal to the amount of real hoarding which takes place in the economy.

Putting the effects on direct absorption aside, we see that the propensity to absorb, or the propensity to hoard, the other side of the same coin, is the all-important factor in this case for the effects of a devaluation on the trade balance (the propensity to hoard is defined as $1 - c$.) As long as c is less than unity, some hoarding will occur, and hence there is a positive effect on the trade balance.

It may be, however, that c is larger than unity. Then a devaluation will have a negative effect on the trade balance, because the induced effects on absorption will be larger than the original effects on production. This case cannot be ignored. We have to remember that we are discussing the case of less than full employment. Devaluation will then have a positive effect on national income. Workers who are employed at this time will probably have a high propensity to consume. Further, the expansion in income may have a positive effect on investment. Together these factors can make the propensity to absorb larger than unity, and devaluation will then have a negative effect on the trade balance.

If the propensity to absorb is less than unity (or made less than unity by policy measures), devaluation is quite an attractive policy for a country in a depression, because it will have both a positive effect on the national income and improve the balance of trade.

That devaluation could have a positive effect on national income was recognized even before the breakthrough of Keynesian analysis. This was probably the main reason, together with balance-of-payments considerations, for the series of devaluations undertaken in the wake of the depression in the first few years of the 1930s.

A successful devaluation by one coutry will usually have adverse effects on other countries, primarily by outcompeting exports from the non-devaluing countries. That is one of the chief reasons devaluations tend to be competitive, and why, if one country devalues, other countries often feel that they must also. The International Monetary Fund has tried to avoid such situations by creating safeguards against competitive devaluations.

It is often argued that devaluation will lead to a deterioration in the terms of trade. Exports are usually much more concentrated than imports, and if devaluation is to have a positive effect, a prerequisite is that export prices, quoted in foreign currency, are lowered. Imports are usually diversified, and import prices, again quoted in foreign currency, are seldom affected to the same degree as export prices. This is the main reason for the deterioration in the terms of trade.

If real income falls, because of adverse terms of trade, so will absorption, and this will have a positive effect on the trade balance. Let us denote by t the reduction in real income because of the deterioration in the terms of trade. Then the fall in absorption will equal ct. This does not constitute a net improvement in the trade balance, however, because the adverse terms of trade imply an initial deterioration in the trade balance with t. Hence the net effect on the trade balance is $t - ct$, or $(1-c)t$. A deterioration in the terms of trade will, therefore, also normally entail a deterioration in the trade balance. Only if c is larger than unity will a deterioration in the terms of trade produce a positive effect on the trade balance.

We have now dealt with the unemployment case. We have now to deal with the case in which there already is full employment when devaluation takes place. In a situation in which the economy is already fully employed or the marginal propensity to absorb is larger than unity, the principal favorable effect of devaluation on the trade balance is through the direct effect on absorption.

The direct effect on absorption is not connected with any change in real national income. It depends on the fact that absorption out of a given real income may change as the price level changes. Let us show how the direct effect may work. Assume a country devalues by 10 per cent and that it has an elasticity of direct absorption of 0.1. This means that a 1 per cent increase in the general price level would induce a 0.1 per cent reduction in absorption at a given level of real income. Let us assume also that the policy environment and substitution conditions in consumption and production between domestic and traded goods are such as to link export and import price changes to changes in the internal price level by a factor of 0.5. This means that a 10 per cent increase of export and import prices in domestic currency leads to an increase of 5 per cent in the general domestic price level. A 10 per cent devaluation would, under these conditions, lead to a decrease in absorption of 0.5 per cent. If the imports of the country consisted of 20 per cent of its G.N.P., it would imply that the trade balance would improve by 2.5 per cent, in terms of imports.

In conventional elasticity analysis it is often taken for granted that devaluation will improve a country's trade balance although the country has full employment. It can only do this by reducing total absorption. We have just given an example of how direct absorption can be reduced at full employment. This was, however, a very mechanical example. Now we have to look into the economics of that example and see which are the economic factors possibly producing an effect on direct absorption.

The most important of the direct absorption effects is the *real balance effect*. If the money supply remains unchanged, and if the holders of cash want to maintain cash holdings of a certain real value, they must, if prices rise, accumulate more cash. The only way they can do this is by cutting down on their real expenditures, i.e. by lowering their absorption.

A single individual may increase his cash by selling assets, but this is not possible for the country as a whole. We have also, by definition, ruled out capital movements. If the behavior of the economic subjects is such that they want to keep their cash holdings at a certain real value, and if the money supply is kept constant, then it follows that a rising price level will imply a fall in absorption.

We hinted that as the real value of cash holdings falls, individuals will try to sell assets to acquire cash. This tends to depress the price of assets and to increase the rate of interest. This is a process which will continue, while the money supply remains constant, until a new equilibrium is reached. It should be observed that the increase in interest rates will also affect investment and consumption, and we would expect the higher interest rates to reinforce the downward pressure on absorption. Hence the real balance effect will set in motion a whole chain of events, leading the economic system to a new equilibrium, at a lower level of absorption.

To illustrate the reasoning above, we give the following example. Assume that the money supply in Britain is £5 billion and that devaluation increases the price level by 5 per cent, cutting the real value of cash balances by 5 per cent, or £250 million. Suppose that before devaluation real balances stood in a desired ratio to real expenditures, and that for every £10 by which real balances were out of adjustment, there is a cut of £1 in expenditure in order to rebuild cash balances. Ignoring secondary effects through an increase in interest rates, there will be a cut in absorption of £25 million yearly, and hence an improvement by £25 million in the trade balance.

It should once more be stressed that the real balance effect is based on the assumption that the money supply remains constant. If this is not the case (if, for instance, the central bank increases the money supply to keep pace with the rise in prices–among other things, in order to neutralize effects on interest rates and keep them stable), then the real balance effect will not come into play.

Other factors can influence direct absorption; one is connected with changes in income distribution. As already pointed out, it is not easy to derive clear-cut effects of devaluation on the income distribution, especially not in the longer run when the effects of a devaluation have worked themselves out and a new equilibrium has been reached. In the short run it is often assumed that devaluation will lead to an increase in profits at the expense of wages. If this were the case, we would expect absorption to fall, because the marginal propensity to consume out of profits can be expected to be smaller than the marginal propensity to consume out of wages. One should, however, keep in mind that an increase in profits may stimulate investment. If a shift of income from wages to profits led to a strong stimulation of investment, the negative effects on absorption might be partially or wholly offset.

Another factor that could lead to a decrease in direct absorption is the presence of *money illusion*. If consumers spend less at higher prices, even though their incomes have also risen, this will have a positive influence on the trade balance.

An increase in prices and money incomes will lead to an increase in government incomes. As taxes in most industrial countries are progressive, the increase in government revenue will be more than proportional. The government's marginal propensity to absorb is usually low, at least in the short run. This mechanism will therefore lead to a fall in direct absorption.

Some of the effects of a devaluation leading to a fall in direct absorption may be of a temporary or transitory nature. They might also depend on whether the devaluation is large or small. The real balance effect, for instance, may initially be quite strong, but later the need for increased cash balances may be met by an increase in the money supply. Wages may to begin with lag behind and the money illusion could work for a time. A small devaluation might take advantage of the money illusion, whereas a larger one might shatter it.

We have already stated that the outcome of devaluation depends to a large degree on the economic policy accompanying devaluation. The absorption approach brings out this fact very clearly. Our discussion of the absorption approach has so far consisted in looking into what in an economy are the 'automatic' factors which could lead to a decrease in absorption in connection with devaluation. These factors can, of course, be strengthened by a conscious economic policy. In the unemployment situation the policy should consist of trimming and expanding supply as fast as possible while restricting expansion in over-all absorption.

In the full-employment situation the policy has to be a more straightforward one of depressing absorption. The decrease in absorption will then leave room for the necessary reallocation of resources, leading to a fall in imports and an increase in exports. The absorption approach is somewhat portmanteau in nature, but it at least firmly keeps the emphasis on aggregated terms.

GENERAL REMARKS ON THE ADJUSTMENT MECHANISM

The time has now come to wind up the discussion about devaluation and to remark more generally on which are the important factors in the adjustment mechanism. What we shall do is comment on typical cases.

Let us start by dealing with a barter economy, a country, let us say, which has only one export good, one import good, and one domestic good, and where money or assets are not present. What would be the effect of a devaluation in this case, and in which way could such an economy achieve an equilibrium in its balance of trade?

In this case a devaluation would lead to a relative increase in the price of traded goods compared with the domestic good, i.e. the prices of imports and exports would rise. This would lead to an increase in the production of both the export and the import-competing good and to a fall in demand for both exports and imports. On balance exports would increase, imports fall, and the trade balance improve in the process.

It is quite easy to see how the adjustment mechanism works in the case of the barter economy. Here the trick consists of a change in relative prices. The change in the relative price structure causes a change in production and consumption, which will erase the deficit in the trade balance and lead to a new equilibrium. It is important to note in this context that the larger the possibilities for substitution between traded and domestic goods both on the production and on the consumption side, the smoother the adjustment mechanism works. Essentially the same factors were at work in connection with the growth and trade models which we studied in Part II. Here the factors important for adaptability were captured by the so-called *elasticity factor*, set out in the denominators of expressions (9A.8) and (9.1).

Let us now introduce money into the model. With a constant supply of money, a deficit in the trade balance implies that there is an excess demand for goods in the economy while people are trying to decrease their holdings of cash. This will have specific implications for relative prices. There will be a tendency for the price of money to fall compared with the price of goods. This tendency is reinforced by devaluation. Because of devaluation the price of traded goods will increase with respect to the price of money.

Money has become cheap because of devaluation, because its price in terms of goods (and especially traded goods) has fallen. Assuming that money has some positive utility for the consumers, devaluation will give them an impetus to acquire cash again. They can only do so by substituting cash for goods, i.e. by decreasing their demand for goods, especially their demand for traded goods. This will lead to a fall in total absorption and to an improvement in the trade balance. From the special viewpoint of monetary theory, this is an example of the workings of the real balance effect.

If assets were introduced into the model, their function would be much the same as that of money. Devaluation would decrease their relative price. As long as there is some substitution between consumed goods and assets, this substitution mechanism will work in the right direction and tend to restore the equilibrium in the trade balance.

We can now sum up the workings of the adjustment mechanism in the case of an economy where only goods are traded, where only domestic money exists, and where assets are not traded.

Devaluation will give rise to a change in the structure of relative prices. A fall in the relative price of money and assets will give rise to a fall in total absorption. this will have a positive influence on the trade balance. Furthermore, the price of non-traded goods will fall in relation to the price of exports and imports, giving rise to a substitution mechanism both on the supply and the demand sides which will cause an expansion in exports and a decrease in imports. This in turn will strengthen the process toward an improvement in the trade balance that was started by the fall in total absorption.

It is obvious that this adjustment mechanism can be smoothened by economic policy measures. A deflationary monetary and fiscal policy will help to cut total absorption. Other measures may help to speed up the adaptability of the economy and bring about the necessary adjustment of exports and imports.

Another observation to make is that the development in the second country (or the rest of the world) will facilitate adjustment. The surplus in the balance of trade created here will lead to an increase in the money supply. This will have a positive effect on absorption. which will help the adjustment. It will also create a tendency for the relative price of traded goods to fall in this country, further reinforcing the adjustment.

If an international currency (for instance, gold) exists which is used in both countries, or if assets are traded internationally, the possibilities for adjustment are increased.

A deficit in the trade balance implies, as usual, an excess demand for goods. As money is now an international commodity, it will flow out of the country as it is used to finance the deficit in the trade balance. As money flows out, the wealth in the hand of the consumers diminishes. This will lead to a fall in total absorption that will help to close the trade deficit.

The existence of internationally traded assets will have much the same implications. To finance a trade deficit the consumers can now sell assets abroad. This will, of course, decrease their wealth, and that will eventually produce a negative effect on absorption.

The adjustment mechanism will also work in the usual fashion: the deficit in the trade balance will be connected with a change in relative prices, and the price of money and assets in terms of goods, especially traded goods, will fall. This will induce a substitution mechanism that will work to close the deficit in the trade balance. Devaluation will accentuate this mechanism.

The existence of an international currency, and the possibility of international mobility of assets, will in short, further facilitate the workings of the adjustment mechanism as we have just described it.

DIRECT CONTROLS

The use of monetary or fiscal policy or of devaluation as a policy means to re-store equilibrium in the balance of payments presupposes that there are possi-bilities for income and price adjustment. The implication is, in other words, that income is sensitive to policy measures or that price changes will lead to changes in consumption and production. This is not always the case. It may be that, even though adjustment through these channels could in principle take place, it would take too long. A country may have to resort to other means to reach equilibrium within a feasible time (before, for instance, the foreign reserves have been com-pletely depleted). Direct controls are an example of other such means.

The word 'control' has a somewhat ambiguous meaning in this context. It is often used in a wide sense to depict not only quantitative restrictions and ex-change restrictions but also to include fiscal means such as taxes and subsidies and also tariffs. We have already dealt with fiscal policy in a general way and we have discussed tariffs at some length in Part III, so we shall here sketch only briefly the effects of direct controls, i.e. quantitative restrictions and exchange restrictions.

Direct controls can be roughly divided into two groups: commercial controls and financial controls. To improve the balance of payments, commercial controls can be used to increase exports and discourage imports. As there is very little that can be done to increase exports directly, commercial controls are usually applied to restrict imports.

The most obvious measure is to limit the volume of imports. This can be done, for instance, by applying quantitative restrictions. The government can, for in-stance, decide that only 80 per cent of the previous year's volume of imports can be imported this year. Such a restriction of imports will make their internal value higher than their external value.

Let us say that in the previous year five cars were imported at a total value of $500. This year only four cars can be imported. What will be the price on the home market for these four cars? (Dollars are assumed to the currency both abroad and at home.)

Let us assume that they each cost $100—and that their price is the same on the foreign market after the restrictions. If the demand is inelastic, the price can now be increased to $125 for a car on the domestic market, and the same total amount will be spent on the cars after as before the restrictions, i.e. $500. The question now is: who will reap the increase of price on the domestic market?

The government may try to pocket the increase by applying a special tax on imported cars. If import restrictions are applied to a wide variety of goods, and if the demand elasticity varies between goods, it will, however, be difficult to apply taxes efficiently. A quite probable outcome is that the whole, or part, of the price increase will go to the importers. This is, of course, especially the case if the govern-ment only introduces quantitative import restrictions without an accompanying means for dealing with the rents or monopoly gains which such restrictions imply.

A system of quantitative restrictions can also be combined with a system of import licenses. The price mechanism may then be applied in a roundabout way and these licenses auctioned off by the government to the importers; or the government can simply give them away (a system, however, easily giving rise to corruption). Alternatively, the government might try to introduce a system of rationing jointly with the import restrictions and establish a quota system for how much of every imported good the consumer can buy.

Another way of implementing direct controls is by the use of exchange restrictions. A government might try to hold complete control over all dealings in foreign exchange by stating that exporters have to sell their foreign earnings to a central board, and that importers have to buy their foreign currency from the same board.

If the government were completely successful in this undertaking, it would also hold complete control over foreign trade. It would then be able to cure any deficit in the balance of payments by selling foreign exchange only to an extent that corresponded to export earnings.

The government could also permit only those imports which it deems desirable (necessities, capital goods, military equipment) and not permit, for example, luxuries.

Import restrictions in the form of foreign exchange restrictions will also create a divergence between domestic and foreign prices on imported goods. This will give an impetus to circumvent the restrictions. A black market will probably be created and the exporters tempted to sell their export earnings on this market to obtain a higher price. Importers who are not able to obtain foreign currency legally may try to buy on this market. Importers who do obtain foreign currency for a specific purpose may try to use it for another purpose, and so on.

Controls of foreign exchange dealings have to be policed very thoroughly in order to be efficient. To neutralize some of these difficulties the government may try to introduce a system of multiple exchange rates.

Let us assume that the U.S. government wants to use exchange restrictions and to apply multiple exchange rates. There may be an official rate of, say, $4 to £1. This rate may be applied to American exporters, and some American importers that import necessities are able to buy British pounds at this rate. Other importers, however, who import goods deemed by the government to be less pertinent, may have to pay $6, $8, or $10 for £1, depending on how vital the imports in question are judged to be. The government can then pocket the difference between the selling and buying price of foreign exchange.

This, in essence, is how a system of multiple exchange rates works. Such a system is to a large extent afflicted by the same difficulties as an ordinary system of exchange control. Exporters still have to be induced not to sell their proceeds of foreign exchange to the highest bidder, and one has to control importers so that they use their allotted foreign exchange for the purpose specified. To work, the system has to be closely controlled.

This will suffice as a sketch of how trade controls work. One can, of course, also try to subsidize exports, but this will only have a positive effect on export earnings if the foreign demand elasticity of exports is larger than unity. If one jointly subsidizes exports and taxes imports in a non-discriminatory fashion, one pursues, in effect, a policy that amounts to a devaluation.

The essence of direct trade controls is usually a wish to restrict imports. If imports are inelastic, such a policy may also be viewed as a tempting alternative to devaluation. It may also be a feasible solution in the short run. In the longer run its effect may often be harmful because of the distortion of prices that it creates and the harmful effects on the allocation of production and consumption that such price distortion implies. There is a degree of optimum trade intervention, as we have seen in connection with the theory of tariffs. Most countries which apply trade restrictions have usually passed beyond this point. Direct trade controls can, under some circumstances at least, be quite a costly way of closing a deficit in the balance of payments. We have already discussed the question of quantitative restrictions in Chapter 14.

INTERNATIONAL CAPITAL MOVEMENTS

In this chapter we have been dealing with various ways of closing a deficit in the balance of payments. Before concluding the chapter it should be mentioned that it is quite possible for a country to continue with a deficit in its balance of payments and to cover it with capital imports.

We said at the beginning of the chapter that it was often difficult to specify the causes of a country's deficit. In a trading system with pegged exchange rates and convertible currencies, disturbances causing deficits will always occur. It is very difficult for a country to pursue a flexible-enough policy which will counteract any such disturbance and produce equilibrium in the balance of payments. This is especially the case if the country also pursues a policy of full employment, a point we shall return to in Chapter 28, where we shall discuss the problem of how a country can achieve external and internal equilibrium at the same time.

Given these circumstances, it may be preferable for a country to make some leeway by using capital imports to cover a deficit. One reason for this may be that the causes of the deficit may disappear and the country automatically return to equilibrium. Another reason may be that the expansionary effects among trading partners which a deficit in one country implies may, given time, work to correct the disequilibrium. The present trading system has, after all, a built-in steering mechanism that always works in the direction of equilibrium. One important aspect of capital movements is that they can give this international adjustment mechanism time to work itself out.

Another aspect of capital movements is that rates of capital accumulation and increases in activity levels may vary between countries. For such 'real' reasons it is quite natural that international capital movements take place. Economic history contains several examples of such long-run capital movements between countries (see Chapter 8). If such a situation occurs, it is natural that a deficit in the trade balance is covered by capital imports.

Viewed from a different angle, it can be argued that the present international monetary system can only function well if it is supported by extensive capital movements. The central banks will play a critical role in this regard. Only if they manage to transform accommodating capital movements into some kind of autonomous capital movements can the present monetary system be expected to work well. Capital movements should not be viewed as exceptional but as a natural complement to other policy means. We shall return to the role played by capital movements in Part V, where we shall deal with the international monetary system.

SELECTED BIBLIOGRAPHY: CHAPTER 25

Classic works on the gold standard are:

> W. A. Brown, jr, *The Gold Standard Re-interpreted, 1914-34*, New York, National Bureau of Economic Research, 1934.

> R. G. Hawtrey, *The Gold Standard in Theory and Practice*, 5th ed., London, Longmans, Green, 1947.

The standard work for discussion of the effects of economic policy on the balance of payments is:

> J. E. Meade, *The Balance of Payments*, London, Oxford University Press, 1951, and its *Mathematical Supplement* (published separately).

Another important paper is:

> H. G. Johnson, 'Towards a General Theory of the Balance of Payments', in *International Trade and Economic Growth: Studies in Pure Theory*, Cambridge, Mass., Harvard University Press, 1961, pp. 153–68 (reprinted in *RIE*).

Early works on the elasticity approach are:

> A. Marshall, *Money, Credit, and Commerce*, New York, 1924, appendix J.

> A. P. Lerner, *The Economics of Control*, New York, Macmillan Co., 1944, ch. 28.

> J. Robinson, 'The Foreign Exchanges', in *Essays in the Theory of Employment*, London, 1937 (reprinted in *RTIT*).

One important essay is:

> A. C. Harberger, 'Currency Depreciation, Income and the Balance of Trade', *JPE*, February 1950 (reprinted in *RIE*).

The first paper to elaborate the absorption approach was:

> S. S. Alexander, 'The Effects of a Devaluation on the Trade Balance', *SP*, April 1952 (reprinted in *RIE*).

For a critical view of the absorption approach and a defence of the elasticity approach, see:

> F. Machlup, 'Relative Prices and Aggregate Spending in the Analysis of Devaluation', *AER*, vol. 45, June 1955.

For attempts to combine the two approaches see:

> S. C. Tsiang, 'The Role of Money in Trade-Balance Stability: Synthesis of the Elasticity and the Absorption Approaches', *AER*, vol. 51, December 1961 (reprinted in *RIE*).

> S. S. Alexander, 'Effects of a Devaluation: A Simplified Synthesis of elasticities and Absorption Approaches', *AER*, vol. 49, March 1959.

The derivation of the complete elasticity formula given in Chapter 25 follows the approach developed by Alexander in the paper cited last.

26
The monetary approach to the balance of payments

The preceding chapter demonstrated the traditional approaches to the analysis of the balance of payments and devaluation. In recent years, important contributions have been made to the monetary side of international economics. This work has primarily concerned with what is commonly called 'the monetary approach' to the balance of payments. The important elements of this analysis are its interpretation of the balance of payments as primarily a monetary phenomenon and its emphasis on hoarding and dishoarding of money (or other assets) as necessary counterparts to surpluses and deficits in the balance of trade. It has stressed the view that the supply and demand for money will be strong forces in determining a country's external position. Normally an increase in the demand for money will lead to a surplus in the balance of payments, while an increase in the supply of money will give rise to deficits. Also important is the view of money as primarily an endogenous variable, which implies that changes in the money supply will be accompanied by changes in external reserves.

The importance of the monetary approach has been disputed and will, undoubtedly, be disputed in the future. It is my view that this approach, regardless of how one evaluates its policy proposals, has created a major breakthrough in international monetary economics. Therefore, it deserves a reasonably thorough exposition. We will in this chapter start by giving a model version that states the basic ingredients and the results of the new approach. Then we will continue by discussing 'the dual' of the monetary approach, the importance of asset markets. One of the messages of the new theory is that changes in both the supply and demand of assets and the expectations about asset prices can have important influences on the determination of exchange rates. This is in sharp contrast to the traditional theory and its stress on trade flows as the basic determinants of exchange rates.

Most writings in the spirit of the new approach tend to be couched in terms of one-sector models. They can give an undue emphasis to changes in aggregate supply and demand and, thereby, to monetary matters. In order to suggest that real, as opposed to monetary, factors can be important, we will in the concluding section use a two-sector model with a traded goods sector and a non-traded goods sector. This exposition can then also be viewed as a partial reconciliation of the new and the more traditional approaches.

THE MONETARY APPROACH

At the heart of the monetary approach is *money*. We learned in Chapter 23 that the balance of payments could be subdivided into the balance of trade, the balance of current account, and the balance of capital account. According to the rules of double-entry book-keeping, the balance of payments will always be in equilibrium. Equilibrium is achieved by offsetting capital movements. We can think of the final part of the capital account as a 'money account', consisting of the change in a country's foreign reserves. If the balance of payments is in surplus, the foreign reserves will increase; if it shows a deficit, they will decrease. Or we could say that any surplus or deficit on the trade balance or balance of current account will be offset by an induced change in the country's asset position that will show up as a change in the capital account.

In contrast to this explanation of the single items or the sub-accounts of the balance of payments, the monetary approach is specifically geared toward an explanation of the over-all settlement of a balance-of-payments deficit or surplus. Thereby it also gives emphasis to the asset position of the country.

Changes in the balance of payments are explained in terms of supply and demand for money. If the supply of money increases, through an expansion of domestic credit, it will cause a deficit in the balance of payments. An increase in the demand for money will, on the contrary, lead to a surplus in the balance of payments as it will lower the demand for goods and various assets, and thereby decrease the aggregate demand in the economy.

The new monetary approach to the balance of payments is essentially an application of monetary analysis to international economics. It assumes, more specifically, that the money supply and the money demand functions are stable. Of special importance is the money demand function. The proponents of the new approach argue that extensive empirical investigations show that the demand for money is a stable function of a few variables. This also implies that the approach is policy-oriented, with a strong emphasis on monetary policy. As it is assumed that the demand for money on the part of firms and households is stable, and that their role in the money supply process also is stable, the monetary policy pursued by the central authorities becomes vital for the outcome of the balance of payments. The central feature is what policy the central authorities carry out with regard to the money supply, or rather the domestic component of the monetary base. A devaluation for instance, has its basic influence on the balance of payments through its effects on the demand for money in the devaluing country.

To gain a more precise insight into the new monetary approach we will first deal with a one-commodity, two-country model where money enters explicitly. This model can be viewed as an application of the new monetary approach with its stress on hoarding and dishoarding as central concepts.[1]

HOARDING, DISHOARDING AND DEVALUATION

We will start by presenting the one-sector model where money enters explicitly. The model demonstrates how changes in the demand for goods and in the demand for money (hoarding) affect the balance of payments. Thereby the model captures an essential aspect of the monetary approach to the balance of payments. It also serves to highlight the difference between the short and the long run and the role of asset changes for the adjustment process.

Following the monetary approach, we assume that there exists a stable demand function for money at the aggregate level:

$$L_1 = k_1 P_1 Y_1 \qquad (26.1a)$$

$$L_2 = k_2 P_2 Y_2 \qquad (26.1b)$$

where k_1 and k_2 are the desired ratios of money to income in country I and country II, where P_1 and P_2 are the price levels in the two countries, and where Y_1 and Y_2 are the national incomes expressed in real terms in the two countries. We assume that the real income (or rather output) is fixed in both countries. (We have given the demand functions for money the simplest possible form so as not to detract from the main line of argument.)

As we assume no tariffs or impediments to trade, the price levels in the two countries are linked to each other by the exchange rate, r:

$$P_1 = P_2 r \qquad (26.2)$$

Furthermore, it is assumed that the nominal quantity of money in each country, M_1 and M_2, consists of one domestic-credit, K, and one international-reserve component, R:

$$M_1 = K_1 + R_1 \qquad (26.3a)$$

$$M_2 = K_2 + R_2 \qquad (26.3b)$$

We assume that the authorities do not change K_1 and K_2. Any change in the money supply will then be caused by imports or exports of money. The money supply in each country then becomes an endogenous variable. The following relationship between changes in the money supply, reserve changes and the balance of payments can then be set out:

$$dM_1 = dR_1 = H_1 = B = -rH_2 = -rdR_2 = -rdM_2 \qquad (26.4)$$

where B is the deficit or surplus in the balance of payments and H_1 and H_2 stand for hoarding in the respective countries.

The nominal demand for (or expenditure on) goods in each country, D_1 and D_2, equals the total money income minus the flow demand for money (or desired hoarding), H_1 and H_2:

$$D_1 = P_1 Y_1 - H_1 \qquad (26.5a)$$

$$D_2 = P_2 Y_2 - H_2 \qquad (26.5b)$$

The hoarding, in its turn, is proportional to the excess *stock* demand for money:

$$H_1 = q_1 (L_1 - M_1) \qquad (26.6a)$$

$$H_2 = q_2 (L_2 - M_2) \qquad (26.6b)$$

Here q_1 and q_2 are rates of adjustment in the two countries. An essential feature of the model is that when the stock demand for money is in equilibrium, then the marginal propensity to spend the income on goods is unity. In the short run, however, when the monetary stock is out of equilibrium, the marginal propensity to spend on goods is less then one.

It might be useful at this stage to point out some of the specific features of this model, and of the monetary approach in general, in order to put them into a broader perspective. The first two equations (26.1a) and (26.1b) embody one essential aspect of the monetary approach. the real income (output) is given in the short run. Furthermore, we live in a 'classical', pre-Keynesian world where wages are fully flexible. Money plays an important 'real' role in the system as there is no money illusion and as demand is a function of the real amount of money available in the two economies.

Another important aspect of the monetary approach is embodied in equation (26.2). Again, the monetary approach alludes to an earlier, pre-Keynesian view of the international economy, the so-called *purchasing-power parity theory*, which Gustav Cassel forcefully put forward just after the First World War.[2] Equation (26.2) states that there is a perfect commodity arbitrage in the world economy: if country I's price level is constant while country II's price level increases by 20 per cent, its exchange rate will also depreciate by the same percentage. This assumption is sometimes fittingly referred to as 'the law of one price'.

At first glance it may look innocent but it is, in fact, a quite stringent assumption. At the microeconomic level, when referring to a single good, it is quite harmless, as it then simply means that we disregard transport costs, trade impediments, etc. At the macro level it is, however, far from innocent, as it means that there is a one-to-one relationship between price *levels* in the two countries via the exchange rate. If country I has technical progress (say of an import-biased kind) while country II is stationary, its exchange rate may well appreciate without any fall in its domestic price level. Likewise, demand shifts or changing asset preferences may well have different impacts on price levels and exchange rates.

It is sometimes argued that the purchasing-power doctrine or the law of one price should hold in the long run but not necessarily in the short run. This is in itself a doubtful proposition. Furthermore, one can argue that balance-of-payments problems are in essence short-run phenomena, and that other parts of this model, like the assumptions of constant real outputs, are of a short-run nature.

Another important feature of the monetary approach is the assertion that money is an endogenous variable. This is reflected in equations (26.3a) and (26.3b), which divide the money supply into two components, one consisting of domestically created credit and the other of international reserves, and demonstrate the feedback from the balance of payments to each country's national stock of money. In Keynesian types of analysis this link was often disregarded. There it was often assumed that changes in international reserves did not affect the money supply but that the influences from the foreign reserves were sterilized by the monetary authorities; sometimes it was assumed that the central bank did hold the interest rate at a fixed level and absorbed whatever changes in the money supply that came via the foreign sector in order to achieve that aim.

Here it seems that the monetary approach is on firm grounds. It is undoubtedly simpler and more straightforward to assume that changes in international reserves will influence the money supply than to rest the analysis on some specific rule for institutional behavior.

The important role played by money in this model is further stressed in equations (26.5) and (26.6). The demand for and supply of money will affect all markets in the economy via the hoarding function. Stock aspects also come into play since equilibrium in the money market is essentially a stock equilibrium. The adjustment to stock equilibrium will, however, not take place immediately as pictured by equation (26.6). There is a partial adjustment mechanism that separates the short-run impact from the long-run effects.

We have set up the model so as to display the essence of the monetary approach.

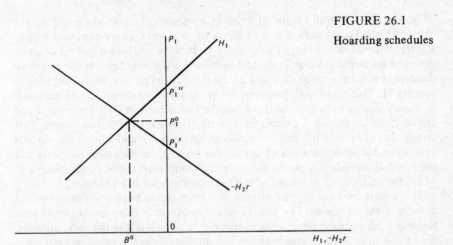

FIGURE 26.1

Hoarding schedules

The income can be spent in essentially two ways: it can either be used to buy goods, or it can be used to build up the stock of money, i.e. it can be used for hoarding. The demand for money is a demand expressed in nominal terms. It is therefore intimately linked to movements in the general price level. If prices go up, then the demand for money will also increase. Thus money serves a real purpose. The agents in the economy, i.e. households and firms, want their cash balances to have a real value that is constant in equilibrium. Therefore, if the price level increases, the demand for money will also increase, i.e. hoarding will take place, and if the price level decreases, dishoarding will occur. It is essential to keep this point in mind in order to understand the monetary approach to the balance of payments.

The interrelationship between hoarding and the price level is expressed in Figure 26.1. The horizontal axis shows the amount of hoarding taking place in the two countries and the vertical axis shows the price level in country I. We have to remember that the nominal quantity of monies is given in the two countries. Then hoarding in country I becomes an increasing function of the price level in that country. As the price level in the country increases, the real value of its stock of money decreases. This gives rise to an excess demand for money and an excess supply of goods. Expenditures on goods fall as the economy tries to restore the real value of its cash balances. The foreign rate of hoarding, $-H_2r$, is by the same type of reasoning a decreasing function of country I's price level, given the exchange rate.

We observe that the hoarding schedules in Figure 26.1 intersect at the price level P_1^0. At this price level the world market for goods is cleared as the world demand for goods equals the world supply of goods. This is illustrated by the fact that the following condition is fulfilled:

$$H_1 = -H_2r \qquad (26.7)$$

so that hoarding in one country equals dishoarding in the other country. At a higher price there would be an excess supply of goods on the world market and at a lower price there would be an excess demand.

We can observe from Figure 26.1 that at a price which clears the world market country I will have a deficit in its balance of payments. This means that money will transferred from country I to country II. In the world which we here describe there are no sterilization policies, and as money is the only asset in the economy the deficit will have to be financed by an outflow of money from country I to country II. This flow will, however, affect the hoarding schedules. As the stock of money decreases in country I its hoarding schedule will shift downwards and as the stock of money increases in country II its schedule shift upwards. This means that they will intersect somewhere between P''_1 and P'_1 on the vertical axis. After this redistribution of monies has taken place the world economy will reach a full equilibrium position where the world market for goods clears and where the balances of payments of the two countries are in equilibrium.

It is now time to study the effects of a devaluation in this one-sector model with its stress on money. The impact of a devaluation in this type of model is by the way it changes the relationship between the price levels in the two countries. We have a strict relationship between the price levels in the two countries given by equation (26.2).

Differentiating this equation gives

$$\frac{dP_1}{P_1} = \frac{dP_2}{P_2} + \frac{dr}{r} \tag{26.8}$$

This equation shows how changes in domestic and foreign price levels are related to each other. Normally, we would expect country I's price level to increase and country II's level to fall, expressed in country I's currency. But other outcomes are also possible. If the prices expressed in terms of foreign currency were to remain constant, then country I's price level would have to increase in the same proportion as the devaluation. If country I's price level did not change, then country II's price level would have to fall in proportion to the devaluation.

Figure 26.2 is helpful in discussing the effects of a devaluation. For the sake of reasoning we can suppose that the foreign prices are constant. Then the domestic price level will have to increase by the same proportion as that which the country has devalued its currency. Or we can assume that the domestic price level is constant. Then the foreign price level will have to decrease by the proportion by which the home country had devalued. These propositions follow directly from equation (26.8).

Let us assume that the domestic hoarding schedule is the one illustrated by H_1 in Figure 26.2. The domestic monetary stock equilibrium would then be at the price level P_1^0. After the devaluation the relation between the two countries' price levels must change. If the domestic price level were to remain at P_1^0, the foreign price level would have to fall. This would imply that the foreign hoarding schedule would have to shift to the right, from $-H_2r$ to $-H_2r'$. This is explained by the fact that a fall in the foreign price level creates a windfall gain for the economic agents in the foreign country. With a given stock of money the value of their real cash balances will go up. They will hoard less in nominal terms and spend more on goods. Hence at an unchanged domestic price level there will be a world excess demand for goods. This will lead to an upward pressure on goods prices, and the price level in country I will increase from P_1^0 to P'_1. Likewise the foreign price level will not fall by the full amount of the devaluation, i.e. by the proportion

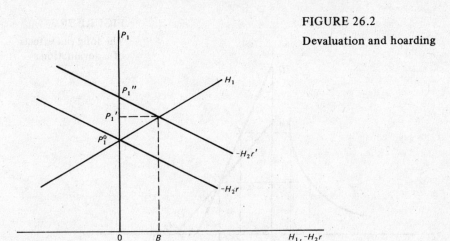

FIGURE 26.2

Devaluation and hoarding

$(P_1'' - P_1^0)/P_1^0$, but by less than this proportion. Thus a process of hoarding will start in the devaluing country and the economic agents in the country will try to exchange goods for money. In the foreign country a process of dishoarding will take place while households and firms try to acquire goods for money. The price level in the devaluing country will increase but by less than the rate of devaluation. So if country I devalues its currency by, say, 20 per cent, we might expect its price level to increase by about 10 per cent. We have earlier (in Chapter 25) hinted that the increase in the domestic price level of a country would depend on its foreign trade share. Here we can see that in this type of model it is primarily determined by monetary factors as expressed by the slope of the hoarding schedules. Likewise the price level in country II will fall, but by less than the proportion with which its trading partner devalues.

We can also observe that the devaluation will have a positive effect on the devaluing country's balance of payments. Since we began from an equilibrium position, in our example country I will have a surplus in its balance of payments. This implies a redistribution of monies between the countries. Country I will have an excess demand for cash balances and will export goods for money. Country II will try to spend part of the capital gains accruing to it because of its trading partner's devaluation and will part with some of its too large stock of money by exchanging it for goods. Hence we can see that the disequilibriums in the balances of payments cause a redistribution of assets between the two countries.

THE EFFECTS OF DEVALUATION IN THE LONG RUN

It is quite obvious that the situation which we have just discussed cannot represent a position of long-run equilibrium. In order for equilibrium in the long run to prevail there must also be equilibria in the balance of payments and in the asset markets. The long-run effects of a devaluation on the supplies of money and on the price levels may be illustrated with the help of Figure 26.3.

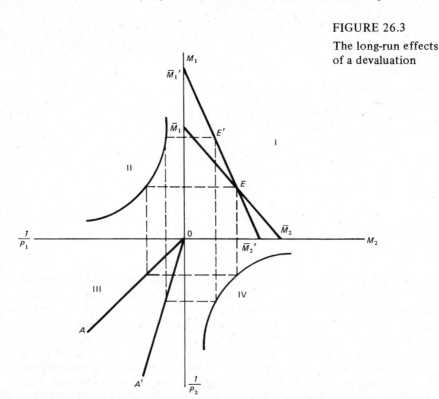

FIGURE 26.3

The long-run effects
of a devaluation

In quadrants II and IV of the figure we show the demand for real balances in country I and country II as hyperbolae. Quadrant III shows the relationship between the price levels ($P_1 r = P_2$) at the original exchange rate as the ray OA. In quadrant I the world money supply evaluated at the initial exchange rate is given by $\bar{M}_1 \bar{M}_2$, where $\bar{M}_2 = \bar{M}_1 / r$.

To begin with, the long-run equilibrium is given at point E, where the real balances held by each country are divided so that the equilibrium relationship between price levels in the two countries is satisfied. Country I now devalues. The devaluation affects both the relationship between price levels in the two countries and the world money supply. For each price level in country I, country II will now have a lower equilibrium price level. This is demonstrated by the fact that the price-level equilibrium line changes from OA to OA'. If the nominal quantities of money are kept unchanged in both countries (i.e. the money supplies underlying the equilibrium at E are kept constant), the world money supply will change in terms of the new price levels. The world money supply will increase when measured in country I's currency and it will fall when measured in country II's currency. Geometrically this means that the 'budget line' relating the money supplies in the two countries will rotate around point E to the new position $\bar{M}_1' \bar{M}_2'$.

Figure 26.3 now demonstrates that the supplies of money which prevailed at point E before devaluation are no longer appropriate as an equilibrium position as they are not compatible with the new relationship between price levels in the two countries. The new equilibrium point is demonstrated by point E'. At this point country I's price level has increased and so has its money supply. The money supply in country II has decreased and so has its price level. The point, however, is that the real balances have remained the same. They have just been adjusted to the new equilibrium price levels.

It is now time to sum up some essential points of the new monetary approach for both short-run and long-run analysis. An essential feature of the new analysis is its stress on hoarding and the real balance effects connected with hoarding. A devaluation will increase the demand for money in the devaluing country. This follows from the fact that it will increase the country's domestic price level and hence cause cash balances to be too low. The only way the residents of the country can build up their real balances is by supplying goods for money. Its trading partner (the rest of the world) will, on the contrary, find that its cash balances are too large as the devaluation will decrease its price level. To take advantage of the cheap goods flowing into the country its residents will exchange some of their now superfluous cash for goods. Thereby they will take advantage of the capital gains which a devaluation abroad will bring them. Hence in the short run the devaluation will bring a surplus in the balance of payments of the devaluing country and an excess demand for goods in the rest of the world.

In the long run assets also must adjust in the two countries. Money will flow from the rest of the world to the devaluing country as long as the latter country's surplus in the balance of payments exists. In the end assets will be redistributed between the countries so as to correspond to the new price levels. The goods market will clear, the demand for money will match the cash balances available in each country, and the balance of payments will be in equilibrium.

The monetary approach in this simplest, but at the same time most basic, formulation strongly emphasizes the presence of a real balance effect. To this extent it is close to the old absorption approach. It is obvious that the positive effects of a devaluation hinge on the fact that a stable demand function for money exists and that the governments and central banks observe some basic rules. It is easy for the authorities to undo the positive effects of a devaluation by following inappropriate monetary policies. This can be demonstrated by reference to Figure 26.4. This demonstrates a case where the authorities in country I increase the money supply in proportion to devaluation. This means, in terms of the figure, that 'the budget line' in quadrant I, describing the world's monetary constraint, now shifts outward from $\bar{M}_2\bar{M}_1$ to $\bar{M}_2\bar{M}'_1$. Thus the world's money supply has remained constant in terms of country II's currency but it has increased in terms of country I's currency. There will be neither positive effects from the devaluation on country I's balance of payments nor any inflow of foreign currency. Hence the traditional, advantageous effects of a devaluation will be absent in the devaluing country. The restoration of an equilibrium in the balance of payments, which we may regard as the main aim of devaluation, will not come about. The end-result will only be an increase in the domestic price level proportionate to the devaluation. The government may, however, count on one beneficial effect: it will be able to run a transitory deficit in its budget without further worsening its balance of payments. (If the balance of payments is in equilibrium before the devaluation *cum* expansion of money supply, it will still be in equilibrium after

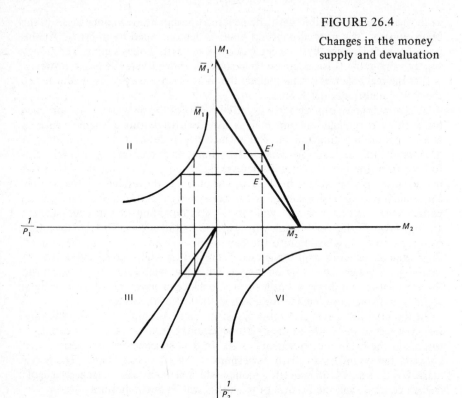

FIGURE 26.4

Changes in the money supply and devaluation

the use of this policy combination.)

This analysis shows that the upshot for the balance of payments depends critically on the monetary policy accompanying a devaluation. Only by keeping the money supply constant can a country be sure that a devaluation will improve its balance of payments.

ASSETS AND FLEXIBLE EXCHANGE RATES

One of the important points of the new monetary approach is its emphasis on the role of assets. As we have seen, to reach full equilibrium following a devaluation assets must be redistributed so as to reach a new equilibrium in asset markets. So far assets have, however, been treated somewhat passively. One important message of the new theory is that considerations of wealth distribution play as powerful a role for determining exchange rates as do monetary and real factors.

In the preceding section we assumed the exchange rates to be pegged and demonstrated the effects of a devaluation, i.e. of a discrete exchange-rate change. In that formulation, money became an endogenous variable. An alternative formulation of the problem takes money as a (fixed) exogenous variable and lets exchange rates be flexible instead. This approach is most amenable for analysing wealth and asset-market considerations.

Which of the two approaches one prefers is to a degree an empirical matter depending on whether one assumes adjustment in the goods market (trade flows) to be faster than adjustment of assets, or vice versa. In the preceding parts of this chapter, a new equilibrium was reached via an adjustment of traded quantities; this implied a redistribution of assets and a new equilibrium in asset markets. Instead, one can assume adjustment in the asset market to be faster. Under flexible exchange rates, changes in the valuation of the stock of assets (including domestic and foreign currencies) can cause a rapid adjustment in the money and asset markets.

Expectations play a great role in the asset approach to exchange rates. When dealing with the effects of real factors on trade flows or the influence of monetary policy on absorption and the balance of payments, expectations can be disregarded. However, they have to be taken into consideration when discussing the formation of asset prices. If everyone expects the German mark to appreciate, the increase in demand for marks will force its appreciation (unless the German central bank increases the supply of marks).

The proponents of the new approach claim that it can explain many of the short-run fluctuations in exchange rates which have taken place since 1971 and which cannot be explained by real factors, i.e. by changes in relative prices of the various national products. An analogy to the stock market may here be appropriate: there it has been observed that the prices of various shares can change greatly over short periods of time due to changing expectations and valuations of various companies. Likewise, expectations about the prices of various monies can cause substantial short-run fluctuations in exchange rates.

It might be useful to state some of the properties of a model where assets play a central role:[3]

$$A = \frac{M}{P} + Q_{FA} \qquad (26.9)$$

This equation states that total assets in country I consists of two parts, the real value of domestic money (M is the money supply and P is the price level) and the supply of foreign assets, Q_{FA}.

The demand for money is a function of the expected rate of inflation, π, the national income, Y (which is constant in the short run), and total assets:

$$\frac{M^d}{P} = L\left(\pi, \bar{Y}, A\right) = \frac{M}{P} \qquad (26.10)$$

We also have a second equilibrium condition:

$$D_{FA} = L_2\left(\pi, \bar{Y}, A\right) = Q_{FA} \qquad (26.11)$$

Due to the wealth constraint, the two equilibrium conditions (26.10) and (26.11) are not independent.

Substituting (26.9) into (26.11) gives the equilibrium condition for the asset market:

$$L_2\left(\pi, \bar{Y}, \frac{M}{P} + Q_{FA}\right) = \frac{M}{P} \qquad (26.12)$$

If the expected rate of inflation, π, the stock of foreign assets, Q_{FA}, and the

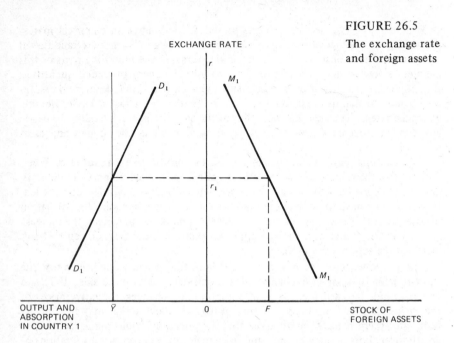

EXCHANGE RATE

FIGURE 26.5

The exchange rate
and foreign assets

OUTPUT AND
ABSORPTION
IN COUNTRY 1

STOCK OF
FOREIGN ASSETS

nominal supply of money, M, are given, the domestic price level is determined. As we further assume that 'the law of one price', or the purchasing-power parity, holds, and if the international price level P_i is taken as given, then the exchange rate is determined thus:

$$P = rP_i \qquad (26.13)$$

Thus the exchange rate is determined by the requirement that the market for foreign assets should be in equilibrium.

It will now be opportune to demonstrate some important points of the asset approach to exchange-rate determination by using the following diagrammatic technique. The more deap-seated implications of a dynamic kind are not easy to convey without the use of a more fully elaborated algebraic analysis which would take us outside the scope of this study. However, we should be able to illustrate some major points of the asset approach by a combination of geometry and the English language.

The vertical axis in Figure 26.5 measures the exchange rate, i.e. number of units of country I's currency per unit of country II's currency. So the further one is from the origin, the more country I's currency depreciates. The horizontal axis to the right of the origin measures the stock of foreign assets. The horizontal axis to the left of the origin measures output and absorption in country I. The $M_1 M_1$ schedule portrays the asset equilibrium line in country I along which there is equilibrium in the asset market in Country I. It has a negative slope since the demand for *foreign* (country II-denominatcd) asscts increases when country I's currency appreciates, i.e. when the relative price of foreign assets falls. The $D_1 D_1$ curve shows absorption in country I as a function of the exchange rate. In ac-

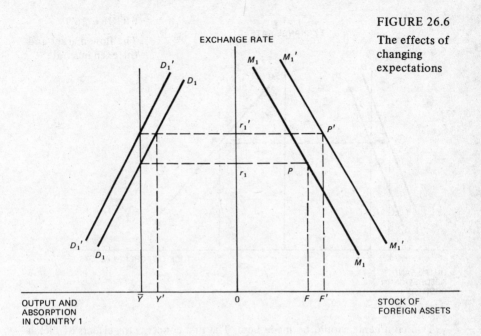

FIGURE 26.6

The effects of changing expectations

cordance with the monetary approach we assume that absorption falls as the exchange rate depreciates (due, for instance, to a real balance effect).

To start with, the citizens of country I hold OF of foreign assets. This gives us the exchange rate Or_1. At this exchange rate domestic absorption amounts to $O\bar{Y}$, $\bar{Y}$ being the full-employment output. This implies that the current-account balance is zero. Hence there is full equilibrium (a stationary-state situation) in the economy as both the capital and current accounts are in equilibrium.

We can now think of various disturbances occurring both in the stock and the flow markets. To highlight the importance of asset considerations, let us assume that the following disturbance occurs in the asset market. Domestic investors change their expectations regarding the exchange rate. They come to believe that it will depreciate. This case is illustrated in Figure 26.6.

Here there will be, as Joan Robinson expressed it, 'an increase in the willingness to lend abroad' as the domestic investors think that the domestic exchange rate is overvalued and expect it to depreciate.[4] This causes the asset equilibrium schedule in country I to shift to $M'_1 M'_1$.

This forces the exchange rate to depreciate and creates a momentary surplus in the balance of current account of $\bar{Y}Y'$ as absorption falls. This fall in absorption will lead to an inflow of foreign capital as the investors try to increase their stock of foreign assets. This wealth effect will again have a positive effect on absorption and will influence the exchange rate in an upwards direction. However, the asset effect will dominate, and we will reach a new full equilibrium (stationary-state equilibrium) at a lower exchange rate (r'_1) and with a larger stock of foreign assets and an absorption of the full-employment output at this new, depreciated exchange rate.

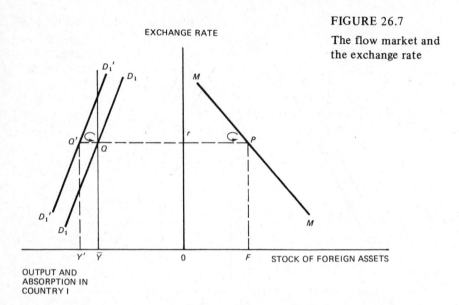

FIGURE 26.7

The flow market and the exchange rate

Two comments should be made here. The first concerns the effects of such a 'psychological' factor as a change in expectations. Such a change can, as the analysis shows, have a powerful effect on the economy. Thus changing expectations on the part of investors are important. They also tend to become self-fulfilling prophecies. If investors think that an exchange rate is over- or undervalued, and act accordingly, they can usually bring about a depreciation or an appreciation. Analogously, if foreign investors had felt that country I's exchange rate had been overvalued, and hence if they had expected a depreciation, they could have brought about such a change by a shift in their demand for assets.

The second comment concerns expectations and dynamic fluctuations of the exchange rate. Our analysis of figure 26.6 led to the conclusion that the exchange rate moved from r_1 to r_1'. These are, however, only two points of equilibria. The path from one to the other will depend in a critical fashion on how expectations are formed. A feature common to many models is that the impact effect of a change in, say, asset preferences is stronger than the long-run effects. This leads to 'overshooting', so that the exchange rate will to begin with depreciate more than what is shown in Figure 26.6. Such over-reactions can create unpleasant disturbances in an economy under flexible exchange rates (see Chapter 30).

We can also study how a change in the flow market affects the exchange rate. This is done in Figure 26.7. We start with an equilibrium exchange rate of Or, a stock of foreign assets of OF, and a national income of OY. Then the government decides to increase its expenditures. This will lead to a shift of the DD schedule to the left, to $D_1'D_1'$, as domestic absorption increases because of the expansionary fiscal policy. The MM curve is, however, not changed as the citizen's demand for foreign assets is not initially affected by the increase in absorption. The exchange rate is not affected either, but the increase in government expenditures causes a deficit in the current account equal to the distance $Y'Y$. This deficit will have to be financed somehow; and it will be financed by sales of foreign assets. This, in turn, causes the exchange rate to depreciate. Because of the depreciation, absorption falls as the price level increases. Both these effects will work to bring the economy back to its original equilibrium, where external balance is also in equilibrium. Hence in this model a change in absorption has no lasting effect on the exchange rate as it does not affect the demand for assets. The asset market is the dominating market. where the rate of exchange is finally determined.

Disturbances which originate in the asset market, for instance because of a shift in demand for assets or changing asset preferences, can have powerful effects on the exchange rate. They can be considered harmful to the real side of the economy, to the activities of exporters and importers, and to stabilization policies and the control of the activity level of the economy. Governments might then want to shield the real side of the economy from influences stemming from the asset market.

There are various ways in which this can be done. One market-oriented approach is to introduce a system of dual exchange rates. Such a system entails an official rate that applies to current-account transactions and a free rate that applies to asset transactions. Another way is simply to control capital movements and not allow movements other than those approved by the authorities. As an example of the first case, Italy has used a two-tier market since the breakdown of the Bretton Woods system in 1971, when a 'financial lira' and a 'commercial lira' were introduced. Sweden, on the other hand, has used regulated capital movements for a long time and has applied quite rigorous restrictions on all capital movements which are not connected with trade flows or direct investments. We now give up the assumption that the money supply is fixed, while we retain the assumption that the supply of foreign assets is fixed.

We now use Figure 26.8 to illustrate the effects of an increase in the money supply on the part of the authorities in country I. To start with, the asset equilibrium line is given by $M_1 M_1$. The supply of foreign assets is OF. Domestic absorption is given by the $D_1 D_1$ schedule. The equilibrium exchange rate is shown by Or_1, where demand for foreign assets equals supply and where the full-employment product OY is completely absorbed.

The authorities now increase domestic money supply by buying $F'F$ of foreign exchange from private domestic citizens. This sharp decline in the holdings of foreign assets on the part of the private sector causes the exchange rate to depreciate to Or'_1. The depreciation of the exchange rate has the usual effects on absorption via a change in the domestic price level, and domestic absorption falls to OY'.

The left part of the figure demonstrates that domestic absorption falls short of domestic production by the amount $\overline{Y}Y'$. Hence a surplus in the current account is created. The surplus in the current account will induce an inflow of foreign assets into the country. Total assets will increase and this will affect both absorption and the demand for foreign assets. The demand schedule for foreign assets shifts out to the right, to $M'_1 M'_1$. The absorption curve shifts out to the left to $D'_1 D'_1$.

The induced capital flows will increase the holdings of foreign assets. By a wealth effect this will appreciate the exchange rate somewhat. Absorption will also gradually increase again until a new equilibrium is reached when the full-

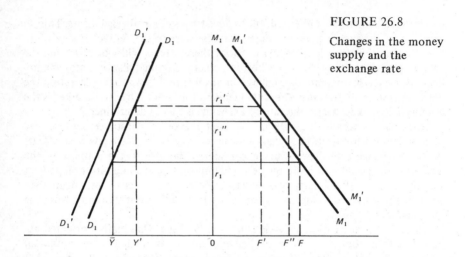

FIGURE 26.8

Changes in the money supply and the exchange rate

employment output is again completely absorbed for domestic purpose. A new equilibrium exchange rate will be established at Or_1''. The asset market is also in equilibrium as the supply of foreign assets OF'' equals the demand for foreign assets as defined by the new asset equilibrium schedule $M'M'$. Hence the economy is again characterized by a new full (stationary-state) equilibrium.

Two important observations should be made in this connection. The first concerns the effects of changes in the money supply. At the new equilibrium, absorption and full-employment output will be the same as before the increase in money supply. The asset mix will, however, differ as foreign assets will be less than before the increase in the money supply, while total assets will have increased. The price level has increased and the exchange rate has depreciated.

To this extent the last model presented in this section is true to the monetary spirit which stresses the absence of money illusion and the operation of the law of one price, i.e. a one-to-one correspondence between the price level and the exchange rate once a full equilibrium has been achieved.

The second observation concerns the adjustment mechanism of the economy. According to our example the impact effect of the increase in the money supply is to depreciate the exchange rate more than proportionately to the change in the money supply. How the economy will be affected by a disturbance in the asset market will depend to a large extent on the formation of expectations. It would take us too far in this connection to venture into a discussion of possible adjustment paths for the economy.[5] The 'overshooting' of the exchange rate that we have referred to above seems to be a result common to several models. Several simple models of how expectations are formed have the common characteristic that the impact effect of a disturbance on the exchange rate will exceed the long-run equilibrium effect.

One important empirical fact since the general floating of exchange rates in 1973 has been the sharp fluctuations in exchange rates. Major exchange rates have fluctuated by 20 per cent or more within a few months, and even weekly fluctuations have been large. We will return to a description of the international monetary system in recent years in Chapter 30. The reader should then keep in mind the analysis of this section.

One of the important themes of the monetary approach to the balance of payments is the stress on stock adjustments and asset markets. This section has demonstrated that changes in supply and demand for assets can have important repercussions on exchange rates and that it can be misleading to view exchange rates as primarily determined by trade flows.

However, one should not forget that real factors are also important for the determination of exchange rates and the development of a country's balance of payments. Before concluding this chapter it should therefore be useful to see how real factors can be included in a monetary framework.

REAL FACTORS AND THE DETERMINATION OF THE EXCHANGE RATE: THE CASE OF NON-TRADED GOODS

In traditional balance-of-payments theory, as expressed by the 'elasticity approach', changes in relative prices and adjustment of supply and demand induced by such changes play an important role. The monetary approach stresses instead the importance of money and hoarding. This is logical as long as the analysis is couched in terms of a one-sector model as in the first part of this chapter. To demonstrate the importance of the adjustment of real factors in a monetary framework, we will now briefly show how the monetary approach can be handled in a two-sector context.

The model that is used for this purpose is a two-sector model which differs from the traditional trade model to the extent that it does not contain one import and one export good but works with one traded good and one non-traded good. In reality we have to think of the sectors as comprising each class of goods. Each class consists of a composite commodity and the relative prices within each class do not change. The relative price between traded and non-traded goods does, however, change. The essence of the model is to show how such changes of relative prices affect absorption.

There are two commodities, S_{1N} and S_{1T}, the non-traded and traded commodity being produced in country I. Production takes place along an ordinary concave transformation curve and production is a function of relative prices:[6]

$$S_{1N} = S_{1N}(P_1) \qquad (26.14)$$

and analogously for the other sector, where P is the relative price of non-traded goods:

$$P = \frac{P_{1N}}{P_{1T}} \qquad (26.15)$$

As in the first section of the chapter, hoarding is a function of the national income and the money supply. It is also a function of the domestic price level:

$$H_1 = H_1(Y_1, M_1, P) \qquad (26.16)$$

The demand for money balances is proportional to money income. Hence the demand for real balances increases with income, and $\delta H_1 / \delta Y_1 > 0$. An increase in

FIGURE 26.9

Hoarding and relative prices

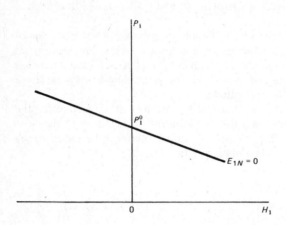

the money supply will decrease real hoarding, and hence $\delta H_1/\delta M_1 < 0$. If the price level increases, the demand for money balances will also increase. The price level can increase because of an increase in the price of either traded or non-traded goods. Hence $\delta H_1/\delta P > 0$.

Equilibrium in the two markets implies that each market clears:

$$E_{1N} = S_{1N}(P_1) - C_{1N}(P_1, D_1) = 0 \qquad (26.17)$$

$$E_{1T} = S_{1T}(P_1) - C_{1T}(P_1, D_1) = 0 \qquad (26.18)$$

where C_{1N} and C_{1T} are the demand for non-traded and traded goods respectively in country I and where D_1 is real expenditure, i.e. $D_1 = Y_1 - H_1$. Equilibrium in the world economy then implies that the planned rate of hoarding in country I equals the planned rate of hoarding in country II, so that:

$$H_1(P_1, M_1) + H_2(P_2, M_2) = 0 \qquad (26.19)$$

In analogy with what was pointed out in the first section of this chapter, the rate of hoarding is intinately linked to a country's balance of payments, and the country can only build up its money balances by running a balance-of-payments surplus. This can be demonstrated by writing the budget constraint for country I in the following way:

$$P_1(S_{1N} - C_{1N}) + (S_{1T} - C_{1T}) = H_1 \qquad (26.20)$$

Equation (26.20) shows that when the market for non-traded goods clears, i.e. $S_{1N} = C_{1N}$, then the excess of traded goods equals the amount of hoarding which takes place in the economy.

It is useful for further exposition to study the interrelationship between hoarding and relative prices. An increase in real hoarding lowers the relative price of non-traded goods. The interconnection between hoarding and relative prices is illustrated in Figure 26.9. The schedule E_{1N} is the market-clearing schedule for the non-traded goods sector. It shows the locus of all the points where the market for non-traded goods is in equilibrium, i.e. where $E_{1N} = 0$. It is downward-slop-

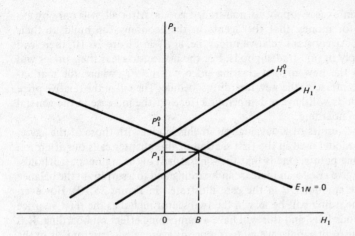

FIGURE 26.10

Devaluation and relative prices

ing. It depends on the fact that an increase in hoarding lowers the demand for goods, *and also* that for non-traded goods. For the market for non-traded goods to clear when hoarding increases, their relative price has to fall, hence the slope of the curve. An increase in hoarding and the fall in over-all demand for goods which accompanies it will force the relative price of non-traded goods to fall and induce people to substitute non-traded goods for traded goods. This will free traded goods for export purposes and traded goods will be exported for cash to be used in order to build up money balances. At point P_1^0 hoarding is zero. At this relative price both markets clear and the balance of payments is in equilibrium. At a lower relative price hoarding will take place and the balance of payments will show a surplus. At a higher relative price dishoarding will occur and the balance of payments will show a deficit. Overspending will take place and will be financed by money balances flowing abroad.

Let us then see how hoarding is related to relative price changes. With a constant nominal quantity of money, hoarding will increase as the relative price of non-traded goods increases. To gain further insight into this relationship, let us assume that the price of traded goods is given. An increase in the price of non-traded goods will then imply an increase in the price level and in the national income in nominal terms. As the income increases, so will the demand for money balances. Hence the hoarding schedule will be upward-sloping, as depicted in Figure 26.10

It is now time to study the effects of a devaluation. We started with the original hoarding schedule H_1^0, which intersects the equilibrium markets schedule for non-traded goods at the price P_1^0. At this price both markets clear, and hoarding is zero. Then country I devalues. The devaluation will lead to an increase in the price of traded goods. In the usual way the price level in the devaluing country will go up. The demand for money balances will increase as the real value of cash balances falls. This means that at *constant relative prices* the demand for cash balances will grow, and hence the hoarding schedule will shift to the right as illustrated by the schedule H_1' in Figure 26.10.

The shift in the hoarding schedule and the accompanying increase in hoard-

ing will lead to an excess supply of non-traded goods. After all, it is only by exchanging goods for money that the agents in the economy can build up their
money balances. At constant relative prices, i.e. at P_1^0 in Figure 26.10, there will
be an excess supply of non-traded goods. For the market to clear their prices will
have to fall and the new market-clearing price will be P_1', where the market-
clearing schedule intersects the new hoarding schedule. The fall in the relative price
of non-traded goods will have a dampening effect on the increase in the general
price level and on hoarding.

Comparing the results of a devaluation in this model with those of the aggregated one-sector model used in the first section of this chapter calls our attention
to some interesting points. One is that the general drift of the argument still holds.
Devaluation will give rise to an increase in hoarding and to a surplus in the balance
of payments (the amount OB in the case illustrated in Figure 26.10). However,
the increase in hoarding will be less in the two-sector model as the relative price
of non-traded goods falls, and this will have a dampening effect on hoarding. It is
important to realize that once we go to a more disaggregated structure, as in the
model with non-traded goods, substitution on the demand and supply side starts
to play a role again. Thus the standard results from the traditional elasticity approach again become relevant. The effects of relative price changes between sectors
will depend on substitution possibilities both on the demand and on the supply
sides.

A devaluation will create a surplus in the balance of payments through an excess supply of traded goods. How large this improvement will be, and how fast
it will take place, depend on how easily resources can be reallocated from the
non-traded to the traded sector. Hence the success of a devaluation will depend
on a combination of real and monetary factors.

SUMMARY AND CONCLUSIONS

One of the essential points of the monetary approach is that a devaluation will
effect the demand for money. A devaluation will cause an inflationary impact in
the devaluing country by raising prices of traded goods denoted in domestic currency. Hence the domestic price level will increase. This will give rise to a real
balance effect as households and firms start to increase their money balances in
nominal terms. They can only do this by exchanging goods for money. This will
lead to an excess supply of goods and a surplus in the balance of payments.

This surplus will, however, be of a transitory nature. Once cash balances have
been restored to an optimal size, the surplus in the balance of payments will
evaporate. When money supplies have been redistributed between countries a
new equilibrium will be reached. In the long run markets will clear, cash balances
will be in equilibrium, and the balance of payments will be in equilibrium. The
only lasting effect of the devaluation will be a change in the nominal price level.
Changes in supply and demand for assets can also have important repercussions
on the exchange rate. If foreign investors expect a country's exchange rate to depreciate, this change in expectations can be self-fulfilling and cause a depreciation
of the currency. Such changes in the exchange rates will then in turn affect real
variables, such as absorption, in the country. Shocks to a country's exchange

rate will often lead to 'overshooting', so that the impact changes on exchange rates will be larger than the long-run effects. This can lead to overly large fluctuations in exchange rates and to unwanted repercussions on domestic economies. Hence governments need to introduce exchange controls or work with dual exchange rates in order to try to shield current-account transactions from disturbances occurring in asset markets. Asset considerations will probably have to be taken into account when explaining the short-run fluctuations in exchange rates which have occurred since 1971.

In the framework of two-sector or more disaggregated models the importance of real factors stands out. It is still true that basic monetary factors affect exchange rates in much the same way as in simpler theoretical structures, but substitution effects on the supply and demand sides of the economy will determine how large a role monetary factors will play.

SELECTED BIBLIOGRAPHY: CHAPTER 26

The literature on the monetary approach to the balance of payments has grown very rapidly in recent years. An authoritative collection of papers is contained in:

J. A. Frenkel and H. G. Johnson (eds), *The monetary Approach to the Balance of payments*, London, University of Toronto Press, 1976.

The reader will observe my indebtedness to the excellent writings of R. Dornbusch contained in his papers published in recent years, among which should be mentioned:

'Devaluation, Money and Non-traded Goods', *AER*, December 1973.

'Currency Depreciation, Hoarding and Relative Prices', *JPE*, July–August 1973.

'Exchange Rates and Fiscal Policy in a Popular Model of International Trade', *AER*, December 1975.

A useful servey article is:

Marina V. N. Whitman, 'Global Monetarism and the Monetary Approach to the Balance of Payments', *Brookings Papers on Economic Activity*, no. 3, 1975.

A valuable collection of papers is contained in no. 2, 1976, of the *Scandinavian Journal of Economics* which is devoted to 'Flexible Exchange Rates and Stabilization Policy'. Here especially contributions by R. N. Cooper, M. Mussa, R. Dornbusch and P. J. K. Kouri should be mentioned. Kouri's analysis of asset markets has greatly influenced the exposition in the chapter.

Valuable background reading is contained in R. A. Mundell's book:

Monetary Theory: Inflation, Interest and Growth in the World Economy, Pacific Palisades, Calif., Goodyear, 1971.

27
Fixed versus flexible exchange rates

In the preceding chapters we have discussed various aspects of fixed and flexible exchange rates. Chapter 22 described the market for foreign exchange under a system of flexible exchange rates, the functioning of forward markets for foreign exchange and the main factors that determine the interrelationships between spot and forward rates. Under a regime of flexible exchange rates, working ideally, markets would be cleared and the balance of payments automatically adjusted. Such a system therefore seemed to provide an elegant solution to the problem of external disequilibrium. A system of flexible exchange rates, however, might give rise to some problems. Chapters 22 and 26 have shown that a depreciation of the exchange rate will increase the price level. One drawback of flexible exchange rates is that they could make an economy prone to inflation and possibly introduce a degree of instability. For the greater part of modern history the major trading countries have had their exchange rates pegged. Floating rates have, however, become common since 1973. It is now opportune to compare the two kinds of systems, to try to evaluate gains and losses connected with either one of them. The relative merits and drawbacks of the two systems have long been a topic for discussion in international economics. This discussion has had a tendency, however, to become rather unfruitful. The debaters have often talked past each other, each being concerned with a limited set of arguments that, despite being of relevance for the problem, presents only part of the picture. The proponents of fixed exchange rates usually assert that flexible rates will be detrimental to the volume of international trade and investment. The proponents of flexible rates usually argue that such a system would make it easier for a country to reach its domestic economic aims and would remove the constraints that could result from concern about external balance.

We will take up some of the main issues. First, the case for flexible exchange rates will be briefly stated. Then some arguments for fixed exchange rates will be given. It is, however, hardly possible to arrive at a straightforward solution to the problem. At a closer look, the question of fixed versus flexible exchange rates consists of several subsets of problems. We will deal with some if those under the headings of *uncertainty, speculation,* and *inflation.* The case against flexible exchange rates has been strengthened by the recently developed theories of optimum currency areas. These theories will be discussed at the end of the chapter.

THE CASE FOR FLEXIBLE EXCHANGE RATES

The fundamental case for flexible exchange rates is built upon the law of supply and demand. According to this law, the price should regulate the quantities supplied and demanded so that the market clears and equilibrium is reached. If the price would rise temporarily over its normal level, supply would increase and demand would decrease, and the price would be driven back by competitive forces to its equilibrium level. Likewise, if the price would fall, supply would also fall, the demand would increase and the price would be driven up to its normal level.

Efforts at government price-fixing will unfailingly create difficulties. If the government sets the price at its equilibrium level, intervention has no effect. Otherwise, the authorities set the price too high or too low. In the first case, supply will exceed demand, and the government, or somebody else, will have to absorb the surplus production. In the second case, the price is set too low, and demand will be larger than supply, forcing the authorities either to meet the excess demand out of their own stocks or to try to restrict demand.

The difficulty with price-fixing is that it will soon create problems in all cases except the one in which the price happens to be fixed at its equilibrium level. That the authorities would happen to pick this one price out of the infinite set of prices is hardly likely. Since the probability of picking a price that is not the equilibrium price is large, the prospects are that price-fixing will cause problems.

If the price is set too high, production will be too large. If the government finds it impossible to lower the price (for instance, because of commitments to producers), it will have to try to restrict production. This can be done by setting production quotas, applying taxes on production, or undertaking some other restrictive measures. Consumption might also be encouraged by distributing surpluses without regard to price, by propaganda, etc.

If the price is fixed too low, shortages will occur and price controls will have to be applied. In a situation of permanent shortage, price controls will hardly be effective in the long run. Rationing might be used, but black markets and various forms of economic disorder will probably emerge. The government might try to use other long-run measures to stimulate production like investments incentives and subsidies for encouraging technical progress. However, such means of over-coming the side-effects of price-fixing are cumbersome, and their effectiveness is open to question. The advocates of flexible exchange rates maintain that exactly these types of problems will occur if the exchange rate is fixed. There is no reason to believe that the government would find the equilibrium price for foreign exchange in terms of the national currency if it tries to fix the exchange rate. Anyway, as soon as the underlying economic conditions change, the exchange rate should also change. As soon as the fixed exchange rate deviates from the equilibrium price of foreign exchange, problems will arise. If the price of foreign currency is set too low, the balance of payments will show a deficit. This means that the currency is overvalued. Imports will then be encouraged, while exports will be placed at a disadvantage. The country will run down its stock of foreign exchange. Sooner or later it will be forced to take some policy action: it will have to deflate the economy to decrease imports, or it will have to apply various restrictions on imports, or it will have to devalue its currency.

If, on the other hand, the price of foreign currency is too high, in other words if the national currency is undervalued, a surplus in the balance of payments will develop. There might be special reasons why a country would want its currency to be undervalued; one might be that the country has nationalistic leanings and wants its currency to be 'strong'. But if the country takes a straightforward economic view of its exchange rate, the bargain price that foreigners will pay for its currency will create problems. The country will have to accumulate foreign reserves. This will expand the country's money supply and stimulate inflation. In order to check the surplus the country can choose between various policies. It might restrict exports or encourage imports. It might foster capital exports or engage in development assistance on a scale that its citizens find undesirable. It might also apply various kinds of controls to check exports and promote imports or try to neutralize the impacts on its money supply. Finally, it might have to appreciate its currency.

According to the advocates of flexible exchange rates, all the troubles that an undervalued or overvalued currency causes could be avoided if the authorities could see the light and begin to float the currency. A flexible exchange rate would not necessarily lead to large fluctuations. It would be stable as long as the underlying economic conditions were not changing. Only if these changed would the price of foreign currency also change. Furthermore, random fluctuations around the 'normal' value would be smoothed out by private speculators. If the currency appreciated above its equilibrium value, if its price fell in terms of foreign currency, speculators would buy the currency; and if it depreciated, speculators would sell the currency. Thereby they would smooth out fluctuations and help to keep the exchange rate stable. If the underlying conditions changed, however, the price of foreign exchange would also change. The same factors which under fixed rates give rise to deficits and surpluses in the balance of payments would under floating rates make the exchange rate depreciate or appreciate. Thereby equilibrium would be preserved and the government could be freed from considerations regarding the external balance.

Central to the arguments for flexible rates is the opinion that government intervention in the economy should be restricted. The controls and the restrictions that often accompany fixed exchange rates are objectionable to those who favor maximum individual freedom. Attempts at fixing or manipulating exchange rates are, according to this view, especially objectionable because the control of exchange rates is often entrusted to experts who are effectively out of reach of any democratic control. The exchange rate is often pegged out of consideration for other economic goals, like preserving a certain market structure or influencing the income distribution. However, such goals can be reached more effectively by the use of more direct means than exchange-rate policy.

The great virtue of flexible exchange rates, according to its proponents, is that such a system will free the government from considerations about the balance of payments. Instead, the government can concentrate its activities on domestic economic policy. Under fixed rates, countries which are averse to inflation will be pitched against countries who view inflation with equanimity. With flexible rates, each country can choose whatever mixture of unemployment and inflation it prefers. Flexible exchange rates should therefore give an increased freedom both to individuals and to countries to pursue whatever aims they have for their economic policies.

We have now stated, albeit in somewhat crude terms, the basic case for flexible exchange rates. We will next look at some important points made by those who favor fixed exchange rates.

THE CASE FOR FIXED EXCHANGE RATES

The case for fixed exchange rates is often stated in rather practical terms. It is seldom presented with the same kind of analytic fervor which characterizes the arguments for flexible exchange rates. It is built upon an analogy with the case for a common national currency. Naturally, a nation derives great advantages from having a common currency; likewise, the world would benefit if it had a single currency. An approximation of this state is a world economy on fixed exchange rates. Within a country, a single currency makes it easier for producers and consumers to survey the market and interpret market signals. It facilitates computations and trade. It promotes economic integration. Markets are less fragmented, producers from all parts of the country are able to compete more effectively, and uncertainty in transactions is reduced. Hence the arguments for fixed exchange rates are part of a more general case for policies aiming at international economic integration.

Those who oppose fixed rates would point out here that this analogy has only a superficial validity. Economic integration is also promoted at the national level by the free movement of factors of production within national boundaries. A worker in Kentucky can move to California and vice versa. This is not the case at the international level. Here the barriers between nations are important. Labor certainly cannot move without restrictions from one country to another. Neither can capital, since various types of restrictions impede movements of goods and services. The presence of such barriers implies that even if fixed rates were to prevail they would not establish the conditions of equality and fair competition that are created by a common currency and unconstrained movements of production factors on the national level.

Furthermore, unequal conditions within a country can prevail for many years even in the presence of a common currency. Many countries have regions that are characterized by states of prolonged distress, while other regions are prosperous. In fact, the adherents of flexible exchange rates would argue that a common currency does not alleviate but rather aggravates such conditions. To get deeper insights into these problems we would have to deal with the theory of the optimum currency area. Here it will suffice simply to state some of the basic pros and cons of fixed exchange rates. We will return to the arguments about optimum currency areas toward the end of this chapter.

Another argument for fixed exchange rates is the so-called 'anchor' argument. Democratically elected governments are greatly tempted to overstimulate their economies. In the short run expansionary economic policies may lower unemployment and create boom conditions – at the expense of a stable price level. Inflation might create a temporary euphoria but it will have harmful effects in the long run. It will lead to arbitrary effects on the distribution of income and wealth and impair a society's morals.

Fixed exchange rates can serve as an anchor. Inflation will cause balance-of-payments deficits and reserve losses. Hence the authorities will have to take counter measures to stop inflation. Fixed exchange rates should therefore impose a 'discipline' on governments and stop them from pursuing inflationary policies which are out of tune with the rest of the world.

The adherents of flexible rates do not agree. They maintain that discipline can be replaced by other, less virtuous means. A government can apply trade restrictions and impose various forms of controls to check the deficits in the balance of payments while the. 'irresponsible' policies continue. Otherwise, the country could avoid restrictive measures by devaluation, but that would strengthen the inflationary forces in the economy.

The interconnection between exchange-rate regime and inflation is a rather subtle one. Therefore, we will briefly return to this question later. At this stage we will have to be content with having given a short presentation of the cases for flexible and fixed exchange rates. It is now time to deal with some of the important analytical issues connected with fixed and flexible exchange rates.

FLEXIBLE EXCHANGE RATES AND UNCERTAINTY

It is often argued that flexible exchange rates would create uncertainty and instability and that this would hamper foreign trade and investment. This would then be a factor to be counted against a system of flexible rates. At the same time, it is also often argued that movements in exchange rates under a system of flexible rates would only reflect changes in underlying economic factors and would therefore give exporters and importers correct signals to guide their behavior. Uncertainty and risk in connection with flexible exchange rates, however, is a very complex problem. That economists arrive at varying results seems to be because they deal only with limited aspects of this complex problem.

To elucidate the problems involved here, we could profitably start with two extreme examples. The first shows how flexible exchange rates decrease instead of aggravate the risks connected with foreign trade.

Assume a country where all prices move together. Further assume that the general price level increases faster than it does abroad. This would, at fixed exchange rates, cause a deficit in the trade balance. The country, however, is under a system of flexible exchange rates, and the exchange rate moves in complete harmony with the price level. If the price level increases by 50 per cent, the exchange rate depreciates correspondingly, which is, by assumption, enough to offset any disequilibria that could arise, and hence the balance of trade is kept in equilibrium.

What must be observed here is that money prices keep changing, but real magnitudes remain unchanged. An Anerican exporter, for example, during one period exports goods to Britain for £100. If the exchange rate is $2 to £1, he will receive $200. Suppose that in the next period the American price level increases by 50 per cent. He still exports the same amount as before, contracted in pounds sterling, and receives £100. His costs have increased by 50 per cent, but the dollar has devalued *pari passu* and he now receives $300 for £100. Hence he is as well off as before and the change in price level and exchange rate will have no effect on the real variables in the economy.

A complication could arise here if there is a discrepancy between delivery of goods and receipt of payments and if the capital market uses contracts reckoned in monetary terms. The solution to this problem would be to have a capital market where contracts are governed by an index clause (stable purchasing-power bonds), so that loans would have to be repaid in constant real amounts. Then a combination of flexible exchange rates and index loans would be the perfect solution to the problem of risk, as it would leave everyone in the same real position despite changes in the general price level. Granted the assumptions, this would, in short, solve the problem of inflation.

The assumptions of the above example, however, are quite restrictive. There is no reason to expect, in a dynamic world where economic growth occurs, that there is a direct relationship between changes in price levels and external disequilibria. Hence there is no reason to expect a direct and close relationship between changes in price levels and exchange rates. Furthermore, all prices in an economy do not move in the same way as the general price level. An institutional fact that we cannot disregard is that contracts in capital markets run in current prices; no major capital markets have so far developed index loans. Flexible exchange rates could conceivably reduce risks connected with foreign trade.

We shall now discuss the case where flexible exchange rates increase rather than reduce the risks of foreign trade. Assume a country where the general price level is stable. The country is under a regime of flexible exchange rates. To begin with, the balance of trade is in equilibrium, but after a time the demand for the country's imports decreases (for instance, because of a change in tastes abroad). This leads to depreciation of the country's currency. The general price level is stable, but importers find that import prices have risen. This leads to a fall in imports and marginal importers will be unable to compete and will become bankrupt. At the same time, exporters will gain because of increased prices but will lose on a decrease in the volume of exports. What the net outcome will be depends on price elasticities, supply functions, and so on. Here we can see that a system of flexible exchange rates introduces an extra risk into the system compared with a regime of fixed exchange rates. The country's importers will be hurt by a change in the exchange rates to which they, through no fault of their own, have fallen victim. With fixed exchange rates, import prices would have been stable and the import volume would not have changed. Under flexible exchanges, import and export prices will show greater variation. An increased risk will be connected with foreign trade, and resources will be reallocated to a greater degree than under fixed exchange rates. Marginally profitable exports and imports will be outcompeted and the volume of foreign trade will be smaller than it would be under a system of fixed exchange rates.

Figure 27.1 should help to illustrate this argument. The α curve shows how the exchange rate will fluctuate under a system of flexible exchange rates; the β line shows the exchange rate under a system of fixed exchange rates. At the beginning, at time t_0, the exchange rate will be the same regardless of systems. At time t_1 the currency will have depreciated under a system of flexible rates, as the rate is not at point A, compared with point A' under a system of fixed rates. Under flexible rates, imports will therefore be discouraged, whereas exports (under normal market conditions) will be encouraged. At time t_2, however, the exchange rate will have appreciated under a system of flexible exchange rates, as it will be at B, whereas it would have been at B' had the country been on a system of fixed rates. At B, exporters will be worse off than they would have

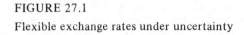

FIGURE 27.1

Flexible exchange rates under uncertainty

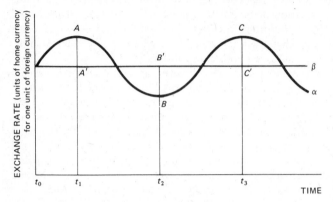

been had the exchange rate stayed at B'. Analogously, importers will be better off at B than at B'. The result of this is that the fluctuation of the exchange rate around a trend value as depicted in Figure 27.1 will cause an increased risk for exporters and importers that will have a dampening effect on foreign trade. Assume that this risk can be represented as a measurable cost.[1] How large this cost could be is difficult to say. In principle, exporters and importers should be able to cover themselves against this risk by hedging, i.e. by buying and selling foreign exchange in a forward market as described in Chapter 22. This risk could then be approximated by the cost of hedging.

Hedging is an important activity in international money markets. But it is not possible to ensure against all risks associated with a system of flexible exchange rates; many economic activities have a longevity that makes hedging difficult. It should be noted that what is involved is not only the risk associated with one single export or import transaction but with export and import activities as a whole. In many instances increasing transaction costs would prohibit constant hedging. A system of flexible exchange rates might therefore considerably dampen the volume of foreign trade.

From this point of view it might therefore be argued that a system of fixed exchange rates implies a subsidy to foreign trade, as it means that society as a whole carries part of the risk connected with foreign trade.[2] If the flexible exchange rate fluctuates in a fairly regular way around a trend value as in Figure 27.1, this subsidy goes to exporters and importers alike. We can observe, however, that if there is an upward or downward trend in the flexible exchange rate, then a system of fixed exchange rates could imply a subsidy to imports and a tax on exports, or vice versa. This is illustrated in Figure 27.2.

The α line shows an exchange rate with a depreciation trend in it. If the exchange rate were kept at the β level, this would imply a subsidy to imports and a tax on exports compared with what would be the case if the exchange rate were permitted to float. The γ line, conversely, shows a flexible exchange rate with an appreciation trend in it. In this case, the fixed rate at the β level would imply a tax on imports and a subsidy to exports.

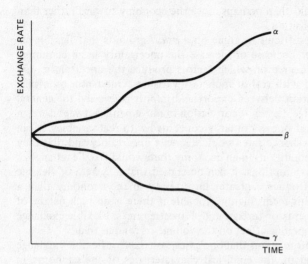

FIGURE 27.2

Flexible exchange rates
with appreciation
and depreciation trends

From quite reasonable assumptions, it can therefore be argued that a pegging of the exchange rate means that a country will get a larger volume of trade than it otherwise would, as a system of fixed exchange rates implies a subsidy to foreign trade. We can then ask, – why should a country subsidize its foreign trade?

This question can be viewed from at least two angles. First, we have the macro-economic or stabilization point of view, from which it could be argued that one of the chief aims of modern economic policy is to stabilize variables such as national income, and the price level of exports and imports. If pegging the exchange rate could facilitate attaining this aim, it could be worth while even though it would be bought at the price of subsidizing foreign trade. For the time being, we will just state the argument; a proper discussion of it belongs to a later part of this chapter, where the macroeconomic costs of pegging the exchange rate will be discussed.

The second angle from which this subsidy can be viewed might be termed the 'microeconomic', or 'resource allocation', point of view. A subsidy to one sector of the economy means that resources will be drawn to that sector. Under a properly functioning price system and with properly functioning markets, there is no reason to engage in such a subsidy, which would merely lead to a misallocation of resources and a lowering of economic welfare.

If, however, imperfections or externalities are involved, the question has a different perspective. It could be, for instance, that foreign trade gives rise to external economies because a wide range of imports give rise to a wider range of choice for consumers. Life could become more varied and pleasant if the consumer had a wide range of goods from which to choose. The very presence of a large assortment of imported goods could increase the level of satisfaction. It could also be argued that a subsidy to foreign trade keeps a pressure on the domestic industry and increases the efficiency of the economy. In a wider calculus, we know that other factors, such as tariffs and taxes, also influence the volume of trade, often in a protectionist direction. An offsetting subsidy in the form of a pegged exchange rate could then perhaps move the economy toward rather than away from an optimum position.

Summing up, it seems difficult to argue on a *priori* grounds that flexible exchange rates would either decrease or increase the uncertainty in an economy. This depends to a large degree on which factors produce the uncertainty, and whether one is concerned with real or monetary variables. One factor of critical importance is the correlation between export and import prices and the general price level. If there is a large degree of correlation in movements between foreign and domestic prices, and if one is primarily concerned with real variables, it can be argued that flexible exchange rates would decrease uncertainty and that they would better reflect real conditions in an economy than would fixed exchanges.

With another set of assumptions, it can be argued that a system of flexible exchange rates would introduce a greater uncertainty in the economy than a system of fixed rates. This seems highly probable if there is no high degree of correlation in the movements of foreign and domestic prices. Flexible exchange rates will then have a dampening effect on the volume of foreign trade.

In this respect, it therefore seems that one's views on fixed or flexible exchange rates must largely depend on the empirical characteristics of the economy in question.

Another question often discussed in connection with stability of the exchange rates is the effect of speculation on flexible exchange rates. We now turn to this problem.

SPECULATION AND THE STABILITY OF THE EXCHANGE RATE

Under a system of flexible exchange rates, many factors influence movements in exchange rates. The most important are connected with supply and demand of exports and imports. But speculation also plays a role. We learned in Chapter 22 that speculation influenced the movements of spot and forward exchange rates and made them move together. Speculation will also affect the supply and demand of foreign exchange. An important question is whether speculation is stabilizing or destabilizing, i.e. whether it tends to smooth out fluctuations in the exchange rate caused by trade or to make them larger than they otherwise would be.

It is often said that speculators see a decline in the exchange rate as a signal for further decline, and that their actions will cause the movement in the exchange rate to be larger than it would be in the absence of speculation. In such a case, speculation is destabilizing. It could be that political motives are also involved, causing capital to leave a country because of political instability or because the ruling class feels threatened by political reform. This has happened in some European countries: France during the popular front government led by Léon Blum in the late 1930s is an example, and the left-center coalition government of Papandreou in Greece in 1964–5 comes close to being another example. Under such circumstances, speculation can easily be destabilizing.

The question of the role speculation plays in the stability of exchange rates is perhaps the most-discussed aspect of the subject. Part of the empirical material that exists to illustrate the question now lies quite far back in time. It originates from the 1920s when several countries allowed their exchange rates to fluctuate. The most interesting example is probably France during the period 1919–26.

The standard work for a discussion of the experiences of the interwar period in this sphere is Ragnar Nurkse's *International Currency Experience,* an investigation carried out for the League of Nations and published in 1944. Nurkse's own attitude is clear. His opinion is that the experiences of the free exchange rates of the 1920s were bad, mainly because speculation was predominantly destabilizing.

Later, Nurkse's interpretation of the development was criticized. Milton Friedman, for example, says without advancing any precise reasons that one can just as well interpret the material so that speculation appears as stabilizing.[3] The most interesting interpretation of the material is that by S. C. Tsiang in an article published in 1959 in the I.M.F.'s *Staff Papers.*[4] He constructs an index of what he calls 'purchasing power' and compares it with the development of the exchange rate. He then finds that the exchange rate fluctuated considerably more than was justified by real factors as measured by the purchasing-power index. He does not wish to explain it solely by speculation, but also advances other explanations such as the easy French monetary policy, the modification in the American monetary policy which forced American exporters to take home their export credits, political anxiety, etc.

Since 1973 many of the leading currencies have been floating against one another, either independently or in groups. The fluctuations of exchange rates have also been quite substantial since 1973. The German mark increased by some 30 per cent compared with the dollar within a few months in the spring of 1973; then it fell by some 20 per cent toward the end of the year. In short, many examples can be found of exchange rates fluctuating up and down by 20 per cent or more within a few months. Extreme short-run fluctuations have also occurred. Speculation seems to have played a role for these exchange-rate changes. Naturally, it is difficult to disentangle the speculative motive from other factors influencing exchange rates. The incidents of speculation in the 1970s do not seem to be radically different from those of the 1920s. Again, it seems that speculation has been destabilizing. A case in point is the bahavior of the German mark in 1973. Germany tried to combat inflation by restrictive monetary policies in the spring of 1973. This caused the German mark to appreciate. If speculation had been stabilizing, private funds should have been transferred to other currencies, with the expectation that the German mark would depreciate after a while, and speculation thereby would have helped to smooth out the fluctuations of the mark. Instead, the opposite seems to have occurred. The upward movement of the mark resulted in further inflows of private capital. Speculation was destabilizing and large fluctuations in exchange rates took place which could not be ascribed to underlying economic forces. (For a further discussion of the experiences of speculation in recent years, see Chapter 30.

Normally one would expect speculation to have a stabilizing influence on exchange rates. It should be noted that if speculation is destabilizing, it implies that the speculators lose money on their activity.[5] This, however, is not too strong an argument in favor of the stabilizing effect of speculation, as the speculators can consist of two groups: one professional, which usually makes a profit; and one a changing body of amateur speculators who make losses.[6]

We should further note that the argument for speculation being stabilizing does not refer to the time period over which profitable speculation is stabilizing. If, for instance, speculation were stabilizing in the long run but destabilizing in the short run, it might be too costly an adjustment mechanism for a government to rely upon.

The question of the effects of speculation on exchange rates is very open. It is perhaps best, therefore, merely to outline the problem and to leave the drawing of inferences to the reader.

FLEXIBLE EXCHANGE RATES AND INFLATION

It is often argued by those who favor fixed exchange rates that flexible exchange rates will have an inflationary impact on an economy, because a depreciation of the exchange rate will cause a rise in the domestic price level. To elucidate this question, we shall begin the discussion with an example.

Depreciation of a currency means that import goods become more expensive, and the increase in import prices leads to an increase in the general price level. That is the argument. Assume that a country's imports amount to 20 per cent of its national income and that its currency depreciates by 15 per cent. This will lead to an increase in import prices of, say, 15 per cent. If this increase is carried through completely, and no secondary effects occur, a general price index in the country will increase by 3 per cent (20 per cent times 15 per cent). Here a depreciation produces an inflationary effect, i.e. causes an increase in the country's internal price level.

This example is based on several critical assumptions. For instance, we assumed that import prices increased by the same percentage as the fall in the exchange rate. This does not necessarily happen. The initial increase in import prices caused by depreciation will lead to a fall in the demand for imported goods. This fall in demand could force foreign exporters to lower their prices. If this happens, the rise in import prices caused by depreciation will be partially offset.

Another important factor to take into account is that as imports become relatively more expensive, they will be substituted by import-competing goods produced at home. This will also tend to restrict the rise in the general price level.

There are, however, several factors working in the opposite direction. Several industries, working for the home market or producing export goods, use imported goods as inputs. When imports become more expensive because of the fall in the exchange rate, the price of these inputs, and the cost of production, will rise. Another factor working in the same direction is an expected increase in the activity level as a result of depreciation. Exporters will receive more in home currency for every unit of foreign currency they earn. This will enable them to lower their prices, reckoned in foreign currency, and to expand production. Producers in import-competing industries will also be in an improved situation, as outlined above. All this will give rise to an increase in the activity level in the country and produce upward pressure on the general price level.

We now recall the analysis of the preceding chapter. According to the monetary approach, the effects of a devaluation are intimately linked to its effects on the

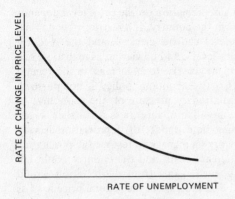

FIGURE 27.3

Relation between changes
in price level and unemployment

price level. We would expect a devaluation to inflate the price level in the de-valuing country. This, in turn, would lead to an increase in the demand for cash balances and a fall in the demand for goods. We need not restate the full analysis of Chapter 26. Suffice it to say that even according to this type of analysis, a depreciation of the exchange rate would produce an increase in the price level.

It is sometimes argued by those who defend flexible exchange rates that a system of flexible exchange rates need have no inflationary impact – that a depreciation should not cause a rise in the general price level. This argument, however, hardly stands up to close scrutiny. Part of the general price level, the prices on import goods, will necessarily rise because of the depreciation. The only way in which the general price level could be kept unchanged would then be if other prices fell. Some substitution, as we have argued, will probably take place. But there is no reason to expect this effect to be so large as to outweigh the rise in import prices. This would, after all, imply (at least for fairly open economies) a drastic fall in the prices of domestic factors of production. But the interest rate cannot be expected to fall as long as the money supply is unchanged and there is little reason to expect a fall in wages. This argument can therefore hardly be sustained.

Another form that this argument sometimes takes is that an exchange de-preciation cannot result in inflation if appropriately restrictive economic policies are pursued. In a limited sense, this argument is correct, but it disregards one critical factor: that in such a case, stable prices have to be bought at the cost of a rise of unemployment. This will necessarily be the case if we assume that there is an inverse relationship between the general price level and the rate of unem-ployment. Such a relationship is set out in Figure 27.3. The curve in the figure is derived from the so-called *Phillips curve,* which shows the relationship between the rate of change of money wages and the rate of unemployment.[7]

Empirical findings from different countries tell us that we would expect to find a relationship of this kind.[8] It is true that some proponents of the monetarist school do not believe in the existence of a long-run Phillips curve.[9] However, in the short run, and that it the relevant time period here, most economists would agree that there is a trade-off between the price level and the unemployment rate.

In general it is true that the effect of a depreciation on the price level depends on the general economic policy pursued in the country. If a restrictive economic policy is pursued, a rise in the price level can be checked, and the recently mentioned figure for the increase in price level could be viewed as realistic, i.e. a fall in the exchange rate of 15 per cent might give rise to an increase in the general price level of only 3 per cent. If a restrictive economic policy is not pursued, depreciation could give rise to strong inflationary pressure on the economy. As the general price level increases, workers will probably press for higher wages. This is very understandable, as the immediate impact of depreciation is very likely to be a fall in real wages. If the workers manage to restore the purchasing power of their wages, this will again increase costs, and the country could fall into a wage – price spiral. If this happened, gains from depreciation would rapidly be destroyed, and there would be an increase in the general price level as large as the depreciation of the currency. A criterion for the success of depreciation is, as we know from Chapter 25, for it to lead to a fall in over-all demand (a fall in total absorption).

It is sometimes asserted that depreciation cannot lead to an increase in the general price level, because it gives rise to an improved allocation of economic resources. Before depreciation (or before the system of flexible exchange rates was introduced), quotas, import licensing, and other trade restrictions were employed in the economy to limit deficits in the balance of payments caused by the overvalued currency. In connection with depreciation, trade restrictions are dismantled, leading to improved allocation of resources and an increase in production. If this increase in production is large enough, depreciation can lead to an excess supply of goods at existing prices, although total absorption has not fallen, and the general price level will fall.

This type of argument, however, is built by stacking the cards in a very definite direction. A situation such as the one described could occur, but if we want to discuss the effects of flexible exchange rates, the logical thing to do is to compare a system of flexible exchange rates with another system (for instance, fixed exchange rates), assuming everything else to be equal. What we must do, in other words, is focus attention on what is relevant and not introduce factors that have no logical connection with a change in the exchange rates. That depreciation gives rise to a drastic change in the over-all efficiency of resource allocation is tantamount to introducing a specific argument into the discussion. (A change in relative prices caused by depreciation will, of course, always produce a change in the production pattern, but this is a different matter.)

A system of flexible exchanges will, under most circumstances, cause changes in the internal price level. If a country has difficulty in coping with inflation, or is averse to it, this could be a strong reason, also, to be averse to a system of flexible exchange rates, because depreciation can normally be expected to cause a rise in the general price level.

It must be stressed, however, that the way one views inflation is primarily a question of value judgments. A higher degree of inflation will probably follow from flexible exchange rates, but at the same time flexible exchanges make policy-makers less constrained by balance-of-payments considerations: it makes it easier to maintain a policy of full employment. How one views this question will therefore ultimately depend on how one values the unfavorable effects of inflation (undesirable redistribution effects and the like) compared with the benefits of a lower rate of unemployment.

Before concluding this section, we should touch on two more subtle effects in connection with inflation that flexible exchange rates might have. If we assume that flexible exchange rates produce greater movements in the exchange rate, this might produce an undesirable 'ratchet effect'.[10] A depreciation in the exchange rate will cause an increase in domestic wages and prices. But an appreciation will not cause a comparable fall in domestic prices and wages, because prices and wages are rigid downward. Hence an asymmetry will occur that produces an upward trend in the price level. Furthermore, if flexible exchange rates produce greater fluctuations in the exchange rate, this could result in overfrequent attempts at reallocation of resources. If there is a cost connected with reallocating resources, flexible exchange rates would perhaps produce a result in this respect that is worse than would be the case under fixed exchange rates.[11]

OPTIMUM CURRENCY AREAS

We can ponder the following question: if the case for flexible exchange rates is really strong, would it not then be appropriate to split up the world into smaller parts and give each region within a country its own currency, and thereby the possibility of pursuing its own stabilization policies?

This question is sometimes raised seriously. It is argued that depressed regions should be allowed to have their own currencies. Bretagne should have its own franc, Southern Italy its own lira, West Virginia its own dollar, etc. They should then pursue their own exchange-rate policies to help achieve their economic aims. At the same time, it is felt that such a division of countries would be absurd. The reasons behind this opposition are intimately linked to the theory of optimum currency areas which was developed during the 1960s.[12] These arguments are of considerable interest for the discussion of fixed versus flexible exchange rates.

It is intuitively felt that splitting up countries into smaller parts would not necessarily be an improvement. On the contrary, there might be strong arguments for linking countries together. We dealt with some of the reasons supporting those arguments in Chapter 20 in connection with the theory of customs unions. The theory of optimum currency areas can be regarded as a branch of the same type of theorizing in which special consideration is paid to monetary factors.

Two countries might want to form a currency area to improve resource allocation. By adopting a common currency the two countries would eliminate exchange-rate risks. Producers would regard not only their own country but the entire common currency area as their marketing territory. If increasing returns to scale are present, producers would expand productive capacities. Capital would be allocated more efficiently and labor would become a more homogeneous factor of production. Hence the creation of an optimum currency area would lead to improved resource allocation. For analogous reasons the same beneficial effects would be obtained with a system of fixed exchange rates. Another important aspect of an optimum currency area is that it would lead to a more stable price level. First, the larger an economic area is, the less disturbance would be caused by random shocks. A decline in incomes in one region would often be compensated by an increase in another region. Moreover, the impact of any single specific disturbance would decrease as the size of the area increases. Second, larger currency areas would be less dependent on external trade. Changes in the foreign exchange rate would have a comparatively minor impact since the share of tradeables would be relatively smaller. Tradeables would carry a smaller weight in the consumption baskets of the citizens and any given change in the exchange rate would be multiplied by a smaller fraction of the national income. These combined facts mean that changes in the exchange rate would have a smaller effect, the larger the optimum currency area is. Hence external price changes would have smaller effects under fixed than flexible exchange rates.

Another, more subtle point concerns the social usefulness of money. Money plays an important economic role as a medium of transactions and as a store of value. It is socially productive because it lowers transaction costs. In the absence of money we would have to switch to a barter economy in which transaction costs would be greatly increased and valuable resources would be spent on an ineffective barter process. The more stable the price level and the better the foresight regarding changes in the price level, the more useful money will become. Since the currency area would improve the stability of the economies joining it, its formation would produce the kind of positive externalities which we have referred to above, i.e. externalities associated with an increased use of money. Hence the welfare of the citizens would also increase. The elimination of speculation and forward exchange brokers would be an obvious positive result of the formation of a currency area. If each country had its own currency, international trade between two countries would have to be conducted by such agents whose activities use up real resources. Furthermore, with currency areas, citizens would no longer need to exchange foreign for domestic currency when travelling within the area, they would not need to worry about exchange risks concerning investments within the currency area, etc. All these factors would have a positive effect on the welfare of the countries joining the optimum currency area.

There are, however, also possible drawbacks from joining a currency area. The most important one is that it would reduce the possibility of pursuing independent monetary policies. Before entering the union each country could apply the remedies that best suited its own situation. After the union, the countries would have to agree on a joint monetary policy. This would usually be a compromise that would not necessarily be optimal for each region. A greater reliance on market forces within the union would take place. If a region had unemployment problems, it is hoped that private entrepreneurs would act as arbitrageurs and move factors of production to the depressed areas. Otherwise, the authorities would have to rely on selective measures, like subsidies to firms or special tax concessions, but the scope for the application of general monetary policies would diminish.

Naturally the union as a whole could establish common exchange-rate policies covering all members. In fact, such instances of natural policy-making may increase. Consider, for example, a devaluation: if successful, it entails a decrease in real income, which is a distinct political drawback. Workers may be unwilling to accept such a decrease, especially if imported goods play a large role in their consumption. Joining the currency area would lower the imported share of goods. If tradeables become less important, workers might be more prone to money illusion and accept with equanimity the fairly small diminution of real wages that a devaluation would cause.

The arguments concerning optimum currency areas are important. They point to the existence of externalities which have usually, been disregarded in the discussion of flexible versus fixed exchange rates. By forming an optimum currency area some of these externalities can be internalized. Thus allocation of resources can be improved and the stability of the partaking economies can be increased. A looser cooperation of countries in the form of fixed exchange rates would provide to a great extent the benefits accruing to an optimum currency area. Hence the arguments for optimum currency areas also strengthen the case for fixed exchange rates.

SUMMARY AND CONCLUSION

The fundamental argument for flexible exchange rates is that they would allow the citizens of a country to pursue their economic interests with a minimum of restrictions. At the same time, they would allow the authorities to work for domestic aims free from balance-of-payments considerations by giving them autonomy with respect to their use of monetary, fiscal and other policy instruments. Because flexible exchange rates would permit the price mechanism to function freely, the need for restriction of international transactions would be minimal. Hence flexible exchange rates would grant autonomy to the national government while being consistent with an efficient organization of the world economy.

The case for fixed exchange rates rests on the argument that they would stabilize trade and improve resource allocation. The advantages of fixed exchanges are much the same as those derived from having a common national currency, and a reasoned case for fixed exchange rates builds substantially on the theory of optimum currency areas. A common currency or fixed exchange rates would also improve the allocation of resources by promoting integration of the economies using fixed exchange rates. The horizon of firms would be larger and they could reap increased returns to scale and allocate capital and labor in a more efficient way. The price level would become more stable and social gains could result from an increased use of money, while the need for currency speculators and forward brokers would diminish. However, the scope for independent monetary policies would decrease.

Important factors to take into account when analysing the pros and cons of exchange-rate regimes are uncertainty, speculation and inflation. In principle, flexible exchange rates might increase or they might decrease uncertainty. For practical purposes, it seems that they would increase uncertainty for traders. This would have a dampening effect on the volume of foreign trade. A decrease in the volume of trade would have to be counted as a cost on the part of flexible rates compared with the benefit that a fixed exchange rate would entail in this respect. A pegged exchange rate could be regarded as a subsidy to those engaged in foreign trade. There can be different views as to who should carry the burden of this subsidy. It must be stressed that the question of exchange rates and uncertainty is very involved and that the implications of a certain exchange-rate regime can vary greatly for different economies.

The effects of speculation are open questions to which no cut-and-dried answers can be given. The limited experiences from the 1920s seem to show that speculation at that time was destabilizing. Since floating rates became common in 1973, fluctuations in exchange rates have been large. It seems that some of the excessive fluctuations have been caused by destabilizing speculation.

Regarding inflation, the problem is more clear cut. A system of flexible exchange rates will give an inflationary bias to an economy. A depreciation of the exchange rate will undoubtedly have a tendency to raise the price level. For most industrial countries, a 'ratchet effect' will probably be at work, which will lead to a depreciation producing its full inflationary impact on the price level, though an appreciation will not have a comparable effect in a downward direction, as prices and wages can be expected to be rigid in a downward direction. To this must also be added the fact that flexible exchange rates might lead to an increase in frictional employment because of a tendency to 'over-reallocate' resources. Flexible exchange rates, therefore, can hardly avoid having an inflationary impact on an economy. This is especially true when there is a depreciation trend in the exchange rate.

If a system of flexible exchange rates has a definite weakness with respect to inflation, it has a strength over fixed rates when it comes to maintaining a high level of employment. As we saw in Chapter 25, a system of fixed exchange rates might make it very difficult for a country to attain both full employment and equilibrium in the balance of payments. Flexible exchange rates have a distinct advantage here as they automatically involve an element of expenditure-switching which will make it easier for a country to reconcile the goals of a high level of employment with external equilibrium.

There is, as we have seen, no neat answer to the question of whether a country should go for a system of fixed or flexible exchange rates. The answer will depend on circumstances. It will depend on the characteristics of the economy, and it will change with time as the economy changes. Value judgments are also involved, and ultimately the answer could depend on values and views of a political nature.

One or two more general comments might be justified. The greater the openness of an economy and the more dependent on foreign trade it is, the larger are the risks connected with flexible exchange rates. The larger, then, will be the inflationary effect and the greater will be the losses connected with Triffin's 'ratchet effect' and the resource-allocation effect. If there is no downward or upward trend in the exchange rate, the country might do well to stay on a system of fixed exchange rates.

If there is a trend in the exchange rate, things might turn out differently. If the cost level of one country rises faster than it does in other countries, this will usually mean that the country runs into balance-of-payments difficulties and that there is a depreciation trend in the exchange rate. If this is the case, fixed exchange rates could put an intolerable pressure on the economy, as a balancing of trade will mean a continually falling rate of employment. For countries that find it difficult to keep their cost level in line with the rest of the world, the attempt to maintain a fixed exchange rate could become a very frustrating undertaking.

This last point hints at a problem of great importance. In a world of fixed exchange rates, external disequilibria will undoubtedly arise. The rate and the pattern of economic growth vary among countries. Rates of inflation vary. Some countries are more ambitious than others as far as domestic economic goals are concerned. These factors will for some countries produce persistent depreciation trends in the exchange rate. These countries will basically have to choose between maintaining a fixed exchange rate until depreciation is forced upon them or going over to a system of flexible exchange rates.

Whether a system of fixed or flexible exchange rates will prevail will depend on economic circumstances. In times of reasonably calm economic development the prospects for fixed exchange rates are good. If the world economy experiences great stress and large disturbances, fixed exchange rates will not be operational and flexible rates are likely to develop. The 1970s have been a time of stress and economic upheaval. Hence floating rates have become common. Chapters 29 and 30 will describe the development of the international monetary system since the Second World War and will analyse how the system has functioned in practice.

SELECTED BIBLIOGRAPHY: CHAPTER 27

The standard arguments in favor of flexible exchange rates are presented in:

M. Friedman, 'The Case for Flexible Rates', in *Essays in Positive Economics,* Chicago, University of Chicago Press, 1953 (reprinted in an abbreviated version in *RIE*).

Another work recommending flexible exchange rates is:

E. Sohmen, *Flexible Exchange Rates: Theory and Controversy,* 2nd ed., Chicago, University of Chicago Press, 1969.

An older work, the implications of which are going in the opposite direction, is:

R. Nurkse, *International Currency Experience: Lessons of the Interwar Period,* Geneva, United Nations, 1944.

Recent experiences are discussed in:

L. B. Yeager, *International Monetary Relations: Theory, History and Policy,* 2nd ed., New York, Harper & Row, 1976.

R. Dornbusch and P. Krugman, 'Flexible Exchange Rates in the Short Run', *Brookings Papers on Economic Activity,* no. 3, 1976.

Among numerous essays treating the subject, the following can be mentioned:

R. E. Caves, 'Flexible Exchange Rates', *AER,* May 1963.

J. E. Meade, 'The Case for Flexible Exchange Rates', *Three Banks Review,* September 1955.

E. V. Morgan, 'The Theory of Flexible Exchange Rates', *AER,* June 1955.

H. G. Johnson, 'The Case for Flexible Exchange Rates, 1969', in *Further Essays in Monetary Economics,* London, Harvard University Press, 1972.

Optimum currency areas are analysed in:

H. G. Johnson and A. K. Swoboda (eds), *The Economics of Common Currencies,* London, Harvard University Press, 1973.

28
The aims–means analysis for reaching internal and external equilibrium

In Part IV we have dealt with problems connected with the external balance of a country. We have seen in what sense the balance of payments can be in disequilibrium and in what sense it will always be in equilibrium, and we have studied the interrelationships among exports, imports, and national income. We have also dealt with the foreign exchange market and with how a country can cure a deficit in the balance of payments.

One of the most important economic questions of many countries is how to keep the external balance in equilibrium. We now know the chief means of economic policy for reaching this goal. External balance is important but it is only one of the aims of a country. Most countries have several goals besides external balance. From an economic point of view, the most important one is usually full employment or internal balance. How a country can achieve jointly external and internal balance, and some of the policy problems connected with reaching these aims, is the subject of this chapter, which concludes our discussion of the balance of payments.

AIMS AND MEANS IN ECONOMIC POLICY

It is perhaps appropriate, before coming to the discussion of concrete cases, to say something about aims and means in economic policy in general.[1]

A country can have more or less specific aims for its economic policy. In capitalist, non-planned economies, aims are usually stated in broad terms, such as 'full employment', 'stable prices', 'equilibrium in the balance of payments', and 'high growth rate'. In planned economies the list of aims can sometimes be very long and very detailed. The aims of economic policy may be stated in terms of tons and liters of commodities, for example. Here we are only concerned with the problem in so far as it bears on economic policy problems in the capitalist or mixed economies with which we are primarily dealing. Therefore, we shall limit ourselves to a few comments which bear on the problem of how to achieve jointly external and internal balance in those types of economies.

On an abstract level we could state the problem in the form of an 'exact' model, consisting of n equations with m means or parameters that determine the values of the n unknowns:[2]

$$f_i(x_1, \ldots, x_n; a_1, \ldots, a_m) = 0 \qquad (i = 1, \ldots, n) \qquad (28.1)$$

Here we have, in other words, a set of aims, symbolized by the x_is, and a set of means or parameters, symbolized by the a_is. We also have a functional relationship between aims and means, symbolized by the f_is. If we knew what these functional relationships were, and if we determined some values to the means, then we would also know what values the aims would take.

This sounds simple. The principle involved is also simple. On a somewhat less abstract level, however, both deep theoretical problems and practical constraints are involved. Let us take a quick look at several of these, so as not to be completely unaware of some of the problems that engage those involved in economic policy.

Sometimes a model may be of such a type that the aims of the model are automatically fulfilled whatever values the means or parameters take. This is a feature quite common to economic models, especially those of a somewhat older date. We can think of a general-equilibrium model of a Walrasian type, where all prices are flexible and where the exchange rate is also flexible. In such a model markets will automatically be cleared, and demand will equal supply. Hence there will always be full employment and external equilibrium, and these two goals will automatically be fulfilled as soon as the system has reached its equilibrium position. From this point of view of economic policy, such a world is the best of all possible worlds, because economic policy is unnecessary.

Another type of model is one where one of two aims is automatically fulfilled but the other is not. Here we can think of a Walrasian type of model for a closed economy, where the two aims are full employment and a constant price level. As prices are flexible, supply will always equal demand and markets be cleared. Relative prices are then determined within the system. Let us assume, however, that the absolute price level is determined by the total money supply.[3] A disturbance in the system, then, will never affect the level of employment – the system will always have full employment – but it may affect the general price level. Hence one means or one parameter is needed to control the price level. Given this parameter, it is possible to achieve the dual aim of stable prices and full employment.

Another case, somewhat resembling, although distinct from, the one just treated, consists of the following. Here neither of two aims is automatically achieved, but if one is reached, so is the other. We assume that price changes are a function of excess supply and demand of goods, that no savings or capital movements take place, and that the two aims are full employment and external equilibrium but that markets are not automatically cleared. Unemployment and disequilibria in the balance of trade are possible in this type of model, but once full employment is reached, external balance is automatically achieved. In this case only one means is necessary to achieve two aims, because full employment implies external balance.

In another type of model two means may be necessary to achieve two aims. In the usual Keynesian model, for instance, full employment does not imply external equilibrium. Here two means are necessary to achieve two aims. Fiscal policy may be used to achieve full employment, and commercial policy (exchange-rate changes) may be used to achieve external equilibrium.

This is, in fact, the general case. Only in specific circumstances can the means used be less than the number of aims. Generally, every aim requires a means. To achieve one aim, one means is required; to reach two aims, two means are required;

for three aims, three means are needed; and so on. If there are more means than aims, an arbitrary combination of the means can be used to realize the aims.

Sometimes the aims are contradictory. In a logical or mathematical sense this can be thought of a system of equations where no solution exists. Or to give a simple example, if, in a closed economy, the aims are for the national income to be $100 billion, investment $30 billion, and consumption $80 billion, then the three aims cannot jointly be achieved.

Usually the situation is less clear cut. If an economist says that the aims are contradictory, this is against a given economic background and with certain means in mind. It is sometimes asserted that the two aims of full employment and stable prices are not compatible. It is then asserted, assuming certain specific relationships between the economic variables, for instance, that prices are inflexible in a downward direction or otherwise assuming that the number of feasible means are restricted. It may also be asserted that external and internal equilibrium are not compatible. This might be done against the background assumption that a means such as devaluation cannot be used.

If an economist concludes that aims similar to those just referred to are incompatible, it is always against a background of his knowledge of, or assumption about, economic relationships and his views on the feasibility of certain means. This state of affairs has deep political implications. What is impossible in a conservative economy (for instance, to reach and maintain full employment) may be possible in a liberal one. And what is impossible in a liberal economy may be possible in a planned socialist economy.

History shows that those means which are permissible change; what is 'impossible' today may be routine tomorrow. If the conflict between aims and performance becomes acute, new means are usually introduced; in the meantime the character of the economy may also change.

Another important point concerns the relationship between aims and means. We have, throughout the book, used the approach of general equilibrium. This indicates, in terms of aims and means, that we cannot change one means or parameter without affecting all the aims; or, to use an example, if a disturbance occurs, all the aims will, except in extraordinary circumstances, be affected. To restore the aims to desired levels, all the means normally have to be used. One should also remember that if one aim moves away from the target, when applying the designated means to achieve the desired level of the aim again, other aims will also normally be affected by the change in this parameter.

Against this background it is important to choose a combination of means and aims (to 'pair them off') in an efficient manner. Let us say that the aims are full employment and a stable price level and that the means are fiscal policy and monetary policy. A change in any of the means will affect both aims. For a policy scheme to work, however, one means (for instance, fiscal policy) must take precedence with regard to one of the aims (for instance, full employment), and the other means must take precedence with respect to the other aim. When designing an optimal policy one must also take into account the secondary effects of a parameter.

In principle we can, of course, have models not of a general equilibrium character, where a change in one aim, one variable, does not affect the other aims. In this case there may also be an isolated relationship between a means

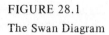

FIGURE 28.1

The Swan Diagram

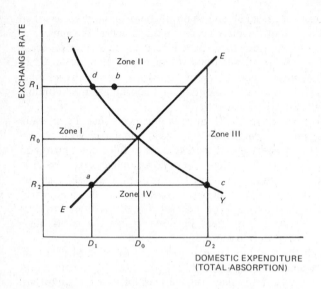

and an aim, so that one means only affects one aim without having any repercussions on other aims. In practice, it can also be the case that although a model
is of general-equilibrium character, the secondary relationships between one
parameter and the aims to which it is not directly related are so unimportant
that they can be neglected.

In a framework of general equilibrium, it is often necessary to use all means
simultaneously to fulfill the aims. An approximate procedure, using one means
at a time, may not lead to a stable solution because of secondary effects. Such a
procedure may lead to an explosion of the system.[4] This can be of great practical
importance if there is, for instance, one authority (the Ministry of Finance)
handling one parameter (fiscal policy), but another authority (the central bank)
handling another means (monetary policy).

After this introduction to means and aims in economic policy, it is time to
discuss internal and external equilibrium in detail.

EXTERNAL AND INTERNAL BALANCE: THE SWAN DIAGRAM

The time has now come to elaborate on the discussion of external and internal
balance by paying more explicit consideration to the fact that a change in exchange rates does not only affect the external balance but also has implications
for the domestic income determination. Hence we will explicitly deal with some
general-equilibrium aspects of aims–means analysis. For this purpose we will
use a diagrammatic technique originally developed by the Australian economist
Trevor Swan.[5]

The vertical axis of Figure 28.1 measures country I's exchange rate. A movement away from the origin means that country I's currency depreciates. The
horizontal axis shows domestic expenditures in real terms. Along the *EE* curve
the external balance is in equilibrium. It combines all the points where the ex-

change rate and domestic absorption match each other and preserve the external balance. The EE curve slopes upward and to the right. At low levels of domestic expenditures like D_1 the equilibrium level of the national income is also low. Hence demand for imports is low. The price of foreign currency must therefore be low, i.e. the amount of domestic currency units one gets for one unit of foreign currency (say the domestic price for 1 Special Drawing Right) must be low, like it is at R_2. This will discourage exports and we will get equilibrium with a small amount of imports and a high value of the domestic currency, such as at point a on the EE curve. If domestic absorption were higher, imports would also be larger. Hence the exchange rate would have to depreciate in order to generate the necessary amount of exports to keep the balance of payments in equilibrium. With domestic absorption at D_0, the exchange rate will have to depreciate to R_0 to keep the external equilibrium.

Points to the left of the EE curve, like b, demonstrate combinations of domestic absorption and exchange rates that give a surplus in the external balance. Points to the right of the EE curve, like point e, show combinations of expenditure patterns and exchange rates that will generate a deficit in the external balance. To sum up, zones I and II show regions of surpluses in the external balance, while zones III and VI show regions of deficits.

The curve YY represents a combination of domestic expenditure and exchange rates that give full employment with stable prices in the domestic economy (internal balance). It slopes downward and to the right. If over-all domestic demand is high, like it is at D_2, export demand from abroad must be kept low. This can be done by maintaining a high price for the domestic currency, such as at the exchange rate R_2. This will discourage exports from the country and hence minimize the foreign injections into the country's income stream. In fact, at a point like c on the YY curve, there is a large external deficit; with such a large amount of domestic expenditure as that depicted by D_2 the terminal balance can only be maintained by running a large import surplus. On the other hand, at a point such as d there is a very low level of domestic absorption. There, full employment can be kept only by depreciating the exchange rate to R_1. This will generate a large export surplus, and as long as this represents a viable alternative, full employment can be maintained despite the low level of domestic expenditures.

Points to the right of the YY curve represent excess demand in the economy. They will manifest themselves in the form of inflation. Points to the left of the YY curve represent deficient aggregate demand in the economy. Hence they are associated with unemployment. Zones II and III, therefore, are zones of inflation, while zones I and IV are zones of unemployment.

The upshot of the analysis so far is that there is only one point that represents bliss: this is point P, where the YY curve intersects the EE curve. There the economy is in both external and internal equilibrium. Outside of point P the economy is in disequilibrium. The various zones are characterized by the following types of imbalances:

Zone I: external surplus, internal unemployment
Zone II: external surplus, internal inflationary pressure
Zone III: external deficit, internal inflationary pressure
Zone IV: external deficit, internal unemployment

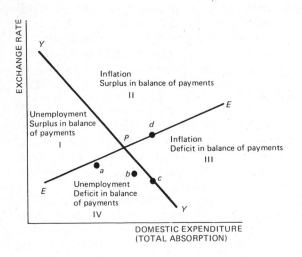

FIGURE 28.2

Disequilibrium in the
balance of payments

For simplicity's sake this analysis is again summarized in Figure 28.2. The characterization of possible economic imbalances into various zones is useful for several purposes. First, it helps to identify clearly the combination of economic ills that a country may suffer from. Second, it helps to point out the appropriate remedies for reaching a full economic equilibrium. Even though this analysis is simplified, it can still contribute significantly to an understanding of the aims–means analysis of economic policy.

Points *a* and *b* in Figure 28.2 both represent a situation with unemployment and a deficit in the balance of payments. At point *a* devaluation combined with an increase in expenditure will be the right medicine. This is a straightforward case. However, point *b* is more complicated. Here devaluation will have to be combined with a *cut* in expenditure.

To understand this it might be useful to compare it with point *c*. At *c* devaluation should be used. This will lead to external equilibrium at *d*. At the same time, it will, however, create inflation. This depends on the fact that a devaluation that takes only the external balance into account will create an export surplus that is too large; excess foreign demand in the domestic economy will produce inflationary pressure. Hence a smaller devaluation will have to be combined with a cut in domestic expenditures if the economy is to be moved to point *P*. The same thing will occur at *b*: a devaluation that leads to equilibrium in the balance of payments will trigger such a large net injection of foreign demand that it will overshoot the internal balance and create inflation. Hence the same policy mix that was needed at *c* should be used at *b*.

When we take the general-equilibrium repercussions into account, policy measures appear more complicated than they were for the model employed early in this chapter. Two situations like *a* and *b*, both initially characterized by unemployment, will need different policies of demand management if full equilibrium is to be reached. In the first case domestic expenditures have to be inflated to get rid of the unemployment, while devaluation takes care of the external balance. In the second case the repercussions of the devaluation on unemployment are so strong that the domestic absorption has to be cut if full equilibrium is to be reached.

Analogous reasoning holds for the other zones. In zone II a policy of appreciation should be followed to take care of the external balance. In most cases, such a policy will have to be combined with inflationary or deflationary measures. In zone I an inflationary policy will help move the economy toward full employment and reduce the trade surplus as well. Again, an appreciation or a depreciation will in most cases be required as a marginal corrective to move the economy to full equilibrium. It should be observed that an exchange-rate change in this zone will help to approach only one of the aims while it will necessarily move the economy away from the other aim. Thus a depreciation of the exchange rate will help to inflate the economy but it will further aggravate the surplus in the balance of payments. An appreciation, on the other hand, will help to get rid of the trade surplus but it will at the same time deflate the economy and aggravate unemployment problems.

The interpretation of the Swan diagram is best viewed as an application of the aims – means analysis introduced at the beginning of this chapter. If there are two targets in the economy, at least two policy means are generally needed if both targets are to be reached. We should observe that any one policy means usually affects both aims. It is therefore important to pair off aims and means to achieve maximum efficiency. This is sometimes referred to as 'the assignment problem'. We have to assign the policy means to the target it can handle most effectively. First, we have to remind ourselves that we need at least as many means as there are aims or targets. If we have two targets, external equilibrium and full employment, we need at least two policy means. In this case we have two: fiscal policy on the one hand, and exchange-rate manipulations on the other.

It is natural to regard changes in the exchange rate as the means most appropriate for producing external equilibrium and to take fiscal policy as more adequate for reaching internal equilibrium. In principle, which of the means should be paired with which of the aims will depend on the empirical characteristics of the economy in question. To further elucidate the assignment problem, Figure 28.3 should be useful.

The figure is similar to Figure 28.2. We start at point *a* in zone II (any point representing disequilibrium can be chosen as an arbitrary point of departure to illustrate the reasoning). Here we have both an inflationary pressure and a trade surplus. The exchange rate is appreciated and we move to point *b*, where there is external equilibrium. Our problem now is to relieve the economy of its inflationary pressure and attain internal equilibrium. This can be done in one of two ways. We can either continue to appreciate the exchange rate or we can deflate the economy by means of a restrictive fiscal policy. Which of the two is chosen is critical for reaching full equilibrium. Let us say that we deflate the economy by lowering domestic expenditure. This will take us to *c*. Now we have full employment and stable prices, but we have created a new surplus in the balance of payments. Again we will have to appreciate the exchange rate, and move to *d*. This time we will have external equilibrium but now we will have some unemployment. However, this will not be very large, and by an appropriate combination of a slight inflation and a small depreciation of the exchange rate we will

FIGURE 28.3

Policy adjustments to
reach internal and
external equilibrium

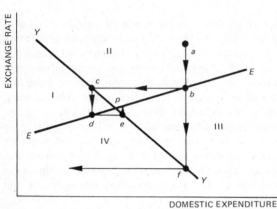

move to *P* and reach the point of bliss.

Had we instead chosen to appreciate when we were at *b* to reach internal equilibrium we would soon have been in dire straights. This would have taken us to *f*, where internal equilibrium reigns but where we would have to confront a huge trade deficit. In order to get rid of that, we would have to deflate, which in turn would create massive unemployment. The policy situation would get out of hand and the economy would be tossed between ever-increasing trade deficits and unemployment disequilibria.

The moral of this story is that it is extremely important how policy means are assigned to targets. In this case, if exchange-rate changes are used for reaching external equilibrium, and if domestic expenditure changes are used to regulate the internal level of demand, everything will work well, and we will soon reach full equilibrium. If, instead, exchange-rate changes had been used for internal equilibrium, and fiscal policy for reaching external equilibrium, the situation would have become explosive. This depends upon the way the curves in the diagram have been drawn. The *EE* curve is flatter than the *YY* curve (disregarding signs). This implies that the effects of exchange-rate changes will be relatively larger on the external balance and expenditure changes will have more powerful effects on the internal equilibrium. There are no *a priori* grounds for assuming one over the other. Some information about the economy in question is required before one can effectively solve the assignment problem. But once we have some knowledge about the behavior relationships of an economy, we can solve the assignment problem with the proper pairing of aims and means, and our theoretical insights should then enable us to hit all the policy targets that have been set for the economy.

There is little doubt that the theory of economic policy has gained ground during the 1960s and 1970s. The aims – means theory is more and more being regarded as a standard tool of analysis. Policy-makers, with varying degrees of understanding of its theoretical underpinnings, have also tried to implement it in various countries.

It is quite common for a country to find itself in zone III, where it has both an inflationary pressure in its economy and a deficit in the balance of payments. An early and illustrative example of such a situation is France in the mid-1950s. The inflationary pressure in the French economy was quite manifest. From the end of 1956 to the middle of 1958 prices rose by 18 per cent. The trade balance showed a deficit. Confidence in the French franc dropped considerably, and the foreign exchange reserves decreased from $2 billion in the beginning of 1956 to $170 million in the middle of 1958. Various forms of trade and currency controls had been tried but with little effect.

In June 1958 Charles de Gaulle became French president and was entrusted with far-reaching powers. He soon appointed a committee of economic experts headed by the well-known economist Jacques Rueff. In December the French franc was devalued by 15 per cent and a monetary reform was introduced that lopped two zeros of all prices and introduced 'the new franc'. The devaluation was accompanied by a restrictive fiscal policy and a tight monetary policy.

A certain fall in real wages took place and a slight slowdown of production occurred. However, exports soon started to rise. They increased in volume by 20 per cent during 1959, and the balance of trade shifted from a deficit of $300 million in 1958 to a surplus of $435 in 1959. The French economy soon began an expansion led by its export sector. The trade deficits were transformed into surpluses and the confidence in the French franc was restored. In the first four years after the reforms of 1958 France's net external assets grew by $4.7 billion.

The French devaluation and its accompanying policies can be viewed as an interesting application of aims–means policies. Devaluation was used to move the economy out of zone III and onto the *EE* curve. At the same time, devaluation *per se* did not solve the country's inflationary pressure. On the contrary, it tended to move the French economy further away from the *YY* curve. Hence it had to be combined by cuts in domestic expenditures. This policy contributed to both dampening the inflationary pressure and relieving the trade deficit. In fact, it can be argued that the restrictive fiscal and monetary policy was even more fundamental than the devaluation for restoring equilibrium in the French economy.

The French case can also be used to illustrate the monetary approach to the balance of payments examined in Chapter 26. There we learned that a restrictive monetary policy (constant money supply) was essential for a successful devaluation. The insights of that chapter, combined with the aims–means analysis of this chapter, should provide us with a thorough understanding of the theory of international economic policy.

Another interesting case is the British devaluation of 1967. The British pound had been weak for long periods during the 1950s and 1960s. When the British tried to expand the economy, the balance of payments often went into deficit. Expectations of a devaluation had been widespread since the Labour Party came to power in 1964 under Harold Wilson. In November 1967, Britain finally devalued the pound sterling by 14.3 per cent.

The positive effects of the devaluation were slow in coming: the year 1968 saw no improvement in the trade balance, as imports rose even faster than in 1967. During the Vietnam war period at the end of the 1960s international capital flows were large and erratic (see Chapter 29 for analysis of the international monetary system in the 1960s). Britain also suffered from continuing speculation against the pound sterling. More stringent policy measures, like a surcharge on imported consumer goods and limits to lendings by the commercial banks, were introduced toward the end of 1968. During 1969 the British trade balance improved and in 1970 Britain recorded the largest surplus on current account in history. The success of the British devaluation can be debated. Prime Minister Harold Wilson headed a rather weak government. Being a Labour leader he had neither the political backing nor the ability to implement the same type of restrictive policies as de Gaulle could during his heyday in the late 1950s. Aims–means analysis along the lines suggested above probably had a more direct relevance for policy formulation in the comparatively calm days of the 1950s and 1960s than it had in the 1970s. The upheavals and great adjustment problems that have followed in the wake of the oil crisis have limited the scope for traditional policy measures (the oil crisis and its effects are analyzed in Chapter 30). Instead, capital movements have gained an increasing importance. We will now continue our analysis by demonstrating how the aims–means analysis can also be applied in two other formulations where capital movements play an essential role.

MONETARY, FISCAL AND EXCHANGE-RATE POLICY:
THE *LM–IS–FE* MODEL

So far we have dealt with real as opposed to monetary aspects of aims–means analysis. Expenditure-reducing policies were used for controlling the national income. Expenditure-switching policies were used to regulate the external balance. However, monetary factors are also important. For instance, capital movements have played a large role during the last two decades in the world economy. One way of keeping the external balance in equilibrium is to induce capital movements by manipulating interest-rate differentials.

Aims–means analysis can help to illustrate how external and internal balance can be achieved in the presence of capital movements. The technique best suited to this kind of analysis is an extended form of the *IS–LM* curve exercise. The *IS–LM* technique was originally developed by two famous economists, J. R. Hicks and Alvin Hansen, as a tool for explaining Keynesian economics.[6] It has been widely used since then and most students are probably familiar with it from elementary macroeconomics.

A given *IS* curve shows the combination of interest rate and national income which gives equilibrium in the goods market (see Figure 28.4). It slopes downward because a fall in the interest rate gives rise to an increase in investment, producing an expansionary effect on the national income. A shift in the *IS* curve, for instance from IS_1 to IS_2, symbolizes a change in investment–savings behavior. It implies that the producers in the economy wish to invest more for any given level of interest rates. If there is, to start with, equilibrium at the interest rate r_1 and national income Y_1 and producers suddenly want to invest more (to take advantage, perhaps, of some new innovations), there will be an expansionary effect on the national income, increasing it from Y_1 to Y_2.

The *LM* curves show the interdependence between the money supply, interest rates, and national income. A point on a given curve shows at what combination of interest rate and national income a given money supply will be demanded and

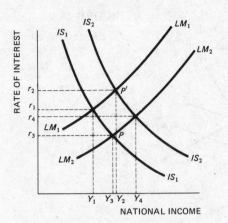

FIGURE 28.4

IS and *LM* curves

hence equilibrium in the money market created. The positive slope of the curve is based on the assumption that if the national income expands, the demand for money will increase, and hence the interest rate will increase if the money supply remains constant. If the money supply is increased, the *LM* curve will shift to the right. This implies that the availability of credit increases, having an expansionary effect on the national income in monetary terms and leading to a fall in the interest rate. This is illustrated in Figure 28.4 by the fact that if the *LM* curve shifts from LM_1 to LM_2 with a given *IS* curve, the national income increases from Y_1 to Y_3 and the interest rate falls from r_1 to r_3. In the open economy it is also important to observe the effects of exchange-rate changes on the *IS* and *LM* curves. It is natural to regard a given *IS* curve as related to a given cost structure. A devaluation changes relative prices and costs. The export industries and the import-competing industries will become more competitive. Hence they will become more profitable and will invest more at any given rate of interest and national income: thus the *IS* curve will shift to the right because of a devaluation.

A devaluation also affects the demand for money. We studied these relationships extensively in Chapter 26. A devaluation increases the price level. This means that a real balance effect will come into play and that the demand for money will increase. This implies that the *LM* curve will shift to the left.

Returning to Figure 28.4 a devaluation will take us from P to P'. The interest rate will rise, while there will be a slight expansionary effect on the national income. An important point already implicit in the analysis of Chapter 26 is illustrated, namely that a devaluation will automatically tighten the money market, and this will have some restrictive influences on the economy, provided, of course, that the authorities do not increase the money supply.

Our next step is to bring the *FE* curve into the analysis. This is done in Figure 28.5. The *FE* curve or foreign exchange schedule, shows the combination of interest rates and national incomes at which the foreign exchange market is in equilibrium. The trick here is to introduce capital flows. We assume that the external balance consists of two parts: the trade balance and the capital balance. A

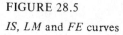

FIGURE 28.5

IS, LM and *FE* curves

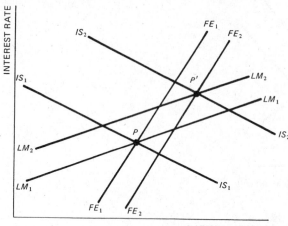

NATIONAL INCOME

deficit on the trade balance can be matched by an inflow of capital and hence the external balance can still be maintained.

Analogously, a trading surplus can be counteracted by an outflow of capital that preserves the external balance. The *FE* curve slopes upward and to the right. This depends on the fact that imports are an increasing function of the national income. Capital, on the other hand, will flow into the country as the interest rate increases; or, rather, capital flows are a function of interest-rate differentials, but it is assumed that the interest rate abroad is constant. Hence if the national income increases, the interest rate will have to go up in order to attract capital inflows so that the external balance can be sustained in equilibrium. Therefore, the *FE* curve, showing the combination of interest rates and nominal incomes at which the foreign exchange market is in equilibrium, will slope upward and to the right.

A devaluation will cause the *FE* schedule to shift downward and to the right. This is illustrated in Figure 28.5 by the shift of the curve from FE_1 to FE_2, the reason being that a devaluation will increase exports at any given level of the national income. Hence any trade deficit will be smaller or any surplus larger at any given rate of interest. This implies that for any given level of national income, a smaller capital inflow will be needed to cover a deficit, since the deficit will be comparatively smaller; hence, the interest rate can be lower. Looking at Figure 28.5 we can observe that the new equilibrium point has moved upward and to the right from P to P'. This means that a devaluation will cause the national income to expand and the interest rate to rise. Generally, economic growth will be stimulated. The foreign trade sector will become relatively more important and profits in the export and import-competing sectors will increase. The Wage-earners might suffer somewhat during a transition period but should be able to keep their relative position once the new equilibrium has been reached. Profits in domestic industries (not involved in foreign trade) may fall, at least in relative terms. Asset owners will be affected somewhat differently, depending on how

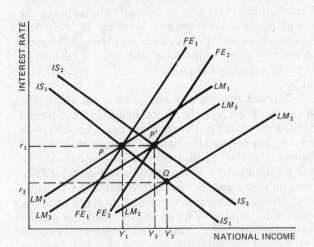

FIGURE 28.6

External and internal
equilibrium in an
IS–LM–FE model

their portfolios are constructed. Assets which give a constant real return will
fall in value, while interest-bearing assets will give an increased yield. People
living on pensions or long-term contractual incomes will suffer. The same will
hold true for owners of 'specific' factors of production which are non-movable
and trapped in industries producing for the home market. In a more complete
dynamic analysis, taking expectations and recursive effects on the price level
into account, the effects will be more difficult to forecast.

The *FE* schedule in Figure 28.5 has been drawn with a steeper slope than the
LM curve. To give the more deep-seated arguments for this would take us outside
the scope of the analysis pursued here. There are, however, good pragmatic
reasons why the slopes should be drawn so. Conventional Keynesian analysis
teaches us that a devaluation will produce a net injection into the income stream.
Hence a devaluation drives our system to a larger national income and, given
a constant money supply, to a higher interest rate. If the slopes were reversed,
the new point of equilibrium would be to the left and above the original one. It
would be difficult to give a meaningful economic interpretation to such a result.

Just as there are strong factors promoting internal equilibrium in the ordinary
IS–LM type of analysis for the closed economy, there are also good reasons to
believe that both external and internal equilibrium can be reached in the extended
IS–LM–FE model. Figure 28.6 can be used to illustrate this proposition.

We start off at point P with the interest rate r_1 and the national income Y_1.
This is the equilibrium spontaneously generated by the economy given the behavior relationships as depicted by the curves in Figure 28.6. Point P represents,
however, a disequilibrium to the extent that there is less than full employment
at Y_1. Let us say that the government wants full employment and uses monetary
policy to reach this policy aim. A policy of easy money is pursued, which means
that the *LM* curve shifts to LM_2. A new point of equilibrium is reached at point
Q and the national income expands to Y_2 while the interest rate falls to r_2 because of the increase in the money supply.

Thus there is internal equilibrium to the extent that saving equals investment, but there is no external equilibrium. Point Q is to the right of and below the schedule which represents equilibrium in the foreign exchange market, FE_1. This means that the national income is so high that it causes a differential between imports and exports which is not offset by capital movements because the interest rate is too low to induce sufficient capital imports. Hence there is a deficit in the balance of payments at Q.

What will happen now? Provided that the government does not interfere, a process of adjustment will come into play. The excess demand in the foreign exchange market will force a depreciation of the exchange rate. This will, as we know, affect all three curves in our system. The demand for cash balances will increase and the LM curve will shift back to the left, from LM_2 to LM_3. At the same time, investment will be stimulated and the IS curve will shift out from IS_1 to IS_2. Exports will also be stimulated by the depreciation of the exchange rate and for any given rate of interest a larger amount of imports can be sustained; thus, as here, the FE schedule shifts out from FE_1 to FE_2. A possible new point of equilibrium is P'. Y_3 is the national income that corresponds to full employment. The combination of Y_3 and the interest rate r_1 produces both internal and external equilibrium as P' is located on the new FE curve compatible with the new exchange rate.

The analysis has so far demonstrated that adjustment of the exchange rate will lead to equilibrium in all three markets. If the balance of payments were not in equilibrium, further exchange-rate changes would be induced which in turn would shift the LM and IS curves until a new equilibrium was reached.

We assumed that full employment was reached above point P'. This is not a necessary outcome. In general we would not expect an exchange-rate change to lead automatically to both external and internal equilibria with full employment. An achievement of this aim would normally imply the explicit use of some further policy means or parameter. Through the use of both monetary and fiscal policy, combined with manipulation of the exchange rate, a country should be able to reach full employment and external equilibrium. However, often governments are constrained in their use of policy parameters. The interest rate or the exchange rate might be pegged, for example. From the policy point of view, such constrained cases are the most interesting ones. We will now turn our attention to these, while keeping the LM–IS–FE technique in mind.

CAPITAL MOVEMENTS AND EXTERNAL BALANCE

The capital markets of the leading industrial countries have become closely integrated during the 1960s and 1970s. This has had important implications for their possibilities of pursuing independent economic policies. Capital movements have also played an increasingly important role as a form of adjustment for removing the huge imbalances in the international economy that followed in the wake of the oil crisis that occurred in 1973.

The best-known application of the LM–IS–FE analysis concerns the role of capital movements under a regime of fixed exchange rates. It is important to study this type of analysis. First, it is essential for an understanding of how the

FIGURE 28.7

Fixed exchange rates with
capital movements

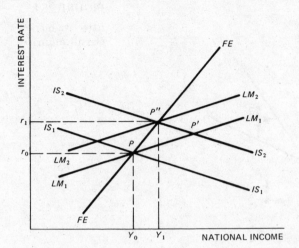

international monetary system worked until 1973, when floating rates become more common. Second, it still has widespread application under the present system since many small countries peg their currencies to larger ones, and even the large countries try to control swings in exchange rates by inducing capital movements. The practical functioning of the international monetary system will be further analyzed in Chapters 29 and 30.

Figure 28.7 illustrates the case of a country with fixed exchange rates. The country is originally at point P with an interest rate of r_0 and a national income of Y_0. The full-employment income, however, is Y_1. We assume that the exchange rate is pegged. How can the country achieve full employment?

In the preceding two sections exchange-rate changes played an essential role for reaching full employment and equilibrium in the balance of payments. Now, such changes are ruled out for political or institutional reasons. However, an important point to remember is that the external balance can be subdivided into two parts: the trade balance and the capital balance. Even though we cannot use expenditure-switching means to steer the trade balance, we can still use monetary policy to control capital movements.

In terms of aims and means we now have two means: monetary policy and fiscal policy. Again we encounter the assignment problem – but this time in a slightly different form. We should pair off our two instruments, monetary and fiscal policy, in an efficient way so that the two targets, internal and external balance, can be reached. In order to do so we should apply the rule of 'efficient market classification'.[7] This is another way of formulating the assignment problem: it says that each policy means should be directed toward that target or aim on which it has relatively the greatest impact. The rule of effective market classification is illustrated in Figure 28.8.

Assume that the economy is initially at point Q. Here the economy is on the *II* line so that internal equilibrium is present. One is, however, to the left of the *EE* schedule – which means that there is a deficit in the balance of payments. If

432   *The Balance of Payments and International Economic Policy*

FIGURE 28.8

Effective market classification

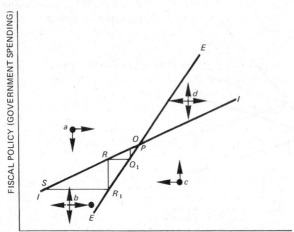

monetary policy is used, and the interest rate is increased, capital inflows will be attracted, while somewhat of a depressive effect on the national income will occur. With 'fine-tuning' fiscal policy we can then reach point P and attain full equilibrium in the economy.

If, instead, fiscal policy had been used at Q to deflate the economy in order to get rid of the external deficit, we would have come to Q_1. Had fiscal policy then been used to achieve full employment, it would have taken us to point R. A continuation of this process would produce wider and wider swings and would clearly lead to an unstable situation. The proper assignment of policies is shown by the solid arrows, while improper ones are illustrated by dotted arrows. This means, in our case, that monetary policy should be directed toward preserving the external balance while fiscal policy should be used for maintaining full employment.

Let us now return to Figure 28.7. The exchange rate is pegged. Hence the FE curve is fixed and cannot be moved. The economy is at point P with a national income of Y_0 and an interest rate of r_0. This is a point of stable equilibrium (Keynesian equilibrium with less than full capacity utilization). Full employment income is at Y_1.

Fiscal policy (an increase in government expenditure or a decrease in taxes) should be used to shift the IS schedule to the right from IS_1 to IS_2. This shift by itself will lead to more than full employment and create a deficit in the balance of payments. Therefore, the expansionary fiscal policy will have to be combined with a restrictive monetary policy which shifts the LM curve to LM_2 and raises the interest rate. Thereby the economy can be moved to P'', which is a point of full equilibrium.

Returning to aims–means analysis, we have seen that monetary policy had its relatively greatest impact on the balance of payments. This is reflected in Figure 28.8 by the fact that the EE line has a steeper slope than the II schedule. Naturally, the slope of these schedules will depend on the behavior relationships of the economy. There are, however, good grounds for assuming the slopes to be of the kind depicted in Figure 28.8.

Normally, capital flows will have a certain interest elasticity. This means that an increase in the interest rate will induce an inflow of capital. The larger the response of capital flows to a given increase in the interest rate, the larger will be the interest elasticity. Both instruments will have an effect on the internal balance, but monetary policy will have an added impact on the balance of payments through its effect on international capital flows. This is the basic reason why monetary policy should be assigned to the external balance in this type of model.

We have now demonstrated how monetary and fiscal policy can be used together to give external and internal equilibrium in a model with fixed exchange rates. It should, however, be observed that no adjustment mechanism of the traditional type is at work here to create both external and internal equilibrium. There is nothing which will eventually restore the relationship between foreign and domestic prices which could give the country external equilibrium at full employment with a more 'neutral' policy mix; everything else being equal, the country will have to restrict its capital exports forever, or, if it is an importer of capital, continue importing capital forever.

Normative aspects of capital movements are difficult to discuss in the abstract. It may be argued, for instance, that if a country has a deficit in its trade balance and covers it with capital imports, it depends on the fact that the country's price level is out of control, that its wages and prices rise faster than its competitors wages and prices. If the country continues to cover its deficits with capital imports, the domestic price level will become more and more out of line with those of competing countries. The interest rate will have to increase more and more in order to attract foreign capital, and finally the country will fall into an untenable position. In this case a policy mix of the type discussed can be said to imply only a postponement of the necessary adjustment.

It may also be, however, that a policy of deficits in the balance of trade and of capital imports leads to an increase in the rate of domestic investment within the country and to more rapid economic growth. If the growth is of a specific kind, it may after some time affect the balance of trade in a positive way. Then the country will get equilibrium in its trade balance, enabling it to lower the interest rate and possibly become a capital exporter. In this case the policy mix has given the economy needed breathing space, permitting the economy to develop in such a fashion that equilibrium in the balance of current account will be reached without any immediate adjustment being required.

CAPITAL MOVEMENTS IN AN INTEGRATED WORLD ECONOMY

Before we end this chapter we should also briefly touch on the case where capital markets are completely integrated and where monetary policy loses its power to influence the domestic activity level. Technological improvements in communication and travel and institutional changes have brought many countries very close together. An important feature of the 1960s and 1970s has been the rapid development of the so-called *euro-dollar market* (see Chapter 30 for a description and analysis

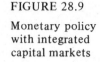

FIGURE 28.9

Monetary policy
with integrated
capital markets

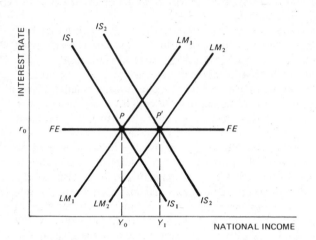

of this). All these factors have led to an integration of capital markets. The supply and demand elasticities which many countries face have become very large. The implications of this development for monetary policy are striking, indeed.

The *LM–IS–FE* model can readily be used to illustrate the lack of power of monetary policy when capital markets are integrated. Figure 28.9 is used to illustrate this case. We start by assuming that the exchange rate is pegged. The *FE* curve is horizontal at the interest rate r_0. This means that at this interest rate the country can import as much capital as it needs because this is the prevailing world rate of interest, and as the country's capital market is integrated with the markets of other countries, its own rate of interest will be determined by the world market rate of interest.

Let us start by assuming that the country is at point P with its national income at Y_0. Full-employment income is at Y_1. The authorities now start an expansionary monetary policy by increasing the money supply. The *LM* schedule shifts to LM_2. The exchange rate is pegged. What will happen now?

The increase in the money supply causes a downward pressure on the interest rate. However, this cannot be realized because the *FE* curve is horizontal, which illustrates the fact that the supply of foreign capital is infinitely elastic. The increase in the money supply will instead give rise to an outflow of short-term capital. The authorities will have to finance this outflow by sales of foreign exchange at the pegged price of foreign exchange. The sales of foreign exchange again decrease the money supply. This means that the *LM* curve again shifts upward and to the left. This process continues until the *LM* curve has shifted back to its initial position.

Thus monetary policy becomes impotent in this case. The effect of the expansionary monetary policy will simply be that the central bank loses foreign reserves. However, this loss of reserves will be matched by private holdings of assets abroad. When the downward pressure on the domestic interest rate occurs and capital flows abroad, that capital will be owned by the private citizens of the home country. So the effect of monetary policy under the assumptions given above will simply be a change in the composition of foreign assets. The monetary authorities will have little chance to implement an expansionary policy in this case. All they will achieve is a loss of foreign reserves. They can, of course, try to change the rules of the game by regulating (perhaps forbidding) exports of capital abroad. But if they live in a world of already integrated capital markets, the prospects for implementing such a policy are probably small.

What the country can do instead is to use fiscal policy to achieve full employment. It can, for instance, shift the *IS* schedule to IS_2 by increasing government expenditure. This will cause an upward pressure on the interest rate. As the interest rate cannot rise, capital will instead be attracted to the country. This will lead to an increase in the money supply as the foreign reserves increase. This means that the *LM* curve is shifted out to LM_2. Hence the country will reach a new equilibrium at P', with full employment and external equilibrium, at fixed exchange rates. It should be noted, of course, that this equilibrium is sustained by an import of capital.

The important conclusion to this story is that the country (in this case) cannot use monetary policy but has to rely on fiscal policy to reach equilibrium. If a country maintains fixed exchange rates and faces a perfectly elastic supply of and demand for foreign capital it will have to rely on fiscal policy as its policy variable.

Let us now change one important assumption of the analysis: the country has floating instead of fixed exchange rates. If it pursues an expansionary monetary policy, a downward pressure on the exchange rate occurs. Capital will flow out of the country. Now, however, this will have an effect on the exchange rate, which will depreciate. This will cause the *IS* curve to shift upward and to the right. The *LM* schedule, on the other hand, will shift to the left. Over-all equilibrium will only be reached when the two intersect on the *FE* line, which is stable as it is determined by conditions in the international capital market. However, the money supply can now be changed so as to reach equilibrium at any desired level of the national income. On the other hand, fiscal policy cannot be used in this case. An expansionary fiscal policy will only lead to an inflow of capital and an appreciation of the exchange rate. This appreciation will shift the *IS* curve back to its original position. Fiscal policy cannot be used to achieve a permanent increase in income if the exchange rate is floating and capital markets integrated.

Practically speaking, the most relevant of the above two cases has been the one with fixed exchange rates and a given international rate of interest. A case in point is West Germany. For a long period during the 1960s it had a surplus in its balance of trade. It tried to pursue restrictive monetary policies to avoid inflationary impulses coming from abroad. The tight monetary policy induced, however, inflows of capital and made it very difficult for the country to control its money supply, and the policy of tight money tended to become inefficient.

Again, we reach the important conclusion that a country must be very careful in pairing off aims and means. It will have to take into account the nature of the problems at hand and the prevailing restrictions, and it will have to choose policy instruments that can be effective for reaching the given targets.

It should also be stressed that the models involving capital movements are only applicable in the short run. No adjustment mechanism leading to a long-run equilibrium is present. For more permanent solutions to imbalances a country will have to rely on the policy means treated in the earlier sections of this chapter. Money, interest rates and short-term capital flows are primarily relevant in the short run.

SUMMARY AND CONCLUSIONS

Usually a country has more than one aim for its economic policy. Countries often want to achieve full employment, a stable price level and equilibrium in their balances of payments. A country then has to design policy means so as to be able to achieve all the aims simultaneously. The basic rule is that the country needs as many policy parameters as it has targets. One means or parameter will in most cases affect more than one of the aims. The authorities, then, have to confront the assignment problem, i.e. they will have to pair off means and aims so as to reach full equilibrium.

Normally, various zones of imbalance can be characterized. The choice of policy means will depend on the types of imbalance that a country confronts. The proper combination of aims and means will depend on the characteristics and behavior relationships of the economy. Most often monetary and fiscal policy should be used to stabilize the national income, while changes in the exchange rate should be used for reaching external balance. The timing and assignment of policy means are important. Both devaluation and deflationary fiscal policy can be used to stimulate the activity level and cure an external deficit. However, which of the two is used and in what combination can be of critical importance for the possibilities of reaching full equilibrium. An improper assignment of policies can create an unstable situation with ever-increasing swings in the national income. As a rule of thumb we can say that changes of exchange rates should be used for reaching external balance while expenditure changes should be applied for getting full employment.

Capital movements can also play an important role for achieving external balance in the short run. If exchange rates are pegged, while capital movements are present, monetary policy can be designed for reaching external equilibrium, while fiscal policy can be used for achieving full employment. Again, the proper timing and assignment of policies are important. According to the principle of 'efficient market classification', monetary policy should be used for reaching equilibrium in the balance of payments and fiscal policy to reach internal equilibrium as long as capital flows have a certain positive interest-rate elasticity.

If capital markets are completely integrated and the interest elasticity of capital movements is infinitely large, and if exchange rates are fixed, then monetary policy loses its effectiveness and fiscal policy will have to be used for reaching full equilibrium. If, instead, exchange rates are floating, fiscal policy will lose its grip while monetary policy should do the job.

It should be remembered that the analysis involving capital movements is only applicable to the short run.

SELECTED BIBLIOGRAPHY: CHAPTER 28

For a general discussion of aims and means in economic policy see:

B. Hansen, *The Economic Theory of Fiscal Policy,* London, Allen & Unwin, 1958.

J. Tinbergen, *On the Theory of Economic Policy,* Amsterdam, North-Holland, 1952.

Important works discussing aims and means primarily in expenditure-switching and expenditure-reducing terms are:

M. Corden, 'The Geometric Representation of Policies to Attain Internal and External Balance', *RES,* October 1960.

H. G. Johnson, 'Theoretical Problems of the International Monetary System', *Pakistan Development Review,* Spring 1967.

J. E. Meade, *The Balance of Payments,* London, Oxford University Press, 1951, chs 9–10.

T. W. Swan, 'Longer-Run Problems of the Balance of Payments', in *RIE,* ch. 27.

Classic discussions of internal and external balance in a world of money are:

M. J. Fleming, 'Domestic Financial Policies under Fixed and under Floating Exchange Rates', *SP,* November 1962.

R. A. Mundell, 'The Appropriate Use of Monetary and Fiscal Policy for Internal and External Stability', *SP,* March 1962.

For extensions and criticisms of this type of analysis, see:

J. E. Floyd, 'International Capital Movements and Monetary Equilibrium', *AER,* September 1969.

R. A. Mundell, *International Economics,* New York, Macmillan Co., chs 11, 14–18.

R. M. Stern, *The Balance of Payments: Theory and Economic Policy,* Chicago, Aldine, 1973.

A. K. Swoboda, 'Equilibrium, Quasi-equilibrium and Macro-economic Stabilization Policy under Fixed Exchange Rates', *QJE,* February 1972.

M. von Neuman-Whitman, *Policies for External and Internal Balance,* Special Papers in Economics No. 9, Princeton, N.J., Princeton University Press, 1970.

PART V

The international monetary system

29
The Bretton Woods system

The final part of the book is devoted to the international monetary system. This part will, due to the nature of the problems involved, be more policy-oriented than the preceding parts of the book. We will now describe the events and analyze the monetary problems that have confronted the world economy since the Second World War. In doing so it is, however, useful to apply methods of analysis developed in the earlier parts of the book, especially those dealt with in Part IV. The approach is therefore still analytical, even if this is less explicit than in the preceding chapters.

This chapter describes the development of the world monetary system from the end of the Second World War until 1971. The system which then prevailed is often referred to as the *Bretton Woods system,* after the name of the meeting place for the conference held in 1944 which established the International Monetary Fund (I.M.F.). This chapter analyzes the principles behind the I.M.F., the role which gold played as a medium for international exchange, and the importance of the dollar for creating the liquidity which the world trading system needed.

Chapter 30 analyzes the system that has evolved since the breakdown of the Bretton Woods system in 1971 and its final kiss of death in 1973. It studies the system of floating exchange rates which has evolved during the 1970s. It deals with the pros and cons of fixed and floating exchange rates and the important role played by euro-dollars and capital movements. The chapter also discusses plans for reform and various options for the future.

THE BACKGROUND OF THE 1930s.

We are all prisoners of the past. In order to understand the principles behind the I.M.F. and the methods used for creating a new world monetary order after the Second World War, we must first consider the events of the 1930s.

The depression of the 1930s affected both the industrial and the primary-producing countries. Production and trade fell. The dollar price of primary products decreased by 50 per cent from 1929 to 1932, and the value of exports fell even more. The G.N.P. of the United States fell by one-third in the period 1929–33.

The Great Depression also created havoc in the international monetary system. Several primary-producing countries devalued their currencies in 1929 and 1930 in an attempt to counteract the decline of their export earnings. Instead of leading to any lasting improvement, an epidemic of exchange depreciations broke out. It gathered momentum in 1931 with the depreciations by Great Britain and countries belonging to the British Commonwealth. Confusion reigned in the world economy. A considerable number of statesmen and economic observers still believed in a return to the gold standard. The final blow to the old system came during 1933-4 when the United States devalued and when an economic conference in London of leading governments failed to organize any early return to the gold standard or to supplant it with any orderly new system.

The depreciations of the 1930s left an impression of capriciousness, not to say chaos, in its wake. Some governments tried to cling to overvalued currencies, while others used competitive exchange rate depreciations for 'beggar-my-neighbor' purposes. The difficulties of maintaining trade and employment which many countries encountered soon led them to erect various types of trade barriers. The system of multilateral trade suffered heavy blows as quotas, import-restrictions and bilateral forms of trade began to be applied. In earlier periods the growth of world trade kept pace with that of world production. Now world trade started to lag behind since its volume increased substantially less than that of industrial production.

THE INTERNATIONAL MONETARY FUND

Plans for an international institution that would organize the international monetary system circulated among the Allied powers during the Second World War. During a conference in 1944 of forty-four nations at Bretton Woods, New Hampshire, in the United States, these plans took a more definite shape. In July of that year the International Monetary Fund was created.

The Bretton Woods system that the I.M.F. was to supervise rested on two pillars: the maintenance of stable exchange rates and a multilateral credit system. The I.M.F. would organize the system, consult with the member countries about exchange-rate changes and create international liquidity when needed.

Principles are one thing, practice another. During the next quarter of a century the I.M.F. played, in fact, a limited role in steering and supervising the system. But an understanding of the principles and functions of the I.M.F. is still a vital prerequisite for evaluating the system's performance and for understanding why the I.M.F. has become more important in recent years.

Fixed exchange rates were deemed desirable against the background of the 1930s. The members of the I.M.F. agreed to keep their exchange rates fixed at agreed par values and not to change them more than 1 per cent below or above parity. A member country could, however, alter the par value. The key concept was then 'fundamental disequilibrium'. A member government could propose a change in its exchange rate if it felt that it had a fundamental disequilibrium in its balance of payments. If the proposed change were less than 10 per cent, the Fund could not object. A country making a larger change was required to obtain the Fund's permission. The Fund could not veto an adjustment of the exchange rate if it were made to correct a 'fundamental disequilibrium'. The I.M.F. might, however, object to the economic and social policies pursued in the country. Often the Fund urged unwilling members, especially less developed countries, to devalue in order to rid themselves of deficits in the balance of payments. The philosophy behind these rules was that exchange-rate changes should take place in an orderly manner and for justifiable economic reasons.

The second important aspect of the Fund's activity concerned its arrangements for international liquidity. Each member had some borrowing rights to help it meet temporary external deficits. This credit system was, in fact, envisaged as an important and integral part of the system which the I.M.F. supervised. In order to understand how it worked it is useful to examine the construction of the Fund.

Each I.M.F. member was allotted a quota. The size of the quota varied according to the importance of the country. The sum of all quotas was established at $8.8 billion in 1944.[1] This can be compared with the figure for total world liquidity, which at the time amounted to approximately $38 billion. It should be noted that each country's quota determines its voting rights, and thereby the influence of the country. The United States was dominant. Its quota at the beginning amounted to 36 per cent of the total holding of the I.M.F. Several general increases of the quotas have taken place, by 50 per cent in 1965 and by 35 per cent in 1970. Some countries have also agreed to larger individual increases, either to reflect more accurately their economic position in the world or to give them greater access to the Fund's resources. In the mid-1970s the sum of the quotas amounted to some 30 billion Special Drawing Rights.[2]

At present (in 1980), 126 nations belong to the Fund. The United States has the largest quota, amounting to 23 per cent of the total. Then come the United Kingdom (9.6 per cent), West Germany (5.5 per cent), France (5.1 per cent), Japan (4.1 per cent), Canada (3.8 per cent), and India (3.2 per cent). Switzerland, the Soviet Union, the countries of Eastern Europe and China are not members of the Fund. (Taiwan has been a member from the beginning.)

A country's quota has three important aspects. First, it specifies how much the country must subscribe to the Fund. Second, the quota defines a country's drawing rights, i.e. how much a country can borrow from the Fund. Third, it indicates the country's voting power.[3]

The most important aspect, from our standpoint, is the *drawing right.* Each country's drawing right is divided into five parts. The first is called the *gold tranche,* because it corresponded to the country's subscription in gold. The next four are called the first, second, third and fourth *credit tranches.* The importance of the drawing right lies in the fact that a country can make drawings on the I.M.F. and use the currency it thereby obtains to cover deficits in its balance of payments. Under I.M.F. practice, a country can automatically make use of its gold tranche. Also, it can usually use its first credit tranche without much difficulty. Thereafter, drawings on the Fund depend on I.M.F. approval. The conditions of approval become more and more stringent as a country applies to go beyond its first credit tranche. Usually, a country must repay the Fund within three to five years, and there is an increasing scale of interest on drawings that go beyond the gold tranche.

The I.M.F. began its operations in 1947. It had been foreseen at the Bretton Woods conference in 1944 that normal conditions in the international monetary field would not be achieved until some time after the war was over. It was 1961 before normalcy returned.

From the outset, the I.M.F. played a conservative role. The Fund feared that its resources would be used for reconstruction purposes and not for solving short-term balance-of-payments problems. Therefore, it laid down stringent conditions for its lending operations (for instance the rule that a country must repay the Fund within three to five years). It also increased charges on its outstanding loans. For a country to get help it had to convince the Fund that its balance-of-payments problems were temporary, and that it could overcome them within a fairly short time.

All this led to the I.M.F. playing quite a passive role during the 1950s. In the late 1940s it stressed the necessity for adjustment in exchange rates and took a positive view of the devaluations by Britain and most other Western European countries in 1949. Later it took the view that changes in major exchange rates were undesirable.

Three main types of adjustment were feasible during this period. A country could reduce its expenditures when confronted with a balance-of-payments deficit, or it could try to rely on expenditure-switching policies by devaluing. A third way was to increase the provision of world liquidity so as to smooth the way for deficit countries. The Fund took a conservative line. It argued that it was each country's own responsibility to maintain a balance in its external transactions. The Fund maintained that a country's first line of defence should be expenditure-reducing policies, and it took a dim view of exchange-rate changes. In 1952, for instance, it stated in its *Annual Report* that 'It is important, therefore, that countries follow commercial policies that will enable them to build up reserves in periods of prosperity which would provide a first cushion to absorb the shock of a recession'.[4] The argument that a country should rely primarily on expenditure reduction was continually reiterated on behalf of the Fund.

It is important to note that the Fund did not try to work for any systematic use of exchange-rate changes during the 1950s and the 1960s. Exchange-rate changes among industrial countries were looked upon with disapproval. They tended to be delayed and were resorted to only when all other means of adjustment had been tried. Thereby they also became overdramatized and governments became unwilling to use them since they were associated with a loss of prestige and a general feeling of failure. When it came to less developed countries, the Fund might tacitly approve of exchange-rate changes, but these were often viewed as the poor man's means of adjustment.

In the 1950s and 1960s, an important growth of world liquidity occurred. However, it was not the I.M.F. that provided this increase in liquidity, but the growth of foreign holdings of U.S. dollars. This phenomenon was intimately connected with the deficits in the balance of payments of the United States, which continued consistently for twenty years. We will soon return to this question as it is important enough to require a section of its own.

During these two decades the world economy was in many ways becoming increasingly integrated. What was noticeable was the integration of capital markets among leading industrial countries. The I.M.F. was also built on the principle of promoting a multilateral credit system. Developments during the 1950s and the 1960s tended, however, to bypass the I.M.F. in this area. In times of crisis the central banks were inclined to cooperate directly, outside the auspices of the I.M.F. So-called 'swap' arrangements between the Federal Reserve System of the United States and the central banks of some Western

European countries and Japan became important. The 'swaps' consist of an exchange of currencies between countries. They are, in fact, short-term credit arrangements. As the two countries taking part in the swap exchange their currencies, the foreign reserves of both increase. Swaps were available on short notice and played a particularly important role in staving off speculative movements of currencies. Part of the reason for the inactivity of the Fund during this period can be explained by the dominance of the United States. The country was by far the most important source of international liquidity. With the cooperation of a few other industrial nations it could control and steer the development of the international system. Under these circumstances it was understandable that the I.M.F. should play second fiddle. Some economists even went so far as to argue that the Fund ought to play a secondary role, that it should primarily concentrate its energies on helping the less developed countries and perhaps assist occasionally when an industrial country came under particular stress. The implication of this line of thought is that 'the club of the rich countries' can better manage their own affairs by direct cooperation. Such arrangements could possibly have been defended during the 1950s and part of the 1960s. But the collapse of the system in 1971 and the gradual development toward a system of floating exchange rates demonstrated that no single country could any longer control the development of the international monetary system.

Recent experiences have shown that the I.M.F. can play an important role in reforming the system's structure. An important step toward revitalizing the Fund was taken in 1967 at the I.M.F. meeting in Rio de Janeiro when Special Drawing Rights were introduced. From relative obscurity the Fund has emerged, at least potentially, as an important supplier of international liquidity and the most important international forum for discussions on international monetary matters.

Special Drawing Rights (S.D.R.s) have the characteristics of international money. They are often referred to as 'paper gold'. The I.M.F. created them by a stroke of the pen, by creating a new account and a new unit of account. The Fund decided that the first issue of S.D.R.s should amount to 9.3 billion units and be made in three instalments: on 1 January in each of the years 1970, 1971 and 1972. The unit of account was originally equal to the gold content of 0.888671 gram, i.e. the same value as 1 U.S. dollar had in 1971 (before the December devaluation of the dollar). On 1 July 1974 the S.D.R. was redefined as a 'basket' that consisted of sixteen various currencies. The weights of the currencies in the basket vary, so that 1 S.D.R. in 1980 consisted of 0.4 U.S. dollars and commensurable fractions of the other fifteen currencies.

It is important to realize that the S.D.R. has the characteristics of a genuine international currency. It is not backed by gold or any other national currency. It derives its strength from the fact that the members of the I.M.F. are willing to accept it and use it as a means of payment between central banks in exchange for existing currencies. The original instalments of the S.D.R.s were distributed to member countries according to their quotas in the Fund. The I.M.F. then designated the countries which should accept S.D.R.s and provided currencies in exchange. No country need accept more than three times its original allocation of S.D.R.s in exchange for its own currency. There are also interest payments connected with being a 'debtor' or a 'creditor' in terms of S.D.R.s.

A country can use S.D.R.s for various reasons: to repay old debts with the I.M.F., to acquire foreign exchange to cover deficits, or to repurchase its own currency from other countries. A country that uses up part of its S.D.R. allotment and becomes a debtor must pay interest on the difference between its original allocation and its present one. Analogously, a creditor country will receive interest on its surplus holdings of S.D.R.s. The interest rate on S.D.R.s was originally 1.5 per cent and was then increased to 5 per cent. The rules surrounding the use of S.D.R.s do limit their usefulness and make them somewhat less than a genuine international currency or 'paper gold'. They do contain, however, important features of such a currency. Contrary to gold, S.D.R. creation does not use up any of the world's scarce resources. Contrary to other forms of international liquidity (like dollars), a creation of S.D.R.s does not require that one country's surplus has to be balanced by another country's deficit. Its use as a unit of account is also spreading: for instance, major international airlines started to use S.D.R.s for accounting purposes on 1 January 1977.

GOLD AND FISCAL RESPONSIBILITY

The emergence of new forms of international liquidity has followed a hazardous course. It has not been controlled by any single government or international organization. Thus it is not difficult to understand that some economists and politicians have argued for a return to what they regard as a more stable and impersonal arrangement: a gold standard.

We have described in chapter 25 the workings of a gold standard and the adjustment mechanism which is its core. Those who support a return to the gold standard contend that gold could serve as an anchor for the world economy. Under a pure gold standard the development of the world price level would depend on the growth of the gold stock on the one hand, and world output on the other. If the supply of world money, i.e. gold, was growing faster than world output, a world inflation would occur, and if the gold stock was growing at a lower rate than world production of goods and services, deflation would take place.[5]

In principle, deflationary and inflationary price movements would also be self-correcting under a gold standard. If growth of output were faster than that of the base money, i.e. gold, the relative price of gold would increase, and that would encourage gold production. With an increase in the price of gold, the profitability of gold-mining would increase and production would go up. An increase in the value of gold might also encourage hoarders to part with their bullion. Hence an increase in the supply of gold used for monetary purposes might also come from traditional hoarding centers.

A fall in world production (or its growth rate) would lead to a fall in the demand for money and hence a fall in the relative price of gold. This would discourage production of gold and encourage hoarding of gold and cause a fall in the rate of growth of the gold stock. Under a gold standard, world output of goods and services would be adjusted to gold production by general equilibrium forces. In equilibrium, under steady-state growth, they would grow by the same rate and the world price level would be stable.

The argument referred to above might seem to be idealized. It contains some rather obvious weaknesses. The link between the gold stock and new production might be weak. The ratio of new production to the existing stock is low. There might be considerable lags between price changes and production changes. Furthermore, demand for industrial purposes and for hoarding could undergo sudden, unforeseen demand shifts; Technical progress in gold production and discovery of new mines might give rise to surpluses; and so on. However, the main weakness in the proposal for restoration of the gold standard is much more fundamental: gold is a commodity money which takes real resources to produce. History has shown that in all national economies, paper monies or credit monies have outcompeted commodity monies. The creation of the latter entails a sterile investment to the extent that it takes real resources to produce the commodity money, in this case gold. Market forces will set to work to economize on gold by providing credit-money substitutes for it. Hence a gold standard will not remain pure for very long. It will gravitate toward a gold reserve standard where some reserve currency will take over the major functionings of gold.

This is a historical fact, with the dollar serving as the major vehicle of currency in the international monetary system since the Second World War. It is still important, however, to understand the argument for a gold standard, both because it pops up now and then and because gold has played an important role in the post-war period.

Let us then study the distribution of gold holdings between various central banks. Large amounts of gold flowed to the United States during the 1930s and the Second World War. The United States guaranteed a stable price of gold by selling and buying it at $35.0875 per ounce. From the beginning of the 1930s to the beginning of the 1950s the United States acquired almost $20 billion-worth of gold and the U.S. holding at Fort Knox amounted to roughly three-quarters of the total monetary gold stock in the world at a value of $25 billion.

However, other countries soon started to rebuild their war-torn economies, and their demand for gold increased. Japan and the industrial countries of Western Europe all had small reserves of gold and foreign exchange in the early 1950s. The attempts to rebuild the economies after the war put a strain on the balance of payments. Holdings of international reserves, which were already small, tended to decrease still further. Direct controls over foreign trade were introduced to avoid deficits in their balances of payments.

Soon an economic resurgence took place and the external balance of most countries improved. This process is illustrated in Table 29.1. As early as 1953, West Germany, for instance, had built up large dollar holdings. Switzerland also had a substantial gold reserve. Most countries, however, had small reserves at the beginning of the 1950s. Naturally, the leading industrial countries outside the communist bloc, which together with the United States dominate world trade, tried to rebuild their depleted reserves of gold and foreign currency. Table 29.1 shows that they were successful. West Germany, Belgium and Switzerland, for instance, had acquired ample reserves in 1958. In the late 1950s and early 1960s, Italy and France generated large export surpluses that enabled them to

TABLE 29.1

Official holdings of gold and foreign exchange ($ billion)

	Gold holdings					Foreign exchange				
	1953	1958	1963	1968	1973	1953	1958	1963	1968	1973
Belgium	0.8	1.3	1.4	1.5	1.8	0.3	0.2	0.4	0.7	3.3
France	0.6	0.8	3.2	3.9	4.3	0.2	0.3	1.3	0.3	4.3
West Germany	0.3	2.6	3.8	4.5	5.0	1.6	3.7	3.3	5.4	28.2
The Netherlands	0.7	1.1	1.6	1.7	2.3	0.5	0.4	0.3	0.8	4.3
Italy	0.3	1.1	2.3	2.9	3.5	0.4	1.0	1.1	2.4	3.0
Sweden	0.2	0.2	0.2	0.2	0.2	0.3	0.3	0.5	0.6	2.2
Switzerland	1.5	1.9	2.8	2.6	3.5	0.3	0.1	0.3	1.2	5.0
Japan	0.0	0.1	0.3	0.4	0.9	0.8	0.8	1.6	2.6	11.4
Great Britain	2.5*	3.1*	2.5	1.5	0.9	–	–	0.2	0.9	5.6

* Including convertible currencies (prior to 1958, U.S. and Canadian dollars only).

SOURCES: United Nations, *Monthly Bulletin of Statistics* and *International Financial Statistics*.

rebuild their gold reserves.

The deficits in the American balance of payments formed a prerequisite for this development. It was only because the United States was running deficits that its main trading partners could generate surpluses which could then be transformed into holdings of gold and foreign exchange.

We will return later to the deficits in the U.S. balance of payments and their importance for international liquidity. It is obvious that they were intimately connected with the international flows of gold. At the beginning of the 1950s the value of the U.S. gold stock amounted to $25 billion. In 1958 its value was 22 billion. In that year came the first massive outflow of gold from the United States. The flow continued. At the beginning of 1968 gold stocks were down to $10.5 billion. In August 1971 President Nixon declared that the dollar was no longer backed by gold. At that time the U.S. gold stock had decreased to 10.2 billion.

At this point we should consider how countries divide their reserves between holdings of gold and holdings of foreign currencies. Part of a country's reserves consist of working balances. A country needs a certain amount of reserves to carry on the daily transactions and to meet seasonal fluctuations. These are usually held in the form of dollars or pounds sterling. When these needs are covered, a country can choose between holding gold or holding dollars.[6]

The central bank is the institution that handles a country's foreign reserves. Central banks vary widely in this respect. Some, such as those in Japan and the Scandinavian countries, have only a small ratio of their reserves in gold, whereas others, for instance the central banks in Switzerland and the E.E.C. countries, have a high ratio of their total reserves in gold. This is illustrated clearly in Table 29.2. It should be added that the reserve countries, the United States and Britain, naturally have a high percentage in gold as they cannot count their own currency as part of their foreign reserves.

TABLE 29.2

Gold as a percentage of total official gold and foreign exchange reserves, September 1966

Over 90	per cent	United States, Switzerland
80–90	per cent	France, South Africa, the Netherlands
70–80	per cent	Belgium, Spain
60–70	per cent	West Germany, Italy, Venezuela, Great Britain, Portugal
40–60	per cent	Austria, Canada
20–40	per cent	India, Mexico, Sweden, Denmark
1–20	per cent	Japan, Australia, Norway

SOURCE: First National City Bank, New York, *Monthly Economic Letter*, January 1967.

Countries whose governments usually have a conservative inclination tend to hold a high proportion of their reserves in gold. These countries usually favor 'fiscal responsibility', support anti-inflationary policy measures and tolerate fairly high levels of unemployment. More progressive countries, like the Scandinavian countries, take a dim view on holdings of gold, 'that barbarous relic', and have a low proportion of their foreign reserves in gold.

The price of gold played an important role in the discussions about a return to a gold standard. The price of $35 an ounce had been set in 1935. Economists and politicians who wanted a return to a gold standard, or who wanted gold to play a more prominent role, argued for an increase in the price of gold. This debate was especially intense in the 1960s. The French, especially, argued for an increase in the price of gold. If the price were increased from $35 to $70 an ounce, it would double the value of the gold stock and lead to an increase in world liquidity. The United States, for instance, held gold worth roughly $10 billion in 1968. At the same time, the outstanding American liabilities amounted roughly to $20 billion. If the price of gold doubled, the value of the U.S. gold stock would cover its liabilities. The U.S. government could then use its gold stock to pay off its liabilities and the world could return to a pure gold standard. This was the French argument. Anyway, the expectation that a world devaluation might occur and that the price of gold might increase caused countries to hold gold.

Already by 1968 foreign holdings of dollars had become so large that the dollar was no longer *de facto* convertible into gold. The largest surplus country in Europe, West Germany, accepted an American request not to demand conversion of its dollars into gold. The gold crisis which occurred in 1968 thus led to the establishment of a two-tier gold market. This meant that in dealings between the central banks, the old price of $35 an ounce still applied. At the same time, a free market was established. In those countries where private ownership of gold was permitted, markets for dealings in gold were established and the determination of the price of gold was left to market forces. After 1968 the world was no longer on a *gold reserve* standard. It had shifted over to a *dollar* standard. No central bank could rely on the United States to exchange its dollars for gold. It became, in fact, a matter of negotiation. This is demonstrated by the fact that major decreases in the U.S. gold stock did not take place after 1968.

The stresses on the international monetary system remained, however, and the previously feeble economic health of the system took a sharp turn for the worse in 1971, when very large outflows of dollars from the United States occurred. On 15 August 1971 President Nixon declared that the dollar was no longer convertible into gold.

In order to understand more fully the development leading up to the inconvertibility of the dollar it is necessary to consider the role of the dollar under the Bretton Woods system.

THE DOLLAR AND THE U.S. BALANCE OF PAYMENTS

The United States had a very strong competitive position in the world economy at the end of the Second World War. This contributed to a very substantial surplus in the country's balance of payments. The strong external position was founded upon a very strong balance of trade. The United States had for a long time been exporting more than it imported. This was especially the case in the late 1940s.

During these years, the United States had a surplus in its balance of trade and services of over $8 billion a year. A surplus of this size could not be maintained for long. Once Western Europe and Japan had built up their damaged economies, their import surpluses decreased. An important correction of cost levels between some of the leading industrial countries also took place in 1949, when the most important countries in Western Europe, including Britain, France and the Scandinavian countries, devalued their currencies by roughly 30 per cent. The United States still had a substantial surplus on its balance of trade and services throughout the 1950s, a surplus that continued until the beginning of the 1970s.

Government transfers also played an important role. In the immediate postwar years the United States launched the Marshall Aid programme to help the Western European countries rebuild their economies. In the 1950s the emphasis shifted to military assistance. In the era of the containment policy practised by the Eisenhower administration, half of the government transfers consisted of military aid and half of loans and aid for civilian purposes. Toward the end of the 1960s the emphasis on military aid increased in connection with the war in Vietnam. However, the balance-of-payments statistics hardly reflect the war effort since the Pentagon disregarded the principles of comparative advantage, by, for example, providing the soldiers with American goods, even cans of beer!

The United States also had an outflow of private capital that partially offset the surplus on current account. The magnitude of this outflow of capital is given in Table 29.3. The outflow of private capital from the United States was fairly limited until 1955. Then a change took place, and during the latter half of the 1950s it increased to over $3 billion annually. It was primarily American investment in Western Europe that increased sharply. We have discussed some of the

TABLE 29.3

	1947-9	1951-6	1958-62	1963-6	1967-71
Balance of trade and services	8.1	2.4	3.4	6.8	2.3
Balance of transfers	−4.3	−2.6	−2.4	−2.8	−3.1
Balance on current account	3.8	−0.2	1.0	4.0	−0.8
Balance of long-term capital	−2.7	−1.0	−2.8	−5.2	−3.8
Basic balance	1.1	−1.2	−1.8	−1.2	−4.6
Balance on short-term capital and errors and omissions	0	0.1	−0.7	0	−3.5
Balance of payments	1.1	−1.1	−2.5	−1.2	−8.1

SOURCES: United Nations, *International Financial Statistics;* and *Statistical Abstract of the United States.*

reasons for this increase in Chapter 21. Here we can add that the establishment of the European Economic Community, the easing of exchange restrictions, and the return to convertibility, plus a climate buoyant with profitable expectations, all made for a rapid increase of American investment in Europe. American investment abroad continued during the 1960s. The main recipients, Canada and Western Europe, received roughly two-thirds of the investments.

During the immediate post-war years, the huge surplus on the balance of trade and services was partially offset by government transfers, while the net outflow of private capital was small. However, the United States still had a surplus in its balance of payments of about $1 billion. This situation put a great strain on the economies of Western Europe. They had large deficits in their external balances which caused them to lose already low reserves of foreign currency. The situation would in all probability have led to a collapse of the international trading system had it not been for the aid from the American government, which was very substantial during these years.

At the beginning of the 1950s, a change took place. The American surplus on the balance of trade and services started to decrease; it was less than $5 billion. At the same time, large government transfers and private investments implied large negative transfer and capital balances. This meant that the surplus in the American balance of payments was transformed into a deficit. The average deficit up to 1956 was not very large; it amounted to roughly $1 billion per year.

The American deficit during this period caused no worries. On the contrary, it was regarded as essential for the proper functioning of the international monetary system. The most important of the U.S. trading partners, the countries of Western Europe and Japan, showed a rapid economic growth, and world trade also grew quickly. International liquidity was necessary to finance world trade. The main reserve currency was the dollar. To help the other leading industrial

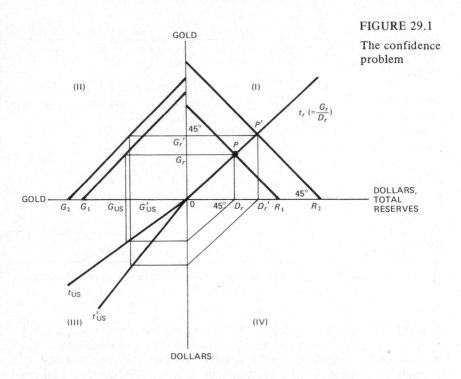

FIGURE 29.1

The confidence problem

nations build up their reserves of foreign currency, i.e. dollars, the United States had to run a deficit in its balance of payments so that its trading partners could transform part of their export surpluses into liquid dollar holdings. This was what took place during the earlier part of the 1950s.

A change in this pattern occurred in 1958. The surplus on the balance of trade and services was still large, but so were government transfers. At the same time, American direct investment abroad, especially in Western Europe, increased sharply to over $3 billion. The deficit in the balance of payments therefore increased to about $3 billion.

In 1958, some Western European countries also started to acquire gold instead of dollars, and the United States lost about $2.3 billion-worth. This greatly disturbed parts of the American business and financial community. The outflow of gold focused attention on the underlying cause, the deficit in the American balance of payments.

That deficit persisted during the 1960s. The picture was remarkably stable during the first half of the decade. A surplus in the balance of trade and services of $7 billion was offset by government transfers of some $3 billion, to which a net outflow of private capital of more than $5 billion had to be added. The U.S. balance of payments continued to weaken during the latter half of the 1960s. In particular, the trade balance showed a persistent deterioration. Capital flows were somewhat volatile, but there could be no doubt that the reserve position of the dollar weakened as domestic inflation in the United States started to make itself felt in connection with the escalation of the Vietnam war.

The outflow of gold continued. At the beginning of the 1950s, the value of the American gold stock amounted to $25 billion. By 1968 it had sunk to $10 billion. This year also marked the end of the *de facto* convertibility of the dollar into gold.

The problems which were inherent in the Bretton Woods system became acute at the end of the 1960s. One of the problems concerned the lack of confidence in the dollar. Another problem arose from the question of *seigniorage* inherent in a gold reserve standard. In order to analyse these problems we must make a slight theoretical detour. As the major goal of our study is to understand the analytics of the international monetary system, not simply to describe its factual development, the time has now come to make that detour, before coming to a description of the forces which made the system collapse.

THE PROBLEMS OF CONFIDENCE AND SEIGNIORAGE

The essential features in a gold exchange standard were that reserves consisted of gold, the basic international reserve, and a national currency, the U.S. dollar, and, furthermore, that countries maintained a fixed parity between their exchange rates. An international monetary system of this kind is inherently unstable. We have seen that the ratio of the U.S. gold reserves to those U.S. dollars held as international reserves was steadily decreasing during the 1950s and 1960s. This undermined the credibility of the system and created the confidence problem as the dollar's strength and the possibility of converting the dollar into gold at a fixed rate were increasingly questioned. The inherent contradiction of the system can be illustrated using Figure 29.1.

The first quadrant in Figure 29.1 shows the international reserve position of countries outside the United States. To start with they are at point P. They hold OG_r of their reserves in gold, and OD_r of their reserves in dollars. Total reserves amount to OR_1, expressed in dollars, as gold can be freely exchanged for dollars at the price or budget line. The rest of the world holds gold and dollars in the desired ratio t_r.

Quadrant II demonstrates how total gold holdings (OG_1) are divided between the United States and the rest of the world. Total gold reserves amounted to OG_1. OG_r was held by the rest of the world. Hence the difference, or OG_{US}, is held by the United States.

The fourth quadrant is used to transform the dollar holdings of the rest of the world by way of a 45° line in order to illustrate the international liquidity position of the United States, which is shown in the third quadrant. To begin with, the United States holds G_{US} of the gold reserves, and its outstanding dollar liabilities amount to OD_r. Its ratio of gold reserves to dollar reserve liabilities is therefore given by the slope of the line t_{US}, with reference to the vertical axis.

Now suppose that, because new gold is mined, the world's monetary gold stock increases from OG_1 to OG_2. At the same time, economic growth occurs and the total reserves demanded by the rest of the world grow by a greater proportion, from OR_1 to OR_2. If the rest of the world does not change its composition of reserves, but wants to hold gold and dollars in the same ratio t_r as before, its gold holdings will increase to OG'_r and its holdings of dollars for international reserve purposes will increase to OD'_r.

At the same time that the rest of the world increases its gold reserves, those of the United States will fall from OG_{US} to OG'_{US}. Its outstanding dollar liabilities will, however, increase from OD_r to OD'_r. Hence the U.S. ratio of gold to outstanding dollar liabilities will fall from t_{US} to t'_{US}. The upshot is that the U.S. international liquidity position will deteriorate; and it will continue to do so as long as the demand for international reserves from the rest of the world grows faster than world supplies of gold, assuming that the rest of the world does not want to change the ratio but rather wants to *keep* the initial ratio of gold to dollars.

Hence the world monetary system seemed to be built on a contradiction when parities were fixed under the gold–dollar standard. Another way of illustrating the problems inherent in the system is by reference to what has sometimes been called 'the dilemma of the deficit'. To provide the rest of the world with its desired increase in international reserves the United States must run a deficit of the same amount.

If the United States runs this deficit, its international reserve position will deteriorate, as its dollar liabilities increase while its holdings of gold fall. On the contrary, if the United States tries to take policy measures to stop the outflow of dollars and correct the deficit, the demand for liquidity by the rest of the world will not be satisfied. This might impair world trade and stop the orderly development of the world economy. This was the essence of 'the dilemma of the deficit'. We have seen that the development of the dollar position *vis-à-vis* gold occurred much as predicted by the model referred to above. The gold position of the United States deteriorated gradually from the end of the 1950s until 1968, when the dollar became in reality inconvertible while the U.S. dollar liabilities to the rest of the world steadily increased.

Another important problem inherent in the use of the dollar reserve standard was the *seigniorage* problem. Some argued that the use of the dollar as an international reserve currency gave the Americans an undue privilege. The problems connected with '*seigniorage*' are due to properties connected with the use of any paper money, be it international or not. As the problem will confront the international monetary system in the future (for instance, in connection with S.D.R.s), it can be worth our while to spell it out explicitly.

Historically, we know that commodity monies have been supplanted by paper monies in all advanced national states, the reason being that paper money can be created at no (or very low) cost.[7] It fills the need for liquidity the same way as commodity money does, but it fulfills this need at a lower social cost. From this fact stems the basic advantage of paper money over commodity money.

The social saving achieved by using paper money instead of commodity money can be approximated as the value of the resources that are freed from the need to create the increase in the stock of the commodity used as money. Let us suppose that the money-printing facility is given as a monopoly to the central bank. The central bank can now extract a monopoly profit from its printing of paper money which is approximately equal to the difference between the resources used in creating the commodity money and the resources used in printing the paper money. This monopoly profit we call *seigniorage*.[8] It is made possible because holders of money are willing to forgo the interest on their holdings of money, as they get in return a means of payment that is fully liquid. Therefore, the central bank that issues the paper money does not have to pay interest on the real resources it gets in return for the paper money. The central bank is free to invest these resources as it sees fit. This discrepancy in behaviour between private persons or institutions and the central bank is the real source of *seigniorage*.

In connection with the international monetary system, the question of *seigniorage* arises from the fact that the country issuing the reserve currency (or currencies) has a certain monopoly power to extract *seigniorage* in a way analogous to that of a central bank.

A country that wanted to increase its international liquidity by obtaining dollars could only get those dollars by creating an export surplus; i.e. it will have to give up real resources in exchange for the dollars. The rate of return on such dollar holdings is zero if the dollars are held in the form of bank-notes or currency. If they are held in another form, they might give some positive rate of return, but this would still be very low. The central bank of the United States, however, can invest at a higher rate of return the resources it has obtained in return for the bank-notes it has issued to foreigners. The *seigniorage* created by this process accrues to the United States because it is the main reserve country of the world.

Many countries objected to the possibility that the United States could extract *seigniorage* because the dollar was used as a reserve currency. President de Gaulle called this property of the system 'an exorbitant privilege' for the Americans. He thus wanted to end the system. The existence of *seigniorage* created irritation which, in the long run, helped to undermine the Bretton Woods system.

WORLD INFLATION AND THE COLLAPSE OF THE SYSTEM

We have now described the evolution of the international monetary system up to the end of the 1960s and studied the inherently unstable features of the system. The late 1960s and the early 1970s did not offer any relief to the system. On the contrary, the pressures on the system that had existed all through the 1960s mounted. The lack of confidence in the dollar became more acute as speculative movements of capital against the dollar started on an unprecedented scale.

One important feature which contributed to the system's collapse was domestic inflation in the United States. The Vietnam war escalated from 1965. First the Johnson administration and then the Nixon administration were unwilling to finance the war efforts by increased taxes. Instead, easy monetary policies were pursued and inflation followed. This in turn weakened the balance of current account during 1968–9.

The surplus countries of Europe grew more and more weary of the situation. They disliked the inflationary pressures of the American economy and feared the transmission of inflation to their own countries, brought about by the combination of fixed exchange rates and surpluses in their own balances of payments which automatically increased their money supplies. They disliked the American intervention in Vietnam and were not particularly pleased with the tough diplomatic line that the Nixon administration followed in its international economic policy. The situation deteriorated in 1970 when the American economy entered a recession. The Nixon administration tried to combat the domestic recession by lowering interest rates. At the same time, the surplus countries of Europe, especially West Germany, tried to stop domestic inflation by pursuing strict monetary policies.

The short-term capital markets of the leading industrial countries were by now well integrated. The change of interest rates therefore produced swift and large capital flows. To an already weak basic balance of around $3 billion were added heavy capital outflows of around $7 billion which led to total outflow of around $10 billion from the United States.

Part of the short-term capital flow was speculative. Speculators had an easy time during the Bretton Woods system as options became 'one way'. Governments with overvalued currencies did not want to depreciate their currencies until forced to do so. Overvalued currencies, like the dollar in 1971, therefore came under extra strain from speculation at a time when everyone knew that a change in parity could only go in one direction.

The outflow of dollars had its counterpart in an inflow of dollars to West Germany and an upward pressure on the German mark. Speculators became more and more anxious to change dollars into marks. The first week of May 1971 saw heavy trading in marks and dollars and the German Bundesbank had to absorb over $2 billion in three days of trading. Trading was then suspended and the Frankfurt foreign exchange market was closed. When the foreign exchange markets opened again the following week, the German Bundesbank had to let the mark float, while the Austrian schilling and the Swiss franc were revalued by 5 and 7 per cent respectively.

However, the speculation against the dollar did not stop. The basic deficit in the U.S. balance of payments (including the current account and long-term capital flows) increased to over $10 billion in 1971. The outflow of short-term capital reached gigantic proportions. Including errors and omissions, roughly $20 billion left the United States in 1971, leaving the country with an over-all deficit of around $30 billion. Several factors brought the situation to a climax in 1971. The confidence problem was not solved; on the contrary, it was obvious that the dollar was overvalued since the deficits in the U.S. balance of current account persisted and, if anything, grew worse. The integration of the world economy in general, and of the capital markets especially, laid the system open to speculation and other various types of disturbances. Firms, especially the large multinational corporations, could, and did, move huge funds around in pursuit of short-run gains. During the 1950s and the early part of the 1960s the central banks had been able to stave off speculation against any single currency by cooperation. But by the beginning of the 1970s the system had become much more vulnerable. These, and the earlier described long-term forces operating in the system, finally took their toll. If one wants to pick a day for the final collapse of the system, one can choose 15 August 1971, the day when President Nixon formally declared that the dollar was no longer even formally convertible into gold.

AN APPRAISAL OF THE BRETTON WOODS SYSTEM

We have looked at some of the shortcomings of the Bretton Woods system. In spite of these, it would be a mistake to conclude that it had been a miserable failure. The 1950s and the 1960s showed a very rapid expansion of international trade. The monetary arrangements could hardly be said to have hampered the development of international trade and investment during this period.

Some of the strong points of the system can easily be mentioned. Compared with the interwar years, the amount of monetary cooperation and rational consideration shown for one another's problems was impressive. Until the mid-1960s the system functioned reasonably well. International liquidity in the form of dollars was created in ample amounts, and the strength of the U.S. economy up to that time gave no great cause for worry about the stability of the system.

One important drawback was obvious almost from the beginning: the lack of an ordinary adjustment mechanism. The I.M.F. played far too weak a role in the early years of the Bretton Woods system. Its insistence on expenditure-reducing policies as the major means for correcting external deficits was poorly founded in economic analysis and unrealistic from a policy point of view. I.M.F. strategies bore overtones too conservative for a world bent on reconstruction and expansion.

One basic flaw of the Bretton Woods system was the reluctance to use expenditure-switching policies for correcting disequilibria. Parities were kept fixed even though basic economic conditions changed. The presumption that the parities of the major currencies were never likely to change gained ground. It was generally assumed that the exchange rate of the dollar would persist unaltered, that in particular the dollar would not be devalued and that no other major currencies would be revalued. The reluctance to use expenditure-switching measures became excessive. Except for the 1949 round of adjustment, the large trading countries did not want to change the exchange rate unless they were well into a monetary crisis. The industrial countries accounted for fewer than ten exchange-rate changes from 1945 to 1971 (disregarding the 1949 adjustments). The confidence problem lurked in the background from the beginning of the 1960s. The U.S. authorities paid little attention to the problem. They preferred to take the attitude of 'benign neglect', assuming that the outflow of dollars showed a preference on the part of the surplus countries for acquiring short-term assets and that any eventual adjustments should be dealt with by the surplus countries themselves through appreciations of their currencies. As long as the United States was the natural leader of the Western World, and the hegemony of the dollar seemed to reflect prevailing and accepted economic conditions, the system worked.

The world inflation emanating from the United States in the late 1960s strained the system unduly. The inherent contradictions of the system, manifested primarily in the confidence problem, became intolerable. The increased integration of capital markets and of international business and banking caused severe disruptions exemplified by the huge flows of short-term capital in 1970-1.

Whatever its defects, the Bretton Woods system taught the leading industrial countries the art of international monetary cooperation. The I.M.F. fostered the habit of consultation, and smaller groupings of the most important countries, like the 'Group of Ten' and the 'Basle Club' became fora for important meetings to coordinate policies and guide the system. When the Bretton Woods system finally broke down in 1971 it had played a vital role for two decades of the fastest growth of international trade that the world has ever seen.

30
The present international monetary system

In the preceding chapter we studied the factors which led to the breakdown of the Bretton Woods system with its stress on fixed parities. On 15 August 1971 President Nixon declared that the dollar was no longer convertible into gold. The following days were characterized by uncertainty. American tourists abroad had difficulties exchanging dollars at all, or had to do so at very unfavorable rates. When the exchange markets were reopened, all major currencies, except the yen, were left to float. The Japanese authorities tried to keep the yen pegged but they were forced to float their currency after two weeks of heavy speculation about a Japanese revaluation.

The following months saw the first more general experience with floating rates. The system was influenced, however, by controls and official interventions. For instance, the United States had applied a 10 per cent surcharge on imports and a wage–price freeze on domestic transactions in connection with the introduction of floating rates. Many statesmen in the leading industrial countries viewed the last months of 1971 as an anomaly: they wanted to return to a system of pegged exchange rates.

THE SMITHSONIAN REALIGNMENT

Most industrial countries regarded the dollar as overvalued and wanted the U.S. authorities to devalue the dollar in terms of gold. The Americans at first rejected the idea of a devaluation. Instead, other countries could, if they wanted to, revalue their currencies against the dollar. Furthermore, U.S. representatives took a broader view on monetary reform. They wanted other countries in the Western world to take on more of the defence costs and they also wanted a discussion of certain aspects of trade policy to be included in talks on monetary reform.

Other countries preferred to concentrate on monetary matters alone and to take a more piecemeal approach. At a meeting between President Nixon and the French President Pompidou the ground was cleared for negotiations.

The leading industrial nations forming the so-called 'Group of Ten' met at the Smithsonian Institution in Washington on 18 and 19 December 1971.[1] The strivings of the major industrial countries toward a new system of stable exchange rates resulted in the *Smithsonian realignment*. The United States devalued the dollar in terms of gold by 8 per cent. The Japanese yen was revalued by 17 per cent and the German mark by 14 per cent. Hence an important adjustment of the leading currencies was made.

The Smithsonian agreement also widened the permissible band of movements of the exchange rates to 2.25 per cent above or below the new parities of 'central rates'. This was an application of 'the band proposal' which meant that the exchange rates should be allowed to vary within a broader band than was permitted under the earlier I.M.F. rules.

The change of parities and the widened band were both steps in the direction of a needed adjustment of exchange rates. The Bretton Woods system had suffered for want of an effective adjustment mechanism. The changes made in the name of the Smithsonian realignment were steps in the right direction. The dollar had been overvalued and the yen and the mark had been undervalued; hence the changes of their parities brought them closer to equilibrium values. The possibility for each currency to fluctuate 4.5 per cent between an upper and a lower limit was also a significant improvement toward increased flexibility. President Nixon, under whose auspices the meeting at the Smithsonian Institution had taken place, referred to the realignment of December 1971 as 'the greatest monetary agreement in history'. But, alas, this turned out to be not quite true.

The agreement lasted only fourteen months. Had steps of the same nature been taken earlier and more frequently during the 1960s, the Bretton Woods system might have lasted longer. Now, even the Smithsonian realignment had primarily the character of a rearguard action to postpone the *coup de grâce* of the system of fixed exchange rates. We know that very heavy capital flows occurred during 1970 and 1971, when $30 billion left the United States. The Smithsonian agreement left the other currencies pegged to a dollar that no longer could be converted into gold. The massive capital flows had also created an 'overhang' of dollars held by various foreign central banks, firms and institutions. This situation made the new system potentially very unstable. In order to understand the nature of this instability it is now appropriate to study the nature of the international capital flows and the development of the international capital market which has taken place since the 1960s.

SHORT-TERM CAPITAL FLOWS AND THE EURO-DOLLAR MARKET

We have seen how very large amounts of capital, 'hot money', could be moved internationally in a matter of a few days. Before the floating of the German mark in May 1971, $2 billion flowed into West Germany during three days in May. In the middle of August the same year, $4 billion flowed into foreign central banks when fears of a dollar devaluation became acute.

The basic reasons for these massive movements of funds were either that firms and other economic agents wanted to protect their funds against possible devaluations or that they wanted to make easy speculative gains because of currency revaluations. One inherent weakness in a system of fixed exchange rates is that speculation tends to become a sure bet, a one-way option.

An important role in the international monetary system was played by the increasing integration of capital markets. Here the rise of the so-called *euro-dollar market* was an interesting phenomenon.

The causes for the existence and growth of the euro-dollar market have been the subject of heated discussion. Economists and bankers tend to have very divergent views about both what the essence of the euro-dollar market is and what its importance has been. We will try to point out some of the essential characteristics of the euro-dollar market.

A basic reason for the existence of the euro-dollar market is the fact that the dollar is a *vehicle currency*. The dollar is the vehicle for financing international trade and investment. Over 35 per cent of world trade, currently running close to $500 billion, is financed in dollars, and an even larger share of trade is denominated in dollars. Firms, institutions and banks have seen many advantages in having part of international trade and investment serviced by a banking system which is working under the most liberal conditions possible and where state interventions and restrictions are few.

Euro-dollars developed as a result of a wish to avoid existing restrictive practices, especially those arising from potential international tensions. In the early post-war years the Soviet Union and various Eastern European countries held their dollar balance in U.S. banks. Because they feared reprisals or blockades during the Cold War, these countries shifted their deposits to European banks that were willing to accept deposits and grant loans denominated in dollars. Such dollar deposits became known as *euro-dollars*.

Both in the United States and in various countries of Western Europe banks were subjected to restrictive practices which were either self-imposed or sponsored by the government. The Federal Reserve System in the United States had imposed the so-called *Regulation Q,* which meant that member banks could not pay interest rates above a certain level on time deposits. Whenever these ceilings became effective, euro-dollar deposits became attractive. As they were unregulated and could pay higher interest rates, European banks received funds and the euro-dollar market expanded.

Banks in several Western European countries used to engage in monopolistic practices. They colluded in upholding lending rates, while they paid substantially lower rates on deposits. As the euro-dollar market grew, its possibilities became more manifest. It appeared as a modern capital market governed by principles of competition, while the old national capital markets were riddled by monopolistic elements and restrictive practices.

Due to the high interest rates on commercial loans in many European countries, and because competition drove down the rates in the euro-dollar market, exporters turned increasingly to the latter market in order to finance trade. As the knowledge and experience of the euro-dollar market increased, many firms also borrowed money for their domestic investments.

The stability of exchange rates increased the importance of the euro-dollar market. The European banks ran hardly any risks in converting national currencies to dollars and lent dollars even for domestic purposes. If they wanted to, they could always cover themselves and purchase dollars in the forward market. During the 1950s and the beginning of the 1960s short-term rates were high in both Italy and West Germany; the banks would not make short-term loans for less than 6 per cent. The foreign currency lending and borrowing were not subject to any restrictions of this kind. Hence German and Italian firms engaged in foreign trade found it advantageous to have both international and domestic needs financed in the euro-dollar market. Competition among the banks increased and interest rates were brought down to 3.5 per cent.

Another, more debatable reason for the growth of the euro-dollar market was the deficit in the U.S. balance of payments. Some maintain that deficits

TABLE 30.1

External positions of reporting European banks in dollars and certain other foreign currencies (in millions of U.S. dollars)

	Liabilities			Assets		
	Dollars	Other foreign currencies	Total	Dollars	Other foreign currencies	Total
1964	9,650	2,570	12,220	9,000	3,030	12,030
1965	11,390	2,820	14,210	11,580	3,550	15,130
1966	14,770	3,570	18,340	16,070	3,840	19,910
1967	18,120	4,150	22,270	19,890	4,570	24,460
1968	26,870	6,660	33,530	30,430	6,980	37,410
1969	46,200	10,170	56,370	47,630	10,190	57,820
1970	58,700	15,870	74,570	60,370	17,880	78,250
1971	70,750	26,980	97,730	71,500	28,630	100,130
1972	96,730	35,200	131,930	98.000	33,840	131,840
1973	131,380	60,720	192,100	132,110	55,510	187,620
1974	156,430	64,340	220,770	156,230	58,940	215,170
1975	189,470	69,200	258,670	190,180	67,950	258,130

SOURCE: Bank for International Settlements, *Annual Reports,* Basel.

caused the outflow of dollars that created the euro-dollar market. This is, however, hardly the case. The presence of U.S. deficits was neither a sufficient nor a necessary prerequisite for the creation of euro-dollars. It could also be demonstrated that even in a year like 1968, when the United States had a surplus in its balance of payments, the euro-dollar market increased by the substantial amount of almost $9 billion. Hence it is hardly correct to argue that the American deficits *caused* the euro-dollar market to expand. A more basic reason was the fact that the dollar was a vehicle currency.

However, one could argue that the availability of dollars for euro-dollar purposes was enhanced by the U.S. deficits. The growth of the euro-dollar market was phenomenal. Table 30.1 gives an illustration of the rapid increase in the creation of euro-dollars which took place, especially in the 1960s.

Another much debated issue was whether there existed a credit multiplier in the euro-dollar market of the same type that we know from domestic credit systems. Let us assume that the banks in a national banking system receive deposits of a certain amount R. Furthermore, they have to abide by a stipulation (implemented by the central bank) that they hold a certain fraction r as the reserve requirement. The possible scope for credit expansion of the banking system will then be $1r \times R$. In other words, if the required reserve ratio is $1/5$, the credit multiplier will be 5.[2]

Does an analogous credit multiplier exist in the euro-dollar market so that the market, as it were, can feed on itself? Opinions vary. It is hardly possible to argue for the existence of a euro-dollar credit multiplier in any strict sense of the word. There are no well-specified reserve assets held by banks in the euro-dollar system. Nor do these banks adhere to any uniform reserve practices or obey any stable reserve requirements. Hence there is no simple way to establish a quantitative value for a multiplier.

What is at issue is, essentially, the amount of leakage that occurs. Will the euro-banking system act as a commerical banking system so that a loan granted to a customer will automatically create other deposits? Or will the euro-banks be more like a savings bank or a building society so that an initial deposit will increase the lending capacity by the same amount but not create any secondary effects? The prevailing opinion denies that the multiplier effects could be very large. Most commentators seem to agree that the euro-banking system is not to be compared with a national banking system when it comes to credit creation. The system is quite fragmented because of its international nature, and there is a widespread interaction between euro-dollar systems and the national banking systems so that a loan granted by a euro-dollar bank often ends up as a deposit in a national bank after having been converted into a national currency. Essentially, the question of the credit multiplier in the euro-dollar system is an empirical question. Unfortunately, there does not, to our knowledge, exist any authoritative empirical investigation of the power of credit creation of the euro-dollar system.

The various central banks play an important role in the operation of the system. If they do redeposit the dollars that they obtain from the euro-dollar market back into the system, this can greatly enhance the possibilities of credit creation. An even more important issue is the role played by the euro-dollar system in the integration of national capital markets and in the influence on the various countries' abilities to pursue independent monetary policies.

We know from Chapter 28 that in a world with fixed exchange rates where capital is internationally mobile, monetary policy loses its power to achieve policy aims. It can be used only to control the reserves of international currency, not to affect the level of domestic activity. The moral is that fiscal policy should be used for stabilizing the domestic activity level while monetary policy should be used to maintain equilibrium in the balance of payments.

As the theoretical argument is simple, we can briefly restate it here. In a two-country world we know that equilibrium requires excess savings in country I to be equal to both a surplus in the trade balance of country I and an excess of investments over savings in country II:

$$I_1 - S_1 = M_1 - X_1 = S_2 - I_2 \tag{30.1}$$

where I and S denote investment and saving respectively, M and X stand for imports and exports, and where subscripts denote countries. Let us now assume that the authorities in country I try to increase the money supply by, for instance, purchasing securities in the domestic market. This will reduce the interest rates and induce an outflow of capital. The authorities will now have to sell foreign currency in order to avoid a depreciation of the exchange rate. This means that the domestic money supply again decreases. A new equilibrium cannot be reached until the interest-rate differential between the two countries has been eliminated. A change in the composition of the monetary base is thus caused so that domestic assets will be substituted for foreign exchange, but the over-all credit base will be unchanged. Hence monetary policy, provided that capital mobility exists and that exchange rates are fixed, cannot influence the activity level.

The European milieu from the beginning of the 1960s up to 1973, when floating exchange rates became common, corresponded essentially to the scenario described above. The various central banks had great difficulties controlling the money supply. A case in point was West Germany. During a very long period the country had a trade surplus. In order to avoid inflationary impulses stemming from the trade surplus, West Germany needed to pursue a restrictive monetary policy which implied high interest rates. These high interest rates, however, induced capital inflows into the country and counteracted the government's attempts at restricting the monetary base. There were other, more sophisticated policies, which the German central bank could use to control the money supply.[3] However, it was very difficult for central banks to control monetary policy effectively as long as fixed exchange rates prevailed.

We saw in the preceding chapter how speculative forces built up to become so strong as to virtually destroy the system in 1971. The same tensions continued after 1971 as well. The Smithsonian realignment only lasted fourteen months. It can be argued that it was not the existence of the euro-dollar market *per se* which gave the final *coup de grâce* to the Bretton Woods system. Table 30.1 above illustrates, however, the enormous magnitudes which euro-dollar deposits had reached by the beginning of the 1970s. Indeed, the scope for speculation was large. It also seems that even some central banks at times tried to take advantage of the euro-dollar market by placing funds there. By the beginning of the 1970s it was clear that the central banks could no longer control the international monetary system and stave off speculative attacks against single currencies the way they had been able to during the 1950s and the early 1960s.[4]

THE CRISIS OF 1973

The same types of forces which had been at work and which finally led the United States to leave the gold standard in 1971 persisted. The Vietnam war continued. The U.S. money supply grew at a high rate in 1972, and inflationary impulses began to be felt in the U.S. economy. The par values of currencies which had been fixed by the Smithsonian Agreement of December 1971 began to be strained and some currencies began more and more to look overvalued while others were felt to be undervalued.

Among the E.E.C. currencies the Italian lira was the weakest. Italy was plagued by a flight of capital which took various forms, among them an export of bank-notes. This suggested that the lira was overvalued. Italy had, at the same time, a surplus in its foreign trade. The country tried to solve its problems by introducing a two-tier market in January 1973, with a 'commercial' lira for trading purposes and a 'financial' lira for capital movements. Immediately upon the introduction of the two-tier market, the 'financial' lira fell 6-7 per cent below the par value established by the Smithsonian realignment. Italian banks tried to cover themselves by buying Swiss francs, and the demand for Swiss francs increased, from this and other various sources. The Swiss authorities felt that they could no longer absorb the inflow of foreign currencies, especially dollars. On 23 January 1973 they gave up their support of the dollar and floated the Swiss franc.

Unrest started to spread to several countries. Toward the end of January 1973, the dollar weakened at the exchanges in Frankfurt, Paris, London, Tokyo and Zurich. The basic problem was that the international monetary system could not find ways to adjust the various countries balances of payments in the face of conflicting policy aims. The countries insisted on pursuing independent monetary policies which could not be reconciled with a system of fixed exchange rates. In some countries price and wage levels rose slowly. In others they rocketed sky high. The differences in price levels tended to create lasting deficits and surpluses. Some currencies were weak, while others were strong.

The field was now left open for speculators to move in. They started to sell the weak currencies and buy the strong ones. They could hardly lose under a system of fixed exchange rates as speculation tended to become a riskless, one-way option. The institutional set-up with the euro-dollar market naturally facilitated speculation. Toward the end of January 1973, speculation started to rise dramatically. Multinational corporations prudently switched out of dollars. During the last week of January the central banks in Europe and Japan absorbed $1 billion. For the time being, the various authorities did nothing. To the contrary, some U.S. congressmen argued that the dollar was 'patently overvalued'. During the first week of February 1973, speculation against the dollar became massive. The German Bundesbank absorbed $6-7 billion in those seven days. It became clear that the situation was untenable and the major exchange markets were closed. On 12 February the U.S. authorities announced that the dollar would be devalued by 10 per cent against the S.D.R. It has been estimated that the speculators made net profits of at least $5 billion during the crisis years 1967-73. These loses were born by the various central banks in their struggle to defend existing parities. The situation in the foreign exchange markets was still nervous. After the devaluation of the dollar, the German Bundesbank was able to sell a substantial part of its dollar holdings. But suspicions about a further devaluation of the dollar lingered on. The speculation against the dollar returned with renewed strength toward the end of February and the beginning of March 1973. On 1 March the German Bundesbank had to buy another $2.5 billion. That night the major foreign exchanges were closed while the finance ministers of the E.E.C. countries started to ponder the situation. Finally, on 11 March, the E.E.C. countries, i.e. West Germany, France, Belgium, Luxemburg, the Netherlands and Denmark, agreed to float their currencies jointly. West Germany decided at the same time to appreciate the mark by 3 per cent. Sweden and Norway, though not members of the E.E.C., decided to join the common European float. By March 1973, the Bretton Woods system had finally come to an end and a new era of floating exchange rates was born. Figures illustrate how the exchange rates have varied during the 1970s. As can be seen, the changes have been especially marked since 1973.

We remember that part of the Smithsonian agreement was 'the band proposal', which permitted a currency to fluctuate 2.25 per cent around its central rate. However, in 1972 the E.E.C. countries decided to limit the

FIGURE 30.1

Exchange rates of major currencies against the Dollar
(percentage devisions with respect to dollar parities of October 1967
end of month figures)*

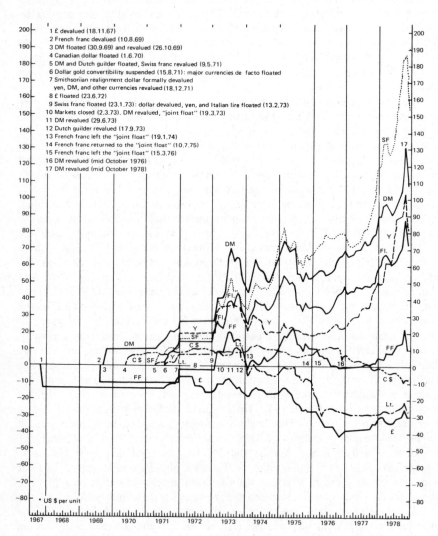

1 £ devalued (18.11.67)
2 French franc devalued (10.8.69)
3 DM floated (30.9.69) and revalued (26.10.69)
4 Canadian dollar floated (1.6.70)
5 DM and Dutch guilder floated, Swiss franc revalued (9.5.71)
6 Dollar gold convertibility suspended (15.8.71): major currencies de facto floated
7 Smithsonian realignment dollar formally devalued
  yen, DM, and other currencies revalued (18.12.71)
8 £ floated (23.6.72)
9 Swiss franc floated (23.1.73): dollar devalued, yen, and Italian lire floated (13.2.73)
10 Markets closed (2.3.73). DM revalued, "joint float" (19.3.73)
11 DM revalued (29.6.73)
12 Dutch guilder revalued (17.9.73)
13 French franc left the "joint float" (19.1.74)
14 French franc returned to the "joint float" (10.7.75)
15 French franc left the "joint float" (15.3.76)
16 DM revalued (mid October 1976)
17 DM revalued (mid October 1978)

* US $ per unit

Reproduced from *O.E.C.D. Economic Outlook,* Paris, December 1978.

FIGURE 30.2
Effective exchange rates
(percentage changes from 1st quarter 1970, weekly averages of daily figures)

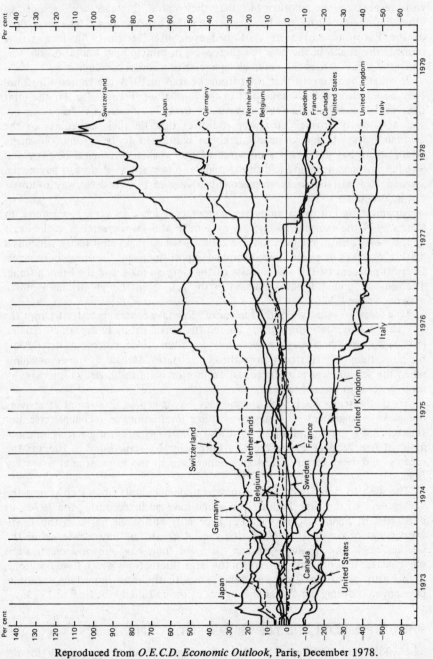

Reproduced from *O.E.C.D. Economic Outlook*, Paris, December 1978.

fluctuations of their currencies relative to each other to a smaller band. This arrangement was called 'the snake in the tunnel'. It meant that the E.E.C. currencies were tied together and could only fluctuate with narrow limits with respect to one another but that they could fluctuate with respect to other currencies within the limits given by the band proposal. The joint float of the European currencies continued even after March 1973. It was now termed 'the snake in the lake', as there was, in principle no limitation on how much the E.E.C. currencies could change relative to other currencies.

It should be observed that right from the start in 1973, the United Kingdom, Italy and Ireland did not take part in the joint float. France also left the joint float in 1974. Hence the 'currency snake' in 1977 consists of West Germany and a group of smaller European countries that tie their currencies to the German mark. As the German mark has continued to be strong, the snake arrangement has put a stress on some of the smaller currencies. Norway and Sweden, for instance, have had substantial deficits in their balances of payments. Sweden also left the snake arrangement in August 1977 and Norway followed suit in December 1978.

Strivings for European monetary cooperation have, however, continued. In March 1979 the European Monetary System (E.M.S.) was created.[5] At the heart of this new form of cooperation is the European currency unit (*ecu*), which is a 'basket' currency of a unit of account made up of the major European currencies. Over 50 per cent of the *ecu* consists of the German mark and the French franc. The English pound is also included in the *ecu*, even though Britain is not a member of the E.M.S.

One essential intention of the European Monetary System is to try to limit the internal exchange-rate movements among the participating European currencies. Hence the members have agreed not to allow their currencies to deviate by more than 2.25 per cent from the central rates, defined as those prevailing when the scheme was introduced; an exemption is Italy, whose lira fluctuate by up to 6 per cent from these rates.

To this extent, the E.M.S. scheme may be viewed as an attempt at reviving the snake arrangement by trying to stabilize fluctuations in exchange rates. But this scheme is more ambitious, as it also aims to establish the *ecu* as an international reserve asset and to create a European Monetary Fund to support the scheme and help foster European cooperation in the international monetary field.

The wish to stabilize currencies may be understandable when seen against the background of the large fluctuations which have occurred during the 1970s, as illustrated in Figures 30.1 and 30.2. Especially noticeable has been the downward trend of the U.S. dollar during the latter part of the decade, while the German mark, the Japanese yen and the Swiss franc have shown strong upward movements. It is not easy to explain the large fluctuations which have occurred. Before turning to that topic, we will deal with the most important economic phenomenon during the 1970s, the effects of the so-called 'oil crisis' of 1973.

THE OIL PROBLEM AND THE TRANSFER OF CAPITAL

The 1950s and 1960s were decades of prosperity and steady growth for the

TABLE 30.2

Posted prices and typical producer–government receipts per barrel of exported oil (in U.S. dollars)*

	Posted prices, f.o.b. Ras Tanura	Saudi Arabia, government take of royalties and taxes
December 1965	1.80	0.83
December 1970	1.80	0.88
June 1971	2.29	1.26
January 1972	2.48	1.45
January 1973	2.59	1.52
October 1973	3.01	1.77
January 1974	11.65	7.00

*The quality is Arabian light crude, $34°$ gravity.

SOURCES: *Petroleum Press Service,* November 1973 and February 1974; and Foster Associates, *Energy Prices 1960–73, A Report to the Energy Policy Project of the Ford Foundation,* Cambridge, Mass., 1974, p.18.

industrial countries. Most of the less-developed countries also had high rates of growth. The world economy of the 1970s has, however, been plagued by severe problems. The pace of development has slackened and unemployment has increased. The expansion of world trade has stopped; the years 1974–5 even witnessed a decline in the volume of international trade.

Some of the disturbances had their origins in Nature. The monsoon rains did not arrive as expected on the Indian subcontinent in 1972. A severe drought hit large parts of Africa and Asia. Even the anchovies disappeared from the shores of Peru; they used to be fished in large amounts, transformed into fishmeal and fed to broilers over a large part of the globe. Agricultural production fell, but consumption needs remained. These developments resulted in heavy price increases, and an inflationary impetus was given to the world economy. The prices of basic foodstuffs increased by 100 per cent from a stable level in 1970 to the beginning of 1974, when the peak of the boom was reached. The price of fertilizer increased by 170 per cent in the same period.

The most spectacular and the most important disturbance was, however, man-made. In connection with the Arab – Israeli war that started in October 1973, the Arab countries embargoed shipments of oil to the United States and the Netherlands. Soon after, the Organization of Petroleum Exporting Countries (OPEC) decided to increase the price of oil drastically.[6] For a long period oil price had been low and stable. World consumption of oil had increased rapidly, and oil as a source of energy had tended to outcompete other energy sources. The increase in price of a representative oil product is given in Table 30.2.

Oil prices started to increase very rapidly in October 1973. Within four months, when a new equilibrium price level was reached, oil prices had increased by almost 300 per cent. The major share of the price rise went to the governments of the oil-producing countries. The essence of the story was that the OPEC countries realized that they could increase both the price of oil and their revenues from exports of oil products by monopoly pricing. The demand for oil was inelastic. Even very large price increases would lead to only small decreases in demand. Hence price rises would entail large increases in revenues. By forming a cartel and dividing up the market, the OPEC countries could guarantee that they all would benefit from the price increase. This they did. Experience has shown that the price boosts were tenable. Oil prices have not fallen from the level they reached in 1974.

Analytically, oil has the characteristics of land, and the revenues accruing from oil can be viewed as a land rent and can best be treated within the context of a Ricardian model. The OPEC countries had been sitting on a scarce resource from which a pure land rent accrued. Before October 1973, they had not, however, realized the potential magnitude of the land rent that they could reap from the oil deposits which they controlled. The Arab – Israeli war of 1973 was the spark that enlightened them. Hence the governments of the oil-producing countries could greatly augment their revenues by reaping the land rents from the oil deposits to the full. Had a world government existed, it could have taxed away all these land rents to the benefit of all mankind. Pure land rents, as Ricardo has already taught us, have the property that they can be taxed away without any negative effects on incentives or the allocative mechanisms of the economy.

We are, however, primarily interested in the effects of the increases in oil prices on the world economy. One very important effect was that the increased oil prices entailed a drastic redistribution of incomes in the international economy. Before 1973, the exports of the oil-producing countries amounted to roughly $30 billion. During 1974 exports from the OPEC countries increased by about $90 billion to a total of around $120 billion. This very large increase in income for the OPEC countries was, for the most part, a pure redistribution. Their increase corresponded to a decrease in incomes for the oil-importing countries. There was no large change in quantities bought and sold, it was only a matter of revaluing exports and imports at new prices. The decrease in incomes had to be borne primarily by the large industrial countries that imported the largest quantities of oil, but many less developed countries that imported oil were also severely hit by this redistribution of income. Table 30.3 shows the development of the trade balance of the OPEC countries.

Their increase in income was so large that they could not even spend it all. Out of total income of around $120 billion in 1974, it has been estimated that the oil producers spent roughly $50 billion, while they saved $70 billion. Three different groups can be distinguished among the oil-producing countries. The first consists of Saudi Arabia and the small emirates around the Persian Gulf. They are all small countries, their joint population amounting to 12 million, but they have large oil deposits and they produce 48 per cent of the current output of oil. The second group consists of four fairly large countries, Algeria, Iran, Iraq and Venezuela. Their total population is 68 million and they provide 41 per cent of the supply of oil. The third group of the OPEC countries are Indonesia and Nigeria, two large countries with a joint population of 200 million and only 11 per cent of the current production of oil.

TABLE 30.3

World current account (in billions of U.S. dollars)

	1970	1971	1972	1973	1974	1975	1976	1977	1978	1979
Trade balance										
O.E.C.D.	8¾	10¼	9¼	8¼	-26¼	5½	-17¼	-23¼	3¾	5¾
OPEC	6½	9	10	21½	77	49½	65	61½	42½	41
Non-oil developing countries	-6	-9½	-6½	-7½	-23½	-38½	-25	-23½	-34	-40
Other	-2¾	-3	-2¾	-4¼	-10¾	-18¾	-12¾	-9	-9¼	-7¾
Total	6½	6¾	10	18	16½	-2¼	10	5¾	3	-1
Services and private transfers, net										
O.E.C.D.	3¼	5¾	6	9¾	9¼	7¼	11¼	10¼	15	16¼
OPEC	-6¾	-8¼	-7¾	-12	-15¼	-19¼	-25½	-28	-30	-32
Non-oil developing countries	-5½	-5	-4½	-5½	-9	-10	-10	-10	-10½	-11
Other	0	0	¾	1	1	¼	0	-1	-1½	-2
Total	-9	-7½	-5½	-6¾	-14	-21¾	-24¼	-28¾	-27	-28¾
Balance on goods, services and private transfers										
O.E.C.D.	12	15¾	15¼	17¾	-16¾	13	-6	-13	18¾	22
OPEC	¼	¾	2¼	9½	61¾	30¼	39½	33½	12½	9
Non-oil developing countries	-11½	-14½	-11	-13	-32½	-48½	-35	-33½	-44½	-51
Other	-2¾	-3	-2	-3¼	-9¾	-18½	-12¾	-10	-10¾	-9¾
Total	-2	-1	4½	11	2¾	-23¾	-14¼	-23	-24	-29¾
Official transfer, net										
O.E.C.D.	-5¼	-6	-7¼	-8¼	-10¾	-12¾	-12¾	-14¾	-19½	-23¼
OPEC	-¼	-¼	-½	-1½	-2½	-3	-2½	-2	-1½	-1½
Non-oil developing countries	3½	4	5	6	8	10	9	9½	10½	12
Other	0	0	0	0	0	0	0	0	0	0
Total	-2	-2¼	-2¾	-3¾	-5¼	-5¾	-6¼	-7¼	-10½	-12¾
Current balance										
O.E.C.D.	6¾	10	7¾	9½	-27½	¼	-18¾	-27½	-¾	-1¼
OPEC	-½	½	1¾	8	59¼	27¼	37	31½	11	7½
Non-oil developing countries	-8	-10½	-6	-7	-24½	-38½	-26	-24	-34	-38
Other	-2¾	-3	-2	-3¼	-9¾	-18½	-12¾	-10	-10¾	-9¾
Total	-4½	-3	1½	7¼	-2½	-29½	-20½	-30	-34½	-41½
Memorandum item										
Soviet Union and Eastern Europe	-1¼	-1	-2¼	-4	-7	-15	-11¼	-9	-9½	-8½

SOURCE: *O.E.C.D. Economic Outlook*, Paris, December 1978.

The economic problem connected with the oil crisis has much to do with the uneven distribution of income both among countries in general, and within the oil-producing countries in particular. The first group of countries will not be able to spend its entire income within the foreseeable future and savings will be consistently larger than domestic investments. The second group of countries will eventually, probably by 1990, be able to spend most of its income for domestic purposes, but they will build up substantial surpluses of savings over investments (and hence on their balances of payments) during the first years after the increase of oil prices. The third group, finally, will not have any difficulties in finding domestic investment outlets and they will simply increase domestic investments at the same rate as their increase in savings.

The large redistribution of income from oil importers to oil exporters had a tremendous impact on the world economy. During 1974, the first year in which the increase in oil prices had its full effect, incomes of the OPEC countries increased by $90 billion and their savings increased by $60 billion. The increase in savings should have led to a corresponding increase in investments. This, in turn, would have led to faster growth and to a more rapid development of the world economy. Events did not go this way. On the contrary, a slump overtook the world economy and the years 1974–5 witnessed the deepest international recession since the 1930s. To understand this course of events we have to invoke both political factors and economic theory.

The OPEC-countries stood with a savings surplus of $70 billion on a yearly basis. This had to be invested somewhere. The only group of countries which could swallow investments of this magnitude, while at the same time offering the investors a reasonable security and return on their investments, were the large industrial countries, i.e. the O.E.C.D. countries.[7] But in order for this to happen an orderly *transfer* of the investible surplus from the OPEC countries to the O.E.C.D. had to take place. Hence the world economy was confronted in 1974 with a variation of the transfer problem which we studied at some length in Chapter 21. The study of traditional transfer processes was usually linked to capital movements or reparations problems, for instances like those that occurred after the First World War. If country A had to transfer a certain sum of money to country B, this transfer of money had to be accompanied by a transfer of real resources. This gave rise to secondary problems concerning the terms of trade and the balances of payments. A successful transfer depends critically on the marginal propensities to import between the two countries. Only if the sum of the two marginal propensities, $m_a + m_b$, equaled 1.0 would a transfer be effected without any secondary repercussions on the two economies. Before the increase of oil prices the rest of the world bought oil products from the OPEC countries to the tune of $30 billion a year. In 1974 oil imports from OPEC increased to $120 billion. It was clear that this increase in imports could not be *effected* by ordinary trade chanels. If we temporarily disregard, for the sake of reasoning, a large number of less developed countries and concentrate our attention to the two main blocs, we can observe that the sum of m_{OPEC} and m_{OECD} was substantially less than 1.0. It appears that the sum of these two critical propensities was somewhere in the neighborhood of 0.5. Out of total OPEC incomes of $120 billion, roughly $50 billion were spent and $70 billion were left as savings, as an investible surplus. How could this transfer of income of $70 billion be accompanied by a transfer of real resources from the O.E.C.D. to OPEC? This was the essential question.

There was no way that an increased $90 billion-worth of resources could be shifted in the short run by way of ordinary trade flows from the O.E.C.D. countries (or, more generally, the non-OPEC countries) to OPEC. The problem had to be viewed as problem of stocks. The extra OPEC savings of $70 billion had to be invested abroad, primarily in the O.E.C.D. area. Hence a transfer of the ownership of part of the capital accumulation financed by oil money has to take place if the transfer problem which lay at the heart of the oil crisis were to be solved.

The transfer problem was also intertwined with a hot political issue: the problem of equilibrium oil prices. In early 1974 an important prerequisite for any solution to the oil problem was whether the new oil prices were feasible equilibrium prices or not. If one believed that the new prices could not be sustained in the long run, there was no hurry to try to solve the transfer problem implied in the new, higher prices. Then prices would come down and the investible surplus generated by the OPEC countries would disappear.

It became obvious that many of the political leaders of the O.E.C.D. countries wanted the oil prices to fall and believed that they *would* come down. There were also economists who argued along those lines. The government of the United States, headed by President Ford and Secretary Kissinger, was vehemently opposed to the new, high oil prices. American threats to occupy the Arab oil fields were circulated, should OPEC not be accommodating and again lower oil prices.

The oil prices did not decrease but were kept at their high 1974 level. In 1977 there was another, though relatively modest, price increase. The political tensions involved were, however, too strong to permit a rational solution to the oil crisis along the lines suggested by transfer analysis. International organizations like the I.M.F. and the World Bank tried to deal with the oil crisis. However, no clear analysis of the essence of the problem at hand emerged from international organizations; nor were any realistic plans advanced to deal with the problem. There was, alas, quite an intense discussion of what was termed the 'recycling' of petro-dollars. The I.M.F. did not, however, succeed in dealing with the transfer problem involved on anything like the scale needed. The fact that the I.M.F. only made credits available for around $12 billion during the years 1974-6 is witness to the failure of international concerted action to solve the problems involved.

The problems created by the oil crisis did not disappear just because the leading industrial nations were unwilling to deal with them by way of sensible, international cooperation built on economic analysis. Since no international solution was possible, the various nations had to deal with the problems on an individual basis as best they could. What appeared, from the point of view of the world economy, as a huge redistribution problem, appeared from the single oil-importing country's point of view as a balance-of-payments problem. Many countries ran very heavy deficits in their balances of payments in 1974 because of the increased oil prices.

The general line taken by the various countries was to deflate their economies. This created, as could be expected, the severe recession that took place in

1974-5. The United States took the lead and unemployment increased to 9 per cent in 1974-5, while G.N.P. fell by around 2 per cent a year in these two years. The rest of the O.E.C.D. countries soon followed suit, with large increases in unemployment, which reached a new record level in 1975 with 18 million people unemployed. For the total O.E.C.D. area the fall of G.N.P. during 1974-5 amounted to 3 per cent. The only two countries where unemployment did not rise were Norway and Sweden, where the deficits in the balances of payments were financed by planned imports of capital. The total welfare cost of the deflationary policies pursued by the O.E.C.D. countries can be estimated at approximately 10 per cent of their total G.N.P. (a direct loss of 3 per cent, plus the loss of normal economic growth of 3.5 per cent per year during 1974-5). In quantitative terms this loss can be estimated at roughly $400 billion, which should be compared with the sum of transfers involved, which was in the neighbourhood of $40 billion a year, between OPEC and the O.E.C.D. countries.

It should be added that even though the transfer problem posed by the increase in oil prices was large, it was in no way unmanageable. The amount of capital which would have to be transferred from the OPEC countries to the O.E.C.D. countries from 1974 to 1980 can be approximated at $250-300 billion. There is no doubt that this sum could be invested profitably in the O.E.C.D. area with the ownership of a corresponding amount of investments (in bonds, shares, etc.) transferred to the OPEC countries. It is absolutely necessary that such transfers be planned and well-organized. The figure $250-300 billion might appear large, but it has to be put into its proper perspective: it only amounts to perhaps 5 per cent of all bonds and shares in the O.E.C.D. countries, or around 2 per cent of their total fixed assets. Only an arrangement along these lines can resolve the oil-importing countries' balance-of-payments problems without jeopardizing the potentional growth of the world economy. Traditional deflationary policies will, as has been demonstrated, lead to secondary burdens that have far more devastating effects on the world economy than the adjustments needed to take care of the original problem.

One of the important consequences of the oil crisis was the recession that followed in its wake. This recession has already had a great impact on the world economy in lowering rates of growth and creating surpluses in the OPEC countries which seem to have a quality of persistence. New disturbances have also occurred, especially in connection with the overthrow of the Shah of Iran in 1978-9, which have tended to push oil prices up again. There is a substantial uncertainty about future oil exports and oil prices. The surpluses are especially concentrated in a small group of OPEC countries which we referred to above, and which is dominated by Saudi Arabia. The deficits are also concentrated. The large industrial countries, especially the United States, Japan and West Germany, have only minor or no deficits, while some other countries, like Britain, France, Italy, Spain, Yugoslavia, Norway and Sweden, carry large deficits. Some of the larger countries have avoided deficits by running their economies at low capacity and fairly high levels of unemployment, while others tend to have undervalued currencies. A large number of less developed countries have also been severely hit by the oil crisis and have been running large deficits. The burden of adjustment has fallen unduly on countries with a weak economic standing.

The need for an orderly operation of the transfer mechanism is still great if the world economy is to adjust to the new circumstances and again develop at the pace it maintained during the two decades preceding the oil crisis.

It was probably advantageous for the workings of the international monetary system that floating exchange rates had become common when the oil crisis broke. It is hardly possible to make any more precise evaluation of how much the system of floating rates may have facilitated the necessary adjustment. Opinions vary, and will continue to vary. It is likely that the effects on both deficits and activity levels would have been even more severe if a system of pegged exchange rates had continued, However, adjustments obviously did not become automatic merely because of the floating rates. For better or worse, the governments tried to manage the float despite their lack of complete faith in the system. The picture has been complicated further by the fact that other factors, like changing preferences for assets and speculation, have influenced exchange rates. The time has now come for a discussion of asset preferences and speculation before we move on to an analysis of the problems connected with the managed float.

ASSET PREFERENCES, SPECULATION, AND MOVEMENTS OF EXCHANGE RATES

We have seen that the forces that brought about the more general floating in 1973 were very strong. It was quite obvious that the international economy could no longer sustain a system of fixed exchange rates, at least not for the time being. However, while objections in principle against a system of floating rates could not be raised, serious doubts about the day-to-day operation of the system remained. Hence, how well the system performed, especially in terms of how large the fluctuations were, became an important question.

Figures 30.1 and 30.2 have already demonstrated that the movements since 1973 have been considerable. Of special importance have been the fluctuations between the dollar and the European snake currencies, headed by the German mark. The German mark reached a peak at the beginning of July 1973 that was 31.2 per cent above its central rate as determined by the devaluation in February. It is true that two small revaluations in March and June (together amounting to 8.7 per cent) had contributed to this result but that does not affect the basic point involved. The French franc and the other E.E.C. currencies also followed suit, even though the swings here were more moderate. By the beginning of July 1973 these currencies had risen roughly 20 per cent above their levels in February. In late July and August, this tendency started to reverse. By the middle of January 1974, the German mark and the Swiss franc had fallen by over 20 per cent against the dollar. The Swiss franc, to take a conspicuous example, fell by 13 per cent during the month of August 1973 alone. The German mark again started to increase substantially during the latter half of 1974 and the first months of 1975. There was a rising trend in the German mark especially, and the other European snake currencies to a smaller degree, against the dollar, but that trend was overshadowed by the large short-run fluctuations. The currency with the clearest appreciating trend against the dollar was the Swiss franc; it appreciated by over 50 per cent from the beginning of 1973 to the end of 1976. But even in the case of the Swiss franc, the fluctuations were large indeed.

The Japanese yen, the English pound and the Italian lira, on the other hand, tended to depreciate against the dollar during these years. Even these currencies experienced marked fluctuations. To sum up; many examples can be found of how exchange rates have fluctuated up and down by 20 per cent or more within a few months. Extreme short-run fluctuations have also occurred as exchange rates have changed by 7-8 per cent in a few weeks. Day-to-day changes of one or two per centage points have also been common. These fluctuations have seemed erratic and difficult to explain. Even by historic standards they must be deemed large. While historic experiences of fluctuating rates are not very prevalent, some examples do exist. The Austrian gulden fluctuated against the pound sterling in the years 1879-91. During this period the maximum yearly fluctuations amounted to 7.7 per cent, while the average monthly fluctuation did not exceed 1.7 per cent. The Canadian dollar fluctuated in the years 1950-61. Its average annual range of fluctuation against the U.S. dollar was 4.17 per cent.

The large fluctuations of the major exchange rates in recent years cannot be explained by real economic factors; and they cannot be explained in terms of the purchasing-power parity or the monetary approach to the balance of payments. Technical progress and changes in demand have not been sufficiently volatile to explain the fluctuations of exchange rates; and they cannot be explained in terms of changes in money supplies and price levels. It is not easy to explain the behavior of exchange rates, but possible causes can be found by reference to changing asset preferences and speculation.

It is convenient here to refer to the theoretical exposition that was given in Chapter 26 of how changes in the asset market could influence exchange rates (the analysis around Figures 26.5 to 26.8 will be especially helpful). A decrease in the demand for one country's assets by foreign investors will lead to a depreciation of its exchange rate. This, in turn, will bring countervailing factors into play on the real side of the economy. Absorption in the country will fall as the exchange rate depreciates and a trade surplus is created. The moral of the story is, however, that changes in asset preferences tend to have the character of a self-fulfilling prophecy. They will have an impact on the exchange rate, and the impact effect will normally have lasting consequences.

Changes in asset preferences are closely related to changes in expectations. If investors believe that a specific currency will appreciate, and if they act accordingly, the increase in demand for that currency will force its appreciation, unless, naturally, the authorities of the country in question increase the money supply so as to neutralize the increase in demand.

The last factor points to an important fact: expectations are greatly influenced by what people believe about various governments and their economic policies. If investors believe that a government will pursue a restrictive monetary policy, they will start demanding that currency. This will force an appreciation quite irrespective of what the short-run policy may be. Sometimes an analogy with the stock market is drawn. The relative price of national monies is determined, it is asserted, by the same types of factors that determine stock market prices. Just as we observe that prices of stocks can change considerably over periods of time, we should similarly expect exchange rates to show marked fluctuations.

The analogy might have some value under specific circumstances and in the short run. The differences between the stock market and the exchange market seem, however, larger than the similarities. A decisive difference is the fact that the concept of a *normal price* is strongly connected to an exchange rate. Unless basic underlying conditions change, there is no reason to expect a long-run change in the exchange rate. Asset considerations might influence short-run behavior, but sooner or later the exchange-rate should return to its 'normal' level unless basic economic conditions change.

It is not possible to demonstrate in any detail how changing asset preferences have influenced the short-run behavior of exchange rates in recent years. However, it is possible, and even probable, that they have played a role in the large fluctuations which have occurred since 1973.

Speculation is closely linked to changing asset preferences. Private speculators naturally want to make a profit on their holdings of various currencies. In theory, profitable speculation should also help to smooth out fluctuations in exchange rates, as analyzed in Chapter 27. It is very doubtful whether speculation has been of a stabilizing character in recent years. Some sceptical analysts thought floating rates would be unstable and by and large speculation would be destabilizing. According to these critics, private capital flows would be capricious and volatile in the absence of the reference point of fixed parity.

Again it is difficult to disentangle the speculative motive from other factors influencing the exchange rates. However, on the whole, one has the impression that private speculation has been destabilizing. One period when the central banks stayed out of the market, the second quarter of 1973, ended in disorder. The German authorities tried to combat inflation by a restrictive monetary policy in the spring of 1973. This caused the German mark to appreciate. Instead of inducing a countervailing speculation that should have stabilized the exchange rate, the upward movement resulted in further inflows of private capital. Exchange-rate movements in one direction induced further movements in the same direction, and the swings were exaggerated. A gross overselling of the dollar took place in the early summer of 1973 and the German mark reached a peak of 42 per cent above its Smithsonian level. It was only after official intervention that the trend in exchange rates changed and the dollar began to climb while the German mark fell.

Yet it was this type of situation that speculation was supposed to take care of under floating rates. In theory, private funds should take positions in currencies that fluctuate heavily because of cyclical, short-run influences. Thereby, speculators could even out cyclical swings by selling the currency when it was dear and buying it when it was cheap. It is doubtful whether that occurred on any significant scale. Firm evidence is hard to come by. The impression is, however, that speculation did not help to stabilize exchange rates. On the contrary, existing evidence suggests that speculative movements of assets might have been one of the factors that contributed to the large fluctuations in exchange rates which took place in the first few years of general floating.

The large fluctuations of exchange rates called for some kind of concerted action on the part of the central banks. After the initial experiences of 1973, the 'clean' float was simply untenable. In one way or another, the float had to be managed. We will now discuss some of the problems connected with the *managed float*.

THE MANAGED FLOAT

A system of free floating has never existed. Not even in early 1973 were exchange rates left to float freely; instead, various forms of cooperation and management took place. The most important example of cooperation was the European countries 'snake' scheme, which consisted of the German mark, the French franc, the Dutch guilder, the Belgium–Luxemburg franc, and the Danish, Norwegian and Swedish kroner. Many other smaller currencies have tied themselves to a larger one, like the dollar, the British pound, or the French franc, depending on geographical or political affinities. Some Middle Eastern currencies are tied to the S.D.R., which is now defined as a weighted average of sixteen major currencies.

The major currencies did float against one another. To this group belonged the U.S. and Canadian dollars, the snake currencies as a group, the Japanese yen, the Swiss franc and the Italian lira. Large swings in exchange rates soon prompted various forms of intervention. The continental countries cooperated closely to keep their currencies within the snake, and also to moderate the swings between their currencies and the dollar.[8] The U.S. Federal Reserve System intervened at times to support the dollar and counteract forces which could produce severe depreciations. This intervention often took the form of 'swap' transactions, i.e. the Federal Reserve sold European currencies that it had acquired from the European central banks, and the European central banks in turn repurchased the dollars later when the currency had regained strength. An example of cooperation has been the control of capital movements. In early 1973 these controls were tightened as the dollar fell. In early 1974 they were lifted to check the appreciation of the dollar which then took place, while at the same time several European countries relaxed their controls over capital imports. Some other countries, for instance, Britain, Japan and Italy, have sold foreign exchange in substantial amounts to avoid an excessive depreciation of their currencies.

Thus cooperation and management have taken place. And despite the great stress on the system, especially in connection with the oil crisis, no significant competitive exchange-rate depreciations have occurred. With the Bretton Woods system the central banks got into the habit of cooperating in order to defend the system of pegged rates. Even though the system has changed, the central banks have continued to cooperate. This is probably the single most important effect of the development of the international monetary system since the Second World War.

Our primary concern here is not with facts but the principles: how should the floating system be managed?

At the bottom of the managed float lies the idea of the 'normal' price, the thought that the exchange rate should fluctuate around some equilibrium value. The managed float could naturally be organized around a system of 'reference

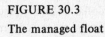

FIGURE 30.3

The managed float

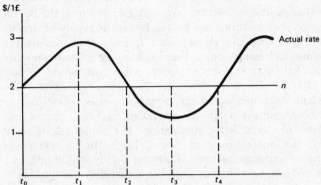

rates', with the various central banks defining the normal level of their exchange rates in terms of S.D.R.s.[9] Such a system would have to revise the reference rates to avoid the rigidity that characterized the Bretton Woods system. This could be accomplished through regular meetings between representatives of the central banks. Supervision of the reference rates could be entrusted to the I.M.F., though the time is not yet ripe for such a step. To start with, these reference rates should probably coincide with the current market rates.

One proposal for intervention has been termed 'leaning against the wind'. According to this proposal, no central bank would sell its currency when the exchange rate depreciates, nor would it buy the currency when its price goes up. The point here is that the central banks should not contribute to the swings in the exchange rate. By buying its own currency when its price falls, and selling it when its price increases, the central bank would help to steady the rate and smooth out fluctuations. It should be observed, however, that the principle of 'leaning against the wind', when it has been advocated, has not yet been connected with any specific system of reference rates. Without any such connection the principle permits ample room for manipulation by central banks. If a central bank wanted its exchange rate to depreciate, it could pursue a policy which naturally leads to depreciation, and then, by reference to the principle of 'leaning against the wind', defend the new value of its currency by selling it whenever it showed a tendency to appreciate again.

A more ambitious proposal is the one suggested by Ethier and Bloomfield.[10] They begin with the idea of a system of reference rates. The structure of these reference rates would then be revised at periodic intervals, so that the agreed rates would not deviate too much from their true equilibrium values. The central rule for management is simply that no central bank shall sell its own currency at a price below its reference rate and that it shall not buy its currency at a price above its reference rate. Figure 30.3 gives an illustration of how the system is supposed to work. We start with a reference, or 'normal', rate, n, at which the dollar exchanges for \$2 for £1. From t_0 to t_1 the dollar depreciates against the pound sterling. During this period the American authorities agree not to sell their own currency. Hence the supply of dollars comes from other sources, presumably from private speculators who are speculating in a depreciation of the dollar and an appreciation of the pound sterling and other currencies. During the period from t_0 to t_1 sterling also appreciates. According to the rule, the British authorities may not buy pounds during this period. Hence the supply of sterling must come from private hands. As we approach t_1 speculation against the American dollar becomes increasingly risky. From t_0 to t_2 the dollar is above its normal rate. After t_2 American authorities switch policy and refuse to buy dollars.

A managed float along these lines would have several advantages. Fluctuations would be dampened around the reference rate. Central banks would not contribute to any kind of destabilizing speculation. The swings taking place would be caused by real, market-oriented forces, like shifts in demand, a temporary fall in export earnings because of adverse supply conditions, etc. Private speculators would not have the one-way option that they had during the Bretton Woods system, since a movement in a depreciatory direction might easily reverse itself as the price of the currency again raises. Central banks have to cooperate and support each other by swap arrangements. Of course, this proposal has its share of difficulties. One is connected with establishing the reference rates. If a currency has a depreciating or an appreciating trend, it might be difficult to adjust it to its 'normal' rate (or true equilibrium value). Surpluses or deficits of long standing might arise if the reference rate deviates too much from the correct equilibrium value of the exchange rate.

Ethier and Bloomfield have thus proposed a simple rule for managing the float. The system of floating rates has performed reasonably well so far. It is unlikely that the authorities will permit a 'clean' float, without interventions, especially because the fluctuations experienced during recent years have been too large and too erratic. The discussion above should have given us some illustration of the problems connected with managing a system of floating rates.

THE I.M.F. AND THE FUTURE OF THE INTERNATIONAL MONETARY SYSTEM

One important aspect of the development of the international monetary system during the 1970s has been the decline in the importance of the dollar. Part of this decline can be explained by the change over to floating exchanges. Since market forces play a larger role, less power is invested in the discretionary actions of national states. Part of the explanation also lies in the increased importance of the I.M.F. As the United States has become less important, more scope has been left for international cooperation under the guidance of the Fund.

The I.M.F. has been active in several areas in recent years. An important meeting of the Fund took place in Jamaica in January 1976. One of the conference's most significant developments concerned the effort to demonetize gold. It was decided that one-sixth of the gold holdings (25 million ounces) should be sold in the world market over a period of four years. The Fund would make some capital gains on these sales, amounting to the difference between the official price of $42.42, or 35 S.D.R.s, and the market price which gold fetches, which has been fluctuating between roughly $100 and $150 an ounce in recent years. By a conservative estimate, putting the prospective market price of gold at

$100 an ounce, the total gains will be roughly $1.5 billion. These gains will be used to help the world's poorest nations, those with a *per capita* annual income of less than $300. Some of these nations have been hard hit by the increase in oil prices and by the world economic recession that followed in its wake and are in desperate need of assistance. Considering the dimensions of the problem, $1.5 billion is only a minor contribution, but it can still have an important effect, especially if used in combination with other forms of support.

In addition to the one-sixth that will be sold on the market, another equally large slice of gold will be redistributed to the member countries which originally subscribed the gold to the Fund. Another measure abolished the official price of gold. In the future there will be no transactions in gold between the Fund and its member countries. Instead, S.D.R.s will become the principal reserve asset.

One can argue about whether the measures undertaken by the Fund have in fact increased or decreased the importance of gold. It is certainly true that gold retains its mystique. Central banks will also be able to hold gold in the future. In fact, they will be allowed to sell and buy gold at market-related prices. This amounts to a very substantial revaluation of gold. From this point of view, the reforms enacted by the Fund might be said to increase the importance of gold. But it is doubtful whether central banks will in the future be very eager to acquire gold since they will have to pay market prices. Acquisitions will entail considerable risks since the price of gold can be expected to fluctuate sharply in terms of any local currency.

Gold will in any case retain its value as an important asset. Central banks will also sell gold when confronted with balance-of-payments problems in the future. How useful gold will be in this role will depend on the willingness of the leading central banks to acquire gold at market-determined prices.

The sheer size of the gold holdings presents a problem. The monetary stock of gold consists of roughly 1 billion ounces. With a market price of gold of around $130 an ounce (which has been the approximate average price of gold in recent years) the world gold stock can be estimated at $130 billion. This is certainly a very important international asset. The daily use of gold by central banks might decrease in importance because of the actions of the I.M.F., but gold remains important as an international asset. In fact, this importance has been increased by the *de facto* revaluation of gold.

It might be useful to compare the importance of gold with that of S.D.R.s. The holdings of international exchange reserves can be estimated at $150 billion. Hence the value of international reserves consisting of gold and currencies amounts to approximately $300 billion. Considering the fact that S.D.R.s now in existence total about $11 billion, it is clear that when the I.M.F. declares that S.D.R.s shall become 'the principal reserve asset' in the future, it is more a statement about intentions than a reflection of existing facts. Even if the amount of S.D.R.s increases, it will take a long time before they will approach gold and international currency reserves in magnitude; nor can we expect the Fund to be invested with the powers of an international central bank that would be able to regulate the increase of international liquidity by open-market operations in S.D.R.s. In steering the international monetary system in the future, the Fund will derive its significance, not as an international central bank, but rather as a forum for international discussion, analysis and negotiation.

Among the interesting developments pursued by the Fund is the so-called *link proposal*. Its basic idea is to link the issue of S.D.R.s. with development assistance. One method would be to distribute a larger share of S.D.R.s to developing countries than what corresponds to their quotas in the I.M.F. Another method would be to issue S.D.R.s to international and regional development banks and institutions. Some arguments along this track go even further. They suggest that some arrangement ought to be found whereby S.D.R.s could be substituted for international liquidity in the form of reserve currencies and be distributed according to the number of inhabitants in various countries. The weakness of all versions of the link proposal is that there is no logical connection between the creation of international reserves and development assistance. The prospects for any such link proposal are therefore dim. This does not mean that many less developed countries are not in desperate need of international reserves. Nor does it imply that the I.M.F. cannot assist them in various ways.

One means of assistance has been to increase the quotas of the I.M.F. At the 1976 Jamaica meeting the members' quotas were increased by 32.5 per cent. The oil-exporting countries had their quotas doubled, while the less developed countries' quotas increased proportionally, and those of industrial countries less than proportionally. This was a scheme expressly designed to help the less developed countries since their possibilities of borrowing from the Fund increased with the increase in their quotas. Another means of assisting the developing countries was to established a compensatory financing facility. It was decided that members of the Fund could borrow up to 75 per cent of their quotas to meet exceptional difficulties, like a sudden shortfall of normal export receipts. We have also seen that the profits on the sales of one-sixth of the gold holdings of the Fund were used to help the poorest of the developing countries. This could, in a way, be viewed as a special case of a link proposal.

Thus the I.M.F. has taken some measures designed specifically to help the less developed countries. It should be noted, however, that the scope for action on the part of the Fund is especially limited in this area. The Fund must first and foremost deal with problems of the international monetary system. Only in rather peripheral ways can it pay special consideration to the problems of the less developed countries. The Fund can best help the poor countries by constructing an efficient monetary system which will function as an instrument for developing the world economy.

The most important problem that the Fund has to deal with concerns the exchange-rate regime. Here, opinions between the major countries have differed. France has preferred a system of pegged exchange rates. The United States, on the other hand, has argued for flexible exchange rates. The I.M.F. took an important step at the Jamaica conference when it sanctioned a system of floating rates. The members of the I.M.F. agreed 'to promote a stable system of exchange rates'. The phrasing is important. They did not agree on a system of stable rates, but on a stable system of rates.

We know that excessive fluctuations of exchange rates have impaired the system of floating rates in recent years. The Fund attended to this problem by stressing that its members should 'seek to promote stability by fostering orderly underlying economic and financial conditions and a monetary system that does not tend to produce erratic disruptions'. The prevailing view seemed to be that instability of exchange rates depended on underlying economic conditions and that attempts at fixing rates would not solve the real problems.

However, the need for stability was emphasized. The Fund bowed to the proponents of fixed exchange rates by providing the means for a restoration of a system of fixed rates. To reintroduce such a system requires 85 per cent of the total votes of the Fund. This implied that the approval of both the United States and the E.E.C. countries is needed for such a restoration. In reality, the I.M.F. condoned the system of floating rates that had evolved after 1973.

Naturally, the role of the I.M.F. in the future will depend on what its members want it to be. The signs are that the Fund will become more active in guiding the international monetary system than it was during the Bretton Woods period. The Fund took some important actions at Jamaica by deciding upon gold sales, which can be viewed as a beginning of its international open-market operations. It has taken a more active attitude in its lending policies by, for instance, liberalizing the use of its *credit tranches*. Admittedly, there are several important areas where little or no progress was made. The long-run role of the S.D.R.s versus gold and international reserves is still unclear. The Fund did not attempt to exercise any control over the euro-currency market. However, it has taken a realistic view of the present exchange-rate system, and the Fund will probably be less rigid in its practice and take more initiatives than it did during the 1950s and 1960s.

SUMMARY AND CONCLUSIONS

The 1970s have seen more tensions in the international economy than the two preceding decades. It became clear during the first few years of the 1970s that the system of pegged exchange rates was no longer feasible. The euro-dollar market grew rapidly. Short-term capital movements were large and there was hardly any possibility for central banks to stave off speculation against a currency during the system of pegged rates. The oil crisis and the increase in oil prices that was at its heart profoundly affected the world economy. No systematic international action was taken to confront the transfer problem that it entailed. When each country had to cope with its adjustment problems separately, a deep recession followed. The presence of the system of floating rates which had gradually evolved in all probability helped to cushion the effects of the oil crisis and smooth out the necessary adjustments. However, the fluctuations of exchange rates have been large. Part of these fluctuations can be explained in terms of speculation and changing asset preferences. The need for supervision of exchange rates has, however, been recognized. The possibilities for a 'clean' float are quite small. Hence a system of managed floating is evolving where the central banks will try to hold the fluctuations of exchange rates around some 'normal' value. The I.M.F. has adjusted its actions and frame of reference to the system which has developed. The Fund has attempted to limit the importance of gold and has been more liberal in its views on lending for adjustment purposes. It will probably play a more active role in the future. The new system that emerges will be less dependent on the dollar than was the old

Bretton Woods system, and the system of floating rates will have a more effective adjustment mechanism.

SELECTED BIBLIOGRAPHY: CHAPTERS 29 AND 30

The literature in this area is voluminous and tends to become dated fast. It is difficult to single out any items at the cost of others; much depends on personal judgment. Valuable discussions of analytical problems of the international monetary system are contained in:

H. G. Johnson, *Further Essays in Monetary Economics,* London, Harvard University Press, 1973.

R. A. Mundell, *Monetary Theory: Inflation, Interest and Growth in the World Economy,* Pacific Palisades, Calif., Goodyear, 1971.

For a wealth of material on the factual development of the international monetary system and the major currencies during this century, see:

L. B. Yeager, *International Monetary Relations: Theory, History and Policy,* 2nd ed., New York, Harper & Row, 1976.

The euro-dollar market is analyzed in:

G. Bell, *The Euro-dollar Market and the International Financial System,* London, Wiley (Halsted Press), 1973.

P. Einzig, *The Euro-dollar System,* 2nd ed., London, Macmillan, 1973.

For a background to and an analysis of the oil problem, see:

P. R. Odell, *Oil and World Power: Background to the Oil Crisis,* 4th ed., London, Penguin Books, 1975.

R. Vernon (ed.), *The Oil Crisis,* New York, Norton, 1976.

H. Chenery, 'Restructuring the World Economy', *Foreign Affairs,* no. 1, 1975.

For the development of exchange rates in recent years see Yeager and:

F. Hirs and D. Higham, 'Floating Rates – Expectations and Experience', *Three Banks Review,* no. 3, 1974.

Theoretical aspects of asset preferences and exchange rates are discussed in a special issue of the *Scandinavian Journal of Economics,* June 1976, devoted to 'Flexible Exchange Rates and Stabilization Policy'.

The problems of the managed float are treated in:

W. Ethier and A. I. Bloomfield, *Managing the Managed Float,* Princeton Essays in International Finance, October 1975.

The role of the I.M.F. in the international monetary system is dealt with in:

E. M. Bernstein *et al., Reflections on Jamaica,* Princeton Essays in International Finance, April 1976.

Useful information on the actual state of the system and differing views on how well it functions can be obtained from various sources. The publications of the

International Finance Section of the Department of Economics at Princeton University should be consulted. Papers like *The Economist*, the *New York Times*, the *London Financial Times*, and the *Wall Street Journal* give timely information. Useful information is also provided by the I.M.F. in its *Annual Reports* and in *Staff Papers, Finance and Development*, and the *I.M.F. Survey*.

Notes and References

CHAPTER 1

1. David Ricardo (1772–1823) accumulated a fortune during the Napoleonic wars as a member of the London stock exchange. He then retired, turning to theoretical economics, and in 1819 became a Member of Parliament. In 1817 he published his main work, *Principles of Political Economy and Taxation,* which contains the first rigorous exposition of the classical theory of value and distribution; in chapter 7, 'On Foreign Trade', Ricardo expounds the theory of comparative advantage.

2. Adam Smith (1723–90) was Professor of Moral Philosophy at Glasgow University. The first major figure of classical economics, he introduced the theory of value and taught the blessings of the unhampered market ('the invisible hand'). His major work, *The Wealth of Nations,* was published in 1776.

3. Robert Torrens (1780–1864), an officer in the British Army during the Napoleonic wars, later turned to economics and published a pamphlet in 1815, *Essay on the External Corn Trade,* which contains what seems to be the earliest formulation of the theory of comparative advantage. He also made significant contributions to classical monetary theory and policy. In 1831 he became a Member of Parliament.

4. For a justification of this statement in modern analytical terms, see J. M. Gransmont and D. McFadden, 'A Technical Note on Classical Gains from Trade', *Journal of International Economics,* vol. 2, May 1972, pp. 109ff.

CHAPTER 2

1. Eli F. Heckscher (1879–1952) was a Swedish economist and economic historian. In 1919 he published in the *Ekonomisk Tidskrift* a paper that contains the core of the Heckscher–Ohlin theory of trade. He is otherwise known primarily for his path-breaking studies on mercantilism and Swedish economic history. Bertil Ohlin (1899–1979), a Swedish economist and politician, was a student of Heckscher's. He published his main work, *Interregional and International Trade,* in 1933. He then turned to politics and became the leader of the Swedish Liberal Party.

2. This has to do with the fact that almost all results in trade theory have been derived using this assumption; it is also necessary if one wants to use geometry as a mode of exposition.

3. The derivation of the production-possibility curve from the box diagram was originally made in K. M. Savosnick, 'The Box Diagram and the Production-Possibility Curve', *Ekonomisk Tidskrift,* vol. 60, September 1958.

CHAPTER 3

1. For a discussion of the role of assumptions in economic theory, see Milton Friedman, *Essays in Positive Economics,* Chicago, University of Chicago Press, 1953; and Ernst Nagel, 'Assumptions in Economic Theory', *American Economic Review,* Papers and Proceedings, vol. 53, May 1963, pp. 211–19.

CHAPTER 6

1. W. W. Leontief, 'Domestic Production and Foreign Trade: the American Capital Position Re-examined', *Proceedings of the American Philosophical Society*, vol. 97, September 1953, pp. 332ff.

2. N. S. Buchanan, 'Lines on the Leontief Paradox', *Economia Internazionale*, vol. 8, November 1955, pp. 791ff.

3. G. A. Loeb, 'A Estrutura do comércio Exterior da América do Norte', *Revista Brasileira de Economia*, vol. 8, December 1954, pp. 81ff.

4. B. C. Swerling, 'Capital Shortage and Labor Surplus in the United States', *Review of Economics and Statistics*, vol. 36, August 1954, pp. 286ff.

5. W. W. Leontief, 'Factor Proportions and the Structure of American Trade: Further Theoretical and Empirical Analysis', *Review of Economics and Statistics*, vol. 38, November 1956, pp. 386ff.

6. The argument about the perverse demand effects as an explanation of the Leontief paradox has been proposed by Stefan Valavanis-Vail, 'Leontief's Scarce Factor Paradox', *Journal of Political Economy*, vol. 52, December 1954, pp. 523ff.

7. H. S. Houthakker, 'An International Comparison of Household Expenditure Patterns, Commemorating the Centenary of Engel's Law', *Econometrica*, vol. 25, October 1957, pp. 532ff.

8. I. B. Kravis, 'Wages and Foreign Trade', *Review of Economics and Statistics*, vol. 38, February 1956, pp. 14ff.

9. Leontief, 'Domestic Production and Foreign Trade: the American Capital Position Re-examined', p. 346.

10. This point is made by R. W. Jones, 'Factor Proportions and the Heckscher–Ohlin Theorem', *Review of Economic Studies*, vol. 24, 1956, pp. 1ff.

11. B. S. Minhas, *An International Comparison of Factor Costs and Factor Use*, Amsterdam, North-Holland, 1963.

12. K. J. Arrow, H. B. Chenery, B. S. Minhas, and R. M. Solow, 'Capital – Labor Substitution and Economic Efficiency', *Review of Economics and Statistics*, vol. 43, August 1961, pp. 225ff. C.E.S. stands for *constant elasticity of substitution*. *Homohypallagic* is compounded from the two Greek words homo ('same') and hypallage ('substitution').

13. Minhas, *International Comparison of Factor Costs and Factor Use*, pp. 32ff.

14. W. W. Leontief, 'An International Comparison of Factor Costs and Factor Use: A Review Article', *American Economic Review*, vol. 54, June 1964, pp. 335ff.

15. Erik Hoffmeyer, 'The Leontief Paradox Critically Examined', *Manchester School of Economic and Social Studies*, vol. 26, May 1958, pp. 160ff.

16. This point has also been made by M. A. Diab, *The United States Capital Position and the Structure of its Foreign Trade*, Amsterdam, North-Holland, 1956.

17. W. P. Travis, *The Theory of Trade and Protection*, Cambridge, Mass, Harvard University Press, 1964, chs 3 and 4.

18. P. B. Kenen, 'Nature, Capital and Trade', *Journal of Political Economy*, vol. 73, October 1965, pp. 437ff.

19. R. E. Baldwin, 'Determinants of the Commodity Structure of U.S. Trade', *American Economic Review*, vol. 61, March 1971, pp. 126ff.

20. D. B. Keesing, 'Labor Skills and Comparative Advantage', *American Economic Review*, vol. 61, May 1966, pp. 249ff.

21. W. H. Branson and N. Monoyios, 'Factor Inputs in U.S. Trade', *Journal of International Economics,* vol. 7, May 1977, pp. 111ff.

22. H. B. Lary, *Imports of Manufacturers from Less Developed Countries,* New York, National Bureau of Economic Research, 1968.

23. G. D. A. MacDougall, 'British and American Exports: A Study Suggested by the Theory of Comparative Costs', *Economic Journal,* December 1951, and September 1952.

24. R. M. Stern, 'British and American Productivity and Comparative Costs in International Trade', *Oxford Economic Papers,* October 1962; B. Balassa, 'An Empirical Demonstration of Classical Comparative Cost Theory', *Review of Economics and Statistics,* August 1963.

CHAPTER 7

1. For an exposition of the vent-for-surplus approach and an application of it to some former British colonies, see H. Myint, 'The Classical Theory of International Trade and the Underdeveloped Countries', *Economic Journal,* vol. 68, June 1958.

2. I. B. Kravis, 'Availability and other Influences on the Composition of Trade', *Journal of Political Economy,* vol. 64, 1956.

3. The concept of *consumers' surplus* builds on the idea that the area below the demand curve measures the largest total amount that the consumers would be willing to pay for a certain quantity of the product. Hence the difference between what they actually pay and what they would be willing to pay measures 'consumers' surplus'. The concept as used here should be regarded as an approximation, since it is based upon some rather stringent assumptions.

4. Some might object to the comparison dollar by dollar of an increase in consumers' surplus with a loss in monopoly profits. Obviously, important effects on income distribution are involved which should be taken into account in a more detailed, thorough-going analysis. Distribution effects are usually disregarded in this type of analysis, however. In most instances the direct comparison of loss of monopoly profits with increase in consumers' welfare should tend to underestimate the gains in terms of national welfare.

5. For a discussion of the importance of length of run for costs of production, see A. A. Alchian, 'Costs and Outputs', in M. Abramowitz *et al.* (eds), *The Allocation of Economic Resources,* Stanford University Press, 1959; and R. J. Wonnacott and P. Wonnacott, *Free Trade between the United States and Canada,* Cambridge, Mass., Harvard University Press, 1967.

6. J. Drèze, 'Quelques reflexions sereins sur l'adaptation de l'industrie Belge au Marché Commun', *Comptes rendues des Travaux de la Société Royale d'Economie Politique de Belgique,* no. 275, 1960.

7. M. V. Posner, 'International Trade and Technical Change', *Oxford Economc Papers,* no. 3, 1961.

8. S. B. Linder, *An Essay on Trade and Transformation,* New York, Wiley.

CHAPTER 8

1. The given figures for the proportion of foreign trade measures the sum of exports and imports related to G.N.P. The figures are taken from Kuznets, *Modern Economic Growth,* pp. 312ff.

2. The terms 'export- and import-biased growth' are explained in Chapter 9, where the theory underlying the concepts is also discussed.

3. Gunnar Myrdal presents a more pessimistic picture of the development of national incomes and *per capita* incomes since the Second World War in Southeast Asia in his *Asian Drama: An Inquiry into the Poverty of Nations,* London, Allen Lane, The Penguin Press, 1968, pp. 473ff.

4. C. P. Kindleberger, *The Terms of Trade,* Cambridge, Mass., Massachusetts Institute of Technology Press, 1956, pp. 232ff.; and GATT, *Trends in International Trade,* Geneva, 1958, pp. 41 and 46ff.

5. R. Nurkse, *Patterns of Trade and Development,* Oxford, Blackwell, 1962, p. 23.

CHAPTER 9

1. J. R. Hicks, 'An Inaugural Lecture', *Oxford Economic Papers,* new series, vol. 5, no. 2, June 1953, pp. 117–135.

2. The following section builds on B. Södersten, *A Study of Economic Growth and International Trade,* Stockholm, Almqvist & Wiksell, 1964.

3. In order to give as simple a formulation of our problem as possible, we assume that Say's Law holds and that everything produced is consumed. We have chosen this formulation because we want to simplify the exposition and concentrate the attention to real factors, i.e. to study the effects of economic growth on real factors such as the terms of trade and the real national income. To introduce savings and money into the model would indeed create great problems. In fact, so far no satisfactory general-equilibrium treatment of the effects of economic growth on the balance of payments has been given.

4. See Södersten, *Study of Economic Growth and International Trade,* pp. 46ff.

5. F. Y. Edgeworth, 'The Theory of International Values', *Economic Journal,* vol. 4, no. 1, March 1894, pp. 35ff.; the quotation is from page 40. See also F. Y. Edgeworth, 'On a Point in the Theory of International Trade', *Economic Journal,* vol. 9, no. 1, March 1899, pp. 125ff.

6. The case of impoverishing growth was discovered anew in the 1950s by H. G. Johnson and J. Bhagwati. See H. G. Johnson, 'Economic Expansion and International Trade', and 'Equilibrium Growth in an International Economy', both reprinted in his *International Trade and Economic Growth,* London, Allen & Unwin, 1958; and J. Bhagwati, 'Immiserizing Growth: A Geometrical Note', *Review of Economic Studies,* vol. 25, no. 68, June 1958.

7. See Södersten, *Study of Economic Growth and International Trade,* pp. 52ff.

8. For a more complete version of the model, see Södersten, *Study of Economic Growth and International Trade,* ch. 2.

CHAPTER 10

1. T. M. Rybczynski, 'Factor Endowment and Relative Commodity Prices', *Economica,* November 1955, pp. 336ff.

2. This section of the chapter builds on the results derived in B. Södersten, *A Study of Economic Growth and International Trade,* Stockholm, Almqvist & Wiksell, 1964, ch. 3.

3. Knut Wicksell (1851–1926), Professor of Economics at the University of Lund, Sweden, was one of the outstanding economists in the neoclassical tradition and made important contributions to many parts of economic theory. Among his main works are *Über Wert, Kapital und Rente*, 1893 (translated as *Value, Capital and Rent*, London, Allen & Unwin, 1954), *Geldzins und Güterpreise*, 1898 (translated as *Interest and Prices*, London, Macmillan, 1936), and *Föreläsningar i national ekonomi*, 1908 (translated as *Lectures on Political Economy*, London, Routledge, 1934–5). The quotation is from *Lectures on Political Economy*, vol. 1, p. 164.

CHAPTER 11

1. Even a great economist like Wicksell was a sworn neo-Malthusian at the beginning of this century. No student of his at the University of Lund could get a degree in economics unless he agreed that the population question was the root of all social evil and that no economic progress could be achieved unless birth control were practised and the increase in population curtailed.

2. J. R. Hicks, *The Theory of Wages*, London, Macmillan, 1932, pp. 131ff. Hicks originally used his classification for discussing the effects of technical progress on the income distribution. It should be observed that Hicks only thought in terms of production functions that are homogeneous of the first degree. We will see later how the Hicksian definitions can be generalized to suit better the study of the effects of technical progress on trade.

3. Strictly speaking, the Hicksian classifications are at constant factor inputs. This is not clearly brought out by the geometric illustration, where we also want to illustrate the fact that an innovation means constant production with less inputs. For illustrative reasons, we let the latter fact take precedence over the former. Nothing substantial in the analysis is changed by this because the critical fact to illustrate is the change in relation between marginal productivities caused by the innovation.

4. This is, in this context, not a critical assumption the way it was when used in connection with factor-price equalization. We will comment upon this fact and upon the use of more general production functions at the end of Chapter 11.

5. This section builds on B. Södersten, *A Study of Economic Growth and International Trade*, Stockholm, Almqvist & Wicksell, 1964, ch. 4. The interested reader will find there a detailed exposition of the results reported in this section.

6. This suggests a reclassification of technical progress better suited to this purpose. The interested reader can consult Södersten, *Study of Economic Growth and International Trade*, pp. 99ff., on this score.

7. If the production function is homogeneous of the first degree, we know that the marginal productivity of at least one of the factors of production will increase because of technical progress. It is still, however, fully conceivable that the marginal productivity of the other factor could fall. See Södersten, *Study of Economic Growth and International Trade*, pp. 103ff. In the more general case of unspecified production functions, it is fully conceivable that both marginal productivities might fall because of the innovation. To understand this it might help to think in geometric terms: technical progress implies an upward shift in the production function, but we do not know anything about the slope of the new production function compared with the old one, and for the marginal productivities it is the slope that matters.

CHAPTER 12

1. Robert Torrens, *Essay on the Production of Wealth,* London, 1821, pp. 96ff.

2. J. M. Keynes, *Economic Journal,* vol. XXII, no. 4, 1912, p. 630.

3. J. M. Keynes, *The Economic Consequences of the Peace,* London, Macmillan, 1920, p. 25.

4. Ibid. p. 10.

5. For an analytic expression for the effects of factor growth given unspecified production functions, see B. Södersten, *A Study of Economic Growth and International Trade,* Stockholm, Almqvist & Wiksell, 1964.

6. Some British economists took a different view. The most notable one is William Beveridge, who forcefully challenged Keynes's views, even though he did not present a more definite theory of his own. See Södersten, *Study of Economic Growth and International Trade,* ch. 6.

7. The main sources for the Singer–Prebisch case are: H. W. Singer, 'The Distribution of Gains Between Investing and Borrowing Countries', *American Economic Review, Papers and Proceedings,* vol. 40, May 1950, pp. 473ff., and 'Economic Progress in Under-Developed Countries', *Social Research,* vol. 16, March 1949, pp. 3ff.; United Nations Economic Commission for Latin America (written by R. Prebisch), *The Economic Development of Latin America and its Principal Problems,* New York, 1950, and R. Prebisch, 'Commercial Policy in the Underdeveloped Countries', *American Economic Review, Papers and Proceedings,* vol. 49, no. 2, May 1959, pp. 251ff. The main partner in the Singer–Prebisch team is undoubtedly Prebisch, and the following discussion is mainly devoted to his writings.

8. Prebisch, 'Commercial Policy in the Underdeveloped Countries', pp. 251ff.

9. United Nations Economic Commission for Latin America, *The Economic Development of Latin America and its Principal Problems,* pp. 12ff.

10. Ibid. pp. 8ff.

11. C. P. Kindleberger gives a survey of the main investigations that have been undertaken in *The Terms of Trade: A European Case Study,* New York, Wiley, 1956, pp. 241ff. His conclusions are quite vague and it seems not to be possible to say anything more definite about the degree of monopoly as between the *center* and the *periphery,* to use Prebisch's language.

12. We do not have to make any sharp distinction here between different types of monopolistic markets. Prebisch *et consortes* presumedly would include under monopolistic markets all market forms where the producer is not a simple price-taker.

13. W. J. Baumol, *Business Behavior, Value and Growth,* New York, Wiley, 1959; J. K. Galbraith, *American Capitalism: the Concept of Countervailing Power,* Boston, Houghton Mifflin, 1952; and P. Sylos-Labini, *Oligopoly and Technical Progress,* Cambridge, Mass., Harvard University Press, 1962.

14. Galbraith, *American Capitalism,* p. 86.

15. Ibid. pp. 84ff.; Sylos-Labini, *Oligopoly and Technical Progress,* pp. 143ff.

16. This point was made in 1911 by Joseph Schumpeter when he first published his *Theorie der wirtschaftlichen Entwicklung,* Munich and Leipzig, Verlag von Duncker & Humblot (2nd ed., 1926); it was on the whole absent from his treat-

ment of short-run problems in *Business Cycles*, New York, McGraw-Hill, 1939, but appeared again in *Capitalism, Socialism and Democracy*, 3rd ed., New York, Harper & Row, 1945.

17. For a similar approach, performed at the same time in a more grand and vague manner, see F. Perroux, 'Esquisse d'une théorie de l'économie dominante', *Economie Appliquée*, April–September 1948, pp. 243ff.

18. Werner Baer, 'The Economics of Prebisch and ECLA', *Economic Development and Cultural Change*, vol. 10, January 1962, pp. 169ff.; the quotation is from page 173.

19. Prebisch, 'Commercial Policy in the Underdeveloped Countries', p. 255.

CHAPTER 13

1. The consumer's surplus obtained from buying Oq_5 of the good at price p is represented by the triangle BDG. The idea is that the total satisfaction which consumers get from consuming Oq_5 of the good is represented by the whole area under the demand curve, i.e. BDq_5O. But they only have to pay the amount GDq_5O for getting this satisfaction. Hence the consumers' surplus equals BDG. Similarly, the consumers' surplus obtained from buying Oq_4 at price $p + t_1$ equals BKE. This Marshallian concept of consumers' surplus has important limitations. It is based on the assumption that the marginal utility of money is constant – that the real income of consumers is not affected by the change in price and consumption of that commodity. It is a partial approach also in the sense that it disregards all cross-effects on the demand for other goods from a change in the relative price structure.

2. The cost for the domestic producers of producing the quantity Oq_1 is measured by the area under the supply curve, i.e. Oq_1IA. Their revenue equals Oq_1IG. The difference is called the producers' surplus. It consists at production Oq_1 of the triangle AIG. When production increases to Oq_2 the producers' surplus increases to AHF. Hence the increase in producers' surplus equals the area $GIHF$.

3. For a proof of this proposition see, for instance, R. G. D. Allen, *Mathematical Analysis for Economists*, London, Macmillan, 1938, pp. 317ff.

4. See Bo Södersten and Karl Vind, 'Tariffs and Trade in General Equilibrium', *American Economic Review*, June 1968, for a formal proof of this proposition.

5. L. A. Metzler, 'Tariffs, the Terms of Trade, and the Distribution of National Income', *Journal of Political Economy*, vol. 57, February 1949.

6. Metzler refined his argument somewhat in a later article, 'Tariffs, International Demand, and Domestic Prices', *Journal of Political Economy*, vol. 57, August 1949. The essence of the argument, however, remains unchanged. For a discussion and criticism of Metzler's two articles, see Södersten and Vind, 'Tariffs and Trade in General Equilibrium'.

7. In principle it could also be explained by the fact that the price elasticity of demand for importables is infinitely large, i.e. that exportables and importables are completely substitutable in consumption.

8. From the point of view of game theory, the optimum tariff is an example of the prisoner's dilemma. See R. D. Luce and H. Raiffa, *Games and Decisions*, New York, Wiley, 1957, pp. 94ff.

9. For an explicit derivation of a formula for the optimum tariff, see Södersten and Vind, 'Tariffs and Trade in General Equilibrium'. The formula they derive for the optimum tariff is

$$t_1^{\text{opt}} = \frac{\left(1 + t_2 \frac{\partial C_{2x}}{\partial Y_2}\right)(S_{1x} - C_{1x})}{(1 + t_2)\left[P(1 + t_2)\frac{\partial S_{2m}}{\partial P} + \frac{\partial C_{2x}}{\partial P} + S_{2m}\frac{\partial C_{2x}}{\partial Y_2}\right]}$$

where t_1^{opt} is country I's optimum tariff and t_2 is country II's tariff. Otherwise the symbols have the same meaning as in Chapter 9, i.e. $S_{1x} - C_{1x}$ is the exports of country I, $\partial S_{2m}/\partial P$ and $\partial C_{2x}/\partial P$ are country II's supply and demand elasticities with respect to relative prices, and $\partial C_{2x}/\partial Y_2$ is the marginal propensity to consume the export good of country II. P is country I's terms of trade and S_{2m} is the supply of import-competing goods in country II.

10. Quantity responses of supply and demand with respect to changes in relative prices play much the same role here as they did in connection with the effects of a tariff on prices and in connection with the effects of economic growth on the terms of trade.

CHAPTER 14

1. A very interesting case for the use of quantative restrictions is made by R. N. Cooper, *The Economics of Interdependence: Economic Policy in the Atlantic Community*, New York, McGraw-Hill, 1968, pp. 227ff.

2. See S. Rosefielde, 'Factor Proportions and Economic Rationality in Soviet International Trade 1955–1968', *American Economic Review*, September 1974, pp. 670–81.

CHAPTER 15

1. Friedrich List (1789–1846), Professor of Economics at Tübingen University. In 1841 he published his main work, *Das Nationale System der Politischen Oekonomie*, containing his thoughts on the need for a protective tariff for less developed countries.

2. List, *Das Nationale System der Politischen Oekonomie*, Jena, 1928, p. 230.

3. John Stuart Mill (1806–1873), English philosopher and economist. His main work in the economic field is *Principles of Political Economy*, published in 1848.

4. See M. C. Kemp, 'The Mill–Bastable Infant Industry Dogma', *Journal of Political Economy*, vol. 68, February 1960.

5. For a penetrating discussion of these problems, see J. Bhagwati and V. K. Ramaswami, 'Domestic Distortions, Tariffs and the Theory of Optimum Subsidy', *Journal of Political Economy*, vol. 71, February 1963.

6. It could also be applicable to a situation with two stationary states of an economy, where in the first state some internal economies were not reaped and the tariff was used to shift the economy over to another stationary state, where these internal economies were then reaped but nothing else happens.

7. The rate of effective protection $(\tau) = (v' - v)/v$, where v' and v are the value added per unit of output with and without protection, respectively. Thus we can

illustrate the concept with the following example:

	Free Trade	With protection
Input	0.50	0.50
Value added	0.50	0.60
Unit price of final output	1.00	1.10

Thus the effective rate of protection, τ, = (0.60−0.50)/0.50 = 0.20 = 20 per cent.

For a further definition and measurement of the concept, see the appendix to this chapter.

8. See B. Balassa, 'Tariff Protection in Industrial Countries: An Evaluation', *Journal of Political Economy*, vol. 73, December 1965, G. Basevi, 'The U.S. Tariff Structure: Estimates of Effective Rates and Protection of U.S. Industries and Industrial Labor', *Review of Economics and Statistics*, 1967; and B. Balassa *et al.*, *The Structure of Protection in Developing Countries*, Baltimore, Johns Hopkins University Press, 1971.

9. Balassa *et al.*, *The Structure of Protection in Developing Countries*, p. 54.

10. See R. Findlay, 'Comparative Advantage, Effective Protection and Domestic Resource Cost of Foreign Exchange', *Journal of International Economics*, no. 1, 1971, for a full presentation of the model.

CHAPTER 16

1. There exist two standard works on import-substitution. One is a six-volume study under the auspices of the O.E.C.D. undertaken in the late 1960s. Another is a twelve-volume study undertaken under the auspices of the National Bureau of Economic Research (N.B.E.R.) in New York in the early 1970s. The major findings of the first study are summarized in I. Little, T. Scitovsky and M. Scott, *Industry and Trade in Some Developing Countries: A Comparative Study*, London, Oxford University Press, 1970, The results of the latter study are surveyed in two volumes, by J. Bhagwati, *Anatomy and Consequences of Exchange Control Regimes* and A. O. Kreuger, *Liberalization Attempts and Consequences*. (Both volumes are to be published by Columbia University Press, New York. Parts of the manuscripts have been made available to the author in mimeographed form. Most of the data presented in the chapter are drawn from these works.)

2. See the works by Bhagwati and Kreuger cited in note 1. They divided control regimes into the five phases treated in the text for the N.B.E.R. ten-country study.

3. Argentina is an exception to this rule. Here incomes of the urban wage-earners are probably lower than the average farm incomes. Hence income distribution (as stressed by Perón in the period leading up to 1955) might have been equalized by a policy of import-substitution.

4. Little, Scitovsky and Scott, *Industry and Trade in Some Developing Countries*, pp. 41ff.

5. Ibid. pp. 93ff.

6. Ibid. pp. 94ff.

7. The figures given here are in U.S. dollars at constant 1960–1 prices.

8. See Carlos E. Diaz-Alejandro, *Essays on the Economic History of the Argentina Republic*, New Haven, Yale University Press, 1970, ch. 6, table 33.

CHAPTER 17

1. Norway established a trade agreement with the E.E.C. after rejection of the terms of full membership by a majority of voters in a referendum.

2. For a full discussion of economic cooperation amongst less developed countries, see K. Morton and P. Tulloch, *Trade and Developing Countries*, London, Croom Helm, 1977, pp. 304ff.

3. See United Nations Economic and Social Council (ECOSOC) Document E.AC 54/L54, 'Economic Cooperation Schemes in Developing Regions: An Appraisal of Mechanisms, Policies and Problems' (1954). The groups studied were the Latin American Free Trade Area (LAFTA), the Central American Common Market (C.A.C.M.), the Caribbean Common Market and Community (CARICOM) – formerly the Caribbean Free Trade Area (CARIFTA), the East African Community (E.A.C.), the Union Douanière et Economique de l'Afrique de l'Ouest (U.D.E.A.O.), the Regional Cooperation for Development (R.C.D.) and the Arab Common Market.

4. The members of LAFTA are Argentina, Brazil, Chile, Columbia, Ecuador, Mexico, Paraguay, Peru, Uruguay and Venezuela.

5. Bolivia, Chile (until 1976), Columbia, Ecuador, Peru and Venezuela.

6. Morton and Tulloch, *Trade and Developing Countries*, London, Croom Helm, 1977, pp. 314ff.

7. Dahomey, Gambia, Ghana, Guinea, Guinea-Bissau, Ivory Coast, Liberia, Mali, Mauritania, Niger, Nigeria, Senegal, Sierra Leone, Togo, Upper Volta.

8. See Robert E. Baldwin, *Non-tariff Distortion of International Trade*, Washington, 1970.

9. Up to the present time (mid-1979) Australia, Austria, Canada, the E.E.C, Finland, Japan, New Zealand, Norway, Sweden, Switzerland and the United States have introduced preferential tariff arrangements.

10. The Declaration of Tokyo, in GATT, *Basic Instruments and Subsidiary Documents*, 20th supplement, 1973, pp. 19–22, para. 5.

11. Ibid. para. 2.

12. For an estimation of the trade benefits to the developing countries of most-favored-nation status versus preferential tariff reductions, see R. E. Baldwin and T. Murray, 'M.F.N. Tariff Reductions and L.D.C. Benefits under the G.S.P.', *Economic Journal*, no. 87, March 1977, pp. 30–46.

CHAPTER 18

1. Raúl Prebisch, *Towards a New Trade Policy for Development*, Geneva, United Nations, 1964, pp. 11ff.

2. Ibid.

3. This argument is presented in Gardner Patterson, *Discrimination in International Trade: The Policy Issues, 1945–1965*, Princeton, N.J., Princeton University Press, 1966.

4. This argument is put forward by I. Little, T. Scitovsky and M. Scott, *Industry and Trade in Some Developing Countries: A Comparative Study*, London, Oxford University Press, 1970.

5. For empirical estimates of effective rates of protection, see B. Balassa, 'Tariff Protection in Industrial Countries: An Evaluation', *Journal of Political Economy*, vol. 73, December 1965; and UNCTAD, *The Kennedy Round: Estimated Effects on Tariff Barriers*, TD/G/Rev. 1, 1968.

6. See Balassa, 'Tariff Protection in Industrial Countries'; and UNCTAD, *The Kennedy Round*.

7. R. E. Baldwin and T. Murray, 'M.F.N..Tariff Reductions and L.D.C. Benefits under the G.S.P.', *Economic Journal*, no. 87, March 1977, p. 44.

8. Morton and Tulloch, *Trade and Developing Countries*, London, Croom Helm, 1977, p. 175.

9. Over three-quarters of the G.S.P. trade can be accounted for by twelve countries: Taiwan, Mexico, Yugoslavia, South Korea, Hong Kong, Brazil, Singapore, India, Peru, Chile, Argentina and Iran. See Baldwin and Murray, 'M.F.N. Tariff Reductions and L.D.C. Benefits under the G.S.P.'.

10. Alisdair MacBean, *Export Instability and Economic Development*, London, Allen & Unwin, 1966.

11. It is interesting to note that Cuba has understood this dilemma. It is now making great efforts to promote agriculture, to concentrate exports on a limited number of products, and to take great care in trying to control supply conditions by implementing scientific agricultural methods.

12. G. F. Erb and S. Schiavo-Campo, 'Export Stability, Level of Development, and Economic Size of Less Developed Countries', *Bulletin of the Oxford University Institute of Economics and Statistics*, vol. 31, November 1969, pp. 263–83.

13. P. B. Kenen and C. S. Voivodas, 'Export Instability and Economic Growth', *Kyklos*, vol. 25, fasc. 4, 1972, pp. 791–805.

14. J. E. Meade, 'International Commodity Agreements', *Lloyds Bank Review*, vol. 73, July 1964.

15. Morton and Tulloch, *Trade and Developing Countries*, London, Croom Helm, 1977, p. 288.

16. UNCTAD, *Liberalization of Tariff and Non-Tariff Barriers*, TD/B/C, 2/R 1, 1969.

CHAPTER 20

1. This chapter builds primarily on R. G. Lipsey's celebrated article 'The Theory of Customs Unions: A General Survey', *Economic Journal*, vol. 70, September 1960.

2. J. Viner, *The Customs Union Issue*, New York, Carnegie Endowment for International Peace, 1953.

3. It should be observed that this gain takes place because the initial tariff was not optimal; otherwise *d* could have been reached initially.

4. This follows from a proposition in the theory of the second best which says that under non-optimum conditions, a complete removal of some taxes or some tariffs might move the economy away from instead of closer to a second-best optimum. See R. G. Lipsey and K. J. Lancaster, 'The General Theory of the Second Best', *Review of Economic Studies*, vol. 24, no. 1, 1956.

5. T. Scitovsky, *Economic Theory and Western European Integration*, London, Allen & Unwin, 1958.

6. H. G. Johnson, 'The Gains from Freer Trade with Europe: An Estimate', *Manchester School of Economic and Social Studies*, vol. 26, September 1958.

7. Scitovsky, *Economic Theory and Western European Integration p. 67.*

8. R. L. Major, 'The Common Market: Production and Trade', *National Institute Economic Review*, August 1962.

9. M. Truman, 'The European Economic Community: Trade Creation and Trade Diversion', *Yale Economic Essays*, vol. 9, Spring 1969, pp. 201–57.

10. J. Williamson and A. Bottrill, 'The Impact of Customs Unions on Trade in Manufactures', *Oxford Economic Papers*, November 1971, pp. 323–51.

11. M. Kreinin, 'Effects of the E.E.C. on Imports of Manufactures', *Economic Journal*, September 1972, p. 916.

12. See L. B. Krause, *European Economic Integration and the United States*, Washington, Brookings Institution, 1968, ch. 2.

13. See Scitovsky, *Economic Theory and Western European Integration*, pp. 110ff.

14. For a vivid description of French business behavior, see D. S. Landes, French Business and the Businessman: A Social and Cultural Analysis', in E. M. Earle (ed.), *Modern France*, Princeton, N.J., Princeton University Press, 1951.

CHAPTER 21

1. This result was first derived by L. A. Metzler, 'The Transfer Problem Reconsidered', *Journal of Political Economy*, vol. 50, June 1942. For further references to the literature, see the bibliographical notes at the end of this chapter.

2. See J. K. Galbraith, *The New Industrial State*, Boston, Houghton Mifflin, 1967.

3. W. Gruber, D. Mehta and R. Vernon, 'The R and D Factor in International Trade and International Investment of U.S. Industries', *Journal of Political Economy*, January–February 1967.

4. U.S. Senate Committee of Finance, *Implications of Multinationals*, 93rd Congress, Washington, 1973.

5. We assume, in other words, that $\partial^2 Q/\partial L\ \partial M$ and $\partial^2 Q/\partial C\ \partial M$ are positive.

6. For a discussion of horizontal and vertical integration in the context of international investment, see Richard E. Caves, 'International Corporations: The Industrial Economics of Foreign Investment', *Econimica*, 1971, pp. 1–27, reprinted in J. Dunning (ed.), *International Investment*, Harmondsworth, Penguin, 1972, pp. 265–301.

7. H. G. Johnson, *Comparative Cost and Commercial Policy Theory for a Developing World Economy*, Wicksell Lectures, Stockholm, Almqvist & Wicksell, 1968.

8. R. Vernon, 'International Investment and International Trade in the Product Cycle', *Quarterly Journal of Economics*, May 1966, pp. 190–207; and R.

Vernon, *Sovereignty at Bay: The Multinational Spread of United States Enterprises,* New York, Basic Books, 1971.

9. G. C. Hufbauer, 'The Multinational Corporation and Direct Investment', in P. B. Kenen (ed.), *International Trade and Finance,* New York, Cambridge University Press, 1975, p. 273.

10. R. Rowthorn, *International Big Business 1957-1967: A Study of Comparative Growth,* Department of Applied Economics, Cambridge University Press, 1971.

11. Caves, 'International Corporations: The Industrial Economics of Foreign Investment', p. 277.

12. J. Robinson, *The New Mercantilism: An Inaugural Lecture,* Cambridge University Press, 1966.

13. This section draws especially on Nils Lundgren, *Internationella koncerner i industriländer,* Stockholm, Liber, 1975, ch. 9.

14. P. Streeten, 'The Theory of Development Policy', in J. Dunning (ed.), *Economic Analysis and the Multinational Enterprise,* London, Praeger, 1974.

15. S. Lall, 'Transfer Pricing by Multinational Manufacturing Firms, *Oxford Bulletin of Economics and Statistics,* August 1973, pp. 173-91.

16. S. de Vylder, *Chile 1970-73: The Political Economy of the Rise and Fall of the Unidad Popular,* Stockholm, Unga Filosofers Förlag, 1974.

17. See A. E. Safarian, 'Foreign Ownership and Control of Canadian Industry', in A. Rostein (ed.), *The Prospect of Change: Proposals for Canada's Future,* Toronto, McGraw-Hill, 1966.

18. K. Morton and P. Tulloch, *Trade and Developing Countries,* London, Croom Helm, 1977, p. 228.

19. This, in concentrated form, was the main message of Jean-Jacques Servan-Schreiber's *The American Challange,* (London, Hamish Hamilton, 1968), which presented an intelligent and well-reasoned argument, even though the author was not a trained economist.

20. J. A. Hobson (1858-1940), British economist. His book *Imperialism* was published in 1902. Lenin's views are contained in *Imperialism: The Highest Stage of Capitalism,* written in 1916 in Zürich and published the following year in Leningrad.

21. This could be concerned with the eminence of the exposer of this theory. Even such a sharp analyst as Oskar Lange becomes unusually vague and elusive when dealing with Lenin's theorizing. See Lange, *Ekonomisk Utweckling och Socialism,* Stockholm, Rabén & Sjögren, 1966, pp. 121ff.

22. An interesting attempt at rescuing the strong version of the theory has been made by an American economist, Harry Magdoff, in *The Age of Imperialism: The Economics of United States Foreign Policy,* New York, Monthly Review Press, 1969. His argument is, essentially, that on the margin, foreign operation of American firms is very important, and that it is from marginal production and sales that profits are primarily derived.

CHAPTER 22

1. This assumption does not restrict the generality of the reasoning. Other forms of speculation can be viewed as a combination of interest arbitrage and forward speculation; see John Spraos, 'The Theory of Forward Exchange and Recent Practice', *Manchester School of Economic and Social Studies,* vol. 21, May 1953.

CHAPTER 25

1. It is assumed in this argument that banks are already at this critical ratio when, with the intention of decreasing liquidity, open-market operations start, and that if they keep a strict ratio, they will have to decrease lending as their liquidity decreases.

2. This need not, strictly speaking, always be the case. This is a pedagogic simplification that will later be restated and refined.

3. An annotated bibliography of the major contributions to the discussion of elasticities is to be found in Hang-Sheng Cheng, 'Statistical Estimates of Elasticities and Propensities in International Trade', *International Monetary Fund Staff Papers,* vol, 7, no. 1, April 1959.

4. Sidney S. Alexander, 'The Effects of a Devaluation on the Trade Balance', *International Monetary Fund Staff Papers,* vol. 2, no. 2, 1952, pp. 263ff.

CHAPTER 26

1. This model was originally proposed by R. Dornbusch, 'Devaluation, Money, and Non-Traded Goods', *American Economic Review,* vol. 63, December 1973, pp. 871ff.

2. Gustav Cassel (1866–1945) was Professor of Economics at Stockholm Unicersity. His major work in theoretical economics is *Theoretische Sozialökonomi,* Leipzig, 1918. Cassel was a vigorous proponent for *laissez-faire* solutions to economic problems and a pronounced anti-Keynesian. His writings on the purchasing-power theory lay at the bottom of his proposals for a reconstruction of the world economy in the interwar period and for a return to the gold standard.

3. For a full presentation of this model, see P. J. K. Kouri, 'The Exchange Rate and the Balance of Payments in the Short Run and in the Long Run: A Monetary Approach', *Scandinavian Journal of Economics,* no. 2, 1976.

4. Joan Robinson, 'The Foreign Exchanges', in H. S. Ellis and L. A. Metzler (eds), *Readings in the Theory of International Trade,* Philadelphia, Allen & Unwin, 1947, pp. 83ff.

5. For a discussion of expectations formation and the dynamic aspects of exchange-rate determination, see R. Dornbusch, 'The Theory of Flexible Exchange Rate Regimes and Macroeconomic Policy', and P. J. K. Kouri, 'The Exchange Rate and the Balance of Payments in the Short Run and the Long Run', both printed in *Scandinavian Journal of Economics,* vol. 78, no. 2, 1976; and J. A. Frenkel and C. A. Rodriguez, 'Portfolio Equilibrium and the Balance of Payments: A monetary Approach', *American Economic Review,* vol. 65, September 1975. The presentation in this section draws especially on Kouri's analysis.

6. For a full exposition of the model, see Dornbusch, 'The Theory of Flexible Exchange Rate Regimes and Maeroeconomic Policy'. For an analogous model, see the appendix to Chapter 9.

CHAPTER 27

1. For a general discussion of risk problems, see K. H. Borch, *The Economics of Uncertainty*, Princeton, N. J., Princeton University Press, 1968.

2. See A. Lanyi, *The Case for Floating Exchange Rates Reconsidered*, Essays in International Finance No. 2, Princeton N. J., Princeton University Press, 1969.

3. M. Friedman, 'The Case for Flexible Exchange Rates', in *Essays in Positive Economics*, Chicago, University of Chicago Press, 1953, pp. 174ff.

4. S. C. Tsiang, 'Fluctuating Exchange Rates in Countries with Relatively Stable Economies: Some European Experience After World War I', *International Monetary Fund Staff Papers*, vol. 7, October 1959.

5. This argument is put forward by Milton Friedman, 'The Case for Flexible Exchange Rates'.

6. M. Farrell, 'Profitable Speculation', *Economica*, May 1966, questions this argument and shows that it might be possible, under what seems to be fairly general assumptions, that speculation can be, at the same time, profitable and destabilizing.

7. See Lanyi, 'Notes on Inflation and the Case for Flexible Exchanges', *The Case for Floating Exchange Rates Reconsidered*, Essays in International Finance No. 2, New York, Princeton, 1969. A. W. Phillips, 'The Relation Between Unemployment and the Rate of Change of Money Wage Rates in the United Kingdom 1861-1957', *Economica*, November 1958.

8. It is quite natural to think of the price level (P) as a function of the exchange rate (r) and the rate of unemployment (U). Then we can set out the following function:

$$P = f(r, U)$$

where $\partial P/\partial r > 0$ and $\partial P/\partial U < 0$. If this relationship holds, depreciation will increase the price level, and an increase in the rate of unemployment will decrease the price level.

9. For a discussion of these problems, see E. S. Phelps (ed.), *The Microeconomic Foundations of Employment and Inflation Theory*, New York, Norton, 1970, and E. S. Phelps, *Inflation Policy and Unemployment Theory*, New York, Norton, 1972.

10. See R. Triffin, *Gold and the Dollar Crisis*, New Haven, Conn., Yale University Press 1961, pp. 82ff.

11. See Lanyi, *The Case for Floating Exchange Rates Reconsidered*, p.13.

12. The pioneering work in this area was done by two American economists, Robert Mundell and Ronald McKinnon. Two classic papers are: R. A. Mundell, 'A Theory of Optimum Currency Areas', *American Economic Review*, September 1961; and R. I. McKinnon, 'Optimum Currency Areas', *American Economic Review*, September 1963.

CHAPTER 28

1. The discussion of aims and means is based especially on Bent Hanson, *The Economic Theory of Fiscal Policy*, London, Allen & Unwin, 1958.

2. We assume that the equations in the system (28.1) are independent and consistent and that the system has a unique solution in the x_is.

3. Whether or not this dichotomy is based on correct theorizing is of no consequence for the example.

4. See Hansen, *The Economic Theory of Fiscal Policy*, pp. 16ff.

5. T. W. Swan, 'Longer-Run Problems of the Balance of Payments', in H. W. Arndt and M. W. Corden (eds), *The Australian Economy: A Volume of Readings*. Melbourne, 1955.

6. J. R. Hicks, 'Mr Keynes and the Classics', *Econometrica*, vol. 5, April 1937; and Alvin Hansen, *Monetary Theory and Fiscal Policy*, New York, McGraw-Hill, 1949.

7. For a pioneering analysis of the principle of 'efficient market classification', see R. A. Mundell, 'The Appropriate Use of Monetary and Fiscal Policy for Internal and External Stability', *International Monetary Fund Staff Papers*, March 1962; and R. A. Mundell, *International Economics*, New York, Macmillan Co., 1968, pp. 201ff.

CHAPTER 29

1. This includes $1.2 billion from the Soviet Union, which, however, never in fact joined the Fund.

2. The special drawing right (S.D.R.) is a unit of account. It was originally equivalent to 0.888671 gram or $^1/_{35}$ troy ounce of gold, i.e. it had the same value as a U.S. dollar until 1971. It has since been redefined in terms of a 'basket of currencies'.

3. There is no nonsense about 'one country, one vote' in the I.M.F. Each member has 250 votes plus one vote for each $100,000 of its subscription.

4. I.M.F., *Annual Report*, Geneva, 1952, p. 46.

5. This argument builds on some rather drastic assumptions, but it may still be useful. It assumes, for instance, that the income elasticity of demand for world money equals 1.0. It disregards changes in demand for gold for other than monetary purposes, technical progress, price effects, etc.

6. We disregard in the future discussion the pound sterling, the minor key currency. Including it would not change anything essential in the argument.

7. It is often assumed that the cost of providing paper money is negligible. This might not be completely true if indirect costs such as precautions against forgery, etc., are also taken into account.

8. *Seigniorage* is the difference between the cost of a mass of bullion and the value as money of the pieces coined from it, usually claimed by a sovereign or feudal superior as a prerogative.

CHAPTER 30

1. The Group of Ten consisted of the following industrial countries: Belgium,

Canada, France, Great Britain, Italy, Japan, the Netherlands, Sweden, the United States and West Germany.

2. This little example should be supplemented by certain assumptions to be correct: the original injection of deposits should consist of 'fresh money'; a small correction might be needed for a necessary increase in the circulation of bank notes; and the money supply abroad should increase *pari passu* to avoid foreign leakages.

3. The central banks could induce the commercial banks to hold dollars forward. By 'swap' transactions the banks were offered attractive rates on forward sales of dollars. This induced them to hold dollars abroad, which helped to absorb excess domestic liquidity.

4. The interested reader can consult the first edition of this work for a discussion of the problems prevailing until the mid-1960s.

5. The members of the E.M.S. were Belgium, Luxemburg, Denmark, France, Ireland, Italy, the Netherlands and West Germany.

6. OPEC consists of the following countries: Abu Dhabi, Algeria, Indonesia, Iran, Iraq, Kuwait, Libya, Nigeria, Qatar, Saudi Arabia and Venezuela.

7. The Organization for Economic Cooperation and Development (O.E.C.D.) consists of the following countries: Australia, Austria, Belgium, Canada, Denmark, Finland, France, Great Britain, Greece, Iceland, Ireland, Italy, Japan, Luxemburg, the Netherlands, New Zealand, Norway, Portugal, Spain, Sweden, Switzerland, Turkey, the United States and West Germany.

8. In January 1974 the French left the European snake scheme and floated the franc independently.

9. For a discussion along these lines, see W. Ethier and A. I. Bloomfield, *Managing the Managed Float*, Princeton Essay in International Finance, No. 112, Princeton, N.J., October 1975.

10. Ibid.

Index